BEFORE HARLEM

AN ANTHOLOGY OF
AFRICAN AMERICAN LITERATURE FROM
THE LONG NINETEENTH CENTURY

Edited by Ajuan Maria Mance

THE UNIVERSITY OF TENNESSEE PRESS / Knoxville

TORCHBEARER TEXTS

The University of Tennessee Press, Knoxville

Library of Congress Cataloging-in-Publication Data

Names: Mance, Ajuan Maria, author.

Title: Before Harlem : an anthology of African American literature from the long nineteenth century / Ajuan Maria Mance.

Description: First edition. | Knoxville : University of Tennessee Press, 2016. | Includes bibliographical references and index.

Identifiers: LCCN 2015035900 | ISBN 9781621902027 (paperback)

Subjects: LCSH: American literature—African American authors. | American literature—19th century. | African Americans—Literary collections. |

BISAC: LITERARY CRITICISM / American / African American. | LITERARY CRITICISM / Reference.

Classification: LCC PS508.N3 M34 2016 | DDC 810.8/0896073—dc23

LC record available at http://lccn.loc.gov/2015035900

In loving memory of my grandparents,
Jennie Vee Hughes Crockett, John Frazier Crockett,
Ernestine English Mance, and William Wilson Mance, Sr.

CONTENTS BY DATE

CONTENTS BY GENRE

ACKNOWLEDGMENTS

I am grateful to those who have supported and assisted me throughout the process of compiling this collection. I would like to thank the staffs of the Northern Regional Library Facility of the University of California; the Newspapers and Microforms Library at the University of California, Berkeley; the Schomburg Center for Research in Black Culture in Harlem; the Beinecke Rare Book and Manuscript Library at Yale University; and the John Hay Library at Brown University. For facilitating my access to the Accessible Archives database of 19th-century newspapers, many thanks to Tom Nagy, Iris Hanney of Unlimited Priorities, and Michael Beller at the Mills College Library. Special thanks, as well, to my graduate and undergraduate research assistants at Mills, Dajanae Barrows, Zenzele Olatunje, Catherine Saunders, and, LaTasha Monique Warmsley, for their energy, enthusiasm, and hard work. I also wish to acknowledge my wonderful colleagues, Diane Cady, Kim Magowan, Kirsten Saxton, and Kara Wittman, whose detailed and thoughtful feedback was a great help to me as I revised key portions of the introduction to this book. I must also acknowledge the exceptional work of Margaret Miller and Kristen Hanley Cardozo, whose assistance in checking the transcribed and edited works collected in this anthology against their 19th-century source texts greatly expedited the final stages of manuscript revision and review. To my parents, Alphonzo C. Mance Sr. and Kathleen A. C. Mance, heartfelt gratitude and appreciation for their advice and for their unwavering faith in my abilities. Finally, I am forever grateful to Cassandra Falby, my fabulous partner, for her support, her sense of humor, and her truly astonishing patience, through years of late-night editing sessions, boxes of books in the dining room, and papers and notepads all over the dining-room table.

INTRODUCTION

The time frame of this collection is based on historian Eric Hobsbawn's notion of a long nineteenth century. In his Marxist analysis of the rise and fall of European political and economic power, he defines the beginning and end of this period based on key developments in the economic and political systems of Europe—the French Revolution and the beginning of World War I—that only loosely conform to its traditional hundred-year span.[1] *Before Harlem* adapts Hobsbawn's basic concept to the specific sociopolitical circumstances and historical conditions that shaped the emergence of African American literature.

For the purposes of this collection, the black nineteenth century begins in the year 1808. While the pioneering black writers of the 1700s—Lucy Terry, Jupiter Hammon, Benjamin Banneker, Phyllis Wheatley, and others—are historically and thematically significant, it is not until 1808 that we first see the emergence of U.S. black literary communities and African American print culture. In that year, black communities in Boston, New York, and Philadelphia commemorated the end of the slave trade in Britain and the United States with speeches, sermons, and brief editorials, many of which were published in pamphlets and progressive newspapers; and it is in these writings and their reception that we see the simultaneous emergence of both a black audience for African American texts and an African American community of literary and textual practice. The period ends in 1910, with the founding of the *Crisis* magazine, the official publication of the National Association for the Advancement of Colored People (NAACP). The launch of the *Crisis,* led by scholar and activist W. E. B. Du Bois, corresponded with a shift in the tone and focus of African American literature and thought, from the late-nineteenth-century interest in "Negro improvement" to the twentieth-century focus on restoring black Americans' basic civil rights and achieving social and political equality.

In July of 1895, a full 15 years before Du Bois's *Crisis* magazine, the First Congress of Colored Women convened in Boston. The culmination of more than a decade of African American women's political organizing, this gathering represented the first attempt by black women to organize at the national level around issues of common concern. The assembled delegates (104 black women, "representing fifty-four clubs from fourteen states and the District of Columbia") heard speeches on a range of subjects, from traditional "women's issues" to education, economics, religion, and more (Logan 133).[2] Principal organizer Josephine Ruffin spoke on the importance of universal academic and moral instruction for African American women; writer and activist T. Thomas Fortune addressed the gathered delegates on the subject of "Political Equality," and, under the leadership of Ida B. Wells-Barnett, the Committee on Resolutions called for employment equality for all African American workers.[3]

Among the invited presenters was New York–based novelist and reporter Victoria Earle Matthews, whose speech, "The Value of Race Literature," established her as one of the earliest African American thinkers to envision the study of U.S. black literature as a discrete field of inquiry. Her address understands the literature of any given race as all of the written expression of its people and is inclusive of creative and scholarly works, as well as journalism and speeches. She offers the following definition: "By race literature we mean ordinarily all the writing emanating from a distinct class—not necessarily race matters; but a general collection of what has been written by men and women of that Race: History, Biographies, Scientific Treatises, Sermons, Addresses, Novels, Poems, Books of Travel, miscellaneous essays, and the contributions to magazines and newspapers" (Matthews 287). Conceived in this way, race literature becomes the fullest and most accessible record of a people's capacity for analysis, reflection, and invention. Its preservation safeguards not only (or even primarily) a body of texts, but a cultural and intellectual legacy. As such, Matthews's call for the preservation and study of race literature is as concerned with safeguarding the African American written tradition as it is with raising awareness of the culture and community out of which that tradition emerged. She writes, "Race Literature does mean [. . .] the preserving of all the records of a Race, and thus cherishing the materials, saving from destruction and obliteration what is good, helpful and stimulating. But for our Race Literature, how will future generations know of the pioneers in Literature, our statesmen, soldiers, divines, musicians, artists, lawyers, critics, and scholars?" (Matthews 187).

It is unlikely that Victoria Earle Matthews herself could have imagined the current state of African American literature studies. Although the last twenty-five years have seen significant progress toward the recovery and authentication of early African American texts, the vast majority of nineteenth-century African

American writers and their work remain largely unknown to contemporary readers.[4] Though little more than a century has passed since Matthews so clearly and thoughtfully mapped out the relationship between race literature, intellectual history, and cultural memory, the richness and breadth of African American literature of the nineteenth century has largely faded from memory, along with all but a vague awareness of the intellectual and cultural debates, political and social struggles, community publications and institutions that fostered and sustained U.S. black writers and their work. Literary historian Elizabeth McHenry sums up the irony of the current state of African American nineteenth-century studies: "[T]he 'recovery' and reprinting of various texts has augmented our access to the nineteenth-century literary creations of African-American writers, [but] we remain less cognizant of the variety of processes of intellectual production and exchange that have existed within African-American communities, processes through which an African-American readership was deliberately coordinated" (McHenry 477).

The failure of increased access to nineteenth-century black texts to bring about a broader awareness of the period's African American intellectual and literary communities is a direct result of the ways that the preferences and concerns of contemporary scholars in the field have shaped and limited the manner in which pre-Harlem Renaissance writers and their work come into view. Contemporary U.S. black literature scholarship highlights those texts that have come to reflect not so much the interests and priorities that shaped the creation of past literatures as the interests and priorities of the current population in looking at the past. One factor shaping the interests of contemporary African American literature scholars is the desire to find and celebrate the progenitors of today's African American writers and texts, as reflected in a 1997 interview with African American literature scholars and *Norton Anthology of African American Literature* (1997) coeditors Henry Louis Gates Jr. and Nellie McKay. McKay explains the impetus behind the anthology's attention to early black texts: "We are interested that people should understand something also that comes from the [beginnings of the African American literature tradition]. Where do we begin to see the quality and the depth of the kind of writing that we now have? Where did it come from? And can we look back to the earlier writers and find it there?" (Gates and McKay, "From the Soil of Suffering").

For the current novel-centered moment in literature, this search for the roots of the "quality and the depth of the kind of writing that we have now" entails, first and foremost, a search for early black novels and novelists, with a similar interest in early book-length memoirs and autobiographical nar-ratives as well as those poets and short-fiction writers who were fortunate enough to see their works collected and republished in book form. In the current moment, in which the most celebrated African American works have been those that seek to interpret African American perspectives and experi-ences in ways that are comprehensible to black and nonblack readers alike, the search for roots has also meant greater attention and visibility to those nineteenth-century African American texts that were most widely embraced by the period's white readership.

NINETEENTH-CENTURY WRITERS
AND THE AFRICAN AMERICAN LITERATURE CANON

The impact of these preferences on the current U.S. black literature canon is apparent in the nineteenth-century selections that appear in influential collec-tions like the *Norton Anthology of African American Literature* (1997, 2003, 2014) and *Call and Response: The Riverside Anthology of the African American Literary Tradition* (1998). Their consecutive release in 1997 and 1998 marked a turning point in African American literature studies. Although these are neither the first nor the most recent general anthologies in the field, the ambitious scale of these volumes (each includes more than two thousand pages of selections spanning more than three hundred years of written and orally-transmitted works) and the canon-making authority of their presses (W. W. Norton and Houghton Mifflin Harcourt, respectively) combined to create what Richard Elliot Fox has described as "the most formidable" anthologies of African American literature ever produced (Fox 2).

As one of the main entry points through which twenty-first-century readers encounter African American writers and their work, these and subsequent anthologies of similar scale (notably the *Prentice Hall Anthology of African Ameri-can Literature,* in 2000, and the *Wiley-Blackwell Anthology of African American Literature,* in 2014) have played a critical role in defining the U.S. Black literature canon; and their influence has been greatest in the subfield of African Ameri-can literature before the Harlem Renaissance. While a number of African American writers from the Harlem Renaissance onward continue to draw a steady audience of mainstream readers, only a handful of nineteenth-century black writers remain consistently in print. Consequently, comprehensive an-thologies like the *Norton* and the *Riverside* are many readers' first and only exposure to African American literature of the period. Among the growing body of nineteenth-century works that are currently available for scholarly research, the *Norton*, the *Riverside*, and similar collections have selected as the most canonical, most essential black texts of the period those poems, novels, and autobiographical narratives distinguished by their effectiveness at conveying African American experiences, aesthetics, and ideas across racial lines, to readers outside of the black community.

To achieve a measure of success beyond the black readership is a significant accomplishment for African American writers of any period. For nineteenth-century black texts in particular, given their emergence against the backdrop of either southern chattel slavery (during the antebellum years) or lynching and Jim Crow (in the decades after Reconstruction), such broad recognition is truly noteworthy. Still, it is important to recognize that broad acceptance of certain black texts reflects not only the willingness of some white readers (and a small number of white, mainstream periodicals and publishers) to embrace a handful of black-authored works, but also their unwillingness to engage with the vast majority of African American writers.

For the overwhelming majority of black writers, the African American readership and the press by which it was served were the only options, whether they aspired to access the larger white readership or not.[5] Ironically, though, while a nineteenth-century black writer's accessibility to white readers did not preclude his or her accessibility to and even popularity among the African American readership, that writer's success or failure in reaching the white readership of his time is often a key factor in determining his status relative to today's African American canon. Albeit inadvertently, contemporary scholars' search for the progenitors of contemporary black genres and texts has, through its greater interest in those cross-racial communications published in book form, extended the influence of the nineteenth-century white readership and its publishers into the present day, where their preferences and sensibilities continue to influence the terms on which nineteenth-century African American writers and their work are made accessible to white and nonwhite readers alike.

As a result, abolitionist poems from book-length collections by George Moses Horton and Frances E. W. Harper have become staples of the African American canon, while pieces like "The New York Riot" (1863), poet Solomon G. Brown's account of the tragic New York Draft Riots of 1863 (originally published in the *Christian Recorder,* a weekly publication of the African

Methodist Episcopal [A.M.E.] Church and one of the most widely circulated publications of the period) remain largely unknown to today's reading audiences. H. Cordelia Ray's "Lincoln: Written for the Occasion of the Unveiling of the Freedman's Monument in Memory of Abraham Lincoln" (1876) has met a similar fate. One of the most widely read poems by any woman of her day, but originally published in pamphlet form, this work has largely been forgotten by both scholars and casual readers.

The interests and preferences of today's readers of nineteenth-century texts have influenced not only which writers make their way into the canon, but also which works by even the most prominent writers gain the widest circulation. This is epitomized by the coverage of Frederick Douglass in today's most prominent African American anthologies. Today, as in his lifetime, Douglass is easily the most widely recognized of all black nineteenth-century authors. However widespread his notoriety among today's readers, the range of works associated with him is nevertheless quite narrow. The inclusion of excerpts from his book-length *Narrative of the Life of Frederick Douglass* in virtually all comprehensive U.S. black anthologies published during the last forty-five years overshadows his participation in African American intellectual, political, and aesthetic debates.[6] The *Norton*, the *Riverside,* and the more recent *Wiley-Blackwell Anthology of African American Literature* (2014) each reprint his *Narrative* in its entirety, along with excerpts from "What to the Negro is the Fourth of July," one of his most celebrated abolitionist speeches.[7] (The *Norton* also includes excerpts from Douglass other two popular autobiographies, *My Bondage and My Freedom,* and *Life and Times of Frederick Douglass.*) Though Douglass was an active participant in nineteenth-century African American literary and intellectual culture, the selections in these anthologies portray him not as a writer shaped in part by the aesthetic practices, ideas, and debates that defined the black literary and intellectual communities of which he was a part, but rather as an isolated respondent to the debates around black freedom and equality that took place among activist whites. Few anthologies include Douglass's editorial pieces on the issues and concerns of northern blacks, even though such pieces appeared regularly in each of his three newspapers. The emphasis in the *Norton*, the *Riverside, Wiley-Blackwell* and other collections on his narrative and his abolitionist speeches obscures the degree to which the aesthetic choices and political perspectives evidenced in Douglass's work were shaped by the ongoing discussions of politics, culture, and education taking place within the period's black readership.

The same patterns of preference that obscure Douglass's participation in the intraracial dialogues and debates that took place in black antebellum communities are evident in contemporary anthologies' treatment of other prominent nineteenth-century black writers. Consider, for example, the case of William Wells Brown, whose inclusion in recent African American anthologies is virtually universal. The selections of his work in recent collections like the *Norton*, the *Riverside*, *Wiley-Blackwell*, and *Prentice Hall* are drawn primarily from his antebellum narrative, his abolitionist novel, *Clotel*, or some combination of the two. A frequent correspondent to several African American-owned newspapers as well as William Lloyd Garrison's *Liberator*, his letters to these publications go wholly unaddressed.[8] Though Brown authored at least six additional books, including a three-volume history of the African American people, these works have received little attention from today's readers and scholars. The portrait of the Brown oeuvre offered up in the U.S. black literature canon and those general anthologies through which its interests and priorities are reinforced reflects, quite simply, the way he was understood and appreciated by the period's mainstream reading audience.[9]

The same interaction between historical biases and contemporary interests that has limited the visibility of all but Dunbar's dialect poetry completely obscures the contributions of most of his peers. One such figure is T. Thomas Fortune, whose remarkable *Black and White* (1884) offers a radical analysis of the impact of wealth distribution on U.S. notions of race and power that would seemingly rank it alongside W. E. B. Du Bois's *The Souls of Black Folk*, but who is virtually untreated in the general anthologies of recent decades. A deeply influential editor and activist who worked with equal passion in a variety of genres, from lyric verse to epic poetry to prose fiction to political philosophy and social theory, Fortune was a frequent contributor to African American newspapers, as well as the founder and co-owner (with father Emmanuel Fortune Jr.) of *The New York Freeman* (later renamed *The New York Age*). Widely recognized as the most distinguished and influential journalist of his time, Fortune was considerably less well known to white readers; and, alas, it is his relationship to the late-nineteenth-century white readership that most closely resembles both his relationship to today's African American canon and his presence in those general anthologies that have served to define its parameters.[10]

Fortune represents what Elizabeth McHenry refers to as the "failed" or only "partially achieved" writer, a label she assigns to those African American writers who failed to realize success "in the conventional senses," by gaining access to mainstream (white-owned and white-run) publication venues (McHenry 383). Such writers are not failures in the traditional understanding of the word. Indeed, many such writers, including McHenry's own example of Mary Church Terrell, were widely published and highly regarded within black print culture, and many never sought publication outside of the black literary establishment. Regardless of these considerations, though, it is their "failure" to attract the interest of white, mainstream editors and publishers that corresponds most closely with the nineteenth-century black writer's inclusion in or exclusion from the African American canon.

Elizabeth McHenry calls for a reengagement with the failed and partially achieved writers and texts of the pre–Harlem Renaissance era. McHenry's own example of the circumstances under which Mary Church Terrell became a "failed" writer points to the importance of revisiting her work and the work of her peers. Terrell's uniform rejection by mainstream (white) publishers was, McHenry asserts, consistently linked to her uncompromising and direct calls for racial justice. The following comment, from Harcourt editor J. E. Springarn is, according to McHenry, a characteristic critique of the author's work: "perhaps you are too intent on reforming this world than on creating an imaginary world of your own, after the artist's fashion" (McHenry 384).

That Terrell was widely published in African American periodicals and pamphlets points to the substantial divide between the kinds of race writing that were embraced by African American readers and those works whose tone and content on issues of race were deemed acceptable for the white readership. One of the side-effects of the last several decades of scholarly focus on prose writers who achieved traction in mainstream (majority white) audiences has been the privileging of those works whose resistance relies on an aesthetics of subtlety, characterized by the subversion, revision, and adaptation of the themes, personae, and settings that were common in mainstream depictions of black subjects and settings; but this preference has developed at the expense of those African American writers and writings, genres and techniques, themes and points of view that developed and thrived in the literary production and intellectual exchange that was taking place within black communities.

It is a distinction well represented in this comparison between Charles Chesnutt's "The Goophered Grapevine," the first African American short fiction ever published in the popular mainstream magazine *Atlantic Monthly* (1887), and David Bryant Fulton's "Henry Berry Lowery, the North Carolina

Outlaw: A Tale of the Reconstruction Period," based on the true story of a popular folk hero, and originally published in *The Citizen,* an African American newspaper (year unknown).[11] Chesnutt's tale manipulates key elements of the white-dominated plantation tradition, overtly deploying its settings and character types, even as it subverts its apologist themes of nostalgia for antebellum culture and society. In Chesnutt's piece, plantation life includes none of the sexual subjugation or crude violence that greets readers of the slave narratives, and the enslaved men and women who populate his tale appear more accepting of than aggrieved by their servitude. Chesnutt's tale does, however, disrupt the plantation tradition's characteristic portrayal of its enslaved characters' happy submission to the will of their masters. Instead, it complicates the presumed hierarchy of white power over black lives by introducing the seminal character of Aun' Peggy, a free black woman whose knowledge and skill as a conjurer grant her the power to effect change in the lives of black and white characters alike. Despite the apparent hierarchy of the owners over the enslaved, both constituencies must humbly submit to the will of Aun' Peggy, and Chesnutt depicts both black and white characters attempting to curry her favor through generous offerings of food and other valuable provisions.

Like Chesnutt's "Goophered Grapevine," David Bryant Fulton's "Henry Berry Lowery" is set in the rural South. Fulton's tale, however, openly rejects the period's white supremacist ethos, replacing the black-white binary on which it depends with a complex racial landscape that includes the "octoroon outlaw" Henry Berry Lowery, his white and Mexican American antagonists, and his racially diverse gang of brawlers and thieves (Fulton, "Henry Berry Lowery" 65).[12] In addition, Fulton's text challenges the exalted status of white outlaw heroes like Jesse James by juxtaposing the similarities between both outlaws' exploits and reputations against the significant disparity in their resources. Writing under the pen name "Jack Thorne," the author explains that, "[j]ust as the name of Jesse James sent an involuntary shudder through the souls of those who heard it, although far removed from the scene of his depredations, so did the name of Henry Berry Lowery awe and terrorize in North Carolina" (66). In addition, Fulton emphasizes that Lowery's gang was able to build their fearsome reputation with considerably fewer arms than the better-equipped and all-white James Gang. He notes, "The James boys and their followers were armed with the most improved firearms of that day; with the exception of the carbine carried by Lowery himself, taken from a Mexican who attempted to capture him, the only weapons these men had were knives and double-barreled shotguns" (66). That he prefaces this comparison with a description of the ethnic makeup of Lowery's gang ("Lowery and his intrepid freebooters were all colored men") implies a relationship between race and access to armaments (66).[13] Both Chesnutt's and Fulton's pieces contribute significantly to our understanding of how questions of race, region, culture, and class intersect in the African American nineteenth-century texts. Alas, though, Chesnutt's embrace by mainstream publications like *The Atlantic Monthly* has been rewarded with a firm place in the African American literature canon, while writers like Fulton, whose works found their greatest audience among black readers, have largely been forgotten.

BLACK PRINT CULTURE AND
THE AFRICAN AMERICAN READERSHIP

The selections in *Before Harlem* are based on a revisionist framework that seeks to contextualize the nineteenth-century black text within the literary and aesthetic sensibilities and concerns of the period's African American readership. This anthology views the Chesnutts and Dunbars of the literary world not as more important than, but alongside and in the context of the Fortunes and the Fultons of the day (that is, those writers who were well regarded among black readers, but otherwise largely unknown). *Before Harlem* does not, then, reject recent anthologies' identification as worthy of preservation and transmission those nineteenth-century African American writers who achieved mainstream recognition. Rather, this collection works from an alternative vision of this period, based on revised selection criteria that take into account the recent canon-making efforts of today's scholars and editors but rely even more heavily on the literary, cultural, and political priorities and interests of black nineteenth-century readers, writers, and editors.[14] While *Before Harlem* includes selections by Douglass, Chesnutt, Dunbar, and others whose works were well received by readers and publishers on both sides of the black-white color line, this volume presents these and other writers as they appeared in the African American press. Where the anthology includes excerpts from their most widely read works, those selections are presented alongside those that were published in black-owned and -edited periodicals, by African American–owned book presses, or in pamphlets or other print media aimed at the black reading audience, including self-published, small-press, and locally distributed volumes.

Before Harlem combines the broad coverage of general anthologies like the *Norton* with the greater interest in works published by African American periodicals and publishing houses found in more specialized collections, like Joan Sherman's influential *African American Poetry of the Nineteenth Century* (1992) and Shirley Wilson Logan's *With Pen and Voice: A Critical Anthology of Nineteenth Century African-American Women* (1995). In combining these features and extending them, this collection challenges prevailing conceptions of genre. Because of its emphasis on the ways that nineteenth-century African American writers engaged and addressed their black readership, *Before Harlem* de-centers the book as the primary vehicle for the transmission of U.S. black literature. This anthology's increased attention to the writers whose works were disseminated through the period's African American magazines, papers, and pamphlets is reflected not only in the inclusion of writers who have often been overlooked, but also in its broader representation of several of the forms that dominated periodical literature of the time. These include rarely treated forms like serialized fiction, the correspondent's letter, and the speech.

This revisionist approach to genre also extends to more familiar (and frequently anthologized) literary forms, certain of which are represented in proportions and contexts that depart from the ways that U.S. black literature of this period has previously been presented. The realignment of the criteria by which to select nineteenth-century texts for anthologizing is perhaps most apparent in the treatment of poetry and autobiography, arguably the two defining genres of this historical subfield. Most often encountered as an antebellum, abolitionist phenomenon, the nineteenth-century African American autobiography takes on compelling and unexpected qualities in the period after Reconstruction. Postbellum autobiographies, like William Wells Brown's *My Southern Home, or The South and Its People* (1880) and the self-titled *An Autobiography: The Story of the Lord's Dealings with Mrs. Amanda Smith, the Colored Evangelist* (1893), draw heavily on the structural and thematic framework of antebellum slave narratives. Yet their creation after the end of U.S. chattel slavery combines with their majority-black reading audience to produce in such texts a level of candor and a breadth of perspectives on the experience of enslavement, the role of white southerners, and the relationship between U.S. black writers, recently emancipated blacks, and black Africans that is largely absent from the more familiar abolitionist works.

Like the post-Reconstruction slave narrative, nineteenth-century African American poetry receives only limited coverage in even the most comprehensive U.S. black literature anthologies.[15] One obstacle confronting efforts to increase the visibility of nineteenth-century black poets, from the pre–Civil War era in particular, is the frequent use of pseudonyms, a trend among writers of all ethnicities, throughout this time. The identities of the period's most prolific writers, especially those whose works appear in a number of periodicals or books or about whom biographical sketches were written, are relatively easy to uncover, like that of the poet and essayist J. Anderson Raymond. During the mid-1860s, his work appeared frequently in the pages of the *Christian Recorder* newspaper. In 1864 and 1865, he published essays and poems on phrenology under his full name. His poems on poetry, literary criticism, philosophical and political subjects, however, appeared under his pseudonym, "RAYMOND." Analyzed in the context of his appearances in that periodical as both a contributor and a topic of discussion (the *Recorder* printed at least three notices of his Philadelphia area lectures), the similarities between his signed and pseudonymous work make clear the link between the lecturer, the essayist, and the poet.

Less easily resolved are cases like the poet "Rosa," whose verses appeared in Samuel Cornish and John B. Russwurm's *Freedom's Journal,* the nation's first African American newspaper, during the fall of 1827. After publishing only four poems, in October and November of that year, Rosa vanished from the paper, prompting a response, also in verse, from a reader identified only as "Frere." Writing in the March 21, 1828, issue, Frere pleads for the return of the "Sweet Minstrel" to "take thy harp again / And breathe upon its chords of fire," and to "Breathe Lady, then again the song . . . Its echoes toning sweet and deep" (Frere 1–2, 17, 20). The exchange between Rosa and Frere (if it may be called an exchange, given that Rosa seems to have offered no response) may well be a snapshot of the early black readership's investment in its writers. Frere was an early reader of *Freedom's Journal,* a newspaper whose outreach and marketing efforts were directed primarily at New York's African American community; and Rosa's work is clearly identified by editors as written especially "For the *Freedom's Journal,*" a designation generally applied to contributions from black writers and readers. Scant information exists, though, to confirm the identity of either the poet or her lyrical admirer; and without such information, it is impossible to establish either writer's ethnicity. Nor does either poet locate himself, herself, or his or her speaker as a racialized "I." Most nineteenth-century periodicals, including those produced by and for African Americans, printed not only original pieces created especially for their pages, but also a significant number of previously published works, many culled from the pages of popular English papers and magazines. White abolitionists were also occasional contributors to black periodicals, and without any evidence that might offer a strong indication that either Rosa or Frere was African American, it is both unwise and irresponsible to assign a particular racial category to either poet.

Still, the challenges posed by the pervasive use of pseudonyms cannot fully account for the limited coverage of nineteenth-century poets in most versions of the African American canon. Here, once again, the selections in those general anthologies of U.S. black literature that have come to define most readers' encounters with nineteenth-century texts reflect a preference for those poets who were successful in achieving publication in forms and avenues that attracted a white, mainstream audience. This focus on that handful of African American poets who did attract a mainstream audience—George Moses Horton, Frances E. W. Harper, and James Monroe Whitfield—obscures the work of African American poets like John Willis Menard, Elymas Payson Rogers, and Henrietta Cordelia Ray, who achieved a measure of notoriety during their lifetimes, but primarily among black readers.

TOWARDS A NEW VISION OF THE BLACK NINETEENTH CENTURY

Once those publications in which nineteenth-century black writers addressed their African American readers are taken into account, a distinctly different vision of pre–Harlem Renaissance black writing begins to emerge. The slave narrative still remains the most influential vehicle through which white readers encounter the work of black writers. Poetry, however, is revealed as both the primary genre through which African Americans entered into literature production and the primary genre through which black readers encountered black writers and their work.

To re-present African American literature of the long nineteenth century as a body of work that represents conversations not only across the racial divide (between marginalized blacks and empowered whites) but within black communities themselves is to highlight not only the role of the rural South but of the urban Northeast in fostering black literary and intellectual production. Only in those cities and towns in which African Americans had stable and defined neighborhoods, well-established churches, access to education, and employment opportunities providing greater than subsistence-level incomes do we see literary culture rise and flourish. African American literature of the nineteenth century is largely the product of free black people living and writing in either the cities of the northeastern and mid-Atlantic states or in those black and multiracial communities that formed around educational institutions in Pennsylvania and Ohio. By the 1920s, the literary, intellectual, and artistic activities of African Americans had become centered in the storied neighborhood of Harlem, in New York City. But, before there was Harlem, there were Philadelphia; Washington, D.C.; the communities of Oberlin and Wilberforce, Ohio; the New York communities of Rochester, Weeksville (in Brooklyn), and Seneca Village (in Manhattan); Boston; New Haven and Hartford, Connecticut; and San Francisco. In a period in which the public response to African American literary and intellectual activity ranged from disbelief to violent suppression, these communities and the publications that linked them were safe havens for black artistic expression and intellectual inquiry. These areas were the earliest incubators of African American literary production. The literature that emerged out of these enclaves is as concerned with the impact of racism on urban and suburban black communities in the North as it is with the effects of chattel slavery and its aftermath on black communities in the agricultural South.

The focus of this anthology on the 19th-century African American works that shaped and were shaped by the debates and exchanges that took place among black writers and readers means that this collection places less emphasis on the racial messages that African American literature of the nineteenth century sought to transmit to the white reading audience and greater emphasis on the racial questions and theories that black writers of the period wished to pose to black readers and to each other. The result is a portrait that reveals black 19th century literature as a body of work whose diverse genres, forms, perspectives, and approaches expose unexpected and sometimes troubling complexities and contradictions.

Before Harlem includes, for example, a small number of texts whose overt critiques of African American morality, piety, and intellect contrast dramatically with the noble and virtuous depictions of black characters—especially enslaved black characters—in those antebellum slave narratives with which 21st-century readers are most familiar. The post-Reconstruction writings of William Hannibal Thomas and William Wells Brown express a general contempt for the mass of rural impoverished African Americans that is rarely more than hinted at in the most common texts of the U.S. black canon.[16] In his 1901 volume, *The American Negro*, for example, Thomas describes "the freeman" as having "neither intuitive nor acquired knowledge of such strength and power as would assure his emergence from hereditary thraldom" (Thomas 136). Brown sounds a similar note in *My Southern Home,* published in 1880, when he asserts that "the negro [...] will sing his old plantation melodies and walk about the cotton fields in July and August, when the toughest white man seeks an awning," that "[h]eat is his element," and the black man "fears no malaria in the rice swamps," an observation that seems to affirm the popular belief in the African American's natural disposition towards agrarian labor (246–47).

However unsettling in their affirmation of several of the anti-black stereotypes of the day, these works by Brown and Thomas are simply the most extreme expressions of a general tone of benign and affectionate curiosity mingled with alienation and distrust that was pervasive throughout African American post-Reconstruction writers' depictions of southern black communities of the previously enslaved. The ambivalence of many northern black writers toward their newly emancipated brethren is reflected in the proliferation of dialect writing during the final decades of the century. Although they were the most highly regarded African American dialect writers of their time and in the present day, with large multi-racial, multi-ethnic audiences in each period, Paul Laurence Dunbar and Charles Chesnutt are only two among many black practitioners in this deeply influential and equally controversial literary sub-genre. There were, however, a number of men and women, mostly from Ohio and the northeastern states, whose invocation of dialect as a symbolic and aesthetic device complicates the positionality (relative to the dominant stereotypes applied to African Americans in this period) of both impoverished rural blacks and the educated black elites who sought to depict them.

The adept and audacious dialect poetry of Maggie Pogue Johnson exemplifies this trend. The Virginia-born poet used dialect to great effect in her renderings of proud and socially independent African American women, like the outspoken title figure in "The Old Maid's Soliloquy." Pogue's use of dialect to create a speaker whose rhythmic language (underscored by the poem's four-line ballad stanzas) and heavy reliance on nature- and agriculture-based metaphors ("I sure is jes' as fine / as any Kershaw pumpkin a-hangin' on the vine") recalls post-Reconstruction white writers who relied on the plantation and other agrarian settings to reinforce their characterizations of African American workers as simple-minded and bestial (7–8). At the same time, the "old maid's" overarching message, that she "rader be a single maid" than settle for a less-than-desirable mate, refutes the very plantation-tradition stereotypes that the language and form of the poem would appear to suggest (29). And although her folksy vernacular and agricultural references might seem to affirm popular stereotypes of the black subject as uneducated rustic, the speaker's principled autonomy and fierce self-reliance boldly challenge white dialect writers' stereotyped presentations of the black rural subject as alternately lustful and childlike, vengeful and fearful, savage and subservient.[17] By including African American writers whose engagement with the question of rural black communities is defined as much by apprehension as by solidarity, this anthology complicates the contemporary understanding of nineteenth-century black literature as characterized by an uncomplicated uniformity of perspective and purpose, a notion perpetuated by canonical nineteenth-century black texts' near unanimity in their uplift of the southern black experience as the rallying point for all African Americans.

This volume's emphasis on that body of work created by African American writers for the black readership brings to light key trends in post-Reconstruction depictions not only of southern black language and culture but also in African American portrayals of whiteness and white racism. In his 1894 essay "The White Problem," for example, Harvard-educated writer and activist Theodore Greener challenges the widespread nineteenth-century understanding of the black other as locus of racial conflict in an essay that de-centers whiteness by highlighting, instead, the black writer's (and his black readers') experience of white people and Anglo-centric perspectives as *other*. Post-Reconstruction anti-lynching texts like Ida B. Wells-Barnett's *Southern Horrors: Lynch Law in All Its Phases* (1892), an investigative essay detailing the horrors of lynching and mob rule in the American South (much of which first appeared in *The New York Age*, an African American-owned newspaper), and David Bryant Fulton's *Hanover* (1900), a fictionalized account of the 1898 Wilmington riots, share with antebellum predecessors like *Narrative of the Life of Frederick Douglass* their strategic use of portrayals of violent anti-black racism to undermine the myth of white southern gentility. Unlike the antebellum slave narratives, however, whose larger goal of appealing to the sensibilities of northern white readers restricted the level of open condemnation their authors could express, writers like Fulton and Wells-Barnett were free to cultivate a tone of outrage and horror equal to the anger and grief of their black readers. Each of their texts uses vivid detail and sentimental excess to heighten the contrast between the moral integrity of African American victims of racial terrorism and the coarse brutality of its white perpetrators. In addition, the juxtaposition of the barbarous white mob against their beleaguered African American victims challenges the basis of all forms of discrimination that depend on the contrasting associations of blackness with brute savagery and whiteness with civilized restraint.

Just as the emphasis in post-Reconstruction texts like *Hanover* and *Southern Horrors* on the antiblack violence of the mob highlights the bigotry and hatred among poor, working-class whites, the "tragic mulatto" and "color-line" stories of the period—especially those published in the African American press—examine and expose racism within the white aristocracy.[18] Late-nineteenth-century black writers' depictions of so-called mulattoes, octoroons, and white Negroes—in works like Ruth D. Todd's "The Octoroon's Revenge," Pauline Hopkins's *Hagar's Daughter,* and other sentimental dramas of racial passing—served as vehicles for the examination and critique of customs and morality among the white aristocracy. In "A Response to Elizabeth McHenry," Alice Deck describes how such writers used the theme of "racial passing . . . to appropriate and subvert the established literary conventions associated with the theme in the mainstream press" (Deck 404). Indeed, even as white novelists of the period linked the presumed tragedy of the mixed-race person of African descent to "an intrinsic, genetic character flaw," African American writers, who often set their passing narratives in the homes and communities of the white upper class, were using their portrayals of racism, miscegenation, and miscegenation anxiety among the elite to undercut the persistent myth of white (especially white upper-class) superiority (Deck 404). "Bernice, the Octoroon" by Marie Louise Burgess-Ware illustrates this trend. The main character's discovery of her African American ancestry allows the author to depict white aristocrats at their most contemptible. The cruel rejection of the "cultured octoroon" protagonist by the very same white aristocrats who once had embraced her as family exposes the existence of hatred and hypocrisy within the American elite (610).

THE BLACK AUTHOR IN CONTEXT AND COMMUNITY

This anthology's emphasis on the period's black print culture also challenges the conception of early black literature as a rare and isolated phenomenon. The focus on book-length prose in the African American literature canon and generally throughout the field reinforces the view that African American writing during the whole of the nineteenth-century was an exceptional act undertaken by exceptional blacks under exceptional circumstances. This characterization of the relationship between writing and race in both the antebellum and postbellum years obscures the everyday uses of literature— to memorialize loved ones, to express religious faith, to honor distinguished individuals, to celebrate beloved institutions—and by a much broader cross-section of the period's black citizens than most versions of the African American canon would suggest.

Throughout the long nineteenth century, black writers used both poetry and prose to explore religious beliefs and the theological concerns of the day. The inclusion of religiously themed work in this anthology is a reflection of both the centrality of religion in the everyday lives of nineteenth-century black readers and the interrelatedness of black religious and intellectual life throughout the period. Each of the nation's earliest black colleges was affiliated with one or another Protestant denomination, and many of the most prominent black church leaders and evangelists (like Sutton E. Griggs, Amanda Smith, and Alexander Crummell) were also noted for their creative and scholarly writing. The active participation of African American religious leaders in the literary and intellectual life of the period reflects the intimate relationship between academic and moral (primarily religious) instruction throughout U.S. higher education at this time.[19] The proliferation of religiously-themed writing in African American literature of the pre-Harlem Renaissance era is also a reflection of the integral role of black churches in the world of nineteenth-century black publishing. From the late antebellum period through the early 1900s, the A.M.E. Church dominated the world of black periodicals. Its weekly newspaper, the *Christian Recorder*, was un-rivaled as a forum for African American literature, scientific tracts, political essays, and religious treatises, from its founding in 1852 until the emergence of Walter W. Wallace's *Colored American* magazine, in 1900.[20] In the 1860s alone, the *Christian Recorder* magazine published works by Frances E. W. Harper, John Willis Menard, Solomon G. Brown, J. Anderson Raymond, and Edmonia Goodelle Highgate, among others. The *Christian Recorder* was joined in 1884 by the *A.M.E. Church Review,* and both publications remain in circulation to this day, with the *Christian Recorder* holding the distinction of being the oldest continuously published African American periodical in the United States.

If the expanded inclusion of religiously themed works in this collection highlights the everyday uses to which literary poetry and prose were applied by African American writers, then the inclusion of black women's writings on motherhood and family highlights the political and aesthetic ends to which black poets and authors applied depictions of the black everyday. In poems like Clara Ann Thompson's "A Lullaby" (1908) and Josephine D. Henderson Heard's "A Mother's Love" (1890), nineteenth-century black poets' portrayals of African American women in the roles and settings associated with ideal or "true" womanhood challenged mainstream conceptions of black female subjectivity as located outside of and in opposition to domesticity, modesty, and other traditionally feminine attributes. Poetry and prose depicting nineteenth-century black family life and domestic concerns were for many years excluded from literary historical accounts of pre-Renaissance writing, due in part to their perceived specificity to women's experience and thus (it was extrapolated) their irrelevance to broader scholarly and aesthetic discussions and aims.

Before Harlem features 142 works by sixty-four of those 19th-century African American writers whose prominence and placement in those pamphlets, periodicals, and presses that served the period's black readers rank them as among the most widely known and highly regarded African American poets and prose writers of their time. As such, the assembled texts present an in-depth portrait of the literary, aesthetic, and intellectual landscape of nineteenth-century African America, as revealed in its most innovative and influential works.

These would include: works aimed at the white reading audience, but which generated considerable discussion within and among the black readership (like *Narrative of the Life of Frederick Douglass*, William Wells Brown's *Clotel; or, The President's Daughter*, Charles W. Chesnutt's "The Goophered Grapevine," and William Hannibal Thomas's *The American Negro: What He Was, What He Is, and What He May Become*); popular self-published volumes (like Peter Randolph's *Sketches of Slave Life: Or, Illustrations of the "Peculiar Institution"*); speeches and poems that were published and distributed in pamphlet form (like H. Cordelia Ray's "Lincoln" and the 1808 speeches of Peter Williams and Absalom Jones); writings published by prominent white abolitionists (in periodicals like William Lloyd Garrison's *The Liberator*, in which the two included sketches by Sarah Mapps Douglass initially appeared); and, most significantly, a wide range of those works that were published in African American–owned newspapers and magazines (like *Freedom's Journal, Frederick Douglass' Paper, The Christian Recorder, The Anglo African,* and others). Selections are organized chronologically, based on the publication date of each author's earliest included work. For each author, I have included a capsule biography emphasizing his or her participation in black literary and intellectual community. Biographies also describe, briefly, the context in which the selection or selections first appeared.

From black men's and women's spiritual and domestic verse to antebellum slave narratives and postbellum miscegenation tales, the depth, breadth, and sheer volume of nineteenth-century African American writing only becomes clear through a thorough examination of those writers, genres, and publications that achieved prominence among the period's black readers. Drawing the greater part of its selections from those periodicals, pamphlets, and presses that targeted and served the period's African American readership, *Before Harlem* calls attention to the significant ways in which U.S. black literature of the nineteenth century was shaped by the preferences, interests, and demands of the communities out of which the period's black writers emerged.

As such, these selections bear witness to the presence of African American literary community and exchange throughout the nineteenth century and as many as 115 years before the Harlem Renaissance began. And yet, despite its unique focus, this collection provides only a glimpse of the wealth and variety of African American literature produced during this vital and turbulent period. It is the portrait of an era many of whose writers and texts remain as yet undiscovered. Let this collection serve as an invitation to read more deeply into the bodies of work that are introduced, as a motivation to locate and explore those writers and texts that did not make their way into this collection, and as a challenge to uncover works as yet unknown.

NOTES

1. See Eric Hobsbawn, *The Age of Revolution, 1789–1848* (1962); *The Age of Capital, 1848–1875* (1975); and *The Age of Empire, 1875–1914* (1987).

2. For more on the sequence of events leading up to the First Congress of Colored Women, see Shirley Logan, *We Are Coming: The Persuasive Discourse of Nineteenth-Century Black Women,* 132–33.

3. For a more detailed description of conference activities, see David Boers, *History of American Education: A Primer,* 71–73.

4. Among the recent decades' most notable recovery and authentication efforts are the 1988 release of *The Schomburg Library of Nineteenth Century Black Women Writers,* a multi-volume compendium of writings by African American women writers of the long nineteenth century produced, in collaboration with Oxford University Press, under the editorial leadership of Henry Louis Gates Jr.; the publication of editor and literary

historian Jean Fagan Yellin's annotated and authenticated edition of Harriet Jacobs's pseudonymously published *Incidents in the Life of a Slave Girl,* in 1987; the 1996 launch of the *Documenting the American South (DocSouth)* digital publishing initiative of the University Library at the University of North Carolina–Chapel Hill; and the emergence of digitized collections of nineteenth-century African American newspapers and other periodicals, like the Pennsylvania-based *Accessible Archives* (founded in 1990), and the award-winning *African American Experience in Ohio,* a project of the Ohio Historical Society and the Library of Congress National Digital Library Program.

5. For the purposes of this anthology, the term "African American press" refers to black-owned and black-edited periodicals, black-owned publishing operations, and those white-owned presses and publishers who issued volumes and editions for black readers.

6. The *Norton* also includes excerpts from Douglass's two subsequent memoirs, *My Bondage and My Freedom* (1855) and *The Life and Times of Frederick Douglass* (1881).

7. Douglass delivered this speech on July 5, 1852, at a gathering held to commemorate the anniversary of the signing of the *Declaration of Independence,* in Rochester, New York.

8. The son of a British Canadian itinerant seaman, William Lloyd Garrison founded the abolitionist newspaper, the *Liberator* in 1831. The paper ceased publication in 1865.

9. For more on the popularity of Dunbar's dialect work, see Michael Norton, *The Dialect of Modernism: Race, Language, and Twentieth-Century Literature* (23); Joseph M. Flora, Lucinda Hardwick MacKethan, and Todd W. Taylor, *The Companion to Southern Literature: Themes, Genres, Places, People, Movements, and Motifs* (esp. 207); and Henry Louis Gates Jr. and Evelyn Brooks Higginbotham, *Harlem Renaissance Lives from the African American National Biography* (174–75).

10. See Eugenia Collier and Richard A. Long, *Afro-American Writing: An Anthology of Poetry and Prose* (129); Paul Finkelman and Cary D. Wintz, *Encyclopedia of the Harlem Renaissance* (405); Manning Marable and Leith Mullings, *Let Nobody Turn Us Around: Voices of Resistance, Reform, and Renewal* (143); and Donald A. Ritchie, *American Journalists: Getting the Story* (156).

11. Fulton's retelling of the Lowery legend was republished in 1907 as part of *"Eagle Clippings" by Jack Thorne, Newspaper Correspondent and Story Teller, A Collection of His Writings to Various Newspapers.*

12. Fulton's description of Lowery (also spelled "Lowry" or, more commonly, "Lowrie") as the "octoroon outlaw" refers to his reputed multiethnic heritage. Lowery was believed to be of Native American (Lumbee), European and, possibly, African descent. While historians dispute the specifics of Lowery's ethnicity, there is a general consensus on the diverse composition of his gang, which included white, Native American, and African American gunslingers and thieves. Late nineteenth- and early twentieth-century accounts of Lowery's activities show a clear fascination with his mixed-ethnic heritage, and most include detailed descriptions of his physical appearance. See Mary Norment, *The Lowrie History, as Acted in Part by Henry Berry Lowrie, the Great North Carolina Bandit, with Biographical Sketch of His Associates* (1909); and George Townsend, *The Swamp Outlaws: or, the North Carolina Bandits. Being a Complete History of the Modern Rob Roys and Robin Hoods* (1872).

13. Sources differ on the makeup of Lowery's gang, specifically around the question of whether any of his followers were white. Norment and Townsend, for example, note two white men among his cohort.

14. My interpretation of the literary interests, aesthetics, and sensibilities of nineteenth-century African Americans is based on the editorial choices, expressed accolades, reviews, and reported public reception for specific writers and texts, both as described by contemporary scholars in the field of nineteenth-century African American literature and as evidenced and reported in black nineteenth-century books and periodicals themselves.

15. Out of its twenty-five nineteenth-century writers, *The Norton Anthology of African American Literature* includes only seven poets. Out of the thirty-five nineteenth-century writers included in *The Riverside Anthology,* only four are presented as poets.

16. Brown's postbellum critiques of culture and morality of enslaved black people are foreshadowed in his scathing depiction, in *Clotel; or, the President's Daughter,* of the "pure Negro" Pompey, the slave trader's accomplice and friend. Writes Brown, "'Pomp' [. . .] was of real negro blood, and would often say, when alluding to himself, 'Dis nigger is no countefit; he is de genewine artekil.' Pompey was of low stature, round face, and, like most of his race, had a set of teeth, which for whiteness and beauty could not be surpassed; his eyes large, lips thick, and hair short and woolly. Pompey had been with [the slave trader] Walker so long, and had seen so much of the buying and selling of slaves, that he appeared perfectly indifferent to the heartrending scenes which daily occurred in his presence" (66).

17. For examples of stereotyped representations of African Americans by white, plantation-tradition writers see Thomas Nelson Page, *In Ole Virginia or Marse Chan and Other Stories* (1887); Thomas Dixon, *The Clansman: An Historical Romance of the Ku Klux Klan* (1905); and Caroline Lee Hentz, *The Planter's Northern Bride* (1854).

18. Readers encounter the same association of mob violence with impoverished, working-class, and middle-class whites in antilynching literature of the mid-twentieth century. See William Faulkner, "Dry September"; and Gwendolyn Brooks; "A Bronzeville Mother Loiters in Mississippi. Meanwhile, a Mississippi Mother Burns Bacon."

19. See John R. Thelin, *A History of American Higher Education* (37, 41–73).

20. The black-owned and -edited *Colored American Magazine* provided a nondenominational alternative to the sectarian *Christian Recorder.* Committed to presenting the greatest cultural and intellectual achievements of the race to a national audience, the Boston-based monthly was deeply invested in disseminating evidence of black excellence in the full range of academic and creative pursuits, including the creation of literature. Writes Nancy Glazener, "Few if any of the contributors to the *Colored American Magazine* (1900–1909) also published work in the *Atlantic* group, yet the magazine manifested a commitment to literature commensurate with the *Atlantic's*" (Glazener 8).

PETER WILLIAMS (1786-1840)

Peter Williams Jr. was born in Brunswick, New Jersey, in 1786. His mother was an indentured servant from St. Kitts. His father, Peter Williams Sr., a former slave and a veteran of the Revolutionary War, was an expert cigar maker and tobacconist as well one of the principal founders of the African Methodist Episcopal Zion (A.M.E.Z.) Church, an independent black denomination distinct from the African Methodist Episcopal (A.M.E.) Church. Peter Williams Jr. was educated at New York's African Free School and by private tutors. As the son of a prominent civil rights activist, the younger Williams was exposed to New York City's burgeoning antiracist movement from an early age. By the age of twenty-two he was recognized as a leader of the city's black community; and when, in late 1807, a group of African American organizers gathered to plan a program of events to celebrate the end of the Atlantic slave trade, they selected him to serve as the keynote speaker. On January 1, 1808, the date on which a new federal law banning the importation of Africans for the purposes of enslavement went into effect, Williams delivered "An Oration on the Abolition of the Slave Trade." Presented in New York's African Church, it was the first abolitionist speech in the United States to be delivered publicly by a black person. His address encouraged both racial pride and abolitionist fervor, through its evocative and contrasting portrayals of precolonial Africa as the Edenic ancestral home and the cruelties of the middle passage and slavery as European violations of the African values of family, culture, and community. Williams would go on to play a central role in New York's African American activist, journalistic, and religious institutions. It is unknown why or when he rejected the Methodist religion of his father, but he would come to play an instrumental role in establishing the city's first black Episcopal church. In 1813, Williams petitioned on behalf of the African Catechetical Institution to permit African American Episcopalians to form their own church. In 1819, St. Philip's Episcopal Church became the first black Episcopal church in New York City. In 1820, Williams was ordained as its deacon, and in 1826, he was ordained as its priest. He was only the second African American ordained by the Episcopal Church, and the first black Episcopal priest in New York. In 1827, Williams joined John Russwurm, Samuel Cornish, and Boston Crummell to form *Freedom's Journal,* the nation's earliest known African American newspaper. Williams died of pneumonia in 1840, leaving behind a legacy of activism that would continue in the work of his daughter Amy Matilda Williams Cassey Remond, a prominent abolitionist in her own right and a member of the Philadelphia Female Anti-Slavery Society.

AN ORATION ON THE ABOLITION OF THE SLAVE TRADE; DELIVERED IN THE AFRICAN CHURCH, IN THE CITY OF NEW YORK, JANUARY 1, 1808

Fathers, Brethren, and Fellow Citizens, At this auspicious moment I felicitate you, on the abolition of the Slave Trade.[1] This inhuman branch of commerce, which, for some centuries past, has been carried on to a considerable extent, is, by the singular interposition of Divine Providence, this day extinguished. An event so important, so pregnant with happy consequences, must be extremely consonant to every philanthropic heart.

But to us, Africans and descendants of Africans, this period is deeply interesting. We have felt, sensibly felt, the sad effects of this abominable traffic. It has made, if not ourselves, our forefathers and kinsmen its unhappy victims; and pronounced on them, and their posterity, the sentence of perpetual slavery. But benevolent men, have voluntarily stepped forward, to obviate the consequences of this injustice and barbarity. They have striven, assiduously, to restore our natural rights; to guaranty them from fresh innovations; to furnish us with necessary information; and to stop the source from whence our evils have flowed.

The fruits of these laudable endeavors have long been visible; each moment they appear more conspicuous; and this day has produced an event which shall ever be memorable and glorious in the annals of history. We are now assembled to celebrate this momentous era; to recognize the beneficial influences of humane exertions; and by suitable demonstrations of joy, thanksgiving, and gratitude, to return to our heavenly Father, and to our earthly benefactors, our sincere acknowledgments.

Review, for a moment, my brethren, the history of the Slave Trade, engendered in the foul recesses of the sordid mind, the unnatural monster inflicted gross evils on the human race. Its baneful footsteps are marked with blood; its infectious breath spreads war and desolation; and its train is composed of the complicated miseries, of cruel and unceasing bondage.

Before the enterprising spirit of European genius explored the western coast of Africa, the state of our forefathers was a state of simplicity, innocence, and contentment. Unskilled in the arts of dissimulation, their bosoms were the seats of confidence; and their lips were the organs of truth. Strangers to the refinements of civilized society, they followed with implicit obedience the (simple) dictates of nature. Peculiarly observant of hospitality, they offered a place of refreshment to the weary, and an asylum to the unfortunate. Ardent in their affections, their minds were susceptible of the warmest emotions of love, friendship, and gratitude.

Although unacquainted with the diversified luxuries and amusements of civilized nations, they enjoyed some singular advantages from the bountiful hand of nature; and from their own innocent and amiable manners, which rendered them a happy people. But, alas! this delightful picture has long since vanished; the angel of bliss has deserted their dwelling; and the demon of indescribable misery, has rioted, uncontrolled, on the fair fields of our ancestors.

After Columbus unfolded to civilized man the vast treasures of this western world, the desire of gain, which had chiefly induced the first colonists of America, to cross the waters of the Atlantic, surpassing the bounds of reasonable acquisition, violated the sacred injunctions of the gospel, frustrated the designs of the pious and humane; and enslaving the harmless aborigines, compelled them to drudge in the mines.

The severities of this employment were so insupportable to men who were unaccustomed to fatigue that, according to Robertson's "History of America," upwards of nine hundred thousand, were destroyed in the space of fifteen years, on the island of Hispaniola. A consumption so rapid, must, in a short period, have deprived them of the instruments of labor; had not the same genius, which first produced it, found out another method to obtain them. This was no other than the importation of slaves, from the coast of Africa.

The Genoese made the first regular importation, in the year 1517, by virtue of a patent granted by Charles, of Austria, to a Flemish favorite;[2] since which, this commerce has increased to an astonishing and almost incredible degree.

After the manner of ancient piracy, descents were first made on the African coast; the towns bordering on the ocean were surprised, and a number of the inhabitants carried into slavery.

Alarmed at these depredations, the natives fled to the interior; and there united to secure themselves from the common foe. But the subtle invaders, were not easily deterred from their purpose. Their experience, corroborated by historical testimony, convinced them, that this spirit of unity, would baffle every violent attempt; and that the most powerful method to dissolve it, would be to diffuse in them, the same avaricious disposition which they themselves possessed; and to afford them the means of gratifying it, by ruining each other. Fatal engine: fatal thou hast proved to man in all ages: where the greatest violence has proved ineffectual, their undermining principles have wrought destruction. By the deadly power, the strong Grecian arm, which bid the world defiance, fell nerveless; by thy potent attacks, the solid pillars of Roman grandeur shook to their base; and, Oh! Africans! by this parent of the Slave Trade, this grandsire of misery, the mortal blow was struck, which crushed the peace and happiness of our country. Affairs now assumed a different aspect; the appearances of war were changed into the most amicable pretensions; presents apparently inestimable were made; and all the bewitching and alluring wiles of the seducer, were practised. The harmless African, taught to believe a friendly countenance, the sure token of a corresponding heart, soon disbanded his fears, and evinced a favorable disposition towards his flattering enemies.

Thus the foe, obtaining an intercourse, by a dazzling display of European finery, bewildered their simple understandings, and corrupted their morals. Mutual agreements were then made; the Europeans were to supply the Africans, with those gaudy trifles which so strongly affected them; and the Africans in return were to grant the Europeans, their prisoners of war, and convicts, as slaves. These stipulations, naturally tending to delude the mind, answered the twofold purpose of enlarging their criminal code, and of exciting incessant war: at the same time, that it furnished a specious pretext, for the prosecution of this inhuman traffic. Bad as this may appear, had it prescribed the bounds of injustice, millions of unhappy victims might have still been spared. But, extending widely beyond measure, and without control, large additions of slaves were made by kidnapping, and the most unpalliated seizures.

Trace the past scenes of Africa, and you will manifestly perceive, these flagrant violations of human rights. The prince who once delighted in the happiness of his people; who felt himself bound by a sacred contract to defend their persons and property; was turned into their tyrant and scourge; he, who once strove to preserve peace, and good understanding with the different nations; who never unsheathed his sword but in the cause of justice, at the signal of a slave ship, assembled his warriors, and rushed furiously upon his unsuspecting friends. What a scene does that town now present, which a few moments past was the abode of tranquility. At the approach of the foe, alarm and confusion pervade every part; horror and dismay are depicted on every countenance; the aged chief, starting from his couch, calls forth his men to repulse the hostile invader: all ages obey the summons; feeble youth and decrepit age join the standard; while the foe, to effect his purpose, fires the town.

Now, with unimaginable terror the battle commences: hear now the shrieks of the women; the cries of the children; the shouts of the warriors; and the groans of the dying. See with what desperation the inhabitants fight in defense of their darling joys. But, alas! Overpowered by a superior foe, their force is broken; their ablest warriors fall; and the wretched remnant are taken captives.

Where are now those pleasant dwellings, where peace and harmony reigned incessant? where those beautiful fields, whose smiling crops, and enchanting verdure, enlivened the heart of every beholder? Alas! those tenements are now enveloped in destructive flames: those fair fields are now bedewed with blood and covered with mangled carcasses. Where are now those sounds of mirth and gladness, which loudly rang throughout the village? where those darling youth, those venerable aged, who mutually animated the festive throng? Alas! those exhilarating peals, are now changed into the dismal groans of inconceivable distress: the survivors of those happy people, are now carried into cruel captivity. Ah! driven from their native soil, they cast their languishing eyes behind, and with aching hearts, bid adieu, to every prospect of joy and comfort.

A spectacle so truly distressing, is sufficient to blow into a blaze, the most latent spark of humanity: but, the adamantine heart of avarice, dead to every sensation of pity, regards not the voice of the sufferers, but hastily drives them to market for sale.

Oh Africa, Africa! to what horrid inhumanities have thy shores been witness; thy shores, which were once the garden of the world, the seat of almost paradisiacal joys, have been transformed into regions of woe; thy sons, who were once the happiest of mortals, are reduced to slavery, and bound in weighty shackles, now fill the trader's ship. But, though defeated in the contest for liberty, their magnanimous souls scorn the gross indignity, and choose death in preference to slavery. Painful; Ah! painful, must be that existence, which the rational mind can deliberately doom to self-destruction. Thus, the poor Africans, robbed of every joy, while they see not the most transient, glimmering, ray of hope, to cheer their saddened hearts, sink into the abyss of consummate misery. Their lives, embittered by reflection, anticipation, and present sorrows, they feel burthensome; and death, (whose dreary mansions appall the stoutest hearts) they view as their only shelter.

You, my brethren, beloved Africans, who had passed the days of infancy when you left your country; you best can tell the aggravated sufferings, of our unfortunate race: your memories can bring to view these scenes of bitter grief. What, my brethren, when dragged from your native land, on board the slave ship; what was the anguish which you saw, which you felt? what the pain, what the dreadful forebodings, which filled your throbbing bosoms?

But you, my brethren, descendants of African forefathers, I call upon you to view a scene of unfathomable distress. Let your imagination carry you back to former days. Behold a vessel, bearing our forefathers and brethren, from the place of their nativity, to a distant and inhospitable clime: behold their dejected countenances, their streaming eyes, their fettered limbs: hear them, with piercing cries, and pitiful moans, deploring their wretched fate. After their arrival in port, see them separated without regard to the ties of blood or friendship: husband from wife; parent from child; brother from sister; friend from friend. See the parting tear rolling down their fallen cheeks; hear the parting sigh, die on their quivering lips.

But, let us no longer pursue a theme of boundless affliction. An enchanting sound now demands your attention. Hail! Hail! glorious day, whose resplendent rising disperseth the clouds, which have hovered with destruction over the land of Africa; and illumines it by the most brilliant rays of future prosperity. Rejoice, Oh! Africans! No longer shall tyranny, war, and injustice, with irresistible sway, desolate your native country; no longer shall torrents of human blood deluge its delightful plains; no longer shall it witness your countrymen, wielding among each other the instruments of death; nor the insidious kidnapper, darting from his midnight haunt, on the feeble and unprotected; no longer shall its shores resound, with the awful howlings of infatuated warriors, the deathlike groans of vanquished innocents, nor the clanking fetters of wo-doomed captives. Rejoice, Oh, ye descendants of Africans! No longer shall the United States of America, nor the extensive colonies of Great Britain, admit the degrading commerce, of the human species: no longer shall they swell the tide of African misery, by the importation of slaves. Rejoice, my brethren, that the channels are obstructed through which slavery, and its direful concomitants, have been entailed on the African race. But let incessant strains of gratitude be mingled with your expressions of joy. Through the infinite mercy of the great Jehovah, this day announces the abolition of the Slave-Trade. Let, therefore, the heart that is warmed by the smallest drop of African blood, glow in grateful transports, and cause the lofty arches of the sky to reverberate eternal praise to his boundless goodness.

Oh, God! we thank thee, that thou didst condescend to listen to the cries of Africa's wretched sons; and that thou didst interfere in their behalf. At thy call humanity sprang forth and espoused the cause of the oppressed: one hand she employed in drawing from their vitals the deadly arrows of injustice; and the other holding a shield, to defend them from fresh assaults: and at that illustrious moment, when the sons of 76 pronounced these United States free and independent; when the spirit of patriotism erected a temple sacred to liberty; when the inspired voice of Americans first uttered those noble sentiments, "we hold these truths to be self-evident, that all men are created equal; that they are endowed by their Creator with certain unalienable rights; among which are life, liberty, and the pursuit of happiness;" and when the bleeding African, lifting his fetters, exclaimed, "am I not a man and a brother;" then, with redoubled efforts, the angel of humanity strove to restore to the African race, the inherent rights of man.

To the instruments of divine goodness, those benevolent men who voluntarily obeyed the dictates of humanity, we owe much. Surrounded with innumerable difficulties, their undaunted spirits, dared to oppose a powerful host of interested men. Heedless to the voice of fame, their independent souls dared to oppose the strong gales of popular prejudice. Actuated by principles of genuine philanthropy, they dared to despise the emoluments of ill gotten wealth, and to sacrifice much of their temporal interests at the shrine of benevolence.

As an American, I glory in informing you, that Columbia[3] boasts the first men, who distinguished themselves eminently, in the vindication of our rights, and the improvement of our state.

Conscious that slavery was unfavorable to the benign influences of christianity, the pious Woolman loudly declaimed against it; and, although destitute of fortune, he resolved to spare neither time nor pains to check its progress. With this view he travelled over several parts of North American on foot, and exhorted his brethren, of the denomination of Friends, to abjure the iniquitous custom. These, convinced by the cogency of his arguments, denied the privileges of their society to the slave-holder, and zealously engaged in destroying the aggravated evil. Thus, through the beneficial labors of this pattern of piety and brotherly kindness, commenced a work which has since been promoted, by the humane of every denomination. His memory ought therefore to be deeply engraved on the tablets of our hearts; and ought ever to inspire us with the most ardent esteem.

Nor less to be prized are the useful exertions of Anthony Benezet.[4] This inestimable person, sensible of the equality of mankind, rose superior to the illiberal opinions of the age; and, disallowing an inferiority in the African genius, established the first school to cultivate our understandings, and to better our condition.

Thus, by enlightening the mind, and implanting the seeds of virtue, he banished, in a degree, the mists of prejudice; and laid the foundations of our future happiness. Let, therefore, a due sense of his meritorious actions, ever create in us, a deep reverence of his beloved name. Justice to the occasion, as well as his merits, forbid me to pass in silence over the name of the honorable William Wilberforce.[5] Possessing talents capable of adorning the greatest subjects, his comprehensive mind found none more worthy his constant attention, than the abolition of the Slave-Trade. For this he soared to the zenith of his towering eloquence, and for this he struggled with perpetual ardour. Thus, anxious in defense of our rights, he pledged himself never to desert the cause; and, by his repeated and strenuous exertions, he finally obtained the desirable end. His extensive services have, therefore, entitled him to a large share of our affections, and to a lasting tribute of our unfeigned thanks.

But think not, my brethren, that I pretend to enumerate the persons who have proved our strenuous advocates, or that I have portrayed the merits of those I have mentioned: No, I have given but a few specimens of a countless number,[6] and no more than the rude outlines of the beneficence of these. Perhaps there never existed a human institution, which has displayed more intrinsic merit, than the societies for the abolition of slavery.

Reared on the pure basis of philanthropy, they extend to different quarters of the globe; and comprise a considerable number of humane and respectable men. These, greatly impressed with the importance of the work, entered into it with such disinterestedness, engagedness, and prudence, as does honor to their wisdom and virtue. To effect the purposes of these societies no legal means were left untried, which afforded the smallest prospects of success. Books were disseminated, and discourses delivered, wherein every argument was employed which the penetrating mind could adduce, from religion, justice or reason, to prove the turpitude of slavery, and numerous instances related, calculated to awaken sentiments of compassion. To further their charitable intentions, applications were constantly made, to different bodies of legislature, and every concession improved to our best possible advantage. Taught by preceding occurrences, that the waves of oppression are ever ready to overwhelm the defenceless, they became the vigilant guardians of all our reinstated joys. Sensible that the inexperienced mind is greatly exposed to the allurements of vice, they cautioned us, by the most salutary precepts, and virtuous examples, against its fatal encroachments; and the better to establish us, in the path of rectitude they instituted schools to instruct us in the knowledge of letters, and the principles of virtue.

By these and similar methods, with divine assistance, they assailed the dark dungeon of slavery; shattered its rugged wall, and enlarging thousands of the captives, bestowed on them the blessings, of civil society. Yes, my brethren, through their efficiency, numbers of us now enjoy the invaluable gem of liberty; numbers have been secured from a relapse into bondage; and numbers have attained a useful education.

I need not, my brethren, take a further view of our present circumstances, to convince you of the providential benefits which we have derived from our patrons; for if you take a retrospect of the past situation of Africans, and descendants of Africans, in this and other countries, to your observation our advancements must be obvious. From these considerations, added to the happy event which we now celebrate, let ever entertain the profoundest veneration for our munificent benefactors, and return to them from the altars of our hearts, the fragrant incense of incessant gratitude. But let not, my brethren, our demonstrations of gratitude, be confined to the mere expression of our lips.

The active part which the friends of humanity have taken to ameliorate our sufferings, has rendered them, in a measure, the pledges of our integrity. You must be well aware, that notwithstanding their endeavors, they have yet remaining, from interest and prejudice, a number of opposers. These, carefully watching for every opportunity to injure the cause, will not fail to augment the smallest defects in our lives and conversation; and reproach our benefactors with them, as the fruits of their actions.

Let us, therefore, by a steady and upright deportment, by a strict obedience and respect to the laws of the land, form an invulnerable bulwark against the shafts of malice. Thus, evincing to the world that our garments are unpolluted by the stains of ingratitude, we shall reap increasing advantages from the favors conferred; the spirits of our departed ancestors shall smile with complacency on the change of our state; and posterity shall exult in the pleasing remembrance.

May the time speedily commence, when Ethiopia shall stretch forth her hands; when the sun of liberty shall beam resplendent on the whole African race; and its genial influences promote the luxuriant growth of knowledge and virtue.

1808

NOTES

1. In 1807, both the United States and Great Britain passed laws banning the importation of black people for the purposes of enslavement. The U.S. ban went into effect on January 1, 1808. The British ban went into effect two months later, on March 1.

2. In 1517, a Genoese company established the first *asiento de negros,* a contract with the Spanish crown to supply Africans for enslavement in Spanish colonies in the Americas.

3. The literary and historical name for the United States, derived from the name of Christopher Columbus, an early European voyager to the Americas.

4. A French-born abolitionist and founder, in 1775, of the Society for the Relief of Free Negroes Unlawfully Held in Bondage, the world's first known antislavery organization.

5. A deeply religious member of the English Parliament, remembered for his regular sponsorship of antislavery legislation throughout his eighteen years in the House of Commons (1784–1812).

6. Among the many eminent defenders of African rights, the reader cannot fail to recognize the Rev. Mr. Thomas Clarkson, whose extensive capacities and unremitting zeal, have classed him with the most conspicuous and useful advocates of the cause. In his essays in defence of injured humanity, he displays a power of argument, which silences every objector. Thus, while Mr. Wilberforce arrested the attention of the national councils on this important subject, the excellent Mr. Clarkson strongly seconded his endeavors, by addressing the community at large; and penetrating the flimsy garb in which sophistry had veiled the evils of slavery, he exploded all its fallacious arguments, exposed this monster of deformity in all its nakedness, and confirmed the principle, that it is not our only duty, but our temporal and eternal interest to "do good unto all men" [Williams' note].

ABSALOM JONES (1746-1818)

Absalom Jones was born into slavery in Sussex, Delaware. As a boy, he taught himself to read using the books he was able to purchase with pocket change. When he was sixteen, he, his six siblings, and his mother were each sold to different owners, at which time he was moved to Philadelphia to work in his new master's store. There he was able to attend evening classes at a school for African American students. In 1770 Jones married, and by 1776 he had saved enough money, from working odd jobs in the evening, to buy his wife's freedom. By 1784, he had saved enough money to purchase his own freedom, as well. After serving as a lay preacher at St. George's Methodist Episcopal Church, Jones helped to establish an "African Church" for Black Philadelphia worshippers. He was joined in this effort by fellow African American lay preacher Richard Allen. In time, Allen would go on to found the A.M.E. Church. Jones remained a part of the Episcopal Church and was welcomed into the priesthood in 1804, the first African American to be ordained as a priest in that denomination. On January 1, 1808, Jones delivered his most famous address, *A Thanksgiving Sermon,* at St. Thomas Episcopal Church in Philadelphia. In it, he gives thanks for the recent abolition of the Atlantic slave trade, and he calls on the members of his congregation to commemorate this event in an annual day of prayer and celebration.

A THANKSGIVING SERMON

At a meeting of the Vestry of St. Thomas's, or the African Episcopal Church,[1] held on Wednesday, February 11, 1808.

Resolved, that the thanks of the Vestry be presented to the Rev. Absalom Jones, for his sermon preached in the said Church, on the first day of January last; and that he be requested to furnish a copy of the same to be printed.

Extract from the Minutes,

WILLIAM COLEMAN, Secretary.

A THANKSGIVING SERMON.

EXODUS, iii. 7–8

And the Lord said, I have surely seen the affliction of my people which are in Egypt, and have heard their cry by reason of their task-masters; for I know their sorrows; and I am come down to deliver them out of the hand of the Egyptians.

These words, my brethren, contain a short account of some of the circumstances which preceded the deliverance of the children of Israel from their captivity and bondage in Egypt.

They mention, in the first place, their *affliction*. This consisted in their privation of liberty: they were slaves to the kings of Egypt, in common with their other subjects; and they were slaves to their fellow slaves. They were compelled to work in the open air, in one of the hottest climates in the world; and, probably, without a covering from the burning rays of the sun. Their work was of a laborious kind: it consisted of making bricks, and travelling, perhaps to a great distance, for the straw, or stubble, that was a component part of them. Their work was dealt out to them in tasks, and performed under the eye of vigilant and rigorous masters, who constantly upbraided them with idleness. The least deficiency, in the product of their labour, was punished by beating. Nor was this all. Their food was of the cheapest kind, and contained but little nourishment: it consisted only of leeks and onions, which grew almost spontaneously in the land of Egypt. Painful and distressing as these sufferings were, they constituted the smallest part of their misery. While the fields resounded with their cries in the day, their huts and hamlets were vocal at night, with their lamentations over their sons; who were dragged from the arms of their mothers, and put to death by drowning, in order to prevent such an increase in their population, as to endanger the safety of the state by an insurrection. In this condition, thus degraded and oppressed, they passed nearly four hundred years. Ah! who can conceive of the measure of their sufferings, during that time? What tongue, or pen, can compute the number of their sorrows? To them no morning or evening sun ever disclosed a single charm: to them, the beauties of spring, and the plenty of autumn had no attractions: even domestick endearments were scarcely known to them: all was misery; all was grief; all was despair.

Our text mentions, in the second place, that, in this situation, they were not forgotten by the God of their fathers, and the Father of the human race.

Though, for wise reasons, he delayed to appear in their behalf for several hundred years; yet he was not indifferent to their sufferings. Our text tells us, that he saw their affliction, and heard their cry: his eye and his ear were constantly open to their complaint: every tear they shed, was preserved, and every groan they uttered, was recorded; in order to testify, at a future day, against the authors of their oppressions. But our text goes further: it describes the Judge of the world to be so much moved, with what he saw and what he heard, that he rises from his throne—not to issue a command to the armies of angels that surrounded him to fly to the relief of his suffering children—but to come down from heaven, in his own person, in order to deliver them out of the hands of the Egyptians. Glory to God for this precious record of his power and goodness: let all the nations of the earth praise him. *Clouds and darkness are round about him,* but *righteousness and judgment are the habitation of his throne. O sing unto the Lord a new song, for he hath done marvelous things: his right hand and his holy arm hath gotten him the victory. He hath remembered his mercy and truth toward the house of Israel, and all the ends of the earth shall see the salvation of God.*

The history of the world shows us, that the deliverance of the children of Israel from their bondage, is not the only instance, in which it has pleased God to appear in behalf of oppressed and distressed nations, as the deliverer of the innocent, and of those who call upon his name. He is as unchangeable in his nature and character, as he is in his wisdom and power. The great and blessed event, which we have this day met to celebrate, is a striking proof, that the God of heaven and earth *is the same, yesterday, and to-day, and for ever.* Yes, my brethren, the nations from which most of us have descended, and the country in which some of us were born, have been visited by the tender mercy of the Common Father of the human race. He has seen the affliction of our countrymen, with an eye of pity. He has seen the wicked arts, by which wars have been fomented among the different tribes of the Africans, in order to procure captives, for the purpose of selling them for slaves. He has seen ships fitted out from different ports in Europe and America, and freighted with trinkets to be exchanged for the bodies and souls of men. He has seen the anguish which has taken place, when parents have been torn from their children, and children from their parents, and conveyed, with their hands and feet bound in fetters, on board of ships prepared to receive them. He has seen them thrust in crowds into the holds of those ships, where many of them have perished from the want of air. He has seen such of them as have escaped from that noxious place of confinement, leap into the ocean, with a faint hope of swimming back to their native shore, or a determination to seek early retreat from their impending misery, in a watery grave. He has seen them exposed for sale, like horses and cattle, upon the wharves; or, like bales of goods, in warehouses of West India[2] and American sea ports. He has seen the pangs of separation between members of the same family. He has seen them driven into the sugar; the rice, and the tobacco fields, and compelled to work—in spite of the habits of ease which they derived from the natural fertility of their own country in the open air, beneath a burning sun, with scarcely as much clothing upon them as modesty required. He has seen them faint beneath the pressure of their labours. He has seen them return to their smoky huts in the evening, with nothing to satisfy their hunger but a scanty allowance of roots; and these, cultivated for themselves, on that day only, which God ordained as a day of rest for man and beast. He has seen the neglect with which their masters have treated their immortal souls; not only in withholding religious instruction from them, but, in some instances, depriving them of access to the means of obtaining it. He has seen all the different modes of torture, by means of the whip, the screw, the pincers, and the red hot iron, which have been exercised upon their bodies, by inhuman overseers: overseers, did I say? Yes: but not by these only. Our God has seen masters and mistresses, educated in fashionable life, sometimes take the instruments of torture into their own hands, and, deaf to the cries and shrieks of their agonizing slaves, exceed even their overseers in cruelty. Inhuman wretches! though You have been deaf to their cries and shrieks, they have been heard in Heaven. The ears of Jehovah have been constantly open to them: He has heard the prayers that have ascended from the hearts of his people; and he has, as in the case of his ancient and chosen people the Jews, *come down to deliver* our suffering country-men from the hands of their oppressors. He *came down* into the United States, when they declared, in the constitution which they framed in 1788, that the trade in our African fellow-men should cease in the year 1808: He *came down* into the British Parliament, when they passed a law to put an end to the same iniquitous trade in May, 1807: He *came down* into the Congress of the United States, the last winter, when they passed a similar law, the operation of which commences on this happy day. Dear land of our ancestors! thou shalt no more be stained with the blood of thy children, shed by British and American hands: the ocean shall no more afford a refuge to their bodies, from impending slavery: nor shall the shores of the British

West India islands, and of the United States, any more witness the anguish of families, parted for ever by a publick sale. For this signal interposition of the God of mercies, in behalf of our brethren, it becomes us this day to offer up our united thanks. Let the song of angels, which was first heard in the air at the birth of our Saviour, be heard this day in our assembly: *Glory to God in the highest,* for these first fruits of *peace upon earth, and good will to man:* O! Let us *give thanks unto the Lord:* let us *call upon his name,* and *make known his deeds among the people.* Let us *sing psalms unto him and talk of all his wondrous works.*

Having enumerated the mercies of God to our nation, it becomes us to ask, what shall we render unto the Lord for them? Sacrifices and burnt offerings are no longer pleasing to him: the pomp of public worship, and the ceremonies of a festive day, will find no acceptance with him, unless they are accompanied with actions that correspond with them. The duties which are inculcated upon us, by the event we are now celebrating, divide themselves into five heads.

In the first place, Let not our expressions of gratitude to God for his late goodness and mercy to our countrymen, be confined to this day, nor to this house: let us carry grateful hearts with us to our places of abode, and to our daily occupations; and let praise and thanksgivings ascend daily to the throne of grace, in our families, and in our closets, for what God has done for our African brethren. Let us not forget to praise him for his mercies to such of our colour as are inhabitants of this country; particularly, for disposing the hearts of the rulers of many of the states to pass laws for the abolition of slavery; for the number and zeal of the friends he has raised up to plead our cause; and for the privileges, we enjoy, of worshiping God, agreeably to our consciences, in churches of our own. This comely building, erected chiefly by the generosity of our friends, is a monument of God's goodness to us, and calls for our gratitude with all the other blessings that have been mentioned.

Secondly, Let us unite, with our thanksgiving, prayer to Almighty God, for the completion of his begun goodness to our brethren in Africa. Let us beseech him to extend to all the nations in Europe, the same humane and just spirit towards them, which he has imparted to the British and American nations. Let us, further, implore the influence of his divine and holy Spirit, to dispose the hearts of our legislatures to pass laws, to ameliorate the condition of our brethren who are still in bondage; also, to dispose their masters to treat them with kindness and humanity; and, above all things, to favour them with the means of acquiring such parts of human knowledge, as will enable them to read the holy scriptures, and understand the doctrines of the Christian religion, whereby they may become, even while they are the slaves of men, the freemen of the Lord.

Thirdly, Let us conduct ourselves in such a manner as to furnish no cause of regret to the deliverers of our nation, for their kindness to us. Let us constantly *remember the rock whence we were hewn, and the pit whence we were digged. Pride was not made for man,*[3] in any situation; and, still less, for persons who have recently emerged from bondage. The Jews, after they entered the promised land, were commanded, when they offered sacrifices to the Lord, never to forget their humble origin; and hence, part of the worship that accompanied their sacrifices consisted in acknowledging, *that a Syrian, ready to perish, was their father:*[4] in like manner, it becomes us, publickly and privately, to acknowledge, that an African slave, ready to perish, was our father or our grandfather. Let our conduct be regulated by the precepts of the gospel; let us be sober minded, humble, peaceable, temperate in our meats and drinks, frugal in our apparel and in the furniture of our houses, industrious in our occupations, just in all our dealings, and ever ready to honour all men. Let us teach our children the rudiments of the English language, in order to enable them to acquire a knowledge of useful trades; and, above all things, let us instruct them in the principles of the gospel of Jesus Christ, whereby they may become *wise unto salvation.* It has always been a mystery, why the impartial Father of the human race should have permitted the transportation of so many millions of our fellow creatures to this country, to endure all the miseries of slavery. Perhaps his design was, that a knowledge of the gospel might be acquired by some of their descendants, in order that they might become qualified to be the messengers of it, to the land of their fathers. Let this thought animate us, when we are teaching our children to love and adore the name of our Redeemer. Who knows but that a Joseph may rise up among them, who shall be the instrument of feeding the African nations with the bread of life, and of saving them, not from earthly bondage, but from the more galling yoke of sin and Satan.

Fourthly, Let us be grateful to our benefactors, who, by enlightening the minds of the rulers of the earth, by means of their publications and remonstrances against the trade in our countrymen, have produced the great event we are this day celebrating. Abolition societies and individuals have equal claims to our gratitude. It would be difficult to mention the names of any of our benefactors, without offending many whom we do not know. Some of them are gone to heaven, to receive the reward of their labours of love towards us; and the kindness and benevolence of the survivors, we hope, are recorded in the book of life, to be mentioned with honour when our Lord shall come to reward his faithful servants before an assembled world.

Fifthly, and lastly, Let the first of January, the day of the abolition of the slave trade in our country, be set apart in every year, as a day of publick thanksgiving for that mercy. Let the history of the sufferings of our brethren, and of their deliverance, descend by this means to our children, to the remotest generations; and when they shall ask, in time to come, saying, What mean the lessons, the psalms, the prayers and the praises in the worship of this day? Let us answer them, by saying, the Lord, on the day of which this is the anniversary, abolished the trade which dragged your fathers from their native country, and sold them as bondmen in the United States of America.

Oh thou God of all the nations upon the earth! We thank thee, that thou art *no respecter of persons,* and that thou *hast made of one blood all nations of men.* [5] *We* thank thee, that thou halt appeared, in the fullness of time, in behalf of the nation from which most of the worshipping people, now before thee, are descended. We thank thee, that the sun of righteousness has at last shed his morning beams upon them. *Rend thy heavens,* O Lord, and *come down* upon the earth; and grant that *the mountains,* which now obstruct the perfect day of thy goodness and mercy towards them, may *flow down at thy presence.* Send thy gospel, we beseech thee, among them. May the nations, which now *sit in darkness,* behold and rejoice in its *light.* May *Ethiopia soon stretch out her hands unto thee,* and lay hold of the gracious promise of thy everlasting covenant. Destroy, we beseech thee, all the false religions which now prevail among them; and grant, that they may soon *cast* their *idols, to the moles and the bats* of the wilderness. O, hasten that glorious time, when the knowledge of the gospel of Jesus Christ, shall cover the *earth, as the waters cover the sea;* when *the wolf shall dwell with the lamb, and the leopard shall lie down with the kid, and the calf and the young lion and the fatling together, and a little child shall lead them;* and, *when, instead of the thorn, shall come up the fir tree, and, instead of the brier, shall come up the myrtle tree: and it shall be to the Lord for a name and for an everlasting sign that shall not be cut off.* [6] We pray, O God, for all our friends and benefactors, in Great Britain, as well as in the United States: reward them, we beseech thee, with blessings upon earth, and prepare them to enjoy the fruits of their kindness to us, in thy everlasting kingdom in heaven: and dispose us, who are assembled in thy presence, to be always thankful for thy mercies, and to act as becomes a people who owe so much to thy goodness. We implore thy blessing, O God, upon the President, and all who are in authority in the United States. Direct them by thy wisdom, in all their deliberations, and O save thy people from the calamities of war. Give peace in our day, we beseech thee, O *thou God of peace!* and grant, that this highly favoured country may continue to afford a safe and peaceful retreat from the calamities of war and slavery, for ages yet to come. We implore all these blessings and mercies, only in the name of thy beloved Son, Jesus Christ, our Lord. And now, O Lord, we desire, with angels and arch-angels, and all the company of heaven, ever more to praise thee, saying, *Holy, holy, holy, Lord God Almighty: the whole earth is full of thy glory.*

Amen.

1808

NOTES

1. The nation's first Episcopal Church for Black worshippers, located in Philadelphia, founded in 1792.

2. The islands of the West Indies.

3. A reference to Isaiah 51:1, which calls upon the ancient Israelites to maintain a sense of humility and to resist the temptations of self-pride.

4. A reference to Deuteronomy 26:5, which describes Jacob, the biblical patriarch, as Aramean or coming from what is now northwest Syria.

5. Acts 10:34 and Acts 17:26, biblical passages widely embraced by antebellum African Americans for their apparent affirmation of the equality of all peoples, in the eyes of God.

6. Refers to Isaiah 11:9, Isaiah 11:6, and Isaiah 55:13.

JAMES FORTEN (1766-1842)

James Forten was born in Philadelphia to Thomas and Margaret Forten. He attended the Friends' African School until the age of eight years, when a change in his family's financial circumstances forced him to abandon his studies. This marked the end of Forten's formal education. During the Revolutionary War, Forten served as a powder boy on the Royal Louis, a privateer vessel from which he was captured by British soldiers. He was sent to the prison ship *Jersey*, anchored off the coast of Long Island. There he spent two weeks as a prisoner of war. Upon returning to the United States, Forten was apprenticed to a prominent Philadelphia sailmaker whose business he eventually purchased. In the early 1800s, Forten invented a device to help control the large and bulky sails used on merchant ships, an innovation he was able to develop into a lucrative manufacturing business. He built a substantial fortune and eventually became one of the wealthiest men in Philadelphia. A committed abolitionist, Forten used his wealth to support antiracist organizations and initiatives, including the *Freedom's Journal* newspaper, for which he provided start-up funds. Not only was Forten a patron of this early publication, but he was also a contributor. His "Letters from a Man of Colour, on a Late Bill before the Senate of Pennsylvania," originally published in pamphlet form in 1813, was reprinted in *Freedom's Journal* in five consecutive issues between February 22 and March 21 of 1828. Forten's title alludes to an effort on the part of key Pennsylvania legislators to limit the migration of black people into the state and to allocate funding for the removal of free blacks to Liberia. Writing under the pseudonym "A Man of Colour," Forten underscores the irony of Philadelphia as the setting for this attack on black liberty and self-determination. The following text is based on the 1828 reprint of Forten's *"Letters"* in the *Freedom's Journal* newspaper.

LETTERS FROM A MAN OF COLOUR, ON A LATE BILL BEFORE THE SENATE OF PENNSYLVANIA

"LETTER I"

O Liberty! thou power supremely bright,
Profuse of bliss and pregnant with delight,
Perpetual pleasures in thy presence reign,
And smiling Plenty leads thy wanton train

—Addison[1]

We hold this truth to be self-evident, that GOD created all men equal, and is one of the most prominent features in the Declaration of Independence, and in that glorious fabric of collected wisdom, our noble Constitution. This idea embraces the Indian and the European, the Savage and the Saint, the Peruvian and the Laplander, the white Man and the African, and whatever measures are adopted subversive of this inestimable privilege, are in direct violation of the letter and spirit of our Constitution, and become subject to the animadversion of all, particularly those who are deeply interested in the measure.

These thoughts were suggested by the promulgation of a late bill, before the Senate of Pennsylvania, to prevent the emigration of people of colour into this state.[2] It was not passed into a law at this session and must in consequence lay over until the next, before when we sincerely hope, the white men, whom we should look upon as our protectors, will have become convinced of the inhumanity and impolicy of such a measure, and forbear to deprive us of those inestimable treasures, Liberty and Independence. This is almost the only state in the Union wherein the African have justly boasted of rational liberty and the protection of the laws, and shall it now be said they have been deprived of that liberty, and publicly exposed for sale to the highest bidder? Shall colonial inhumanity that has marked many of us with shameful stripes, become the practice of the people of Pennsylvania, while Mercy stands weeping at the miserable spectacle? People of Pennsylvania, descendants of the immortal Penn, doom us not to the unhappy fate of thousands of our countrymen in the Southern States and the West Indies; despise the traffic in blood, and the blessing of the African will forever be around you. Many of us are men of property, for the security of which, we have hitherto looked to the laws of our blessed state, but should this become a law, our property is jeopardized, since the same power which can expose to sale an unfortunate fellow creature, can wrest from him those estates which years of honest industry have accumulated. Where shall the poor African look for protection, should the people of Pennsylvania consent to oppress him? We grant there are a number of worthless men belonging to our colour, but there are laws of sufficient rigour for their punishment, if properly and duly enforced. We wish not to screen the guilty do not permit the innocent to suffer. If there are worthless men, there also men of merit among the African race, who are useful members of Society. The truth of this let their benevolent institutions and the numbers clothed and fed by them witness. Punish the guilty man of colour to the utmost limit of the laws, but sell him not to slavery! If he is in danger of becoming a public charge prevent him! If he is too indolent to labour for his own subsistence, compel him to do so; but sell him not slavery. By selling him you do not make him better, but commit a wrong, without benefiting the object of it or society at large. Many of our ancestors were brought here more than one hundred years ago; many of our fathers, many of ourselves, have fought and bled for the independence of our country. Do not then expose us to sale. Let not the spirit of the father behold the son robbed of that liberty which he died to establish, but let the motto of our legislators, be—"The Law knows no distinction."

These are only a few desultory remarks on the subject and intend to succeed this effervescence of feeling, by a series of essays, tending to prove the impolicy and unconstitutionality of the law in question.

For the present, I leave the public to the consideration of the above observations, in which I hope they will see so much truth, that they will never consent to sell to slavery

A Man of Colour.

1813

NOTES

1. From "Extract from The Letter from Italy: The Blessings of Liberty" by English poet Joseph Addison (1672–1719).

2. The bill would prohibit the migration of free black men and women into the state of Pennsylvania.

SAMUEL CORNISH (1795-1858) AND JOHN RUSSWURM (1799-1851)

Samuel Cornish was born to free black parents in Sussex County, Delaware. A founder and one of two coeditors of *Freedom's Journal,* he was educated at the Free African School in Philadelphia before entering ministerial training with the Philadelphia Presbytery. Cornish was the first African American to complete the highly structured training and examination process to become a Presbyterian minister. He was ordained in 1822. He soon moved to New York, where he would establish the city's first Black Presbyterian Church. A staunch advocate for the abolition of slavery in the South as well as for the full enfranchisement of free blacks in the North, Cornish was among a group of African Americans who met at the home of Boston Crummell, a local community organizer and the father of the noted scholar and minister Alexander Crummell. It was there, in the home of the senior Crummell, that the assembled activists resolved to establish an independent black newspaper to serve as the voice for New York City's African American population. The first issue of *Freedom's Journal* appeared on March 16, 1827, with Cornish as senior editor and John B. Russwurm as the junior editor. Cornish left the paper after only six months, however, reportedly over a rift with Russwurm over the issue of colonization. Cornish opposed the emigration of free black people to the U.S.-controlled African colony of Liberia, while Russwurm, who hailed from a family with considerably greater privilege than that of his senior editor, was an apparent supporter of the scheme. Cornish would return to *Freedom's Journal* briefly in 1829, after Russwurm announced his appointment as superintendent of Liberia's school system. Cornish briefly revived the paper, renamed *The Rights of All,* releasing only a handful of issues before shutting down all operations, in 1830.

Freedom's Journal coeditor John Brown Russwurm was born in Port Antonia, Jamaica, to an enslaved black woman and a white American merchant. Russwurm's father, for whom the editor was named, considered his son a free citizen. In 1807, he enrolled his son at a boarding school in Montreal, Canada. A defining moment in young Russwurm's education took place when his father moved to Portland, Maine, and married Susan Blanchard, a white woman. She quickly embraced her black stepson as a full member of the family and, in 1819, four years after her husband's death, she oversaw young Russwurm's enrollment at Maine's Hebron Academy. There he completed his secondary education. By 1824, she had remarried, and she and her new husband helped facilitate Russwurm's admission to Bowdoin College. When he graduated in 1826, he became only the second African American known to have earned a bachelor's degree from a U.S. college or university. After Bowdoin, Russwurm relocated to New York City, where he quickly became involved in antiracist and abolitionist activism. Within a year of graduating from college, he was appointed the junior editor of *Freedom's Journal.* His involvement with the paper ceased in 1829, after Russwurm announced his intentions to migrate to Liberia. There he served as the superintendent of schools as well as the editor of the *Liberia Herald,* one of the colony's most widely read periodicals. In 1836, he became the governor of Liberia's Maryland Settlement. He would remain in that post until his death, in 1851.

The following editorial statement, published on the front page of *Freedom's Journal*'s inaugural issue, conceives of African American writing not only as intellectual and artistic expression, but also as the medium through which New York's black community might begin to set the terms on which black interests, experiences, and conditions are debated and understood.

TO OUR PATRONS

In presenting our first number to our Patrons, we feel all the diffidence of persons entering upon a new and untried line of business. But a moment's reflection upon the noble objects, which we have in view by the publication of this Journal; the expediency of its appearance at this time, when so many schemes are in action concerning our people—encourage us to come boldly before an enlightened publick. For we believe, that a paper devoted to the dissemination of useful knowledge among our brethren, and to their moral and religious improvement, must meet with the cordial approbation of every friend to humanity.

The peculiarities of this Journal, render it important that we should advertise to the world the motives by which we are actuated, and the objects which we contemplate.

We wish to plead our own cause. Too long have others spoken for us. Too long has the publick been deceived by misrepresentations, in things which concern us dearly, though in the estimation of some mere trifles; for though there are many in society who exercise towards us benevolent feelings; still (with sorrow we confess it) there are others who make it their business to enlarge upon the least trifle, which tends to the discredit of any person of colour; and pronounce anathemas and denounce our whole body for the misconduct of this guilty one. We are aware that there are many instances of vice among us, but we avow that it is because no one has taught its subjects to be virtuous; many instances of poverty, because no sufficient efforts accommodated to minds contracted by slavery, and deprived of early education have been made, to teach them how to husband their hard earnings, and to secure to themselves comforts.

Education being an object of the highest importance to the welfare of society, we shall endeavour to present just and adequate views of it, and to urge upon our brethren the necessity and expediency of training their children, whole young, to habits of industry, and thus forming them for becoming useful members of society. It is surely time that we should awake from this lethargy of years, and make a concentrated effort for the education of our youth. We form a spoke in the human wheel, and it is necessary that we should understand our pendence on the different parts, and theirs on us, in order to perform our part with propriety.

Though not desirous of dictating, we shall feel it our incumbent duty to dwell occasionally upon the general principles and rules of economy. The world has grown too enlightened, to estimate any man's character by his personal appearance. Though all men acknowledge the excellency of Franklin's maxims, yet comparatively few practise upon them. We may deplore when it is too late, the neglect of these self-evident truths, but it avails little to mourn. Ours will be the task of admonishing our brethren on these points.

The civil rights of a people being of the greatest value, it shall ever be our duty to vindicate our brethren, when oppressed, and to lay the case before the publick. We shall also urge upon our brethren, (who are qualified by the laws of the different states, the expediency of using their elective franchise; and of making an independent use of the same. We wish them not to become the tools of party.

And as much time is frequently lost, and wrong principles instilled, by the perusal of works of trivial importance, we shall consider it a part of our duty to recommend to our young readers, such authors as will not only enlarge their stock of useful knowledge, but such as will also serve to stimulate them to higher attainments in science.

We trust also, that through the columns of the FREEDOM'S JOURNAL, many practical pieces, having for their bases, the improvement of our brethren, will be presented to them, from the pens of many of our respected friends, who have kindly promised their assistance.

It is our earnest wish to make our Journal a medium of intercourse between our brethren in the different states of this great confederacy: that through its columns an expression of our sentiments, on many interesting subjects which concern us, may be offered to the publick: that plans which apparently are beneficial may be candidly discussed and properly weighed; if worthy, receive our cordial approbation; if not, our marked disapprobation.

Useful knowledge of every kind, and every thing that relates to Africa, shall find a ready admission into our columns; and as that vast continent becomes daily more known, we trust that many things will come to light, proving that the natives of it are neither so ignorant nor stupid as they have generally been supposed to be.

And while these important subjects shall occupy the columns of the FREEDOM'S JOURNAL, we would not be unmindful of our brethren who are still in the iron fetters of bondage. They are our kindred by all the ties of nature; and though but little can be effected by us, still let our sympathies be poured forth, and our prayers in their behalf, ascend to Him who is able to succour them.

From the press and the pulpit we have suffered much by being incorrectly represented. Men, whom we equally love and admire have not hesitated to represent us disadvantageously, without becoming personally acquainted with the true state of their honor discerning between virtue and vice among us. The virtuous part of our people feel themselves sorely aggrieved under the existing state of things—they are not appreciated.

Our vices and our degradation are ever arrayed against us, but our virtues are passed by unnoticed. And what is still more lamentable, our friends, to whom we concede all the principles of humanity and religion, from these very causes seem to have fallen into the current of popular feeling and are imperceptibly floating on the stream—actually living in the practice of prejudice, while they abjure it in theory, and feel it not in their hearts. Is it not very desirable that such should know more of our actual condition, and of our efforts and feelings, that in forming or advocating plans for our amelioration, they may do it more understandingly? In the spirit of candor and humility we intend by a simple representation of facts to lay our case before the publick, with a view to arrest the progress of prejudice, and to shield ourselves against the consequent evils. We wish to conciliate all and to irritate none, yet we must be firm and unwavering in our principles, and persevering in our efforts.

If ignorance, poverty and degradation have hitherto been our unhappy lot; has the Eternal decree gone forth, that our race alone, are to remain in this state, while knowledge and civilization are shedding their enlivening rays over the rest of the human family? The recent travels of Denham and Clapperton[1] in the interior of Africa, and the interesting narrative which they have published; the establishment of the republic of Hayti after years of sanguinary warfare; its subsequent progress in all the arts of civilization; and the advancement of liberal ideas in South America, where despotism has given place to free governments, and where many of our brethren now fill important civil and military stations, prove the contrary.

The interesting fact that there are FIVE HUNDRED THOUSAND[2] free persons of colour, one half of whom might peruse, and the whole be benefited by the publication of the Journal; that no publication, as yet, has been devoted exclusively to their improvement—that many selections from approved standard authors, which are within the reach of few, may occasionally be made—and more important still, that this large body of our citizens have no public channel—all serve to prove the real necessity, at present, for the appearance of the FREEDOM'S JOURNAL.

It shall ever be our desire to conduct the editorial department of our paper as to give offence to none of our patrons; as nothing is farther from us than to make it the advocate of any partial views, either in politics or religion. What few days we can number, have been devoted to the improvement of our brethren; and it is our earnest wish that the remainder may be spent in the same delightful service.

In conclusion, whatever concerns us as a people, will ever find a ready admission into the FREEDOM'S JOURNAL, interwoven with all the principal news of the day.

And while every thing in our power shall be performed to support the character of our Journal, we would respectfully invite our numerous friends to assist by their communications, and our coloured brethren to strengthen our hands by their subscriptions, as our labour is one of common cause, and worthy of their consideration and support. And we do most earnestly solicit the latter, that if at any time we should seem to be zealous, or too pointed in the inculcation of any important lesson, they will remember, that they are equally interested in the cause in which we are engaged, and attribute our zeal to the peculiarities of our situation, and our earnest engagedness in their well-being.

THE EDITORS

1827

NOTES

1. English adventurers who traveled extensively in West and Central Africa during the 1820s.

2. The 1830 census recorded a total U.S. population of 12,866,020, including a black population of 2,328,842, of whom 319,599 were free.

AMOS BEMAN (1812-1874)

Amos Gerry Beman was born in Colchester, Connecticut, to free black parents Fanny Condol Beman and the noted minister and abolitionist Jehiel Beman. One of at least seven children, he received his early education in Middletown, Connecticut, schools. Beman's options for post-secondary education were very limited, and he began his college studies on an informal basis, meeting with young abolitionist and Wesleyan University student Samuel Dole for tutorial sessions in Dole's dormitory room. This arrangement was short-lived due to threats and harassment directed at both Beman and his tutor. In time he would enroll at Beriah Green's Oneida Institute in Whitesboro, New York, one of only two U.S. baccalaureate institutions open to African Americans during this period. At Oneida, he was one of four black entering students, along with Alexander Crummell, Thomas Sidney, and William G. Allen. Beman left Oneida after one year, most likely due to an absence of funds. He served briefly as a schoolteacher in Hartford, Connecticut, before successfully completing the licensing exam to become a Congregational minster. In 1838, Beman was appointed full-time minister of the Temple Congregational Church in New Haven. He was the first African American in the city's history to occupy that post. He would serve there for nineteen years, during which time he traveled throughout the United States, speaking on abolitionism, voting rights, and other issues of interest to African Americans. Between 1856 and 1857, Beman's family was stricken with typhoid. He would lose his wife, his oldest son, and his oldest daughter to the disease. In 1858 he resigned his post at Temple Congregational Church and accepted a new position as pastor of the Abyssinian Congregational Church in Portland, Maine. Though his second marriage—to Eliza Kennedy, a white New Haven resident—sparked controversy in the African American communities of both Maine and Connecticut, Beman remained a popular speaker on abolitionism and civil rights. In the following poem, published in *The Christian Recorder* under the pseudonym "Africus," Beman writes from the perspective of the enslaved black men and women of the American South.

Adieu, to my dear native shore,
To toss on the boisterous wave;
To enjoy my kindred no more,
But to weep—the tears of a SLAVE!

By the sons of freemen I'm borne,
To a land of the free and the brave;
From my wife and children I'm torn,
To weep—the sad tears of a SLAVE!

When, I think on mother and friends,
And the joy their countenance gave;
Ah! how my sad bosom it rends,
While weeping—the tears of a SLAVE!

Ah! now, I must labour for gold,
To pamper the pride of a knave;
Ah! now, I am shackled and sold
To weep—the sad tears of a SLAVE!

Keen sorrow so presses my heart,
That often I sigh for my grave;
While feeling the lash'—cruel smart!
And weeping—the tears of a SLAVE!

Ye sons, of the free and the wise,
Your tender compassion I crave;
Alas! can your bosoms despise?
The pitiful tears of a SLAVE!

Can a land of Christians so pure!
Let demons of slavery rave!
Can the angel of mercy endure,
The pitiless—tears of a SLAVE!

Just Heaven, to thee I appeal;
Hast thou not the power to save?
In mercy thy power reveal,
And dry—the sad tears of a SLAVE.

1828

AMOS BEMAN   29

S. (?-?)

Scholars have offered a number of hypotheses about the true identity of "S.," the pseudonym used by the author of the pioneering short story "Theresa— A Haytien Tale." For example, Dickson D. Bruce proposes journalist and physician James McCune Smith as a possible author (though he would have been a teenager at the time), while Frances Smith Foster suggests the U.S.-born Haitian émigré Prince Saunders as the likely scribe. Serialized in *Freedom's Journal* between January 18 and February 15 of 1828, "Theresa" is very likely the first piece of short fiction ever published by an African American author. Though it is, as yet, impossible to identify with any certainty the story's author, contextual evidence from *Freedom's Journal* strongly indicates that the writer is African American. The story of a black family's flight from French troops sent to crush the rebellion in Haiti, "Theresa—A Haytien Tale" offers a title character whose physical stamina, emotional fortitude, and unimpeachable morality combine to create an idealized portrait of black womanhood that emphasizes feminine humility and heroic resilience, attributes largely absent from white writers' depictions of female protagonists of African descent.

THERESA, — A HAYTIEN TALE

During the long and bloody contest, in St. Domingo,[1] between the white man, who flourished the child of sensuality, rioting on the miseries of his slaves; had the sons of Africa, who, provoked to madness, and armed themselves against French barbarity; Madame Paulina was left a widow, unhappy—unprotected, and exposed to all the horrors of the revolution. Not without much unhappiness, she saw that if she would save her life from the inhumanity of her country's enemy, she must depart from the endeared village of her innocent childhood; still dear to her, though now it was become a theatre of many tragic scenes. The once verdant plains, round its environs had been crimsoned with the blood of innocence, and the nature of the times afforded no security to the oppressed natives of Saint Nicholas.[2]

Famine which had usurped the place of plenty and happiness, with her associate security, were banished from the humble dwellings of the injured Haytiens.

After much unpleasant reflections on her pitiable situation, Madame Paulina resolved to address a letter, soliciting the advice of her brother, then at Cape Marié,[3] and at the head of a party of his patriot brethren, who like him, disdained slavery, and were determined to live free men, or expire in their attempts for liberty and independence. But reason had scarce approved this suggestion of her mind, when suddenly she heard a simultaneous volley of musketry, and the appalling roaring of heavy artillery rumbling along the mountain's ridge, like terrifying thunders to this distant warfare, the lapse of fifteen minutes brought a cessation, which announced, that on either side, many that were, had ceased to be. Silence having ensued, there was a stillness in the air. All at Saint Nicholas, desirous to know the issue of the combat, remained in doubtful anxiety.

Each one's heart was the abode of fear and doubt, while the dense smoke, escaping the despot's fury, and evading the implacable resentment of those armed in the justice of their cause, was seen to overtop the dusky hills, winding its way upwards in sulphureous columns, as if, to supplicate at the Eternal's Throne, and plead the cause of the injured.

The French in this combat with the Revolutionists, suffered much, both from the extreme sultriness of the day, and the courage of those with whom they contended; disappointed and harassed by the Islanders; they thought it a principle of policy, to resort to acts of cruelty; and to intimidate them, resolved, that none of them should be spared; but that the sword should annihilate, or compel them to submit to their wonted degradations; and St. Nicholas was the unfortunate village, first to be devoted to the resentful rage of the cruel enemy. All the natives were doomed to suffer; the mother and the infant that reposed on her bosom, fell by the same sword, while groans of the sick served only as the guides which discovered them to the inhumanity of the inexorable, at whose hands they met a miserable death.

The sun was fast receding to the west, as if ashamed of man's transactions, boasting itself in the dark mantle of twilight, when Gen. Leclerc[4] fired the few dwellings, then remaining in the village. Misery was now garbed in her most terrifying robes, and terror possessed itself the heart of all, except the French, in whose hands were placed the weapons of destruction. The intelligence of the defeat of the army recently stationed at Cape Marie, reached the ears of the unhappy Paulina, and with horror she heard that her beloved brother in his attempt to regain St. Nicholas, breathed out his valuable life in the cause of freedom, and for his country. But it was now no time to indulge in grief—Safety was the object of the wretched villagers.

To effect an escape from the horrors of this ominous night, was difficult in the extreme; for the passes leading out into the country were all occupied by the enemy's troops, who were not only vigilant, but relentless and cruel. Madame Paulina apprehended her own danger, but her greatest solicitude was for the safety of her daughters, who in the morning of life, were expanding, like the foliages of the rose into elegance and beauty. She had kept them long concealed from the knowledge of the enemy, whose will she knew was their law, and whose law was injustice—the mother's wretchedness, and the daughter's shame and ruin. In happier days, when peace blessed her native island, she had seen a small hut, during a summer's excursion, in an unfrequented spot, in the delightful valley of Vega Real, and on the eastern bank of the beautiful Yuma; and now she resolved if possible, to retreat thither with both her daughters.

Necessity being the source of human inventions, was now ready to commune with her mind on subjects of moment, and to give birth to the events of its decision—and in the midst of the general uproar in which the village now was—The shrieks of the defenceless, the horrible clashing of arms, and the expiring groans of the aged, Paulina hurried herself in the execution of her plans for escaping.

With a feigned passport and letter, she ingeniously contrived to pass out of the village conducting her daughters, like the pious Aeneas, through all the horrors, in which St. Nicholas was now involved.

But though protected by the mantle of night, Madame was hastening on her way to safety and quiet; she frequently would turn her eyes bathed with the dew of sorrow, and heave her farewell sigh towards her ill-fated village; and like Lot when departing out of Sodom, Paulina prayed for mercy for the enemies of her country, and the destroyers of her peace. She and her daughters, driven by cruel ambition, from their peaceful abodes were wretched. Their souls were occupied by fearful doubts and anxiety. Every whisper of the winds among the leaves of the plantain and orange trees caused her daughters to apprehend the approach of danger, and she to heave the anxious sigh.

The green lizard crossed not the road in the way to its hole, at the noise of the fugitives feet, but they beheld through the shade of the night a body of the enemy; the distant glare of the firefly, was a light which pointed to the enemies camps; while the bat beating the ... in its nocturnal ranges, often was the false messenger of danger to the fair adventurers. Every tree kissed by the zephyrs, that ruffled its leaves, was an army approaching, and in the trunk of every decored mahogany, was seen a Frenchman in ambush—not less alarming to the fugitives, were the ripe fruit that frequently fell to the earth. Then having turned into a by-path, Paulina felt herself more secure; and with a soul oppressed with mingled grief and joy, she with maternal affection embraced her daughters, and observed to them, that however just may be the cause which induces us to practice duplicity, or the laudable object which gives birth to hypocrisy. Truth alone can make us happy, and prevent the Internal Judge of the human mind, filling us with fearful apprehensions, and painting to our imaginations the result which would attend detection.

Morning had just began to peep forth, and the golden rays of the returning sun were seen to burnish the tops of the majestic Cibao mountains, when the bewildered adventurers were suddenly startled by the shrill blast of a bugle; their surprise was not less than their wretchedness, when at no great distance, they beheld approaching them a detachment of the enemy's cavalry. At this unexpected crisis Madame Paulina overcome with fearful apprehensions, trembled lest she should be wanting in the discharge of her difficult undertaking. But it was now too late; she must either act well her part or be reconducted by the foe to St. Nicholas, and there, after witnessing the destruction of those for whose happiness, she was more concerned, than for her own, receive a cruel and ignominious death.

The party of horsemen being now very near, she gave some necessary instructions to her daughters, and conducted them onward with no little confidence in her success. The lieutenant, by whom the French were commanded, observing her attired in the uniform of a French officer, took her for what she so well affected to be—(a captain of the French army) he made to her the order of the day, and enquired the time she left St. Nicholas, and whether conducting the two prisoners, (for Paulina had the presence of mind to disguise her daughters as such) she replied, and taking forth her letter, she handed it to the lieutenant. Succeeding thus far admirably, our adventuress was led to make some enquiries relative to the welfare of the French troops, stationed west of St. Nicholas, and having collected much valuable information, they parted, and Madame Paulina favoured by a ready address, and with much fortitude, escaped death—conducting the dear objects of her tender solicitude far, from the ill-fated village of their infancy.

Being informed by the lieutenant, that at the distance of a few miles, there were encamped a company of the French, she thought it judicious to avoid all public roads, and having turned into a thick grove of the Pimento trees, she proposed to her daughters to rest in this spot until darkness again should unfold her mantle.

In this grove of quiet security, the troubled souls of the fugitives ceased partially to be oppressed with fear—the milky juice of the cocoanut allayed their thirst and moistened their parched lips, and the delicious orange, and luxurious mango, in spontaneous abundance, yielded a support to their nearly exhausted natures.

Madame Paulina and her daughters were now seated under the shade of a majestic spreading Guava. The day was fast declining, and though the heat of July was intensely oppressive; in this secluded spot, the air was rendered fragrant with the variety of aromatic shrubs, that grew spontaneously in this grove of peace. The hummingbird skipping capriciously from blossom to blossom, displayed its magnificent plumage, and for a while diverted the minds of the unhappy fugitives from grief and from ominous forebodings; wearied and fatigued by a journey which was not less tiresome than hazardous, their much exhausted natures were greatly refreshed by the cool breeze which gave to their whole bodies a calm sensation, in which their souls soon participated and Madame and her eldest daughter were now lost in the arms of sleep, the kind restorer of vigour to the minds and bodies of men. All around was now still, save the western woodpecker was heard at times to peck the hollow trunk of some decayed tree, or the distant roaring of heavy cannon, which announced that all creative beings were born to enjoy peace, but man who, stimulated by ambition, is more cruel than the beasts of the forest, which soil he ever renders fertile with the blood of his victims. But Mademoiselle Theresa, the youngest of the three adventurers, greeted not sleep. The vigour of her body was indeed much exhausted, but the emotions of her mind were more active than ever; she saw with the mind's eye the great services which might be rendered to her country; she brought to her imagination the once delightful fields of her native Hayti, now dy'd with the blood of her countrymen in their righteous struggle for liberty and for independence.

Not less did she contemplate the once flourishing plantations ruined and Santa Domingo once the granary of the West Indies, reduced to famine, now the island of misery, and the abode of wretchedness.

It was but the last night, that she witnessed the most terrifying scenes of her life—when the shrieks of her dying friends made her apprehend justly what her own fate must be, should she fail to effect an escape from the village of her happiest days. Theresa thought of the brave St. Clair; she imagined she saw her beloved uncle weltering in his blood, and the barbarous French fixing his venerable head on a pole, and it exposed on a cross road, as the head of a rebel. She shuddered at this thought; her soul was subdued, and the fount of grief issued from her eyes in copious streams, bathing her febrile cheeks with the dews of sorrow. "Why," said she, "O, my God! hast thou suffered thy creatures to be thus afflicted in all thy spacious earth? Are not we too thy children? And didst thou not cover us with this sable exterior, by which our race is distinguished, and for which they are contemned and ever been cruelly persecuted! O, my God—my God!—be propitious to the cause of justice—Be near to the Haytiens in their righteous struggle, to obtain those rights which thou hast graciously bestowed on all thy children. Raise up some few of those, who have been long degraded—give to them dominion, and enable them to govern a state of their own—so that the proud and cruel may know that thou art alike the Father of the native of the burning desert, and of the more temperate, region."

It was in the presence of Theresa that the conversation between M. L'Motelle and her heroic mother took place. Madame Paulina, on her part leaving nothing undone, which might serve to accomplish the object for which she had been induced to practice duplicity; M. L'Motelle regarded her for what she really appeared to be; and unhesitatingly spoke of matters concerning the nature of the times; of the military and local situations of the French troops: their condition and strength were topics of interest; and Theresa learned that the distance to the camp of the brave Toussaint, L'Ouverture,[5] was a single league from the place where he communicated the intelligence. Seeming to be inattentive, she pensively bent her eyes towards the earth, listening the while as he unconsciously developed many military schemes, which were about being executed, and if successful, would, in all probability, terminate in the destruction of the Revolutionists, and, in the final success of the French power in this island. These were invaluable discoveries, and could they be made known in due time to those against whose rights, their injustice was intended, it would not fail to give success to Haytien independence, disappoint the arch-enemy, and aid the cause of humanity. But, alas! important as they were to the cause of freedom, by whom shall they be carried?

Who shall reveal them to the Revolutionists? No one interested was near, and they were in the possession of none friendly to the cause of justice, except the three defenceless ones. Theresa herself must be the bearer, or survive only to witness them executed agreeably to the desires of the enemy. In what manner must she act? The salvation of her oppressed country to her was an object of no little concern; but she also owed a duty to that mother, whose tender solicitude for her happiness, could not be surpassed by any parent, and a sister too, whom she tenderly loved, and whose attachment to her was undivided. Her absence from the grove, she was confidently assured, would be to them their greatest source of affliction; it would probably terminate the already much exhausted life of her dear mother, and complete the measure of Amanda's wretchedness. Her own inexperience in the manner, should she conduct in an affair so important and hazardous, was an obstacle which in connection with her sense of duty, and care for her mother's happiness, would deter her from embarking in it. She paused; then, as if aroused by some internal agent, exclaimed, "Oh Hayti!—be independent, and let Theresa be the unworthy sacrifice offered to that God, who shall raise his mighty arm in defence of thy injured children. She drew from her bosom a pencil and wrote on a piece of bark of the Gourd tree, telling her mother and Amanda, whither she was gone—her errand; begged that, they would not be unhappy on account of her absence; that they would remain at their place of peace and quiet, until she should return to them with an escort, who should conduct them to a safer retreat, and commit them to the protection of friends. This scroll, Theresa pinned on her mother's coat, while she and Amanda were yet indulging in repose, and like a heroine of the age of chivalry, she forsook the grove of Pimento and hastened on her way to the camp of L'Ouverture. She had scarce reached the third part of her journey, when her mother, dreaming that one of her daughters had been borne off by an officer of the enemy, awoke from sleep and, missing Theresa, believed her dream prophetic. It was now that the keenest anguish filled her soul. Paulina wished not to live. Life to a mother thus sorely afflicted, is misery—she would go in search of the dear object of all her affliction, but where, she knew not. Keen is the grief of a mother, whose child has been forced from her. She is extremely wretched, and her affliction then, cannot be less severe, than it was when in the anguish and sorrow of her soul, the dear object of her tenderest solicitude was introduced into the world, to take its station among the Probationers for eternity. Amanda was now awakened by the unhappy and pitiful grief of her bewildered mother. Hastily she enquired for her sister; Paulina in a burst of grief and wild despair, told her, she had been borne off while they slept; with half articulated accents, she related her ominous dream, and the fact was now realized in her absence from the grove. An icy chillness pervaded her whole nature—a dark mist covered her eyes—all the objects by which she was surrounded seemed to recede—her senses were bewildered, and Amanda, unobserved by her mother, swooned and fell to the earth. But soon recovering, she beheld the piece of Gourd bark pinned to the skirt of her mother's coat—she hastened to unpin—it was the hand writing of Theresa—they read it with avidity—joyful in the happy discovery, the mother and the daughter embraced each other. From neither, words found utterance. Silence was perched upon their tongues, while the tears of mingled joy and sorrow poured from their eyes; the troubles of their souls were greatly subsided, but happiness could not be restored, until the success of Theresa be ascertained, and she again be encircled in their arms.

It was uncertain whether she could, in safety reach the camp of the Revolutionists; the roads were at all times travelled by reconnoitering parties of the French; and what would be the fate of the heroic Theresa, if taken by any of them! How cruel would be her usage, particularly, if her intentions and the circumstances, which gave them birth be known. Death inevitable would deprive the world of one so fair, virtuous, and so noble.

Such were the thoughts of the mother and sister of the noble adventuress. But while they were thus grieving, Theresa, favoured by fortune, had safely arrived at the military quarters of the great Toussaint: had communicated to the chieftain the object of her visit to his camp, and was receiving all the distinctions due her exalted virtue, and which her dauntless resolution so justly merited.

The sun was now fast receding behind the lofty Cibao, whose rugged summits in the morning, appeared burnished by its resplendent rays, and darkness was out-stretching her spacious mantle. The orange and citron groves, and all the rich enameled luxuriance of torrid luxuries, now began to wear a somber aspect, while the chattering Paroquet[6] ceased to imitate man, and disturb the sweets of solitude, with prating garrulity, had retired to her roost on the sturdy logwood. Now it was, that Theresa, under a strong military escort, left the general's camp of hospitality, retracing her steps towards the grove of Pimento, where, at her departure, she left her dear mother and Amanda, enjoying calm repose; seated in a close carriage, her thoughts reverted to the deplorable state of her country; with a prophetic eye she saw the destruction of the French, and their final expulsion from her native island. She entreated the Creator, that he would bless the means, which through her agency, he had been pleased to put in the possession of her too long oppressed country-men, and that all might be made useful to the cause of freedom. But turning her thoughts toward her mother and sister, Theresa was conscious that her absence from the grove could not fail to have given them extreme sorrow and unhappiness; her gentle nature recoiled at the recollection, and she gave way to a flood of tears. But recollecting again the important services she had rendered her aggrieved country and to the Haytien people—the objects which prompted her to disobedience, which induced her to overstep the bounds of modesty, and expose to immediate dangers her life and sex. She felt that her conduct was exculpated, and self-reproach was lost in the consciousness of her laudable efforts to save St. Domingo. Her noble soul re-animated, recovered its wonted calm, as the ocean its quiet motion when the gentle breeze, and the returned sunshine, succeed a tempestuous sky and boisterous winds.

Fated to experience trials, she was now to be made more wretched than ever. St. Lewis was now near the forward progressing company of his brethren in arms. He had been dispatched to the Pimento grove, to acquaint Madame Paulina and Amanda of the approach of their dear Theresa. But, alas! by whom, or how was the doleful news to be reported to the heroine? Her mother and sister were not to be found at the place where she had left them: and who shall keep the shocking intelligence from her! Already she saw him approaching; he was now near. She observed the gloomy melancholy which settled on his brow, that plainly foretold all were not well. She inquired into the result of his journey to the grove, and as an earthquake rends the bosom of the earth, so the intelligence of her gentle soul.

"Oh! Theresa!—Theresa!" said she in bitter grief, "thou art the murderer of a mother and a loving sister! Where! where shall I hide me from the dis-pleasure of heaven and the curse of man!—Oh, matricide! Matricide! Whither shalt thou flee from thy accusing conscience! In life I shall be wretched, after death, oh! Who shall release this soul from the bonds of self-condemnation! Oh my affectionate mother! Hast Theresa rewarded thee thus, for thy tender solicitude for her; was it for this, that thou saved me from the devouring flames of my native St. Nicholas! Was it for this, that thou didst exert all thy ingenuity, and saved me from the uplifted sword of the enemy of St. Domingo!—Oh God! forgive this matricide! Forgive Theresa, who to save her country, sacrificed a mother and a sister—Wretched Amanda! And thrice wretched is thy sister, who devoted thee to misery and death!"

The body of escorts were now arrived at the Pimento grove—Theresa sprang from her carriage; hastened to the place where her mother and sister reposed at her departure. She cried in the anguish of her soul, "My mother, my mother! Where art thou!—Come forth—let Theresa embrace thee to her wretched bosom. Come Amanda! Dear Amanda, come, and save thy loving sister from black despair! Where, cruel enemy, where have ye conducted them! If ye have murdered my dear mother and sister, let Theresa but embrace their clayey bodies, and while I bless the enemies of the Haytiens!" But her grief was unheard by those, the loss of whom she bitterly deplored; solemn silence occupied the grove, interrupted only by intervals with the moans and sobs of the men of arms, who marked her anguish of soul, and were absorbed into pity. Whither now shall Theresa bend her steps! No kind mother to guide her in life, or affectionate sister, to whom to impart the sorrow of her soul, or participate with in innocent pleasure; friendless and disconsolate, she was now left exposed to may evils, and at a time too when the assiduous care of a mother was most essential in the preservation of her wellbeing. Theresa was on her way back to the camp of the kind Toussaint L'Ouverture, to claim his fatherly protection, and seek a home in the bosom of those to whom she had rendered herself dear by her wisdom and virtue. The trampling of many horses was heard rapidly approaching, and bending its way towards the same direction. It was a party of the French troops, and she was now to witness war in all its horrors. The enemy of Haytien freedom was now near. The war trumpet now sounded the terrible blast for the engagement, and the Revolutionists like lions, rushed on to the fight with a simultaneous cry of "Freedom or Death!" The French, great in number, fought in obedience to a cruel master; the Haytiens for liberty and independence and to obtain their rights of which they long have been unjustly deprived.

The pass between the Mole and the village St. Nicholas, drank up the lives of hundreds in their blood. The French retreated with precipitance, leaving their baggage with their gasping friends, on the spot where victory perched on the standard of freedom: and now the conquerors had began to examine the property deserted by the vanquished. A faint but mournful groan issued from a baggage cart forsaken by the enemy; directed by the light of a flambeau, Captain Inginac bent thither his nimble steps. Curiosity is lost in surprise—joy succeeds sorrow—the lost ones are regained. It was Madame Paulina and Amanda, the mother and sister of the unhappy Theresa.

1828

NOTES

1. The Haitian Revolution (1791–1804) pitted the French colonizers of Saint-Domingue against the enslaved Africans who lived there. The victorious Africans named their new nation the Republic of Haiti.

2. The name of both an arrondissement (district) in the northwest region of Haiti and its central commune (town).

3. Cape Dame Marie is a small seaside commune located at the westernmost tip of Haiti.

4. The French general who captured Haitian rebel leader Toussaint L'Ouverture and deported him to France.

5. Leader of the Haitian rebellion against French colonial rule.

6. An obsolete term for parakeet.

GEORGE MOSES HORTON (1797-1883?)

George Moses Horton was born into slavery in Northampton County, North Carolina. As a child, Horton taught himself to read and, shortly after began composing rhymes in his head, based on the meter and language of Methodist hymns. Around 1815, Horton began making regular trips to the city of Chapel Hill, North Carolina, to sell produce, and it was during this time that he began to make his first contact with the University of North Carolina community. Students were impressed with his ability to compose verses without the aid of pen and paper, and the young men at the University began paying him to compose love poems for the people they were courting. Horton was particularly well known for his skill at creating acrostics based on young women's names. Eventually, his reputation attracted the attention of novelist Caroline Lee Hentz, wife of a University of North Carolina professor. Hentz taught Horton how to write and helped facilitate the publication of his first book. She was the first of several supporters and mentors who would aid Horton in his attempt to raise enough money from the sale of his work to buy his way out of slavery. Alas, none were successful in helping him achieve this goal. Neither his first book, *The Hope of Liberty* (1829), nor his second, *The Poetical Works of George M. Horton, the Colored Bard of North-Carolina* (1845), generated sufficient funds to enable the author to purchase his freedom. Horton would remain enslaved until 1865, when Union troops reached the Raleigh-Durham area. His third volume, *Naked Genius,* was published that same year, with the aid and support of Captain William H. S. Banks, a Union officer. Horton settled in Philadelphia, where he continued to write poems, creating at least one additional manuscript, of which no existing copies have been found. The place and time of his death are unknown, though recent evidence suggests that he may have emigrated to Liberia as early as 1866. Each of the poems included in this collection appeared in African American periodicals during Horton's lifetime. "Gratitude," "Lines, on the Evening and the Morning," and "Slavery" were first published in 1828, in *Freedom's Journal,* on July 18, August 15, and September 5, respectively. All three would later appear in Horton's first collection, *The Hope of Liberty* (1829). "Forbidden to Ride on the Street Cars," a critique of racism in the postbellum North, was published in the *Christian Recorder* in 1866.

GRATITUDE

Dedicated to the Gentleman who takes so kind an interest in his behalf.

Joy kindles by thy vital gale,
And breathes true philanthropy;
Thus with delight I hail
The dawn of Liberty.

The song of Gratitude I owe
To thee from whom these pleasures rise,
And strains of praise to thee shall flow,
Until my memory dies.

Far from this dark inclement place
Unto thy sacred beams I'll flee;
Unto the soothing smiles of grace,
The smiles of liberty.

Enraptur'd by the pleasing charm,
Aloud will I my joys proclaim;
And soar above oppression's storm,
And triumph in thy name.

Philanthropy, thou feeling dove,
Whose voice can sound the vassal free,
Upon thy wing of humane love
I'll fly to liberty.

Through inclement seas distress'd,
Where all the storms of hardship roar,
Ere long I humbly hope to rest,
On freedom's peaceful shore.

May Providence reward each man
Who feels such safe regard for me,
And in his breast enroll a plan
Devis'd for liberty.

May all the smiles of Heaven attend
Thy life who thus relieves the poor,
And showers of blessings down descend
To amplify thy store.

Thus may thy feeling heart rejoice,
And cause me to rejoice with thee,
And triumph with a cheerful voice,
The voice of liberty.

1828

LINES: ON THE EVENING AND THE MORNING

When evening bids the sun to rest retire,
Unwearied Ether sets her lamps on fire,
Lit by one torch, each is supplied in turn,
'Till all the candles in the concave burn.

The right hawk now with his nocturnal tone
Wakes up, and all the owls begin to moan,
Or heave from dreary vales their dismal song,
Whilst in the air the meteors play along.

At length the silver queen begins to rise
And spread her glowing mantle in the skies,
And from the smiling chamber of the east,
Invites the eye to her resplendent feast.

What joy is this into the rustic swain
Who from the mount surveys the moonlight plain,
Who with the spirit of a dauntless Pan.
Controls his fleecy train and leads the van;

Or pensive, muses on the water's side,
Which purling doth thro' green meanders glide
With watchful care he broods his heart away
Till night is swallowed in the flood of day.

The meteors cease to play, that mov'd so fleet
And spectres from the murky groves retreat,
The prowling wolf withdraws, which howl'd so bold,
And bleating lambs may venture from their fold

The night-hawk's din deserts the shepherd's ear,
Succeeded by the huntsman's trumpet clear,

O come Diana start the morning chase
Thou ancient goddess of the hunting race.

Aurora's smiles adorn the mountain's brow,
The peasant hums delighted at his plow,
And lo, the dairy maid salutes her bounteous cow.

1828

SLAVERY

When first my bosom glowed with hope,
I gaz'd as from a mountain top
On some delightful plain;
But oh! how transient was the scene—
It fled as though it had not been,
And all my hopes were vain.

How oft this tantalizing blaze
Has led me through deception's maze;
My friend became my foe—
Then like a plaintive dove I mourn'd,
To bitter all my sweets were turn'd,
And tears began to flow.

Why was the dawning of my birth
Upon this vile accursed earth,
Which is but pain to me?
Oh! that my soul had winged its flight,
When first I saw the morning light,
To worlds of liberty!

Come, melting Pity 'from afar'
And break this vast, enormous bar
Between a wretch and thee;
Purchase a few short days of time,
And bid a vassal rise sublime
On wings of liberty.

Is it because my skin is black,
That thou should'st be so dull and slack,

And scorn to set me free?
Then let me hasten to the grave,
The only refuge for the slave,
Who mourns for liberty.

The wicked cease from trouble there:
No more I'd languish or despair—
The weary there can rest?
Oppression's voice is heard no more,
Drudg'ry, and pain, and toil are o'er,
Yes! there I shall be blest.

1828

FORBIDDEN TO RIDE ON THE STREET CARS

*(The writer, widely known as "The Slave Poet," recently saw a colored person enter
a Philadelphia passenger railway car, which had stopped for a passenger, but the
conductor immediately compelled her to leave. The following lines were suggested.)*

Why wilt thou from the right revolt?
    I wish to ride not far;
Why wilt thou fear the mild result,
Nor bid the humble horses halt,
    But spare me from the car?

And though I wish to travel fleet,
    Regardless of a jar,
A short mile's journey to complete,
I dare not ride along the street,
    Within a rattling car.

What retribution wilt thou meet,
    When summoned to the bar!
Wilt thou not from the call retreat?
Leave not the traveler on his feet,
    Alone to watch the car.

Like thee, we bravely fought our way,
    Before the shafts of war;
Lest thou shouldn't fall the rebels' prey;

Why canst thou not a moment stay,
 And take one on the car?

E'er long, we trust, the time will come,
 We'll ride, however far;
And all ride on together home,
When freedom will be in full bloom,
 Regardless of the car!

1866

DAVID WALKER (1796?-1830)

David Walker was born in Wilmington, North Carolina, to an enslaved father and a free mother. Because North Carolina law stipulated that children of African descent inherit the status of their mother, Walker was freeborn. In addition to her relationship to slavery, his mother also passed on to him her deeply held belief in the injustice of that institution. Walker's antislavery position was reinforced by the abuses and deprivations that he witnessed during his extensive travels throughout the slaveholding South. Lacking access to formal education, Walker was tutored by his mother in the rudiments of literacy, but was otherwise self-taught. Around 1824 or 1825, Walker left the South, eventually settling in Boston. There, he launched a small clothing business, selling new and used garments. By the end of 1826 he had made a number of key connections within the city's African American community. In February of that year, he married Eliza Butler, daughter of a prominent family in Boston's African American elite. Shortly after, in July, he was inducted into the city's most prestigious African Masonic Lodge. During the same period, he joined the city's May Street Methodist Episcopal Church, pastored by Rev. Samuel Snowden, one of Boston's most outspoken black abolitionists. Over the next three years, Walker became increasingly active as an organizer of the African American community, serving as the Boston-area agent for *Freedom's Journal* and as a founding member of the Massachusetts General Colored Association. Increasingly respected and trusted as a spokesperson for the local black community, Walker wrote and published the first edition of his *Appeal to the Coloured Citizens of the World* in 1829. A stinging, seventy-six-page indictment of the cruel and inhuman treatment of African Americans, his *Appeal* was especially forthright in its characterization of Christian supporters of slavery as unscrupulous and hypocritical. Walker highlighted and extended his treatment of this theme in its second and third editions. Widely embraced by African American readers up and down the Eastern Seaboard, the *Appeal* was met with criticism by most white readers; and, in several of the slave states, dramatic efforts were made to suppress the work. The following excerpt from his appeal was taken from the third and final edition, published in 1830 and including revisions made after the first two editions had been published. Walker died during the summer of 1830 and, at the time, was believed by many to be the victim of a southern conspiracy to silence the writer, possibly through the use of a poison. That his daughter had passed away from tuberculosis only one week prior and that city records list his cause of death as "consumption" points to the possibility that he was but another casualty of a then common infectious disease.

APPEAL TO THE COLOURED CITIZENS OF THE WORLD

Article I: Our Wretchedness in Consequence of Slavery

My beloved brethren:—The Indians of North and of South America—the Greeks—the Irish, subjected under the king of Great Britain—the Jews, that ancient people of the Lord—the inhabitants of the islands of the sea—in fine, all the inhabitants of the earth, (except however, the sons of Africa) are called men, and of course are, and *ought to* be free. But we, (coloured people) and our children are *brutes*!! and of course are, and ought to be SLAVES to the American people and their children forever!! to dig their mines and work their farms; and thus go on enriching them, from one generation to another with our *blood* and our *tears*!!!!

I promised in a preceding page to demonstrate to the satisfaction of the most incredulous, that we, (coloured people of these United States of America) are the most *wretched*, *degraded* and *abject* set of beings that *ever lived* since the world began, and that the white Americans having reduced us to the wretched state of *slavery*, treat us in that condition *more cruel* (they being an enlightened and Christian people), than any heathen nation did any people whom it had reduced to our condition. These affirmations are so well confirmed in the minds of all unprejudiced men, who have taken the trouble to read histories, that they need no elucidation from me. But to put them beyond all doubt, I refer you in the first place to the children of Jacob, or of Israel in Egypt, under Pharaoh and his people. Some of my brethren do not know who Pharaoh and the Egyptians were—I know it to be a fact, that some of them take the Egyptians to have been a gang of *devils*, not knowing any better, and that they (Egyptians) having got possession of the Lord's people, treated them *nearly* as cruel as *Christian Americans* do us, at the present day. For the information of such, I would only mention that the Egyptians, were Africans or coloured people, such as we are—some of them yellow[1] and others dark—a mixture of Ethiopians and the natives of Egypt—about the same as you see the coloured people of the United States at the present day.—I say, I call your attention then, to the children of Jacob, while I point out particularly to you his son, among the rest, in Egypt.

"And Pharaoh said unto Joseph, thou shalt be over my house, and according unto thy word shall all my people be ruled: only in the throne will I be greater than thou.[2]

"And Pharaoh said unto Joseph, see, I have set thee over all the land of Egypt."[3]

"And Pharaoh said unto Joseph, I am Pharaoh, and without thee shall no man lift up his hand or foot in all the land of Egypt."[4]

Now I appeal to heaven and to earth, and particularly to the American people themselves, who cease not to declare that our condition is not hard, and that we are comparatively satisfied to rest in wretchedness and misery, under them and their children. Not, indeed, to show me a coloured President, a Governor, a Legislator, a Senator, a Mayor, or an Attorney at the Bar.—But to show me a man of colour, who holds the low office of Constable, or one who sits in a Juror Box, even on a case of one of his wretched brethren, throughout this great Republic!!—But let us pass Joseph the son of Israel a little farther in review, as he existed with that heathen nation.

"And Pharaoh called Joseph's name Zaphnath-Paaneah; and he gave him to wife Senath the daughter of Potipherah priest of On. And Joseph went out over all the land of Egypt."[5]

Compare the above, with the American institutions. Do they not institute laws to prohibit us from marrying among the whites? I would wish, candidly, however, before the Lord, to be understood, that I would not give a *pinch* of *snuff* to be married to any white person I ever saw in all the days of my life. And I do say it, that the black man, or man of colour, who will leave his own colour (provided he can get one, who is good for any thing) and marry a white woman, to be a double slave to her, just because she is *white*, ought to be treated by her as he surely will be, viz: as a NIGGER!!!! It is not, indeed, what I care about inter-marriages with the whites, which induced me to pass this subject in review; for the Lord knows, that there is a day coming when they will be glad enough to get into the company of the blacks, notwithstanding, we are, in this generation, leveled by them, almost on a level with the brute creation: and some of us they treat even worse than they do the brutes that perish. I only made this extract to show how much lower we are held, and how much more cruel we are treated by the Americans, than were the children of Jacob, by the Egyptians.—We will notice the sufferings of Israel some further, under *heathen Pharaoh*, compared with ours under the *enlightened Christians of America*.

"And Pharaoh spoke unto Joseph, saying, thy father and thy brethren are come unto thee:

"The land of Egypt is before thee: in the best of the land make thy father and brethren to dwell; in the land of Goshen let them dwell: and if thou knowest any men of activity among them, then make them rulers over my cattle."[6]

I ask those people who treat us so *well*, Oh! I ask them, where is the most barren spot of land which they have given unto us? Israel had the most fertile land in all Egypt. Need I mention the very notorious fact, that I have known a poor man of colour, who laboured night and day, to acquire a little money, and having acquired it, he vested it in a small piece of land, and got him a house erected thereon, and having paid for the whole, he moved his family into it, where he was suffered to remain but nine months, when he was cheated out of his property by a white man, and driven out of door! And is not this the case generally? Can a man of colour buy a piece of land and keep it peaceably? Will not some white man try to get it from him, even if it is in a *mud hole*? I need not comment any farther on a subject, which all both black and white, will readily admit. But I must, really, observe that in this very city, when a man of colour dies, if he owned any real estate it most generally falls into the hands of some white person. The wife and children of the deceased may weep and lament if they please, but the estate will be kept snug enough by its white possessor.

But to prove farther that the condition of the Israelites was better under the Egyptians than ours is under the whites, I call upon the professing Christians, I call upon the philanthropist, I call upon the very tyrant himself, to show me a page of history, either sacred or profane, on which a verse can be found, which maintains, that the Egyptians heaped the *insupportable insult* upon the children of Israel, by telling them that they were not of the *human family*. Can the whites deny this charge? Have they not, after having reduced us to the deplorable condition of slaves under their feet, held us up as descending originally from the tribes of *Monkeys* or *Orang-Outangs*? O! My God! I appeal to every man of feeling—is not this insupportable? Is it not heaping the most gross insult upon our miseries, because they have got us under their feet and we cannot help ourselves? Oh! pity us we pray thee, Lord Jesus, Master.—Has Mr. Jefferson declared to the world, that we are inferior to the whites, both in the endowments of our bodies and our minds? It is indeed surprising, that a man of such great learning, combined with such excellent natural parts, should speak so of a set of men in chains. I do not know what to compare it to, unless, like putting one wild deer in an iron cage, where it will be secured, and hold another by the side of the same, then let it go, and expect the one in the cage to run as fast as the one at liberty. So far, my brethren, were the Egyptians from heaping these insults upon their slaves, that Pharaoh's daughter took Moses, a son of Israel, for her own, as will appear by the following.

"And Pharaoh's daughter said unto her [Moses's mother], take this child away, and nurse it for me, and I will pay thee thy wages. And the woman took the child [Moses] and nursed it.

"And the child grew, and she brought him unto Pharaoh's daughter and he became her son. And she called his name Moses: and she said because I drew him out of the water."[7]

In all probability, Moses would have become Prince Regent to the throne, and no doubt, in process of time but he would have been seated on the throne of Egypt. But he had rather suffer shame, with the people of God, than to enjoy pleasures with that wicked people for a season. O! that the coloured people were long since of Moses' excellent disposition, instead of courting favour with, and telling news and lies to our *natural enemies*, against each other—aiding them to keep their hellish chains of slavery upon us. Would we not long before this time have been respectable men, instead of such wretched victims of oppression as we are? Would they be able to drag our mothers, our fathers, our wives, our children and ourselves, around the world in chains and handcuffs as they do, to dig up gold and silver for them and theirs? This question, my brethren, I leave for you to digest: and may God Almighty force it home to your hearts. Remember that unless you are united, keeping your tongues within your teeth, you will be afraid to trust your secrets to each other, and thus perpetuate our miseries under the *Christians*!!!!

ADDITION.—Remember, also to lay humble at the feet of our Lord and Master Jesus Christ, with prayers and fastings. Let our enemies go on with their butcheries, and at once fill up their cup. Never make an attempt to gain our freedom or *natural right*, from under our cruel oppressor, and murderers, until you see your way clear[8]—when that hour arrives and you move, be not afraid or dismayed; for be you assured that Jesus Christ the King of heaven and of earth who is the God of justice and of armies, will surely go before you. And those enemies who have for hundreds of years stolen our rights, and kept us ignorant of Him and His divine worship, he will remove. Millions of whom, are this day, so ignorant and avaricious, that they cannot conceive how God can have an attribute of justice, and show mercy to us because it pleased Him to make us black—which colour, Mr. Jefferson calls unfortunate!!!!!! As though we are not as thankful to our God, for having made us as it pleased himself, as they, (the whites,) [sic] are for having made them white. They think because they hold us in their infernal chains of slavery, that we wish to be white, or of their color—but they are dreadfully deceived—we wish to be just as it pleased our Creator to have made us, and no avaricious and unmerciful wretches, have any business to make slaves of, or hold us in slavery. How would they like for us to make slaves of, and hold them in cruel slavery, and murder them as they do us?—But is Mr. Jefferson's assertions true? viz. "that it is unfortunate for us that our Creator has been pleased to make us *black*." We will not take his say so for the fact. The world will have an opportunity to see whether it is unfortunate for us that our Creator *has made us* darker than the *whites*.

Fear not the number and education of our enemies, against whom we shall have to contend for our lawful right, guaranteed to us by our Maker; for why should we be afraid, when God is, and will continue, (if we continue humble) to be on our side?

The man who would not fight under our Lord and Master Jesus Christ, in the glorious and heavenly cause of freedom and of God—to be delivered from the most wretched, abject and servile slavery, that ever a people was afflicted with since the foundation of the world, to the present day—ought to be kept with all of his children or family, in slavery, or in chains, to be butchered by his *cruel enemies*.

I saw a paragraph, a few years since, in a South Carolina paper, which, speaking of the barbarity of the Turks, it said: "The Turks are the most barbarous people in the world—they treat the Greeks more like *brutes* than human beings." And in the same paper was an advertisement, which said: "Eight well built Virginia and Maryland *Negro fellows* and four *wenches* will positively be sold this day, to the *highest bidder!*" And what astonished me still more was, to see in this same *humane* paper, the cuts of three men, with clubs and budgets on their backs, and an advertisement offering a considerable sum of money for their apprehension and delivery. I declare, it is really so amusing to hear the Southerners and Westerners of this country talk about *barbarity*, that it is positively enough to make a man *smile*.

The sufferings of the Helots[9] among the Spartans, were somewhat severe, it is true, but to say that theirs were as severe as ours among the Americans, I do most strenuously deny—for instance, can any man show me an article on a page of ancient history which specifies that the Spartans chained and handcuffed the Helots, and dragged them from their wives and children, children from their parents, mothers from their suckling babes, wives from their husbands, driving them from one end of the country to the other? Notice the Spartans were heathens, who lived long before our Divine Master made his appearance in the flesh. Can Christian Americans deny these barbarous cruelties? Have you not, Americans, having subjected us under you, added to these miseries, by insulting us in telling us to our face, because we are helpless, that we are not of the human family? I ask you, O! Americans, I ask you, in the name of the Lord, can you deny these charges? Some perhaps may deny, by saying that they never thought or said that we were not men. But do not actions speak louder than words?—Have they not made provisions for the Greeks, and Irish? Nations who have never done the least thing for them, while we, who have enriched their country with our blood and tears—have dug up gold and silver for them and their children, from generation to generation, and are in more miseries than any other people under heaven, are not seen, but by comparatively, a handful of the American people? There are indeed, more ways to kill a dog, besides choking it to death with butter. Further—The Spartans or Lacedaemonians[10] had some frivolous pretext for enslaving the Helots, for they (Helots) while being free inhabitants of Sparta, stirred up an intestine commotion, and were, by the Spartans subdued, and made prisoners of war. Consequently, they and their children were condemned to perpetual slavery.[11]

I have been for years troubling the pages of historians, to find out what our fathers have done to the white Christians of America, to merit such condign punishment as they have inflicted on them, and do continue to inflict on us their children. But I must aver that my researches have hitherto been to no effect. I have therefore, come to the immoveable conclusion, that they (Americans) have, and do continue to punish us for nothing else, but for enriching them and their country. For I cannot conceive of anything else. Nor will I ever believe otherwise, until the Lord shall convince me.

The world knows, that slavery as it existed among the Romans, (which was the primary cause of their destruction) was, comparatively speaking, no more than a *cypher*, when compared with ours under the Americans. Indeed I should not have noticed the Roman slaves, had not the very learned and penetrating Mr. Jefferson said, "When a master was murdered, all his slaves in the same house, or within hearing, were condemned to death."[12]—Here let me ask Mr. Jefferson, (but he is gone to answer at the bar of God, for the deeds done in his body while living); I therefore ask the whole American people, had I not rather die, or be put to death, than to be a slave to any tyrant, who takes not only my own, but my wife and children's lives by the inches? Yea, would I meet death with avidity far! far!! in preference to such servile submission to the murderous hands of tyrants. Mr. Jefferson's very severe remarks on us have been so extensively argued upon by men whose attainments in literature, I shall never be able to reach, that I would not have meddled with it, were it not to solicit each of my brethren, who has the spirit of a man, to buy a copy of Mr. Jefferson's "Notes on Virginia," and put it in the hand of his son. For let no one of us suppose that the refutations which have been written by our white friends are enough—they are whites—we are blacks. We and the world wish to see the charges of Mr. Jefferson refuted by the blacks themselves, according to their chance; for we must remember that what the whites have written respecting this subject is other men's labours, and did not emanate from the blacks. I know well, that there are some talents and learning among the coloured people of this country, which we have not a chance to develop, in consequence of oppression; but our oppression ought not to hinder us from acquiring all we can. For we will have a chance to develop them by and by. God will not suffer us, always to be oppressed. Our sufferings will come to an *end*, in spite of all the Americans this side of *eternity*. Then we will want all the learning and talents among ourselves, and perhaps more, to govern ourselves.—"Every dog must have its day"; the American's is coming to an end.

But let us review Mr. Jefferson's remarks respecting us some further. Comparing our miserable fathers, with the learned philosophers of Greece, he says: "Yet notwithstanding these and other discouraging circumstances among the Romans, their slaves were often their rarest artists. They excelled too, in science, insomuch as to be usually employed as tutors to their master's children; Epictetus, Terence and Phaedrus, were slaves,—but they were of the race of whites. It is not their *condition* then, but *nature*, which has produced the distinction."[13] See this, my brethren!! Do you believe that this assertion is swallowed by millions of the whites? Do you know that Mr. Jefferson was one of as great characters as ever lived among the whites? See his writings for the world, and public labours for the United States of America. Do you believe that the assertions of such a man will pass away into oblivion unobserved by this people and the world? If you do you are much mistaken—See how the American people treat us—have we souls in our bodies? Are we men who have any spirits at all? I know that there are many *swell-bellied* fellows among us, whose greatest object is to fill their stomachs. Such I do not mean—I am after those who know and feel, that we are MEN, as well as other people; to them, I say, that unless we try to refute Mr. Jefferson's arguments respecting us, we will only establish them.

But the slaves among the Romans. Everybody who has read history, knows, that as soon as a slave among the Romans obtained his freedom, he could rise to the greatest eminence in the State, and there was no law instituted to hinder a slave from buying his freedom. Have not the Americans instituted laws to hinder us from obtaining our freedom? Do any deny this charge? Read the laws of Virginia, North Carolina, &c. Further: have not the Americans instituted laws to prohibit a man of colour from obtaining and holding any office whatever, under the government of the United States of America? Now, Mr. Jefferson tells us, that our condition is not so hard, as the slaves were under the Romans!!!!!!

It is time for me to bring this article to a close. But before I close it, I must observe to my brethren that at the close of the first Revolution in this country, with Great Britain, there were but thirteen States in the Union, now there are twenty four, most of which are slave-holding States, and the whites are dragging us around in chains and in handcuffs, to their new States and Territories to work their mines and farms, to enrich them and their children—and millions of them believing firmly that we being a little darker than they, were made by our Creator to be an inheritance to them and their children for ever—the same as a parcel of *brutes*.

Are we MEN!!—I ask you, O my brethren! are we MEN? Did our Creator make us to be slaves to dust and ashes like ourselves? Are they not dying worms as well as we? Have they not to make their appearance before the tribunal of Heaven, to answer for the deeds done in the body, as well as we? Have we any other Master but Jesus Christ alone? Is he not their Master as well as ours?—What right then, have we to obey and call any other Master, but Himself? How we could be so *submissive* to a gang of men, whom we cannot tell whether they are as good as ourselves or not, I never could conceive. However, this is shut up with the Lord, and we cannot precisely tell—but I declare, we judge men by their works.

The whites have always been an unjust, jealous, unmerciful, avaricious and blood-thirsty set of beings, always seeking after power and authority.—We view them all over the confederacy of Greece, where they were first known to be anything, (in consequence of education) we see them there, cutting each other's throats—trying to subject each other to wretchedness and misery—to effect which, they used all kinds of deceitful, unfair, and unmerciful means. We view them next in Rome, where the spirit of tyranny and deceit raged still higher. We view them in Gaul, Spain, and in Britain.—In fine, we view them all over Europe, together with what were scattered about in Asia and Africa, as heathens, and we see them acting more like devils than accountable men. But some may ask, did not the blacks of Africa, and the mulattoes of Asia, go on in the same way as did the whites of Europe. I answer, no—they never were half so avaricious, deceitful and unmerciful as the whites, according to their knowledge.

But we will leave the whites or Europeans as heathens, and take a view of them as Christians, in which capacity we see them as cruel, if not more so than ever. In fact, take them as a body, they are ten times more cruel, avaricious and unmerciful than ever they were; for while they were heathens, they were bad enough it is true, but it is positively a fact that they were not quite so audacious as to go and take vessel loads of men, women and children, and in cold blood, and through devilishness, throw them into the sea, and murder them in all kind of ways. While they were heathens, they were too ignorant for such barbarity. But being Christians, enlightened and sensible, they are completely prepared for such hellish cruelties. Now suppose God were to give them more sense, what would they do? If it were possible, would they not dethrone Jehovah and seat themselves upon his throne? I therefore, in the name and fear of the Lord God of Heaven and of earth, divested of prejudice either on the side of my colour or that of the whites, advance my suspicion of them, whether they are as good by nature as we are or not. Their actions, since they were known as a people, have been the reverse, I do indeed suspect them, but this, as I before observed, is shut up with the Lord, we cannot exactly tell, it will be proved in succeeding generations.—The whites have had the essence of the gospel as it was preached by my master and his apostles—the Ethiopians have not, who are to have it in its meridian splendor—the Lord will give it to them to their satisfaction. I hope and pray my God, that they will make good use of it, that it may be well with them."[14]

1830

1. A reference to people of African descent with lighter skin, used primarily in the United States.

2. See Genesis, chap. xli [Walker's note; citation refers to Genesis 41: 39–40].

3. Xli. 41 [Walker's reference to Genesis 41:41].

4. Xli. 44 [Walker's reference to Genesis 41:44].

5. Xli. 45 [Walker's reference to Genesis 41:45, highlighted for its implicit support of cross-cultural marriages].

6. Genesis, chap. xlvii. 5, 6 [Walker's note].

7. See Exodus, chap. ii., 9, 10 [Walker's note].

8. It is not to be understood here, that I mean for us to wait until God shall take us by the hair of our heads and drag us out of abject wretchedness and slavery, nor do I mean to convey the idea for us to wait until our enemies shall make preparations, and call us to seize those preparations, take it away from them, and put every thing before us to death, in order to gain our freedom which God has given us. For you must remember that we are men as well as they. God has been pleased to give us two eyes, two hands, two feet, and some sense in our heads as well as they. They have no more right to hold us in slavery than we have to hold them, we have just as much right, in the sight of God, to hold them and their children in slavery and wretchedness, as they have to hold us, and no more [Walker's note].

9. The servant class of ancient Sparta.

10. Another term for Spartans (the free citizens of Sparta).

11. See Dr. Goldsmith's History of Greece—page 9. See also, Plutarch's Lives. The Helots subdued by Agis, king of *Sparta*.

12. See his Notes on Virginia, 210 [Walker's note].

13. See his Notes on Virginia, 211 [Walker's note].

14. It is my solemn belief, that if ever the world becomes Christianized (which must certainly take place before long) it will be through the means, under God of the *Blacks,* who are now held in wretchedness, and degradation, by the white *Christians* of the world, who before they learn to do justice to us before our Maker—and be reconciled to us, and reconcile us to them, and by that means have clear consciences before God and man.—Send out Missionaries to convert the Heathens, many of whom after they cease to worship gods, which neither see nor hear, become ten times more the children of Hell, then ever they were, why what is the reason? Why the reason is obvious, they must learn to do justice at home, before they go into distant lands, to display their charity, Christianity, and benevolence; when they learn to do justice, God will accept their offering, (no man may think that I am against Missionaries for I am not, my object is to see justice done at home, before we go to convert the Heathens) [Walker's note].

MARIA W. STEWART (1803-1879)

Maria W. Stewart was born Maria Miller in Hartford, Connecticut. Orphaned by the age of five, she was bound out as a domestic servant for what she would later describe as "a clergyman's family," until the age of fifteen. She had little formal education, slowly building her literacy skills in the occasional Sabbath school class. In 1826, she married James W. Stewart, a Boston shipping agent, and she settled into life as part of the city's growing black middle class. At her husband's request, she adopted both his surname and his middle initial and was henceforth known as Maria W. Stewart. After her husband's death in 1829, she began writing essays and speeches on issues related to race and the status of women. In 1861, Stewart moved to Washington, DC, where she established a school for newly freed African American migrants. Today, Stewart is revered as a pioneering speaker and activist on issues pertaining to both racism and sexism. Her speeches, which predate those of both Sojourner Truth and Frederick Douglass, place Stewart among such early black abolitionist voices as Prince Hall, David Walker, Sarah Mapps Douglass, and William Whipper. Sources differ on the specific year and location, but historians agree that in either 1832 (on September 12, at Boston's Franklin Hall) or 1833 (on February 27, at Boston's African Masonic Hall) Stewart became the first American woman of any race or ethnicity to deliver a speech to a mixed audience of women and men. A pioneer in many areas, Stewart is also the first American woman to leave a written record of her speeches, which were gathered and published in pamphlet form in 1835. Titled *Productions of Mrs. Maria W. Stewart,* this collection of her Boston-area speeches is the source for the lecture included below.

AN ADDRESS, DELIVERED AT THE AFRICAN MASONIC HALL, BOSTON, FEBRUARY 27, 1833

African rights and liberty is a subject that ought to fire the breast of every free man of color in these United States, and excite in his bosom a lively, deep, decided and heart-felt interest. When I cast my eyes on the long list of illustrious names that are enrolled on the bright annals of fame among the whites, I turn my eyes within, and ask my thoughts, "Where are the names of our illustrious ones?" It must certainly have been for the want of energy on the part of the free people of color, that they have been long willing to bear the yoke of oppression. It must have been the want of ambition and force that has given the whites occasion to say, that our natural abilities are not as good, and our capacities by nature inferior to theirs. They boldly assert, that, did we possess a natural independence of soul, and feel a love for liberty within our breasts, some one of our sable race, long before this, would have testified it, notwithstanding the disadvantages under which we labor. We have made ourselves appear altogether unqualified to speak in our own defence, and are therefore looked upon as objects of pity and commiseration. We have been imposed upon, insulted and derided on every side; and now, if we complain, it is considered as the height of impertinence. We have suffered ourselves to be considered as Bastards, cowards, mean, faint-hearted wretches; and on this account, (not because of our complexion) many despise us, and would gladly spurn us from their presence.

These things have fired my soul with a holy indignation, and compelled me thus to come forward; and endeavor to turn their attention to knowledge and improvement; for knowledge is power. I would ask, is it blindness of mind, or at stupidity of soul, or the want of education, that has caused our men who are 60 to 70 years of age, never to let their voices be heard, or nor their hands be raised in behalf of their color? Or has it been for the fear of offering the whites? If it has, O ye fearful ones, throw off your fearfulness, and come forth in the name of the Lord, and in the strength of the God of Justice, and make yourselves useful and active members in society; for they admire a noble and patriotic spirit in others; and should they not admire it in us? If you are men, convince them that you possess the spirit of men; and as your day, so shall your strength be. Have the sons of Africa no souls? Feel they no ambitious desires? Shall the chains of ignorance forever confine them? Shall the insipid appellation of "clever negroes," or "good creatures," any longer content them? Where can we find among ourselves the man of science, or a philosopher, or an able statesman, or a counselor at law? Show me our fearless and brave, our noble and gallant ones. Where are our lecturers on natural history, and our critics in useful knowledge? There may be a few such men among us, but they are rare. It is true, our fathers bled and died in the revolutionary war, and others fought bravely under the command of Jackson, in defence of liberty.

But where is the man that has distinguished himself in these modern days by acting wholly in the defence of African rights and liberty? There was one; although he sleeps, his memory lives.

I am sensible that there are many highly intelligent gentlemen of color in those United States, in the force of whose arguments, doubtless, I should discover my inferiority; but if they are blest with wit and talent, friends and fortune, why have they not made themselves men of eminence, by striving to take all the reproach that is cast upon the people of color, and in endeavoring to alleviate the woes of their brethren in bondage? Talk, without effort, is nothing; you are abundantly capable, gentlemen, of making yourselves men of distinction; and this gross neglect, on your part, causes my blood to boil within me. Here is the grand cause which hinders the rise and progress of the people of color. It is their want of laudable ambition and requisite courage.

Individuals have been distinguished according to their genius and talents, ever since the first formation of man, and will continue to be while the world stands. The different grades rise to honor and respectability as their merits may deserve. History informs us that we sprung from one of the most learned nations of the whole earth; from the seat, if not the parent of science; yes, poor, despised Africa was once the resort of sages and legislators of other nations, was esteemed the school for learning, and the most illustrious men in Greece flocked thither for instruction. But it was our gross sins and abominations that provoked the Almighty to frown thus heavily upon us, and give our glory unto others. Sin and prodigality have caused the downfall of nations, kings and emperors; and were it not that God in wrath remembers mercy, we might indeed despair; but a promise is left us; "Ethiopia shall again stretch forth her hands unto God."[1]

But it is of no use for us to boast that we sprung from this learned and enlightened nation, for this day a thick mist of moral gloom hangs over millions of our race. Our condition as a people has been low for hundreds of years, and it will continue to be so, unless, by true piety and virtue, we strive to regain that which we have lost. White Americans, by their prudence, economy and exertions, have sprung up and become one of the most flourishing nations in the world, distinguished for their knowledge of the arts and sciences, for their polite literature. While our minds are vacant, and starving for want of knowledge, theirs are filled to overflowing. Most of our color have been taught to stand in fear of the white man, from their earliest infancy, to work as soon as they could walk, and call "master," before they scarce could lisp the name of mother. Continual fear and laborious servitude have in some degree lessened in us that natural force and energy which belong to man; or else, in defiance of opposition, our men, before this, would have nobly and boldly contended for their rights. But give the man of color an equal opportunity with the white from the cradle to manhood, and from manhood to the grave, and you would discover the dignified statesman, the man of science, and the philosopher. But there is no such opportunity for the sons of Africa, and I fear that our powerful ones are fully determined that there never shall be. For bid, ye Powers on high, that it should any longer be said that our men possess no force. O ye sons of Africa, when will your voices be heard in our legislative halls, in defiance of your enemies, contending for equal rights and liberty? How can you, when you reflect from what you have fallen, refrain from crying mightily unto God, to turn away from us the fierceness of his anger, and remember our transgressions against us no more forever. But a God of infinite purity will not regard the prayers of those who hold religion in one hand, and prejudice, sin and pollution in the other; he will not regard the prayers of self-righteousness and hypocrisy. Is it possible, I exclaim, that for the want of knowledge, we have labored for hundreds of years to support others, and been content to receive what they chose to give us in return? Cast your eyes about, look as far as you can see; all, all is owned by the lordly white, except here and there a lowly dwelling which the man of color, midst deprivations, fraud and opposition, has been scarce able to procure. Like king Solomon, who put neither nail nor hammer to the temple, yet received the praise; so also have the white Americans gained themselves a name, like the names of the great men that are in the earth, while in reality we have been their principal foundation and support. We have pursued the shadow, they have obtained the substance; we have performed the labor they have received the profits; we have planted the vines, they have eaten the fruits of them.

I would implore our men, and especially our rising youth, to flee from the gambling board and the dance-hall; for we are poor, and have no money to throw away. I do not consider dancing as criminal in itself, but it is astonishing to me that our young men are so blind to their own interest and the future welfare of their children, as to spend their hard earnings for this frivolous amusement; for it has been carried on among us to such an unbecoming extent, that it has became absolutely disgusting. "Faithful are the wounds of a friend, but the kisses of an enemy are deceitful." Had those men among us, who have had an opportunity, turned their attention as assiduously to mental and moral improvement as they have to gambling and dancing, I might have remained quietly at home, and they stood contending in my place. These polite accomplishments will never enroll your names on the bright annals of tune, who admire the belle void of intellectual knowledge, or applaud the dandy that talks largely on politics, without striving to assist his fellow in the revolution, when the nerves and muscles of every other man forced him into the field of action. You have a right to rejoice, and to let your hearts cheer you in the days of your youth; yet remember that for all these things, God will bring you into judgment. Then, O ye sons of Africa, turn your mind from these perishable objects, and contend for the cause of God and the rights of man. Form yourselves into temperance societies. There are temperate men among you; then why will you any longer neglect to strive, by your example, to suppress vice in all its abhorrent forms? You have been told repeatedly of the glorious results arising from temperance, and can you bear to see the whites arising in honor and respectability, without endeavoring to grasp after that honor and respectability also?

But I forbear. Let our money, instead of being thrown away as heretofore, be appropriated for schools and seminaries of learning for our children and youth. We ought to follow the example of the whites in this respect. Nothing would raise our respectability, add to our peace and happiness, and reflect so much honor upon us, as to be ourselves the promoters of temperance, and the supporters, as far as we are able, of useful and scientific knowledge. The rays of light and knowledge have been hid from our view; we have been taught to consider ourselves as scarce superior to the brute creation; and have performed the most laborious part of American drudgery. Had we as a people received one half the early advantages the whites have received, I would defy the government of these United States to deprive us any longer of our rights.

I am informed that the agent of the Colonization Society[2] has recently formed an association of young men, for the purpose of influencing those of us to go to Liberia who may feel disposed. The colonizationists are blind to their own interest, for should the nations of the earth make war with America, they would find their forces much weakened by our absence; or should we remain here, can our "brave soldiers," and "fellow-citizens," as they were termed in time of calamity, condescend to defend the rights of the whites, and be again deprived of own, or sent to Liberia in return? Or, if the colonizationists are real friends to Africa, let them expend the money which they collect, in erecting a college to educate her injured sons in this land of gospel light and liberty; for it would be most thankfully received on our part, and convince us of the truth of their professions, and save time, expense and anxiety. Let them place before us noble objects, worthy of pursuit, and see if we prove ourselves to be those unambitious Negroes they term us. But ah! methinks their hearts are so frozen towards us, they had rather their money should be sunk in the ocean than to administer it to our relief; and I fear, if they dared, like Pharaoh, king of Egypt, they would order every male child among us to be drowned. But the most high God is still as able to subdue the lofty pride of these white Americans, as He was the heart of that ancient rebel. They say, though we are looked upon as things, yet we sprang from a scientific people. Had our men the requisite force and energy, they would soon convince them by their efforts both in public and private, that they were men, or things in the shape of men. Well may the colonizationists laugh us to scorn for our negligence; well may they cry, "Shame to the sons of Africa." As the burden of the Israelites was too great for Moses to bear, so also is our burden too great for Moses to bear, so also is our burden too great for our noble advocate to bear. You must feel interested, my brethren, in what he undertakes, and hold up his hands by your good works, or in spite of himself, his soul will become discouraged, and his heart will die within him; for he has, as it were, the strong bulls of Bashan[3] to contend with.

It is of no use for us to wait any longer for a generation of well educated men to arise. We have slumbered and slept too long already; the day is far spent; the night of death approaches; and you have sound sense and good judgment sufficient to begin with, if you feel disposed to make a right use of it.

Let every man of color throughout the United States, who possesses the spirit and principles of a man, sign a petition to Congress, to abolish slavery in the District of Columbia, and grant you the rights and privileges of common free citizens; for if you had had faith as a grain of mustard seed, long before this the mountains of prejudice might have been removed. We are all sensible that the Anti-Slavery Society has taken hold of the arm of our whole population, in order to raise them out of the mire. Now all we have to do is, by a spirit of virtuous ambition to strive to raise ourselves; and I am happy to have it in my power thus publicly to say, that the colored inhabitants of this city, in some respects, are beginning to improve. Had the free people of color in these United States nobly and boldly contended for their rights, and showed a natural genius and talent, although not so brilliant as some; had they help up, encouraged and patronized each other, nothing could have hindered us from being a thriving and flourishing people. There has been a fault among us. The reason why our distinguished men have not made themselves more influential is, because they fear that the strong current of opposition through which they must pass, would cause their downfall and prove their overthrew. And what gives rise to this opposition? Envy. And what has it amounted to? Nothing. And who are the cause of it? Our whited sepulchers, who want to be great, and don't know how; who love to be called of men "Rabbi, Rabbi, who put on false sanctity, and humble themselves to their brethren, for the sake of acquiring the highest place in the synagogue, and the uppermost seats at the feast."[4] You, dearly beloved, who are the genuine followers of our Lord Jesus Christ, the salt of the earth and the light of the world, are not so culpable. As I told you, in the very first of my writing, I tell you again, I am but as a drop in the bucket—as one particle of the small dust of the earth. God will surely raise up those among who will plead the cause of virtue, and the pure principles of morality, more eloquently than I am able to do.

It appears to me that America has become like the great city of Babylon, for she has boasted in her heart,—I sit a queen, and am no widow, and shall see no sorrow.[5] She is indeed a seller of slaves and the souls of men; she has made the Africans drunk with the wine of her fornication; she has put them completely beneath her feet, and she means to keep them there; her right hand supports the reins of government, and her left hand the wheel of power, and she is determined not to let go her grasp. But many powerful sons and daughters of Africa will shortly arise, who will put down vice and immorality among us, and declare by Him that sitteth upon the throne, that they will have their rights; and if refused,' I am afraid they will spread horror and devastation around. I believe that the oppression of injured Africa has come up before the Majesty of Heaven; and when our cries shall have reached the ears of the Most High, it will be a tremendous day for the people of this land; for strong is the arm of the Lord God Almighty.

Life has almost lost its charms for me; death has lost its sting and the grave its terrors; and at times I have a strong desire to depart and dwell with Christ, which is far better. Let me entreat my white brethren to awake and save our sons from dissipation, and our daughters from ruin. Lend the hand of assistance to feeble merit, plead the cause of virtue among our sable race; so shall our curses upon you be turned into blessings; and though you should endeavor to drive us from these shores, still we will cling to you the more firmly; nor will we attempt to rise above you: we will presume to be called your equals only.

The unfriendly whites first drove the Native American from his much loved home. Then they stole our fathers from their peaceful and quiet dwellings, and brought them hither, and made bond-men and bond-women of them and their little ones; they have obliged our brethren to labor, kept them in utter ignorance, nourished them in vice, and raised them in degradation; and now that we have enriched their soil, and filled their coffers, they say that we are not capable of becoming like white men, and that we never can rise to respectability in this country. They would drive us to a strange land. But before I go, the bayonet shall pierce me through. African rights and liberty is a subject that ought to fire the breast of every free man of color in these United States, and excite in his bosom a lively, deep, decided and heart-felt interest.

1833

NOTES

1. Psalms 68:31.

2. The Society for the Colonization of Free People of Color of America, founded in 1816 for the express purpose of hastening the expatriation of free black people in the United States to British-ruled Sierra Leone and U.S.-ruled Liberia.

3. A reference to Psalms 22:12.

4. Matthew 23:7.

5. Revelation 18:7.

SARAH MAPPS DOUGLASS (1806–1882)

Sarah Mapps Douglass was born to free parents in Philadelphia. The daughter of prominent abolitionists Robert Douglass and Grace Bustill Douglass and the granddaughter of Cyrus Bustill, the owner of a prosperous bakery, young Sarah received tutoring at home, as well as more formal instruction at the African American children's school founded and run by her mother. A teacher and antislavery activist, Douglass is believed to have either taken over the operations of her mother's school or to have established a school of her own. In 1853, she joined the faculty of Philadelphia's Institute for Colored Youth (later renamed Cheyney University), where she taught for twenty years. In addition to her achievements as an educator, she was also a founding member of several women's literary and antislavery organizations, including the Female Literary Association of Philadelphia, the Philadelphia Anti-Slavery Circle, and the Sarah M. Douglass Literary Circle. A passionate supporter of the abolitionist movement, she may have been the first black woman to deliver a speech on the issue of slavery (to the Female Literary Society of Philadelphia, during the summer of 1832). She was a prolific writer, and her primary medium was the correspondent's letter. Her sketches and opinion pieces appeared in *The Liberator, The North Star, The Pennsylvania Freeman,* and other mid-century periodicals, usually under a pseudonym. Douglass's "Ella: A Sketch" was published in the *Liberator* in August of 1832, under the name "Sophanisba." "Family Worship," another of Douglass's short sketches, first appeared in the September 8, 1832 issue of the *Liberator*.

ELLA: A SKETCH

"Welcome peaceful, happy Sabbath morning!" said Ella, as she sat in the low door-way of her humble cottage. "Welcome peaceful morning, faint type of that rest which my heavenly Father has prepared for his Christian children! My heart rejoices in thy blest return—the sun shines with a peculiar brightness—the flowers send forth a sweet perfume—the birds sing melodiously in the trees—and my heart is filled with love to God.

"I look abroad, and my eye rests upon the silent repository of the dead. Truly the grave is a leveler of distinctions: there the despised black reposes in undisturbed serenity by the side of the lordly white: 'the small and the great are there, and the slave is free from his master.'[1] I think of the time when this frail body shall be a tenant of the same silent mansion, and the soul, I humbly trust, through the atoning blood of Christ, be arrayed in the white robe. I look on this fertile spot, my home, and can say of a truth, 'the lines have fallen to me in pleasant places'[2]—blessings, unmerited blessings are mine. But while I thus repose, as under my own vine and fig tree, my heart is filled with sorrow for my enslaved sisters. The Sabbath is no day of rest to the poor slave—she hears no hymn, no prayer, upon this holy morning. She has no Bible in which to read the matchless love of Jesus. Alas! She has never been taught to read: no ray of light penetrates the darkness of her mental vision. Sister slave, fainting with toil and sickness in the burning sun, cheer up! Christ is near thee, even in thy heart! Seek him—he will be found of thee—he has undertaken they cause—he will plead with thy oppressors himself. 'Call upon him from amidst thy bonds, for assuredly he will hear thee.'[3] Cheer up—a few of the noblest and best of thy country-women have acknowledged that thou are their sister: the time of thy deliverance draweth nigh. The time is approaching when Christ shall reign king of nations: then look to him alone.

He hears thy sighs and counts thy tears

He shall lift up thy head."[4]

The sounds of the church bell now broke the stillness of the morning, and Ella arose and went forth to the. . . .

Sophanisba

Philadelphia, July 20th, 1832

1832

FAMILY WORSHIP

Come, gentle lady, let us screen ourselves with this luxuriant honeysuckle, and look through the open window into the cottage of Albert Lindsey. Step lightly, for the family are assembled to offer their morning sacrifice; and now the voice of the mother falls like sweet music on the ear, as she reads a portion from the book of books, and the meek and loving expression on the countenances of her children bears witness, that it is happiness to be thus employed. Now heart and knees are bowed, and the humble prayer ascends like holy incense to the throne of the Eternal; but as the prayer proceeds, the manly voice of the father falters, and a tear is on the cheek of the mother. Is the emotion caused by joy? Let us listen. He prays that the lamb who has strayed from the fold may be restored. Their eldest son is absent. O, surely, the remembrance of hours spent in this delightful exercise sometimes comes over the soul of the wayward boy, in the midst of his wanderings, causing tears to flow and a resolution to spring up, that he will ere long seek his home.

I feel as if I should again see him kneeling at his parent's knees, waving their blessing as he was wont to do when a happy and sinless child. I believe 'there is no part of the Christian religion productive of more good than that of family worship, if performed with regularity and due solemnity. O, lady, would that we might see all the families of our people so engaged! How would the sunshine of such an example disperse the mists of prejudice which surround us! Yes, religion and education would raise us to an equality with the fairest in our land. The voice of prayer has ceased: let us lift the latch, and enter the abode of humble, unostentatious piety.

Sophanisba

Philadelphia, Aug. 28th, 1832.

1832

NOTES

1. Job 3:19.

2. Psalms 16:6.

3. From "Hymn VIII" by the English poet Anna Letitia Barbaud (1743–1825).

4. Lyrics from a popular Protestant hymn, written by German lyricist Paul Gerhardt in 1656 and translated into English by John Wesley in 1737.

ANN PLATO (1824-?)

Little is known about the life of Ann Plato, the second African American woman known to have published a book. She was born in Hartford, Connecticut, to free parents, farmer Henry Plato and his wife, Deborah Plato, a seamstress. A member of the Hartford Colored Congregational Church and a student at its affiliated school, Plato was encouraged to write by her pastor, the formerly enslaved author and abolitionist Rev. James W. C. Pennington. After completing her education, she accepted a teaching post at Hartford's South African School. She remained on its faculty from 1842 until 1847. In 1841, Plato published her only known work, *Essays: Including Biographies and Miscellaneous Pieces, in Prose and Poetry.* The volume consists of inspirational poems and instructional essays, and features an introduction by Pennington. He attests to the piety and virtue of the young poet and to the quality of her work. The following selections are reprinted from that collection.

ADVICE TO YOUNG LADIES

Day after day I sit and write,
    And thus the moments spend—
The thought that occupies my mind,—
    Compose to please my friend.

And then I think I will compose,
    And thus myself engage—
To try to please young ladies' minds,
    Which are about my age.

The greatest word that I can say,—
    I think to please, will be,
To try and get your learning young,
    And write it back to me.

But this is not the only thing
    That I can recommend;

Religion is most needful for
    To make in us a friend.

At thirteen years I found a hope,
    And did embrace the Lord;
And since, I've found a blessing great,
    Within his holy word.

Perchance that we may ne'er fulfill,
    The place of aged sires,
But may it with God's holy will,
    Be ever our desires.

1841

LINES UPON BEING EXAMINED IN SCHOOL STUDIES FOR THE PREPARATION OF A TEACHER

Teach me, O! Lord, the secret errors of my way,
Teach me the paths wherein I go astray,
Learn me the way to teach the word of love,
For that's the pure intelligence above.
As well as learning, give me that truth forever—
Which a mere worldly tie can never sever,
For though our bodies die, our souls will live forever.
To cultivate in every youthful mind,
Habitual grace, and sentiments refined.
Thus while I strive to govern human heart,
May I the heavenly precepts still impart;
Oh! may each youthful bosom, catch the sacred fire,
And youthful mind to virtue's throne aspire.
Now fifteen years their destined course have run,
In fast succession round the central sun;
How did the follies of that period pass,
I ask myself—are they inscribed in brass!
Oh! Recollection, speed their fresh return,
And sure 'tis mine to be ashamed and mourn.
"What shall I ask, or what refrain to say?
Where shall I point, or how conclude my lay?

So much my weakness needs—so oft thy voice,
Assures that weakness, and confirms my choice.
Oh, grant me active days of peace and truth,
Strength to my heart, and wisdom to my youth,
A sphere of usefulness—a soul to fill
That sphere with duty, and perform thy will."

1841

THE INFANT CLASS: WRITTEN IN SCHOOL

This, my youngest class in school,
    Is what I do admire;
      Their sweetest, ever perfect praise,
    Their eyes as sparkling fire.

How oft I've blessed them in my heart,
    Besought that every grace
      And consolation, might there dwell,
    To cheer each youthful face.

I love them all as children each,
    How happy they appear:
      O, may no dull unclouded path,
    Make happiness to fear.

How sweet their prayerful voices join,
    To say what I do teach:
      Their infant voices, how adorn'd,
    How full of music each.

When out of school, how oft I think
    Of these, my little ones,
      But when in school, how glances all,
    They shine like many suns.

They gather round me, one by one,
    Like darlings to be taught;
      Ah, there behold my orphan dear,
    For me she now has sought.

Dearest, we soon must say farewell,
    May God your steps approve,
    If then on earth we no more meet,
    Or nev'er do this course more greet,
    May we in Christ e'er move.

1841

FREDERICK DOUGLASS (1818-1895)

Frederick Douglass was born Frederick Augustus Washington Bailey, in Talbot County, Maryland. His mother was Harriet Bailey, an enslaved African American woman. The identity of his father is unknown. Douglass escaped slavery in 1838 and went on to become the foremost African American leader of the nineteenth century and one of the most famous living Americans of his time. Largely self-educated, both prior to and after his escape, Douglass quickly involved himself in the growing abolitionist movement. Choosing Rochester, New York, as his base, he quickly became a popular and well-respected lecturer. In addition to drawing large audiences, his speeches on abolitionism and the plight of enslaved blacks were also distributed as popular pamphlets. Douglass also published numerous letters, editorials, and even a small amount of short fiction, most of which appeared in his own newspaper. Known under three different names during its sixteen-year run, the *North Star* (later *Frederick Douglass' Paper* and, finally, the *Douglass Monthly*) published many of the most important African American writers and thinkers of the day, including James McCune Smith, Frances E. W. Harper, William J. Wilson, Joseph C. Holly, William Whipper, William James Watkins, and Samuel Ringgold Ward. After emancipation, Douglass remained an outspoken advocate of equality and basic civil rights, especially for African Americans and women. Today, Douglass is remembered primarily for his deeply affecting *Narrative of the Life of Frederick Douglas, an American Slave* (1845), the first of three autobiographies that he published during his lifetime. Indeed, Douglass's autobiographical writings, including the subsequent volumes, *My Bondage and My Freedom* (1855) and *The Life and Times of Frederick Douglass* (1881), have long overshadowed his shorter essays and opinion pieces, two of which are included here, alongside his one piece of short fiction, "The Heroic Slave," serialized in *Frederick Douglass' Paper* in 1853.

WHAT ARE THE COLORED PEOPLE DOING FOR THEMSELVES?

The present is a time when every colored man in the land should bring this important question home to his own heart. It is not enough to know that white men and women are nobly devoting themselves to our cause; we should know what is being done among ourselves. That our white friends have done, and are still doing, a great and good work for us, is a fact which ought to excite in us sentiments of the profoundest gratitude; but it must never be forgotten that when they have exerted all their energies, devised every scheme, and done all they can do in asserting our rights, proclaiming our wrongs, and rebuking our foes, their labor is lost—yea, worse than lost, unless we are found in the faithful discharge of our anti-slavery duties. If there be one evil spirit among us, for the casting out of which we pray more earnestly than another, it is that lazy, mean and cowardly spirit, that robs us of all manly self-reliance, and teaches us to depend upon others for the accomplishment of that which we should achieve with our own hands. Our white friends can and are rapidly removing the barriers to our improvement, which themselves have set up; but the main work must be commenced, carried on, and concluded by ourselves. While in no circumstances should we undervalue or fail to appreciate the self-sacrificing efforts of our friends, it should never be lost sight of, that our destiny, for good or for evil, for time and for eternity, is, by an all-wise God, committed to us; and that all the helps or hindrances with which we may meet on earth, can never please us from this high and heaven-imposed responsibility. It is evident that we can be improved and elevated only just so fast and far as we shall improve and elevate ourselves. We must rise or fall, succeed or fail, by our own merits. If we are careless and unconcerned about our own rights and interests, it is not within the power of all the earth combined to raise us from our present degraded condition.

"Hereditary bondsmen, know ye not

Who would be free, themselves must strike the blow?"[1]

We say the present is a time when every colored man should ask himself the question, What am I doing to elevate and improve my condition, and that of my brethren at large? While the oppressed of the old world are making efforts, by holding public meetings, putting forth addresses, passing resolutions, and in various other ways making their wishes known to the world, and the working men of our own country are pressing their cause upon popular attention, it is a shame that we, who are enduring wrongs far more grievous than any other portion of the great family of man, are comparatively idle and indifferent about our welfare. We confess, with the deepest mortification, that out of the five hundred thousand free colored people in this country, not more than two thousand can be supposed to take any special interest in measures for our own elevation; and probably not more than fifteen hundred take, read and pay for an anti-slavery paper. We say this in sorrow, not in anger. It cannot be said that we are too poor to patronize our own press to any greater extent than we now do; for in popular demonstrations of odd-fellowship, free-masonry and the like, we expend annually from ten to twelve thousand dollars. If we put forth a call for a National Convention, for the purpose of considering our wrongs, and asserting our rights, and adopting measures for our mutual elevation and the emancipation of our enslaved fellow-countrymen, we shall bring together about fifty; but if we call a grand celebration of odd-fellowship, or free-masonry,[2] we shall assemble, as was the case a few days ago in New York, from four to five thousand—the expense of which alone would be from seventeen to twenty thousand dollars, a sum sufficient to maintain four or five efficient presses, devoted to our elevation and improvement. We should not say this of odd-fellowship and free-masonry, but that it is swallowing up the best energies of many of our best men, contenting them with the glittering follies of artificial display, and indisposing them to seek for solid and important realities. The enemies of our people see this tendency in us, and encourage it. The same persons who would puff such demonstrations in the newspapers, would mob us if we met to adopt measures for obtaining our just rights. They see our weak points, and avail themselves of them to crush us. We are imitating the inferior qualities and examples of white men, and neglecting superior ones. We do not pretend that all the members of odd-fellow societies and Masonic lodges are indifferent to their rights and the means of obtaining them; for we know the fact to be otherwise. Some of the best and brightest among us are numbered with those societies; and it is on this account that we make these remarks. We desire to see these noble men expending their time, talents and strength for higher and nobler objects than any that can be attained by the weak and glittering follies of odd-fellowship and free-masonry.

We speak plainly on this point, for we feel deeply. We have dedicated ourself, heart and soul, without reserve, to the elevation and improvement of our race, and have resolved to sink or swim with them. Our inmost soul is fired with a sense of the various forms of injustice to which we are daily subjected, and we must and will speak out against anything, within ourselves or our guilty oppressors, which may tend to prolong this reign of injustice. To be faithful to our oppressors, we must be faithful to ourselves; and shame on any colored man who would have us do otherwise. For this very purpose the *North Star* was established—that it might be as faithful to ourselves as to our oppressors. In this respect, we intend that it shall be different from most of its predecessors, and if it cannot be sustained in its high position, its death will be welcomed by us. But to return.

It is a doctrine held by many good men, in Europe as well as in America; that every oppressed people will gain their rights just as soon as they prove themselves worthy of them; and although we may justly object to the extent to which this doctrine is carried, especially in reference to ourselves as a people, it must still be evident to all that there is a great truth in it.

One of the first things necessary to prove the colored man worthy of equal freedom, is an earnest and persevering effort on his part to gain it. We deserve no earthly or heavenly blessing, for which we are unwilling to labor. For our part, we despise a freedom and equality obtained for us by others, and for which we have been unwilling to labor. A man who will not labor to gain his rights, is a man who would not, if he had them, prize and defend them. What is the use of standing a man on his feet, if, when we let him go, his head is again brought to the pavement? Look out of ourselves as we will—beg and pray to our white friends for assistance as much as we will—and that assistance may come, and come at the needed time; but unless we, the colored people of America, shall set about the work of our own regeneration and improvement, we are doomed to drag on in our present miserable and degraded condition for ages. Would that we could speak to every colored man, woman and child in the land, and, with the help of Heaven, we would thunder into their ears their duties and responsibilities, until a spirit should be roused, among them, never to be lulled till the last chain is broken.—But here we are mortified to think that we are now speaking to tens where we ought to speak to thousands. Unfortunately, those who have the ear of our people on Sundays, have little sympathy with the anti-slavery cause, or the cause of progress in any of its phases. They are too frequently disposed to follow the beaten paths of their fathers.—The most they aim at, is to get to heaven when they die. They reason thus: Our fathers got along pretty well through the world without learning and without meddling with abolitionism, and we can do the same.—We have in our minds three pulpits among the colored people in the North, which have the power to produce a revolution in the condition of the colored people in this country in three years.

First among these, we may mention the great Bethel Church in Philadelphia.[3] That church is the largest colored church in this Union, and from two to three thousand persons worship there every Sabbath. It has its branches in nearly all parts of the North and West, and a few in the south. It is surrounded by numerous little congregations in Philadelphia. Its ministers and bishops travel in all directions, and vast numbers of colored people belong to its branches all over the country. The Bethel pulpit in Philadelphia may be said to give tone to the entire denomination—"as goes large Bethel, so go the small Bethels throughout the Union." Here is concentrated the talent of the church, and here is the central and ruling power.—Now, if that pulpit would but speak the right word—the word for progress—the word for mental culture—encourage reading, and would occasionally take up contributions to aid those who are laboring for their elevation, as the white churches do to aid the colonization society to send us out of the country—there is no telling the good that would result from such labors. An entire change might soon take place in that denomination; loftier views of truth and duty would be presented; a nobler destiny would be opened up to them, and a deeper happiness would at once be enjoyed through all the ramifications of that church.

Similarly situated is the "Zion Church" in New York.[4] That church exerts a controlling influence over the next largest colored denomination in this country. It, too, is a unit—had its branches in all directions in the North rather than in the South. Its ministers are zealous men, and some of them powerful preachers. There is no estimating the good these men might do, if they would only encourage their congregations to take an interest in the subject of reform.

The next church in importance, is St. Phillip's, in New York.[5] This church is more important on account of the talent and respectability which it comprises, than for its numbers. Now, could the influence of these churches be enlisted in exciting our people to a constant and persevering effort at self-elevation, a joyful change would soon come over us.

What we, the colored people, want, is character, and this nobody can give us. It is a thing we must get for ourselves. We must labor for it. It is gained by toil—hard toil. Neither the sympathy nor the generosity of our friends can give it to us. It is attainable—yes, thank God, it is attainable. "There is gold in the earth, but we must DIG it"—so with character. It is attainable; but we must attain it, and attain it each for himself. I cannot for you, and you cannot for me.—What matters it to the mass of colored people of this country that they are able to point to their Penningtons, Garnets, Remonds, Wards, Purvises, Smiths, Whippers, Sandersons,[6] and a respectable list of other men of character, which we might name, while our general ignorance makes these men exceptions to our race? Their talents can do little to give us character in the eyes of the world. We must get character for ourselves, as a people. A change in our political condition would do very little for us without this. Character is the important thing, and without it we must continue to be marked for degradation and stamped with the brand of inferiority. With character, we shall be powerful. Nothing can harm us long when we get character.—There are certain great elements of character in us which may be hated, but never despised. Industry, sobriety, honesty, combined with intelligence and a due self-respect, find them where you will, among black or white, must be looked up to—can never be looked down upon. In their presence, prejudice is abashed, confused and mortified. Encountering this solid mass of living character, our vile oppressors are ground to atoms. In its presence, the sneers of a caricaturing press, the taunts of natural inferiority, the mischievous assertions of Clay,[7] and fine-spun sophisms of Calhoun,[8] are innoxious, powerless and unavailing. In answer to these men and the sneers of the multitude, there is nothing in the wide world half so effective as the presentation of a character precisely to the opposite of all their representations. We have it in our power to convert the weapons intended for our injury into positive blessings. That we may sustain temporary injury from gross and general misrepresentation, is most true; but the injury is but temporary, and must disappear at the approach of light, like mist from the vale. The offensive traits of character imputed to us, can only be injurious while they are true of us. For a man to say that sweet is bitter—that right is wrong—that light is darkness—is not to injure the truth, but to stamp himself a liar; and the like is true when they impute to us that of which we are not guilty. We have the power of making our enemies slanderers, and this we must do by showing ourselves worthy and respectable men.

We are not insensible to the various obstacles that throng the colored man's pathway to respectability. Embarrassments and perplexities, unknown to other men, are common to us. Though born on American soil, we have fewer privileges than aliens. The school-house, the work-shop, counting-house, attorney's office, and various professions, are opened to them, but closed to us. This, and much more, is true. A general and withering prejudice—a malignant and active hate, pursues us even in the best parts of this country. But a few days ago, one of our best and most talented men—and he a lame man, having lost an important limb—was furiously hurled from a car on the Niagara &

Buffalo Railroad, by a band of white ruffians, who claim impunity for their atrocious outrage on the plea that New York law does not protect the rights of colored against a company of white men, and the sequel has proved them right; for the case, it appears, was brought before the grand jury, but that jury found no bill. We cannot at this time dwell on this aspect of the subject.

The fact that we are limited and circumscribed, ought rather to incite us to a more vigorous and persevering use of the elevating means within our reach, than to dishearten us. The means of education, though not so free and open to us as to white persons, are nevertheless at our command to such an extent as to make education possible; and these, thank God, are increasing. Let us educate our children, even though it should us subject to a coarser and scantier diet, and disrobe us of our few fine garments. "For the want of knowledge we are killed all the day."[9] Get wisdom—get understanding, is a peculiarly valuable exhortation to us, and the compliance with it is our only hope in this land.—It is idle, a hollow mockery, for us to pray to God to break the oppressor's power, while we neglect the means of knowledge which will give us the ability to break this power.—God will help us when we help ourselves. Our oppressors have divested us of many valuable blessings and facilities for improvement and elevation; but, thank heaven, they have not yet been able to take from us the privilege of being honest, industrious, sober and intelligent. We may read and understand—we may speak and write—we may expose our wrongs—we may appeal to the sense of justice yet alive in the public mind, and by an honest, upright life, we may at last wring from a reluctant public the all-important confession, that we are men, worthy men, good citizens, good Christians, and ought to be treated as such.

1848

TO MY OLD MASTER

THOMAS AULD—SIR:—[10]

The long and intimate, though by no means friendly, relation which unhappily subsisted between you and myself, leads me to hope that you will easily account for the great liberty which I now take in addressing you in this open and public manner. The same fact may possibly remove any disagreeable surprise which you may experience on again finding your name coupled with mine, in any other way than in an advertisement, accurately describing my person, and offering a large sum for my arrest. In thus dragging you again before the public, I am aware that I shall subject myself to no inconsiderable amount of censure. I shall probably be charged with an unwarrantable if not a wanton and reckless disregard of the rights and proprieties of private life. There are those North as well as South, who entertain a much higher respect for rights which are merely conventional, than they do for rights which are personal and essential. Not a few there are in our country who, while they have no scruples against robbing the laborer of the hard-earned results of his patient industry, will be shocked by the extremely indelicate manner of bringing your name before the public. Believing this to be the case, and wishing to meet every reasonable or plausible objection to my conduct, I will frankly state the ground upon which I justify myself in this instance, as well as on former occasions when I have thought proper to mention your name in public. All will agree that a man guilty of theft, robbery or murder, has forfeited the right to concealment and private life; that the community have a right to subject such persons to the most complete exposure. However much they may desire retirement, and aim to conceal themselves and their movements from the popular gaze, the public have a right to ferret them out, and bring their conduct before the proper tribunals of the country for investigation. Sir, you will undoubtedly make the proper application of these generally-admitted principles, and will easily see the light in which you are regarded by me. I will not, therefore, manifest ill-temper, by calling you hard names. I know you to be a man of some intelligence, and can readily determine the precise estimate which I entertain of your character. I may therefore indulge in language which may seem to others indirect and ambiguous, and yet be quite well understood by yourself.

I have selected this day on which to address you, because it is the anniversary of my emancipation; and knowing of no better way, I am led to this as the best mode of celebrating that truly important event. Just ten years ago this beautiful September morning, yon bright sun beheld me a slave—a poor degraded chattel—trembling at the sound of your voice, lamenting that I was a man, and wishing myself a brute. The hopes which I had treasured up for weeks of a safe and successful escape from your grasp, were powerfully confronted at this last hour by dark clouds of doubt and fear, making my person shake and my bosom to heave with the heavy contest between hope and fear. I have no words to describe to you the deep agony of soul which I experienced on that never-to-be-forgotten morning—(for I left by daylight)—I was taking a leap in the dark. The probabilities, so far as I could by reason determine them, were stoutly against the undertaking. The preliminaries and precautions I had adopted previously, all worked badly. I was like one going to war without weapons—ten chances of defeat to one of victory. One in whom I had confided, and one who had promised me assistance, appalled by fear at the trial-hour, deserted me, thus leaving the responsibility of success or failure solely with myself. You, sir, can never know my feelings. As I look back to them, I can scarcely realize that I have passed through a scene so trying. Trying however as they were, and gloomy as was the prospect, thanks be to the Most High, who is ever the God of the oppressed, at the moment which was to determine my whole earthly career, His grace was sufficient, my mind was made up. I embraced the golden opportunity, took the morning tide at the flood; and a free man, young, active, and strong, is the result.

I have often thought I should like to explain to you the grounds upon which I have justified myself in running away from you. I am almost ashamed to do so now, for by this time you may have discovered them yourself. I will, however, glance at them. When yet but a child about six years old, I imbibed the determination to run away. The very first mental effort that I now remember on my part, was an attempt to solve the mystery, Why am I a slave? and with this question my youthful mind was troubled for many days, pressing upon me more heavily at times than others. When I saw the slave-driver whip a slave-woman, cut the blood out of her neck, and heard her piteous cries, I went away into the corner of the fence, wept and pondered over this mystery. I had, through some medium, I know not what, got some idea of God, the Creator of all mankind, the black and the white, and that he had made the blacks to serve the whites as slaves.[11] How he could do this and be good, I could not tell. I was not satisfied with this theory, which made God responsible for slavery, for it pained me greatly, and I have wept over it long and often. At one time, your first wife, Mrs. Lucretia, heard me singing and saw me shedding tears, and asked of me the matter, but I was afraid to tell her. I was puzzled with this question, till one night, while sitting in the kitchen, I heard some of the old slaves talking of their parents having been stolen from Africa by white men, and were sold here as slaves. The whole mystery was solved at once. Very soon after this, my aunt Jinny and Uncle Noah ran away, and the great noise made about it by your father-in-law, made me for the first time acquainted with the fact, that there were free States as well as slave States. From that time, I resolved that I would some day run away. The morality of the act, I dispose of as follows: I am myself; you are yourself; we are two distinct persons, equal persons. What you are I am. You are a man, and so am I.—God created both, and made us separate beings. I am not by nature bound to you, or you to me. Nature does not make your existence depend upon me, or mine to depend upon yours. I cannot walk upon your legs, or you upon mine. I cannot breathe for you, or you for me; I must breathe for myself, and you for yourself. We are distinct persons, and are each equally provided with faculties necessary to our individual existence. In leaving you, I took nothing but what belonged to me, and in no way lessened your means of obtaining an honest living. Your faculties remained yours, and mine became useful to their rightful owner. I therefore see no wrong in any part of the transaction. It is true, I went off secretly, but that was more your fault than mine. Had I let you into the secret, you would have defeated the enterprise entirely; but for this, I should have been really glad to have made you acquainted with my intention to leave.

You may perhaps want to know how I like my present condition. I am free to say, I greatly prefer it to that which I occupied in Maryland. I am, however, by no means prejudiced against that State as such. Its geography, climate, fertility and products, are such as to make it a very desirable abode for any man; and but for the existence of slavery there, it is not impossible that I might again take up my abode in that State. It is not that I love Maryland less, but freedom more. You will be surprised to learn that people at the North labor under the strange delusion that if the slaves were emancipated at the South, they would all flock to the North. So far from this being the case, in that event, you would see many old and familiar faces back again at the South. The fact is, there are few here who would not return to the South in the event of emancipation. We want to live in the land of our birth, and to lay our bones by the side of our fathers'; and nothing short of an intense love of personal freedom keeps us from the South. For the sake of this, most of us would live on a crust of bread and a cup of cold water.

Since I left you, I have had a rich experience. I have occupied stations which I never dreamed of when a slave. Three out of the ten years since I left you, I spent as a common laborer on the wharves of New Bedford, Massachusetts. It was there I earned my first free dollar. It was mine. I could spend it as I pleased. I could buy hams or herring with it, without asking any odds of anybody. That was a precious dollar to me. You remember when I used to make seven or eight, and even nine dollars a week in Baltimore, you would take every cent of it from me every Saturday night, saying that I belonged to you, and my earnings also. I never liked this conduct on your part—to say the best, I thought it a little mean. I would not have served you so. But let that pass. I was a little awkward about counting money in New England fashion when I first landed in New Bedford. I like to have betrayed myself several times. I caught myself saying phip, for fourpence;[12] and one time a man actually charged me with being a runaway, whereupon I was silly enough to become one by running away from him, for I was greatly afraid he might adopt measures to get me again into slavery, a condition I then dreaded more than death.

I soon, however, learned to count money, as well as to make it, and got on swimmingly. I married soon after leaving you: in fact, I was engaged to be married before I left you; and instead of finding my companion a burden, she was truly a helpmeet. She went to live at service, and I to work on the wharf, and though we toiled hard the first winter, we never lived more happily. After remaining in New Bedford for three years, I met with Wm. Lloyd Garrison,[13] a person of whom you have possibly heard, as he is pretty generally known among slaveholders. He put it into my head that I might make myself serviceable to the cause of the slave by devoting a portion of my time to telling my own sorrows, and those of other slaves which had come under my observation. This was the commencement of a higher state of existence than any to which I had ever aspired. I was thrown into society the most pure, enlightened and benevolent that the country affords. Among these, I have never forgotten you, but have invariably made you the topic of conversation—thus giving you all the notoriety I could do. I need not tell you that the opinion formed of you in these circles, is far from being favorable. They have little respect for your honesty, and less for your religion.

But I was going on to relate to you something of my interesting experience. I had not long enjoyed the excellent society to which I have referred, before the light of its excellence exerted a beneficial influence on my mind and heart. Much of my early dislike of white persons was removed, and their manners, habits and customs, so entirely unlike what I had been used to in the kitchen-quarters on the plantations of the South, fairly charmed me, and gave me a strong disrelish for the coarse and degrading customs of my former condition. I therefore made an effort so to improve my mind and deportment, as to be somewhat fitted to the station to which I seemed almost Providentially called. The transition from degradation to respectability was indeed great, and to get from one to the other without carrying some marks of one's former condition, is truly a difficult matter.—I would not have you think that I am now entirely clear of all plantation peculiarities, but my friends here, while they entertain the strongest dislike to them, regard me with that charity to which my past life somewhat entitles me, so that my condition in this respect is exceedingly pleasant. So far as my domestic affairs are concerned, I can boast of as comfortable a dwelling as your own. I have an industrious and neat companion, and four dear children—the oldest a girl of nine years, and three fine boys, the oldest eight, the next six, and the youngest four years old. The three oldest are now going regularly to school—two can read and write, and the other can spell with tolerable correctness words of two syllables. Dear fellows! They are all in comfortable beds, and are sound asleep, perfectly secure under my own roof. There are no slaveholders here to rend my heart by snatching them from my arms, or blast a proud mother's dearest hopes by tearing them from her bosom. These dear children are ours—not to work up into rice, sugar and tobacco, but to watch over, regard, and protect, and to rear them up in the nurture and admonition of the gospel—to train them up in the paths of wisdom and virtue, and, as far as we can, to make them useful to the world and to themselves. Oh! Sir, a slaveholder never appears to me so completely an agent of hell, as when I think of and look upon my dear children. It is then that my feelings rise above my control. I meant to have said more with respect to my own prosperity and happiness, but thoughts and feelings which this recital has quickened, unfits me to proceed further in that direction. The grim horrors of slavery rise in all their ghastly terror before me, the wails of millions pierce my heart, and chill my blood. I remember the chain, the gag, the bloody whip, the deathlike gloom overshadowing the broken spirit of the fettered bondman, the appalling liability of his being torn away from wife and children and sold like a beast in the market. Say not that this is a picture of fancy. You well know that I wear stripes on my back inflicted by your direction; and that you, while we were brothers in the same church, caused this right hand, with which I am now penning this letter, to be closely tied to my left, and my person dragged at the pistol's mouth, fifteen miles, from the Bay side to Easton, to be sold like a beast in the market, for the alleged crime of intending to escape from your possession. All this and more you remember, and know to be perfectly true, not only of yourself, but of nearly all the slaveholders around you.

At this moment, you are probably the guilty holder of at least three of my own dear sisters, and my only brother in bondage. These you regard as your property. They are recorded on your ledger, or perhaps have been sold to human flesh mongers, with a view to filling your own ever-hungry purse. Sir, I desire to know how and where these dear sisters are. Have you sold them? or are they still in your possession? What has become of them? Are they living or dead? And my dear old grandmother, whom you turned out like an old horse, to die in the woods—is she still alive? Write and let me know all about them. If my grandmother be still alive, she is of no service to you, for by this time she must be nearly eighty years old—too old to be cared for by one whom she has ceased to be of service, send her to me at Rochester, or bring her to Philadelphia, and it shall be the crowning happiness of my life to take care of her in her old age. Oh! She was to me a mother, and a father, so far as hard toil for my comfort could make her such. Send me my grandmother! That I may watch over and take care of her in her old age. And my sisters, let me know all about them. I would write to them, and learn all I want to know of them without disturbing you in any way, but that, through your unrighteous conduct, they have been entirely deprived of the power to read and write. You have kept them in utter ignorance, and have therefore robbed them of the sweet enjoyments of writing or receiving letters from absent friends and relatives. Your wickedness and cruelty committed in this respect on your own fellow-creatures, are greater than all the stripes you have laid upon my back, or theirs. It is an outrage upon the soul—a war upon the immortal spirit, and one for which you must give account at the bar of our common Father and Creator.

The responsibility which you have assumed in this regard is truly awful— and how you could stagger under it these many years is marvelous. Your mind must have become darkened, your heart hardened, your conscience seared and petrified, or you would have long since thrown off the accursed load and sought relief at the hands of a sin forgiving God. How, let me ask, would you look upon me, were I some dark night in company with a band of hardened villains, to enter the precincts of your own elegant dwelling and seize the person of your own lovely daughter Amanda, and carry her off from your family, friends and all the loved ones of her youth—make her my slave—compel her to work, and I take her wages—place her name on my ledger as property—disregard her personal rights—fetter the powers of her immortal soul by denying her the right and privilege of learning to read and write—feed her coarsely—clothe her scantily, and whip her on the naked back occasionally; more and still more horrible, leave her unprotected—a degraded victim to the brutal lust of fiendish overseers who would pollute, blight, and blast her fair soul—rob her of all dignity—destroy her virtue, and annihilate all in her person the graces that adorn the character of virtuous womanhood? I ask how would you regard me, if such were my conduct? Oh! The vocabulary of the damned would not afford a word sufficiently infernal, to express your idea of my God-provoking wickedness. Yet sir, your treatment of my beloved sisters is in all essential points, precisely like the case I have now supposed. Damning as would be such a deed on my part, it would be no more so than that which you have committed against me and my sisters.

I will now bring this letter to a close; you shall hear from me again unless you let me hear from you. I intend to make use of you as a weapon with which to assail the system of slavery—as a means of concentrating public attention on the system, and deepening their horror of trafficking in the souls and bodies of men. I shall make use of you as a means of exposing the character of the American church and clergy—and as a means of bringing this guilty nation with yourself to repentance. In doing this I entertain no malice towards you personally. There is no roof under which you would be more safe than mine, and there is nothing in my house which you might need for your comfort, which I would not readily grant. Indeed, I should esteem it a privilege, to set you an example as to how mankind ought to treat each other.

I am your fellow man but not your slave,

FREDERICK DOUGLASS.

1848

THE HEROIC SLAVE

Part I.

> Oh! child of grief, why weepest thou?
> Why droops thy sad and mournful brow?
> Why is thy look so like despair?
> What deep, and sorrow lingers there?[14]

The State of Virginia is famous in American annals for the multitudinous array of her statesmen and heroes. She has been dignified by some the mother of statesmen. History has not been sparing in recording their names, or in blazoning their deeds.—Her high position in this respect, has given her an enviable distinction among her sister States. With Virginia for his birthplace, even a man of ordinary parts, on account of the general partiality for her sons, easily rises to eminent stations. Men, not great enough to attract special attention in their native States, have, like a certain distinguished citizen in the State of New York, sighed and repined that they were not born in Virginia. Yet not all the great ones of the Old Dominion[15] have, by the fact of their birth-place, escaped undeserved obscurity. By some strange neglect, *one* of the truest, manliest, and bravest of her children—one who, in after years, will, I think, command the pen of genius to set his merits forth, holds now no higher place in the records of that grand old Commonwealth than is held by a horse or an ox. Let those account for it who can, but there stands the fact, that a man who loved liberty as well as did Patrick Henry—who deserved it as much as Thomas Jefferson—and who fought for it with a valor as high, an arm as strong, and against odds as great, as he who led all the armies of the American colonies through the great war for freedom and independence, lives now only in the chattel records of his native State.

Glimpses of this great character are all that can now be presented. He is brought to view only by a few transient incidents, and these afford but partial satisfaction. Like a guiding star on a stormy night, he is seen through the parted clouds and the howling tempests; or, like the gray peak of a menacing rock on a perilous cost, he is seen by the quivering flash of angry lightning, and he again disappears covered with mystery.

Curiously, earnestly, anxiously we peer into the dark, and wish even for the blinding flash, or the light of northern skies to reveal him. But alas! he is still enveloped in darkness, and we return from the pursuit like a wearied and disheartened mother, (after a tedious and unsuccessful search for a lost child,) who returns weighed down with disappointment and sorrow. Speaking of marks, traces, possibles, and probabilities, we come before our readers.

In the spring of 1835, on a Sabbath morning, within hearing of the solemn peals of the church bells at a distant village, a Northern traveller through the State of Virginia drew up his horse to drink at a sparkling brook, near the edge of a dark pine forest.—While his weary and thirsty steed drew in the grateful water, the rider caught the sound of human voice, apparently engaged in earnest conversation.

Following the direction of the sound, he descried, among the tall pines, the man whose voice had arrested his attention. "To whom can he be speaking?" thought the traveller. "He seems to be alone." The circumstance interested him much, and he became intensely curious to know what thoughts and feelings, or, it might be, high asperations, guided those rich and mellow accents.

Tying his horse at a short distance from the brook, he stealthily drew near the solitary speaker; and, concealing himself by the side of a huge fallen tree, he distinctly heard the following soliloquy:

"What, then, is life to me? it is aimless and worthless, and worse than worthless.—Those birds, perched on yon swinging boughs, in friendly conclave, sounding forth their merry notes in seeming worship of the rising sun, though liable to the sportsman's fowling-piece, are still my superiors. They *live free,* though they may die slaves. They fly where they list by day, and retire in freedom at night. But what is freedom to me, or I to it? I am a *slave*—born a slave, an abject slave—even before I made part of this breathing world, the scourge was plated for my back; the fetters were forged for my limbs. How mean a thing I am. That accursed and crawling snake, that miserable reptile, that has just glided into a slimy home, is freer and better off than I. He escaped my blow, and is safe. But here am I, a man—yes, *a man!*—with thoughts and wishes, with powers and faculties as far as angel's flight above that hated reptile—yet he is my superior, and scorns to own me as his master, or to stop to take my blows—When he saw my uplifted arm, he darted beyond my reach, and turned to give me battle. I dare not do as much as that. I neither run nor fight, but do meanly stand, answering each heavy blow of a cruel master with doleful wails and piteous cries. I am galled with irons; but even these are more tolerable than the consciousness, the *galling* consciousness of cowardice and indecision.—Can it be that I *dare* run away? *Perish the thought, I dare do* any thing which may be done by another. When that young man struggled with the waves *for life,* and others stood appalled in helpless horror, did I not plunge in, forgetful of life, to save his?—The raging bull from whom all others fled, pale with fright, did I not keep at bay with a single pitchfork? Could a coward do that? *No—no*—I wrong myself; I am no coward. *Liberty* I will have, or die in the attempt to gain it. This working that others may live in idleness! this cringing submission to insolence and curses? this living under the constant dread and apprehension of being sold and transferred like a mere brute, is *too* much for me. I will stand it no longer.—What others have done, I will do. These trusty legs, or these sinewy arms shall place me among the free. Tom escaped; so can I. The North Star will not be less kind to me than to him. I will follow it. I will at least make the trial. I have nothing to lose. If I am caught, I shall only be a slave. If I am shot, I shall only lose a life which is a burden and a curse. If I get clear, (as something tells me I shall,) liberty, the inalienable birth-right of every man, precious and priceless, will be mine. My resolution is fixed. *I shall be free.*"

At these words the traveller raised his head cautiously and noiselessly, and caught, from his hiding-place, a full view of the unsuspecting speaker. Madison (for that was the name of our hero) was standing erect, a smile of satisfaction rippled upon his expressive countenance, like that which plays upon the face of one who has but just solved a difficult problem, or vanquished a malignant foe; for at that moment he was free, at least in spirit. The future gleamed bright before him, and his fetters lay broken at his feet.—His air was triumphant.

Madison was of manly form. Tall, symmetrical, round and strong. In his movements he seemed to combine, with the strength of the lion, the lion's elasticity.—His torn sleeves disclosed arms like polished iron. His face was "black, but comely."[16]—His eye, lit with emotion, kept guard under a brow as dark and as glossy as the raven's wing. His whole appearance betokened Herculean strength; yet there was nothing savage or forbidding in his aspect. A child might play in his arms, or dance on his shoulders. A giant's strength, but not a giant's heart was in him. His broad mouth and nose spoke only of good nature and kindness. But his voice, that unfailing index of the soul, though full and melodius, had that in it which could terrify as well as charm.—He was just the man who would choose when hardships were to be endured, or danger to be encountered,—intelligent and brave. He had the head to conceive, and the hand to execute. In a word, he was one to be sought as a friend, but to be dreaded as an enemy.

As our traveller gazed upon him, he almost trembled at the thought of his dangerous intrusion. Still he could not quit the place.—He had long desired to sound the mysterious depths of the thoughts and feelings of a slave. He was not, therefore, disposed to allow so providential an opportunity to pass unimproved. He resolved to hear more; so he listened again for those mellow and mournful accents which, he says, made such an impression upon him as can never be erased. He did not have to wait long. There came another gush from the same full fountain; now bitter, and now sweet. Scathing denunciations of the cruelty and injustice of slavery; heart-touching narrations of his own personal suffering, intermingled with prayers to the God of the oppressed for help and deliverance, were followed by presentations of the dangers and difficulties of escape, and formed the burden of his eloquent utterances; but his high resolution clung to him,—for he ended each speech by an emphatic declaration of his purpose to be free. It seemed that the very repetition of this, imparted a glow to his countenance.—The hope of freedom seemed to sweeten, for a season, the bitter cup of slavery, and to make it, for a time, tolerable; for when in the very whirlwind of anguish,—when his heart's cord seemed screwed up to snapping tension, hope sprung up and soothed his troubled spirit. Fitfully he would exclaim, "How can I leave her? Poor thing! what can she do when I am gone? Oh! oh! 'tis impossible that I can leave poor Susan!"

A brief pause intervened. Our traveller raised his head, and saw again the sorrow-smitten slave. His eye was fixed upon the ground. The strong man staggered under a heavy load. Recovering himself, he argued thus aloud: "All is uncertain here. Tomorrow's sun may not rise before I am sold, and separated from her I love. What, then, could I do for her? I should be in more hopeless slavery, and she no nearer to liberty,—whereas if I were free,—my arms my own,—I might devise the means to rescue her."

This said, Madison cast around a searching glance, as if the thought of being overheard had flashed across his mind. He said no more, but, with measured steps, walked away, and was lost to the eye of our traveller amidst the wildering woods.

Long after Madison had left the ground, Mr. Listwell (our traveller) remained in motionless silence, meditating on the extra-ordinary revelations to which he had listened. He seemed fastened to the spot, and stood half hoping, half fearing the return of the sable preacher to his solitary temple. The speech of Madison rung through the chambers of his soul, and vibrated through his entire frame. "Here is indeed a man," thought he, "of rare endowments,—a child of God,—guilty of no crime but the color of his skin,—hiding away from the face of humanity, and pouring out his thoughts and feelings, his hopes and resolutions to the lonely woods; to him those distant church bells have no grateful music. He shuns the church, the altar, and the great congregation of Christian worshippers, and wanders away to the gloomy forest, to utter in the vacant air complaints and griefs, which the religions of his times and his country can neither console nor relieve. Goaded almost to madness by the sense of the injustice done him, he resorts hither to give vent to his pent up feelings, and to debate with himself the feasibility of plans, plans of his own invention, for his own deliverance. From this hour I am an abolitionist. I have seen enough and heard enough, and I shall go to my home in Ohio resolved to atone for my past indifference to this ill-starred race, by making such exertions as I shall be able to do, for the speedy emancipation of every slave in the land."

Part II.

"The gaudy, blabbling and remorseful day
Is crept into the bosom of the sea:
And now loud-howling wolves arouse the jades
That drag the tragic melancholy night;
Who with their drowsy, slow, and flagging wings
Clip dead men's graves, and from their misty jaws
Breathe foul contagions, darkness in the air."

—*Shakespeare.*[17]

Five years after the foregoing singular occurrence, in the winter of 1840, Mr. and Mrs. Listwell sat together by the fireside of their own happy home, in the State of Ohio. The children were all gone to bed. A single lamp burned brightly on the centre-table.—All was still and comfortable within; but the night was cold and dark; a heavy wind sighed and moaned sorrowfully around the house and barn, occasionally bringing against the clattering windows a stray leaf from the large oak trees that embowered their dwelling. It was a night for strange noises and for strange fancies. A whole wilderness of thought might pass through one's mind during such an evening. The smouldering embers, partaking of the spirit of the restless night, became fruitful of varied and fantastic pictures, and revived many bygone scenes and old impressions. The happy pair seemed to sit in silent fascination, gazing on the fire. Suddenly this *reverie* was interrupted by a heavy growl. Ordinarily such an occurrence would have scarcely provoked a single word or excited the least apprehension. But there are certain seasons when the slightest sound sends a jar through all the subtle chambers of the mind; and such a season was this. The happy pair started up, as if some sudden danger had come upon them. The growl was from their trusty watch-dog.

"What can it mean? certainly no one can be out on such a night as this," said Mrs. Listwell.

"The wind has deceived the dog, my dear; he has mistaken the noise of falling branches, brought down by the wind, for that of the footsteps of persons coming to the house. I have several times tonight thought that I heard the sound of footsteps. I am sure, however, that it was but the wind. Friends would not be likely to come out at such an hour, or such a night; and thieves are too lazy and self-indulgent to expose themselves to this biting frost; but should there be any one about, our brave old Monte, who is on the look-out, will not be slow in sounding the alarm."

Saying this they quietly left the window, whither they had gone to learn the cause of the menacing growl, and reseated themselves by the fire, as if reluctant to leave the slowly expiring embers, although the hour was late. A few minutes only intervened after resuming their seats, when again their sober meditations were disturbed. Their faithful dog now growled and barked furiously, as if assailed by an advancing foe. Simultaneously the good couple arose, and stood in mute expectation. The contest without seemed fierce and violent. It was, however, soon over—the barking ceased, for, with true canine instinct, Monte quickly discovered that a friend, not an enemy of the family, was coming to the house, and instead of rushing to repel the supposed intruder, he was now at the door, whimpering and dancing for the admission of himself and his newly made friend.

Mr. Listwell knew by this movement that all was well; he advanced and opened the door, and saw by the light that streamed out into the darkness, a tall man advancing slowly towards the house, with a stick in one hand, and a small bundle in the other. "It is a traveller," thought he, "who has missed his way, and is coming to inquire the road.—I am glad we did not go to bed earlier—I have felt all the evening as if somebody would be here tonight."

The man had now halted a short distance from the door, and looked prepared alike for flight or battle. "Come in, sir, don't be alarmed, you have probably lost your way."

Slightly hesitating the traveller walked in; not, however, without regarding his host with a scrutinizing glance. "No, sir," said he, "I have come to ask you a greater favor."

Instantly Mr. Listwell exclaimed, (as the recollection of the Virginia forest scene flashed upon him,) "Oh, sir, I know not your name, but I have seen your face and heard your voice before. I am glad to see you. *I know all.* You are flying for your liberty—be seated—be seated—banish all fear. You are safe under my roof."

This recognition, so unexpected, rather disconcerted and disquieted the noble fugitive. The timidity and suspicion of persons escaping from slavery are easily awakened, and often what is intended to dispel the one, and to allay the other, has precisely the opposite effect. It was so in this case. Quickly observing the unhappy impression made by his words and action, Mr. Listwell assumed a more quiet and inquiring aspect, and finally succeeded in removing the apprehensions which his very natural and generous salutation had aroused.

Thus assured, the stranger said, "Sir, you have rightly guessed, I am, indeed, a fugitive from slavery. My name is Madison—Madison Washington my mother used to call me. I am on my way to Canada, where I learn that persons of my color are protected in all the rights of men; and my object in calling upon you was, to beg the privilege of resting my weary limbs for the night in your barn. It was my purpose to have continued my journey till morning; but the piercing cold, and the frowning darkness compelled me to seek shelter; and, seeing a light through the lattice of your window, I was encouraged to come here to beg the privilege named.—You will do me a great favor by affording me shelter for the night."

"A resting-place, indeed, sir, you shall have; not, however, in my barn, but in the best room of my house. Consider yourself, if you please, under the roof of a friend; for such am I to you, and to all your deeply injured race."

While this introductory conversation was going on, the kind lady had revived the fire, and was diligently preparing supper; for she, not less than her husband, felt for the sorrows of the oppressed and hunted ones of earth, and was always glad of an opportunity to do them a service. A bountiful repast was quickly prepared, and the hungry and toil-worn bondman was cordially invited to partake thereof. Gratefully he acknowledged the favor of his benevolent benefactress; but appeared scarcely to understand what such hospitality could mean. It was the first time in his life that he had met so humane and friendly a greeting at the hands of persons whose color was unlike his own; yet it was impossible for him to doubt the charitableness of his new friends, or the genuineness of the welcome so freely given; and he therefore, with many thanks, took his seat at the table with Mrs. and Mr. Listwell, who, desirous to make him feel at home, took a cup of tea themselves, while urging upon Madison the best that the house could afford.

Supper over, all doubts, and apprehensions banished, the three drew around the blazing fire, and a conversation commenced, which lasted till long after midnight.

"Now," said Madison to Mr. Listwell, "I was a little surprised and alarmed when I came in, by what you said; do tell me, sir, *why* you thought you had seen my face before, and by what you knew me to be a fugitive from slavery; for I am sure that I never was before in this neighborhood, and I certainly sought to conceal what I supposed to be the manner of a fugitive slave."

Mr. Listwell at once frankly disclosed the secret; rehearsing the language which he (Madison) had used; referring to the effect which his manner and speech had made upon him; declaring the resolution he there formed to be an abolitionist; telling how often he had spoken of the circumstance, and the deep concern he had ever since felt to know what had become of him; and whether he had carried out the purpose to make his escape, as in the woods he declared he would do.

"Ever since that morning," said Mr. Listwell, "you have seldom been absent from my mind, and though now I dare not to hope that I should ever see you again, I have often wished that such might be my fortune; for, from that hour, your face seemed to be daguerreotyped on my memory."

Madison looked quite astonished, and felt amazed at the narration to which he had listened. After recovering himself he said, "I well remember that morning, and the bitter anguish that wrung my heart; I will state the occasion of it. I had, on the previous Saturday, suffered a cruel lashing; had been tied up to the limb of a tree, with my feet chained together, and a heavy iron bar placed between my ankles. Thus suspended, I received on my naked back forty stripes, and was kept in this distressing position three or four hours, and was then let down, only to have my torture increased; for my bleeding back, gashed by the cow-skin, was washed by the overseer with old brine, partly to augment my suffering, and partly, as he said, to prevent inflammation. My crime was that I had staid longer at the mill, the day previous, than it was thought I ought to have done, which, I assured my master and the overseer, was no fault of mine; but no excuses were allowed. 'Hold your tongue, you impudent rascal,' met every explanation. Slave-holders are so imperious when their passions are excited, as to construe every word of the slave into insolence. I could do nothing but submit to the agonizing infliction. Smarting still from the wounds, as well as from the consciousness of being whipped for no cause, I took advantage of the absence of my master, who had gone to church, to spend the time in the woods, and brood over my wretched lot. Oh, sir, I remember it well,—and can never forget it."

"But this was five years ago; where have you been since?"

"I will try to tell you," said Madison.—"Just four weeks after that Sabbath morning, I gathered up the few rags of clothing I had, and started, as I supposed, for the North and for freedom. I must not stop to describe my feelings on taking this step. It seemed like taking a leap into the dark.—The thought of leaving my poor wife and two little children caused me indescribable anguish;

but consoling myself with the reflection that once free, I could, possibly, devise ways and means to gain their freedom also, I nerved myself up to make the attempt. I started, but ill-luck attended me; for after being out a whole week, strange to say, I still found myself on my master's grounds; the third night after being out, a season of clouds and rain set in, wholly preventing me from seeing the North Star, which I had trusted as my guide, not dreaming that clouds might intervene between us.

"This circumstance was fatal to my project, for in losing my star, I lost my way; so when I supposed I was far towards the North, and had almost gained my freedom, I discovered myself at the very point from which I had started. It was a severe trial, for I arrived at home in great destitution; my feet were sore, and in travelling in the dark, I had dashed my foot against a stump, and started a nail, and lamed myself. I was wet and cold; one week had exhausted all my stores; and when I landed on my master's plantation, with all my work to do over again,—hungry, tired, lame, and bewildered,—I almost cursed the day that I was born. In this extremity I approached the quarters. I did so stealthily, although in my desperation I hardly cared whether I was discovered or not. Peeping through the rents of the quarters, I saw my fellow-slaves seated by a warm fire, merrily passing away the time, as though their hearts knew no sorrow. Altho' I envied their seeming contentment, all wretched as I was, I despised the cowardly acquiescence in their own degradation which it implied, and felt a kind of pride and glory in my own desperate lot. I dared not enter the quarters,—for where there is seeming contentment with slavery, there is certain treachery to freedom. I proceeded towards the great house, in the hope of catching a glimpse of my poor wife, whom I knew might be trusted with my secret even on the scaffold. Just as I reached the fence which divided the field from the garden, I saw a woman in the yard, who in the darkness I took to be my wife; but a nearer approach told me it was not she. I was about to speak; had I done so, I would not have been here this night; for the alarm would have been sounded, and the hunters been put on my track. Here were hunger, cold, thirst, disappointment, and chagrin, confronted only by the dim hope of liberty. I tremble to think of that dreadful hour. To face the deadly cannon's mouth in warm blood unterrified, is, I think, a small achievement, compared with a conflict like this with gaunt starvation. The gnawings of hunger conquers by degrees, till all that a man has he would give in exchange for a single crust of bread. Thank God, I was not quite reduced to this extremity.

"Happily for me, before the fatal moment of utter despair, my good wife made her appearance in the yard. It was she; I knew her step. All was well now. I was, however, afraid to speak lest I should frighten her.—Yet speak I did; and, to my great joy, my voice was known. Our meeting can be more easily imagined than described. For a time hunger, thirst, weariness, and lameness were forgotten. But it was soon necessary for her to return to the house. She being a house-servant, her absence from the kitchen, if discovered, might have excited suspicion. Our parting was like tearing the flesh from my bones; yet it was the part of wisdom for her to go. She left me with the purpose of meeting me at midnight in the very forest where you last saw me. She knew the place well, as one of my melancholy resorts, and could easily find it, though, the night was dark.

"I hastened away, therefore, and concealed myself, to await the arrival of my good angel. As I lay there among the leaves, I was strongly tempted to return again to the house of my master and give myself up; but remembering my solemn pledge on that memorable Sunday morning, I was able to linger out the two long hours between ten and midnight. I may well call them long hours. I have endured much hardships; I have encountered many perils; but the anxiety of those two hours, was the bitterest I ever experienced. True to her word, my wife came laden with provisions, and we sat down on the side of a log at that dark and lonesome hour of the night. I cannot say we talked; our feelings were too great for that; yet we came to an understanding that I should make the woods my home, for if I gave myself up, I should be whipped and sold away; and if I started for the North, I should leave a wife doubly dear to me. We mutually determined, therefore, that I should remain in the vicinity. In the dismal swamps I lived, sir, five long years,—a cave for my home during the day. I wandered about at night with the wolf and the bear,—sustained by the promise that my good Susan would meet me in the pine woods at least once a week. This promise was redeemed, I assure you, to the letter, greatly to my relief. I had partly become contented with my mode of life, and made up my mind to spend my days there; but the wilderness that sheltered me thus long took fire, and refused longer to be my hiding-place.

"I will not harrow up your feelings by portraying the terrific scene of this awful conflagration. There is nothing to which I can liken it. It was horribly and indiscribably grand. The whole world seemed on fire, and it appeared to me that the day of judgment had come; that the burning bowels of the earth had burst forth, and that the end of all things was at hand. Bears and wolves, scorched from their mysterious hiding-places in the earth, and all the wild inhabitants of the untrodden forest, filled with a common dismay, ran forth, yelling, howling, bewildered amidst the smoke and flame. The very heavens seemed to rain down fire through the towering trees; it was by the merest chance that I escaped the devouring element. Running before it, and stopping occasionally to take breath, I looked back to behold its frightful ravages, and to drink in its savage magnificence. It was awful, thrilling, solemn beyond compare. When aided by the fitful wind, the merciless tempest of fire swept on, sparkling, creaking, cracking, curling, roaring, out-doing in its dreadful splendor a thousand thunderstorms at once. From tree to tree it leaped, swallowing them up in its lurid, baleful glare; and leaving them leafless, limbless, charred, and lifeless behind. The scene was overwhelming, stunning,—nothing was spared,—cattle, tame and wild, herds of swine and of deer, wild beasts of every name and kind,—huge night-birds, bats, and owls, that had retired to their homes in lofty tree-tops to rest, perished in that fiery storm. The long-winged buzzard and croaking raven mingled their dismal cries with those of the countless myriads of small birds that rose up to the skies, and were lost to the sight in clouds of smoke and flame. Oh, I shudder when I think of it!—Many a poor wandering fugitive, who, like myself, had sought among wild beasts the mercy denied by our fellow men, saw, in helpless consternation, his dwelling-place and city of refuge reduced to ashes forever. It was this grand conflagration that drove me hither; I ran alike from fire and from slavery."

After a slight pause, (for both speaker and hearers were deeply moved by the above recital,) Mr. Listwell, addressing Madison, said, "If it does not weary you too much, do tell us something of your journeyings since this disastrous burning,—we are deeply interested in everything which can throw light on the hardships of persons escaping from slavery; we could hear you talk all night; are there no incidents that you could relate of your travels hither? or are they such that you do not like to mention them?"

"For the most part, sir, my course has been uninterrupted; and, considering the circumstances, at times even pleasant. I have suffered little for want of food; but I need not tell you how I got it. Your moral code may differ from mine, as your customs and usages are different. The fact is, sir, during my flight, I felt myself robbed by society of all just rights; that I was in an enemy's land, who sought both my life and my liberty. They had transformed me into a brute; made merchandise of my body, and, for all the purposes of my flight, turned day into night,—and guided by my own necessities, and in contempt of their conventionalities, I did not scruple to take bread where I could get it."

"And just there you were right," said Mr. Listwell; "I once had doubts on this point myself, but a conversation with Gerrit Smith,[18] (a man, by the way, that I wish you could see, for he is a devoted friend of your race, and I knew he would receive you gladly,) put an end to all my doubts on this point.—But do not let me interrupt you."

"I had but one narrow escape during my whole journey," said Madison.

"Do let us hear of it," said Mr. Listwell.

"Two weeks ago," continued Madison, "after travelling all night, I was overtaken by daybreak, in what seemed to me an almost interminable wood. I deemed it unsafe to go farther, and, as usual, I looked around for a suitable tree in which to spend the day. I liked one with a bushy top, and found one just to my mind. Up I climbed, and hiding myself as well as I could, I, with this strap, (pulling one out of his old coat-pocket,) lashed myself to a bough, and flattered myself that I should get a *good night's* sleep that day; but in this I was soon disappointed. I had scarcely got fastened to my natural hammock, when heard the voices of a number of persons, apparently approaching the part of the woods where I was. Upon my word, sir, I dreaded more these human voices than I should have done those of wild beasts. I was to a loss to know what to do. If I descended, I should probably be discovered by the men; and if they had dogs should, doubtless, be ' *treed.*' It was an anxious moment, but hardships and dangers had been the accompaniments of my life; and have, perhaps, imparted to me a certain hardness of character, which, to some extent, adapts me to them. In my present predicament, I decided to hold my place in the tree-top, and abide the consequences. But here I must disappoint you; for the men, who were all colored, halted at least a hundred yards from me, and began with their axes, in right good earnest, to attack the trees. The sound of their laughing axes was like the report of so many well-charged pistols. By and by there came down at least a dozen trees with a terrible crash. They leaped upon the fallen trees with an air of victory. I could see no dog with them, and felt myself comparatively safe, though I could not forget the possibility that some freak or fancy might bring the axe a little nearer my dwelling than comported with my safety.

"There was no sleep for me that day, and I wished for night. You may imagine that the thought of having the tree attacked under me was far from agreeable, and that it very easily kept me on the look-out. The day was not without diversion. The men at work seemed to be a gay set, and they would often make the woods resound with that uncontrolled laughter for which we, as a race, are remarkable. I held my place in the tree till sunset,—saw the men put on their jackets to be off. I observed that all left the ground but one, whom I saw sitting on the side of a stump, with his head bowed, and his eyes apparently fixed on the ground. I became interested in him. After sitting in the position to which I have alluded ten or fifteen minutes, he left the stump, walked directly towards the tree in which I was secreted, and halted almost under the same. He stood for a moment and looked around, deliberately and reverently took off his hat, by which I saw that he was a man in the evening of life, slightly bald and quite gray. After laying down his hat carefully, he knelt and prayed aloud, and such a prayer, the most fervent, earnest, and solemn, to which I think I ever listened. After reverently addressing the Almighty, as the all-wise, all-good, and the common Father of all mankind, he besought God for grace, for strength, to bear up under, and to endure, as a good soldier, all the hardships and trials which beset the journey of life, and to enable him to live in a manner which accorded with the gospel of Christ.—His soul now broke out in humble supplication for deliverance from bondage. 'O thou,' said he, 'that hearest the raven's cry, take pity on poor me! O deliver me! O deliver me! in mercy, O God, deliver me from the chains and manifold hardships of slavery!—With thee, O Father, all things are possible. Thou canst stand and measure the earth—Thou hast beheld and drove asunder the nations—all power is in thy hand,—thou didst say of old, 'I have seen the affliction of my people, and am come to deliver them,'—'Oh look down upon our afflictions, and have mercy upon us.' But I cannot repeat his prayer, nor can I give you an idea of its deep pathos. I had given but little attention to religion, and had but little faith in it; yet, as the old man prayed, I felt almost like coming down and kneel by his side, and mingle my broken complaint with his.

"He had already gained my confidence; as how could it be otherwise? I knew enough of religion to know that the man who prays in secret is far more likely to be sincere than he who loves to pray standing in the street, or in the great congregation. When he arose from his knees, like another Zacheus, I came down from the tree. He seemed a little alarmed at first, but I told him my story, and the good man embraced me in his arms, and assured me of his sympathy.

"I was now about out of provisions, and thought I might safely ask him to help me replenish my store. He said he had no money; but if he had, he would freely give it me. I told him I had *one dollar;* it was all the money I had in the world. I gave it to him, and asked him to purchase some crackers and cheese, and to kindly bring me the balance; that I would remain in or near that place, and would come to him on his return, if he would whistle. He was gone only about an hour. Meanwhile, from some cause or other, I know not what, (but as you shall see very wisely,) I changed my place. On his return I started to meet him; but it seemed as if the shadow of approaching danger fell upon my spirit, and checked my progress.—In a very few minutes, closely on the heels of the old man, I distinctly saw *fourteen men,* with something like guns in their hands."

"Oh! the old wretch!" exclaimed Mrs. Listwell, "he had betrayed you, had he?"

"I think not," said Madison, "I cannot believe that the old man was to blame. He probably went into a store, asked for the articles for which I sent, and presented the bill I gave him; and it is so unusual for slaves in the country to have money, that fact, doubtless, excited suspicion, and gave rise to inquiry. I can easily believe that the truthfulness of the old man's character compelled him to disclose the facts; and thus were these blood-thirsty men put on my track. Of course I did not present myself; but hugged my hiding-place securely. If discovered and attacked, I resolved to sell my life as dearly as possible."

"After searching about the woods silently for a time, the whole company gathered around the old man; one charged him with lying, and called him an old villain; said he was a thief; charged him with stealing money; said if he did not instantly tell where he got it, they would take the shirt from his old back, and give him thirty-nine lashes.

"'I did *not* steal the money,' said the old man, 'it was given me, as I told you at the store; and if the man who gave it me is not here, it is not my fault.'

"'Hush! you lying old rascal; we'll make you smart for it. You shall not leave this spot until you have told where you got that money.'

"They now took hold of him, and began to strip him; while others went to get sticks with which to beat him. I felt, at the moment, like rushing out in the midst of them; but considering that the old man would be whipped the more for having aided a fugitive slave, and that, perhaps, in the *melee* he might be killed outright, I disobeyed this impulse. They tied him to a tree, and began to whip him. My own flesh crept at every blow, and I seem to hear the old man's piteous cries even now. They laid thirty-nine lashes on his bare back, and were going to repeat that number, when one of the company besought his comrades to desist. 'You'll kill the d—d old scoundrel! You've already whipt a dollar's worth out of him, even if he stole it!' 'O yes,' said another, 'let him down. He'll never tell us another lie, I'll warrant ye!' With this, one of the company untied the old man, and bid him go about his business.

The old man left, but the company remained as much as an hour, scouring the woods. Round and round they went, turning up the underbrush, and peering about like so many bloodhounds. Two or three times they came within six feet of where I lay. I tell you I held my stick with a firmer grasp than I did in coming up to your house tonight. I expected to level one of them at least. Fortunately, however, I eluded their pursuit, and they left me alone in the woods.

"My last dollar was now gone, and you may well suppose I felt the loss of it; but the thought of being once again free to pursue my journey, prevented that depression which a sense of destitution causes; so swinging my little bundle on my back, I caught a glimpse of the *Great Bear* (which ever points the way to my beloved star,) and I started again on my journey. What I lost in money I made up at a hen-roost that same night, upon which I fortunately came."

"But you did'nt eat your food raw? How did you cook it?" said Mrs. Listwell.

"O no, Madam," said Madison, turning to his little bundle;—"I had the means of cooking." Here he took out of his bundle an old-fashioned tinder-box, and taking up a piece of a file, which he brought with him, he struck it with a heavy flint, and brought out at least a dozen sparks at once." "I have had this old box," said he, "more than five years. It is the *only* property saved from the fire in the dismal swamp. It has done me good service. It has given me the means of broiling many a chicken!"

It seemed quite a relief to Mrs. Listwell to know that Madison had, at least, lived upon cooked food. Women have a perfect horror of eating uncooked food.

By this time thoughts of what was best to be done about getting Madison to Canada, began to trouble Mr. Listwell; for the laws of Ohio were very stringent against any one who should aid, or who were found aiding a slave to escape through that State. A citizen, for the simple act of taking a fugitive slave in his carriage, had just been stripped of all his property, and thrown penniless upon the world. Notwithstanding this, Mr. Listwell was determined to see Madison on his way to Canada. "Give yourself no uneasiness," said he to Madison, "for if it cost my farm, I shall see you safely out of the States, and on your way to a land of liberty. Thank God that there is *such* a land so near us!—You will spend tomorrow with us, and tomorrow night I will take you in my carriage to the Lake. Once upon that, and you are safe."

"Thank you! thank you," said the fugitive; "I will commit myself to your care."

For the *first* time during *five* years, Madison enjoyed the luxury of resting his limbs on a comfortable bed, and inside a human habitation. Looking at the white sheets, he said to Mr. Listwell, "What, sir! you don't mean that I shall sleep in that bed?"

"Oh yes, oh yes."

After Mr. Listwell left the room, Madison said he really hesitated whether or not he should lie on the floor; for that was *far* more comfortable and inviting than any bed to which he had been used.

We pass over the thoughts and feelings, the hopes and fears, the plans and purposes, that revolved in the mind of Madison during the day that he was secreted at the house of Mr. Listwell. The reader will be content to know that nothing occurred to endanger his liberty, or to excite alarm. Many were the little attentions bestowed upon him in his quiet retreat and hiding-place. In the evening, Mr. Listwell, after treating Madison to a new suit of winter clothes, and replenishing his exhausted purse with five dollars, all in silver, brought out his two-horse wagon, well provided with buffaloes,[19] and silently started off with him to Cleveland. They arrived there without any interruption, a few minutes before sunrise the next morning. Fortunately the steamer admiral lay at the wharf, and was to start for Canada at nine o'clock. Here the last anticipated danger was surmounted. It was feared that just at this point the hunters of men might be on the look-out, and, possibly, pounce upon their victim. Mr. Listwell saw the captain of the boat; cautiously sounded him on the matter of carrying liberty-loving passengers, before he introduced his precious charge. This done, Madison was conducted on board.—With usual generosity this true subject of the emancipating queen welcomed Madison, and assured him that he should be safely landed in Canada, free of charge. Madison now felt himself no more a piece of merchandise, but a passenger, and, like any other passenger, going about his business, carrying with him what belonged to him and nothing which rightfully belonged to anybody else.

Wrapped in his new winter suit, snug and comfortable, a pocket full of silver, safe from his pursuers, embarked for a free country, Madison gave every sign of sincere gratitude, and bade his kind benefactor farewell, with such a grip of the hand as bespoke a heart full of honest manliness, and a soul that knew how to appreciate kindness. It need scarcely be said that Mr. Listwell was deeply moved by the gratitude and friendship he had excited in a nature so noble as that of the fugitive. He went to his home that day with a joy and gratification which knew no bounds. He had done something "to deliver the spoiled out of the hands of the spoiler," he had given bread to the hungry, and clothes to the naked; he had befriended a man to whom the laws of his country forbade all friendship,—and in proportion to the odds against his righteous deed, was the delightful satisfaction that gladdened his heart. On reaching home, he exclaimed,—"*He is safe,—he is safe,—he is safe,*"—and the cup of his joy was shared by his excellent lady. The following letter was received from Madison a few days after:

"WINDSOR, C.W., Dec. 16, 1840.

My dear Friend,—for such you truly are:—

Madison is out of the woods at last; I nestle in the mane of the British lion, protected by his mighty paw from the talons and the beak of the American eagle. I AM FREE, and breathe an atmosphere too pure for *slaves*, slavehunters, or slaveholders. My heart is full. As many thanks to you, sir, and to your kind lady, as there are pebbles on the shores of the Lake Erie; and may the blessing of God rest upon you both. You will never be forgotten by your profoundly grateful friend,

MADISON WASHINGTON."

1853

NOTES

1. From *Childe Harold's Pilgrimage,* Canto the Second, Stanza 76, by the English Romantic poet George Gordon, Lord Byron (1788–1824).

2. Refers to the Prince Hall Masons and the Grand United Order of Odd Fellows, fraternal organizations whose African American lodges were popular primarily among the northern black elite.

3. The mother church of the A.M.E. denomination, established in 1794 by Rev. Richard Allen, the denomination's founder.

4. The A.M.E. Zion denomination was founded in New York City in 1796 and chartered in 1801 by African Americans seeking an alternative to the discrimination they experienced in predominately white congregations.

5. The first African American Episcopal church in New York, founded in 1809 as the Free African Church of St. Philip and dedicated as St. Philip's Episcopal Church in 1818.

6. Prominent African American abolitionists of the early nineteenth century, including Presbyterian pastor James William Charles Pennington (1807–1870), Presbyterian

pastor Henry Highland Garnet (1815–1882), activist and lecturer Charles Lenox Remond (1810–1873), Congregational pastor and newspaper editor Samuel Ringgold Ward (1817–1866), Amherst alumnus and philanthropist Robert Purvis (1810–1898), physician and journalist James McCune Smith, investor and entrepreneur William Whipper (1804–1876), and educator Jeremiah Sanderson (1821–1875), the first black principal in San Francisco.

7. Kentucky Congressman (and later Senator) Henry Clay (1777–1852), a staunch supporter of colonization (the expatriation of free African Americans to British- and American-ruled territories in West African).

8. John C. Calhoun (1782–1850), representative and senator from South Carolina, a vice-president of the United States, and a strong supporter of U.S. slavery.

9. An amalgamation of Hosea 4:6 and Psalms 44:22.

10. Brother-in-law to the daughter of Douglass's owner, infamous for his role in Douglass's narrative, in which he responded to learning of Douglass's ability to read by sending him away to labor under the cruel slave master Edward Covey.

11. Genesis 9:25–27, Colossians 3:22, Ephesians 6:5, and 1 Peter 2:18, each instruct the enslaved to obey their masters.

12. Four pennies, U.S. currency.

13. Renowned abolitionist and founder of *The Liberator*, a prominent antislavery newspaper, in 1831.

14. A popular sacred poem published under various titles throughout the nineteenth century, including "God Is Love," "Why Weepest Thou," and "For I Know Their Sorrows."

15. A nickname for the State of Virginia.

16. In Song of Solomon 1:5, the self-description of a young woman appealing to her lover.

17. William Shakespeare, *King Henry VI, Part Two*, Act 4, Scene 1.

18. Gerrit Smith (1797–1874), U.S. politician, abolitionist, and advocate for women's suffrage.

19. Another name for buffalo robes, blankets made from tanned, hair-on buffalo hides.

WILLIAM WELLS BROWN
(CA. 1814-1884)

William Wells Brown was born in Lexington, Kentucky, in either the fall of 1814 or the spring of 1815, the son of an enslaved African American woman and a close relative of his owner. Brown received little education in his youth, gaining virtually all his formal instruction at the hands of Elijah P. Lovejoy, a print shop proprietor and abolitionist activist to whom the young Kentucky slave was hired out. Brown escaped slavery on January 1, 1834, after which he worked at a number of positions throughout Ohio and New York. This was a period of great transformation in the life of the newly freed bondsman, as he undertook to educate himself, reading broadly and deeply in a variety of subjects. During this time, Brown also became involved in the abolitionist movement. In 1843 he became a traveling speaker, touring throughout western New York State and strengthening his ties to and reputation within and among antislavery activist circles. Brown was widely known for his skills as an orator, but his deepest passion was for the written word; and he published his first book, *Narrative of William W. Brown, a Fugitive Slave, and Written by Himself,* in 1847. In 1852, Brown published *Three Years in Europe; or, Places I Have Seen and People I Have Met,* the first known travel book by an African American writer. William Wells Brown is best known to contemporary readers, however, for his 1853 novel, *Clotel; or, The President's Daughter: A Narrative of Slave Life in the United States,* the first full-length novel ever published by an African American author. In addition to the first travel book and the first novel, William Wells Brown is also author of *The Escape; or, A Leap for Freedom; A Drama in Five Acts,* the first published African American play. Brown remained a prolific writer even after slavery was abolished, and between 1863 and 1874 he published three books on the subject of U.S. black history. His last published volume was *My Southern Home: or, The South and Its People* (1880) a retrospective consideration of the antebellum black culture in which he was raised. Though most widely remembered for his pioneering book-length texts, Brown first became known to the African American readership through his early correspondence with Frederick Douglass's *North Star,* beginning in the early 1850s. During this period he was living in Western Europe, effectively exiled from the United States when the 1850 Fugitive Slave Law was passed. The following works include two such letters, along with chapters from *Clotel* and *My Southern Home*, and an essay from the 1854 anthology *Autographs for Freedom*.

LETTER FROM WILLIAM W. BROWN, ADELPHI HOTEL, YORK, MARCH 26, 1851

DEAR DOUGLASS:

—I closed my last letter in the ancient town of Melrose, on the banks of the Tweed, and within a stone's throw of the celebrated ruins from which the town derives its name.[1] The valley in which Melrose is situated, and the surrounding hills, together with the Monastery, have so often been made a theme for the most interesting part of Scotland. Of the many gifted writers who have taken up the pen, none have done more to bring the Eildon Hills and Melrose Abbey into note, than the author of Waverly.[2] But one cannot read his writings without a regret that he should have so woven fact and fiction together, that it is almost impossible to discriminate between the one and the other.

We arrived at Melrose in the evening, and proceeded to the chapel where our meeting was to be held, and where our friends, the Crafts, were warmly greeted. On returning from the meeting, we passed close by the ruins of Melrose, and, very fortunately, it was a moonlight night. There is considerable difference of opinion among the inhabitants of the place as regards the best time to view the Abbey. The author of the "Lay of the Last Minstrel,"[3] says

"If thou wouldst view fair Melrose aright,
Go visit it by the pale moonlight:
For the gay beams of lightsome day
Gild but to flout the ruins gray."

In consequence of this admonition, I was informed that many persons remain in town to see the ruins by moonlight. Aware that the moon did not send its rays upon the old building every night in the year, I asked the keeper what he did on dark nights. He replied that he had a large lantern, which he put upon the end of a long pole, and with this he succeeded in lighting up the ruins.—This good man labored hard to convince me that his invention was nearly if not quite as good as nature's own moon. But having no need of an application of his invention to the Abbey, I had no opportunity of judging of its effect. I thought, however, that he had made a moon to some purpose, when he informed me that some nights, with his pole and lantern, he earned his four or five shillings. Not being content with a view by "moonlight alone," I was up the next morning before the sun, and paid my respects to the Abbey. I was too early for the keeper, and he handed me the key through the window, and I entered the rooms alone. It is one labyrinth of gigantic arches and dilapidated halls, the ivy growing and clinging wherever it can fasten its roots, and the whole as fine a picture of decay as imagination could create. This was the favorite resort of Sir Walter Scott, and furnished him much matter for the "Lay of the Last Minstrel." He could not have selected a more fitting place for solitary thought than this ancient abode of monks and priests. In passing through the cloisters, I could but remark the carvings of leaves and flowers, wrought in stone in the most exquisite manner, looking as fresh as if they were just from the hands of the artist. The lapse of centuries seems not to have made any impression upon them or changed their appearance in the least. I sat down among the ruins of the Abbey.—The ground about was piled up with magnificent fragments of stone, representing various texts of scripture, and the quaint ideas of the priests and monks of that age. Scene after scene swept through my fancy as I looked upon the surrounding objects. I could almost imagine I saw the bearded monks going from hall to hall, and from cell to cell. In visiting these dark cells, the mind becomes oppressed by a sense of the utter helplessness of the victim who once passed over the threshold and entered one of these religious prisons.—There was no help or hope but in the will that ordered their fate. How painful it is to gaze upon those walls, and to think how many tears have been shed by their inmates, when this old Monastery was in its glory. I ascended to the top of the ruin by a circuitous stairway, whose stone steps were worn deep from use, many of whom, like myself, had visited them to gratify a curiosity. From the top of the Abbey, I had a splendid view of the surrounding hills and the beautiful valley through which flows the Gala Water[4] and Tweed. This is unquestionably the most splendid specimen of Gothic architectural ruin in Scotland. But any description of mine conveys but a poor idea to the fancy. To be realized, it must be seen.

During the day, we paid a visit to Abbotsford, the splendid mansion of the late Sir Walter Scott, Bart. This beautiful seat is situated on the banks of the Tweed, just below its junction with the Gala Water. It is a dreary looking spot, and the house from the opposite side of the river has the appearance of a small, low castle. In a single day's ride through England, one may see half a dozen cottages larger than Abbotsford House. I was much disappointed in finding the premises undergoing repairs and alterations, and that all the trees between the house and the river had been cut down. This is to be regretted the more, because they were planted, nearly every one of them, by the same hand that waved its wand of enchantment over the world. The fountain had been removed from where it had been placed by the hands of the poet, to the centre of the yard; and even a small stone that had been placed over the favorite dog "Percy," had been taken up and thrown among some loose stone. One visits Abbotsford because of the genius of the man that once presided over it. Everything connected with the great poet is of interest to his admirers, and anything altered or removed, tends to diminish that interest. We entered the house, and were conducted through the great hall, which is hung all round with massive armor of all descriptions, and other memorials of ancient times. The floor is of white and black marble. In passing through the hall, we entered a narrow arched room, stretching quite across the building, having a window at each end. This little or rather narrow room is filled with all kinds of armor, which is arranged with great taste. We were next shown into the dining-room, whose roof is of black oak, richly carved. In this room is a painting of the head of Queen Mary, in a charger, taken the day after the execution. Many other interesting portraits grace the walls of this room. But by far the finest apartment in the building is the drawing-room, with a lofty ceiling, and furnished with antique ebony furniture. After passing thro' the library, with its twenty thousand volumes, we found ourselves in the study, and I sat down in the same chair where once sat the poet, while before me was the table upon which was written the "Lady of the Lake,"[5] "Waverly," and other productions of this gifted writer. The clothes last worn by the poet were shown to us. There was the broad skirted blue coat, with its large buttons, the plaid trousers, the heavy shoes, the black vest and white hat. These were all in a glass case, and all looked the poet and novelist.—But the inside of the buildings had undergone alterations as well as the outside. In passing through the library, we saw a grand-daughter of the poet. She was from London, and was only on a visit of a few days. She looked pale and dejected, and seemed as if she longed to leave this secluded spot and return to the metropolis. She looked for all the world like a hot-house plant. I don't think the Scotch could do better than to purchase Abbotsford, while it has some imprint of the great magician, and secure its preservation, for I am sure that, a hundred years hence, no place will be more frequently visited in Scotland than the home of the late Sir Walter Scott. After sauntering three hours about the premises, I left, but not without feeling that I had been well paid for my trouble in visiting Abbotsford.

In the afternoon of the same day, in company with the Crafts, I took a drive to Dryburgh Abbey. It is a ruin of little interest, except its being the burial place of Scott. The poet lies buried in St. Mary's Aisle.—His grave is in the left transept of the cross, and close to where the high altar formerly stood. Sir Walter Scott chose his own grave, and he could not have selected a sunnier spot if he had roamed the wide world over. A shaded window breaks the sun as it falls upon his grave. The ivy is creeping and clinging wherever it can, as if it would shelter the poet's grave from the weather.—The author lies between his wife and eldest son, and there is only room enough for one grave more, and the son's wife has the choice of being buried here.

The four o'clock train took us to Harwich; and after a pleasant visit in this place, and the people registering their names against American slavery, and the Fugitive Bill in particular, we set out for Carlisle, passing through the antique town of Longholme. After leaving the latter place, we had to travel by coach. But no matter how one travels here, he travels at a more rapid rate than in America. The distance from Longholme to Carlisle, twenty miles, occupied only two and a half hours in the journey. It was a cold day and I had to ride on the outside, as the inside had been taken up. We changed horses, and took in and put out passengers with a rapidity which seems almost incredible. The road was as smooth as a mirror.

We bid farewell to Scotland, as we reached the little town of Gretna Green. This town being on the line between England and Scotland, is noted as the place where a little cross-eyed, red-faced blacksmith, by the name of Priestly, first set up his own altar to Hymen, and married all who came to him, without regard to rank or station, and at prices to suit all. It was worth a ride through this part of the country, if for no other purpose than to see the town where more clandestine marriages have taken place than in any other port in the world.[6] A ride of eight or nine miles brought us in sight of the Eden, winding its way slowly through a beautiful valley, with farms on either side, covered with sheep and cattle. There are four very tall chimneys, sending forth dense columns of black smoke, announcing to us that we were near Carlisle. I was really glad of this, for Ulysses was never more tired of the shores of Ilion[7] than I of the top of that coach.

We remained over night at Carlisle, partaking of the hospitality of the prince of bakers, and left the next day for the Lakes, where we had a standing invitation to pay a visit to a distinguished literary lady. A cold ride of about fifty miles brought us to the foot of Lake Windermere, a beautiful sheet of water, surrounded by mountains that seemed to vie with each other which should approach nearest the sky. The margin of the lake is carved out and built up into terrace above terrace, until the slopes and windings are lost in the snow-capped peaks of the mountains. It is not surprising that such men as Southey, Coleridge, Wordsworth[8] and others, resorted to this region for inspiration. After a coach ride of five miles, (passing on our journey the "Dove's Nest," home of the late Mrs. Hemans,) we were put down at the door of the Salutation Hotel, Ambleside, and a few minutes after found ourselves under the roof of the authoress of "Society in America." I know not how it is with others, but for my own part, I always form an opinion of an author whose writings I am at all familiar with, or a statesman whose speeches I have read. I had pictured in my own mind a tall, stately-looking lady of about sixty years, as the authoress of "Travels in the East," and for once I was right, with the single exception that I had added on too many years by twelve. The evening was spent in talking about the United States; and William Craft[9] had to go through the narrative of his escape from slavery. When I retired for the night, I found it almost impossible to sleep. The idea that I was under the roof of the authoress of the "Hour and the Man," and that I was on the banks of the sweetest lake in Great Britain, within half a mile of the residence of the late poet Wordsworth, drove sleep from my pillow. But I must leave an account of my visit to the Lakes for a future letter.

When I look around and see the happiness here, even among the poorer classes, and that too in a country where the soil is not at all to be compared with our own, I mourn for our downtrodden countrymen, who are plundered, oppressed, and made chattels of, to enable an ostentatious aristocracy to vie with each other in splendid extravagance.

I am holding meetings, in company with the Crafts, on the Fugitive Slave Law, and we also hope to get up an interest against the slaveholders who may make their appearance at the great Exhibition. But of this, more in my next. Until then, believe me to be

Yours, right truly,

WM. W. BROWN.

1851

LETTER FROM WILLIAM WELLS BROWN, OXFORD, SEPTEMBER 10TH, 1851

DEAR DOUGLASS:—

I have just finished a short visit to the far famed city of Oxford,[10] which has not unaptly been styled, the city of palaces.

Aside from this being one of the principal seats of learning in the world, it is distinguished alike for its religious, and political changes in times past. At one time it was the seat of popery; at another, the uncompromising enemy of Rome. Here the tyrant, Richard the Third, held his court, and when James the First, and his son Charles the First found their capital too hot to hold them, they removed to their loyal city of Oxford.

The writings of the great Republicans were here committed to the flames.[11] At one time popery sent Protestants to the stake and faggot;[12] at another, a papist King found no favor with the people.[13] A noble monument now stands where Cranmer, Ridley, and Latimer, proclaimed their sentiments and faith, and sealed it with their blood.[14] And we read upon the town treasurer's book,—for three loads of wood, one load of faggots, one post, two chains and staples, to burn Ridley and Latimer, L1 5s 2p.

Such is the information one gets by looking over the records of books written three centuries ago.

It was a beautiful day on which I arrived at Oxford, and instead of remaining in my hotel, I sallied forth to take a survey of the beauties of the city. I strolled into Christ Church Meadows, and there spent the evening in viewing the numerous halls of learning, which surrounds that splendid promenade.

And fine old buildings they are; centuries have rolled over many of them, hallowing the old walls and making them gray with age.—They have been for ages the chosen homes of piety, and philosophy. Heroes and scholars, have gone forth from their studies here, into the great field of the world, to seek their fortunes, and to conquer and be conquered.

As I surveyed the exterior of the different Colleges, I could here and there see the reflection of the light from the window of some student, who was busy at his studies, or throwing away his time over some trashy novel, too many of which find their way into the trunks or carpet bags of the young man on setting out for College. As I looked upon the walls of these buildings, I thought as the rough stone is taken from the quarry to the finisher, there to be made into an ornament, so was the young mind brought here to be cultivated and developed.

Many a poor unobtrusive young man with the appearance of little or no ability, is here moulded into a hero, a scholar, a tyrant, or a friend of humanity.

I never look upon these monuments of education, without a feeling of regret, that so few of our own race can find a place within their walls.

And this being the fact, I see more and more the need of our people being encouraged to turn their attention more seriously to self-education, and thus to take a respectable position before the world, by virtue of their own cultivated minds, and moral standing.

Education, though obtained by a little at a time, and that, too, over the midnight lamp, will place its owner in a position to be respected by all, even though he be black.

I know that the obstacles which the laws of the land, and of society, places between the colored man and education in the United States, is very great, yet if one can break through these barriers, more can, and if our people would only place the right appreciation upon education, they would find these obstacles are easier to be overcome than appears at first sight. A young man once asked Carlyle, what was the secret of success. His reply was, "Energy; whatever you undertake, do it with all your might."

Had it not been for the possession of energy, I might now have been working as a servant for some brainless fellow who might be able to command my labour with his money, or I might have been yet toiling in chains and slavery. But thanks to energy, not only for my being to day in a land of freedom, but also for my dear girls being in one of the best Seminaries in France,[15] instead of being in an American school, where the finger of scorn would be pointed at them, by those whose superiority rests entirely upon their having a whiter skin.

But I am straying too far from the purpose of this letter.

Oxford is indeed one of the finest located places in the Kingdom, and every inch of ground about it, seems hallowed by interesting associations. The University founded by the good King Alfred,[16] still throws its shadow upon the side walk; and the lapse of ten centuries seems to have made but little impression upon it. Other seats of learning may be entitled to our admiration, but Oxford claims our veneration. Although the lateness of the night compelled me to, yet I felt an unwillingness to tear myself from the scene of such surpassing interest. Few places in any country as noted as Oxford is, but that has some distinguished person residing within its precincts. And knowing that the city of palaces was not an exception to this rule, I resolved to see some of its Visions.

Here of course is the head quarters of the Bishop of Oxford,[17] a son of the late William Wilberforce, Africa's noble champion.

I should have been glad to have seen this distinguished pillar of the Church, but I soon learned that the Bishop's residence was out of town, and that he seldom visited the city, except on business.

I then determined to see one, who, although, a lesser dignitary in the church, is nevertheless, scarcely less known than the Bishop of Oxford. This was the Rev. Dr. Pusey,[18] a divine whose name is known wherever the religion of Jesus is known and taught, and the acknowledged head of the Puseyites.[19]

On the second morning of my visit, I proceeded to Christ Church Chapel, where the Rev. Gentleman officiates.

Fortunately I had an opportunity of seeing the Dr., and following close in his footsteps to the church.

His personal appearance is anything but that of one who is the leader of a growing, and powerful party in the church.

He is rather under the middle size, and is round shouldered, or rather stoops. His profile is more striking than his front face, the nose being very large and prominent.—As a matter of course, I expected to see a large nose, for all great men have them.

He has a thoughtful, and somewhat sullen brow, a firm, and somewhat pensive mouth, a cheek pale, thin, and deeply furrowed.

A monk fresh from the cloisters of Tintern Abbey,[20] in its proudest days, could scarcely have made a more ascetic and solemn appearance than did Dr. Pusey on this occasion.

He is not apparently above forty-five, or at most fifty years of age, and his whole aspect renders him an admirable study for an artist.

Dr. Pusey's style of preaching is cold and tame, and one looking at him would scarcely believe that such an uninteresting appearing man could cause such an eruption in the church as he has.[21] I was glad to find that a colored young man was among the students at Oxford.[22]

A few months since, I paid a visit to our countryman, Alexander Crummell,[23] who is still pursuing his studies at Cambridge,[24] a place, though far inferior to Oxford, as far as appearance is concerned, is said to be greatly its superior as a place of learning. In an hour's walk through the Strand, Regent, or Piccadilly streets in London, one may meet a half a dozen colored young men, who are inmates of the various Colleges in the metropolis. These are all signs of progress in the cause of the sons of Africa.

Then let our people take courage, and with that courage let them apply themselves to learning.

A determination to excel, is the secret road to greatness, and that is as open to the black man as the white.

It was that which has accomplished the mightiest and noblest triumphs in the intellectual and physical world. It was that which has made such rapid strides towards civilization, and broken the chains of ignorance, and superstition, which has so long fettered the human intellect.

It was determination which raised so many worthy individuals from the humble walks of society, and from poverty, and placed them in positions of trust and renown. It is no slight barrier that can effectually oppose the determination of the will; success must ultimately crown its efforts.

"The world shall hear of me," was the exclamation of one whose name has become as familiar as household words. A Toussaint, once laboured in the sugar field with his spelling book in his pocket, and the combined efforts of a nation to keep him in ignorance. His name is now recorded among the list of Statesmen of the past. A Soulouque[25] was once a slave, and knew not how to read. He now sits upon the throne of an Empire.

In our own country, there are men who once held the plough, and that too without any compensation, that are now presiding at the editor's table.

It was determination that brought out the genius of a Franklin, a Fulton,[26] and that has distinguished many of the American Statesmen, who but for their energy and determination would never have had a name beyond the precincts of their own homes.

It is not always those who have the best advantages, or the greatest talents, that eventually succeed in their undertakings, but it is those who strive with untiring diligence to remove all obstacles to success, and with unconquerable resolution to labour on until the rich reward of perseverance is within their grasp.

Then again let me say to our young men, Take courage, "There is a good time coming." The darkness of the night appears greatest, just before the dawn of day.

Yours, right truly,

W. W. BROWN.

1851

Chapter I: The Negro Sale

"WHY stands she near the auction stand,
That girl so young and fair?
What brings her to this dismal place,
Why stands she weeping there?"[27]

With the growing population of slaves in the Southern States of America, there is a fearful increase of half whites, most of whose fathers are slave-owners, and their mothers slaves. Society does not frown upon the man who sits with his mulatto child upon his knee, whilst its mother stands a slave behind his chair. The late Henry Clay, some years since, predicted that the abolition of negro slavery would be brought about by the amalgamation of the races. John Randolph,[28] a distinguished slaveholder of Virginia, and a prominent statesman, said in a speech in the legislature of his native state, that "the blood of the first American statesmen coursed through the veins of the slave of the South." In all the cities and towns of the slave states, the real negro, or clear black, does not amount to more than one in every four of the slave population. This fact is, of itself, the best evidence of the degraded and immoral condition of the relation of master and slave in the United States of America.

In all the slave states, the law says:—"Slaves shall be deemed, sold, taken, reputed, and adjudged in law to be chattels personal in the hands of their owners and possessors, and their executors, administrators and assigns, to all intents, constructions, and purposes whatsoever." A slave is one who is in the power of a master to whom he belongs. The master may sell him, dispose of his person, his industry, and his labour. He can do nothing, possess nothing, nor acquire anything, but what must belong to his master. The slave is entirely subject to the will of his master, who may correct and chastise him, though not with unusual rigour, or so as to maim and mutilate him, or expose him to the danger of loss of life, or to cause his death. The slave, to remain a slave, must be sensible that there is no appeal from his master." Where the slave is placed by law entirely under the control of the man who claims him, body and soul, as property, what else could be expected than the most depraved social condition? The marriage relation, the oldest and most sacred institution given to man by his Creator, is unknown and unrecognised in the slave laws of the United

States. Would that we could say, that the moral and religious teaching in the slave states were better than the laws; but, alas! we cannot. A few years since, some slaveholders became a little uneasy in their minds about the rightfulness of permitting slaves to take to themselves husbands and wives, while they still had others living, and applied to their religious teachers for advice; and the following will show how this grave and important subject was treated:—

"Is a servant, whose husband or wife has been sold by his or her master into a distant country, to be permitted to marry again?"

The query was referred to a committee, who made the following report; which, after discussion, was adopted:—

That, in view of the circumstances in which servants in this country are placed, the committee are unanimous in the opinion, that it is better to permit servants thus circumstanced to take another husband or wife.

Such was the answer from a committee of the "Shiloh Baptist Association;" and instead of receiving light, those who asked the question were plunged into deeper darkness!

A similar question was put to the "Savannah River Association," and the answer, as the following will show, did not materially differ from the one we have already given:—

"Whether, in a case of involuntary separation, of such a character as to preclude all prospect of future intercourse, the parties ought to be allowed to marry again."

Answer—

"That such separation among persons situated as our slaves are, is civilly a separation by death; and they believe that, in the sight of God, it would be so viewed. To forbid second marriages in such cases would be to expose the parties, not only to stronger hardships and strong temptation, but to church-censure for acting in obedience to their masters, who cannot be expected to acquiesce in a regulation at variance with justice to the slaves, and to the spirit of that command which regulates marriage among Christians. The slaves are not free agents; and a dissolution by death is not more entirely without their consent, and beyond their control, than by such separation."

Although marriage, as the above indicates, is a matter which the slaveholders do not think is of any importance, or of any binding force with their slaves; yet it would be doing that degraded class an injustice, not to acknowledge that many of them do regard it as a sacred obligation, and show a willingness to obey the commands of God on this subject. Marriage is, indeed, the first and most important institution of human existence—the foundation of all civilization and culture—the root of church and state. It is the most intimate covenant of heart formed among mankind; and for many persons the only relation in which they feel the true sentiments of humanity. It gives scope for every human virtue, since each of these is developed from the love and confidence which here predominate. It unites all which ennobles and beautifies life,—sympathy, kindness of will and deed, gratitude, devotion, and every delicate, intimate feeling. As the only asylum for true education, it is the first and last sanctuary of human culture. As husband and wife through each other become conscious of complete humanity, and every human feeling, and every human virtue; so children, at their first awakening in the fond covenant of love between parents, both of whom are tenderly concerned for the same object, find an image of complete humanity leagued in free love. The spirit of love which prevails between them acts with creative power upon the young mind, and awakens every germ of goodness within it. This invisible and incalculable influence of parental life acts more upon the child than all the efforts of education, whether by means of instruction, precept, or exhortation. If this be a true picture of the vast influence for good of the institution of marriage, what must be the moral degradation of that people to whom marriage is denied? Not content with depriving them of all the higher and holier enjoyments of this relation, by degrading and darkening their souls, the slaveholder denies to his victim even that slight alleviation of his misery, which would result from the marriage relation being protected by law and public opinion. Such is the influence of slavery in the United States, that the ministers of religion, even in the so-called free states, are the mere echoes, instead of the correctors, of public sentiment.

We have thought it advisable to show that the present system of chattel slavery in America undermines the entire social condition of man, so as to prepare the reader for the following narrative of slave life, in that otherwise happy and prosperous country.

In all the large towns in the Southern States, there is a class of slaves who are permitted to hire their time of their owners, and for which they pay a high price. These are mulatto women, or quadroons,[29] as they are familiarly known, and are distinguished for their fascinating beauty. The handsomest usually pays the highest price for her time. Many of these women are the favourites of persons who furnish them with the means of paying their owners, and not a few are dressed in the most extravagant manner. Reader, when you take into consideration the fact, that amongst the slave population no safeguard is thrown around virtue, and no inducement held out to slave women to be chaste, you will not be surprised when we tell you that immorality and vice pervade the cities of the Southern States in a manner unknown in the cities and towns of the Northern States. Indeed most of the slave women have no higher aspiration than that of becoming the finely-dressed mistress of some white man. And at negro balls and parties, this class of women usually cut the greatest figure.

At the close of the year—the following advertisement appeared in a newspaper published in Richmond, the capital of the state of Virginia:—"Notice: Thirty-eight negroes will be offered for sale on Monday, November 10th, at twelve o'clock, being the entire stock of the late John Graves, Esq. The negroes are in good condition, some of them very prime; among them are several mechanics, able-bodied field hands, plough-boys, and women with children at the breast, and some of them very prolific in their generating qualities, affording a rare opportunity to any one who wishes to raise a strong and healthy lot of servants for their own use. Also several mulatto girls of rare personal qualities: two of them very superior. Any gentleman or lady wishing to purchase, can take any of the above slaves on trial for a week, for which no charge will be made." Amongst the above slaves to be sold were Currer and her two daughters, Clotel and Althesa; the latter were the girls spoken of in the advertisement as "very superior." Currer was a bright mulatto, and of prepossessing appearance, though then nearly forty years of age. She had hired her time for more than twenty years, during which time she had lived in Richmond. In her younger days Currer had been the housekeeper of a young slaveholder; but of later years had been a laundress or washerwoman, and was considered to be a woman of great taste in getting up linen. The gentleman for whom she had kept house was Thomas Jefferson, by whom she had two daughters. Jefferson being called to Washington to fill a government appointment, Currer was left behind, and thus she took herself to the business of washing, by which means she paid her master, Mr. Graves, and supported herself and two children. At the time of the decease of her master, Currer's daughters, Clotel and Althesa, were aged respectively sixteen and fourteen years, and both, like most of their own sex in America, were well grown. Currer early resolved to bring her daughters up as ladies, as she termed it, and therefore imposed little or no work upon them. As her daughters grew older, Currer had to pay a stipulated price for them; yet her notoriety as a laundress of the first class enabled her to put an extra price upon her charges, and thus she and her daughters lived in comparative luxury. To bring up Clotel and Althesa to attract attention, and especially at balls and parties, was the great aim of Currer. Although the term "negro ball" is applied to most of these gatherings, yet a majority of the attendants are often whites. Nearly all the negro parties in the cities and towns of the Southern States are made up of quadroon and mulatto girls, and white men. These are democratic gatherings, where gentlemen, shopkeepers, and their clerks, all appear upon terms of perfect equality. And there is a degree of gentility and decorum in these companies that is not surpassed by similar gatherings of white people in the Slave States. It was at one of these parties that Horatio Green, the son of a wealthy gentleman of Richmond, was first introduced to Clotel. The young man had just returned from college, and was in his twenty-second year. Clotel was sixteen, and was admitted by all to be the most beautiful girl, coloured or white, in the city. So attentive was the young man to the quadroon during the evening that it was noticed by all, and became a matter of general conversation; while Currer appeared delighted beyond measure at her daughter's conquest. From that evening, young Green became the favourite visitor at Currer's house. He soon promised to purchase Clotel, as speedily as it could be effected, and make her mistress of her own dwelling; and Currer looked forward with pride to the time when she should see her daughter emancipated and free. It was a beautiful moonlight night in August, when all who reside in tropical climes are eagerly gasping for a breath of fresh air, that Horatio Green was seated in the small garden behind Currer's cottage, with the object of his affections by his side. And it was here that Horatio drew from his pocket the newspaper, wet from the press, and read the advertisement for the sale of the slaves to which we have alluded; Currer and her two daughters being of the number. At the close of the evening's visit, and as the young man was leaving, he said to the girl, "You shall soon be free and your own mistress."

As might have been expected, the day of sale brought an unusual large number together to compete for the property to be sold. Farmers who make a business of raising slaves for the market were there; slave-traders and speculators were also numerously represented; and in the midst of this throng was one who felt a deeper interest in the result of the sale than any other of the bystanders; this was young Green. True to his promise, he was there with a blank bank check in his pocket, awaiting with impatience to enter the list as a bidder for the beautiful slave. The less valuable slaves were first placed upon the auction block, one after another, and sold to the highest bidder. Husbands and wives were separated with a degree of indifference that is unknown in any other relation of life, except that of slavery. Brothers and sisters were torn from each other; and mothers saw their children leave them for the last time on this earth.

It was late in the day, when the greatest number of persons were thought to be present, that Currer and her daughters were brought forward to the place of sale. Currer was first ordered to ascend the auction stand, which she did with a trembling step. The slave mother was sold to a trader. Althesa, the youngest, and who was scarcely less beautiful than her sister, was sold to the same trader for one thousand dollars. Clotel was the last, and, as was expected, commanded a higher price than any that had been offered for sale that day. The appearance of Clotel on the auction block created a deep sensation amongst the crowd. There she stood, with a complexion as white as most of those who were waiting with a wish to become her purchasers; her features as finely defined as any of her sex of pure Anglo-Saxon; her long black wavy hair done up in the neatest manner; her form tall and graceful, and her whole appearance indicating one superior to her position. The auctioneer commenced by saying, that "Miss Clotel had been reserved for the last, because she was the most valuable. How much gentlemen? Real Albino, fit for a fancy girl for any one. She enjoys good health, and has a sweet temper. How much do you say?" "Five hundred dollars." "Only five hundred for such a girl as this? Gentlemen, she is worth a deal more than that sum; you certainly don't know the value of the article you are bidding upon. Here, gentlemen, I hold in my hand a paper certifying that she has a good moral character." "Seven hundred." "Ah, gentlemen, that is something like. This paper also states that she is very intelligent." "Eight hundred." "She is a devoted Christian, and perfectly trustworthy." "Nine hundred." "Nine fifty." "Ten." "Eleven." "Twelve hundred." Here the sale came to a dead stand. The auctioneer stopped, looked around, and began in a rough manner to relate some anecdotes relative to the sale of slaves, which, he said, had come under his own observation. At this juncture the scene was indeed strange. Laughing, joking, swearing, smoking, spitting, and talking kept up a continual hum and noise amongst the crowd; while the slave-girl stood with tears in her eyes, at one time looking towards her mother and sister, and at another towards the young man whom she hoped would become her purchaser. "The chastity of this girl is pure; she has never been from under her mother's care, she is a virtuous creature." "Thirteen." "Fourteen." "Fifteen." "Fifteen hundred dollars," cried the auctioneer, and the maiden was struck for that sum. This was a Southern auction, at which the bones, muscles, sinews, blood, and nerves of a young lady of sixteen were sold for five hundred dollars; her moral character for two hundred; her improved intellect for one hundred; her Christianity for three hundred; and her chastity and virtue for four hundred dollars more. And this, too, in a city thronged with churches, whose tall spires look like so many signals pointing to heaven, and whose ministers preach that slavery is a God-ordained institution!

What words can tell the inhumanity, the atrocity, and the immorality of that doctrine which, from exalted office, commends such a crime to the favour of enlightened and Christian people? What indignation from all the world is not due to the government and people who put forth all their strength and power to keep in existence such an institution? Nature abhors it; the age repels it; and Christianity needs all her meekness to forgive it.

Clotel was sold for fifteen hundred dollars, but her purchaser was Horatio Green. Thus closed a negro sale, at which two daughters of Thomas Jefferson, the writer of the Declaration of American Independence, and one of the presidents of the great republic, were disposed of to the highest bidder!

"O God! my every heart-string cries,
Dost thou these scenes behold
In this our boasted Christian land,
And must the truth be told?

"Blush, Christian, blush! for e'en the dark,
Untutored heathen see
Thy inconsistency; and, lo!
They scorn thy God, and thee!"[30]

1853

VISIT OF A FUGITIVE SLAVE TO THE GRAVE OF WILBERFORCE

On a beautiful morning in the month of June, while strolling about Trafalgar Square, I was attracted to the base of the Nelson column,[31] where a crowd was standing gazing at the bas-relief representations of some of the great naval exploits of the man whose statue stands on the top of the pillar. The death-wound which the hero received on board the Victory,[32] and his being carried from the ship's deck by his companions, is executed with great skill. Being no admirer of warlike heroes, I was on the point of turning away, when I perceived among the figures (which were as large as life) a full-blooded African, with as white a set of teeth as ever I had seen, and all the other peculiarities of feature that distinguish that race from the rest of the human family, with musket in hand and a dejected countenance, which told that he had been in the heat of the battle, and shared with the other soldiers the pain in the loss of their commander. However, as soon as I saw my sable brother, I felt more at home, and remained longer than I had intended. Here was the Negro, as black a man as was ever imported from the coast of Africa, represented in his proper place by the side of Lord Nelson, on one of England's proudest monuments. How different, thought I, was the position assigned to the colored man on similar monuments in the United States. Some years since, while standing under the shade of the monument erected to the memory of the brave Americans who fell at the storming of Fort Griswold, Connecticut,[33] I felt a degree of pride as I beheld the names of two Africans who had fallen in the fight,[34] yet I was grieved but not surprised to find their names colonized off, and a line drawn between them and the whites. This was in keeping with American historical injustice to its colored heroes.

The conspicuous place assigned to this representative of an injured race, by the side of one of England's greatest heroes, brought vividly before my eye the wrongs of Africa and the philanthropic man of Great Britain, who had labored so long and so successfully for the abolition of the slave trade, and the emancipation of the slaves of the West Indies; and I at once resolved to pay a visit to the grave of Wilberforce.

A half an hour after, I entered Westminster Abbey, at Poets' Corner,[35] and proceeded in search of the patriot's tomb; I had, however, gone but a few steps, when I found myself in front of the tablet erected to the memory of Granville Sharpe,[36] by the African Institution of London, in 1816; upon the marble was a long inscription, recapitulating many of the deeds of this benevolent man, and from which I copied the following:—"He aimed to rescue his native country from the guilt and inconsistency of employing the arm of freedom to rivet the fetters of bondage, and establish for the negro race, in the person of Somerset,[37] the long-disputed rights of human nature. Having in this glorious cause triumphed over the combined resistance of interest, prejudice, and pride, he took his post among the foremost of the honorable band associated to deliver Africa from the rapacity of Europe, by the abolition of the slave-trade; nor was death permitted to interrupt his career of usefulness, till he had witnessed that act of the British Parliament by which the abolition was decreed." After viewing minutely the profile of this able defender of the negro's rights, which was finely chiseled on the tablet, I took a hasty glance at

Shakespeare, on the one side, and Dryden on the other, and then passed on, and was soon in the north aisle, looking upon the mementoes placed in honor of genius. There stood a grand and expressive monument to Sir Isaac Newton, which was in every way worthy of the great man to whose memory it was erected. A short distance from that was a statue to Addison, representing the great writer clad in his morning gown, looking as if he had just left the study, after finishing some chosen article for the Spectator. The stately monument to the Earl of Chatham is the most attractive in this part of the Abbey. Fox, Pitt, Grattan,[38] and many others, are here represented by monuments. I had to stop at the splendid marble erected to the memory of Sir Fowell Buxton, Bart.[39] A long inscription enumerates his many good qualities, and concludes by saying:—"This monument is erected by his friends and fellow-laborers, at home and abroad, assisted by the grateful contributions of many thousands of the African race." A few steps further and I was standing over the ashes of Wilberforce. In no other place so small do so many great men lie together. The following is the inscription on the monument erected to the memory of this devoted friend of the oppressed and degraded negro race:—

> To the memory of William Wilberforce, born in Hull, August 24, 1759, died in London, July 29, 1833. For nearly half a century a member of the House of Commons, and for six parliaments during that period, one of the two representatives for Yorkshire. In an age and country fertile in great and good men, he was among the foremost of those who fixed the character of their times; because to high and various talents, to warm benevolence, and to universal candor, he added the abiding eloquence of a Christian life. Eminent as he was in every department of public labor, and a leader in every work of charity, whether to relieve the temporal or the spiritual wants of his fellow men, his name will ever be specially-identified with those exertions which, by the blessings of God, removed from England the guilt of the African slave-trade, and prepared the way for the abolition of slavery in every colony of the empire. In the prosecution of these objects, he relied not in vain on God; but, in the progress, he was called to endure great obloquy and great opposition. He outlived, however, all enmity, and, in the evening of his days, withdrew from public life and public observation, to the bosom of his family. Yet he died not unnoticed or forgotten by his country; the Peers and Commons of England, with the Lord Chancellor and the Speaker at their head, in solemn procession from their respective houses, carried him to his fitting place among the mighty dead around, here to repose, till, through the merits of Jesus Christ his only Redeemer and Saviour, whom in his life and in his writings he had desired to glorify, he shall rise in the resurrection of the just.

The monument is a fine one; his figure is seated on a pedestal, very ingeniously done, and truly expressive of his age, and the pleasure he seemed to derive from his own thoughts. Either the orator or the poet have said or sung the praises of most of the great men who lie buried in Westminster Abbey, in enchanting strains. The statues of heroes, princes, and statesmen are there to proclaim their power, worth, or brilliant genius, to posterity. But as time shall step between them and the future, none will be sought after with more enthusiasm or greater pleasure than that of Wilberforce. No man's philosophy was ever moulded in a nobler cast than his; it was founded in the school of Christianity, which was, that all men are by nature equal; that they are wisely and justly endowed by their Creator with certain rights which are irrefragable, and no matter how human pride and avarice may depress and debase, still God is the author of good to man; and of evil, man is the artificer to himself and to his species. Unlike Plato and Socrates, his mind was free from the gloom that surrounded theirs. Let the name, the worth, the zeal, and other excellent qualifications of this noble man, ever live in our hearts, let his deeds ever be the theme of our praise, and let us teach our children to honor and love the name of William Wilberforce.

1854

MY SOUTHERN HOME: OR, THE SOUTH AND ITS PEOPLE

Chapter IX

While the "peculiar institution" was a great injury to both master and slaves, yet there was considerable truth in the oft-repeated saying that the slave "was happy."[40] It was indeed, a low kind of happiness, existing only where masters were disposed to treat their servants kindly, and where the proverbial light-heartedness of the latter prevailed. History shows that of all races, the African was best adapted to be the "hewers of wood, and drawers of water."[41]

Sympathetic in his nature, thoughtless in his feelings, both alimentativeness and amativeness large, the negro is better adapted to follow than to lead. His wants easily supplied, generous to a fault, large fund of humor, brimful of music, he has ever been found the best and most accommodating of servants. The slave would often get rid of punishment by his wit; and even when being flogged, the master's heart has been moved to pity, by the humorous appeals of his victim. House servants in the cities and villages, and even on plantations, were considered privileged classes. Nevertheless, the field hands were not without their happy hours.

An old-fashioned corn-shucking took place once a year, on "Poplar Farm," which afforded pleasant amusement for the out-door negroes for miles around. On these occasions, the servants, on all plantations, were allowed to attend by mere invitation of the blacks where the corn was to be shucked.

As the grain was brought in from the field, it was left in a pile near the corn-cribs. The night appointed, and invitations sent out, slaves from plantations five or six miles away, would assemble and join on the road, and in large bodies march along, singing their melodious plantation songs.

To hear three or four of these gangs coming from different directions, their leaders giving out the words, and the whole company joining in the chorus, would indeed surpass anything ever produced by "Haverly's Minstrels,"[42] and many of their jokes and witticisms were never equaled by Sam Lucas or Billy Kersands.[43]

A supper was always supplied by the planter on whose farm the shucking was to take place. Often when approaching the place, the singers would speculate on what they were going to have for supper. The following song was frequently sung:—

"All dem puty gals will be dar,
   Shuck dat corn before you eat.
Dey will fix it fer us rare,
   Shuck dat corn before you eat.
I know dat supper will be big,
   Shuck dat corn before you eat.
I think I smell a fine roast pig,
   Shuck dat corn before you eat.
A supper is provided, so dey said,
   Shuck dat corn before you eat.
I hope dey'll have some nice wheat bread,
   Shuck dat corn before you eat.
I hope dey'll have some coffee dar,
   Shuck dat corn before you eat.

I hope dey'll have some whisky dar,
   Shuck dat corn before you eat.
I think I'll fill my pockets full,

Shuck dat corn before you eat.
Stuff dat coon an' bake him down,
   Shuck dat corn before you eat.
I speck some niggers dar from town,
   Shuck dat corn before you eat.
Please cook dat turkey nice an' brown.
   Shuck dat corn before you eat.
By de side of dat turkey I'll be foun,
   Shuck dat corn before you eat.
I smell de supper, dat I do,
   Shuck dat corn before you eat.
On de table will be a stew,
   Shuck dat corn, etc."

Burning pine knots, held by some of the boys, usually furnished light for the occasion. Two hours is generally sufficient time to finish up a large shucking; where five hundred bushels of corn is thrown into the cribs as the shuck is taken off. The work is made comparatively light by the singing, which never ceases till they go to the supper table. Something like the following is sung during the evening:

"De possum meat am good to eat,
   Carve him to de heart;
You'll always find him good and sweet,
   Carve him to de heart;
My dog did bark, and I went to see,
   Carve him to de heart.
And dar was a possum up dat tree,
   Carve him to de heart.

CHORUS.—"Carve dat possum, carve dat possum children,
   Carve dat possum, carve him to de heart;
Oh, carve dat possum, carve dat possum children,
   Carve dat possum, carve him to de heart.

"I reached up for to pull him in,
   Carve him to de heart;
De possum he began to grin,
   Carve him to de heart;

I carried him home and dressed him off,
  Carve him to de heart;
I hung him dat night in de frost,
  Carve him to de heart.

CHORUS.—"Carve dat possum, etc.

"De way to cook de possum sound,
  Carve him to de heart;
Fust par-bile him, den bake him brown,
  Carve him to de heart;
Lay sweet potatoes in de pan,
  Carve him to de heart;
De sweetest eatin' in de lan,'
  Carve him to de heart.

CHORUS.—Carve dat possum, etc."

Should a poor supper be furnished, on such an occasion, you would hear remarks from all parts of the table,—

"Take dat rose pig 'way from dis table."
"What rose pig? you see any rose pig here?"
"Ha, ha, ha! Dis ain't de place to see rose pig."
"Pass up some dat turkey wid clam sauce."
"Don't talk about dat turkey; he was gone afore we come."
"Dis is de las' time I shucks corn at dis farm."
"Dis is a cheap farm, cheap owner, an' a cheap supper."
"He's talkin' it, ain't he?"
"Dis is de tuffest meat dat I is been called upon to eat fer many a day;
    you's got to have teeth sharp as a saw to eat dis meat."
"Spose you ain't got no teef, den what you gwine to do?"
"Why, ef you ain't got no teef you muss *gum it!*"
"Ha, ha, ha!" from the whole company, was heard.

On leaving the corn-shucking farm, each gang of men, headed by their leader, would sing during the entire journey home. Some few, however, having their dogs with them, would start on the trail of a coon, possum, or some other game, which might keep them out till nearly morning.

To the Christmas holidays, the slaves were greatly indebted for winter rec-reation; for long custom had given to them the whole week from Christmas day to the coming in of the New Year.

On "Poplar Farm," the hands drew their share of clothing on Christmas day for the year. The clothing for both men and women was made up by women kept for general sewing and housework. One pair of pants, and two shirts, made the entire stock for a male field hand.

The women's garments were manufactured from the same goods that the men received. Many of the men worked at night for themselves, making splint and corn brooms, baskets, shuck mats, and axe-handles, which they would sell in the city during Christmas week. Each slave was furnished with a pass, something like the following:—

> "*Please let my boy, Jim, pass anywhere in this county, until Jan. 1, 1834,*
> *   and oblige*
> *Respectfully,*
> "JOHN GAINES, M.D.
> "'*Poplar Farm,*' *St. Louis County, Mo.*"

With the above precious document in his pocket, a load of baskets, brooms, mats, and axe-handles on his back, a bag hanging across his shoulders, with a jug in each end,—one for the whiskey, and the other for the molasses,—the slaves trudged off to town at night, singing,—

> "Hurra, for good ole massa,
>   He give me de pass to go to de city.
> Hurra, for good ole missis,
>   She bile de pot, and giv me de licker.
>   Hurra, I'm goin to de city."

> "When de sun rise in de mornin',
>   Jes' above de yaller corn,
> You'll fin' dis nigger has take warnin',
>   An's gone when de driver blows his horn.

> Hurra, for good ole massa,
>   He giv me de pass to go to de city.
> Hurra for good ole missis,

> She bile de pot, and give me de licker.
> Hurra, I'm goin to de city."

Both the Methodists and Baptists,—the religious denominations to which the blacks generally belong,—never fail to be in the midst of a revival meeting during the holidays, and, most of the slaves from the country hasten to these gatherings. Some, however, spend their time at the dances, raffles, cock-fights, foot-races, and other amusements that present themselves.

1880

NOTES

1. The ruins of St. Mary's Abbey, founded in 1136, located in Melrose, Roxburghshire, Scotland.

2. Sir Walter Scott (1771–1832), author of the popular novels *Waverly,* published in 1814, and *Ivanhoe,* 1820.

3. The narrative poem by Sir. Walter Scott, published in 1805, in which the speaker describes a visit to the St. Mary's Abbey ruins.

4. A tributary of the River Tweed, flowing east to west through the Scottish Borders region just north of the English counties of Cumbria and Northumberland.

5. A narrative poem in six cantos, published in 1810 by Sir Walter Scott.

6. Refers to the historic tradition of Gretna Green marriages, dating back to 1754, when young couples seeking a way around the tightening parental consent requirements for unions in England and Wales chose instead to marry in the Scottish border village of Gretna Green, where English laws did not apply.

7. The Greek name for Troy, the setting of the Trojan war, described in Homer's *Iliad,* on whose shores the Achaean (Greek) forces landed, led by Odysseus (also known by the Roman name Ulysses).

8. Robert Southey (1774–1843), Samuel Taylor Coleridge (1772–1834), and William Wordsworth (1770–1850), English Romantic poets who lived in the Lake District of Northwest England and, consequently, were called the Lake Poets. In the next sentence, he reports passing the home of the prominent woman writer and Wordsworth associate Felicia Dorothea Browne Hemans (1793–1858).

9. In 1848, he and his wife escaped from enslavement in Macon, Georgia, to freedom in the North, with Craft (1824–1900) posing as a personal valet and his wife (Ellen Craft, 1826–1891) masquerading as his white male owner.

10. Home of the University of Oxford, the oldest university in the English-speaking world, offering instruction since the late eleventh century.

11. A reference to University of Oxford's status as one of several sites where, during the seventeenth century, the writings of John Milton, John Goodwin, and other English Republicans were burned by order of King Charles II.

12. In 1555, the Anglican bishops Hugh Latimer, Nicholas Ridley, and Thomas Cranmer, the Archbishop of Canterbury, were convicted of heresy at Oxford's University Church of St. Mary the Virgin and burned at the stake just outside the city walls.

13. King James II, the last Catholic King of England, alienated many of his Anglican subjects by encouraging tolerance for the practice of the Catholic faith (in 1687) and by appointing a several Catholics to prominent positions at the University of Oxford, as fellows, professors, and even a dean (in 1688).

14. Today a memorial stands where Cranmer, Ridley, and Latimer, also known as the Oxford Martyrs, were burned at the stake.

15. Brown's daughters were enrolled in a girl's boarding school at Calais.

16. Legend has long held that King Alfred the Great (849–899) was the founder of the University of Oxford. Today the university traces its origins to the gathering of teachers and students there beginning as early as 1096, with the formal establishment of the institution funded, in part, by a bequest from the estate of William of Durham (d. 1249).

17. Samuel Wilberforce (1805–1873), Bishop of Oxford, Christ Church Cathedral, Christ Church College, University of Oxford.

18. Edward Bouverie Pusey (1800–1882), for more than fifty years the Regius Professor of Hebrew at Christ Church College, University of Oxford.

19. A nineteenth-century movement advocating the reincorporation of aspects of Catholicism into Anglican faith and ritual.

20. The famous ruins of first Cistercian abbey, founded in 1131 at Tintern, Monmouthshire, Wales.

21. Refers to the Gorham Controversy, a theological debate within the Anglican Church in England around the doctrine of baptismal regeneration (the idea that baptism is a prerequisite for spiritual salvation).

22. Christian Frederick Cole, Oxford's earliest known black student, entered the university in 1873, though anecdotal evidence suggests that students of African descent were in attendance as early as the first part of the sixteenth century.

23. Noted African American writer, activist, and speaker, and the first known black graduate of the University of Cambridge, English (Queens' College, 1853).

24. The second oldest university in the English-speaking world, founded in 1209.

25. Faustin-Élie Soulouque (1782–1867), elected the seventh president of Haiti, in 1847, and proclaimed the emperor of Haiti in 1849.

26. Benjamin Franklin (1706–1790), U.S. inventor and statesman, and Robert Fulton (1765–1815), U.S. engineer and inventor of the steamboat.

27. The opening stanza of the poem "The Slave-Auction—A Fact," written by the pseudonymous Anonymous Americas and first published in *The Anti-Slavery Harp,* a collection of abolitionist songs compiled and edited by William Wells Brown and published in 1848.

28. A member of the U.S. House of Representatives from Virginia, later elected to the Senate, and also a founding member of the American Colonization Society.

29. A term applied to persons believed to have three-quarters European ancestry and one-quarter African or black ancestry, used in the United States to distinguish enslaved

mixed-race men and women from so-called clear blacks (people of African descent with no known European ancestry).

30. The final two stanzas of "The Slave Auction—A Fact," written by the pseudonymous Anonymous Americas and first published in *The Anti-Slavery Harp*.

31. A monument in central London's Trafalgar Square, commemorating Vice-Admiral Horatio Nelson, the commander-in-chief of Britain's Mediterranean fleet, who led the Royal Navy to victory in the Battle of Trafalgar.

32. The H.M.S. Victory, Admiral Nelson's ship.

33. Site of the Battle of Groton Heights, September 6, 1781, the last battle of the Revolutionary War to take place in the North.

34. Jordan Freeman, a free black man and orderly to Colonel William Ledyard, and Lambert "Lambo" Latham, an enslaved servant to the family of Continental Army Captain William Latham.

35. An area of the South Transept of London's Westminster Abbey, named for the large number of writers buried or memorialized there.

36. Author of *A Representation of the Injustice and Dangerous Tendency of Tolerating Slavery* (1769), the first book-length abolitionist text by an English author, later appointed chairman of England's first antislavery organization, the Society for Effecting the Abolition of the Slave Trade (in May of 1787).

37. James Somerset, an enslaved black man who, after being transported from Boston to England and through the advocacy of English abolitionist Granville Sharpe, won the right to resist resale to Jamaica and, eventually, his freedom.

38. Henry Grattan (1746–1820), William Pitt the Younger (1759–1806), and Charles James Fox (1749–1806), late Georgian-era politicians each of whom served, for a time, in the English Parliament.

39. Cofounder (in 1823) of the Society for the Mitigation and Gradual Abolition of Slavery and member of the English Parliament, who led the antislavery movement of the British House of Commons through the abolition of slavery throughout the British Empire, in 1833.

40. A central theme in southern postbellum plantation tradition literature and apologist thought.

41. Joshua 9:23.

42. Haverly's Mastodon Minstrels, a popular late-nineteenth-century blackface minstrel troupe comprised exclusively of white American performers.

43. Sam Lucas (1850–1916) and Billy Kersands (1942?–1915) were popular African American entertainers who performed in blackface.

JAMES MCCUNE SMITH (1813-1865)

James McCune Smith was born in New York City. He attended Manhattan's
African Free School, but was eventually forced to leave the country in order to
pursue post-secondary education. He completed his studies at the University
of Glasgow in Scotland, where he earned a BA (in 1835), an MA (in 1836), and
an MD (in 1837). The first African American to hold an MD, Smith was a much
sought-after physician and pharmacist within the African American community
of greater New York. In addition to his career in the medical sciences, McCune
was also a prolific writer. He was the author of several books and pamphlets,
including *The Destiny of the People of Color* (1843), in which he argues in favor
of African Americans' aggressive pursuit of full social and political equality.
Smith may well have been best known, however, for his regular contributions to
Frederick Douglass' Paper, submitted under the pseudonym "Communipaw."
In his "Heads of the Colored People," published in Douglass's paper between
1852 and 1854, in ten installments, Smith uses character sketches of African
American residents of New York to comment on social and political attitudes
of his day. Four installments from this series are reprinted here.

"HEADS OF THE COLORED PEOPLE,"
DONE WITH A WHITEWASH BRUSH

"Age Zographon ariste
Graphe Zographon ariste
Best of Painters, come away
Paint me the *whitewash brush,* I pray."

If Daniel Webster,[1] in search of the presidency, quoted New Testament Greek,
why may not Communipaw draw upon old Anacreon[2] in his endeavor to win
the post of door keeper, not to the Senate, (heaven save the mark!) but to the
outermost enclosure leading to the Republic of Letters? That glorious commonwealth, perpetually progressive, free from *caste,* and Cass and Fillmores,
which smiles upon all her citizens, if they be but true, which holds triumphant sway and is crowned with perennial laurel in the *coming ages!* Dear old

musical Anacreon! If any doubts the music, let them read the above motto, pronouncing the first word *"agge"* and the *"o"* as in zone.

The Black News-Vender, March 25, 1852

Any Sunday morning, in West Broadway, on the West side, between Anthony and Lemard streets, mid-way the block, may be seen arranged in piles, the *Sunday Herald, Sunday Dispatch, Sunday Times, Sunday Atlas,* &c., &c., lying on the flat stone stoop, before the white butcher's door, which is closed, and behind a colored fisherman's stand, which is just closing up. Behind the papers, and almost part of them, is the figure of a black man, razed to the knees, as if for the convenient handling of his literary peltry. Rain or shine, summer and winter, sure as Sunday morning comes, there stands that figure, and the papers. He does not, like the news boys, shout out *Sunday Herald, Times and Courier,* not he. He's none of your nomad criers in the literary world. He is a stationed vender, or, perhaps, like his class, the colored people, he noiselessly does his mission and leaves it to others to find out who and what he is. Our colored news vendor *kneels* about four feet ten; black transparent skin, broad and swelling chest, whose symmetry proclaims Virginia birth, fine long hooked nose, evidently from the first families, wide loose mouth, sharpish face, clean cut hazel eyes, buried beneath luxuriantly folded lids, and prominent perceptive faculties. I did not ask time to pull off cloth cap with long greasy ears, lest his brow should prove him the incontestible descendent of Thomas Jefferson and Black Sal. But *nil de mortus nise*—black babies and yellow, so far as Tom Jefferson is concerned; for notwithstanding the respectable and pious *N.Y. Tribune,* publishes, at the request of a Southern planter, (himself no doubt a literal follower of Jefferson in these matters,) all the stale anti-negroisms of Jefferson's notes. It is well known, as stated in Dr. Bacon's "Wanderings on the shores of Africa,"[3]—I mean the Dr. Bacon who wrote the lives of the apostles—it is well known that Jefferson contradicted his philosophy of negro hate, by seeking the dalliance of black women as often as he could, and by leaving so many descendants of mixed blood, that they are to be found as widely scattered as his own writings throughout the world. One at least, a granddaughter, is a shouting Methodist, in Liberia.

I have heard, from an eye witness, that on more than one occasion, when the sage of Monticello[4] left that retreat, for the Presidential abode, at Washington, there would be on the top of the same coach, a yellow boy of his own begetting, "running away." And when told that one of his slaves was going off without leave, Jefferson said, well! let him go, his right is as good as his father's! And, somehow, *that* boy would get a douceur before the "parting of the ways." Ah me! The pride of old Virginia! I might exclaim of it as Black Dan[5] did of our Republic *Epese, Epese.* "Thou hast fallen, thou hast fallen!" These crocus colored products of unphilosophical lust, are now reared, and penned up, and branded, and sold, by slaveholding fathers in Old Dominion,[6] who go to Presbyterian and Methodist churches, and to the altars of Episcopacy, and drink the "blood which Christ shed for all;" and thank God that they are not heathen Circassians[7] who sell their daughters as prostitutes to *Mahommedan,* not *Christian,* lust! But our black news-vender! He has sold nearly all his stock, poor, black, silent, and maimed as he is, (having lost both his legs by frost, and the surgeon's knife), fastened near the ground by this terrific misfortune, the true heart of the American people beats kindly, and with warm sympathy towards him! and many a "b'hoy," half covered from last night's debauch, staggers a square out of the way, to deal with him, and many a child, with half tearful eye-lid, runs across the way, passing a dozen vociferous newsboys, to buy a paper from the poor legless *man;* and many a dandy, who thinks, in a political sense, the negro almost a dog, snatches up a paper, and with half-averted face, throws down four times its worth, and rushes away from the *human sympathy* that has stolen away into his heart, in spite of, and through the chinks of the thrice-ribbed armor with which American Church and American state, "the droppings of the pulpit," and of the Senate, have endeavored to encase his affections. Merciful God! what a living fountain of human sympathy hast thou planted on that stone stoop, linking human creature to human creature, in spite of all the bars which society has vainly placed between them! Our black news-vender has nearly sold out, and has a few moments leisure; let us have a chat.

Com.: Good morning, sir; have you a family?

News Vender: Yes: a wife and two children; one of them, you recollect, was sick, and—What's the news in the flats?

Com.: Sharp, last night. (Here, a customer asks for the *Sunday Times*—all gone.—Another asks for the Life of Kate Hastings;[8] all sold, yesterday, and the demand large, at an advanced price.) Where was you born?

News Vender: In Virginia; came from there some years ago, and followed the sea, until two years and a half ago, since which time I have sold papers. In the week-days I keep on the corner, of Broadway and Duane Streets. I sell more *Heralds* than any other paper; and of the Sunday papers, the *Dispatch* and *Times* are most called for; next, the *Atlas,* &c. What papers are left unsold,

I dispose of, at thirty-one cents a hundred, for waste paper. My profits on the dailies are from one-fourth, to a cent each; on the Sunday papers, one cent. My wife goes down in the mornings, to buy the papers, and I can judge very nearly, of the quantity that will sell."

Com.: You *came* from Virginia—free, of course?

News Vender: Why—yes—I—made myself free.

Com.: Have you no fears of being arrested and taken back!

News Vender: Not now, (sadly looking at his maimed legs.) When I stood six feet two in my stockings, and heard talk of Virginians hereabouts, I would go straight to the dock, take ship, and be away two or three months; but now—what would they want with me?

Com.: Do you deal in policies?

News Vender: No. Or I should not be free.

Com.: Do you save any money?

News Vender: Yes. Last summer, a year ago, and winter, I saved up fifteen dollars; but was taken sick and most of it went; but now I am coming up again. I wish to get a place, a stand or shop in doors to sell papers and stationery; when the weather is cold and frosty, my stump troubles me and may lay me up.

Com.: How did you lose your legs?

News Vender: On board ship Tuscarora,[9] on her passage from Liverpool to New York. We were cast away on the coast of New Jersey; three were lost, and two others, with myself, badly frozen. The ship was a total loss: my legs were so badly frozen that I was obliged to have them amputated below the knees.

Com.: When did this happen—what month?

News Vender: I—let me see—forget the time exactly, but it was Christmas Eve, two years ago. *"Christmas Eve, two years ago! 1849!"*

The tears rushed from my eyes: for on that very night, when the poor sailor struggled with the cold and storm, and met his terrible misfortune, there came into my household a messenger for my first born: sweet, patient little sufferer, after a year of hopes and fears, and deep agony; in the intervals from distress, that day her young hopes were gladdened with tomorrow's Christmas tree and the expected adornings from a mother's loving hand. But long ere midnight came,

There sat the Shadow feared of man;
. . .
And spread his mantle, dark and cold,
And wrapped her formless in the fold,
And dulled the murmur on her lip.[10]

News Vender! You must have a shop. Your story must be printed and sold. A little place must be hired. And your first stock in trade shall be purchased from the sum left behind by the little girl who found rest in heaven, while you manfully met and battled with your severest ill on earth. Forgive me, dear Douglass, for writing so much; but I cannot close without drawing attention to the moral which grows out of the black News Vender's history. There is hope in it for all who, like him, are battling against slavery and caste. There need be no fear in particularizing his whereabouts, for I defy all Virginia to 'come and take' his trunk and arms—legs he has none. Compliments to Ethiop.

Yours affectionately,

COMMUNIPAW. NEW YORK, March 21st, 1852.

The Washerwoman, June 17, 1852

Saturday night! *Dunk!* goes the smoothing-iron, then a swift gliding sound as it passes smoothly over starched bosom and collar, and wrist-bands, of one of the many dozen shirts that hang round the room on horses, chairs, lines and every other thing capable of being hanged on. *Dunk! dunk!* goes the iron, sadly, wearily, but steadily, as if the very heart of toil were throbbing its penultimate beats! *Dunk! dunk!* and that small and delicately formed hand and wrist swell up with knotted muscles and bursting veins! And the eye and brow, chiselled out for stern resolve and high thought, the one now dull and haggard, and the other, seamed and blistered with deep furrows and great drops of sweat wrung out by over toil. The apartment is small, hot as an oven, the air in it thick and misty with the steam rising from the ironing table; in the corners, under the tables, and in all out-of-the-way places, are stowed tubs of various sizes, some empty, some full of clothes soaking for next week's labor.

On the walls hang pictures of old Pappy Thompson, or Brother Paul, or Sammy Cornish:[11] in one corner of the room, a newly varnished mahogany table is partly filled with books—Bunyan's *Pilgrim's Progress*, Watts' *Hymns*, the *Life of Christ*, and a nice 'greasy novel' just in from the circulating library; between the windows stand an old bureau, the big drawer of which is the larder, containing sundry slices of cold meat, second handed toast, 'with butter on it,' and the carcass of a turkey, the return cargo of a basket of clothes sent down town that morning. But even this food is untasted; for, the Sabbath approaches, and old Zion, and the vivid doses of hell fire ready to be showered from the pulpit, on all who do labor (saving the parson, who *does* pound the reading board in a style which, to the unsanctified, looks like hard work) on the Day of Rest. *Dunk! dunk!!* goes the smoothing-iron, the frame of the washerwoman bends again to her task, her mind is "far away" in the sunny South, with her sisters and their children who toil as hard but without any pay! And she fancies the smiles which will gladden their faces, when receiving the things she sent them in a box by the last Georgetown packet. *Dunk! dunk!! dunk!!!* goes the iron, this time right swift and cheerily, shot away and back, under thy smile, Oh Freedom! No *Prie Dieu*,[12] in reverential corner, no crucifix and lugubrious beads pendent from the sidewall, no outward and visible sign, but the great impulse of progressive humanity has touched her heart as with flame, and her tried muscles forget all weariness, the iron flies as a weaver's shuttle, shirts appear and disappear with rapidity from the heated blanket and at a quarter to twelve, the groaning table is cleared, and the poor washerwoman sink upon her knees in prayer for them, that they also may soon partake of that freedom which, however toilsome, is yet so sweet.

Once lighted up, the imagination ranges over the possibilities of their enfranchisement. Each one of her three sisters had been brought North with the white family, and went back, for their children's sake, into bondage. She alone had remained North, from her girlhood, as a slave, until one day, when she had reached woman's years, her so-called master, with much bustle, with whip in hand, had called her up stairs for punishment. The scene was short and decisive: the tall, stout man had raised his arm to strike—"see here!" fiercely exclaimed the frail being before him, "if you dare touch me with that lash, I will tear you to pieces!" The whipper, whipped, dropt his uplifted arm, and quietly slunk down stairs. There had been, unseen by either of them, a silent witness of the scene, who, looking through a glass door, ready to stay the arm of his uncle, had felt a terrible fear, and a terrible triumph. Yes! well, I had forgotten to say, that, alongside the ironing table, was a good-for-nothing looking quarter grown, bushy-headed boy, a shade or two lighter than his mother, so intent upon "Aladdin; or, the Wonderful Lamp," that he had to be called three or four times before he sprang to put fresh wood on the fire, or light another candle, or bring a pail of water. A boy there, but no evidence around the room, that he called any one father, nor had he, ever, except the unseen, universal "our Father, which art in Heaven!" A sort of social Pariah, he had come into the world, after the fashion which so stirs up Ethiop's pious honor. And yet, genial, forgiving Nature, with a healthy forgetfulness of priests and the rituals, had stamped this boy's face with no lineament particularly hideous, nor yet remarkable, except a 'laughing devil' in his eye that seemed ready to "face the devil" without Burn's prophylactic.[13]

Sunday evening! Can it be the same apartment? No sign of toil is there; everything tidy, neat and clean; all the signs of the hard week's work stowed away in drawers or in the cellar. The washerwoman dressed up in neat, even expensive, garments; and her boy with his Sunday go-to-meetin's on, one of the pockets stuffed with sixpence worth of 'pieces,' (candy,) which he had made Stuart the Confectioner (corner of Chamber and Greenwich, father of the present millionaires) rouse up, at day light, and sell him, as he came back from carrying home clothes, that morning. But I must break off this sketch half way, lest Ethiop should 'tire' wading through it. By the way, how long will it be before we have a titled nobility among our colored American-dom? Our friend, Ethiop, for example, tries to make out that he came into New York, *a la* Benjamin Franklin, with a blue coat on, and a roll of bread under his arm; when everybody knows that he just came from Shrewsbury River, in a Jersey oyster boat, and spent his first half hour in New York dancing for eels at Catharine Market,[14] on Sunday morning at that! As to the coat, why the fellow had only *one* garment on. We must be down upon this aristocracy, dear Fred: let us mount on our 'scutcheon, a broken chain, and get some one to do up the Latin stating, *"if we are slave born, we have ever earned our own living,* and do not, and never did, lay off *(sterquilinire)* or any dead man's earnings North or South."* I only wish that I could add to my escutcheon that noblest bar on yours, *"Egomet me liberavil"* "I have set myself free!" The most remarkable thing at the May Anniversary was said by Mr. Latrobe of Baltimore,[15] the main speaker, at the Colonization meeting, "that although he had been very earnestly urged by a leading member of the New York State Colonization Society, to say nothing about the impossibility of the blacks and whites living together, in equality and harmony in the same land and under the same political rule," yet he would advert to that subject, &c., &c. This is very remarkable and very cheering, and indicates light breaking where it is much wanted. It was also remarkable, that, when Mr. Latrobe stated the hideous old doctrine of "incompatibility, &c.," in the loudest, and most cheer-beseeching terms, his New York audience received the outburst in cold silence.

Mrs. Mary Lundie Duncan,[16] in her book on America devotes a chapter to the colored race, in which she paints our condition so abject and non-resisting, that I could only wish her within ear-shot of where I write, that she might learn that colored men and boys too can "strike back" when insulted by whites. But here comes P. Awning Bell,[17] and I must close.

Yours, COMMUNIPAW.

The Sexton, July 16, 1852

Years ago, when the idea of turning church and churchyard into houses and lots, would have brought down a volley of oaths in low Dutch, French and English, all along Nassau street, there lived and flourished the most remarkable of New York sextons.—All the sextons in those days were colored men, John Mace[18] and a thousand other funerals were *nondum*.[19] Our hero was of gigantic height, with broad double-jointed shoulders, bowed legs and a head to match: he seemed to have grown up under the church, part of its support, one of its under-ground pillars, so much a part of it, that whenever he crept out of the vaults into the open air, it seemed clear that he must have braced up a huge stone pillar, to take his place 'until his return,' else *that* side of the edifice must have caved in. His mother must have brooded in charnel houses,[20] fascinated with vampire fancies, or he never would have come into the world with that huge, misshapen head! His eyes were large, prominent and staring, with the whites visible all round, and seemed to have been placed at different times and unsymmetrical places in his head; they were no more a pair than if they had belonged to different persons. His hair, on week days, lay close to his head, carefully done up in five closely plaited pig-tails which lay close to the scalp, from the natural disposition to 'grow in again,' manifested by 'each partic'lar hair.' But on Sundays, his whole scalp passed from the grub to the butterfly state—the pig-tails expanded into whirls, elaborately combed out, into prow, *alae*,[21] *naviculum*,[22] in short, decidedly papilionaceous; thus affording a tempting subject for urchin's laughter, and for the minister's illustration of the doctrine of euthanasia.[23] Such was

> "The sexton he, whose strenuous arm
>   Dug all the graves, and tolled the bell,"
> All else appeared to him as dead,
>   Awaiting but the shroud and pall,
> It seemed that to himself he said,
>   "I shall soon dig the graves of all."[24]

He held a plurality of offices; sexton to the French church, and grave-digger to St. Philips.[25] On Sundays, he assisted the French minister in rob-ing, and about mid sermon, walked softly up the aisle to whisper a word to Dr. P——, one of the church wardens: the Doctor would hasten out, hat in hand, under the earnest gaze of half the congregation, then in a little while would return, with a peculiar beam of satisfaction in his face, that allayed all anxiety about the 'danger of the case.' He happened so regularly, that inquiry was set on foot, when it was discovered that the patient was in the doctor's own stomach first, then in the sexton's, for they both had visited Niblo's coffee house, then located just over the way. But it was in the old Chrystie street grave-yard[26] that our sexton most did flourish. There he had buried all the colored population for quarter of a century; at first with the aid of two assistants, but latterly, as the ground grew full, alone. People enough were buried there every six months, to fill any ground of the same area, but our sexton's sharp spade, and skill in packing, made room for more.—With a huge wall, or pestle, and a convenient corner in the vault, skulls and other bones not quite dry, were hastened in the process of turning into dust. His labors extended far into the night, and there are persons living who attest that they have seen him crawl out of the old Chrystie street yard, at crow of cock, licking his chops, and with suspicious bits of flesh adhering to his frowsy garments; and one lady bought a bureau the veneering of which she was sure was the exact grain of the lid of her husband's coffin! When they built the tallow melting establishment next door to the graveyard, coffins were found shoved under the old foundations like drawers in a druggist's store. And most strange to say, when this establishment went into operation, the graveyard grew more roomy, whilst the order from the bone boiling-factory grew horridly human. Fierce rumors grew apace, and even reached the dull ears of the vestry of St. Philips, in the shape of threats; but that stolid body quietly looked at the account-book, found that the grave-yard yielded them plenty of money, which being all they wanted from live niggers, was all they could expect from dead ones. "Was not the liturgy read?—Was not the minister paid? What further had the vestry to do with the matter?"—"This grumbling must be the doing of envious outsiders who wished to disturb the peace of the church." Such were the replies of the vestry.

Our sexton was a public man of some note. He helped to organize the New York African Society for mutual relief in 1809: on the occurrence of the first death in that body, he, along with a leading sweep-master, kept watch over the corpse the first night.—As these two compared notes and reckoned profits in business, towards midnight, they heard a series of raps! One went to the door, called, but no one answered nor appeared. They resumed talk-ing when the raps came again! Again going to the door, and finding no one, the sweep-master locked the door and laid the key on the table. The raps oc-curred again and again, as horror crept through the bones of the two setters up! Finding one of the eyes of the sexton resting on the sheet-covered corpse, saw the linen rise and fall as the raps came; with a shriek and howl he pointed to the spot, when the sweep-master also caught sight, and both made for the chimney, the sweep-master up first and the other clenching to his heels. Their uproar stirred the neighbors, who, finding the door locked, burst it open, sure (from his reputation that way) to find the sexton feasting on the corpse! Someone snatched the sheet from the body and found—the deceased man's favorite spaniel—the cause of the rappings sadly crouched near his dead masters remains. The rumors against our sexton at length reached the ears of the corporation of the city of New York. He was notified that on a certain day, the city Inspector would visit the grave-yard in Chrystie street; on the morning of that day at daylight, the sexton's wife missed him from her side, (he always came home at cock crowing,) and he has never been heard of since. Rewards were offered, the city and the vaults ransacked, and although everybody knew him, no one had witnessed his exit. About twenty years after, in 1850, a man came to my house, hardly over the fright, for he declared that he had seen and spoken to this very sexton in Detroit, in a barber's shop. But the sexton's wife, yet living, did not believe him, the vestry of St. Philips *did* believe him, and *that* is regarded as proof that the man must have been mistaken.

The Schoolmaster, November 3, 1854

The leaves are falling in our lane; and the trees, stripped and gaunt, seem prepared to wrestle with the coming storms; and the blossoms are withered, and the little feet no longer patter in our door-way, and

"Oh, I am a-weary, a-weary!"

"Close up!" they say, when the ranks are thinned in battle; "close up!" already exclaims the human tide, from which is missed those who sank in the *Arctic*.[27] "What of Sevastopol?[28] The eighteen thousand *not slain?*" How curiously this war has educated the public mind; even those who condemn war in the abstract, blatant peace men, have been worried up to blood heat by the merciful delays of fleets and armies; Napier[29] is grown cowardly, and the allies at Varna[30] waste *precious time* when they haste not to mingle in the slaughter; nowhere have I seen it upheld as praiseworthy that ministers in London and Paris have tried to avoid bloodshed and substitute diplomacy. So feel we outsiders. But they who are mingled in the fight—Englishmen—especially seem differently affected; when they walk over the field covered with the dead of the *enemy*, they find nothing *to hate*; they see upturned faces, with fair skins, and blue eyes, and light hair, that in their looks, for the most part youthful, reminds them of brothers, perhaps sons, at home; and the voice of Abel cries to them from the ground.

There would be some hope for these soldiers, could they be left to their own reflections; it might lead to a spectacle not yet dreamed of in the world's progress of ten thousand men, in battle array, grounding their arms, and asking of their chief, *why* they must shoot down, bayonet and stab their ten thousand brothers on the other side of the stream. It would not be taken by them as a good reason, that "the Queen, or the Emperor (plagued with an indigestion, or overdosed with Brown Stout) says you must fight." After the fight was over, at Alma,[31] Sir William Young, Bart, an English captain, was shot dead by a wounded Russian, to whom he was offering a cup of water. The Russian soldier serf, had fought in earnest, what he believed to be his foe; he could conceive of no other relation which an English soldier in that field could bear to him; he was not sufficiently *enlightened* to know that the man who had just shot him down, could humanely alleviate the suffering he had inflicted.

And here the question arises, how far was the free-born English baronet in advance of the serf-born Russian? Do they represent distinct phases of human progress? Which of them was in advance of the other? Sir William Young, thoroughly educated in a most Christian university, had just left in England, a young, equally accomplished and most beautiful wife—the Russian, ignorant, a serf, from the Don or the Volga:

"There were his young barbarians all at play, And there their Dacian mother!"[32]

Our daily papers make much comment on the fact that not a single woman was saved from the wreck of the *Arctic*: there is no reason why they should writhe under this imputation: does it reflect any disgrace on a nation of women whippers?[33] There is not much room for her worship, in the loss of that noble steamer. There was young HOLLAND[34] on deck, who went down with the wreaths of the signal gun circling his brow, performing his self-imposed duty to the last; and there was below, as Captain Luce tells us, ANNA DOWNER, alone, working at the pumps, and exclaiming, *"Captain, I am willing to pump as long as I can work my arms!"*

Young Holland will probably have a monument at Washington: he was white as well as brave. Mrs. Downer, beautiful and prepossessing, was brave; but she was a *woman,* and a *colored* woman. Who would think of erecting a monument to her? It is true that she kept at the pump, when there was no hope of relief therefrom; but in this she did the best duty she knew of, and acted as intelligently as Holland, and as wisely as the Captain himself, whose views of his responsibility and duty were summed up in his often repeated determination to sink with the ship.

Mrs. ANNA DOWNER, was carefully brought up and fairly educated in Connecticut where she was born: she was married early, and, it was thought, well. After several years of prosperous wedded life, she was suddenly thrown upon the world penniless and with an aged mother to support, by the misconduct of her husband. Young and in the midst of this great Babylon, she went bravely to work, sought employment, and secured a berth, as under stewardess of the *Arctic*—on the retirement of her senior three years ago, she succeeded to the chief office, by virtue of the energy of character she had displayed as subordinate. And now it was the joy of her heart and the aim of her being to make her aged mother comfortable and happy—and each return voyage of the *Arctic* found her adding something new to accomplish this purpose. One day last winter, I asked her playfully, "what she, such a little body, would do if her big ship were wrecked." She replied, energetically, "work at the pumps as hard as I could!"

The last time I saw her, was at my door, when I gave her a sad, sad message to take to a mutual friend in Liverpool. The next day she sailed to return no more; and others too have since gone from that door, to return no more.

And Mrs. Anna Downer, has left a word worth remembering, by all, and especially by those with whom oppression identified her. The *Arctic* was sinking; her machinery was no longer able to pump; strong men had wrought at the breaks and given up to despair; "she had," said Mr. Baahlam, to her mother, "run from pump to pump cheering the workers and lending a hand." Everybody had run to the upper deck; a few frantic with fear, all paralyzed; one or two folding their clothes decently to die: the Captain stepped below and found her alone at the pump: with resolute and aforethought purpose there she labored: and when told to desist, exclaimed, *"Captain, I am willing to pump as long as I can work my arms!"* Brethren! This great ship of state in which we are, is no fairer to look at, nor of better material, nor statelier mould than the ill-starred *Arctic*: she sails too, at fullest speed without signal, through sunshine and fog: do not her sides already gape, and the wild tide of damning oppression rush in? These quarter boats of Anti-Slavery (old organization) and Liberty Party, with its tackle slipped, have already sheared off with no room for black men, the raft of Kansas migration would hold as many of us,[35] and as safely as poor McCabe's did and yet it is our duty to work as dying Anna Downer did, as long *as we can move our arms.* We may not save the ship, but like that noble woman we may leave a deathless name.

What I have to say 'bout the Schoolmaster, Mr. Editor, must be reserved to another occasion. I hope my friend, the Elder on the Heights, will keep calm.[36]

Yours, COMMUNIPAW.

1852–1854

NOTES

1. A congressman and, later, senator from Massachusetts, eventually serving as secretary of state under President Millard Fillmore (from 1850 to 1852).

2. A Greek poet of the fifth century BCE.

3. David Francis Bacon, MD, served for three years as principal colonial physician in Liberia. He is also the author of *Wanderings on the Seas and Shores of Africa,* a highly regarded and popular memoir of his time in the West African colony.

4. President Thomas Jefferson's plantation home, located in Charlottesville, Virginia.

5. A popular name for Daniel Webster, adopted both his supports and his detractors.

6. A popular nickname for the State of Virginia.

7. A central Asian ethnic group who, during the mid-nineteenth century, made its home in the North Caucasus region of Russia and whose ethnic religion, Adyghe Khabze, is monotheistic, but with elements of transcendentalist thought.

8. *The Life and Death of Kate Hastings; Being a Complete History of Her Eventful Life and Melancholy Death in the Charitable Hospital, Paris,* a popular risqué novel by prolific genre author George Thompson (writing as Amy Morton), likely based on the life of a real-life New York sex worker, Katherine Hastings.

9. In 1849, the packet ship Tuscarora went aground just south of Cape Henlopen, Delaware, en route from Liverpool to Pennsylvania.

10. A passage from Alfred, Lord Tennyson's long poem, *In Memoriam A.H.H.,* published in 1849.

11. A possible reference to George Donisthorpe Thompson (1804–1878), English antislavery activist and noted orator; Captain Paul Cuffee (1759–1812), African American and Wampanoag shipping magnate, abolitionist, and pro-colonization activist; and Samuel Cornish (1795–1858), African American journalist, Presbyterian minister, and cofounder of the nation's first black newspaper.

12. A wooden kneeling bench fitted with a shelf for Bibles, prayer books, or other devotional materials.

13. A reference to "Address to the Devil," a satirical challenge to Calvinist views on Satan and original sin, by Scottish Romantic poet Robert Burns (1759–1796).

14. Refers to the late-eighteenth and early nineteenth-century tradition in which enslaved black men and women would gather at the Catherine Market on Sunday mornings and do traditional regional dances in exchange for small amounts of money or bunches of eels, considered an inedible or throwaway fish by more affluent shoppers.

15. Baltimore attorney John H. B. Latrobe (1803–1891), chief counsel for the B&O Railroad, founder of the American Bar Association and the Maryland Historical Society, and a staunch supporter of African colonization.

16. *America as I Found It* (1852) by Scottish author Mary Grey Lundie Duncan.

17. New York–based African American journalist Phillip Alexander Bell (1808–1889), a correspondent to *Frederick Douglass' Paper.*

18. A mid-nineteenth-century undertaker and coffin dealer operating out of a warehouse on Carmine Street in lower Manhattan.

19. Latin term meaning "not yet."

20. A building, vault, or chamber in which human remains are stored.

21. A wing-like protrusion from a bone, a shell, or other hardened material.

22. An incense boat used in Catholic religious ceremonies, often made of bronze, noted here for the ornamental lip that turns up from one edge.

23. The belief that it is, in some cases, permissible and even just to aid suffering patients in hastening their deaths.

24. From Scottish poet John Sterling's long poem "The Sexton's Daughter," first published in the July 1838 issue of *Blackwood's Edinburgh Magazine.*

25. St. Philip's Episcopal Church, the first African American Episcopal parish in the City of New York, established in 1818.

26. Between 1795 and 1853 as many as five thousand of New York City's black residents were interred in this cemetery, which once extended from what is now Bowery Street on the west edge to Forsyth Street on the east and from Stanton Street on the north edge to Rivington Street on the south.

27. A paddle steamer in the Collins Line that collided with the French steamer *Vesta,* in September of 1854, on a return voyage from Liverpool to New York. Of the roughly 400 passengers on board, only 85 survived, 61 of whom were members of the crew. None of the women and children on the ship were saved.

28. The Siege of Sevastopol (September 1854–September 1855), an early campaign in the Crimean War.

29. William Napier, a British Army sergeant in the allied forces during the Siege of Sevastopol.

30. A Bulgarian resort city used as a headquarters for naval operations by the French and British allies during the Crimean War.

31. The Alma River, in what is now the Crimean Peninsula of Ukraine, site of the Battle of Alma (September 1854), considered the first battle of the Crimean War.

32. From Lord Byron's "The Dying Gladiator," Canto the Fourth, Stanza 141, *Childe Harold's Pilgrimage.*

33. A term used by many in the North to call attention to the brutality of slavery in the South, but used here as an indictment of misogynist violence through the United States.

34. Stewart Holland, an apprentice engineer on the crew of the *Arctic* who died working to fire the ship's signal gun.

35. A reference to the Kansas-Nebraska Act of May 1854. This legislation established the Kansas and Nebraska territories under the provision that the status of each region as slave territory or free would be decided by those U.S. citizens who migrated there.

36. A reference to Smith's fellow correspondent William J. Wilson (Ethiop).

WILLIAM J. WILSON (1818-?)

A schoolteacher and abolitionist, William J. Wilson was also a prolific writer, publishing articles and correspondence in many African American-owned periodicals, throughout the mid-nineteenth century. Wilson's greatest notoriety, though, came as a result of his work as the Brooklyn correspondent for *Frederick Douglass' Paper.* Known to his readers by the pen name "Ethiop," Wilson engaged in a lively correspondence with the playfully antagonistic "Communipaw" (physician and author James McCune Smith), throughout the first half of the 1850s. Their spirited debates on the key issues of the day were equal parts politics and performance, informing their readers of the nuances surrounding issues like colonization, abolitionism, and racial equality, each writing as highbrow sophisticate and brash illuminato, respectively and in turn. Of the following selections, the first appeared in *Frederick Douglass' Paper* in 1852. In it, Wilson responds to the first installment of James McCune Smith's "Heads of the Colored People." Wilson's "Afric-American Picture Gallery" (1859) imagines an art exhibition through whose images the author is able to describe and comment on the condition of black people in the United States and beyond. Once again taking up the pseudonym of "Ethiop," the writer published the piece in the *Anglo-African Magazine.* It was released in seven installments. This, the first of those, appeared in the February 1859 issue.

FROM OUR BROOKLYN CORRESPONDENT

Published on May 13, 1852

MY DEAR DOUGLASS:

When a boy, nothing to me was more refreshing than to wade the stream that passed in gentle ripples, near by the home of my childhood.

At Summer eve, or morn—or—when—

Upon the strength of day, reclined the sunny hours.

It was equally refreshing, even at this day of life, to wade, last week, through some two columns, nearly, of my neighbor Communipaw's cogitations, in your paper, tending to show that a determined man, no matter how low his condition, or what his color, despite all opposition, may, if he persevere, raise himself up to the highest *niche* in the profession he marks out for himself; and, at the same time, have not only a name and a praise among men, but something more substantial for himself and children. I own, I labored, but failed to show it so conclusively as he has done; and all who are anxious about *our* welfare, as I am, heartily thank him for it.

As I, my dear sir, proposed in the onset, to *Crayon* for you and your numerous subscribers, with a *charcoal,* Afric-America, giving a faithful picture, with all its lights and shades, I am, upon the whole, rather pleased with neighbor Communipaw's *"Heads* of the *Blacks,* with a *white-wash brush,"* since it leaves me free to sketch more faithfully their HANDS, and HOMES, and HEARTS, as time and occasion present themselves for doing.

Encased in my best coat (not blue) and pants, and gloves, I crossed over to Gotham the other Sunday, to attend worship at St. Philip's Church. Old St. Philip's!!! As I entered her portals, the atmosphere seemed cold and strange; and as I stood in the aisle, and one after another swiftly passed by me, none recognized me. I listened—but heard not, as once, the short quick-step of the little old man, as his goose-quilled shoes squeakingly glided up the *aisle,* announcing, by their presence, to everybody, that "meeting was now in." He was not, there!!! And as I bowed my head in silence, I heard a voice; but oh! it was not the meek and heavenly voice of the *Rev. Peter Williams;* it was another's, whose feet were occupying that place, where, for so many years, that venerable father so faithfully proclaimed the gospel of Christ to his flock. I looked, and lo!! it was a *white* man!!! a *dictator* sent to dictate to his flock; and he did dictate; and they, I fear, alas! have learned too well how to submissively obey. Why is this? Where is Bery? Where the talented Crummell?[1] Would any black man have dared to utter an hundredth part of what this white man has, upon a matter so vital to the people of color, and have retained that pulpit a day, or even an hour? Would he have dared to utter such language, and found New York sufficiently large for his trembling feet twenty-four hours? How is it, then, that *blacks* will submit to so much from *whites* and bear nothing from one of themselves, even though it be proper? A colored man, whose pretension to respectability is about equal to most of ours, informed me the other day, that it was his solemn conviction, that it was highly improper for blacks to employ whites in menial stations, such as servants, &c., while they ought to fill all important stations among us, such as preaching, and in otherwise overseeing, &c.; or in other words, we should look up to *them* solely for all these things, and they should look down to, and hand to us such as they think proper, and at such times as they think mete. The idea with him, of receiving instruction *from* black lips, no matter how valuable, was not to be thought of; or a black head "wagging in a pulpit," was scarcely to be endured; or the feeling a pulse with shady fingers, or attending to our law cases, by a limb of the *law* encased in colored skin, to him was monstrous; and I am not sure that there are not more in this region, of the same opinion; nay, not very certain that it is not in consonance with "the feelings" of many, the growing fashionable idea of the day, among us, however singular it may seem when on paper.

Confidence, my dear sir, in our own *capacities,* is one of the ingredients needed in our composition for the moulding of us into the proper shape for progress; and Ethiop's opinion is, (all things considered) that it will be the proper time for white men to preach to, and teach the blacks, when black men can be permitted to preach to, and teach the *whites.* Till then, the matter is exceedingly lop-sided, resembling very much the handle of a jug, and fraught with much evil.

But to return to St. Philip's. The Rev. Peter Williams was not there. Neither the shrill *Tenor,* fina *Alto,* nor the rich, full round *Bass,* mingling in harmony with the pealing notes of the well-played organ, came to my ear as was their wont in days that are passed; nor yet the sharp voice, leading in prayer, or ringing out in response high above the rest, *A-a-m-e-n,* as the little old man, with intelligent face and *spects,* would lock up, and his fine countenance gleam out through his huge glasses—he (counterpart of him of the goose-quilled shoes), he was not there. My eyes ran around the pews for others I once knew, but I saw them not; and then came the thought that they were gone! all gone! and then stole the silent tear down my face. I looked for some relief of the past, and could find but the old hanging chandeliers. I lingered long in the aisle for someone to show me a seat; but none came. I was but an indifferent looking stranger. True, one of the present dignitaries, who ought to have recognized me much better than I did the old hanging chandeliers, cast on me an inquiring, but hurried glance, and passed on. As my eyes ran round the wall, I discovered on either side of the pulpit projected a tablet of marble. From the remote seat into which I had groped my way, I could make out only that one was in memory of the lamented Isaiah G. DeGrasse,[2] and the other, a medallion of the once beloved and faithful pastor, Peter Williams, whose mild face, when on earth, beamed so much of heaven, seemed still to beam out from the cold marble, rebuking the teachings that now emanate from his once-beloved desk. My foot long lingered after the stately congregation had passed out. Finding my way at length to the street, with a sigh I looked back upon poor old St. Philip's,

> And then again the silent tear
> Stole stealthily down my rigid cheek;
> First one by one, and then they came
> Both thick and fast, though silent still.

'Twas here, in old St. Philip's, I heard my first sermon when first I came to Gotham. 'Twas here I first saw one whose shadow ever walketh by my side; and *from* hence, with a heavy heart, I now wended my way to my quiet home. Yours truly,

ETHIOP.

BROOKLYN HEIGHTS, May 1st, 1852.

1852

AFRIC-AMERICAN PICTURE GALLERY

Number I

I always had a *penchant* for pictures. From a chit of a boy till now, my love for beautiful, or quaint old pictures has been unquenched.

If an ever abiding love for any branch of Art is indicative of a fitness to pursue it, then I should have been a painter. Even when so small as to be almost imperceptible, I used to climb up, by the aid of a stool, to my mother's mantle piece, take down the old family almanac and study its pictures with a greater relish than ever a fat alderman partook of a good dinner including a bountiful supply of the choicest wines. All this however, never made me a painter. Fate marked out a rougher, sterner destiny for me. But the habit of rambling in search of, and hunting up curious, old, or rare and beautiful pictures, is as strong as ever.

It was in one of these rambles, that I stumbled over the Afric-American Picture Gallery, which has since become one of my dearest retreats wherein to spend many an otherwise weary hour, with profit and pleasure.

The collection is quite numerous, having been sought from every quarter of the American continent, and some from abroad; and though as a *Gallery of Art,* if not highly meritorious, still from its wide range of subjects and the ingenuity with which many of them are presented, it must, to the lover and curious in such matters, afford much for amusement, and to the careful observer and the thinker much that is valuable and interesting.

In style and excellence these pictures vary according to the fancy or skill of the artist. Some are finely executed, while others are mere rough sketches. Some are in oil, some in water colors, and India. Ink shadings, a few statues, statuettes, and a few Crayons and Pencilings possessing a high degree of merit; others are mere charcoal sketches and of little worth beyond the subjects they portray.

But without pursuing this general outline further, let the reader, with me, enter into this almost unknown Gallery. Well, here we are, and looking about us.

The first thing noticeable, is the unstudied arrangement of these pictures. They seem rather to have been put up out of the way, many of them, than hung for any effect.

The walls are spacious, and contain ample room for more, and, in many instances, better paintings; and many niches yet vacant for busts and statues; and just here, let me make an humble petition in behalf of this our newly discovered Gallery—It is that generous artists, will, at their convenience, have the goodness to paint an occasional picture, or chisel a statue or bust, and we will be sure to assign it to its appropriate place. But let us take a survey, and speak only of what strikes us most forcibly in our present mood.

PICTURE NUMBER 1.—THE SLAVE SHIP.

This picture hangs near the entrance, on the south side of the Gallery, and in rather an unfavorable light. The view is of course Jamestown harbor, Virginia,[3] in 1609, and has all the Wild surroundings of that portion of our country at that period; the artist having been faithful even to every shrub, crag and nook. Off in the mooring lays the slave ship, Dutch-modeled and ugly, even hideous to look upon, as a slave-ship ought to be. On the shore is a group of emaciated Africans, heavily manacled, the first slaves that ever trod the American continent; while in the fierce and angry waters of the bay, which seem to meet the black and dismal and storm-clad sky, is seen a small boat containing another lot of these human beings, just nearing the shore.

If the artist's general conception of this picture may be regarded a success, in its details, beyond all question, this is its crowning point. The small boat struck by, and contending with a huge breaker, is so near the shore that you can behold, and startle as you behold, the emaciated and death-like faces of the unfortunate victims, and the hideous countenances of their captors; and high and above all, perched upon the stern, with foot, tail and horns, and the chief insignias of his office, is his Satanic Majesty, gloating over the whole scene. What is more truthful than that the devil is ever the firm friend and companion of the slave ship?

PICTURE NUMBER 2.—

TIIE FIRST AND THE LAST COLORED EDITOR.

This small, but neat picture hangs on the north side of the gallery; and though simple in its details, is so well executed that it has much attracted me. The Last Colored Editor, quite a young man, with a finely formed head and ample brow—thoughtful, earnest, resolute—sits in chair editorial, with the first number of the *Freedom's Journal,* the first journal ever edited by, and devoted to the cause of the colored man in America, held in one hand and outspread before him, while the other, as though expressive of his resolve, is firmly clenched.

Surrounding him are piles of all the journals edited by colored men from the commencement up till the present, among which the *Freedom's Journal, Colored American, People's Press, North Star,* and *Frederic Douglass'* paper are the more prominent. The First Editor is represented as a venerable old man, with whitened locks and placid face, leaning on a staff, and unperceived by the Last Editor, is looking intently over his shoulder on the outspread journal.

It is his own first editorial, and the first ever penned and published by a colored man in America. The scene is the linking together of our once scarcely hopeful past with the now bright present.

PICTURE NO. 3—THE FIRST MARTYR OF THE REVOLUTION.

This is a head of Attucks. It may not be generally known, and it may not be particularly desirable that the public should know, that the First Martyr of the American Revolution was a colored man; that the first bosom that was bared to the blast of war was black; the first blood that drenched the path-way which led up to American liberty, was from the veins of a colored man.

And yet such is the fact; and the artist has done a service in the execution of this head. It hangs at the north east end of the Gallery, and is a fine likeness of a bold, vigorous man,—just such as would be likely to head a revolution to throw off oppression. May the name of Attucks and the facts connected therewith never perish.

PICTURE NO. 4. SUNSET IN ABBEOKUTA.

This is a fine painting. The landscape is rich, varied, beautiful. The sky has all the warmth of hue and softness of tint, and all that gorgeousness (changing seemingly with every instant) for which an African sky is so much noted. No rainbow with us, in its full splendor, is so variegated or so wide in its range of colors.

The last touches of the artist's pencil has made the glow of the coming evening to softly spread itself over here and there a dusky inhabitant reclining upon the banks of an unrippled lake. The effect is fine, and the whole scene is so charming that one could almost wish to be there.

PICTURES 5 AND 6.—THE UNDERGROUND RAILROAD.

In these two pictures the artist is certainly quite up to our idea. They are of large size and represent both the Southern and Northern portions of that mysterious road. They hang beside each other on the south side of the Gallery and are marked A and B. I would suggest that B be changed over to the north wall, as a more appropriate place. Picture A, or the south view represents a dark road leading through a darker forest, along which is seen merely some twenty pairs of fine stalwart human feet and legs—male and female—of all sizes, hurrying northward. Every muscle and limb indicates firmness and resolution. The scene is night-time, and far distant through the forest is faintly seen the north star—small but bright and unfailing, and to the fugitive, unerring.

Picture B on the north view consists of some twenty bold heads and fine robust faces, each of which is lit up with a joy no pen can portray, and nothing but the pencil of the master could have reached. The exclamation of each must be we have found it!!!

In the foreground is a lake and the background is a Canadian forest, through which here and there you can perceive a small rustic cottage. Both of these pictures sustain well that air of mystery which envelopes the Under Ground Rail Road.

In the first view we have but the feet and legs, indicating the mysterious manner in which those feet and legs move bodies towards freedom, or pass along that undefined and undefinable Road that leads to liberty. There is another thought. The head, the recognized seat of the mind, is useless to the slave, or, if of service to him, this thinking apparatus is not his own; it belongs to his owner; hence he makes use of his feet and legs, or the physical machinery; while in the second view, at the northern end of this undefinable Road, where liberty is, the head or mental part is presented to view. The slave,—the chattel,—the thing is a man.

1859

NOTES

1. African American professor, abolitionist, and antiracist activist Alexander Crummell (1819–1898).

2. Isaiah George DeGrasse (1813–1841), African American abolitionist and missionary, ordained a deacon at St. Philip's, New York City's oldest Episcopal church for black worshippers.

3. Site of the arrival of the first African captives brought to serve as slaves in the United States.

JAMES MONROE WHITFIELD (1822–1871)

James Monroe Whitfield was born to free African American parents in Exeter, New Hampshire. He attended local Exeter schools as a child, but it is unclear whether he had any additional academic training. In 1839, he relocated to Buffalo, New York. There he married, and he established a successful barbershop. Through his work as a barber, he encountered many members of the area's black elite, including Frederick Douglass. During this period, Whitfield began writing poetry, and by the middle of the century his work had begun to appear in African American and abolitionist periodicals, including the *North Star, Frederick Douglass' Paper,* and the *Liberator.* His earliest works took up the themes that would define his career as a writer, including race pride and antiracist critique. In 1853, Whitfield published *America and Other Poems,* his only collection. A staunch advocate of African American emigration, he dedicated this volume to abolitionist and emigration advocate Martin Delany, at the time a contributing editor to *Frederick Douglass' Paper.* From 1858 to 1860, Whitfield traveled in Central America, most likely as fact-finding commissioner for a group of emigration and colonization advocates led by Congressman Frank P. Blair. In 1860, he returned to the United States and relocated to San Francisco. In 1867, Whitfield published his longest work, the four-hundred-line *Poem,* in celebration of the fourth anniversary of the Emancipation Proclamation. Originally written for and delivered at the Emancipation Proclamation anniversary celebration at San Francisco's Platt's Hall, the piece examined the curious relationship between the ideal of constitutional freedoms and the reality of their application in the lives of African American people. The following versions of "America" and "Prayer of the Oppressed" were taken from Whitfield's 1853 collection, *America and other Poems*. His *Poem, Written for the Celebration of the Fourth Anniversary of Abraham Lincoln's Emancipation Proclamation* was first published in pamphlet form by the *San Francisco Elevator,* an African American newspaper, under the auspices of founder and editor Phillip A. Bell.

AMERICA

America, it is to thee,
Thou boasted land of liberty,—
It is to thee I raise my song,
Thou land of blood, and crime, and wrong.
It is to thee, my native land,
From whence has issued many a band
To tear the black man from his soil,
And force him here to delve and toil;
Chained on your blood-bemoistened sod,
Cringing beneath a tyrant's rod,
Stripped of those rights which Nature's God
    Bequeathed to all the human race,
Bound to a petty tyrant's nod,
    Because he wears a paler face.
Was it for this, that freedom's fires
Were kindled by your patriot sires?
Was it for this, they shed their blood,
On hill and plain, on field and flood?
Was it for this, that wealth and life
Were staked upon that desperate strife,
Which drenched this land for seven long years
With blood of men, and women's tears?
When black and white fought side by side,
    Upon the well-contested field,—
Turned back the fierce opposing tide,
    And made the proud invader yield—
When, wounded, side by side they lay,
    And heard with joy the proud hurrah
From their victorious comrades say
    That they had waged successful war,
The thought ne'er entered in their brains
That they endured those toils and pains,
To forge fresh fetters, heavier chains
For their own children, in whose veins

Should flow that patriotic blood,
So freely shed on field and flood.
Oh no; they fought, as they believed,
    For the inherent rights of man;
But mark, how they have been deceived
    By slavery's accursed plan.
They never thought, when thus they shed
    Their heart's best blood, in freedom's cause.
That their own sons would live in dread,
    Under unjust, oppressive laws:
That those who quietly enjoyed
    The rights for which they fought and fell,
Could be the framers of a code,
    That would disgrace the fiends of hell!
Could they have looked, with prophet's ken,
    Down to the present evil time,
    Seen free-born men, uncharged with crime,
Consigned unto a slaver's pen,—
Or thrust into a prison cell,
With thieves and murderers to dwell—
While that same flag whose stripes and stars
Had been their guide through freedom's wars
As proudly waved above the pen
Of dealers in the souls of men!
Or could the shades of all the dead,
    Who fell beneath that starry flag,
Visit the scenes where they once bled,
    On hill and plain, on vale and crag,
By peaceful brook, or ocean's strand,
    By inland lake, or dark green wood,
Where'er the soil of this wide land
    Was moistened by their patriot blood,—
And then survey the country o'er,
    From north to south, from east to west,
And hear the agonizing cry
Ascending up to God on high,
From western wilds to ocean's shore,
    The fervent prayer of the oppressed;

The cry of helpless infancy
    Torn from the parent's fond caress
By some base tool of tyranny,
    And doomed to woe and wretchedness;
The indignant wail of fiery youth,
    Its noble aspirations crushed,
Its generous zeal, its love of truth,
    Trampled by tyrants in the dust;
The aerial piles which fancy reared,
    And hopes too bright to be enjoyed,
Have passed and left his young heart seared,
    And all its dreams of bliss destroyed.
The shriek of virgin purity,
    Doomed to some libertine's embrace,
Should rouse the strongest sympathy
    Of each one of the human race;
And weak old age, oppressed with care,
    As he reviews the scene of strife,
Puts up to God a fervent prayer,
    To close his dark and troubled life.
The cry of fathers, mothers, wives,
    Severed from all their hearts hold dear,
And doomed to spend their wretched lives
    In gloom, and doubt, and hate, and fear;
And manhood, too, with soul of fire,
And arm of strength, and smothered ire,
Stands pondering with brow of gloom,
Upon his dark unhappy doom,
Whether to plunge in battle's strife,
And buy his freedom with his life,
And with stout heart and weapon strong,
Pay back the tyrant wrong for wrong,
Or wait the promised time of God,
    When his Almighty ire shall wake,
And smite the oppressor in his wrath,
And hurl red ruin in his path,
And with the terrors of his rod,
    Cause adamantine hearts to quake.

Here Christian writhes in bondage still,
    Beneath his brother Christian's rod,
And pastors trample down at will,
    The image of the living God.
While prayers go up in lofty strains,
    And pealing hymns ascend to heaven,
The captive, toiling in his chains,
    With tortured limbs and bosom riven,
Raises his fettered hand on high,
    And in the accents of despair,
To him who rules both earth and sky,
    Puts up a sad, a fervent prayer,
To free him from the awful blast
    Of slavery's bitter galling shame—
Although his portion should be cast
    With demons in eternal flame!
Almighty God! 'tis this they call
    The land of liberty and law;
Part of its sons in baser thrall
    Than Babylon or Egypt saw—
Worse scenes of rapine, lust and shame,
    Than Babylonian ever knew,
Are perpetrated in the name
    Of God, the holy, just, and true;
And darker doom than Egypt felt,
May yet repay this nation's guilt.
Almighty God! thy aid impart,
And fire anew each faltering heart,
And strengthen every patriot's hand,
Who aims to save our native land.
We do not come before thy throne,
    With carnal weapons drenched in gore,
Although our blood has freely flown,
    In adding to the tyrant's store.
Father! before thy throne we come,
    Not in the panoply of war,
With pealing trump, and rolling drum,
    And cannon booming loud and far;

Striving in blood to wash out blood,
　　Through wrong to seek redress for wrong;
For while thou'rt holy, just and good,
　　The battle is not to the strong;
But in the sacred name of peace,
　　Of justice, virtue, love and truth,
We pray, and never mean to cease,
　　Till weak old age and fiery youth
In freedom's cause their voices raise,
And burst the bonds of every slave;
Till, north and south, and east and west,
The wrongs we bear shall be redressed.

1853

PRAYER OF THE OPPRESSED

Oh great Jehovah! God of love,
　　Thou monarch of the earth and sky,
Canst thou from thy great throne above
　　Look down with an unpitying eye?—

See Afric's sons and daughters toil,
　　Day after day, year after year,
Upon this blood-bemoistened soil,
　　And to their cries turn a deaf ear?

Canst thou the white oppressor bless
　　With verdant hills and fruitful plains,
Regardless of the slave's distress,
　　Unmindful of the black man's chains.

How long, oh Lord! ere thou wilt speak
　　In thy Almighty thundering voice,
To bid the oppressor's fetters break,
　　And Ethiopia's sons rejoice.

How long shall Slavery's iron grip,
　　And Prejudice's guilty hand,
Send forth, like blood-hounds from the slip,
　　Foul persecutions o'er the land?

How long shall puny mortals dare
   To violate thy just decree,
And force their fellow-men to wear
   The galling chain on land and sea?

Hasten, oh Lord! the glorious time
   When everywhere beneath the skies,
From every land and every clime,
   Peans to Liberty shall rise!

When the bright sun of liberty
   Shall shine o'er each despotic land,
And all mankind, from bondage free,
   Adore the wonders of thy hand.

1853

A POEM

*Written for the Celebration of the Fourth Anniversary
of President Lincoln's Emancipation Proclamation.*

*To P. A. Bell, Esq., a Pioneer in the Intellectual Elevation of His Race,
these Lines Are Respectfully Inscribed by the Author*

More than two centuries have passed
   Since, holding on their stormy way,
Before the furious wintry blast,
   Upon a dark December day,
Two sails, with different intent,[1]
   Approached the Western Continent.
One vessel bore as rich a freight
   As ever yet has crossed the wave;
The living germs to form a State
   That knows no master, owns no slave.
She bore the pilgrims to that strand
   Which since is rendered classic soil,
Where all the honors of the land
   May reach the hardy sons of toil.

The other bore the baleful seeds
    Of future fratricidal strife,
The germ of dark and bloody deeds,
    Which prey upon a nation's life.
The trafficker in human souls
    Had gathered up and chained his prey,
And stood prepared to call the rolls,
When, anchored in Virginia's Bay—
    His captives landed on her soil,
Doomed without recompense to toil,
    Should spread abroad such deadly blight,
    That the deep gloom of mental night
    Spreading its darkness o'er the land,
And paralizing every hand
      Raised in defense of Liberty,
    Should throw the chains of slavery
    O'er thought and limb, and mind and soul,
    And bend them all to its control.
    New England's cold and sterile land
    Gave shelter to the pilgrim band;
    Virginia's rich and fertile soil
    Received the dusky sons of toil.
The one bore men whose lives were passed
    In fierce contests for liberty—
Men who had struggled to the last
    'Gainst every form of tyranny.
Vanquished in many a bloody fight,
    Yet still in spirit unsubdued;
Though crushed by overwhelming might,
    With love of freedom still imbued,
They bore unto their Western home,
    The same ideas which drove them forth,
As houseless fugitives to roam
    In endless exile o'er the earth.
And, on New England's sterile shore,
    Those few and feeble germs took root,

To after generations bore
    Abundance of the glorious fruit—
    Freedom of thought, and of the pen,
    Free schools, free speech, free soil, free men.
    Thus in that world beyond the seas,
    Found by the daring Genoese,[2]
    More than two centuries ago
    A sower wandered forth to sow.
He planted deep the grains of wheat,
    That generations yet unborn,
When e'er they came to reap and eat,
    Might bless the hand that gave the corn;
    And find it yield that priceless bread
    With which the starving soul is fed;
    The food which fills the hungry mind,
    Gives mental growth to human kind,
    And nerves the sinews of the free
    To strike for Truth and Liberty.
Yet, planted at the self-same time
    Was other seed by different hands,
To propagate the deadliest crime
    That ever swept o'er guilty lands—
    The crime of human slavery,
    With all its want and misery—
    The harrowing scenes of woe and pain,
    Which follow in its ghastly train.
The same old feud that cursed the earth
    Through all the ages of the past,
In this new world obtained new birth,
    And built again its walls of caste,
More high and deep, more broad and strong,
    On ancient prejudice and wrong.
The same old strife of every age,
    Inherited by son from sire,
Which darkens each historic page,
    And sends a discord through the lyre
Of every bard, who frames his song
    In praise of Freedom, Truth, and Right,

Rebukes the gathered hosts of wrong,
　　And spreads the rays of Freedom's light—
　　That strife, long fought in Eastern lands,
　　Was transferred to the Western strand.
　　The same old seeds of endless strife,
　　Deep in the Nation's inmost life
　　Were sown, to yield in after years
　　A plenteous crop of blood and tears.
'Twas here the dragon's teeth were sown,
　　And crops of armed men sprang up;
Here the Republic, mighty grown,
　　Drank deep rebellion's bitter cup;
Here, where her founders sowed the wind,
　　They reaped the whirlwind's furious blast—
Proudly refusing to rescind
　　The deadly errors of the past,
They drew the sword, by deed and word
　　To rivet slavery's bloody chain,
And, slaughtered by th' avenging sword,
　　Their bones strew many a battle plain.
　　The strife of aristocracy
　　In conflict with democracy,
　　Was here renewed, with greater zeal,
　　And danger to the common weal.
One century and a half had flown
　　When Freedom gained the first great fight;
Defied the power of the throne,
　　And bravely proved the people's might,
　　　　When banded in a righteous cause,
　　　　To overthrow oppressive laws.
'Twas then, when struggling at its birth,
　　To take its proper place beside
The other Nations of the earth,
　　The rule of justice was applied;
　　And all mankind declared to be
　　Inheritors of Liberty;
　　With right to make their freedom known,
　　By choosing rulers of their own.

But when it came t' enforce the right,
   Gained on the well-contested field,
Slavery's dark intrigues won the fight,
   And made victorious Freedom yield;
   Giving each place of power and trust,
   To those who, groveling in the dust,
   Seek to extend the giant crime
   Of Slavery through all coming time.
   The victory won at fearful cost,
   Over a mighty monarch's host,
   By which oppression's power seem'd foiled
     On the Atlantic's western shore,
   And those who through long years had toiled,
     The burden of the battle bore,
   In order that this land might be
   A home and refuge for the free,
   Were doomed to see their labor lost—
   Their victory won at fearful cost,
   Over oppression's mighty power,
   Surrendered in the trying hour;
   And made to strengthen slavery's hand,
   Ruling with iron rod the land.
   The power the warrior's hand had lost,
     The politician's skill restored;
   And slavery's votaries could boast
     Intrigue was mightier than the sword.
   But fraud and force in vain combined
   To check the progress of the mind;
   And every effort proved in vain
   T' enslave the cultivated brain.
   The same ideas the pilgrim's brought
     When first they crossed the wintry wave,
   Spreading throughout the land were fraught
     With light and freedom to the slave:
And hence where slavery bore the rule,
   It labored to suppress the school,
   Muzzle the tongue, the press, the pen,

As means by which the rights of men
Might be discussed, and Freedom's light
Break up the gloom of slavery's night,
Efforts which, in a better cause
    Had brought their authors deathless fame,
Were made to frame oppressive laws,
    And to arouse, excite, inflame,
The vilest passions of the throng,
    And stir that bitter prejudice
Which makes men blind to right and wrong,
    And opens wide that deep abyss
Where pride of rank, and caste, and race,
    Have left such marks of bitter hate,
As nought but time can e'er efface,
    To foment discord in the State.
    But vain their efforts to control
    The aspirations of the soul;
For still a faithful few were found
    Who would not bend the servile knee,
But in each conflict stood their ground,
    And boldly struck for Liberty.
From year to year the contest grew,
    Till slavery, glorying in her strength,
Again war's bloody falchion drew,
    And sluggish freedom, roused at length,
Waked from her stupor, seized the shield,
And called her followers to the field.
And at that call they thronging came,
With arms of strength, and hearts on flame;
Answering the nation's call to arms,
The northern hive poured forth its swarms;
The lumbermen of Maine threw down
    The axe, and seized the bayonet;
The Bay State's sons from every town,
    Left loom and anvil, forge and net;
The Granite State sent forth its sons,
    With hearts as steadfast as her rocks;

The stern Vermonters took their guns,
    And left to others' care their flocks;
Rhode Island and Connecticut
    Helped to fill up New England's roll,
And showed the pilgrim spirit yet
    Could animate the Yankee soul.
The Empire State sent forth a host,
    Such as might seal an empire's fate;
Even New Jersey held her post,
    And proved herself a Union State.
The Key-Stone of the Union arch
    Sent forth an army true and tried;
Ohio joined the Union march,
    And added to the Nation's side
    A force three hundred thousand strong,
    While Michigan took up the song;
Wisconsin also, like the lakes,
When the autumnal gale awakes,
And rolls its surges on the shore,
Poured forth its sons to battle's roar.
The gallant State of Illinois
Sent forth in swarms its warlike boys.
On Indiana's teeming plain,
    Thick as the sheaves of ripened grain,
    Were soldiers hurrying to the wars
    To battle for the Stripes and Stars.
From Iowa fresh numbers came,
    While Minnesota joined the tide,
And Kansas helped to spread the flame,
    And carry o'er the border side
    The torch the ruffians once applied
    When fiercely, but in vain, they tried
    The people of their rights to spoil,
    And fasten slavery on her soil.
From East unto remotest West,
    From every portion of the North,

The true, the bravest, and the best,
    Forsook their homes and sallied forth;
    And men from every foreign land
    Were also reckoned in that band.
    The Scandinavians swelled the train,
    The brave Norwegian, Swede, and Dane,
    And struck as though Thor[3] rained his blows
    Upon the heads of haughty foes;
    Or Odin's self had sought the field
    To make all opposition yield.
Italia's sons, who once had cried
    Loud for united Italy,
And struck by Garibaldi's side
    For union and equality—
Obtained another chance to fight
    For nationality and right.
The Germans came, a sturdy throng,
    And to the bleeding country brought
Friends of the right, foes of the wrong,
    Heroes in action as in thought,
Sigel, and Schurz,[4] and many others,
    Whose names shall live among the brave,
Till all men are acknowledged brothers,
    Without a master or a slave.
Ireland's sons, as usual, came
    To battle strife with shouts of joy,
With Meagher and Corcoran[5] won such fame
    As well might rival Fontenoy.[6]
Briton and Frank, for centuries foes,
    Forgot their struggles, veiled their scars,
To deal on slavery's head their blows,
    Fighting beneath the Stripes and Stars.
From the Atlantic's stormy coast,
    Unto the broad Pacific's strand,
Came pouring forth a martial host,
    From every portion of the land.

They came, as flocking sea birds swarm,
    Whene'er the cloud-king mounts his throne
And calls the warriors of the storm
    To sweep the earth from zone to zone.
They came as come the rushing waves
    When o'er the sea the tempest raves,
    They came as storm clouds quickly fly
    When lightnings flash along the sky,
    And on the Southern plains afar
    Soon burst the thunderbolts of war.
    In quick and fierce succession fell
    The furious showers of shot and shell.
Though East, and West, and North combined,
    And foreigners from every land
With all that art and skill could find,
    They could not crush the rebel band.
They clung unto th' accursed thing,
    That which they knew accursed of God,
Nor strength, nor skill could victory bring
    With that accursed thing abroad.
When Abraham, the poor man's friend,
    Assumed the power to break the chain.
Obey the Lord, and put an end
    To slavery's dark and bloody reign,
To make the nation shield from harm
    Its loyal sons of every hue,
In its defence receive and arm
    All those who to its flag were true,
    He found the touchstone of success,
    For then Jehovah deigned to bless,
    And smile upon the nation's arms,
    And give it rest from war's alarms.
    Thus men of every land and tongue,
        Of every station, every hue,
    Were found the Union hosts among,
        Enlisted with the boys in blue;
    And all mankind should freely draw
        The prize for which their lives were given;

"Equality before the law,"
    To every person under heaven.
As storms and tempests pass away,
    And leave the sun's enlivening light,
Our war-cloud brought the opening day
    To slavery's long and gloomy night.
As storms and thunder help to clear
And purify the atmosphere,
E'en so the thunders of the war,
Driving malaria afar,
Have purged the moral atmosphere,
And made the dawn of freedom clear.
From swamps and marshes left undrained
    Malarious vapors will arise,
From human passions, unrestrained,
    Rise fogs to cloud our moral skies:
So now, from portions of the land
    Where lately slavery reigned supreme,
Its conquered chiefs together band,
    Concocting many an artful scheme,
By which Oppression's tottering throne
    May be restored to pristine power,
And those who now its rule disown
    Be made submissive to its power.
The self-styled Moses brings the aid
    Of power and place to help them through,
To crush the race by him betrayed,
    And every man who, loyal, true,
    And faithful to his country's laws—
    Declines to aid the tyrant's cause.
Our real Moses,[7] stretched his rod
    Four years ago across the sea,
And through its blood-dyed waves we trod
    The path that leads to Liberty.
His was the fiery column's light,
    That through the desert showed the way,
Out of oppression's gloomy night,
    Toward the light of Freedom's day;

And, like his prototype of old,
    Who used his power, as Heaven had told,
    To God and to the people true,
    Died with the promised land in view.
And we may well deplore his loss,
    For never was a ruler given,
More free from taint of sinful dross,
    To any Nation under Heaven.
And ever while the earth remains,
    His name among the first shall stand
Who freed four million slaves from chains,
    And saved thereby his native land.
Though Achans[8] rise within the camp,
    And covet slavery's cursed spoil,
Invent oppressive laws, to cramp
    The energies of men who toil
Through hardship, danger, sickness, health,
To add unto the Nation's wealth—
Some Joshua shall yet arise,
    Whose hand shall extirpate the seeds
Sown by this worst of tyrannies,
    Which ripen into bloody deeds
Such fiendish murders as of late
    Occur in every rebel State.
While Freedom falters, once again
    The fogs and mists begin to rise,
And cast their shadows o'er the plain,
    Vailing the issue from our eyes,
On which the nation yet must stand,—
Impartial freedom through the land.
Yet once again our moral air
    Is tainted by that poisonous breath,
Which Freedom's lungs can never bear,
    Which surely ends in moral death.
Then let the people in their might
    Arise, and send the fiat forth,
That every man shall have the right
    To rank according to his worth;

That north and south, and west and east,

All, from the greatest to the least,

Who rally to the nation's cause,

Shall have the shield of equal laws,

Wipe out the errors of the past,

Nursed by the barbarous pride of caste,

And o'er the nation's wide domain,

Where once was heard the clanking chain,

And timorous bondmen crouched in fear,

Before the brutal overseer,

Proclaim the truth that equal laws

Can best sustain the righteous cause;

And let this nation henceforth be

In truth the country of the free.

[During the delivery of the Oration and Poem the speakers were frequently interrupted by loud bursts of applause.]

1867

NOTES

1. The *Mayflower,* whose free English passengers arrived in Massachusetts in late November of 1620, and the *White Lion,* a Dutch ship whose cargo of roughly twenty enslaved Africans arrived at Jamestown, Virginia, in August of 1619.

2. Christopher Columbus, whose voyages to what are now the Antilles, Venezuela, Honduras, Nicaragua, Costa Rica, and Panama launched the Spanish colonization of the Americas.

3. The Norse god of thunder.

4. Majors General Franz Sigel (1824–1902) and Carl Christian Schurz (1829–1906), German-born immigrants who served as Union officers during the American Civil War.

5. Irish-born Union officers Brigadier General Michael Corcoran and General Thomas Meagher fought in the American Civil War as part of New York's Sixty-ninth Militia, with Meagher succeeding Corcoran as leader of the regiment following Corcoran's capture at the Battle of Bull Run.

6. The Battle of Fontenoy, May 1745, in which the Irish Brigade, fighting alongside the French, played a decisive role in the French victory over the allied Dutch, Hanoverian, and British forces.

7. U.S. President Abraham Lincoln (1809–1865).

8. A reference to the biblical story of Achan, who was sentenced to humiliation and death as punishment for stealing a portion of the spoils of the Israelites' victory against the city of Jericho (Joshua 7:1).

JOSEPH C. HOLLY (1825-1855)

Joseph Cephas Holly was born to free African American parents in Washington, DC. In 1844, he relocated with his brother James to Burlington, Vermont, where the two established a boot-making business. Both men became increasingly involved in the region's abolitionist movement, traveling together as antislavery lecturers until they came to odds around the issue of black emigration to Liberia. James was a staunch supporter of black emigration, while Joseph believed that African Americans should strive for full citizenship and enfranchisement in the country of their birth. In 1852, Joseph Holly relocated to Rochester, New York, an abolitionist stronghold and the home of Frederick Douglass. There he published his only collection, *Freedom's Offering,* in 1853. Throughout the first half of the 1850s, Holly's poems appeared in *Frederick Douglass' Paper;* and when his book was released, the paper recognized it with a positive review. His marriage produced one child, a son who died in infancy. Holly continued to write and publish his poems until shortly before his death from tuberculosis.

TO MRS. HARRIET B. STOWE

Thy magic pen a power wields,
More potent than the steel-clad hosts,
With glittering swords, and myriad shields;
Who guard around Oppression's posts.
Thou sawest thy brother, bruised, and bow'd,
Tho' clothed in Afric's hated hue;
Thou heard'st him groan, and cry aloud,
And to thy woman's heart proved true.
Unto his wrongs thou gav'st an ear;
Unto his wounds thou gav'st a tongue;
A list'ning world, came nigh to hear
Thee sing the burthen of his song.

The Britton heard it on the strand,
The Frank upon the Elysee,
The Arab on his Arid sand,
The Russ upon the Baltic sea,
The Greek upon his Island home,
The German at his classic lore;
'Twas heard along the streets of Rome,
And e'en on Afric's dusky shore,
In Birmah, China and Japan,
Myriads thy magic power own;
And long the streets of Ispahan,[1]
Thy "Uncle Tom" and Cassy's known[2]
Truth, mighty is the falchion bright:
Which thou with mystic arm doth wield,
And her attendants love, and light
These are thy buckler and thy shield.

1853

ON THE DEATH OF MY SISTER CECILIA — THE LAST OF FIVE MEMBERS OF THE FAMILY, WHO DIED SUCCESSIVELY

Our family tree is in the sear
   And yellow leaf of life;
Branch after branch, year after year,
   Yields to death's pruning knife.
First, youngest born, as if 'twere meet,
   The sacrifice should be,
"The last of earth," the first to meet
   Th' unknown eternity.'
'Twas God who gave, 'twas He who took,
   His voice let us obey,
So that in his eternal book,
   Our names shine bright as day.

1853

AN EPITAPH

Let no fond parent shed a tear upon my head,
Nor sister on my grave, sweet flowers spread,
Nor loving brother mourn when I depart,
But for me breathe a prayer with fervent heart.
No! life is but a transitory gleam,
And we but bask within a sunny beam;
But pause alas! 'tis but a vale of tears—
A day of human sorrow, toil, and cares.
Then why should I within this vale delay,
When heavenly spirits call my soul away?
And why should parents—friends my demise mourn?
'Tis but the fate of all of woman born.
Let tears for pious prayers be quick exchanged;
Let wisdom, guide the mind that's most deranged,
With resignation to the makers will,
He died for thee, and he will love thee still.

1853

NOTES

1. The ancient capital of Persia.
2. African American characters in Harriet Beecher Stowe's *Uncle Tom's Cabin*.

FRANCES ELLEN WATKINS HARPER (1825-1911)

Orphaned shortly after her birth in Baltimore, poet and novelist Frances Ellen Watkins Harper was raised by her uncle, William Watkins, a prominent educator and frequent correspondent to the African American newspapers of the day. Harper was educated at Baltimore's Watkins Academy for Colored Youth. After several years of domestic labor in that city, she accepted a teaching post at Ohio's Union Seminary (later renamed Wilberforce University), where she was the first woman to serve on the faculty. During her years there, Harper became increasingly involved in antislavery activism. From Union Seminary, she moved to Philadelphia where, for a brief period, she worked on the Underground Railroad. From Philadelphia, Harper relocated to New England, where she began a demanding schedule as a lecturer for the Maine Anti-Slavery Society. Harper was a wildly popular speaker, attracting audiences throughout the northeast. Her lectures were covered extensively in the *Colored American* and other African American newspapers of the period. After Emancipation, Harper continued her activist work, becoming increasingly involved in women's rights organizations, campaigning on behalf of women's suffrage, publishing essays, and speaking on the rights and responsibilities of black women. Throughout her life, Harper remained a prolific writer. Her first book, a collection of poems titled *Forest Leaves,* appeared in 1846. There are no known surviving copies. Eighteen fifty-four saw the publication of her most popular volume. The aptly titled *Poems on Various Subjects* was a selection of verses on topics ranging from the cruelty of slavery to religious and domestic themes. A wildly successful book by any standard, this collection sold more than twenty thousand copies before the end of the century. In the years between the publication of her first collection of poetry and her death in 1911, Harper published several collections of poetry, at least one serialized novella, numerous pamphlets, and three serialized novels. But she is most widely remembered by twenty-first-century readers for her antebellum, abolitionist poetry and for *Iola Leroy, or Shadows Uplifted* (1892), her one novel that was not published in serial form. Each of the following three poems appeared in both Harper's 1854 collection, *Poems on Various Subjects,* and in *Frederick Douglass' Paper,* though "Eliza Harris" was identified as having been written especially for the paper. The speech "Enlightened Motherhood" was initially published in 1892, in pamphlet form.

ELIZA HARRIS

Like a fawn from the arrow, startled and wild,
A woman swept by us, bearing a child,[1]
In her eye was the night of a settled despair,
And her brow was o'ershadowed with anguish and care.

She was nearing the river, in reaching the brink,
She heeded no danger, she paused not to drink,
For she is a mother, her child is a slave,
And she'll give him his freedom or find him a grave.

'Twas a vision to haunt us, that innocent face,
So pale in its fear, so fair in its grace,
As the tramp of the horses and the bay of the hound,
With the fetters that gall, were trailing the ground.

She was nerved by despair and strengthened by woe,
And she leaped o'er the chasms that yawned from below;
Death howl'd in the tempest, and raced in the blast;
But she heard not the sound till the danger was past.

Oh how shall I speak of my proud country's shame—
Of the spots of her banners, how give them their name?
How say that her flag in proud mockery waves
O'er thousands of bondmen, and millions of slaves?

How say that by law we may torture and chase
A woman whose crime is the hue of her face?
How the depths of the forests may echo around,
With the shrieks of despair, and the bay of the hound.

With her step on the ice, and her arm on the child,
The danger was fearful, the pathway was wild;

But aided by heaven, she gained a free shore,
Where the friends of humanity opened their door.

So fragile and lovely, so fearfully pale,
Like a lily that bends to the breath of the gale,
Save the heave of her breast, and the sway of her hair,
You'd have thought her a statue of fear and despair.

In agony close to her bosom she pressed
The life of her life, the child of her breast.
Oh! Love from its tenderness, gathering might,
Had strengthened her soul for the dangers of flight.

But she's free!—yes, free from the land where the slave
From the hand of oppression must rest in the grave;
Where bondage and blood, where scourges and chains,
Have placed on our banner indelible stains.

Did a fever e'er burning through bosom and brain,
Send a lava-like flood through every vein,
Till it suddenly cooled 'neath a healing spell,
And you knew, oh! the joy, you knew you were well?

So felt this young mother, as a sense of the rest,
Stole gently and sweetly o'er her weary breast,
As her boy look'd up and wondering smiled,
On the mother whose love had freed her child.

The blood hounds have missed the scent of her way,
The hunter is rifled and foiled of his prey,
The cursing of men and clanking of chains,
Make sound of strange discord on liberty's plains.

With the rapture of love and fullness of bliss,
She placed on his brow a mother's fond kiss.
Oh! Poverty, danger and death she can brave,
For the child of her love is no longer a slave.

1853

THE SLAVE AUCTION

The sale began—young girls were there,
    Defenseless in their wretchedness,
Whose stifled sobs of deep despair
    Revealed their anguish and distress.

And mothers stood, with streaming eyes,
    And saw their dearest children sold;
Unheeded rose their bitter cries,
    While tyrants bartered them for gold.

And woman, with her love and truth—
    For these in sable forms may dwell—
Gazed on the husband of her youth,
    With anguish none may paint or tell.

And men, whose sole crime was their hue,
    The impress of their Maker's hand,
And frail and shrinking children too,
    Were gathered in that mournful band.

Ye who have laid your loved to rest,
    And wept above their lifeless clay,
Know not the anguish of that breast,
    Whose loved are rudely torn away.

Ye may not know how desolate
    Are bosoms rudely forced to part,
And how a dull and heavy weight
    Will press the life-drops from the heart.

1854

BURY ME IN A FREE LAND

Make me a grave where'er you will,
In a lowly plain, or a lofty hill;
Make it among earth's humblest graves,
But not in a land where men are slaves.

I could not rest if around my grave
I heard the steps of a trembling slave;
His shadow above my silent tomb
Would make it a place of fearful gloom.

I could not rest if I heard the tread
Of a coffle gang to the shambles led,
And the mother's shriek of wild despair
Rise like a curse on the trembling air.

I could not sleep if I saw the lash
Drinking her blood at each fearful gash,
And I saw her babes torn from her breast,
Like trembling doves from their parent nest.

I'd shudder and start if I heard the bay
Of bloodhounds seizing their human prey,
And I heard the captive plead in vain
As they bound afresh his galling chain.

If I saw young girls from their mother's arms
Bartered and sold for their youthful charms,
My eye would flash with a mournful flame,
My death-paled cheek grow red with shame.

I would sleep, dear friends, where bloated might
Can rob no man of his dearest right;
My rest shall be calm in any grave
Where none can call his brother a slave.

I ask no monument, proud and high,
To arrest the gaze of the passers-by;
All that my yearning spirit craves,
Is bury me not in a land of slaves.

1854

ENLIGHTENED MOTHERHOOD: AN ADDRESS . . .
BEFORE THE BROOKLYN LITERARY SOCIETY,
NOVEMBER 15, 1892

It is nearly thirty years since an emancipated people stood on the threshold of
a new era, facing an uncertain future—a legally unmarried race, to be taught
the sacredness of the marriage relations; an ignorant people, to be taught to
read of the Christian law and to learn to comprehend more fully the claims
of the gospel of the Christ of Calvary.[2] A homeless race, to be gathered into
homes of peaceful security and to be instructed how to plant around their
firesides the strongest batteries against sins that degrade and the race vices that
demoralize. A race unversed in the science of government and unskilled in the
just administration of law, to be translated from the old oligarchy of slavery
into the new commonwealth of freedom, and to whose men came the right
to exchange the fetters on their wrists for the ballots in their right hands—a
ballot which, if not vitiated by fraud or restrained by intimidation, counts
just as much as that of the most talented and influential man in the land.

While politicians may stumble on the barren mountain of fretful controversy, and men, lacking faith in God and the invisible forces which make for
righteousness, may shrink from the unsolved problems of the hour, into the
hands of Christian women comes the opportunity of serving the ever blessed
Christ, by ministering to His little ones and striving to make their homes
the brightest spots on earth and the fairest types of heaven. The school may
instruct and the church may teach, but the home is an institution older than
the church and antedates schools, and that is the place where children should
be trained for useful citizenship on earth and a hope of holy companionship
in heaven.

Every mother should endeavor to be a true artist. I do not mean by this
that every woman should be a painter, sculptor, musician, poet, or writer, but
the artist who will write on the tablet of childish innocence thoughts she will
not blush to see read in the light of eternity and printed amid the archives
of heaven, that the young may learn to wear them as amulets around their
hearts and throw them as bulwarks around their lives, and that in the hour
of temptation and trial the voices from home may linger around their paths
as angels of guidance, around their steps, and be incentives to deeds of high
and holy worth.

The home may be a humble spot, where there are no velvet carpets to
hush your tread, no magnificence to surround your way, nor costly creations

of painter's art or sculptor's skill to please your conceptions or gratify your tastes; but what are the costliest gifts of fortune when placed in the balance with the confiding love of dear children or the devotion of a noble and manly husband whose heart can safely trust in his wife? You may place upon the brow of a true wife and mother the greenest laurels; you may crowd her hands with civic honors; but, after all, to her there will be no place like home, and the crown of her motherhood will be more precious than the diadem of a queen.

As a marriage is the mother of homes, it is important that the duties and responsibilities of this relation should be understood before it is entered on. A mistake made here may run through every avenue of the future, cast its shadow over all our coming years, and enter the lives of those whom we should shield with our love and defend with our care. We may be versed in ancient lore and modern learning, may be able to trace the path of worlds that roll in light and power on high, and to tell when comets shall cast their trail over our evening skies. We may understand the laws of stratification well enough to judge where lies the vein of silver and where nature has hidden her virgin gold. We may be able to tell the story of departed nations and conquering chieftains who have added pages of tears and blood to the world's history; but our education is deficient if we are perfectly ignorant how to guide the little feet that are springing up so gladly in our path, and to see in undeveloped possibilities gold more fine than the pavements of heaven and gems more precious than the foundations of the holy city. Marriage should not be a blind rushing together of tastes and fancies, a mere union of fortunes or an affair of convenience. It should be "a tie that only love and truth should weave and nothing but death should part."

Marriage between two youthful and loving hearts means the laying the foundation stones of a new home, and the woman who helps erect that home should be careful not to build it above the reeling brain of a drunkard or the weakened fibre of a debauchee. If it be folly for a merchant to send an argosy, laden with the richest treasures, at midnight on a moonless sea, without a rudder, compass, or guide, is it not madness for a woman to trust her future happiness, and the welfare of the dear children who may yet nestle in her arms and make music and sunshine around her fireside, in the unsteady hands of a characterless man, too lacking in self-respect and self-control to hold the helm and rudder of his own life; who drifts where he ought to steer, and only lasts when he ought to live?

The moment the crown of motherhood falls on the brow of a young wife, God gives her a new interest in the welfare of the home and the good of society. If hitherto she had been content to trip through life a lighthearted girl, or to tread amid the halls of wealth and fashion the gayest of the gay, life holds for her now a high and noble service. She must be more than the child of pleasure or the devotee of fashion. Her work is grandly constructive. A helpless and ignorant babe lies smiling in her arms. God has trusted her with a child, and it is her privilege to help that child develop the most precious thing a man or woman can possess on earth, and that is a good character. Moth may devour our finest garments, fire may consume and floods destroy our fairest homes, rust may gather on our silver and tarnish our gold, but there is an asbestos that no fire can destroy, a treasure which shall be richer for its service and better for its use, and that is a good character.

But the question arises, "What constitutes an enlightened motherhood?" I do not pretend that I will give you an exhaustive analysis of all that a mother should learn and of all she should teach. In the Christian scriptures the story is told of a mother of whom it was said: "From henceforth all nations shall call her blessed." While, in these days of religious unrest, criticism, and investigation, numbers are ready to relegate this story to the limbo of myth and fiction; whether that story be regarded as fact or fiction, there are lessons in it which we could not take into our lives without its making life higher, better, and more grandly significant. It is the teaching of a divine overshadowing and a touching self-surrender which still floats down the ages, fragrant with the aroma of a sweet submission. "The handmaid of the Lord, be it done unto me according to Thy word."[3]

We read that Christ left us an example that we should tread in His footsteps; but does not the majority of the Christian world hold it as a sacred creed that the first print of His feet in the flesh began in the days of His antenatal life; and is not the same spirit in the world now which was there when our Lord made His advent among us, bone of our bone and flesh of our flesh; and do we not need the incarnation of God's love and light in our hearts as much now as it was ever needed in any preceding generation? Do we not need to hold it as a sacred thing, amid sorrow, pain, and wrong, that only through the love of God are human hearts made strong? And has not every prospective mother the right to ask for the overshadowing of the same spirit, that her child may be one of whom it may be truly said, "Of such is the kingdom of heaven," and all his life he shall be lent to the Lord? Had all the mothers of this present generation dwelt beneath the shadow of the Almighty, would it have been possible for slavery to have cursed us with its crimes, or intemperance degraded us with its vices? Would the social evil still have power to send to our streets women whose laughter is sadder than their tears, and over whose wasted lives death draws the curtains of the grave and silently hides their sin and shame? Are there not women, respectable women, who feel that it would wring their hearts with untold anguish, and bring their gray hairs in sorrow to the grave, if their daughters should trail the robes of their womanhood in the dust, yet who would say of their sons, if they were trampling their manhood down and fettering their souls with cords of vice, "O, well, boys will be boys, and young men will sow their wild oats."

I hold that no woman loves social purity as it deserves to be loved and valued, if she cares for the purity of her daughters and not her sons; who would gather her dainty robes from contact with the fallen woman and yet greet with smiling lips and clasp with warm and welcoming hands the author of her wrong and ruin. How many mothers to-day shrink from a double standard for society which can ostracise the woman and condone the offense of the man? How many mothers say within their hearts, "I intend to teach my boy to be as pure in his life, as chaste in his conversation, as the young girl who sits at my side encircled in the warm clasp of loving arms?" How many mothers strive to have their boys shun the gilded saloon as they would the den of a deadly serpent? Not the mother who thoughtlessly sends her child to the saloon for a beverage to make merry with her friends. How many mothers teach their boys to shrink in horror from the fascinations of women, not as God made them, but as sin has degraded them?

To-night, if you and I could walk through the wards of various hospitals at home and abroad, perhaps we would find hundreds, it may be thousands, of young men awaiting death as physical wrecks, having burned the candle of their lives at both ends. Were we to bend over their dying couches with pitying glances, and question them of their lives, perhaps numbers of them could tell you sad stories of careless words from thoughtless lips, that tainted their imaginations and sent their virus through their lives; of young eyes, above which God has made the heavens so eloquent with His praise, and the earth around so poetic with His ideas, turning from the splendor of the magnificent sunsets or glorious early dawns, and finding allurement in the dreadful fascinations of sin, or learning to gloat over impure pictures and vile literature. Then, later on, perhaps many of them could say, "The first time I went to a house where there were revelry and song, and the dead were there and I knew it not, I went with men who were older than myself; men, who should have showed me how to avoid the pitfalls which lie in the path of the young, the tempted, and inexperienced, taught me to gather the flowers of sin that blossom around the borders of hell."

Suppose we dared to question a little further, not from idle curiosity, but for the sake of getting, from the dying, object lessons for the living, and say, "God gave you, an ignorant child, into the hands of a mother. Did she never warn you of your dangers and teach you how to avoid them?" How many could truthfully say, "My mother was wise enough to teach me and faithful enough to warn me." If the cholera or yellow-fever were raging in any part of this city, and to enter that section meant peril to health and life, what mother would permit her child to walk carelessly through a district where pestilence was breathing its bane upon the morning air and distilling its poison upon the midnight dews? And yet, when boys go from the fireside into the arena of life, how many ever go there forewarned and forearmed against the soft seductions of vice, against moral conditions which are worse than "fever, plague and palsy, and madness *all* combined?"

Among the things I would present for the enlightenment of mothers are attention to the laws of heredity and environment. Mrs. Winslow,[4] in a paper on social purity, speaks of a package of letters she had received from a young man of talent, good education, and a strong desire to live a pure and useful life. In boyhood he ignorantly ruined his health, and, when he resolved to rise above his depressed condition, his own folly, his heredity and environment, weighed him down like an incubus. His appeals, she says, are most touching. He says: "If you cannot help me, what can I do? My mother cursed me with illegitimacy and hereditary insanity. I have left only the alternative of suicide or madness." A fearful legacy! For stolen money and slandered character we may make reparation, but the opportunity of putting the right stamp on an antenatal life, if once gone, is gone forever; and there never was an angel of God, however bright, terrible, or strong he may be, who was ever strong enough to roll away the stone from the grave of a dead opportunity.

In the annals of this State may be found a record of six generations of debased manhood and womanhood, and prominent among them stands the name of Margaret,[5] the mother of criminals. She is reported as having five sisters, the greater number of whom trailed the robes of their womanhood in the dust, and became fallen women. Some time since, their posterity was traced out, and five hundred and forty persons are represented as sharing the blood of these unfortunate women; and it is remarkable, as well as very sad, to see the lines of debasement and weakness, vice and crime, which are displayed in their record. In the generation of Margaret, fifty percent of the women were placed among the fallen, and in all the generations succeeding, including only those of twelve years of age and over, to the extent of fifty per cent.; and of this trail of weakness there were three families in the sixth generation who had six children sent to the house of refuge. Out of seven hundred and nine members of this family, nearly one-ninth have been criminals, and nearly one-tenth paupers; twenty-two had acquired property, and eight had lost property; nearly one-seventh were illegitimate, and one sister was the mother of distinctively pauperized lines.

Or, take another line of thought. Would it not be well for us women to introduce into all of our literary circles, for the purpose of gaining knowledge, topics on this subject of heredity and the influence of good and bad conditions upon the home life of the race, and study this subject in the light of science for our own and the benefit of others? For instance, may we not seriously ask the question: Can a mother or father be an habitual tippler, or break God's law of social purity, and yet impart to their children, at the same time, abundant physical vitality and strong moral fibre? Can a father dash away the reins of moral restraint, and, at the same time, impart strong will-power to his offspring?

A generation since, there lived in a Western city a wealthy English gentleman who was what is called a high liver. He drank his toddy in the morning, washed down his lunch with champagne, and finished a bottle of port for dinner, though he complained that the heavy wines here did not agree with him, owing to the climate. He died of gout at fifty years, leaving four sons. One of them became an epileptic, two died from drinking. Called good fellows, generous, witty, honorable young men, but before middle age miserable sots. The oldest of the brothers was a man of fixed habits, occupying a leading place in the community, from his keen intelligence, integrity, and irreproachable morals. He watched over his brothers, laid them in their graves, and never ceased to denounce the vice which had ruined them; and when he was long past middle age, financial trouble threw him into a low, nervous condition, for which wine was prescribed. He drank but one bottle. Shortly after, his affairs were righted and his health and spirits returned, but it was observed that once or twice a year he mysteriously disappeared for a month or six weeks. Nor wife, nor children, nor even his partner, knew where he went; but at last, when he was old and gray headed, his wife was telegraphed from an obscure neighboring village, where she found him dying of mania à potu.[6] He had been in the habit of hiding there when the desire for liquor became maddening, and when there he drank like a brute.

May Wright Sewall, president of the Woman's National Council, writing of disinherited children, tells of a country school where health and joyousness and purity were the rule, vulgarity and coarseness the exception, and morbid and mysterious manners quite unknown. There came one morning, in her childhood, two little girls, sisters, of ten and twelve years. They were comfortably dressed. At the noonday meal their baskets opened to an abundant and appetizing lunch. But they were not like other children. They had thin, pinched faces, with vulgar mouths, and a sidelong look from their always downcast eyes which made her shudder; and skin, so wrinkled and yellow, that her childish fears fancied them to be witches' children. They held themselves aloof from all the rest. For two or three years they sat in the same places in that quiet school doing very little work, but, not being disorderly, they were allowed to stay. One day, when my father had visited the school, as we walked home together, I questioned him as to what made Annie and Minnie so different from all the other little girls at the school, and the grave man answered: "Before they were born their father sold their birthright, and they must feed on pottage all their lives." She felt that an undefined mystery hovered around their blighted lives. She knew, she says, that they were blighted, as the simplest child knows the withered leaf of November from the glowing green of May, and she questioned no more, half conscious that the mystery was sin and that knowledge of it would be sinful too.

But we turn from these sad pictures to brighter pages in the great books of human life. To Benjamin West[7] saying: "My mother's kiss made me a painter." To John Randolph[8] saying: "I should have been an atheist, or it had not been for one recollection, and that was the memory of the time when my departed mother used to take my little hands in hers and sank me on my knees to say: 'Our Father, who art in heaven.'" Amid the cold of an Arctic expedition, Adam Isles found sickness had settled on part of his comrades, and the request came to him, I think from one of the officers of the ship, saying: "Isles, for God's sake, take some spirits, or we will be lost." Then the memory of the dear mother came back, and looking the entreaty in the face, he said, "I promised my mother I would not do it, and I wouldn't do it if I die in the ice."

I would ask, in conclusion, is there a branch of the human race in the Western Hemisphere which has greater need of the inspiring and uplifting influence that can flow out of the lives and examples of the truly enlightened than ourselves? Mothers who can teach their sons not to love pleasure or fear death; mothers who can teach their children to embrace every opportunity, employ every power, and use every means to build up a future to contrast with the old sad past. Men may boast of the aristocracy of blood; they may glory in the aristocracy of the talent, and be proud of the aristocracy of wealth, but there is an aristocracy which must ever outrank them all, and that is the aristocracy of character.

The work of the mothers of our race is grandly constructive. It is for us to build above the wreck and ruin of the past more stately temples of thought and action. Some races have been overthrown, dashed in pieces, and destroyed; but to-day the world is needing, fainting, for something better than the results of arrogance, aggressiveness, and indomitable power. We need mothers who are capable of being character builders, patient, loving, strong, and true, whose homes will be uplifting power in the race. This is one of the greatest needs of the hour. No race can afford to neglect the enlightenment of its mothers. If you would have a clergy without virtue or morality, a manhood without honor, and a womanhood frivolous, mocking, and ignorant, neglect the education of your daughters. But if, on the other hand, you would have strong men, virtuous women, and good homes, then enlighten your women, so that they may be able to bless their homes by the purity of their lives, the tenderness of their hearts, and the strength of their intellects. From schools and colleges your children may come well versed in ancient lore and modern learning, but it is for us to learn and teach, within the shadow of our own homes, the highest and best of all sciences, the science of a true life. When the last lay of the minstrel shall die upon his ashy lips, and the sweetest numbers of the poet cease to charm his death-dulled ear; when the eye of the astronomer shall be too dim to mark the path of worlds that roll in light and power on high; and when all our earthly knowledge has performed for us its mission, and we are ready to lay aside our environments garments we have outworn and outgrown: if we have learned that science of a true life, we may rest assured that this acquirement will go with us through the valley and shadow of death, only to grow lighter and brighter through the eternities.

1892

NOTES

1. Eliza Harris was central character in Harriet Beecher Stowe's *Uncle Tom's Cabin*, whose enslavement dramatized the plight of mothers and their children under slavery in the South and fugitive slave law in the North.

2. Identified in the four canonical Gospels as the site of Christ's crucifixion, also called Golgotha.

3. A reference to Luke 1:38.

4. Dr. Caroline Winslow (1822–1896) was a physician and supporter of Social Purity, a movement that opposed sexual intercourse for any purposes other than procreation.

5. Margaret Juke (both Margaret and the surname Juke are pseudonyms), whose extended family and descendants were the subjects of extensive study for evidence of either environment or heredity as the cause of criminality.

6. An alcohol-induced psychosis.

7. American-born painter Benjamin West (1738–1820), president of London's Royal Academy of Arts, was best known for his dramatic portrayals of scenes from history and classical mythology.

8. A Virginia congressman, who served in both the House and the Senate, and who experienced a religious conversion in 1818, after a brief period of spiritual ambivalence.

PETER RANDOLPH (1825?-1897)

Peter Randolph was born into slavery on the Brandon Plantation. Located in Prince George County, Virginia, the estate was owned by Carter U. Edloe. Randolph's mother was owned by Edloe, and his father was owned by George Harrison, a neighbor. Edloe died in 1843, leaving instructions in his will to free all of those enslaved on his plantation. Although the will was disputed in court by his relatives, Edloe's wishes were finally carried out in 1847, and Randolph migrated to Boston along with sixty-six of the men, women, and children with whom he had been enslaved. Though he had little formal education, Randolph was self-taught in the areas of reading, writing, and theology, and he was eventually licensed as a minister in the Baptist Church. He would go on to become the founder of Boston's Ebenezer Baptist Church, one of the largest and most influential African American churches in the city. An abolitionist as well as a clergyman, Randolph published his *Sketches of Slave Life: Or, Illustrations of the "Peculiar Institution"* in order to correct northern misconceptions about the practice of slavery in the South. Released in 1855, the forty-page first edition consists of brief vignettes depicting various aspects of slave life. Randolph's book was an immediate success, selling out its first edition within a few months of its release. The expanded second edition, which appeared later the same year, includes additional sketches on the living and working conditions experienced by enslaved blacks. In 1893, Randolph published *From Slave Cabin to the Pulpit: The Autobiography of Rev. Peter Randolph: the Southern Question Illustrated,* a spiritual autobiography that adds to his previous works a lengthy description of both his religious awakening and his achievements in the ministry. The following selections are taken from the first edition of his 1855 volume.

SKETCHES OF SLAVE LIFE: OR, ILLUSTRATIONS OF THE "PECULIAR INSTITUTION"

The Blood of the Slave

> The blood of the slave cries unto God from the ground, and it calls loudly for vengeance on his adversaries.

The blood of the slave cries unto God from the rice swamps.

The blood of the slave cries unto God from the cotton plantations.

The blood of the slave cries unto God from the tobacco farms.

The blood of the slave cries unto God from the sugar fields.

The blood of the slave cries unto God from the corn fields.

The blood of the slave cries unto God from the whipping-post.

The blood of the slave cries unto God from the auction-block.

The blood of the slave cries unto God from the gallows.

The blood of the slave cries unto God from the hunting-dogs that run down the poor fugitive.

The blood of men, women and babes cries unto God from Texas to Maine. Wherever the Fugitive Slave Law reaches, the voice of its victims is heard.

The mighty God, the great Jehovah, speaks to the consciences of men, and says, "LET MY PEOPLE GO FREE!" And the slaveholder answers, "Who is Jehovah, that we should obey him?" Then the Anti-Slavery voice is heard, calling, Awake! AWAKE! and cry aloud against this great evil; lift up your voice like a trumpet, and show the people their sins, and the nation its guilt. Pray that God may have mercy upon us. O, forgive us this great evil,—the evil of selling, whipping, and killing men, women and children! O, God of justice! give us hearts and consciences to feel the deep sorrows of this great evil that we have so long indulged in! Lo! we have sinned against Heaven; we have sinned against light,—against the civilized world. We have sinned against that declaration which our fathers put forth to the world, "All men are created equal."

O God! forgive us this great sin! O let this prayer be heard!

Slaves on the Auction Block

The auctioneer is crying the slave to the highest bidder. "Gentlemen, here is a very fine boy for sale. He is worth twelve hundred dollars. His name is Emanuel. He belongs to Dea.[1] William Harrison, who wants to sell him because his overseer don't like him. How much, gentlemen—how much for this boy? He's a fine, hearty nigger. Bid up, bid up, gentlemen; he must be sold." Some come up to look at him, pull open his mouth to examine his teeth, and see if they are good. Poor fellow! he is handled and examined like any piece of merchandize; but he must bear it. Neither tongue nor hand, nor any other member, is his own,—why should he attempt to use another's property?

Again the bidding goes on: "I will give one thousand dollars for that boy." The auctioneer says, "Sir, he is worth twelve hundred at the lowest. Bid up, gentlemen, bid up; going, going—are you all done?—once, twice, three times—all done?—GONE!"

See the slaveholder, who just bought the image of God, come to his victim, and take possession of him. Poor Emanuel must go away from his wife, never to see her again. All the ties of love are severed; the declaration of the Almighty, which said, "What God hath joined together, let not man put asunder," is unheeded, and he must leave all to follow his *Christian* master,— a member of the Episcopal Church,—a partaker, from time to time, of the Lord's sacrament! Such men mock religion and insult God. O that God would rend the heavens, and appear unto these heartless men!

Next come Jenny and her five children. Her husband was sold and gone. The oldest of her children is a girl seventeen years old,—her name, Lucy.

Auctioneer—"Here, gentlemen, is a fine girl for sale: how much for her? Gentlemen, she will be a fortune for any one who buys her that wants to raise niggers. Bid up gentlemen, bid up! Fine girl; very hearty; good health; only seventeen years old; she's worth fifteen hundred dollars to any one who wants to raise niggers. Here's her mother; she's had nine children; the rest of them are sold. How much, gentlemen,—how much? Bid up! bid up!"

Poor Lucy is sold away from all the loved ones, and goes to receive the worst of insults from her cruel taskmaster. Her poor mother stands by heartbroken, with tears streaming down her face. O! is there a heart not all brutish, that can witness such a scene without falling to the earth with shame, that the rights of his fellow-creatures are so basely trampled upon? The seller or buyer of a human being, for purposes of slavery, is not human, and has no right to the name.

The next "article" sold is Harry, a boy of fifteen.

Auctioneer—"Gentlemen, how much for this boy? He is an honest boy, can be trusted with any thing you wish; how much for him?"

Harry is sold from his mother, who is standing watching for her turn. She began to scream out, "O, my child! my child!" Here the old slaveholder said, "Ah my girl, if you do not stop that hollering, I will give you something to holler for." Poor Jenny, the mother, tried to suppress her grief, but all in vain. Harry was gone, and the children cried out, "Good by, Harry; good by!" The broken-hearted mother sobbed forth, "Farewell, my boy; try to meet me in heaven."

The next of the children was Mary. She was put upon the block and sold. Then the mother became so much affected that she seemed like one crazy. So the old rough slaveholder went to the mother, and began to lay the lash upon her; but it mattered not to her—her little Mary was gone, and now her turn had come. O, mothers, who sit in your comfortable homes, surrounded by your happy children, think of the poor slave mother, robbed so cruelly of her all by a fate worse than death! O, think of her, pray for her, toil for her, even; teach your blooming daughters to think with compassion of their far-off colored sisters, and train them up anti-slavery women! Teach your sons the woes and burning wrongs of slavery; make them grow up earnest, hard-working anti-slavery men. When mothers all do this, we may hope yet to live in a *free country*.

Wretched, childless, widowed Jenny was placed upon the block for sale.

Auctioneer—"Gentlemen, here is Jenny,—how much for her? She can do good work. Now, gentlemen, her master says he believes her to be a Christian, a very pious old woman; and she will keep every thing straight around her. You may depend on her. She will neither lie nor steal: what she says may be believed. Just let her pray, and she will keep right."

Here Jesus Christ was sold to the highest bidder; sold in Jenny to keep her honest, to bring gold to the slaveholder. Jenny was sold away from all her little children, never to see them again. Poor mother! who had toiled day and night to raise her little children, feeling all a mother's affection for them, she must see them no more in this world! She feels like great mourning,—"like Rachel weeping for her children, and would not be comforted, because they were not." So she commends them to the care of the God of the widow and the fatherless, by bathing her bosom in tears, and giving them the last affectionate embrace, with the advice to meet her in heaven. O, the tears of the poor slave that are in bottles, to be poured out upon this blood-stained nation, as soon as the cup of wrath of the almighty Avenger is full, when He shall say, "I have heard the groanings of my people, and I will deliver them from the oppressor!"

Slaveholders carry the price of blood upon their backs and in their pockets; the very bread they eat is the price of blood; the houses they live in are bought with blood; all the education they have is paid for by the blood and sorrows of the poor slaves.

In parting with their friends at the auction-block, the poor blacks have the anticipation of meeting them again in the heavenly Canaan, and sing—

"O fare you well, O fare you well,

God bless you until we meet again;

Hope to meet you in heaven, to part no more.

CHORUS—Sisters fare you well; sisters, fare you well;

        God Almighty bless you, until we meet again."

Among the slaves, there is a great amount of talent, given by the hand of inspiration; talent, too, which, if cultivated, would be of great benefit to the world of mankind. If these large minds are kept sealed up, so that they cannot answer the end for which they were made, somebody must answer for it on the great day of account. O think of this, my readers! Think of that great day when it shall be said to all the world, "Give an account of thy stewardship!" Among the slaves may be found talents which, if improved, would be instrumental in carrying the blessed Gospel of truth to distant lands, and in bringing the people to acknowledge the true and living God. But all has been crushed down by a Christian world, and by the Christian Church. With these solemn facts written against this nation, see to it, my readers, before this iniquity overthrow you, and it be too late to repent.

The sin of holding slaves is not only against one nation, but against the whole world, because we are here to do one another good, in treating each other well; and this is to be done by having right ideas of God and his religion. But this privilege is denied to three millions and a half of the people of this, our own "free" land. The slaveholders say we have not a true knowledge of religion; but the great Teacher said, when he came on his mission, "The spirit of the Lord is upon me, because he hath anointed me to preach the gospel to the poor. He hath sent me to heal the broken-hearted; to preach deliverance to the captive, and recovering of sight to the blind; to set at liberty them that are bruised, and to preach the acceptable year of the Lord." This ought to be the work of the ministers and the churches. Any thing short of this is not the true religion of Jesus.

This is the great command of the New Testament—"Love the Lord thy God with all thy heart, and thy neighbor as thyself."[2] "Do unto others as ye would that they should do to you," is the golden rule for all men to follow. By this rule shall all men be judged. We have got to hear, "Come, ye blessed; depart, ye cursed!" These are my convictions, and my belief of the religion of Jesus, the wonderful Counsellor of the children of the created Adam, our great progenitor.

This I respectfully submit to my readers, and earnestly beg of them to renew their interest in the anti-slavery cause, never turning a deaf ear to the pleadings of the poor slave, or to those who speak, however feebly, for him. The antislavery cause is the cause of HUMANITY, the cause of RELIGION, the cause of GOD!

1855

NOTES

1. Deacon.
2. Luke 10:27.
3. Refers to Matthew 7:12 and Luke 6:31.
4. Refers Matthew 25:34 and 25:41.

ELYMAS PAYSON ROGERS (1815-1861)

Elymas Payson Rogers was born in Madison, Connecticut, to Abel and Chloe Ladue Rogers. When he was fifteen or sixteen years old, Rogers moved to Hartford, Connecticut. Once there, he paid his way through school using his earnings as a live-in laborer for the family of Major John Caldwell, the first president of the Hartford Bank. After two years, Rogers relocated to Peterboro, New York, where he studied for eighteen months at a school for young men, established by abolitionist and future U.S. Representative Gerritt Smith. In 1836, Rogers enrolled at the Oneida Institute, graduating in 1841. He was ordained as a Presbyterian minister in 1845 and soon after was appointed pastor of the Plane Street Church in Newark, New Jersey. He would remain in this post until shortly before his death. A proponent of African American emigration to Liberia, Rogers traveled to West Africa in 1860, where he died within less than two months of his arrival. He was eulogized by pro-emigration activist Henry Highland Garnet. As a writer, he was best known for his political poems, including "A Poem on the Fugitive Slave Law," published as a pamphlet in 1855, and "The Repeal of the Missouri Compromise Considered," released in a similar format in 1856. He also authored both a poem and a testimonial letter affirming the character and achievements of Jermaine Wesley Loguen. Both pieces are included as an appendix to Loguen's autobiography, *Rev. J. W. Loguen, as a Slave and as a Freeman,* published in 1859. The following selections include "Loguen's Position," first published in Reverend Loguen's autobiography, and excerpts from the long poem "The Repeal of the Missouri Compromise Considered." The latter poem, written in the alternating voices of Freedom, Slavery, and an unnamed antislavery advocate (perhaps Rogers himself), condemns northern legislators whose self-interest, the piece argues, is responsible for the 1854 vote that effectively removed most strictures on the expansion of slavery into the newly organized territories of Kansas and Nebraska.

FROM *THE REPEAL OF THE MISSOURI COMPROMISE CONSIDERED*

'Tis done! the treach'rous deed is done;[1]
Eternal infamy is won
By Legislators, who've decreed
The direful and unrighteous deed.

'Tis done! the fearful die is cast,
The dreadful rubicon is past;
Nor will the deadly strife be o'er
'Till Freedom bleeds at every pore.

The grave Nebraska leaders feel
That by their treacherous repeal
Of the Missouri Compromise,
They've plucked away from Freedom's skies
The glorious sun revolving there,
And buried hope in deep despair.
That sun, long partially obscured,
They think eternally immured
Within the darkest, foulest night,
No more to shed her glorious light.

They've summoned their nefarious bands,
With whom they've struck polluted hands,
And compassed Freedom's altar round
And sought to raze it to the ground;
That altar of unbounded worth
Bequeathed by gracious heaven to earth,
Like as a monument to stand
As a design for every land,
That in each clime and realm might be
A beautiful facsimile;
That unto each there might be brought
The off'ring of the patriot,
Composed of treasure and of blood,
And offered in the name of God.

It is at such an altar, where
The ardent patriot should swear
By all that's good, by all that's great,
Eternal, unrelenting hate
To all unjust, oppressive laws,
And there espouse the righteous cause
Of Freedom, justice and the right,
And take his armor for the fight.

At such an altar let him stand
Until he feel both heart and hand
Nerved with extraordinary power
To battle in the trying hour.

Then let him quickly turn away
And seek to win a glorious day,
And let his watchword ever be
Almighty God and Liberty.
When battling for inherent right
Our honored sires, both black and white,
Upon this self-same altar swore
To wear a foreign yoke no more.

They by this self-same altar fought,
And sacred liberty was bought,—
Bought by the brav'ry and the blood
Of those who near the altar stood.

This altar, 'round which patriots kneel,
Inspires them with peculiar zeal,
And fills them with resistless might,
Enabling them to put to flight
Ten thousand of the vile and base,
And one a thousand foes to chase.

The covetous Nebraskaites[2]
Have near extinguished Freedom's lights,
Have thrown her altars to the ground
And hurled the hallowed parts around.

And then, their treason to complete,
They've leaped with their unhallowed feet
Upon the fragments on the sand,
(Still both magnificent and grand,)
And in their wild delirium swore
That liberty should be no more.
The dignified and lofty tree,
Of heaven-descending liberty,
No longer tow'ring upward stands,
But, prostrate by Vandalic hands,
Lies where the faithless act was done,
And withers in the noon-tide sun.

They think that liberty is doomed,
That she forever is entombed,
Nor will her cold and languid ear
The voice of resurrection hear.

Though sacred Freedom bleeds, we said,
She is not terrified nor dead;
For truth's her everlasting prop
And bears her gentle spirit up.

When truth is girded for the fight
And draws her weapons keen and bright,
And lifts aloft her burnished shield,
Her God-like influence to wield,
If vict'ry in that self-same hour
Is not accomplished by her power,
She'll not retreat nor flee away,
But win the field another day.
She will with majesty arise,
Seize her traducers by surprise,
And by her overwhelming might
Will put her deadly foes to flight.
. . . .
"I want the land," was Freedom's cry;
And Slavery answered, "So do I!
By all that's sacred, I declare

I'll have my just and lawful share.
The Northern cheek should glow with shame
To think to rob me of my claim:
And if my claim you dare deny,
I'll knock the Union into pi."
The Northern faces did not glow,
Because they were composed of dough:
But such a tall and horrid threat
Their equilibrium upset.
"O gracious heavens!" the patriot said,
As nervously he shook his head,
And quickly moved his tangled hair
To feel the bump of firmness there:
But how distracted was his mind,
When searching long he could not find
This stately organ of the brain,
Nor could the mystery explain,
Or make a fit apology
For this freak of phrenology.
The reason why the bump was low
Was it was fashioned out of dough;
And Slavery's bold and fearless threat
Had crushed the lofty organ flat.

This horrid threat from Southern men,
In Congress was all powerful then;
And when the North opposed the South,
This remedy sealed up their mouth,
And made them quickly toe the mark
And sanction schemes however dark.
The Union breaking threat prevailed,
When every other measure failed.

But recently the North drove back
The Southern tyrants from the track,
And put to flight their boasting ranks,
And gave the speaker's chair to Banks.

In twenty tyranny prevailed,[3]
And Northern men before it quailed
And bowed to Slavery—sad mistake—
But all was for the Union's sake.
The glorious Union, they declared,
Must never, never be impaired!
It is, said they, a sacred thing,
And to it we will ever cling;
The Union is above all price.
'Tis wisdom to convey a slice
Of territory, thus to save
The Union from a dismal grave.
And if God's righteous law we break,
'Twill all be for the Union's sake!
We must support the Constitution
And if we sin seek absolution.

A few, of never-dying fame,
Would never yield to Slavery's claim,
Would have no fellowship with it,
And now their wisdom we admit.
But these were a minority,
The others a majority;
And hence the Compromise was made,
And Slavery's claim was duly paid.

And, after gaining his desire,
He scarce was willing to retire,
And, as he turned to take his leave,
He laughed immoderate in his sleeve,
And said he'd surely call for more
In eighteen hundred fifty-four.
"The rest," quoth he, "I cannot get,
I am not strong enough as yet;
But when I am maturely strong,
I'll seize the balance, right or wrong."
But Freedom cried, "Wo worth the day
When such a treacherous game you play;

And such a treacherous game to win
Would be a most atrocious sin.
The act would gracious heaven defy,
And tempt the Majesty on high;
And then would ruin most complete
Accompany your sad defeat."

"But hold!" said Slavery; "you're too fast;
I judge the future by the past.
I always have high heaven defied,
And man's authority denied;
I always have securely seized
And borne away whate'er I pleased,
And, if my numerous games be sin,
Whene'er I play, I always win:
And I control the legislation
Of this great democratic nation,
And to my tried and cordial friends
My lib'ral patronage extends;
I raise them up to seats of power,
Although unworthy, base, and poor.
O'er each department I preside,
And all official actions guide;
I send ambassadors afar,
And, when I please, provoke a war
Ostensibly for public weal,
But 'tis in fact my burning zeal
To multiply my territory,
Instead of for the nation's glory.
And presidents I nominate
For confirmation by each State,
And no Chief-Magistrate is made
Without my all-sufficient aid.
Of politics, I am the pope
To whom each candidate must stoop,
And there devoutly kneeling low
Do homage to my sacred toe.

All these are facts which I defy
My sanguine scoffers to deny.

"I know that Northern freemen might
Upon one platform all unite,
And freedom's banner there unfurl,
And through the ballot-boxes hurl
Me from my proud and lofty station,
And send throughout this mighty nation
A grand and glorious jubilee,
Which would the wretched captive free:
They might construe the Constitution
So as to crush my institution;
So as to break the iron bands
From every human chattel's hands.
The power of Congress regulates
Commercial acts between the States,
And, hence, can with the utmost ease
Confine me wheresoe'er they please.
Were I forbidden to migrate
From place to place, from State to State,
I soon should lack sufficient room,
Which would accelerate my doom.
I'm so much like a roving herd,
That it is perfectly absurd
To think to tarry in one place,
Deprived of new and ample space.
Without new fertile territory,
I soon must part with all my glory.

"Some Northern men despise me much
And fear pollution from my touch,
And cry to heaven both night and day
To smite me dead without delay;
Then from their altars turn away,
The painted hypocrite to play,
And to my filthy garments cling
And seek to crown me as their king.

If I but gain their votes at last,
I care not how they pray and fast;
Their prayers are but the merest hoax—
But daring and blasphemous jokes.
When I am privileged to see
Their words and actions both agree,
I then may tremble, not before,
Upon my lofty seat of power."

                    1856

LOGUEN'S POSITION

They say I have a daring look—[4]
A bold and fearless mien:
For this I'm not accountable,
As shortly will be seen.

I am athletic, they declare,
And strong in every part,
With lurid vengeance in my eye,
And mischief in my heart.

But let each one be slow to judge,
Until my tale is told,
In which the reason will appear
Why I am tart and bold.

I am a panting fugitive—
I fled from Tennessee,
From chains, and whips, and bloodhounds, too,
In search of Liberty.

'Twas There I saw my sister flogged,
And heard her thrilling prayer,
Oh! spare me, master! Master! Oh,
For God's sake, master, spare!

I and my mother felt the lash—
Our sufferings who can tell!

O Slavery! thou bloody fiend,
I hate thee worse than hell!

And now they wish to drag me back
To servitude again;
But never, no! so help me God!
Will I endure the chain.

I would not turn upon my heel
To flee my master's power;
But if he comes within my grasp,
He falls the self-same hour!

I know 'tis God-like to forgive—
Perhaps I may be wrong;
But, were your soul in my soul's stead,
You'd doubtless feel as strong.

Hasten, O God! the joyful day
When Slavery shall not be;
When millions now confined in chains,
Shall sound a jubilee.

1859

NOTES

1. The passage of the Kansas-Nebraska Act of 1854 effectively nullified those portions of the Missouri Compromise of 1820 that prohibited slavery in the northern portion of the former Louisiana Territory.

2. Supporters of the Kansas-Nebraska Act and its nullification of the strict prohibition of slavery north of the 36°30' line.

3. Refers to the passage of the Missouri Compromise, in 1820, by the U.S. Congress.

4. "Loguen's Position" refers to Rev. J. W. Loguen's antislavery beliefs and his status as an escaped slave who was once recaptured under fugitive slave law.

J. W. LOGUEN (1813-1872)

Jermaine Wesley Loguen was born in Davidson County, Tennessee. One of three known offspring of his mother, an enslaved African American woman named Jane, and her owner, David Logue, Loguen was raised with the full knowledge that his master was also his father. Acknowledged by his father and accepted as his son, the author received privileged treatment throughout much of his childhood. Over time, though, he witnessed his father and owner becoming ever more violent toward his mother and less affectionate toward Loguen, himself. Around 1835, Loguen escaped to Canada, where he began his formal education. In 1839, he returned to the United States to continue his studies at the Oneida Institute, in Whitesboro, New York. In 1842, he was ordained as a minister of the African Methodist Episcopal Zion (A.M.E.Z.) Church. Loguen spent several years in Syracuse, New York, where, in addition to working as a clergyman and teacher, he also served as a conductor on the Underground Railroad. In 1859, he published his autobiography. *The Rev. J. W. Loguen, as a Slave and as a Freeman* is a third-person narrative recounting the author's life under slavery, his escape to the North, and his involvement in the abolitionist movement. The early chapters of his biography describe the circumstances of his birth and early rearing. In 1860, his autobiography was revised to include a letter from the wife of Loguen's father and former owner, along with Loguen's written reply. This exchange, in which Mrs. Sarah Logue casts Loguen's escape as the theft of a valuable asset, includes her appeal to the author for reimbursement. In his response, Loguen makes a passionate and compelling argument in favor of abolitionism, offering Mrs. Logue's own text as evidence of the damage that slavery has done to her sense of justice and compassion. The transcript of these letters was printed in African American and progressive white-owned newspapers throughout the New York region. The first paper to reprint this exchange was William Lloyd Garrison's *Liberator,* during the winter of 1860.

Chapter I

We must devote a brief chapter to the parents of Mr. Loguen.

The genealogy of an American Slave may be traced with certainty to the mother, rarely to the father, never beyond them on the male line. It is the condition of the mother *de facto* that makes the slave. She is mother *de lege* only to the intent that her offspring may be an outlaw. As to the progenitor on the male side, he is rarely known as the father in fact, never in law. The slave has no father. Slave legislation has no use of a paternal line, and refuses to acknowledge one. It acknowledges a mother, not in respect to any natural relation, but for accommodation, as the medium of titles, not of affections and obligations. Legally speaking, the slave has neither father or mother.

Slavery, of course, has no records of conjugal relations. Should the Clairvoyant translate and publish the secrets of its history, the domestic relations of the South would be broken up, and society sink in the abyss of vulgar passions. It owes its existence to the fact that its sexual history is faintly shadowed in the varied colors of the abused race.

It is hardly proper to pass by those familiar truths, while placing upon the record the life and character of Jermain W. Loguen. It is to be presumed that his physical, intellectual and moral qualities, partake of the character of his ancestors, and that they were modified by the influences that surrounded his childhood.

The mother of Mr. Loguen is a pure African. Her skin is jet black, and her hair short and curled to the head. She is now, if living, near as can be determined, about seventy years of age. In her youth and maturity her face was fair, and her features marked and regular—her bodily proportions large, symmetrical, round, and muscular—presenting a model of health and strength, and a specimen of the best of her race.

Of her parents and kindred of any kind, she is perfectly ignorant. The extent of her recollection is that she was free in her infancy, in the guardianship of a man in Ohio, by the name of McCoy, with whom she lived until about seven years of age. She remembers that she was out of sight and hearing of Mr. McCoy's house, alone, when she was such little girl, and that a bad man got out of a covered wagon and took her into it with one hand about her body and the other upon her mouth to prevent her screams—that when she got into the wagon, he held her in his lap, and told the teamster to drive on—that there were several other little colored children in the wagon with her—and that they were taken over the river together in a boat; probably into Kentucky.

This story she often repeated to her son, and kindled in his boyhood the intensest indignation against the institution which so outraged the mother he loved. All other memories were drowned in the sorrows and terrors, which at that time overwhelmed her spirit, and the brutal associations and treatment she received afterwards.

Thus all recollection of parents, kindred and friends of every kind, were merged in the clouds which the kidnappers drew about her; and she has not heard the name of any one of them pronounced from that day to this. She is as if she never had any parents, or kindred, or, as if they were all buried and forgotten. That she was once free, she has the most distinct remembrance, and a flickering recollection of happy days in early childhood, still faintly illumines the dark horizon of her memory.

She does not remember the precise number of wretched little children, boys and girls, who were in the wagon with her, but thinks they were about her age, and all involved in the intensest grief. She remembers that their cries and sobs, like her own, were silenced by the terrors of the lawless villains who had them in charge.

We may be allowed to remark that these colored orphans illustrate the helplessness of the whole colored race, in a country where slavery is guarded as lawful and sacred. In proportion as slavery has the protection of law, do the persons of all colored men, women and children, lose the protection of law? As the condition of the former is hopeful and secure, is the latter desperate and exposed to outrage. Not only does the colored man suffer from the contempt and insolence of the favored class, but his or her person is outlawed to the limited and unlimited abuses of the conscienceless men who make them their prey. Developments of such enormities, incidentally and occasionally appear, as specks of light through "the blanket of the dark" upon the black volume which is out of sight.

These unhappy little ones were at the age, when childhood carols its joys with the birds, and bounds like lambs in the pastures at the touch of angels. For long and weary days and nights, not a motion or sound of delight, not a joyous look or laugh varied their depression and wretchedness. The oblivion of sleep was the only solace of the little sufferers; and even this was often tortured by the pressure of misery, and the silence of night broken by their sighs and sobs. Whether, like the mother of Mr. Loguen, they were stolen from their parents, or purchased from those who should have protected them, is unknown. Their story is untold or it is forgotten, and their history is a secret only to him who gathered little children in his arms to represent the kingdom of God.

After they passed the river, the kidnappers sold them, one after another, as they could light of purchasers on the road. The mother of Mr. Loguen was left or sold to three brothers, David, Carnes, and Manasseth Logue, who lived in a small log house on Manscoe's Creek, (so called) in Davidson county, about sixteen miles from Nashville, Tennessee. They were large, rough, and demi-civilized young men, the unmarried owners of a miserably cultivated plantation, and (what was at that time in that part of the country of better repute than a school or meeting house,) a whiskey distillery.

Whether these brothers were a link of a chain of kidnappers, extending through a part or the whole of the free and slave states, and claimed the poor girl as a Pirate's portion; or whether they purchased her for money or other thing, she does not know. Of one thing she is certain, so soon as the ruffians left her, she had an interview with her purchasers which made a lasting impression upon her person and memory.

There was nothing in the aspect or conduct of the Logues that showed aught but sympathy for her manifest wretchedness. Such was the tenderness and concern with which, at first, they seemed to be touched, and the obvious natural humanity which in their countenances, concealed and gilded the quiet ferocity of their natures, that she ventured to tell them how she was stolen, in the hope that they would return her back to her friends in Ohio. She had but begun the story when every expression of sympathy vanished, and their faces were covered with frowns. Their kind words changed into threats and curses. Nor was this all, or the worst. One of them took a slave whip that hung on the wall of the cabin and whipped her. Of course she could but beg and suffer, and at the conclusion promise she would never again repeat the offensive fact of her freedom.

Thus was this innocent child, according to the customary mode in such cases, metamorphosed from a human being into a chattel. To cover the transaction and make the change more complete, the name by which she had always been called, "Jane," was taken from her, and that of "Cherry," the name by which she has ever since been called and known, was given her.

Of course it is not the intent to give more of the history of this woman than shall serve to illustrate the maternal influences which nourished the spirit of her son. Though the enchanter's wand touched and changed her into a slave *de facto*, the terrible lesson did but adjust her habits to a prudential exterior. While it checked the growth of the sympathies and virtues of artless childhood, it awakened and strengthened animal energies, which under better influences had ever slept. The Logues intended her for a useful slave. The whipping and threats and extorted promise were designed for that end—and whether they were aware she had been stolen or not, her treatment would have been the same. They had no unkindness farther than they intended that neither her tongue or name should lead to evidence, by accident or intent, by which they might be deprived of their property; all memory of which they hoped would be overgrown by the habits of servile life.

Free colored persons have no right or privilege beyond a permitted residence in slave states, and such residence gives them nothing that deserves the name of protection from the wrongs of white men. The kidnapping and enslaving of this little girl therefore, could not be looked upon as very bad, by men like the Logues, and the body of slaveholders, whose morals and humanity are so inverted, is to suppose, that by making her a slave, they raised her from the lowest to a higher condition, and furnished her with protection and privileges not to be enjoyed in a state of freedom. This fact will be illustrated in the course of our history, and we have mentioned it, incidentally, to relieve the Logues from the inference that their principles and habits were barbarous beyond public sentiment and the laws of the land.

Not slaveholders only, but slaves in the slave breeding States, as a general truth, regard theirs as a favored position, compared with the condition of free colored men and women at the South. Mr. Loguen, whose biography we write, is not the only one who says from experience, "If I must live in a slave State, let me be a slave."

Thus was Jane, who we shall hereafter call "Cherry, at the age of seven, robbed of all her rights, even of a knowledge or the names of her parents, and every one of her kindred, and placed under the tutelage of the rude habits and passions, and unscrupulous avarice of David, Carnes, and Manasseth Logue. These three brothers, lived with their widowed mother in a small log house, and Cherry was put in a pretty cabin, with other slaves, a little distance from them.

As her physical strength developed, she became their main dependence, in the house, the distillery, and in the field. Without losing her feminine proportions, she grew to a masculine hardihood. Among her other accomplishments, she became expert in the art of manufacturing whiskey, and was often employed day and night with other slaves in the distillery. On the plantation there was no hard service, whether it was driving the oxen, loading, lifting, plowing, hoeing or any other thing, to which she did not do a man's days work. There was no man on the plantation, upon whom her masters more depended in all the departments of labor, and at all times, and in all weathers.

Cherry had now arrived at the condition her masters desired her to occupy. She was a faithful, skilful and able slave. She however felt the condition as a necessity, and submitted to it with the same contentment that the young Leopard feels under the restraints that cages and tames him. Her natural disposition was gentle, affectionate, kind, and confiding; but these qualities reposed upon a spirit, which, when roused and chafed, was as resolute and indomitable as the tigress in the jungles. She knew no fear, and submitted only to passion, interest, and necessity. Nothing but the lamb-like sympathies she always manifested under decent treatment, and her inestimable personal services, saved her from the legal and usual consequences of desperate resistance to those who would outrage her person.

It is believed that ten thousand slaves have been whipped to death, shot, or otherwise murdered, for transgressions not half so offensive as hers. But ignorant and brutal as were her masters, they respected alike the natural loveliness of her affections, and her indomitable impulses under wrongs, which no chastisement could subdue. But what most contributed to her safety, was the fact, that she was a first class laborer and slave breeder, and finally the mistress of David Logue, the youngest of the three.

This spirit of resistance caused her many and some bloody battles and scourgings—the marks of which she will carry on her person while she lives. She would never allow a woman or any number of women to whip her. Nor could she be subdued by any ordinary man. When women sometimes inconsiderately engaged with her, they were obliged to call in a posse of stout men to bind her.

Jermain W. Loguen, whose heart even now, is as tender as a child to the touch of pity, when a little boy, and afterwards, has seen her knocked down with clubs, stripped and bound, and flogged with sticks, ox whips and rawhide, until the blood streamed down the gashes upon her body. When released from the place of torture, she never retired with a subdued spirit, but passed from a scourging to her labors like a sullen tigress. Her habits and character in this regard will be more unfolded in connection with the life of her son.

Compelled, as she was, to endure violence from her masters, and comparatively cautious in resisting them, she never endured it from others. White or black, male or female, if they attempted liberties with her person, against her consent, she not only resisted, but fought with a spirit and force proportioned to her own estimate of her rights and wrongs.

In describing the person of Cherry in the ripeness of robust youthful development, it may be inferred she was not destitute of attractions for the casual lust of the vulgar slaveholders who lived along the banks of Manscoe's Creek. The black distillery was the common resort of that class of lawless men. David, Manasseth, and Carnes Logue, her masters, were of the same class. They were all hard drinkers, and the distillery was a convenient place for coarse enjoyment and low carousals.

Though Cherry made the fire-water, she never drank it. Her nights and days were often spent at work in the distillery, and of course she was in the sight and hearing of these vulgar men, and often the subject of their brutal remarks. But outside the family of Logues, woe to the hand laid upon her person with lascivious intent. The body of a female Slave is outlawed of course to the white man. All the law she has is her own arm, and how Cherry appreciated that law may be illustrated by the following incident.

When she was about the age of twenty-four or five, a neighboring planter, finding her alone at the distillery and presuming upon the privileges of his position, made insulting advances, which she promptly repelled.

He pursued her with gentle force, and was still repelled. He then resorted to a slaveholder's violence and threats. These stirred all tiger's blood in her veins. She broke from his embrace, and stood before him in bold defiance.

He attempted again to lay hold of her—and careless of caste and slave laws, she grasped the heavy stick used to stir the malt, and dealt him a blow which made him reel and retire. But he retired only to recover and return with the fatal knife, and threats of vengeance and death. Again, she aimed the club with unmeasured force at him, and hit the hand which held the weapon, and dashed it to a distance from him. Again he rushed upon her with the fury of a madman, and she then plied a blow upon his temple, which laid him, as was supposed, dead at her feet.

This incident, though no portion of the biography of her son, is introduced to show the qualities of the woman who bore him, and which those acquainted with him will infer she imparted to him. This, and like scenes, formed the cradle in which the infant spirit of Jermain W. Loguen was rocked.

Cherry, unterrified by the deed we have related, did not flee to escape the application of the severe laws she had violated by striking a white man. She left the now passionless and apparently lifeless villain, bleeding not only from the wound inflicted, but from his nose and ears also, to inform her masters of the encounter, and meet the consequences. She told them she had killed the wretch, and the whole family of Logues hastened to the distillery to look, as they supposed, upon the face of their dead neighbor. They found him laying in his gore. But upon raising him and washing his wounds, he showed signs of life, though it seemed likely he would die.

To curtail a story which may seem an interpolation, after the most unremitting care and skilful attention of the best surgeons and physicians they could procure—and after the lapse of many weeks, during which time he was stretched on a sick bed, and racked by pains and fevers—after drinking to the dregs as severe a cup as ever touched a slaveholder's lips, he recovered.

In the meantime Cherry was shielded from harm, partly by the shame of her violator—partly by her masters' sense of justice—more because they had a beastly affection for her as a family chattel—more still because they prized her as property—but most of all because she was the admitted mistress of David Logue, the father of Jermain, then about six years of age.

He (Jermain) well remembers the case and the excitement produced by it in the family and neighborhood. His memory was refreshed with the rehearsal of it for years by the family and the negroes.

When Cherry arrived at about the age of twenty-eight, she was the mother of three children. To this period, she had never passed through the ceremonial sham of a negro marriage, but for years, as stated above, had been the admitted mistress of David Logue, the father of her children.

Here we may be permitted to record a fact well known at the south, and allowed by most white men, and by all slaves, to wit: that a young negress is often her master's mistress, until childbearing and years render it tasteful or convenient to sell the offspring from his sight, and exchange her for another victim. Such was the relation Cherry sustained to David Logue, and such too her fate.

At this point we drop the mother to consider briefly the character of the father.

It is rarely possible for a slave to identify his father with so much certainty as in this case. In a society where promiscuous intercourse is allowable, as at Manscoe's Creek, the chastity of white men of course does not transcend the chastity of black women; and the conspicuity of virtue, is apparent, only, in the fidelity of the slave girl to her condition of mistress. On this point the conduct of Cherry was a bright example, and her fidelity to that relation was confessed and allowed, not by the parties only, but by the family and neighborhood.

Jarm, as Mr. Loguen was called when a slave, remembers when a very little child he was the pet of Dave, as his father was also nicknamed, that he slept in his bed sometimes, and was caressed by him—he also received from him many little favors and kindnesses which won his young heart. As his body and features grew to fixedness and maturity, all who knew them both, instantly recognized a personal, and even a spiritual resemblance.

On his recent visit to the fugitive slaves in Canada, Mr. Loguen met a fugitive from the neighborhood of his old master in Tennessee. She informed him that she was struck with his resemblance to his father— that his size and form—his walk and motions, every thing but his hair and complexion, was a striking expression of him—that from his walk, alone, she should take him for the same man at a distance, if his face was concealed.

Thus was Mr. Loguen taught by his mother, by the treatment of his infancy, by the admitted fact in the family and neighborhood, by family resemblance, not of person only, but as we shall see by the impulses of his spirit, that David Logue was his veritable father.

With his other brothers, David lived at the paternal mansion of their widowed mother, when Cherry came into their possession. They were all three, young men, David, the youngest, probably not over eighteen years of age. Jermain never saw or heard of a schoolhouse or school, or meeting house, at Manscoe's Creek, nor does he believe there were either. Many of the planters were ignorant of letters. Their Sundays were spent in sport and dissipation. Their agriculture resembled the Indian culture on the Onondaga Reservation in the State of New York. Mr. Loguen never passes through that Reservation in the Summer, without being sensibly reminded of the scenes of his childhood. The houses were all log houses, and the people even more destitute than the Indians of the means of intellectual, moral, and religious culture.

Nevertheless, the father of Mr. Loguen was not devoid of noble and generous impulses. He was full six feet high, sprightly in the use of abundant muscle; an impulsive, drinking, and chivalrous rowdy—unscrupulous in his pleasures—but ever ready to help a friend or smite a foe. Had he been cast amid the privileges of northern culture, instead of the creature of passion and indulgence that he was, his excellent physical and intellectual qualities might have blossomed into the highest use—the public might have honored him as a benefactor, and Jermain loved and revered him as a father. Even now, bowed down, as it is said he is, by poverty and dissipation, it would be a real pleasure to Mr. Loguen to contribute to his father's necessities—and help the infirmities of his sin smitten and rapidly declining age.

We need not dwell longer upon the father and mother of Mr. Loguen. We have given enough for the purposes of our story, and their character and condition, will, of course, be further illustrated by facts to appear in the history.

Chapter II

In the ordinary and acknowledged relations of life, the mere naked facts attending the infancy of any man or woman are the farthest removed from romance or interest. They must be the result of an individual or social departure from the order of nature, to claim a slight attention. Nevertheless, we must devote a little, attention to the infancy of Loguen.

The fact that shocks us in the infancy of a southern slave, is, that its story cannot be told. No facilities are provided to mark its steps or preserve its memories. A slave baby is the offspring of brute passion and the subject of brute neglect and suffering. It claims no greater sympathy and care than any other animal of the sty or the field. The angels, who delight to touch the delicate fibres of the brain, and communicate the joys of heaven, and paint them on an infant's face, are driven away by oppression, that the most perfect medium of Gods, converse ... conjunction, with man may be tortured and distorted by devils. Black and damning will be the record of the crimes and cruelties by which thousands of these little innocents are let into heaven.

The above remarks are made, not because they apply to the infancy of Mr. Loguen, for they do not—but because they do apply, as a general truth, to the great body of children who are born as Mr. Loguen was. We should do injustice to history, did we present his infancy or childhood other than as an exception to the general rule. He has every reason to believe that his infancy was cared for by the strongest maternal affection consistent with his mother's servitude, guarded as he believes it was by the instincts of a lawless, but naturally susceptible father. Multitudes of kindnesses partialities, and unquestionable loves, are indelibly written upon his memory, which he thinks contributed to the formation of his character. They are lessons which even now temper and mollify his passions, as he sees them through the sorrows and trials and outrages and storms that are piled upon his pathway.

"Jump on my back, Jarm," half whispered Dave, as, rifle in hand, he stepped lightly down the bank of the creek where little Jarm was playing with the pebbles, suiting his bulky frame to the body of a child three or four years old.

Well did the child understand the accustomed ceremony, and he clasped his little arms upon his father's shoulders.

"Be still now—say not a word and you shall see me shoot a deer."

"Where is a deer?" said the child, while Dave neared a bunch of bushes, and pointed to an animal the former took for a pet calf which had grown up under his eye, and for which he cherished a child's regard.

"Don't say a word now—you will scare the deer away if you do," repeated Dave.

Jarm was obedient, while Dave with his load, which was scarce more than a fly on a giant's shoulder, crept slyly into the jungle, and crouching by a log, rested his rifle on it, and drove a bullet through the body of the beautiful animal. The deer with dying energy, leaped and poured his mortal bleat upon the air, then staggered and fell.

Poor little Jarm was in an exstacy of grief, and made the plantation echo with his screams, and brought the whole swarm of whites and blacks to his relief. His cry was "He has killed the calf, he has killed the calf." Even old "Granny," as Jarm called the mother of the Logues, hearing the screams, came to see what mattered the little favorite chattel.

Ere they assembled, Dave had the game, bleeding from the deep gash his knife had made in the throat, at the feet of the child, and was soothing him with the tenderness of a father's love.

The boy soon saw his mistake, and was laughed and petted into a tremulous composure; but the shock of seeming cruelty made an indelible impression on his spirit and memory. To others, it was an amusing and vanishing incident—to Jarm, it was a lesson of life.

Life, truly and philosophically speaking, is the form and embodiment of thoughts and affections. In its uninterrupted current from the uncreated fountain, it creates and vivifies material receptacles in the form of angels, and also of all that is healthful, beautiful, lovely, innocent and correspondent of heaven, in animal and vegetable nature. But when that current is intercepted, and passes through the medium of infernal loves, it creates and vivifies other receptacles of monstrous forms. Hence all the noxious plants, and loathsome insects, and poisonous reptiles, and ferocious animals, and hateful men, correspondent, all, to the varied passions of Hell. Hence the slaveholder and the slave.

The life of little Jarm blossomed in the shape of an angel, but receptive of the disordered affections and monster passions around him. The problem must be solved, whether he should resist those surrounding affections and passions, and preserve his virgin life, or be deformed into a monster. The incident just related was the first shock upon his spirit which he remembers. It is introduced to show the condition of his childhood, but may be noted as the commencement of incidents which were to form his manhood. The forms of feeling and consequent combinations of thought, which are the life of a child, manufacture the spiritual cable which holds him amidst the storms and tempests of the world, or leaves him a wreck upon its waves. To change the figure, they are the causes which ultimate the hero, the despot and the slave.

The first ten years of Jarm's life was to him a period of much freedom. He was as well fed and housed as any other little savage. A single loose, coarse cotton garment covered his burly body, and he was left in summer to hunt mice and chipmunks, catch little fishes, or play with the ducks and geese in the creek, and tumble down and sleep in the sun or shade if he was weary; and in the winter, covered only by the same garment, to sit in the corner and parch corn, scatter it among the fowls and pigs, (his peers in the sphere of plantation rights) and occasionally ride on Dave's back or trot by his side, to the great house, (about the size of a moderate log cabin on the Onondaga Reserve) and have a frolic with him and "Granny," and perhaps stay over night.

It was the only schooling he ever enjoyed—for he was left to his own thoughts and invisible instructors. And though doubtless he came to as valuable intellectual results as any boy, it must be confessed the school was better adapted to physical than mental development. His tender muscles swelled and hardened with the severity of his voluntary exercise, and no boy on the plantation or in the neighborhood, black or white, could measure strength with him. Personally, he suffered no treatment from his masters which hinted to him that he was a slave.

But he was at school, and was not to eat and drink, and sleep and grow only—but to think also. The story of the deer was the first item in life's reality, gently pictured on the Canvas, which, ere long, was to be covered with black, ugly, and unendurable forms. As the days and months increased, the items multiplied. He saw little boys and girls brutally handled for deeds, and even no deeds, which he knew would not attract censure had he been the subject. In his day dreams, it puzzled him to know why he was secure and petted, while they were insecure and abused.

Forbearance and forgiveness, or any of the virtues of charity, find little root in the soil of slavery; but passion, revenge and violence come up as in a hot bed, and are familiar to every eye. The oft repeated sights, instead of darkening, sharpened the eye of Jarm, and stimulated his enquiry. They made him think the more. When, as near as he can guess, he arrived at the age of seven or eight years, loitering on the bank of the creek at the close of a summer's day, he saw his mother coming with unusual steps. It was obvious to Jarm that she was in distress, for her head, usually erect, was downcast, and her sighs and sobs were borne almost noiselessly on the light wind to the heart of her son.

"What is the matter?" with animated voice exclaimed Jarm.

The poor woman, absorbed by grief, had not noticed her darling; and was even thinking not to shock his young heart by appearing before him, until the depression which bent her down, and the crimson signals upon her person, had disappeared in the waters of Manscoe's Creek. The idea came too late. All trembling with indignant sorrow, surprise and love, at the sight of her boy, she rushed towards him, raised him from the ground, and pressing him to her bosom exclaimed in a voice of hysteric earnestness:

"Oh my poor boy, what will become of you?"

Jarm felt there was sadness and significance in her emphasis, altogether unusual, which, with the tremulous pressure of her embrace communicated a nervous sympathy to his heart, and was already changing his spirit by the influx of a new idea.

"What is the matter, mother, and what makes you bloody?" instantly asked the little boy.

"You will understand such things too soon. Don't ask me about it," replied the mother, as she sat him on his feet again, and let fall a drop of blood from her brow on the face of the child.

He wiped the stain away on his coarse shirt, and plied the enquiry with a concern which could not be resisted.

Fearing he would pursue the subject at the house, with the slaves, with Dave, and even with Carnes, and thereby involve himself and perhaps forfeit his future security by an alarming independence which was increasing with his years, and which was less likely to be indulged as her attractions and intimacy with Dave were failing, she determined to improve the occasion for his benefit. She trembled lest his unrestrained spirit should be an inconvenience to her oppressors, and that Dave would consent to the breaking it, by the same brutal treatment that other little colored children of the plantation suffered— or what was worse, that they would sell him at a distance to rid themselves of an annoyance—therefore she determined to satisfy his enquiries, and if possible, determine him to a prudent silence.

"Where is Jane?" a little girl two years younger than Jarm.

"I have just sent her to the house with the babe," replied Jarm—"but what is the matter, mother? Do tell me."

"Well, I will tell you" said she, "and I tell you that you may not speak of it to anybody, and especially that you do not let Mannasseth, Carnes, or even Dave, know that you know it. If you should speak to them about it, they will not treat you so well as they have done; and I fear they may whip you as they whip me; and what is very dreadful, I fear they will sell you to the slave drivers and I shall never see you again."

Cherry had not yet known the deep grief of parting with any of her children, and the fear of that heart-rending experience often tortured her spirit. She knew there was no dependence upon Manasseth and Carnes, and that her peril increased with the increasing dissipation and consequent embarrassment of all the white Logues.

Jarm had never seen his mother stricken, and his blood boiled when she gave the cause of her wounds and misery, and he asked fiercely "who whipped you?"

Cherry had effectually roused the indignation of her boy, and saw before her precisely the presence she feared he would one day exhibit to her masters, in view of the outrages inflicted on her or on himself. A change of relations which was being more apparent every day, made it not unlikely he would manifest the same spirit to them, and bring on himself one of those awful flagellations employed to crush the budding manhood of a slave. No premonition warns the undisciplined wretch of his fate. A display of just feeling and manly spirit, precisely what Cherry now saw in the swelling muscles of her son, was sufficient to subject him to cruel torture. To be a slave, he must cease to feel that he is a man.

The evidence of deep feeling which her words and appearance produced in the child induced her to make him acquainted with his true condition, so far as he could comprehend it, and if possible set him on guard against invisible dangers.

In answer to his enquiry, "who whipped you?" she said Carnes struck her on the head, and made the wound from which the blood dropped. She said that

Mannasseth and Carnes often whipped her, and even Dave had lately treated her roughly. She explained to him, his and her helpless condition—how she was stolen when a little child like himself, and left with "Granny," and the white Logues—how she was cruelly whipped for innocently stating her case to excite their justice and pity—and again charged him, with great earnestness, not to let it be known at the house that she had told him this, or that he knew anything about it—assuring him, that if the white Logues knew she had told him these things, they would whip him also, and may be sell him to the slave drivers, as they did little "Charley and Fanny," a few weeks previous. She told him that though Dave and old Granny now loved him, they would certainly hate him, if he pestered them with complaints regarding her wrongs—and that his doing so would bring upon her greater wrongs, and in the end upon himself the most terrible chastisement, and perhaps they would sell him away from her forever.

Jarm was now fully possessed of one other shocking idea, which though it determined his prudence as it excited his pity and fear, did not repress the swelling and burning current in his veins, which swept before it every lamb-like feeling. The case of the deer, shocked his pity deeply, but did not forbid utterance—but now, at the sight of his mother brutally mutilated, suffering, and bleeding, he was taught to stifle his sympathies and passions, clamoring, swelling, and almost bursting his heart for utterance. The incident was burned into his memory by the fire it kindled, and the incident and the fire will remain there forever.

Cherry went with him to the creek and washed the stains away as well as she could, then assuming an erect and cheerful position as possible, took her course, towards the cabin, requesting him to wait a while, and then follow on. Her interview with Jarm was a relief to her sad heart—she partook of her coarse meal, hugged her babe to her breast, and then care-worn and weary, cast herself on her bed of straw, and lapsed into oblivious and healing sleep.

Not so Jarm. This second chapter in the slave's life weighed upon his spirits and disturbed him. He was not old enough to comprehend its full import, but his understanding was sufficiently mature to receive and plant it deep in his memory, and shape his manners to its terrible demands. It had full possession of him, and it was sometime ere sleep closed his memory, and laid the surges of sorrow and anger that swelled within him.

The morning found Cherry composed, and Jarm too was soothed and refreshed by disturbed slumber. She went to her usual labors in the field, and he, after a breakfast of corn bread and bacon, sauntered away alone, to reconsider the lesson which was taught him, and study its philosophy and bearings. His daydreams and buoyancy were laid aside, and that day was spent in studying the alarming reality which stared him in the face.

Thus early was he forced to revolve matters of grave importance. His treatment by the white Logues was most difficult to reconcile with the perils which his mother thought was present with him. To his inexperience, the enigma was inscrutable—but the conclusion was irresistible, that he and his mother were linked to a common destiny, and he felt his heart grappled to hers with a force greatly increased by sympathy for her sorrows, and a strong conviction of common dangers. The causes which attached him to her weakened his attachment to her oppressors, which no evidence of kindness or affection on their part could prevent.

From this time forward, though left to dispose of his time and body as he willed, the clouds increased and thickened around him. Dave's favors and caresses were less frequent as the months and years came on, and in perfect recklessness of his presence, the most shocking and brutal outrages were inflicted on his mother. His masters were late at their carousals, and became more and more embruited as their affairs became embarrassed.

It was about this time that the family and neighborhood were agitated by Cherry's brave resistance and almost death of the licentious villain at the distillery, which were circumstantially related in the last chapter. This also served to confirm the story of his unhappy mother regarding the condition and danger of both, in the mind of her precocious and considerate child. The conversation among the slaves as well as among the whites, assured him, that not only his mother, but himself also, was at the mercy of every white man, and in case he or she resisted them, be their intents never so murderous, the whole power of Tennessee was pledged to their destruction. It was much talked of and well understood at Manscoe's Creek, that poor Cherry had forfeited her life to the law, and that she held it at the mercy of the ignorant, and passionate, and unscrupulous people about her.

The distance between Jarm and Dave widened as the intimacy between Cherry and Dave ceased. He soon brought to his home a white woman, who resided with him as a wife or a mistress, and by whom he afterwards had children. Nor did Jarm regret the separation from his mother. The events of every day convinced him that their intimacy and connection was forced and unnatural. His boyhood was social and buoyant, but it revolted from family relations which seemed pregnant with evil, and obviously destitute of mutual trust, affection and support. The current of causes was forcing the affections of the mother and son to a common center, and fusing them into one. He felt that she and their little ones were all the world to him.

He sympathised deeply with those who were in like condition with himself, but to his mother, brother and sisters he was attached by ties which none can appreciate, but those, who, in like condition, have felt them.

The spiritual changes which were now gradually forming the great gulph between him and the white Logues, allowed him more leisure for thought and physical development. His time was nearly all his own; and with maturer judgment, and greater strength, he pursued his game on the land and in the water. The harmony of woods and fields, of birds and flowers and bounding animals, gave birth to ideas that chimed with the angelic counsels of his mother but which, in the family of his oppressors were never felt or imagined.

1859

LETTER TO REV. J. W. LOGUEN, FROM HIS OLD MISTRESS, AND MR. LOGUEN'S REPLY

The following letter was received a day or two since by Rev. J.W. LOGUEN, of this city, from his old mistress 'way down in Tennessee.' The old lady is evidently 'hard up,' financially, and attempts to frighten her former servant into the payment of $1,000 as 'hush money.' We imagine she sent to the wrong man, as Mr. Loguen needs no 'bill of sale' to secure himself from capture in this section of the State. Besides his own stalwart arm, he has hosts of friends who would make this region too hot to hold the man-hunters who would venture on such an errand as the old lady hints at in her somewhat singular epistle. Her lamentations about the old mare are decidedly funny, (we may add womanly,) and all the misfortunes of the family are traced directly to the escape of 'Jarm.' But here is her letter:

MC,[1] State of Tennessee, Feb. 20, 1860.

To J:—

I now take my pen to write you a few lines, to let you know how we all are. I am a cripple, but I am still able to get about. The rest of the family are all well. Cherry is as well as common. I write you these lines to let you know the situation we are in,—partly in consequence of your running a way and stealing Old Rock, our fine mare. Though we got the mare back, she never was worth much after you took her;— and, as I now stand in need of some funds, I have determined to sell you, and I have had an offer for you, but did not see fit to take it. If you will send me one thousand dollars, and pay for the old mare, I will give up all claim I have to you. Write to me as soon as you get these lines, and let me know if you will accept my proposition. In consequence of your running away, we had to sell Abe and Ann and twelve acres of land; and I want you to send me the money, that I may be able to redeem the land that you was the cause of our selling, and on receipt of the above-named sum of money, I will send you your bill of sale. If you do not comply with my request, I will sell you to some one else, and you may rest assured that the time is not far distant when things will be changed with you. Write to me as soon as you get these lines. Direct your letter to Bigbyville, Maury County, Tennessee. You had better comply with my request.

I understand that you are a preacher. As the Southern people are so bad, you had better come and preach to your old acquaintances. I would like to know if you read your Bible. If so, can you tell what will become of the thief if he does not repent? And, if the blind lead the blind, what will the consequence be? I deem it unnecessary to say much more at present. A word to the wise is sufficient. You know where the liar has his part. You know that we reared you as we reared our own children; that you was never abused, and that shortly before you ran away, when your master asked you if you would like to be sold, you said you would not leave him to go with any body.

Sarah Logue

Rev. LOGUEN'S REPLY:

Mrs. Sarah Logue:—Yours of the 20th of February is duly received, and I thank you for it. It is a longtime since I heard from my poor old mother, and I am glad to know she is yet alive, and as you say, "as well as common." What that means I don't know. I wish you had said more about her.

You are a woman; but had you a woman's heart you could never have insulted a brother by telling him you sold his only remaining brother and sister, because he put himself beyond your power to convert him into money.

You sold my brother and sister, ABE and ANN, and 12 acres of land, you say, because I ran away. Now you have the unutterable meanness to ask me to return and be your miserable chattel, or in lieu thereof send you $1,000 to enable you to redeem the land, but not to redeem my poor brother and sister! If I were to send you money it would be to get my brother and sister, and not that you should get land. You say you are a cripple, and doubtless you say it to stir my pity, for you know I was susceptible in that direction. I do pity you from the bottom of my heart. Nevertheless I am indignant beyond the power of words to express, that you should be so sunken and cruel as to tear the hearts I love so much all in pieces; that you should be willing to impale and crucify us out of all compassion for your poor foot or leg. Wretched woman! Be it known to you that I value my freedom, to say nothing of my mother, brothers and sisters, more than your whole body; more, indeed, than my own life; more than all the lives of all the slaveholders and tyrants under Heaven.

You say you have offers to buy me, and that you shall sell me if I do not send you $1,000, and in the same breath and almost in the same sentence, you say, "you know we raised you as we did our own children." Woman, did you raise your own children for the market? Did you raise them for the whipping-post? Did you raise them to be drove off in a coffle in chains? Where are my poor bleeding brothers and sisters? Can you tell? Who was it that sent them off into sugar and cotton fields, to be kicked, and cuffed, and whipped, and to groan and die; and where no kin can hear their groans, or attend and sympathize at their dying bed, or follow in their funeral? Wretched woman! Do you say you did not do it? Then I reply, your husband did, and you approved the deed—and the very letter you sent me shows that your heart approves it all. Shame on you.

But, by the way, where is your husband? You don't speak of him. I infer, therefore, that he is dead; that he has gone to his great account, with all his sins against my poor family upon his head. Poor man! gone to meet the spirits of my poor, outraged and murdered people, in a world where Liberty and Justice are MASTERS.

But you say I am a thief, because I took the old mare along with me. Have you got to learn that I had a better right to the old mare, as you called her, than MANASSETH LOGUE had to me? Is it a greater sin for me to steal his horse, than it was for him to rob my mother's cradle and steal me? If he and you infer that I forfeit all my rights to you, shall not I infer that you forfeit all your rights to me? Have you got to learn that human rights are mutual and reciprocal, and if you take my liberty and life, you forfeit me your own liberty and life? Before God and High Heaven, is there a law for one man which is not law for every other man?

If you or any other speculator on my body and rights, wish to know how I regard my rights, they need but come here and lay their hands on me to enslave me. Did you think to terrify me by presenting the alternative to give my money to you, or give my body to Slavery? Then let me say to you, that I meet the proposition with unutterable scorn and contempt. The proposition is an outrage and an insult. I will not budge one hair's breadth. I will not breathe a shorter breath, even to save me from your persecutions. I stand among a free people, who, I thank God, sympathize with my rights, and the rights of mankind; and if your emissaries and venders come here to re-enslave me, and escape the unshrinking vigor of my own right arm, I trust my strong and brave friends, in this City and State, will be my rescuers and avengers.

Yours, &c.,

J. W. Loguen.

1860

NOTE

1. Maury County.

MARTIN R. DELANY (1812-1885)

Martin Robison Delany was born to an enslaved father and a free mother in what is now Charleston, West Virginia. In 1822, Delany's mother relocated with her children to Pennsylvania so that her children would have access to school. Delany pursued many occupations over the course of his lifetime. Apprenticed to a Pittsburgh physician in 1833, Delany practiced rudimentary medicine for several years before entering Harvard Medical School to complete his studies in the field. He was one of three African American men to enter the program; they were the first black students ever admitted. He was forced to withdraw after only two weeks, however, when the college capitulated to the will of white students who petitioned the administration to dismiss their black peers. During the Civil War, after meeting with President Abraham Lincoln, he was commissioned at the rank of Major in the Fifty-second U.S. Colored Troops Regiment, becoming the first African American line officer in the history of the U.S. military. Throughout his life, and whatever his occupation, Delany maintained a commitment to the creation and dissemination of anti-racist literature. In 1843, while living in Pittsburgh, he founded and edited *The Mystery,* a weekly newspaper that promoted black equality and civil rights. In 1847, he joined Frederick Douglass as coeditor of *The North Star.* Over the course of his lifetime, Delany would publish extensively on the subject of civil rights, including *The Condition, Elevation, Emigration, and Destiny of the Colored People of the United States, Politically Considered* (1852), considered by many to be the nation's first Black Nationalist text. Indeed, Delany's enthusiastic support for the colonization of West Africa by free U.S. blacks grew in large part out of his deeply held belief in African American political and economic self-determination and the related belief that such freedom could only be achieved through the establishment of an independent black nation. The following excerpt is reprinted from *Blake; or, the Huts of America* (1859), Delany's only novel. Serialized in early black publisher Thomas Hamilton's *Anglo-African Magazine, Blake* tells the story of Henry, an enslaved African American who returns from an out-of-town assignment to find that Maggie, his wife, has been sold. Written partially in response to the docile piety of the title character in Harriet Beecher Stowe's *Uncle Tom's Cabin, Blake* portrays both free and enslaved African Americans engaged in active resistance. In the following excerpt, protagonist Henry Blake, upon learning that his wife has been sold, escapes and begins organizing a slave rebellion.

BLAKE; OR, THE HUTS OF AMERICA

Chapter VI: Henry's Return

Early on Monday morning, a steamer was heard puffing up the Mississippi. Many who reside near the river, by custom can tell the name of every approaching boat by the peculiar sound of the steam-pipe, the one in the present instance being the Sultana.[1]

Daddy Joe had risen and just leaving for the plantation, but stopped a moment to be certain.

"Hush!" admonished mammy Judy, "Hush! Sho chile, do'n yeh heah how she hollah? Sholy dat's de wat's name! wat dat yeh call eh? 'Suckana,' wat not; sho! I ain' gwine bautha my head long so—sho! See, ole man see! Dah she come! See dat now! I tole yeh so, but yeh uden bleve me!" And the old man and woman stood for some minutes in breathless silence, although the boat must have been some five miles distant, as the escape of steam can be heard on the western waters a great way off.

The approach toward sunrise admonished daddy Joe of demands for him at the cotton farm, when after bidding "good monin' ole umin," he hurried to the daily task which lay before him.

Mammy Judy had learned--by the boy Tony--that Henry was expected on the "Sultana," and at the approach of every steamer, her head had been thrust out of the door or window to catch a distinct sound. In motionless attitude after the departure of her husband this morning, the old woman stood awaiting the steamer, when presently the boat arrived. But then to be certain that it was the expected vessel—now came the suspense.

The old woman was soon relieved from this most disagreeable of all emotions, by the cry of news boys returning from the wharf.

"'Ere's the Picayune, Atlas, Delta![2] lates' news from New Orleans by the swift steamer Sultana!"

"Dah now!" exclaimed mammy Judy in soliloquy; "Dah now! I tole yeh so! —de wat's name come!" Hurrying into the kitchen, she waited with anxiety the arrival of Henry.

Busying about the breakfast for herself and other servants about the house—the white members of the family all being absent—mammy Judy for a time lost sight of the expected arrival. Soon however, a hasty footstep arrested her attention, when on looking around it proved to be Henry who came smiling up the yard.

"How'd you do mammy! How's Mag' and the boy?" inquired he, grasping the old woman by the hand.

She burst into a flood of tears, throwing herself upon him.

"What is the matter!" exclaimed Henry. "Is Maggie dead?"

"No chile," with increased sobs she replied, "much betteh she wah."

"My God! Has she disgraced herself?"

"No chile, may be betteh she dun so, den she bin heah now an' not sole. Maus Stephen sell eh case she!—I dun'o, reckon dat's da reason!"

"What!—Do you tell me, mammy, she had better disgraced herself than been sold! By the—!"

"So, Henry! yeh ain' gwine swah! hope yeh ain' gwine lose yeh 'ligion? Do'n do so; put yeh trus' in de Laud, he is suffishen fah all!"

"Don't tell me about religion! What's religion to me? My wife is sold away from me by a man who is one of the leading members of the very church to which both she and I belong! Put my trust in the Lord! I have done so all my life nearly, and of what use is it to me? My wife is sold from me just the same as if I didn't. I'll—"

"Come, come, Henry, yeh mus'n talk so; we is po'weak an' bline cretehs, an' cah see de way uh da Laud. He move' in a mystus way, his wundahs to puhfaum."

"So he may, and what is all that to me? I don't gain anything by it, and—"

"Stop, Henry, stop! Ain' de Laud bless yo' soul? Ain' he take yeh foot out de miah an' clay, an' gib yeh hope da uddah side dis vale ub teahs?"

"I'm tired looking the other side; I want a hope this side of the vale of tears. I want something on this earth as well as a promise of things in another world. I and my wife have been both robbed of our liberty, and you want me to be satisfied with a hope of heaven. I won't do any such thing; I have waited long enough on heavenly promises; I'll wait no longer. I—"

"Henry, wat do mauttah wid yeh? I neveh heah yeh talk so fo'—yeh sin in de sight ub God; yeh gone clean back, I reckon. De good Book tell us, a tousan' yeahs wid man am but a day wid de Laud. Boy, yeh got wait de Laud own pinted time."

"Well mammy, it is useless for me to stand here and have the same gospel preached into my ears by you, that I have all my life time heard from my enslavers. My mind is made up, my course is laid out, and if life last, I'll carry it out: I'll go out to the place to-day, and let them know that I have returned."

"Sho boy! What yeh gwine do, bun house down? Bettah put yeh trus' in de Laud!" concluded the old woman.

"You have too much religion, mammy, for me to tell you what I intend doing," said Henry in conclusion.

After taking up his little son, impressing on his lips and cheeks kisses for himself and tears for his mother, the intelligent slave left the abode of the care-worn old woman, for that of his master at the cotton place.

Henry was a black—a pure negro—handsome, manly and intelligent, in size comparing well with his master, but neither so fleshy nor heavy built in person. A man of good literary attainments—unknown to Col. Franks, though he was aware he could read and write—having been educated in the West Indies, and decoyed away when young. His affection for wife and child was not excelled by Colonel Franks for his. He was bold, determined and courageous, but always mild, gentle and courteous, though impulsive when an occasion demanded his opposition.

Going immediately to the place, he presented himself before his master. Much conversation ensued concerning the business which had been entrusted to his charge, all of which was satisfactorily transacted, and full explanations concerning the horses, but not a word was uttered concerning the fate of Maggie, the Colonel barely remarking "your mistress is unwell."

After conversing till a late hour, Henry was assigned a bed in the great house, but sleep was far from his eyes. He turned and changed upon his bed with restlessness and anxiety, impatiently awaiting a return of the morning.

Chapter VII: Master and Slave

Early on Tuesday morning, in obedience to his master's orders, Henry was on his way to the city to get the house in readiness for the reception of his mistress, Mrs. Franks having much improved in three or four days. Mammy Judy had not yet risen when he knocked at the door.

"Hi Henry! Yeh heah ready! Huccum yeh git up so soon; arter some mischif I reckon? Do'n reckon yeh arter any good!" saluted Mammy Judy.

"No mammy," replied he; "no mischief, but like a good slave such as you wish me to be, come to obey my master's will, just what you like to see."

"Sho boy! None yeh nonsens'; huccum I want yeh bey maus Stephen? Git dat nonsens' in yeh head las' night long so, I reckon! Wat dat yeh gwine do now?"

"I have come to dust and air the mansion for their reception. They have sold my wife away from we, and who else would do her work?" This reply excited the apprehension of Mammy Judy.

"Wat yeh gwine do Henry? Yeh arter no good; yeh ain' gwine 'tack maus Stephen is yeh?"

"What do you mean mammy, strike him?"

"Yes! reckon yeh ain' gwine hit 'im?"

"Curse—!"

"Henry, Henry, membeh wat ye 'fess! Fah de Laud sake, yeh ain gwine take to swahin?" interrupted the old woman.

"I make no profession, mammy. I once did believe in religion, but now I have no confidence in it. My faith has been wrecked on the stony hearts of such pretended Christians as Stephen Franks, while passing through the stormy sea of trouble and oppression! And—"

"Hay, boy! Yeh is gittin high! Yeh call maussa 'Stephen?'"

"Yes, and I'll never call him 'master' again, except when compelled to do so."

"Bettah g'long ten' t' de house fo' wite folks come, an' nebeh mine talkin' 'bout fightin' 'long wid maus Stephen. Wat yeh gwine do wid white folks? Sho!"

"I don't intend to fight him, mammy Judy, but I'll attack him concerning my wife, if the words be my last. Yes, I'll—!" and pressing his lips to suppress the words, the outraged man turned away from the old slave mother, with such feelings as only an intelligent slave could realize.

The orders of the morning were barely executed, when the carriage came to the door. The bright eyes of the foot boy Tony sparkled when he saw Henry approaching the carriage.

"Well Henry! ready for us?" enquired his master.

"Yes sir, " was the simple reply. "Mistress!" he saluted, politely bowing as he took her hand to assist her from the carriage.

"Come Henry, my man, get out the riding horses," ordered Franks after a little rest.

"Yes sir."

A horse for the Colonel and lady each, was soon in readiness at the door, but none for himself, it always having been the custom in their morning rides, for the maid and man-servant to accompany the mistress and master.

"Ready did you say?" enquired Franks on seeing but two horses standing at the stile.

"Yes sir."

"Where's the other horse?"

"What for sir?"

"What for? yourself to be sure!"

"Colonel Franks!" said Henry, looking him sternly in the face, "when I last rode that horse in company with you and lady, my wife was at my side, and I will not now go without her! Pardon me—my life for it, I won't go!"

"Not another word you black imp!" exclaimed Franks, with an uplifted staff in a rage, "or I'll strike you down in an instant!"

"Strike away if you will sir, I dont care—I wont go without my wife!"

"You impudent scoundrel! I'll soon put an end to your conduct! I'll put you on the auction block, and sell you to the negro traders."

"Just as soon as you please sir, the sooner the better, as I dont want to live with you any longer!"

"Hold your tongue sir, or I'll cut it out of your head! you ungrateful black dog! Really things have come to a pretty pass, when I must take impudence off my own negro! By gracious!—God forgive me for the expression—I'll sell every negro I have first! I'll dispose of him to the hardest negro trader I can find!" said Franks in a rage.

"You may do your mightiest, colonel Franks. I'm not your slave, nor never was, and you know it! and but for my wife and her people, I never would have stayed with you till now. I was decoyed away when young, and then became entangled in such domestic relations as to induce me to remain with you; but now the tie is broken! I know that the odds are against me, but never mind!"

"Do you threaten me, sir! Hold your tongue, or I'll take your life instantly, you villain!"

"No sir, I dont threaten you, colonel Franks, but I do say that I won't be treated like a dog. You sold my wife away from me, after always promising that she should be free. And more than that, you sold her because—! and now you talk about whipping me. Shoot me, sell me, or do anything else you please, but dont lay your hands on me, as I will not suffer you to whip me!"

Running up to his chamber, colonel Franks seized a revolver, when Mrs. Franks grasping hold of his arm exclaimed—

"Colonel! what does all this mean?"

"Mean, my dear? It's rebellion! a plot—this is but the shadow of a cloud that's fast gathering around us! I see it plainly, I see it!" responded the Colonel, starting for the stairs.

"Stop Colonel!" admonished his lady, "I hope you'll not be rash. For Heaven's sake, do not stain your hands in blood!"

"I do not mean to, my dear! I take this for protection!" Franks hastening down stairs, when Henry had gone into the back part of the premises.

"Dah now! dah now!" exclaimed mammy Judy as Henry entered the kitchen, "see wat dis gwine back done foh yeh! Bettah put yo' trus' in de Laud! Henry, yeh gone clean back t'de wuhl ghin, yeh knows it!"

"You're mistaken mammy, I do trust the Lord as much as ever, but I now understand him better than I use to, that's all. I dont intend to be made a fool of any longer by false preaching."

"Henry!" interrogated Daddy Joe, who apprehending difficulties in the case, had managed to get back to the house, "yeh gwine lose all yo' ligion? Wat yeh, mean boy!"

"Religion!" replied Henry rebukingly, "that's always the cry with black people. Tell me nothing about religion when the very man who hands you the bread at communion, has sold your daughter away from you!"

"Den yeh 'fen' God case man 'fen' yeh! Take cah Henry, take cah! mine wat yeh 'bout; God is lookin' at yeh, an' if yeh no' willin' trus' 'im, yeh need'n call on 'im in time o' trouble."

"I dont intend, unless He does more for me then than he has done before. 'Time of need!' If ever man needed his assistance, I'm sure I need it now."

"Yeh do'n know wat yeh need; de Laud knows bes.' On'y trus' in 'im, an' 'e bring yeh out mo' nah conkah. By de help o' God I's heah dis day, to gib yeh cumfut!"

"I have trusted in Him daddy Joe, all my life, as I told mammy Judy this morning, but—"

"Ah boy, yeh's gwine back! Dat on't do Henry, dat on't do!"

"Going, back from what? my oppressor's religion! If I could only get rid of his inflictions as easily as I can his religion, I would be this day a free man, when you might then talk to me about 'trusting.'"

"Dis Henry, am one uh de ways ob de Laud; 'e fus 'flicks us an' den he bless us."

"Then it's a way I dont like."

"Mine how yeh talk, boy!"

"God moves in a myst'us way

His wundahs to pehfaum, an—"

"He moves too slow for me daddy Joe; I'm tired waiting so—"

"Come Henry, I hab no sich talk like dat! yeh is gittin' rale weaked; yeh gwine let de debil take full 'session on yeh! Take cah boy, mine how yeh talk!"

"It is not wickedness, daddy Joe; you dont understand these things at all. If a thousand years with us is but a day with God, do you think that I am required to wait all that time?"

"Dont Henry, dont! de wud say 'Stan' still an' see de salbation.'"

"That's no talk for me daddy Joe, I've been 'standing still' long enough; I'll 'stand still' no longer."

"Den yeh no call t' bey God wud? Take cah boy, take cah!"

"Yes I have, and I intend to obey it, but that part was intended for the Jews, a people long since dead. I'll obey that intended for me."

"How yeh gwine bey it?"

"Now is the accepted time, to-day is the day of salvation." So you see, daddy Joe, this is very different to standing still."

"Ah boy, I's feahed yeh's losen yeh 'ligion!"

"I tell you once and for all daddy Joe, that I'm not only 'losing,' but I have altogether lost my faith in the religion of my oppressors, As they are our religious teachers, my estimate of the things they give, is no greater than it is for those who give it."

With elbows upon his knees, and face resting in the palms of his hands, daddy Joe for some time sat with his eyes steadily fixed on the floor, whilst Ailcey who for a part of the time had been an auditor to the conversation, went into the house about her domestic duties.

"Never mind Henry! I hope it will not always be so with you. You have been kind and faithful to me and the Colonel, and I'll do anything I can for you!" sympathetically said Mrs. Franks, who having been a concealed spectator of the interview between Henry and the old people, had just appeared before them.

Wiping away the emblems of grief which stole down his face with a deep toned voice, upgushing from the recesses of a more than iron-pierced soul, he enquired—

"Madam, what can you do! Where is my wife?" To this, Mrs. Franks gave a deep sigh. "Never mind, never mind!" continued he, "yes, I will mind, and by—!"

"O! Henry, I hope you've not taken to swearing! I do hope you will not give over to wickedness! Our afflictions should only make, our faith the stronger."

"'Wickedness!' Let the righteous correct the wicked, and the Christian condemn the sinner!"

"That is uncharitable in you Henry! as you know I have always treated you kindly, and God forbid that I should consider myself any less than a Christian! and I claim as much at least for the Colonel, though like frail mortals he is liable to err at times."

"Madam!" said he with suppressed emotion—starting back a pace or two— "do you think there is anything either in or out of hell so wicked, as that which Colonel Franks has done to my wife, and now about to do to me? For myself I care not—my wife!"

"Henry!" said Mrs. Franks, gently placing her hand upon his shoulder, "there is yet a hope left for you, and you will be faithful enough I know, not to implicate any person; it is this: Mrs. Van Winter, a true friend of your race, is shortly going to Cuba on a visit, and I will arrange with her to purchase you through an agent on the day of your sale, and by that means you can get to Cuba, where probably you may be fortunate enough to get the master of your wife to become your purchaser."

"Then I have two chances!" replied Henry.

Just then Ailcey, thrusting her head in the door, requested the presence of her mistress in the parlor.

Chapter VIII: The Sale

"Dah now, dah now!" exclaimed mammy Judy; "jis wat ole man been-tellin' on yeh! Yeh go out yandah, yeh kick up yeh heel, git yeh head clean full proclamation an' sich like dat, an' let debil fool yeh, den go fool long wid wite folks long so, sho! Bettah go 'bout yeh bisness; been sahvin' God right, yeh no call t'do so eh reckon!"

"I dont care what comes! My course is laid out and my determination fixed, and nothing they can do can alter it. So you and daddy Joe, mammy, had just as well quit your preaching to me the religion you have got from your oppressors."

"Soul-driveh git yeh, yeh cah git way fom dem eh doh reckon! Sho chile, yeh, ain' dat mighty!" admonished mammy Judy.

"Henry my chile, look to de Laud! look to de Laud? case 'e 'lone am able t' bah us up in ouah trouble! An—"

"Go directly sir, to captain John Harris' office and ask him to call immediately to see me at my house!" ordered Franks.

Politely bowing, Henry immediately left the premises on his errand.

"Laud a' messy maus Stephen!" exclaimed mammy Judy, on hearing the name of John Harris the negro-trader; "hope yeh arteh no haum! gwine sell all on us to de tradehs?"

"Hoot-toot, hoot-toot! Judy, give yourself no uneasiness about that, till you have some cause for it. So you and Joe may rest contented Judy," admonished Franks.

"Tank'e maus Stephen! case ah heahn yeh tell Henry dat yeh sell de las' nig—"

"Hush! ole umin, hush! yeh tongue too long! Put yeh trus' in de Laud!" interrupted daddy Joe.

"I treat my black folks well," replied Franks; "and all they have to—"

Here the door bell having been rung, he was interrupted with a message from Ailcey, that a gentleman awaited his presence in the parlor.

At the moment which the Colonel left the kitchen, Henry stepped over the style into the yard, which at once disclosed who the gentleman was to whom the master had been summoned. Henry passed directly around and behind the house.

"See, ole man, see! reckon 'e gwine dah now!" whispered mammy Judy, on seeing Henry pass through the yard without going into the kitchen.

"Whah?" enquired daddy Joe.

"Dun'o out yandah, whah 'e gwine way from wite folks!" she replied.

The interview between Franks and the trader Harris was not over half an hour duration, the trader retiring, Franks being prompt and decisive in all of his transactions, making little ceremony.

So soon as the front door was closed, Ailcey smiling bore into the kitchen a half pint glass of brandy, saying that her master had sent it to the old people.

The old man received it with compliments to his master, pouring it into a black jug in which there was both tansy and garlic, highly recommending it as a "bitters" and certain antidote for worms, for which purpose he and the old woman took of it as long as it lasted, though neither had been troubled with that particular disease since the days of their childhood.

"Wat de gwine do wid yeh meh son?" enquired mammy Judy as Henry entered the kitchen.

"Sell me to the soul-drivers! what else would they do?"

"Yeh gwin 'tay 'bout till de git yeh?"

"I shant move a step! and let them do their—"

"Maus wants to see yeh in da front house Henry," interrupted Ailcey, he immediately obeying the summons.

"Heah dat now!" said mammy Judy, as Henry followed the maid out of the kitchen.

"Carry this note sir, directly to captain Jack Harris!" ordered Franks, handing to Henry a sealed note. Receiving it, he bowed politely, going out of the front door, directly to the slave prison of Harris.

"Eh heh! I see," said Harris on opening the note; "Colonel Frank's boy; walk in here;" passing through the office into a room which proved to be the first department of the slave-prison. "No common negro I see! you're a shade higher. A pretty deep shade too! Can read, write cipher; a good religious fellow, and has a Christian and sir name. The devil you say! Who's your father? Can you preach?"

"I have never tried," was the only reply.

"Have you ever been a member of Congress?" continued Harris with ridicule.

To this Henry made no reply.

"Wont answer hey! beneath your dignity. I understand that you're of that class of gentry who dont speak to common folks! You're not quite well enough dressed for a gentleman of your cloth. Here! Mr. Henry, I'll present you with a set of ruffles: give yourself no trouble sir, as I'll dress you! I'm here for that purpose," said Harris, fastening upon the wrists of the manly bondman, a heavy pair of handcuffs.

"You hurt my wrist!" admonished Henry.

"New clothing will be a little tight when first put on. Now sir!" continued the trader, taking him to the back door and pointing into the yard at the slave gang there confined; "as you have been respectably dressed, walk out and enjoy yourself among the ladies and gentleman there; you'll find them quite a select company."

Shortly after this the sound of the bell-ringers voice was heard—a sound which usually spread terror among the slaves: "Will be sold this afternoon at three o'clock by public outcry, at the slave-prison of captain John Harris, a likely choice negro-fellow, the best trained body servant in the state, trained to the business by the most accomplished lady and gentleman negro-trainers in the Mississippi Valley. Sale positive without a proviso."

"Dah, dah! did'n eh tell yeh so? Ole man, ole man! heah dat now! Come heah. Dat jis what I been tellin on im, but 'e uden blieve me!" ejaculated old mammy Judy on hearing the bell ring and the hand bill read.

Falling upon their knees, the two old slaves prayed fervently to God, thanking him that it was as "well with them" as it was.

"Bless de Laud! my soul is happy!" cried out mammy Judy being overcome with devotion, clapping her hands.

"Tang God, fah wat I feels in my soul!" responded daddy Joe.

Rising from their knees with tears trickling down their checks, the old slaves endeavored to case their troubled souls by singing—

Oh, when shall my sorrows subside,
And when shall my troubles be ended;
And when to the bosom of Christ be conveyed,
To the mansions of joy and bliss;
To the mansions of joy and bliss!

"Wuhthy to be praise! blessed be de name uh de Laud! Po' black folks, de Laud o'ny knows wats t' come ob us!" exclaimed mammy Judy.

"Look to de Laud ole umin, 'e's able t' bah us out mo' neh conkeh. Keep de monin stah in sight!" advised daddy Joe.

"Yes ole man yes, dat I is done dis many long day, an' ah' ain' gwine lose sight uh it now! No, God bein' my helpeh, I is gwine keep my eyes right on it, dat I is!"

As the hour of three drew near, many there were going in the direction of the slave-prison, a large number of persons having assembled at the sale.

"Draw near, gentlemen! draw near!" cried Harris; "the hour of sale is arrived: a positive sale with no proviso, cash down, or no sale at all!" A general laugh succeeded the introduction of the auctioneer.

"Come up here my lad!" continued the auctioneer, wielding a long red rawhide; "mount this block, stand beside me, an let's see which is the best looking man! We have met before, but I never had the pleasure of introducing you. Gentlemen one and all, I take pleasure in introducing to you Henry— pardon me sir—Mr. Henry Holland, I, believe—am I right sir?—Mr. Henry Holland, a good looking fellow you will admit."

"I am offered one thousand dollars; one thousand dollars for the best looking negro in all Mississippi! If all the negro boys in the state was as good looking as him, I'd give two thousand dollars for 'em all myself!"

This caused another laugh. "Who'll give me one thousand five—"

Just then a shower of rain came on.

"Gentlemen!" exclaimed the auctioneer; "without a place can be obtained large enough to shelter the people here assembled, the sale will have to be postponed. This is a proviso we could'nt foresee, an' therefore is not responsible for it." There was another hearty laugh.

A whisper went through the crowd, when presently a gentleman came forward saying, that those concerned had kindly tendered the use of the Church which stood near by, in which to continue the sale.

"Here we are again, gentlemen! Who bids five hundred more for the likely negro fellow? I am offered fifteen hundred dollars for the finest negro servant in the state! Come my boy bestir yourself an' dont stan' there like a statue; cant you give us a jig? whistle us a song! I forgot, the negro fellow is religious; by the by, an excellent recommendation gentlemen. Perhaps he'll give us a sermon. Say, git up there old fellow, an' hold forth. Cant you give us a sermon on Abolition? I'm only offered fifteen hundred dollars for the likely negro boy! Fifteen, sixteen, sixteen hundred dollars, seventeen hundred, just agoing at—eighteen, eighteen, nineteen hundred, nineteen nineteen! Just agoing at nineteen hundred dollars for the best body servant in the State; just a-going; at nineteen and without a better bid I'll—going! going! Go—!"

Just at this point a note was passed up the aisle to the auctioneer, who after reading it said:

"Gentlemen! circumstances beyond my control, make it necessary that the sale be postponed until one day next week; the time of continuance will be duly announced," when bowing he left the stand.

"That's another proviso not in the original bill!" exclaimed a voice as the auctioneer left the stand, at which there were peals of laughter.

To secure himself against contingency, Harris immediately delivered Henry over to Franks.

There were present at the sale, Crow, Slider, Walker, Borbridge, Simpson, Hurst, Spangler and Williams, all noted slave traders, eager to purchase, some on their return home, and some with their gangs en route for the southern markets.

The note handed the auctioneer read thus:

CAPT. HARRIS:—Having learned that there are private individuals at the sale, who design purchasing my negro man, Harry, for his own personal advantage, you will peremptorily postpone the sale—making such apology as the occasion demands—and effect a private sale with Richard Crow, Esq., who offers me two thousand dollars for him. Let the boy return to me. Believe me to be,

Very Respectfully,
STEPHEN FRANKS.
Capt. John Harris.
Natchez, Nov. 20th, 1852.'

"Now sir," said Franks to Henry, who had barely reached the house from the auction block; "take this pass and go to Jackson and Woodville, or anywhere else you wish to see your friends, so that you be back against Monday afternoon. I ordered a postponement of the sale, thinking that I would try you awhile longer, as I never had cause before to part with you, Now see if you can't be a better boy!"

Eagerly taking the note, thanking him with a low bow, turning away, Henry opened the paper, which read:

Permit the bearer, my boy Henry, sometimes calling himself Henry Holland—a kind of negro pride he has—to pass and repass wherever he wants to go, he behaving himself properly.

STEPHEN FRANKS.
To all whom it may concern.
Natchez, Nov. 29th 1852.

Carefully depositing the charte volante in his pocket wallet, Henry quietly entered the hut of mammy Judy and daddy Joe.

Chapter IX: The Runaway

"De Laud's good—bless his name!" exclaimed mammy Judy wringing her hands as Henry entered their hut, "'e heahs do prahs ob 'is chilen. Yeh hab reason t' tang God yeh is heah dis day!"

"Yes Henry, see wat de Laud's done fah yeh. Tis true's I's heah dis day! Tang God fah dat!" added daddy Joe.

"I think," replied he after listening with patience to the old people, "I have reason to thank our Ailcey and Van Winter's Biddy; they, it seems to me should have some credit in the matter."

"Sho boy, g' long whah yeh gwine! Yo' backslidin, gwine git yeh in trouble ghin eh reckon?" replied mammy Judy.

Having heard the conversation between her mistress and Henry, Ailcey as a secret, informed Van Winter's Derba, who informed her fellow servant Biddy, who imparted it to her acquaintance Nelly, the slave of esquire Potter, Nelly informing her mistress, who told the 'Squire, who led Franks into the secret of the whole matter.

"Mus'n blame me, Henry!" said Ailcey in an undertone, "I did'n mean de wite folks to know wat I tole Derba, nor she di'n mean it nether, but dat devil, Pottah's Nell! us gals mean da fus time we ketch uh out, to duck uh in da rivah! She's rale wite folk's nigga, dat's jus' wat she is. Nevah mine, we'll ketch her yit!"

"I dont blame you Ailcey, nor either of Mrs. Van Winter's girls, as I know that you are my friends, neither of whom would do anything knowingly to injure me. I know Ailcey that you are a good girl, and believe you would tell me—"

"Yes Henry, I is yo' fren' an' come to tell yell now wat da wite folks goin' to do."

"What is it Ailcey; what do you know?"

"Wy dat ugly ole devil Dick Crow— God fah gim me! but I hate 'im so, case he nothin' but po' wite man, no how— I know 'im he come from Fagina on—"

"Never mind his origin, Ailcey, tell me what you know concerning his visit in the house."

"I is goin' to, but da ugly ole devil, I hates 'im so! Maus Stephen had 'im in da pahla, an' 'e sole yeh to 'im, dat ugly ole po' wite devil, fah—God knows how much—a hole heap a money; 'two' somethin."

"I know what it was, two thousand dollars, for that was his selling price to Jack Harris."

"Yes, dat was da sum, Henry."

"I am satisfied as to how much he can be relied on. Even was I to take the advice of the old people here, and become reconciled to drag out a miserable life of degradation and bondage under them, I would not be permitted to do so by this man, who seeks every opportunity to crush out my lingering manhood, and reduce my free spirit to the submission of a slave. He cannot do it, I will not submit to it, and I defy his power to make me submit."

"Laus a messy, Henry, yeh free man! huccum yeh not tell me long'o? Sho boy, bettah go long whah yeh gwine, out yandah, an' not fool long wid wite folks!" said mammy Judy with surprise, "wat bring yeh heah anyhow?"

"That's best known to myself, mammy."

"Wat make yeh keep heah so long den, dat yeh ain' gone fo' dis?"

"Your questions become rather pressing mammy; I cant tell you that either."

"Laud, Laud, Laud! So yeh free man? Well, well, well!"

"Once for all, I now tell you old people, what I never told you before, nor never expected to tell you under such circumstances; that I never intend, to serve any white man again. I'll die first!"

"De Laud a' messy on my po' soul! An' huccum yeh not gone befo'?"

"Carrying out the principles and advice of you old people 'standing still, to see the salvation.' But with me, 'now is the accepted time, to-day is the day of salvation.'"

"Well, well, well!" sighed mammy Judy.

"I am satisfied that I am sold, and the wretch who did it, seeks to conceal his perfidy by deception. Now if ever you old people did anything in your lives, you must do it now."

"Wat dat yeh want wid us?"

"Why, if you'll go, I'll take you on Saturday night, and make our escape to a free country."

"Wat place yeh call dat?"

"Canada!" replied Henry, with emotion.

"How fah yeh gwine take me?" earnestly enquired the old woman.

"I cant just now tell the distance, probably some two or three thousand miles from here, the way we'd have to go."

"De Laus a messy on me! an' wat yeh gwine do wid little Joe; ain gwine leave 'im behine?"

"No, mammy Judy, I'd bury him in the bottom of the river first! I intend carrying him in a bundle on my back, as the Indians carry their babies."

"Wat yeh gwine do fah money; yeh ain' gwine rob folks on de road?"

"No mammy, I'll starve first. Have you and daddy Joe saved nothing from your black-eye peas and poultry selling for many years?"

"Ole man, how much in dat pot undeh de flo' dah; how long since yeh count it?"

"Don'o," replied daddy Joe, "las' time ah count it, da, wah faughty guinea."[3]

"uh sich a mauttah, an' ah put in some six-seven guinea mo' since dat."

"Then you have some two hundred and fifty dollars in money."

"Dat do yeh?" enquired mammy Judy.

"Yes, that of itself is enough, but—"

"Den take it an' go long whah yeh gwine; we ole folks too ole fah gwine headlong out yandah an' don'o whah we gwine. Sho boy! take de money an' g'long!" decisively replied the old woman after all her inquisitiveness.

"If you dont know, I do mammy, and that will answer for all."

"Dat ain' gwine do us. We ole folks ain' politishon an' undehstan' de graumma uh dese places, an' w'en we git dah den maybe do'n like it an cahn' git back. Sho chile, go long whah yeh gwine!"

"What do you say, daddy Joe? Whatever you have to say, must be said quick, as time with me is precious."

"We is too ole dis time a-day chile, t'go way out yauah de Laud knows whah; bettah whah we is."

"You'll not be too old to go if these whites once take a notion to sell you. What will you do then?"

"Trus' to de Laud!"

"Yes, the same old slave song—'Trust to the Lord.' Then I must go and—"

"Ain' yeh gwine take de money Henry?" interrupted the old woman.

"No mammy, since you will not go, I leave it for you and daddy Joe, as you may yet have use for it, or those may desire to use it, who better understand what use to make of it than you and daddy Joe seem willing to be instructed in."

"Den yeh 'ont have de money?"

"I thank you and daddy most kindly, mammy Judy, for your offer, and only refuse because I have two hundred guineas about me."

"Sho boy, yeh got all dat, yeh no call t'want dat little we got. Whah yeh git all dat money? Do'n reckon yeh gwine tell me! Did'n steal from maus Stephen, do'n reckon?"

"No mammy I'm incapable of stealing from any one, but I have, from time to time, taken by littles, some of the earnings due me for more than eighteen years' service to this man Franks, which at the low rate of two hundred dollars a year, would amount to sixteen hundred dollars more than I secured, exclusive of the interest, which would have more than supplied my clothing, to say nothing of the injury done me by degrading me as a slave. 'Steal' indeed! I would that when I had an opportunity, I had taken fifty thousand instead of two. I am to understand you old people as positively declining to go, am I?"

"No no, chile, we cahn go! We put ouh trus' in de Laud, he bring us out mo' nah conkah."

"Then from this time hence, I become a runaway. Take care of my poor boy while he's with you. When I leave the swamps, or where I'll go, will never be known to you. Should my boy be suddenly missed, and you find three notches cut in the bark of the big willow tree, on the side away from your hut, then give yourself no uneasiness; but if you don't find these notches in the tree, then I know nothing about him. Good bye!" and Henry strode directly for the road to Woodville.

"Fahwell me son, fah well, an' may God a'mighty go wid you! May de Laud guide an tect yeh on de way!"

The child, contrary to his custom, commenced crying, desiring to see mama Maggie and dadda Henry. Every effort to quiet him was unavailing. This brought sorrow to the old people's hearts and tears to their eyes, which they endeavored to soothe in a touching lamentation:

See wives and husbands torn apart,
Their children's screams, they grieve my heart.
They are torn away to Georgia!
Come and go along with me—
They are torn away to Georgia!
Go sound the Jubilee!

1859

NOTES

1. One of several steamers of the same name that traveled the route between St. Louis and New Orleans.

2. New Orleans area newspapers of the mid- to late-nineteenth century.

3. "Guinea" with the slave, is a five dollar gold piece [Delany's note].

HARRIET E. WILSON (1825?–1863?)

Harriet E. Wilson was born in Milford, New Hampshire, to Joshua Green, an African American barrel maker, and Margaret Adams, a white laundress. At the age of four or five, following the death of her father, she was bound out as a servant to the family of Nehemiah Hayward, a local landholder. Wilson had little formal education, attending Milford's District School Number Three sporadically, from the age of seven to the age of nine. Wilson is best known for her 1859 novella *Our Nig, or, Sketches from the Life of a Free Black,* published by the Boston-based Geo. C. Rand and Avery Company. The novel was rediscovered and authenticated in the early 1980s by prominent African American literature scholar Henry Louis Gates Jr. However, the relationship between events in the text and the life of the writer, remains unclear. The details of Wilson's childhood seem to correspond with the experiences of her young protagonist. After she reaches adulthood, however, the trajectory of Wilson's life becomes more difficult to discern. For example, it is possible that Wilson remained a domestic servant in northern New England for the balance of her working life. Some evidence, however, seems to suggest that she went on to establish a successful career as a Boston spiritualist and medium. That Wilson's novel was published in Boston has led many to conclude that she did, in fact, settle in that city, but literary historian R. J. Ellis points out that the location of a writer's publisher does not necessarily correspond with the location of the writer. The following excerpt from the novella describes the early life of Wilson's protagonist who, like the author herself, was abandoned by her mother.

OUR NIG: SKETCHES FROM THE LIFE OF A FREE BLACK

Chapter I: Mag Smith, My Mother

> Oh, Grief beyond all other griefs, when fate
> First leaves the young heart lone and desolate
> In the wide world, without that only tie

For which it loved to live or feared to die;
Lorn as the hung-up lute, that ne'er hath spoken
Since the sad day its master-chord was broken!
    MOORE.[1]

Lonely Mag Smith! See her as she walks with downcast eyes and heavy heart. It was not always thus. She had a loving, trusting heart. Early deprived of parental guardianship, far removed from relatives, she was left to guide her tiny boat over life's surges alone and inexperienced. As she merged into womanhood, unprotected, uncherished, uncared for, there fell on her ear the music of love, awakening an intensity of emotion long dormant. It whispered of an elevation before unaspired to; of ease and plenty her simple heart had never dreamed of as hers. She knew the voice of her charmer, so ravishing, sounded far above her. It seemed like an angel's, alluring her upward and onward. She thought she could ascend to him and become an equal. She surrendered to him a priceless gem, which he proudly garnered as a trophy, with those of other victims, and left her to her fate. The world seemed full of hateful deceivers and crushing arrogance. Conscious that the great bond of union to her former companions was severed, that the disdain of others would be insupportable, she determined to leave the few friends she possessed, and seek an asylum among strangers. Her offspring came unwelcomed, and before its nativity numbered weeks, it passed from earth, ascending to a purer and better life.

"God be thanked," ejaculated Mag, as she saw its breathing cease; "no one can taunt her with my ruin."

Blessed release! may we all respond. How many pure, innocent children not only inherit a wicked heart of their own, claiming life-long scrutiny and restraint, but are heirs also of parental disgrace and calumny, from which only long years of patient endurance in paths of rectitude can disencumber them.

Mag's new home was soon contaminated by the publicity of her fall; she had a feeling of degradation oppressing her; but she resolved to be circumspect, and try to regain in a measure what she had lost. Then some foul tongue would jest of her shame, and averted looks and cold greetings disheartened her. She saw she could not bury in forgetfulness her misdeed, so she resolved to leave her home and seek another in the place she at first fled from.

Alas, how fearful are we to be first in extending a helping hand to those who stagger in the mires of infamy; to speak the first words of hope and warning to those emerging into the sunlight of morality! Who can tell what numbers, advancing just far enough to hear a cold welcome and join in the reserved converse of professed reformers, disappointed, disheartened, have chosen to dwell in unclean places, rather than encounter these "holier-than-thou" of the great brotherhood of man!

Such was Mag's experience; and disdaining to ask favor or friendship from a sneering world, she resolved to shut herself up in a hovel she had often passed in better days, and which she knew to be untenanted. She vowed to ask no favors of familiar faces; to die neglected and forgotten before she would be dependent on any. Removed from the village, she was seldom seen except as upon your introduction, gentle reader, with downcast visage, returning her work to her employer, and thus providing herself with the means of subsistence. In two years many hands craved the same avocation; foreigners who cheapened toil and clamored for a livelihood, competed with her, and she could not thus sustain herself. She was now above no drudgery. Occasionally old acquaintances called to be favored with help of some kind, which she was glad to bestow for the sake of the money it would bring her; but the association with them was such a painful reminder of by-gones, she returned to her hut morose and revengeful, refusing all offers of a better home than she possessed. Thus she lived for years, hugging her wrongs, but making no effort to escape. She had never known plenty, scarcely competency; but the present was beyond comparison with those innocent years when the coronet of virtue was hers.

Every year her melancholy increased, her means diminished. At last no one seemed to notice her, save a kind-hearted African, who often called to inquire after her health and to see if she needed any fuel, he having the responsibility of furnishing that article, and she in return mending or making garments.

"How much you earn dis week, Mag?" asked he one Saturday evening.

"Little enough, Jim. Two or three days without any dinner. I washed for the Reeds, and did a small job for Mrs. Bellmont; that's all. I shall starve soon, unless I can get more to do. Folks seem as afraid to come here as if they expected to get some awful disease. I don't believe there is a person in the world but would be glad to have me dead and out of the way."

"No, no, Mag! don't talk so. You shan't starve so long as I have barrels to hoop. Peter Greene boards me cheap. I'll help you, if nobody else will."

A tear stood in Mag's faded eye. "I'm glad," she said, with a softer tone than before, "if there is one who isn't glad to see me suffer. I b'lieve all Singleton wants to see me punished, and feel as if they could tell when I've been punished long enough. It's a long day ahead they'll set it, I reckon."

After the usual supply of fuel was prepared, Jim returned home. Full of pity for Mag, he set about devising measures for her relief. "By golly!" said he to himself one day—for he had become so absorbed in Mag's interest that he had fallen into a habit of musing aloud—"By golly! I wish she'd marry me."

"Who?" shouted Pete Greene, suddenly starting from an unobserved corner of the rude shop.

"Where you come from, you sly nigger!" exclaimed Jim.

"Come, tell me, who is't?" said Pete; "Mag Smith, you want to marry?"

"Git out, Pete! and when you come in dis shop again, let a nigger know it. Don't steal in like a thief."

Pity and love know little severance. One attends the other. Jim acknowledged the presence of the former, and his efforts in Mag's behalf told also of a finer principle.

This sudden expedient which he had unintentionally disclosed, roused his thinking and inventive powers to study upon the best method of introducing the subject to Mag.

He belted his barrels, with many a scheme revolving in his mind, none of which quite satisfied him, or seemed, on the whole, expedient. He thought of the pleasing contrast between her fair face and his own dark skin; the smooth, straight hair, which he had once, in expression of pity, kindly stroked on her now wrinkled but once fair brow. There was a tempest gathering in his heart, and at last, to ease his pent-up passion, he exclaimed aloud, "By golly!" Recollecting his former exposure, he glanced around to see if Pete was in hearing again. Satisfied on this point, he continued: "She'd be as much of a prize to me as she'd fall short of coming up to the mark with white folks. I don't care for past things. I've done things 'fore now I's 'shamed of. She's good enough for me, any how."

One more glance about the premises to be sure Pete was away.

The next Saturday night brought Jim to the hovel again. The cold was fast coming to tarry its apportioned time. Mag was nearly despairing of meeting its rigor.

"How's the wood, Mag?" asked Jim.

"All gone; and no more to cut, any how," was the reply.

"Too bad!" Jim said. His truthful reply would have been, I'm glad.

"Anything to eat in the house?" continued he.

"No," replied Mag.

"Too bad!" again, orally, with the same *inward* gratulation as before.

"Well, Mag," said Jim, after a short pause, "you's down low enough. I don't see but I've got to take care of ye. 'Sposin' we marry!"

Mag raised her eyes, full of amazement, and uttered a sonorous "What?"

Jim felt abashed for a moment. He knew well what were her objections.

"You's had trial of white folks any how. They run off and left ye, and now none of 'em come near ye to see if you's dead or alive. I's black outside, I know, but I's got a white heart inside. Which you rather have, a black heart in a white skin, or a white heart in a black one?"

"Oh, dear!" sighed Mag; "Nobody on earth cares for me—"

"I do," interrupted Jim.

"I can do but two things," said she, "beg my living, or get it from you."

"Take me, Mag. I can give you a better home than this, and not let you suffer so."

He prevailed; they married. You can philosophize, gentle reader, upon the impropriety of such unions, and preach dozens of sermons on the evils of amalgamation. Want is a more powerful philosopher and preacher. Poor Mag. She has sundered another bond which held her to her fellows. She has descended another step down the ladder of infamy.

Chapter II: My Father's Death

Misery! we have known each other,
Like a sister and a brother,
Living in the same lone home
Many years—we must live some
Hours or ages yet to come.
    SHELLEY.[2]

Jim, proud of his treasure,—a white wife,—tried hard to fulfill his promises; and furnished her with a more comfortable dwelling, diet, and apparel. It was comparatively a comfortable winter she passed after her marriage. When Jim could work, all went on well. Industrious, and fond of Mag, he was determined she should not regret her union to him. Time levied an additional charge upon him, in the form of two pretty mulattos, whose infantile pranks amply repaid the additional toil. A few years, and a severe cough and pain in his side compelled him to be an idler for weeks together, and Mag had thus a reminder of by-gones. She cared for him only as a means to subserve her own comfort; yet she nursed him faithfully and true to marriage vows till death released her. He became the victim of consumption. He loved Mag to the last. So long as life continued, he stifled his sensibility to pain, and toiled for her sustenance long after he was able to do so.

A few expressive wishes for her welfare; a hope of better days for her; an anxiety lest they should not all go to the "good place;" brief advice about their children; a hope expressed that Mag would not be neglected as she used to be; the manifestation of Christian patience; these were all the legacy of miserable Mag. A feeling of cold desolation came over her, as she turned from the grave of one who had been truly faithful to her.

She was now expelled from companionship with white people; this last step—her union with a black—was the climax of repulsion.

Seth Shipley, a partner in Jim's business, wished her to remain in her present home; but she declined, and returned to her hovel again, with obstacles threefold more insurmountable than before. Seth accompanied her, giving her a weekly allowance which furnished most of the food necessary for the four inmates. After a time, work failed; their means were reduced.

How Mag toiled and suffered, yielding to fits of desperation, bursts of anger, and uttering curses too fearful to repeat. When both were supplied with work, they prospered; if idle, they were hungry together. In this way their interests became united; they planned for the future together. Mag had lived an outcast for years. She had ceased to feel the gushings of penitence; she had crushed the sharp agonies of an awakened conscience. She had no longings for a purer heart, a better life. Far easier to descend lower. She entered the darkness of perpetual infamy. She asked not the rite of civilization or Christianity. Her will made her the wife of Seth. Soon followed scenes familiar and trying.

"It's no use," said Seth one day; "we must give the children away, and try to get work in some other place."

"Who'll take the black devils?" snarled Mag.

"They're none of mine," said Seth; "what you growling about?"

"Nobody will want any thing of mine, or yours either," she replied.

"We'll make 'em, p'r'aps," he said. "There's Frado's six years old, and pretty, if she is yours, and white folks'll say so. She'd be a prize somewhere," he continued, tipping his chair back against the wall, and placing his feet upon the rounds, as if he had much more to say when in the right position.

Frado, as they called one of Mag's children, was a beautiful mulatto, with long, curly black hair, and handsome, roguish eyes, sparkling with an exuberance of spirit almost beyond restraint.

Hearing her name mentioned, she looked up from her play, to see what Seth had to say of her.

"Wouldn't the Bellmonts take her?" asked Seth.

"Bellmonts?" shouted Mag. "His wife is a right she-devil! and if—"

"Hadn't they better be all together?" interrupted Seth, reminding her of a like epithet used in reference to her little ones.

Without seeming to notice him, she continued, "She can't keep a girl in the house over a week; and Mr. Bellmont wants to hire a boy to work for him, but he can't find one that will live in the house with her; she's so ugly, they can't."

"Well, we've got to make a move soon," answered Seth; "if you go with me, we shall go right off. Had you rather spare the other one?" asked Seth, after a short pause.

"One's as bad as t'other," replied Mag. "Frado is such a wild, frolicky thing, and means to do jest as she's a mind to; she won't go if she don't want to. I don't want to tell her she is to be given away."

"I will," said Seth. "Come here, Frado?"

The child seemed to have some dim foreshadowing of evil, and declined.

"Come here," he continued; "I want to tell you something."

She came reluctantly. He took her hand and said: "We're going to move, by-'m-bye; will you go?"

"No!" screamed she; and giving a sudden jerk which destroyed Seth's equilibrium, left him sprawling on the floor, while she escaped through the open door.

"She's a hard one," said Seth, brushing his patched coat sleeve. "I'd risk her at Bellmont's."

They discussed the expediency of a speedy departure. Seth would first seek employment, and then return for Mag. They would take with them what they could carry, and leave the rest with Pete Greene, and come for them when they were wanted. They were long in arranging affairs satisfactorily, and were not a little startled at the close of their conference to find Frado missing. They thought approaching night would bring her. Twilight passed into darkness, and she did not come. They thought she had understood their plans, and had, perhaps, permanently withdrawn. They could not rest without making some effort to ascertain her retreat. Seth went in pursuit, and returned without her. They rallied others when they discovered that another little colored girl was missing, a favorite playmate of Frado's. All effort proved unavailing. Mag felt sure her fears were realized, and that she might never see her again. Before her anxieties became realities, both were safely returned, and from them and their attendant they learned that they went to walk, and not minding the direction soon found themselves lost. They had climbed fences and walls, passed through thickets and marshes, and when night approached selected a thick cluster of shrubbery as a covert for the night. They were discovered by the person who now restored them, chatting of their prospects, Frado attempting to banish the childish fears of her companion. As they were some miles from home, they were kindly cared for until morning. Mag was relieved to know her child was not driven to desperation by their intentions to relieve themselves of her, and she was inclined to think severe restraint would be healthful.

The removal was all arranged; the few days necessary for such migrations passed quickly, and one bright summer morning they bade fare-well to their Singleton hovel, and with budgets and bundles commenced their weary march. As they neared the village, they heard the merry shouts of children gathered around the schoolroom, awaiting the coming of their teacher.

"Halloo!" screamed one, "Black, white and yeller!" "Black, white and yeller," echoed a dozen voices.

It did not grate so harshly on poor Mag as once it would. She did not even turn her head to look at them. She had passed into an insensibility no childish taunt could penetrate, else she would have reproached herself as she passed familiar scenes, for extending the separation once so easily annihilated by steadfast integrity. Two miles beyond lived the Bellmonts, in a large, old fashioned, two-story white house, environed by fruitful acres, and embellished by shrubbery and shade trees. Years ago a youthful couple consecrated it as home; and after many little feet had worn paths to favorite fruit trees, and over its green hills, and mingled at last with brother man in the race which belongs neither to the swift or strong, the sire became grey-haired and decrepit, and went to his last repose. His aged consort soon followed him. The old homestead thus passed into the hands of a son, to whose wife Mag had applied the epithet "she-devil," as may be remembered. John, the son, had not in his family arrangements departed from the example of the father. The pastimes of his boyhood were ever freshly revived by witnessing the games of his own sons as they rallied about the same goal his youthful feet had often won; as well as by the amusements of his daughters in their imitations of maternal duties.

At the time we introduce them, however, John is wearing the badge of age. Most of his children were from home; some seeking employment; some were already settled in homes of their own. A maiden sister shared with him the estate on which he resided, and occupied a portion of the house.

Within sight of the house, Seth seated himself with his bundles and the child he had been leading, while Mag walked onward to the house leading Frado. A knock at the door brought Mrs. Bellmont, and Mag asked if she would be willing to let that child stop there while she went to the Reed's house to wash, and when she came back she would call and get her. It seemed a novel request, but she consented. Why the impetuous child entered the house, we cannot tell; the door closed, and Mag hastily departed. Frado waited for the close of day, which was to bring back her mother. Alas! it never came. It was the last time she ever saw or heard of her mother.

Chapter III: A New Home for Me

Oh! did we but know of the shadows so nigh,
The world would indeed be a prison of gloom;
All light would be quenched in youth's eloquent eye,
And the prayer-lisping infant would ask for the tomb.

For if Hope be a star that may lead us astray,
And "deceiveth the heart," as the aged ones preach;
Yet 'twas Mercy that gave it, to beacon our way,
Though its halo illumes where it never can reach.
    ELIZA COOK[3]

As the day closed and Mag did not appear, surmises were expressed by the family that she never intended to return. Mr. Bellmont was a kind, humane man, who would not grudge hospitality to the poorest wanderer, nor fail to sympathize with any sufferer, however humble. The child's desertion by her mother appealed to his sympathy, and he felt inclined to succor her. To do this in opposition to Mrs. Bellmont's wishes, would be like encountering a whirlwind charged with fire, daggers and spikes. She was not as susceptible of fine emotions as her spouse. Mag's opinion of her was not without foundation. She was self-willed, haughty, undisciplined, arbitrary and severe. In common parlance, she was a scold, a thorough one. Mr. B. remained silent during the consultation which follows, engaged in by mother, Mary and John, or Jack, as he was familiarly called.

"Send her to the County House," said Mary, in reply to the query what should be done with her, in a tone which indicated self-importance in the speaker. She was indeed the idol of her mother, and more nearly resembled her in disposition and manners than the others.

Jane, an invalid daughter, the eldest of those at home, was reclining on a sofa apparently uninterested.

"Keep her," said Jack. "She's real handsome and bright, and not very black, either."

"Yes," rejoined Mary; "that's just like you, Jack. She'll be of no use at all these three years, right under foot all the time."

"Poh! Miss Mary; if she should stay, it wouldn't be two days before you would be telling the girls about our nig, our nig!" retorted Jack.

"I don't want a nigger 'round me, do you, mother?" asked Mary.

"I don't mind the nigger in the child. I should like a dozen better than one," replied her mother. "If I could make her do my work in a few years, I would keep her. I have so much trouble with girls I hire, I am almost persuaded if I have one to train up in my way from a child, I shall be able to keep them awhile. I am tired of changing every few months."

"Where could she sleep?" asked Mary. "I don't want her near me."

"In the L chamber," answered the mother.

"How'll she get there?" asked Jack. "She'll be afraid to go through that dark passage, and she can't climb the ladder safely."

"She'll have to go there; it's good enough for a nigger," was the reply.

Jack was sent on horseback to ascertain if Mag was at her home. He returned with the testimony of Pete Greene that they were fairly departed, and that the child was intentionally thrust upon their family.

The imposition was not at all relished by Mrs. B., or the pert, haughty Mary, who had just glided into her teens.

"Show the child to bed, Jack," said his mother. "You seem most pleased with the little nigger, so you may introduce her to her room."

He went to the kitchen, and, taking Frado gently by the hand, told her he would put her in bed now; perhaps her mother would come the next night after her.

It was not yet quite dark, so they ascended the stairs without any light, passing through nicely furnished rooms, which were a source of great amazement to the child. He opened the door which connected with her room by a dark, unfinished passage-way. "Don't bump your head," said Jack, and stepped before to open the door leading into her apartment,—an unfinished chamber over the kitchen, the roof slanting nearly to the floor, so that the bed could stand only in the middle of the room. A small half window furnished light and air. Jack returned to the sitting room with the remark that the child would soon outgrow those quarters.

"When she does, she'll outgrow the house," remarked the mother.

"What can she do to help you?" asked Mary. "She came just in the right time, didn't she? Just the very day after Bridget left," continued she.

"I'll see what she can do in the morning," was the answer.

While this conversation was passing below, Frado lay, revolving in her little mind whether she would remain or not until her mother's return. She was of willful, determined nature, a stranger to fear, and would not hesitate to wander away should she decide to. She remembered the conversation of her mother with Seth, the words "given away" which she heard used in reference to herself; and though she did not know their full import, she thought she should, by remaining, be in some relation to white people she was never favored with before. So she resolved to tarry, with the hope that mother would come and get her some time. The hot sun had penetrated her room, and it was long before a cooling breeze reduced the temperature so that she could sleep.

Frado was called early in the morning by her new mistress. Her first work was to feed the hens. She was shown how it was always to be done, and in no other way; any departure from this rule to be punished by a whipping. She was then accompanied by Jack to drive the cows to pasture, so she might learn the way. Upon her return she was allowed to eat her breakfast, consisting of a bowl of skimmed milk, with brown bread crusts, which she was told to eat, standing, by the kitchen table, and must not be over ten minutes about it. Meanwhile the family were taking their morning meal in the dining-room. This over, she was placed on a cricket[4] to wash the common dishes; she was to be in waiting always to bring wood and chips, to run hither and thither from room to room.

A large amount of dish-washing for small hands followed dinner. Then the same after tea and going after the cows finished her first day's work. It was a new discipline to the child. She found some attractions about the place, and she retired to rest at night more willing to remain. The same routine followed day after day, with slight variation; adding a little more work, and spicing the toil with "words that burn," and frequent blows on her head. These were great annoyances to Frado, and had she known where her mother was, she would have gone at once to her. She was often greatly wearied, and silently wept over her sad fate. At first she wept aloud, which Mrs. Bellmont noticed by applying a rawhide, always at hand in the kitchen. It was a symptom of discontent and complaining which must be "nipped in the bud," she said.

Thus passed a year. No intelligence of Mag. It was now certain Frado was to become a permanent member of the family. Her labors were multiplied; she was quite indispensable, although but seven years old. She had never learned to read, never heard of a school until her residence in the family.

Mrs. Bellmont was in doubt about the utility of attempting to educate people of color, who were incapable of elevation. This subject occasioned a lengthy discussion in the family, Mr. Bellmont, Jane and Jack arguing for Frado's education; Mary and her mother objecting. At last Mr. Bellmont declared decisively that she should go to school. He was a man who seldom decided controversies at home. The word once spoken admitted of no appeal; so, notwithstanding Mary's objection that she would have to attend the same school she did, the word became law.

It was to be a new scene to Frado, and Jack had many queries and conjectures to answer. He was himself too far advanced to attend the summer school, which Frado regretted, having had too many opportunities of witnessing Miss Mary's temper to feel safe in her company alone.

The opening day of school came. Frado sauntered on far in the rear of Mary, who was ashamed to be seen "walking with a nigger." As soon as she appeared, with scanty clothing and bared feet, the children assembled, noisily published her approach: "See that nigger," shouted one. "Look! look!" cried another. "I won't play with her," said one little girl. "Nor I neither," replied another.

Mary evidently relished these sharp attacks, and saw a fair prospect of lowering Nig where, according to her views, she belonged. Poor Frado, chagrined and grieved, felt that her anticipations of pleasure at such a place were far from being realized. She was just deciding to return home, and never come there again, when the teacher appeared, and observing the downcast looks of the child, took her by the hand, and led her into the school-room. All followed, and, after the bustle of securing seats was over, Miss Marsh inquired if the children knew "any cause for the sorrow of that little girl?" pointing to

Frado. It was soon all told. She then reminded them of their duties to the poor and friendless; their cowardice in attacking a young innocent child; referred them to one who looks not on outward appearances, but on the heart. "She looks like a good girl; I think I shall love her, so lay aside all prejudice, and vie with each other in showing kindness and good-will to one who seems different from you," were the closing remarks of the kind lady. Those kind words! The most agreeable sound which ever meets the ear of sorrowing, grieving childhood.

Example rendered her words efficacious. Day by day there was a manifest change of deportment towards "Nig." Her speeches often drew merriment from the children; no one could do more to enliven their favorite pastimes than Frado. Mary could not endure to see her thus noticed, yet knew not how to prevent it. She could not influence her schoolmates as she wished. She had not gained their affections by winning ways and yielding points of controversy. On the contrary, she was self-willed, domineering; every day reported "mad" by some of her companions. She availed herself of the only alternative, abuse and taunts, as they returned from school. This was not satisfactory; she wanted to use physical force "to subdue her," to "keep her down."

There was, on their way home, a field intersected by a stream over which a single plank was placed for a crossing. It occurred to Mary that it would be a punishment to Nig to compel her to cross over; so she dragged her to the edge, and told her authoritatively to go over. Nig hesitated, resisted. Mary placed herself behind the child, and, in the struggle to force her over, lost her footing and plunged into the stream. Some of the larger scholars being in sight, ran, and thus prevented Mary from drowning and Frado from falling. Nig scampered home fast as possible, and Mary went to the nearest house, dripping, to procure a change of garments. She came loitering home, half crying, exclaiming, "Nig pushed me into the stream!" She then related the particulars. Nig was called from the kitchen. Mary stood with anger flashing in her eyes. Mr. Bellmont sat quietly reading his paper. He had witnessed too many of Miss Mary's outbreaks to be startled. Mrs. Bellmont interrogated Nig.

"I didn't do it! I didn't do it!" answered Nig, passionately, and then related the occurrence truthfully.

The discrepancy greatly enraged Mrs. Bellmont. With loud accusations and angry gestures she approached the child. Turning to her husband, she asked,

"Will you sit still, there, and hear that black nigger call Mary a liar?"

"How do we know but she has told the truth? I shall not punish her," he replied, and left the house, as he usually did when a tempest threatened to envelop him. No sooner was he out of sight than Mrs. B. and Mary commenced beating her inhumanly; then propping her mouth open with a piece of wood, shut her up in a dark room, without any supper. For employment, while the tempest raged within, Mr. Bellmont went for the cows, a task belonging to Frado, and thus unintentionally prolonged her pain. At dark Jack came in, and seeing Mary, accosted her with, "So you thought you'd vent your spite on Nig, did you? Why can't you let her alone? It was good enough for you to get a ducking, only you did not stay in half long enough."

"Stop!" said his mother. "You shall never talk so before me. You would have that little nigger trample on Mary, would you? She came home with a lie; it made Mary's story false."

"What was Mary's story?" asked Jack.

It was related.

"Now," said Jack, sallying into a chair, "the school-children happened to see it all, and they tell the same story Nig does. Which is most likely to be true, what a dozen agree they saw, or the contrary?"

"It is very strange you will believe what others say against your sister," retorted his mother, with flashing eye. "I think it is time your father subdued you."

"Father is a sensible man," argued Jack. "He would not wrong a dog. Where is Frado?" he continued.

"Mother gave her a good whipping and shut her up," replied Mary.

Just then Mr. Bellmont entered, and asked if Frado was "shut up yet."

The knowledge of her innocence, the perfidy of his sister, worked fearfully on Jack. He bounded from his chair, searched every room till he found the child; her mouth wedged apart, her face swollen, and full of pain.

How Jack pitied her! He relieved her jaws, brought her some supper, took her to her room, comforted her as well as he knew how, sat by her till she fell asleep, and then left for the sitting room. As he passed his mother, he remarked, "If that was the way Frado was to be treated, he hoped she would never wake again!" He then imparted her situation to his father, who seemed untouched, till a glance at Jack exposed a tearful eye. Jack went early to her next morning. She awoke sad, but refreshed. After breakfast Jack took her with him to the field, and kept her through the day. But it could not be so generally. She must return to school, to her household duties. He resolved to do what he could to protect her from Mary and his mother. He bought her a dog, which became a great favorite with both. The invalid, Jane, would gladly befriend her; but she had not the strength to brave the iron will of her mother. Kind words and affectionate glances were the only expressions of sympathy she could safely indulge in. The men employed on the farm were always glad to hear her prattle; she was a great favorite with them. Mrs. Bellmont allowed them the privilege of talking with her in the kitchen. She did not fear but she should have ample opportunity of subduing her when they were away. Three months of schooling, summer and winter, she enjoyed for three years. Her winter over-dress was a cast-off overcoat, once worn by Jack, and a sun-bonnet. It was a source of great merriment to the scholars, but Nig's retorts were so mirthful, and their satisfaction so evident in attributing the selection to "Old Granny Bellmont," that it was not painful to Nig or pleasurable to Mary. Her jollity was not to be quenched by whipping or scolding. In Mrs. Bellmont's presence she was under restraint; but in the kitchen, and among her schoolmates, the pent up fires burst forth. She was ever at some sly prank when unseen by her teacher, in school hours; not unfrequently some out-burst of merriment, of which she was the original, was charged upon some innocent mate, and punishment inflicted which she merited. They enjoyed her antics so fully that any of them would suffer wrongfully to keep open the avenues of mirth. She would venture far beyond propriety, thus shielded and countenanced.

The teacher's desk was supplied with drawers, in which were stored his books and other et ceteras of the profession. The children observed Nig very busy there one morning before school, as they flitted in occasionally from their play outside. The master came; called the children to order; opened a drawer to take the book the occasion required; when out poured a volume of smoke. "Fire! fire!" screamed he, at the top of his voice. By this time he had become sufficiently acquainted with the peculiar odor, to know he was imposed upon. The scholars shouted with laughter to see the terror of the dupe, who, feeling abashed at the needless fright, made no very strict inves-tigation, and Nig once more escaped punishment. She had provided herself with cigars, and puffing, puffing away at the crack of the drawer, had filled it with smoke, and then closed it tightly to deceive the teacher, and amuse the scholars. The interim of terms was filled up with a variety of duties new and peculiar. At home, no matter how powerful the heat when sent to rake hay or guard the grazing herd, she was never permitted to shield her skin from the sun. She was not many shades darker than Mary now; what a calamity it would be ever to hear the contrast spoken of. Mrs. Bellmont was determined the sun should have full power to darken the shade which nature had first bestowed upon her as best befitting.

1859

NOTES

1. From the best-selling *Lalla Rookh* by Thomas Moore (1817), a romance of Central and South Asia, told in verse.

2. From "Invocation to Misery," first published in 1818, by English poet Percy Bysshe Shelley.

3. From the English poet's widely published poem, "The Future," which appeared in popular periodicals between the 1840s and the 1860s.

4. A footstool sometimes used as a low stool for children.

HARRIET JACOBS (1813-1897)

Harriet Ann Jacobs was born to enslaved parents Delilah and Elijah Jacobs, in Edenton, Chowan County, North Carolina. Jacobs's mother died when she was six years old, at which point she was sent to live in the home of her mother's owner. In the household of Margaret Horniblow, Jacobs was taught to read and write, and she remained relatively comfortable until her mistress's death in 1825. At that time, she was transferred to the home of Dr. James Norcom, to whose daughter Jacobs had been bequeathed. There she was subject to frequent sexual harassment from the master of the house. Consistently rejecting her owner's advances, Jacobs entered into a consensual relationship with a white member of the local aristocracy, attorney and future congressman Samuel Treadwell Sawyer. He would father two children with Jacobs, a son (in 1829) and a daughter (in 1833). Sawyer purchased his children's freedom and sent both to be cared for in the North. In the interim, Jacobs planned and executed a daring escape, feigning her flight north by taking refuge in the crawlspace above her grandmother's home. After seven years in hiding, she escaped to the free state of New York, where she found employment with the family of poet Nathaniel Willis. Once in the North, Jacobs was reunited with her children and her brother John, at the time a Rochester, New York-based abolitionist. With her brother's encouragement, Jacobs began to give public addresses on slavery and the need for greater investment in the abolitionist cause. In 1852, Quaker abolitionist Amy Post encouraged Jacobs to consider writing her life story. In late 1853, Jacobs began work on her narrative, advised by her editor, writer and antislavery activist Lydia Maria Child. The book, called *Incidents in the Life of a Slave Girl,* was published for the author by a Boston printer, in 1861. The following year a condensed version of Jacobs's story, titled *A Deeper Wrong,* was published in England. The book achieved a modest measure of popularity among U.S. abolitionists but was more enthusiastically received in England. As the nation moved toward Civil War, Jacobs relocated to Washington, DC, where she helped to provide relief aid for the newly freed black migrants to that city. She would eventually settle there with her daughter, with whom she lived out the remainder of her life. In the following chapters from Jacobs' narrative, she describes the circumstances of her birth and early childhood, as well as the plight of enslaved women and girls.

INCIDENTS IN THE LIFE OF A SLAVE GIRL

Chapter I: Childhood

I was born a slave; but I never knew it till six years of happy childhood had passed away. My father was a carpenter, and considered so intelligent and skilful in his trade, that, when buildings out of the common line were to be erected, he was sent for from long distances, to be head workman. On condition of paying his mistress two hundred dollars a year, and supporting himself, he was allowed to work at his trade, and manage his own affairs. His strongest wish was to purchase his children; but, though he several times offered his hard earnings for that purpose, he never succeeded. In complexion my parents were a light shade of brownish yellow, and were termed mulattoes. They lived together in a comfortable home; and, though we were all slaves, I was so fondly shielded that I never dreamed I was a piece of merchandise, trusted to them for safe keeping, and liable to be demanded of them at any moment. I had one brother, William, who was two years younger than myself—a bright, affectionate child. I had also a great treasure in my maternal grandmother, who was a remarkable woman in many respects. She was the daughter of a planter in South Carolina, who, at his death, left her mother and his three children free, with money to go to St. Augustine, where they had relatives. It was during the Revolutionary War; and they were captured on their passage, carried back, and sold to different purchasers. Such was the story my grandmother used to tell me; but I do not remember all the particulars. She was a little girl when she was captured and sold to the keeper of a large hotel. I have often heard her tell how hard she fared during childhood. But as she grew older she evinced so much intelligence, and was so faithful, that her master and mistress could not help seeing it was for their interest to take care of such a valuable piece of property. She became an indispensable personage in the household, officiating in all capacities, from cook and wet nurse to seamstress. She was much praised for her cooking; and her nice crackers became so famous in the neighborhood that many people were desirous of obtaining them. In consequence of numerous requests of this kind, she asked permission of her mistress to bake crackers at night, after all the household work was done; and she obtained leave to do it, provided she would clothe herself and her children from the profits. Upon these terms, after working hard all day for her mistress, she began her midnight bakings, assisted by her two oldest children. The business proved profitable; and each year she laid by a little, which was saved for a fund to purchase her children. Her master died, and the property was divided among his heirs. The widow had her dower in the hotel which she continued to keep open. My grandmother remained in her service as a slave; but her children were divided among her master's children. As she had five, Benjamin, the youngest one, was sold, in order that each heir might have an equal portion of dollars and cents. There was so little difference in our ages that he seemed more like my brother than my uncle. He was a bright, handsome lad, nearly white; for he inherited the complexion my grandmother had derived from Anglo-Saxon ancestors. Though only ten years old, seven hundred and twenty dollars were paid for him. His sale was a terrible blow to my grandmother; but she was naturally hopeful, and she went to work with renewed energy, trusting in time to be able to purchase some of her children. She had laid up three hundred dollars, which her mistress one day begged as a loan, promising to pay her soon. The reader probably knows that no promise or writing given to a slave is legally binding; for, according to Southern laws, a slave, being property, can hold no property. When my grandmother lent her hard earnings to her mistress, she trusted solely to her honor. The honor of a slaveholder to a slave!

To this good grandmother I was indebted for many comforts. My brother Willie and I often received portions of the crackers, cakes, and preserves, she made to sell; and after we ceased to be children we were indebted to her for many more important services.

Such were the unusually fortunate circumstances of my early childhood. When I was six years old, my mother died; and then, for the first time, I learned, by the talk around me, that I was a slave. My mother's mistress was the daughter of my grandmother's mistress. She was the foster sister of my mother; they were both nourished at my grandmother's breast. In fact, my mother had been weaned at three months old, that the babe of the mistress might obtain sufficient food. They played together as children; and, when they became women, my mother was a most faithful servant to her whiter foster sister. On her death-bed her mistress promised that her children should never suffer for any thing; and during her lifetime she kept her word. They all spoke kindly of my dead mother, who had been a slave merely in name, but in nature was noble and womanly. I grieved for her, and my young mind was troubled with the thought who would now take care of me and my little brother. I was told that my home was now to be with her mistress; and I found it a happy one. No toilsome or disagreeable duties were imposed on me. My mistress was so kind to me that I was always glad to do her bidding, and proud to labor for her as much as my young years would permit. I would sit by her side for hours, sewing diligently, with a heart as free from care as that of any free-born white child. When she thought I was tired, she would send me out to run and jump; and away I bounded, to gather berries or flowers to decorate her room. Those were happy days—too happy to last. The slave child had no thought for the morrow; but there came that blight, which too surely waits on every human being born to be a chattel.

When I was nearly twelve years old, my kind mistress sickened and died. As I saw the cheek grow paler, and the eye more glassy, how earnestly I prayed in my heart that she might live! I loved her; for she had been almost like a mother to me. My prayers were not answered. She died, and they buried her in the little churchyard, where, day after day, my tears fell upon her grave.

I was sent to spend a week with my grandmother. I was now old enough to begin to think of the future; and again and again I asked myself what they would do with me. I felt sure I should never find another mistress so kind as the one who was gone. She had promised my dying mother that her children should never suffer for any thing; and when I remembered that, and recalled her many proofs of attachment to me, I could not help having some hopes that she had left me free. My friends were almost certain it would be so. They thought she would be sure to do it, on account of my mother's love and faithful service. But, alas! we all know that the memory of a faithful slave does not avail much to save her children from the auction block.

After a brief period of suspense, the will of my mistress was read, and we learned that she had bequeathed me to her sister's daughter, a child of five years old. So vanished our hopes. My mistress had taught me the precepts of God's Word: "Thou shalt love thy neighbor as thyself."[1] "Whatsoever ye would that men should do unto you, do ye even so unto them."[2] But I was her slave, and I suppose she did not recognize me as her neighbor. I would give much to blot out from my memory that one great wrong. As a child, I loved my mistress; and, looking back on the happy days I spent with her, I try to think with less bitterness of this act of injustice. While I was with her, she taught me to read and spell; and for this privilege, which so rarely falls to the lot of a slave, I bless her memory.

She possessed but few slaves; and at her death those were all distributed among her relatives. Five of them were my grandmother's children, and had shared the same milk that nourished her mother's children. Notwithstanding my grandmother's long and faithful service to her owners, not one of her children escaped the auction block. These God-breathing machines are no more, in the sight of their masters, than the cotton they plant, or the horses they tend.

Chapter II: The New Master and Mistress

Dr. Flint, a physician in the neighborhood, had married the sister of my mistress, and I was now the property of their little daughter. It was not without murmuring that I prepared for my new home; and what added to my unhappiness, was the fact that my brother William was purchased by the same family. My father, by his nature, as well as by the habit of transacting business as a skillful mechanic, had more of the feelings of a freeman than is common among slaves. My brother was a spirited boy; and being brought up under such influences, he daily detested the name of master and mistress. One day, when his father and his mistress both happened to call him at the same time, he hesitated between the two; being perplexed to know which had the strongest claim upon his obedience. He finally concluded to go to his mistress. When my father reproved him for it, he said, "You both called me, and I didn't know which I ought to go to first."

"You are my child," replied our father, "and when I call you, you should come immediately, if you have to pass through fire and water."

Poor Willie! He was now to learn his first lesson of obedience to a master. Grandmother tried to cheer us with hopeful words, and they found an echo in the credulous hearts of youth.

When we entered our new home we encountered cold looks, cold words, and cold treatment. We were glad when the night came. On my narrow bed I moaned and wept, I felt so desolate and alone.

I had been there nearly a year, when a dear little friend of mine was buried. I heard her mother sob, as the clods fell on the coffin of her only child, and I turned away from the grave, feeling thankful that I still had something left to love. I met my grandmother, who said, "Come with me, Linda;" and from her tone I knew that something sad had happened. She led me apart from the people, and then said, "My child, your father is dead." Dead! How could I believe it? He had died so suddenly I had not even heard that he was sick. I went home with my grandmother. My heart rebelled against God, who had taken from me mother, father, mistress, and friend. The good grandmother tried to comfort me. "Who knows the ways of God?" said she. "Perhaps they have been kindly taken from the evil days to come." Years afterwards I often thought of this. She promised to be a mother to her grandchildren, so far as she might be permitted to do so; and strengthened by her love, I returned to my master's. I thought I should be allowed to go to my father's house the next morning; but I was ordered to go for flowers, that my mistress's house might be decorated for an evening party. I spent the day gathering flowers and weaving them into festoons,[3] while the dead body of my father was lying within a mile of me. What cared my owners for that? He was merely a piece of property. Moreover, they thought he had spoiled his children, by teaching them to feel that they were human beings. This was blasphemous doctrine for a slave to teach; presumptuous in him, and dangerous to the masters.

The next day I followed his remains to a humble grave beside that of my dear mother. There were those who knew my father's worth, and respected his memory.

My home now seemed more dreary than ever. The laugh of the little slave-children sounded harsh and cruel. It was selfish to feel so about the joy of others. My brother moved about with a very grave face. I tried to comfort him, by saying, "Take courage, Willie; brighter days will come by and by."

"You don't know any thing about it, Linda," he replied. "We shall have to stay here all our days; we shall never be free."

I argued that we were growing older and stronger, and that perhaps we might, before long, be allowed to hire our own time, and then we could earn money to buy our freedom. William declared this was much easier to say than to do; moreover, he did not intend to buy his freedom. We held daily controversies upon this subject.

Little attention was paid to the slaves' meals in Dr. Flint's house. If they could catch a bit of food while it was going, well and good. I gave myself no trouble on that score, for on my various errands I passed my grandmother's house, where there was always something to spare for me. I was frequently threatened with punishment if I stopped there; and my grandmother, to avoid detaining me, often stood at the gate with something for my breakfast or dinner. I was indebted to her for all my comforts, spiritual or temporal. It was her labor that supplied my scanty wardrobe. I have a vivid recollection of the linsey-woolsey[4] dress given me every winter by Mrs. Flint. How I hated it! It was one of the badges of slavery.

While my grandmother was thus helping to support me from her hard earnings, the three hundred dollars she had lent her mistress were never repaid. When her mistress died, her son-in-law, Dr. Flint, was appointed executor. When grandmother applied to him for payment, he said the estate was insolvent, and the law prohibited payment. It did not, however, prohibit him from retaining the silver candelabra, which had been purchased with that money. I presume they will be handed down in the family, from generation to generation.

My grandmother's mistress had always promised her that, at her death, she should be free; and it was said that in her will she made good the promise. But when the estate was settled, Dr. Hint told the faithful old servant that, under existing circumstances, it was necessary she should be sold.

On the appointed day, the customary advertisement was posted up, proclaiming that there would be a "public sale of negroes, horses, &c. " Dr. Flint called to tell my grandmother that he was unwilling to wound her feelings by putting her up at auction, and that he would prefer to dispose of her at private sale. My grandmother saw through his hypocrisy; she understood very well that he was ashamed of the job. She was a very spirited woman, and if he was base enough to sell her, when her mistress intended she should be free, she was determined the public should know it. She had for a long time supplied many families with crackers and preserves; consequently, "Aunt Marthy," as she was called, was generally known, and every body who knew her respected her intelligence and good character. Her long and faithful service in the family was also well known, and the intention of her mistress to leave her free. When the day of sale came, she took her place among the chattels, and at the first call she sprang upon the auction-block. Many voices called out, "Shame! Shame! Who is going to sell you, aunt Marthy? Don't stand there! That is no place for you." Without saying a word, she quietly awaited her fate. No one bid for her. At last, a feeble voice said, "Fifty dollars." It came from a maiden lady, seventy years old, the sister of my grandmother's deceased mistress. She had lived forty years under the same roof with my grandmother; she knew how faithfully she had served her owners, and how cruelly she had been defrauded of her rights; and she resolved to protect her. The auctioneer waited for a higher bid; but her wishes were respected; no one bid above her. She could neither read nor write; and when the bill of sale was made out, she signed it with a cross. But what consequence was that, when she had a big heart overflowing with human kindness? She gave the old servant her freedom.

At that time, my grandmother was just fifty years old. Laborious years had passed since then; and now my brother and I were slaves to the man who had defrauded her of her money, and tried to defraud her of her freedom. One of my mother's sisters, called Aunt Nancy, was also a slave in his family. She was a kind, good aunt to me; and supplied the place of both housekeeper and waiting maid to her mistress. She was, in fact, at the beginning and end of every thing.

Mrs. Flint, like many southern women, was totally deficient in energy. She had not strength to superintend her household affairs; but her nerves were so strong, that she could sit in her easy chair and see a woman whipped, till the blood trickled from every stroke of the lash. She was a member of the church; but partaking of the Lord's supper did not seem to put her in a Christian frame of mind. If dinner was not served at the exact time on that particular Sunday, she would station herself in the kitchen, and wait till it was dished, and then spit in all the kettles and pans that had been used for cooking. She did this to prevent the cook and her children from eking out their meagre fare with the remains of the gravy and other scrapings. The slaves could get nothing to eat except what she chose to give them. Provisions were weighed out by the pound and ounce, three times a day. I can assure you she gave them no chance to eat wheat bread from her flour barrel. She knew how many biscuits a quart of flour would make, and exactly what size they ought to be.

Dr. Flint was an epicure. The cook never sent a dinner to his table without fear and trembling; for if there happened to be a dish not to his liking, he would either order her to be whipped, or compel her to eat every mouthful of it in his presence. The poor, hungry creature might not have objected to eating it; but she did object to having her master cram it down her throat till she choked.

They had a pet dog that was a nuisance in the house. The cook was ordered to make some Indian mush for him. He refused to eat, and when his head was held over it, the froth flowed from his mouth into the basin. He died a few minutes after. When Dr. Flint came in, he said the mush had not been well cooked, and that was the reason the animal would not eat it. He sent for the cook, and compelled her to eat it. He thought that the woman's stomach was stronger than the dog's; but her sufferings afterwards proved that he was mistaken. This poor woman endured many cruelties from her master and mistress; sometimes she was locked up, away from her nursing baby, for a whole day and night.

When I had been in the family a few weeks, one of the plantation slaves was brought to town, by order of his master. It was near night when he arrived, and Dr. Flint ordered him to be taken to the work house, and tied up to the joist, so that his feet would just escape the ground. In that situation he was to wait till the doctor had taken his tea. I shall never forget that night. Never before, in my life, had I heard hundreds of blows fall, in succession, on a human being. His piteous groans, and his "O, pray don't, massa," rang in my ear for months afterwards. There were many conjectures as to the cause of this terrible punishment. Some said master accused him of stealing corn; others said the slave had quarreled with his wife, in presence of the overseer, and had accused his master of being the father of her child. They were both black, and the child was very fair.

I went into the work house next morning, and saw the cowhide still wet with blood, and the boards all covered with gore. The poor man lived, and continued to quarrel with his wife. A few months afterwards Dr. Flint handed them both over to a slave-trader. The guilty man put their value into his pocket, and had the satisfaction of knowing that they were out of sight and hearing. When the mother was delivered into the trader's hands, she said, "You promised to treat me well." To which he replied, "You have let your tongue run too far; damn you!" She had forgotten that it was a crime for a slave to tell who was the father of her child.

From others than the master persecution also comes in such cases. I once saw a young slave girl dying soon after the birth of a child nearly white. In her agony she cried out, "O Lord, come and take me!" Her mistress stood by, and mocked at her like an incarnate fiend. "You suffer, do you?" she exclaimed. "I am glad of it. You deserve it all, and more too."

The girl's mother said, "The baby is dead, thank God; and I hope my poor child will soon be in heaven, too."

"Heaven!" retorted the mistress. "There is no such place for the like of her and her bastard."

The poor mother turned away, sobbing. Her dying daughter called her, feebly, and as she bent over her, I heard her say, "Don't grieve so, mother; God knows all about it; and HE will have mercy upon me."

Her sufferings, afterwards, became so intense, that her mistress felt unable to stay; but when she left the room, the scornful smile was still on her lips. Seven children called her mother. The poor black woman had but the one child, whose eyes she saw closing in death, while she thanked God for taking her away from the greater bitterness of life.

Chapter V: The Trials of Girlhood

During the first years of my service in Dr. Flint's family, I was accustomed to share some indulgences with the children of my mistress. Though this seemed to me no more than right, I was grateful for it, and tried to merit the kindness by the faithful discharge of my duties. But I now entered on my fifteenth year—a sad epoch in the life of a slave girl. My master began to whisper foul words in my ear. Young as I was, I could not remain ignorant of their import. I tried to treat them with indifference or contempt. The master's age, my extreme youth, and the fear that his conduct would be reported to my grandmother, made him bear this treatment for many months. He was a crafty man, and resorted to many means to accomplish his purposes. Sometimes he had stormy, terrific ways that made his victims tremble; sometimes he assumed a gentleness that he thought must surely subdue. Of the two, I preferred his stormy moods, although they left me trembling. He tried his utmost to corrupt the pure principles my grandmother had instilled. He peopled my young mind with unclean images, such as only a vile monster could think of. I turned from him with disgust and hatred. But he was my master. I was compelled to live under the same roof with him—where I saw a man forty years my senior daily violating the most sacred commandments of nature. He told me I was his property; that I must be subject to his will in all things. My soul revolted against the mean tyranny. But where could I turn for protection? No matter whether the slave girl be as black as ebony or as fair as her mistress. In either case, there is no shadow of law to protect her from insult, from violence, or even from death; all these are inflicted by fiends who bear the shape of men. The mistress, who ought to protect the helpless victim, has no other feelings towards her but those of jealousy and rage. The degradation, the wrongs, the vices that grow out of slavery are more than I can describe. They are greater than you would willingly believe. Surely, if you credited one half the truths that are told you concerning the helpless millions suffering in this cruel bondage, you at the north would not help to tighten the yoke. You surely would refuse to do for the master, on your own soil, the mean and cruel work which trained bloodhounds and the lowest class of whites do for him at the south.

Every where the years bring to all enough of sin and sorrow; but in slavery the very dawn of life is darkened by these shadows. Even the little child, who is accustomed to wait on her mistress and her children, will learn, before she is twelve years old, why it is that her mistress hates such and such a one among the slaves. Perhaps the child's own mother is among those hated ones. She listens to violent outbreaks of jealous passion, and cannot help understanding what is the cause. She will become prematurely knowing in evil things. Soon she will learn to tremble when she hears her master's footfall. She will be compelled to realize that she is no longer a child. If God has bestowed beauty upon her, it will prove her greatest curse. That which commands admiration in the white woman only hastens the degradation of the female slave. I know that some are too much brutalized by slavery to feel the humiliation of their position; but many slaves feel it most acutely, and shrink from the memory of it. I cannot tell how much I suffered in the presence of these wrongs, nor how I am still pained by the retrospect. My master met me at every turn, reminding me that I belonged to him, and swearing by heaven and earth that he would compel me to submit to him. If I went out for a breath of fresh air, after a day of unwearied toil, his footsteps dogged me. If I knelt by my mother's grave, his dark shadow fell on me even there. The light heart which nature had given me became heavy with sad forebodings. The other slaves in my master's house noticed the change. Many of them pitied me; but none dared to ask the cause. They had no need to inquire. They knew too well the guilty practices under that roof, and they were aware that to speak of them was an offence that never went unpunished.

I longed for some one to confide in. I would have given the world to have laid my head on my grandmother's faithful bosom, and told her all my troubles. But Dr. Flint swore he would kill me, if I was not as silent as the grave. Then, although my grandmother was all in all to me, I feared her as well as loved her. I had been accustomed to look up to her with a respect bordering upon awe. I was very young, and felt shamefaced about telling her such impure things, especially as I knew her to be very strict on such subjects. Moreover, she was a woman of a high spirit. She was usually very quiet in her demeanor; but if her indignation was once roused, it was not very easily quelled. I had been told that she once chased a white gentleman with a loaded pistol, because he insulted one of her daughters. I dreaded the consequences of a violent outbreak; and both pride and fear kept me silent. But though I did not confide in my grandmother, and even evaded her vigilant watchfulness and inquiry, her presence in the neighborhood was some protection to me. Though she had been a slave, Dr. Flint was afraid of her. He dreaded her scorching rebukes. Moreover, she was known and patronized by many people; and he did not wish to have his villainy made public. It was lucky for me that I did not live on a distant plantation, but in a town not so large that the inhabitants were ignorant of each other's affairs. Bad as are the laws and customs in a slaveholding community, the doctor, as a professional man, deemed it prudent to keep up some outward show of decency.

O, what days and nights of fear and sorrow that man caused me! Reader, it is not to awaken sympathy for myself that I am telling you truthfully what I suffered in slavery. I do it to kindle a flame of compassion in your hearts for my sisters who are still in bondage, suffering as I once suffered.

I once saw two beautiful children playing together. One was a fair white child; the other was her slave, and also her sister. When I saw them embracing each other, and heard their joyous laughter, I turned sadly away from the lovely sight. I foresaw the inevitable blight that would fall on the little slave's heart. I knew how soon her laughter would be changed to sighs. The fair child grew up to be a still fairer woman. From childhood to womanhood her pathway was blooming with flowers, and overarched by a sunny sky. Scarcely one day of her life had been clouded when the sun rose on her happy bridal morning.

How had those years dealt with her slave sister, the little playmate of her childhood? She, also, was very beautiful; but the flowers and sunshine of love were not for her. She drank the cup of sin, and shame, and misery, whereof her persecuted race are compelled to drink.

In view of these things, why are ye silent, ye free men and women of the north? Why do your tongues falter in maintenance of the right? Would that I had more ability! But my heart is so full, and my pen is so weak! There are noble men, and women who plead for us, striving to help those who cannot help themselves. God bless them! God give them strength and courage to go on! God bless those, every where, who are laboring to advance the cause of humanity!

Chapter VI: The Jealous Mistress

I would ten thousand times rather that my children should be the half-starved paupers of Ireland than to be the most pampered among the slaves of America. I would rather drudge out my life on a cotton plantation, till the grave opened to give me rest, than to live with an unprincipled master and a jealous mistress. The felon's home in a penitentiary is preferable. He may repent, and turn from the error of his ways, and so find peace; but it is not so with a favorite slave. She is not allowed to have any pride of character. It is deemed a crime in her to wish to be virtuous.

Mrs. Flint possessed the key to her husband's character before I was born. She might have used this knowledge to counsel and to screen the young and the innocent among her slaves; but for them she had no sympathy. They were the objects of her constant suspicion and malevolence. She watched her husband with unceasing vigilance; but he was well practised in means to evade it. What he could not find opportunity to say in words he manifested in signs. He invented more than were ever thought of in a deaf and dumb asylum. I let them pass, as if I did not understand what he meant; and many were the curses and threats bestowed on me for my stupidity. One day he caught me teaching myself to write. He frowned, as if he was not well pleased; but I suppose he came to the conclusion that such an accomplishment might help to advance his favorite scheme. Before long, notes were often slipped into my hand. I would return them, saying, "I can't read them, sir." "Can't you?" he replied; "then I must read them to you." He always finished the reading by asking, "Do you understand?" Sometimes he would complain of the heat of the tea room, and order his supper to be placed on a small table in the piazza. He would seat himself there with a well-satisfied smile, and tell me to stand by and brush away the flies. He would eat very slowly, pausing between the mouthfuls. These intervals were employed in describing the happiness I was so foolishly throwing away, and in threatening me with the penalty that finally awaited my stubborn disobedience. He boasted much of the forbearance he had exercised towards me, and reminded me that there was a limit to his patience. When I succeeded in avoiding opportunities for him to talk to me at home, I was ordered to come to his office, to do some errand. When there, I was obliged to stand and listen to such language as he saw fit to address to me. Sometimes I so openly expressed my contempt for him that he would become violently enraged, and I wondered why he did not strike me. Circumstanced as he was, he probably thought it was better policy to be forebearing. But the state of things grew worse and worse daily. In desperation I told him that I must and would apply to my grandmother for protection. He threatened me with death, and worse than death, if I made any complaint to her. Strange to say, I did not despair. I was naturally of a buoyant disposition, and always I had a hope of somehow getting out of his clutches. Like many a poor, simple slave before me, I trusted that some threads of joy would yet be woven into my dark destiny.

I had entered my sixteenth year, and every day it became more apparent that my presence was intolerable to Mrs. Flint. Angry words frequently passed between her and her husband. He had never punished me himself, and he would not allow any body else to punish me. In that respect, she was never satisfied; but, in her angry moods, no terms were too vile for her to bestow upon me. Yet

I, whom she detested so bitterly, had far more pity for her than he had, whose duty it was to make her life happy. I never wronged her, or wished to wrong her; and one word of kindness from her would have brought me to her feet.

After repeated quarrels between the doctor and his wife, he announced his intention to take his youngest daughter, then four years old, to sleep in his apartment. It was necessary that a servant should sleep in the same room, to be on hand if the child stirred. I was selected for that office, and informed for what purpose that arrangement had been made. By managing to keep within sight of people, as much as possible, during the day time, I had hitherto succeeded in eluding my master, though a razor was often held to my throat to force me to change this line of policy. At night I slept by the side of my great aunt, where I felt safe. He was too prudent to come into her room. She was an old woman, and had been in the family many years. Moreover, as a married man, and a professional man, he deemed it necessary to save appearances in some degree. But he resolved to remove the obstacle in the way of his scheme; and he thought he had planned it so that he should evade suspicion. He was well aware how much I prized my refuge by the side of my old aunt, and he determined to dispossess me of it. The first night the doctor had the little child in his room alone. The next morning, I was ordered to take my station as nurse the following night. A kind Providence interposed in my favor. During the day Mrs. Flint heard of this new arrangement, and a storm followed. I rejoiced to hear it rage.

After a while my mistress sent for me to come to her room. Her first question was, "Did you know you were to sleep in the doctor's room?"

"Yes, ma'am."

"Who told you?"

"My master."

"Will you answer truly all the questions I ask?"

"Yes, ma'am."

"Tell me, then, as you hope to be forgiven, are you innocent of what I have accused you?"

"I am."

She handed me a Bible, and said, "Lay your hand on your heart, kiss this holy book, and swear before God that you tell me the truth."

I took the oath she required, and I did it with a clear conscience.

"You have taken God's holy word to testify your innocence," said she. "If you have deceived me, beware! Now take this stool, sit down, look me directly in the face, and tell me all that has passed between your master and you."

I did as she ordered. As I went on with my account her color changed frequently, she wept, and sometimes groaned. She spoke in tones so sad, that I was touched by her grief. The tears came to my eyes; but I was soon convinced that her emotions arose from anger and wounded pride. She felt that her marriage vows were desecrated, her dignity insulted; but she had no compassion for the poor victim of her husband's perfidy. She pitied herself as a martyr; but she was incapable of feeling for the condition of shame and misery in which her unfortunate, helpless slave was placed.

Yet perhaps she had some touch of feeling for me; for when the conference was ended, she spoke kindly, and promised to protect me. I should have been much comforted by this assurance if I could have had confidence in it; but my experiences in slavery had filled me with distrust. She was not a very refined woman, and had not much control over her passions. I was an object of her jealousy, and, consequently, of her hatred; and I knew I could not expect kindness or confidence from her under the circumstances in which I was placed. I could not blame her. Slaveholders' wives feel as other women would under similar circumstances. The fire of her temper kindled from small-sparks, and now the flame became so intense that the doctor was obliged to give up his intended arrangement.

I knew I had ignited the torch, and I expected to suffer for it afterwards; but I felt too thankful to my mistress for the timely aid she rendered me to care much about that. She now took me to sleep in a room adjoining her own. There I was an object of her especial care, though not of her especial comfort, for she spent many a sleepless night to watch over me. Sometimes I woke up, and found her bending over me. At other times she whispered in my ear, as though it was her husband who was speaking to me, and listened to hear what I would answer. If she startled me, on such occasions, she would glide stealthily away; and the next morning she would tell me I had been talking in my sleep, and ask who I was talking to. At last, I began to be fearful for my life. It had been often threatened; and you can imagine, better than I can describe, what an unpleasant sensation it must produce to wake up in the dead of night and find a jealous woman bending over you. Terrible as this experience was, I had fears that it would give place to one more terrible.

My mistress grew weary of her vigils; they did not prove satisfactory. She changed her tactics. She now tried the trick of accusing my master of crime, in my presence, and gave my name as the author of the accusation. To my utter astonishment, he replied, "I don't believe it; but if she did acknowledge it, you tortured her into exposing me." Tortured into exposing him! Truly, Satan had no difficulty in distinguishing the color of his soul! I understood his object in making this false representation. It was to show me that I gained nothing by seeking the protection of my mistress; that the power was still all in his own hands. I pitied Mrs. Flint. She was a second wife, many years the junior of her husband; and the hoary-headed miscreant was enough to try the patience of a wiser and better woman. She was completely foiled, and knew not how to proceed. She would gladly have had me flogged for my supposed false oath; but, as I have already stated, the doctor never allowed any one to whip me. The old sinner was politic. The application of the lash might have led to remarks that would have exposed him in the eyes of his children and grandchildren. How often did I rejoice that I lived in a town where all the inhabitants knew each other! If I had been on a remote plantation, or lost among the multitude of a crowded city, I should not be a living woman at this day.

The secrets of slavery are concealed like those of the Inquisition. My master was, to my knowledge, the father of eleven slaves. But did the mothers dare to tell who was the father of their children? Did the other slaves dare to allude to it, except in whispers among themselves? No, indeed! They knew too well the terrible consequences.

My grandmother could not avoid seeing things which excited her suspicions. She was uneasy about me, and tried various ways to buy me; but the never-changing answer was always repeated: "Linda does not belong to me. She is my daughter's property, and I have no legal right to sell her." The conscientious man! He was too scrupulous to sell me; but he had no scruples whatever about committing a much greater wrong against the helpless young girl placed under his guardianship, as his daughter's property. Sometimes my persecutor would ask me whether I would like to be sold. I told him I would rather be sold to any body than to lead such a life as I did. On such occasions he would assume the air of a very injured individual, and reproach me for my ingratitude. "Did I not take you into the house, and make you the companion of my own children?" he would say. "Have I ever treated you like a negro? I have never allowed you to be punished, not even to please your mistress. And this is the recompense I get, you ungrateful girl!" I answered that he had reasons of his own for screening me from punishment, and that the course he pursued made my mistress hate me and persecute me. If I wept, he would say, "Poor child! Don't cry! Don't cry! I will make peace for you with your mistress. Only let me arrange matters in my own way. Poor, foolish girl! You don't know what is for your own good. I would cherish you. I would make a lady of you. Now go, and think of all I have promised you."

I did think of it.

Reader, I draw no imaginary pictures of southern homes. I am telling you the plain truth. Yet when victims make their escape from this wild beast of Slavery, northerners consent to act the part of bloodhounds, and hunt the poor fugitive back into his den, "full of dead men's bones, and all uncleanness." Nay, more, they are not only willing, but proud, to give their daughters in marriage to slaveholders. The poor girls have romantic notions of a sunny clime, and of the flowering vines that all the year round shade a happy home. To what disappointments are they destined! The young wife soon learns that the husband in whose hands she has placed her happiness pays no regard to his marriage vows. Children of every shade of complexion play with her own fair babies, and too well she knows that they are born unto him of his own household. Jealousy and hatred enter the flowery home, and it is ravaged of its loveliness.

Southern women often marry a man knowing that he is the father of many little slaves. They do not trouble themselves about it. They regard such children as property, as marketable as the pigs on the plantation; and it is seldom that they do not make them aware of this by passing them into the slave-trader's hands as soon as possible, and thus getting them out of their sight. I am glad to say there are some honorable exceptions.

I have myself known two southern wives who exhorted their husbands to free those slaves towards whom they stood in a "parental relation;" and their request was granted. These husbands blushed before the superior nobleness of their wives' natures. Though they had only counseled them to do that which it was their duty to do, it commanded their respect, and rendered their conduct more exemplary. Concealment was at an end, and confidence took the place of distrust.

Though this bad institution deadens the moral sense, even in white women, to a fearful extent, it is not altogether extinct. I have heard southern ladies say of Mr. Such-a-one, "He not only thinks it no disgrace to be the father of those little niggers, but he is not ashamed to call himself their master. I declare, such things ought not to be tolerated in any decent society!"

1861

NOTES

1. Mark 12:31.

2. Matthew 7:12.

3. A chain or garland of flowers, leaves, ribbons, or other material.

4. A coarse woven fabric, usually made of linen and wool.

JOHN WILLIS MENARD (1838-1893)

Poet John Willis Menard was born in Kaskaskia, Illinois, to French Creole parents. Educated at Iberia College in Ohio, he was a staunch advocate for abolitionism as well as for African American emigration to Liberia. During the Civil War, Menard moved to Washington, DC, where he accepted a post in the Bureau of Emigration. In so doing, he became the first African American to hold a clerkship in the U.S. Department of the Interior. In 1863, on orders from President Abraham Lincoln, he traveled to British Honduras to investigate the possibility of establishing a settlement there for America's newly freed blacks. In 1865, Menard relocated to New Orleans, where he was appointed to serve as one of the city's street commissioners. In 1868, in a special election held to replace a recently deceased congressman, John Willis Menard became the first African American ever elected to the U.S. House of Representatives. His opponent refused to concede, however, and after making an eloquent appeal on the floor of the House, the first ever by a black man or woman, Menard remained unseated. In 1871, he relocated to Jacksonville, Florida, where his loyalty to the Republican Party was rewarded with a position in the city post office. There he started *The Florida Sun,* the first of several African American newspapers for which he would serve as founding editor. In the coming years he would establish three additional papers, including *The Radical Standard, Key West News,* and *Florida News* (later renamed the *Southern Leader*). In 1889, he returned to Washington, DC, where he founded the *National American* magazine. Menard first gained acclaim as a writer in 1860, when he published the abolitionist tract *An Address to the Free Colored People of Illinois.* Around that time, his poems also began appearing in the *Christian Recorder.* In 1879, Menard released his only volume of poetry, *Lays in Summer Lands.* The book achieved significant notoriety and was hailed for its uncompromising expression of pro-Republican and antiracist sentiments. The poem "Liberia" was first published in the *Christian Recorder,* in March of 1863. The poem "To Madame Selika" celebrates the African American soprano Madame Marie Selika Williams, who, on November 13, 1878, became the first African American to perform at the White House.

Liberia! O, immortal name!
To Afric's sons and daughters;
It glows like an undying flame
Upon their hearts and altars!

Oh, country 'neath the torrid skies,
With hills and placid rivers;
And sons that scorn to *compromise*
With friends and *nigger-drivers!*—

I love thee for thy verdant brow,—
Thy sunny vales and mountains;
I love thy woodland choir that swells
The music of thy fountains!

The light-winged zephyrs from the sea
Are in thy bowers sighing;
And FREEDOM, RIGHT and LIBERTY,
Upon thy plains are vying!

Beneath the gospel's potent voice,
Thy native tribes are crying;
And heathenism's rugged voice
Has ceased its plaintive sighing.

Oh! country of the sable race—
The germ of Freedom's dower;
The stubborn nations of the earth
Ere long will *feel* thy power.

LIBERIA, rise!—no longer sigh—
Thy *night* is nearly over;
For *Freedom, Liberty* and *Right*
Over thy plains doth hover!

1863

TO MADAME SELIKA

O siren of the colored race,[1]
    With matchless voice and queenly grace!
'Tis thine to move the heart to tears,
    And lift it to the upper spheres!

Sweet heavenly gifts to thee belong,
    To heal our ills with magic song;
And make our drooping hearts rejoice
    With the sweet pathos of thy voice!

Enchantress from the sunset glow!
    Thy notes in mellow cadence flow;
Like music from a hidden lyre,
    Or echoes from the heavenly choir!

Selika! thou art sent to shame,
    The scoffers of our race, who blame,
And curse the Negro for his skin,—
    And wrong him for this God-sent sin!

1879

NOTE

1. Marie Selika Williams (1849?–1937), a concert soprano soloist and the first African American to perform at the White House (in 1878).

SOLOMON G. BROWN (1829-1906)

Solomon G. Brown was born in Washington, DC, to former slaves Isaac and Rachel Brown. The fourth of six children, he was unable to afford a formal education. Instead, Brown worked form an early age to supplement his family's earnings. A turning point in both his economic fortunes and his intellectual life came in 1844, when he secured employment at the Washington, DC, post office. There he worked under the direct supervision of scientists Joseph Henry, inventor of the electromagnetic relay, and Samuel Morse, the inventor of the telegraph. Employed as their assistant, Brown helped established the nation's first telegraph line, from the District of Colombia to Baltimore. In 1856, Joseph Henry, the first director of the Smithsonian Institution, invited Brown to become its first African American employee. There Brown would spend the next fifty-four years, the remainder of his working life. By the mid-1850s, Brown was delivering public lectures on the sciences, and by 1869 he was solely responsible for registering all specimens and other materials received by the museum. In addition to his work as a lecturer and registrar, Brown was also a poet, with works appearing in some of the major African American papers of the day, including *The Washington Bee* and the *Christian Recorder.* The following poem is reprinted from the August 22, 1863, issue of the *Christian Recorder*.

THE NEW YORK RIOT

The white man boasts that he is white,[1]
He also boasts that he has light,
That's not possessed by black men.

He boasts of whites of by-gone days,
And on their acts much grandeur lays:
He calls them his relations.

They swell around, like they were king,
To their own glory oft do sing,
But must lie down and die.

They also boast of education,
And lift to glory his fair nation;
And yet behave so mean.

They boast quite loud of their inventions,
And do make known some new intentions
To rid this land of negroes.

They gather up tremendous bands,
Attack the blacks on every hand,
But can't exterminate them.

They murder fathers and children too,
And many whom they never knew,
Because their skin is colored.

If black men go upon the street
Some white men there they sure will meet,
For this they're ofttimes murdered.

Our people sold like hogs and sheep,
Some dear one stole, while we lay asleep—
And bartered off like cattle.

The white men say they truly think
That all the negroes greatly stink,
But seem to like the odour.

The black men work from day to day,
Receive just what they choose to pay;
And humbly they retire.

Their wives must have subsistence, too,
Their children's feet must have the shoe,
And they must have their living.

The people give us much abuse,
Declare the negro is no use,—
Except on their plantations.

They sing, the blacks can never be
Such as in themselves they see,
They never could be human.

The saying we have put to flight,
Our people running to the fight,
Receiving education.

And thus we live from month to month,
And pass along without a grunt,
We do not give offences.

One glorious hope the blacks possess,
The God who sees and knows all best,
One day the trouble settles.

This glorious Being none can defraud,
But each receives his own reward,
For all their past offences.

Then when all's been said and done,
The white man finds it is no fun,
What he has done to negroes.

The Lord, who made all living beings,
Has all their wicked actions seen,
And will correct this nation.

The white men boast of New York State,
The wrongs that have been done of late
To a defenceless people.

Who never did them any harm,
In early days did work their farms,
And brought the State to riches.

To carry out this hellish plan,
A mob was raised with clubs in hand,
They started Monday morning.

The Government had planned a draft
At this command the rabble laughed,
And burned the conscript office.

They burned the orphan asylum down,
The highest brick lay on the ground,
The orphan children scattered.

Three hundred children out of doors,
Who could not save a piece of clothes,
For all they had were stolen.

If one black man went to the door,
They on him set, and bruised him sore,
That he could not recover.

A colored man his way had lost,
Was being carried by his horse,
Was set upon and murdered.

When little life in him they see,
They bring his body to a tree,
And tried their best to burn it.

By day the street was in a haze,
By night the town was in a blaze,
The work of these vile wretches.

This mob increased from street to street,
Destroying all they chanced to meet,
Until restrained by soldiers.

The colored men were set upon,
And shot like dogs, if they should run,
By these outlaw'd assassins.

I do not think when danger's nigh,
Because I'm black that I should fly,
But try and save my people.

The blacks had chances which were good,
To show to all mankind they would
Fight like men and demons.

If you get scared at such a few,
To go down South would never do,
To face so many rebels.

Our men did not defend their lives,
Paid no attention to their wives,
Nor would they fight the rabble.

Ah, shame on you who boast you could
Ten thousand raise, who freely would
Come down with John C. Fremont.[2]

A man that's brave will risk his life,
Or stay at home, protect his wife,
And try to save his children.

A man who will from danger fly,
And leave his dear ones thus to die,
Would never make a soldier.

Some men were chased till out of breath,
And some were smashed or choked to death,
And some were thrown in rivers.

Although this crowd was large and low,
God knows each man who struck a blow,
In his own time avenge them.

The Roman Bishop did proclaim,[3]
Invites the rabble in his name,
And said he would address them.

The white man boasts that he possest
The traits that suit the negro best,
And thinks to treat him badly.

He also boasts of his high station,
And thinks he's classed to rule the nation,
And sell all those that's black.

To all white men I don't allude,
For some of them have given us food,
When we knew not where to get it.

They ofttimes come to our relief,
When our dear ones have been bereaved,
And knew not where to look to.

On us their last cent they would spend,
Indeed they have been our best friend,
When our own race forsook us.

And now adieu I bid to all,

In his own time the Lord will call

All men up to judgment.

Washington, Aug. 8, 1863

NOTES

1. The New York City Draft Riots took place from July 13 to July 16, 1863. The four days of violent upheaval began as a working-class rebellion against the Civil War draft. However, the insurrection quickly took on racial and ethnic overtones, as the largely Irish crowd turned its anger against the African Americans of the city. More than one hundred black people were killed, and the Colored Orphan Asylum at Forty-fourth Street and Fifth Avenue was raided, looted, and then burned down.

2. The antislavery Republican candidate for the U.S. presidency in 1856 and the commander of the Western Armies during the American Civil War.

3. Archbishop John Hughes, whose address to four thousand of the rioters was harshly criticized by Horace Greeley and other journalists for its failure to quell the mob.

J. ANDERSON RAYMOND (?-?)

Few details are known about the life of J. Anderson Raymond. During the mid-1860s, he contributed several poems and pieces of prose to the *Christian Recorder*. A resident of Philadelphia, Pennsylvania, Raymond wrote passionately against both southern slavery and northern racism. He also published meditations on the role of the poet, as well as a six-part series on "Phrenology." During the same period, he gained some notice as an orator, delivering sermons and scientific talks in local area Baptist churches. The following selections appeared in the *Christian Recorder* between July and November of 1864.

POETRY AND POETS: PART I

Gentle as the summer breeze
Glides softly on like running streams;
Then, like the lightning through the trees,
Its lurid glare in rapture gleams.

Valleys, and hills, and running rills,
Have poems stored within their breast:
The empty mind with music fills,
The rambling thought is hushed to rest.

Flits calmly as the zephyr's breath,
Then, like the thunder's sound o'erhead;
Still'd like the quiet sleep of death,
Her song is hushed—her voice hath fled!

The meadows green, the bleating sheep,
The tall tree-top that hangs above,
The ocean blue, the briny deep,
The thoughts that frame sweet words of love;

Each tells to me of poetry:
She dwells in all earth's precious goods.

The merry birds chime glad and free
Poetic notes in leafy woods.

There's poetry in leafy groves,
In limpid streams and landscapes wild;
There's poetry in words of love
That Jesus spoke, so meek and mild.

In lands of dreams, where thoughts traverse,
When slumber weighs our eyelids down,
The soul its prison-home deserts,
And revels in poetic ground.

There's poetry in heighten'd spires
That point to where resides a God;
There's poetry in ancient sires,
Whose home is 'neath the sacred sod.

The wheel of time doth hasten on
There's poetry in time that's fled;
There's poetry in saddened song,
That sounds like the requiem of the dead.

Judge all who will of poets' song,
I wish no other path to tread.
How many the great pathway throng
Of HOMER—muses' fountain head!

Oh, that my thoughts could drink the stream
That muses drank in days of yore—
A spark of MILTON in me gleam,
And feed my soul from heaven's store.

Let POPE and SHAKSPEARE in me build
Sublime and noble thoughts, to trace
The great poetic flame instill'd
By HOMER in the human race.

1864

O, could I grasp thee, gem of worth;
Could I but stand where *Milton* stood,
And drink sublimest things of Earth,
I'd have achieved my greatest good.

My busy mind in vain calls in
Its rambling thoughts which flutter free,
What would I give if I could swim
The mystic sea of poetry?

Profoundest thoughts did *Herbert*[1] place
Upon the page of sacred worth,
Of God, the Church of holy grace,
And treasures hidden deep in earth.

Pope[2] lent to us a sweeter song,
Than birds that warble in the trees;
The vesper hymns at twilight throng,
And flutter in the evening breeze.

How soft the pen of *Moore* could glide,
When *Lalla's*[3] beauty he portrayed;
How grand the great, the swelling tide,
Of poesy in even's shade.

Scott's Lady of the Lake enchants,
He paints her charms with master hand;
Those noble lines my soul entrance,
That fell from thoughts of *Sheridan*.

Burns loved to pen his Scottish lays;
Though gone from earth, does he not live
In hearts of those that sound his praise?
Yes:—him their blessing still they give.

The *Thanatopsis*—*Bryant's* boon—
So full of nature's flaming fire!
Lord Byron. Ah! he fell so soon
To ruined nature's direful ire!

Longfellow[4] soon his laurels won,
And *Goldsmith*[5] too deserves our praise,
While I, a youth, have just begun
To tread the path of poet's lays.

May I yet hope to scale the heights,
Of Heaven's brightest gift to man?
May I yet revel in delight,
At works constructed by my hand?

With nature for my tutor, I
Will glean my share of knowledge too;
No gem of worth shall flutter by
Unread, uncared for,—old or new.

Months, years, may lapse before the day
Arrives for me to show my worth.
Before the time I sing my lay,
My spirit may have flown from earth.

1864

POETRY AND POETS: PART IV (CONCLUDED)

Some power unseen beyond the scope of sight,
Did shed on *Pope* its mystic ray of light;
The treasure-house of knowledge opened wide,
And bathed his reason in its swelling tide.
Earth holds within her bosom one whose name
Shall ever float upon the sea of fame;
A family word, kept dear in every breast,
Shall be the name of him that's flown to rest.
As calm, as meek, as placid as a child,
His natural mood, (although so helpless,) mild;
When roused a lion in its might of power!
His nature changed within the fleeting hour.
Great *Dryden,*[6] like the lurid lightning's flash,
Burst unexpected with a fearful crash!
He seldom swam in sweet tranquility,

Or bowed to sip the stream humility.
The strain of *Wallace*,[7] filled with fire
From nature's spark, but not with dire
Essays and words that oft inflame
The passions—*Dryden!*—honored name!
Saxe[8] oft excites our merry mirth,
And wakes our dullness to new birth;
His briefless *Barrister*[9] in rhyme
Is filled with wit and thoughts sublime.
Prentice[10] was truly on the wing of flight,
And gleamed upon him that great orb of light;
His lines on "time," remorseless, flying thing,
Doth tell me *Prentice* once was on the wing.
But sensual pleasure oft destroys the man,
And leads him captive in destruction's van.
What pleasure men endowed with God's great gift,
Can find on folly's fitful sea, and drift
Down with the swell
Of ruin's dismal, howling wilderness,
Where God forever will their souls dismiss,
I ne'er could tell.
Thus many, stored with knowledge rich and rare,
Have thrown aside the pearl, and sought the fare
Of fools, though hardly fit for heav'n nor hell!
Our greatest bards, and men of priceless worth,
Were meanest worms that ever pressed the earth.
I could, nor would not give my soul to hell,
For all the knowledge that could in me dwell.
While God is master of this sinking world,
Shall I into the depths of hell be hurled?
No! Hell may rage in vain; I have a place,
Not made with hands, but in the realms of grace.
But I digress; I wander from my theme;
The sword of truth hath waked me from a dream.
But I must cease—my poet's lay is done;
Alas! 'tis plain, no boasting fame I've won.

1864

And if the fruit fall not, the trunk that bears
May sink beneath the load of earthly cares.
Although the fruit be not of tempting nature—
Although 'tis minus form and given stature,
I can but do what others do—my best—
And to the gazing critic leave the rest.
Now if he choose my lines to ruminate,
He must not grumble at the tasteless bait,
Where'er you turn, where'er your eyes are cast,
The critic's first will meet your gaze, and last.
Their venom slang is freely given,
They spare not even the saints in heaven.
Do what you will—no matter whom you please,
He's sworn to criticise you at his ease.
Should effort fail, he still will make attempts—
Tries to condemn even such as Heav'n exempts.
Each Sabbath critic to the house of God repairs—
Not to drink in the light of knowledge there—
But to condemn the preacher in the stand.
His faults are numerous as the countless sands.
If preachers would be learned in Bible lore,
In College they must spend five years or more.
And learn of men what none but God can teach,—
If learned not thus, the preacher cannot preach.
How authors tremble when censorious sages
Lay ruthless hands upon their guileless pages!
The volume which with care was penn'd,
Is hardly read before it is condemned.
Thus years of labor does he crush to earth—
The bud is nipped just in its opening birth.
The rhymester toils to put his thoughts in rhyme,
And dreams of glory in the future time—
Dreams of a future which will bring success—
Of glory, which will all his labors bless,—
Dreams that his Muse's magisterial god—

Dreams that his pen is mightier than the sword,—
Dreams of his conquest o'er his fallen foe—
Dreams that his Muse hath laid each rival low.
Poet, seek not to free thy fettered mind;
Let all thy dreams of glory be resigned.
Remove the film that intercepts thy sight,
Or else still grope thy way in starless night.
Oh, spare thyself the tidings of defeat;
Let not thy Muse the cynic's vigils meet!
Or else he'll strike thee dumb. 'Tis true,
Poor poet,—here's the fate of me and you.
Perhaps 'tis well I close this rhapsody;
For if 'twere long as vast eternity,
There still would be a portion undefined
Of this great master-piece of human-kind.
A Lexicon of words could not describe
Him who'd betray his Master for a bribe.
The modern cynic I supremely hate,
Heaven save me from the vicious censor's fate!

1864

NOTES

1. George Herbert (1693–1633), an English poet and Anglican priest.

2. English poet Alexander Pope (1688–1744).

3. A reference to the protagonist and title character of Thomas Moore's *Lalla Rookh*.

4. U.S. poet Henry Wadsworth Longfellow (1807–1882).

5. Irish novelist and poet Oliver Goldsmith (1730–1774).

6. English poet and playwright John Dryden (1631–1700).

7. *The Actes and Deidis of the Illustre and Vallyeant Campioun Schir William Wallace* (more commonly known as *The Wallace*), a fifteenth-century Scottish epic by the poet Blind Harry (1440–1492).

8. Popular American poet and humorist John Godfrey Saxe (1816–1887).

9. "The Briefless Barrister," one of John Godfrey Saxe's most popular poems.

10. U.S. poet and publisher George Dennison Prentice (1802–1870).

EDMONIA GOODELLE HIGHGATE (1844–1870)

Author and educator Edmonia Goodelle Highgate was born in Virginia. The daughter of Hannah and Charles Highgate, a barber, she was raised in Syracuse, New York, and was educated in the local schools. Barred from teaching in Syracuse because of her race, Highgate instead began her career at an African American school in Montrose, Pennsylvania. In 1864, under the auspices of the American Missionary Association, she assumed a teaching post at a school for newly freed blacks, in Norfolk, Virginia. Though her stay was cut short by illness and exhaustion, her efforts on behalf of formerly enslaved African Americans attracted the attention of prominent thinkers and activists, and, in 1864, she was one of only two women invited to address the National Convention of Colored Men (the other was poet and novelist Frances E. W. Harper). The following year she established a school for black students in Darlington, Maryland, before moving on to New Orleans to organize African American schools in that city. Highgate was one of only a small number of female correspondents writing for African American newspapers. She is known to have published only one piece of fiction, the short story "Congojoco," in which the young heroine chooses a life of service over the promise of romance. To mid-century readers, though, she was best known for her lively and thoughtful dispatches from the newly liberated South. The essay "Neglected Opportunities" was published in the *Christian Recorder* on July 14, 1866. "On Horse Back—Saddle Dash, No. 1" appeared in the *Recorder*'s November 3, 1866, edition.

NEGLECTED OPPORTUNITIES

In the sober light of reason, one is often led to wonder what punishment the great Dealer of justice has in store for that class of persons who have amber-hued opportunities, and never develop in their lives—a purpose—never make themselves felt in their own State, County, town, village or ward.

Some girls and boys at twenty-two or five,—good-rate, graduate from an academic course, possibly before thirty, from a collegiate course—come out into the earnest, hard-working world of realities, without ever feeling that they have a role to enact. Without realizing that their advantages have made them liable to be the grand starter in some move that could draw thousands with them. Too many males and females, with an ambition equal to Caesar's, or Napoleon's, or Margaret Fuller's,[1] or Frederick Douglass's, never make any thing of themselves. Do not even become energetic tradesmen. Why is it? Some of our elaborately educated young men dash all their energy upon some love-sick penchant for some imperious, handsome-faced, brainless girl, who for want of other avenues, uses efforts at passing cupid darts through their gizzards. Excuse me, "embryo hearts" I meant. Some of our men that might have been good physicians, lawyers, orators, professors and essayists, have been lost to the higher cause of literature or sacred manhood, by this dashing against Charybdis. Too many friends spoil this, and give abortive developments of their own personal ruin. A rich father has made too many earth-encumbering sons, or useless lady shadows. All things alternately will be tried by the test of ability, and I would not have it otherwise. It is more than a fancy that many of these people, who have been like good gardens, which contain weeds and nothing else, all their fifty or sixty years of earth—death will have exquisite Tantales hereafter in punishment for lost opportunities. A real man or woman makes circumstances and controls them. *They* be deterred from doing what duty calls them to! Never! They control their destiny and observe every weaker mind within the square of the distance. I find it easier to coalesce with a person who has been guilty of ennui, and whose lives are proof of their repentance, than these good-for-nothing aspirants! Any thing which you young pump-strutters earnestly wish to be, you can be. God gives every key to a sober demander. All that you ought to be, pretty beau-catcher[2] wearer, you can be, if you have to wait till you are thirty-five to attain your goal, and do without Mr. Exquisite for your partner in an aimless non-existence. I hate a weak man or woman. I fling them from me as I do half-drowned, clinging cats. Yet no one sooner than I would be a strong friend to one who has determined to reform—to be definitely something. I don't believe in world-saving—but I do in self-making—No—I am no shining light; but I have a reverence for a real every-inch-man, or a whole woman, who earnestly is a definite something besides a fawning husband—liver and corset lacer, and liver and dier by this eternal "style." Come out into the glory of God's world of functions and uses—Create something. Aspire to leave something immortal behind you. That's the life test at last. The monument you leave—I don't mean granite or marble—but something that will stand the corruption of the ages. A principle well developed will in science or ethics—A cause will—An immortal healthy soul. Ah! the gods would any of these! Have I said too much? Is it inelegant? Does it not breathe balm of a thousand flowers? Opopinax, excuse me,—but I never wear perfumed kids,[3] especially when I have to touch wads. Up! work, make something out of yourself, even if it is like getting blood from a turnip. Try! The race needs living, working demonstrations—the world does. Young man, the master in world-reconstruction has called; is calling, but will not enact, for you and your sister.

New Orleans, June 21st.

1866

ON HORSE BACK — SADDLE DASH, NO. 1

Who that has taught school, the elementary branches year in and year out, don't know what teacher's ennui is? I always thought I did, but find that I have just found out. Here I am in the western interior of Louisiana trying with my might to instruct these very French, little and large Creoles, in the simplest English, and in morals. But for my roan,[4] I would break down as a harp unstrung; but as soon as day-school is out I am on his back, and off on a quick gallop for these grand old October woods. I took my first ride of six miles to a famous old spring,[5] at which the rebel General Morton drank with his wretchedly demoralized command in their retreat after the battle of Shiloh. My horse, like everything else here, was Creole, and I am afraid rather *confederate* in his tendencies; for when I was feeling lost, almost to my surroundings in some meditations of an intensely union cast, he had the bad taste to get into a fence leaping mood. Of course I conquered, and made myself mistress of the situation. Then I plunged into the thickest of the oak tree forest with its exquisite drapery of *gray* hanging moss. The old dame must have anticipated some children visitors, for she had swings readymade, formed of the thick inter-lapping vine-like branches, reaching from treetop to treetop all through these woods. What delightful order! Oh, if dear Henry D. Thoreau were here, wouldn't he go into a rhapsody! But he is here in spirit.

Nature's admiring children, who perseveringly labor to know her secrets while in earth form, only learn more after they "cross the river Jordan," and they hover around beautiful retreats. Yes, they are "ministering spirits." They don't imagine me a modern spiritualist after the "affinity-seeking," "wife and husband leaving" strife. No, I detest "table rappings and crockery breaking," especially the last; for I have broken so much. But those who are of the same mind do coalesce whether in the spirit or out. Oh, what a cluster of scarlet blossoms! All negroes like red; so push on, pony, I must have those flowers! How I wish my Philadelphia friends had these! Why they are handsomer than either "fuchsias or bleeding heart." But I have left my botany in the city; so I can't trace their genera.

Oh, how independent one feels in the saddle! One thing, I can't imagine why one needs to wear such long riding skirts. They are so inconvenient when you have to ford streams or dash through briers. Oh, fashion, will no Emancipation Proclamation free us from thee!

My . . . "American horse," so-called because he came from the North. Creoles . . . call northern horses "American horses." Really it is a compliment. They are so much more reliable that creole horses. One of the latter must have its own slow gait, like a mule's pass, or else run away on a wild gipsy chase.

Now for the matter in this saddle-dash. I had to keep off horseback several days in order to recover from extreme fatigue and soreness, but my bay is at the door this glorious Saturday morning, and I am off till noon. Some rebel equestrians just passed, and fired four times almost in my face. But who is going to let grape keep them off horseback or off duty? Hasn't He promised to keep His workers? "Then to doubt would be disloyal; to falter would be sin."

Oh! I forgot to say my roan did not understand English any better than my scholars do When I said, "Whoa, pony," he would gallop.

Au revoir. I am home again from my canter. We passed through several cotton and cornfields worked on shares. The former owners are giving half what the crops yield to the hands in payment. Besides, there is five per cent tax levied to pay for the school privilege for the children of the hands. These men work well. Their employers say; "better than slaves did." But they work all day Sunday of their own accord on land they have rented; so anxious are they to get places of their own. Cotton is worth from 40 to 50 cents per pound here. One would soon get rich with one of these plantations. Oh! It is time for my night school. Believe me,

Votre Amie des Chevaux.
Oct. 13th, Vermillionville,
Lafayette Parish, La.

1866

NOTES

1. Sarah Margaret Fuller Ossoli (1810–1850), American feminist, journalist, and historian.

2. A circular curl of hair worn flat against the forehead or cheek.

3. Perfumed leather gloves, popular women's accessories in the mid-nineteenth century.

4. A horse with an evenly mixed coat of white and colored hairs.

5. The notorious "Bloody Pond," a spring-fed body of water—one of the few water sources for the fighters at Shiloh—reported by witnesses to have turned red with the blood of soldiers who died in that battle.

ALEXANDER CRUMMELL (1819-1898)

Alexander Crummell was born in New York City to Boston and Charity Hicks Crummell. His mother was freeborn. His father, a prosperous oysterman and former slave, was brought from Africa to the United States at the age of thirteen. Crummell's parents were well acquainted with many of New York's most influential African American writers and activists, and Crummell was exposed early on to the potential for black men and women to use literature as a tool for social change. The newspaper *Freedom's Journal* was founded in their home when Alexander was just eight years old. Crummell began his education at New York City's African Free School. In 1836, he enrolled at the Oneida Institute in Whitesboro, New York, where he was one of four black entering students. In subsequent decades, he and his African American classmates, Amos Beman, Henry Highland Garnet, and Thomas Sidney, would all go on to distinguish themselves in the burgeoning movement for black civil rights. He left Oneida after two years, attending courses in theology at Yale University and receiving private tutoring from Episcopal clergymen. He was ordained an Episcopal priest in 1844. Crummell completed his baccalaureate studies at Queens College, University of Cambridge, England. In later life, Crummell settled in Washington, DC, where he would eventually establish and lead St. Luke's Episcopal Church. A supporter of the colonization of Liberia by free African Americans, Crummell traveled to the colony in 1853 to serve as a missionary. While there, he also served on the faculty of Liberia College, located in the capital city of Monrovia. Upon his return in 1862, Crummell published *The Future of Africa: Being Addresses, Sermons, etc. Delivered in the Republic of Liberia.* In 1897, he established the American Negro Academy in order to foster the development and productivity of African American writers and scholars. This he undertook in deliberate opposition to Booker T. Washington and other black leaders who advocated for vocational education as the pathway to Negro improvement. As a writer, Crummell was best known for his sermons and political tracts. The following selection, Crummell's "Thanksgiving Day Sermon," advances the themes of racial uplift and self-improvement through racial and ethnic solidarity. Delivered in 1875, on Thanksgiving Day, the sermon appeared in pamphlet form in 1882.

THANKSGIVING DAY SERMON:
THE SOCIAL PRINCIPLE AMONG A PEOPLE AND
ITS BEARING ON THEIR PROGRESS AND DEVELOPMENT

Isaiah XLI, 6, 7

> They helped every one his neighbor, and every one said to his brother, Be
> of good courage. So the carpenter encouraged the goldsmith, and he that
> smootheth with the hammer him that smote the anvil, saying, It is ready
> for the soldering; and he fastened it with nails that it should not be moved.

More than a month has passed away since we received the proclamation
of our Chief Magistrate, appointing the 25th of November a day of public
thanksgiving to Almighty God.[1]

And, in accordance with this pious custom, we, in common with millions
of our fellow-citizens, have met together this morning, to offer up our tribute
of praise and thankfulness to our common Parent in heaven, for all the gifts,
favors, blessings, and benefactions, civil, domestic, religious, and educational,
which have been bestowed upon us during the year; for the blessings of
heaven above; for the precious fruits brought forth by the sun; for the precious things of the earth and the fullness thereof; for the golden harvests of
peace, unstained by blood, and unbroken by strife; for the constant stream
of health which has flowed through our veins and households, untainted by
plague or pestilence; for the babes whom the Lord has laid upon your arms
and given to your hearts; for the plentiful supply of food which has been
granted us from the fields, and which has laden our boards; for the goodly
instruction which trains the mind and corrects the hearts of our children, and
prepares them for responsibility, for duty, and eternity; for the civil privileges
and the national freedom, in which we are permitted to participate; for the
measure of success which God has given His Gospel, and for the hope that
is ours that the Cross shall yet conquer everywhere beneath the sun, and that
JESUS shall rule and reign through all the world. For these and all other gifts
and blessings we render our tribute of praise and gratitude to the Lord, our
Maker, Preserver, and Benefactor, through JESUS CHRIST our Lord!

Grateful as is this theme of gratitude, and inviting as it is for thought and
further expression, it is not my purpose to pursue it today. I feel that we should
turn the occasion into an opportunity for improvement and progress.

Especially is this the duty of a people situated as we are in this country;
cut loose, blessed be GOD, for ever-more, from the dark moorings of servitude

and oppression; but not fully arrived at—only drifting towards, the deep, quiet waters of fullest freedom and equality. Few, comparatively, in numbers; limited in resources; the inheritors of prodigious disasters; the heirs of ancestral woes and sorrows; burdened with most manifest duties and destinies; anxious for our children; thoughtful for our race; culpability and guilt of the deepest dye will be ours, if we do not most seriously consider the means and instruments by which we shall be enabled to go forward, and to rise upward. It is peculiarly a duty at this time when there is evidently an ebb-tide of indifference in the country, with regard to our race; and when the anxiety for union neutralizes the interest in the black man.

The agencies to the high ends I have referred to are various; but the text I have chosen suggests a train of thought, in a distinct and peculiar line. It shows us that spirit of unity which the world exhibits, when it would fain accomplish its great, commanding ends.

The prophet shows us here the notable sight, that is, that GOD comes down from heaven to put an end to the devices of the wicked. Whatever discord and strife may have before existed among them, at once it comes to an end. A common danger awaits them; a common peril menaces. At once they join hands; immediately their hearts are united. "They helped every one his neighbor, and every one said to his neighbor, be of good courage."

The lesson is one which we shall do well to learn with diligence; that it comes from the wicked, does not detract from its value. The world acts on many a principle which Christians would do well to lay to heart. Our Saviour tells us that "the children of this world are wiser in their generation than the children of light." So here, this principle of united effort, and of generous concord, is worthy of the imitation of the colored people of this country, if they would fain rise to superiority of both character and achievement. I shall speak, therefore, of the "Social principle among a people; and its bearing on their progress and development."

What I mean by the social principle, is the disposition which leads men to associate and join together for specific purposes; the principle which makes families and societies, and which binds men in unity and brotherhood, in races and churches and nations.

For man, you will observe, is a social being. In his mental and moral constitution God has planted certain sympathies and affections, from which spring the desire for companionship. It is with reference to these principles that God declared of the single and solitary Adam, "It is not good for the man to live alone."' It was no newly discovered affinity of the Maker, no after-thought of the Almighty. He had formed His creature with a fitness and proclivity for association. He had made him with a nature that demanded society. And from this principle flows, as from a fountain, the loves, friendships, families, and combinations which tie men together, in union and concord. A wider and more imposing result of this principle is the welding of men in races and nationalities. All the fruit and flower of these organisms come from the coalescence of diverse faculties and powers, tending to specific ends. For no one man can effect anything important alone. There never was a great building, a magnificent city, a noble temple, a grand cathedral, a stately senate-house which was the work of one single individual. We know of no important event in history, no imposing scheme, no great and notable occurrence which stands as an epoch in the annals of the race, which was accomplished by a single, isolated individual. Whether it is the upbuilding of Imperial Rome; or the retreat of the Ten Thousand;[2] or the discovery of America; or Cook's or Anson's voyages[3] around the globe; or the conquest of India; or the battle of Waterloo; everywhere we find that the great things of history have been accomplished by the combination of men.

Not less is this the case in those more humane and genial endeavors which have been for the moral good of men, and wherein the individuality of eminent leaders has been more conspicuous. We read of the evangelization of Europe,[4] from the confines of Asia to Britain; and, in more modern times, we have the abolition of the Slave Trade and Slavery, the grand efforts for the relief of prisoners, the Temperance Reformation, the Sunday-school system. These were noble schemes, which originated in the fruitful brains and sprung from the generous hearts of single individuals, and which, in their gracious results, have made the names of Howard[5] and Wilberforce, of Clarkson[6] and Robert Raikes,[7] bright and conspicuous. But yet we know that even they of themselves did not achieve the victories which are associated with their names. Thousands, nay, tens of thousands of the good and pious were aroused by their passionate appeals to stirring energy; and only when the masses of the godly were marshalled to earnest warfare, were those evils doomed; and they fell, never to rise again!

The application of this truth to the interests and the destiny of the colored race of America is manifest. We are living in this country, a part of its population, and yet, in diverse respects, we are as foreign to its inhabitants as though we were living in the Sandwich Islands.[8] It is this, our actual separation from the real life of the nation, which constitutes us "a nation within a nation:" thrown very considerably upon ourselves for many of the largest interests of life, and for nearly all our social and religious advantages. As a consequence on this state of things, all the stimulants of ambition and self-love should lead this people to united effort for personal superiority and the uplifting of the race; but, instead thereof, overshadowed by a more powerful race of people; wanting in the cohesion which comes from racial enthusiasm; lacking in the confidence which is the root of a people's stability; disintegration, doubt, and distrust almost universally prevail, and distract all their business and policies.

Among a people, as in a nation, we find farmers, mechanics, sailors, servants, business men, trades. For life, energy, and progress in a people, it is necessary that all these various departments of activity should be carried on with spirit, skill, and unity. It is the cooperative principle, working in trades, business, and manufacturing, which is the great lever that is lifting up the million masses in great nations, and giving those nations themselves a more masterly superiority than they have ever known, in all their past histories. No people can discard this principle, and achieve greatness. Already I have shown that it cannot be done in the confined sphere of individual, personal effort. The social principle prevails in the uprearing of a nation, as in the establishing of a family. Men must associate and combine energies in order to produce large results. In the same way that a family becomes strong, influential, and wealthy by uniting the energies of parents and children, so a people go on to honor and glory, in the proportion and extent that they combine their powers to definite and productive ends.

Two principles are implied in the remarks I have made, that is, the *one* of mutuality, and the *other* of dependence.

By mutuality I mean the reciprocal tendencies and desires which interact between large bodies of men, aiming at single and definite ends. I mean the several sentiments of sympathy, cheer, encouragement, and combination, among any special body of people; which are needed and required in distinct departments of labor. Solitude, in any matter, is alien to the human heart. We need, we call for the aid of our fellow-creatures. The beating heart of man waits for the answering heart of his brother.

It is the courageous voice of the venturesome soldier that leads on a whole column to the heart of the fray. It is the cheering song of the hardy sailor as he hangs upon the shrouds, amid the fierceness of the tempest, that lifts up the heart of his timid messmates, and stimulates to boldness and noble daring. On the broad fields of labor, where the scythe, the plough, and the spade work out those wondrous transformations which change the wild face of nature to order and beauty, and in the end, bring forth those mighty cargoes of grain which gladden the hearts and sustain the frames of millions; there the anthems of toil invigorate the brawny arms of labor; while the sun pours down its fiery rays, and the midday heat allures in vain to the shade and to rest. Deep down in the dark caves of earth, where the light of the sun never enters, tens of thousands of men and children delve away in the coal beds, or iron mines, buried in the bowels of the earth; cheered on in their toilsome labor by the joyous voices and the gladdening songs of their companions. What is it, in these several cases, that serves at once to lighten toil, and to stimulate to hardier effort? Several principles indeed concur; but it is evident that what I call mutuality, i.e., sympathy and unison of feeling, act upon the hearts of soldiers, sailors, laborers, and miners, and spur them on to duty and endurance.

So, likewise, we may not pass by the other motive, *i.e.,* the feeling of *dependence*. We need the skill, the energy, the achievement of our fellow-creatures. No man stands up entirely alone, self-sufficient in the entire circle of human needs. Even in a state of barbarism the rude native man feels the need of the right arm of his brother. How much more with those who are civilized and enlightened! If you or I determine upon absolute independency of life and action, rejecting the arm and the aid of all other men, into how many departments of labor should we not at once have to multiply ourselves?

It is the recognition of this principle of association, which has made Great Britain, France, the United States, Holland, and Belgium the greatest nations of the earth. There are more partnerships, combinations; trades unions, banking-houses, and insurance companies in those countries than in all the rest of the world together. The mere handful of men in these nations, numbering but one hundred millions, sway and dominate all the other nine hundred millions of men on the globe. Or just look at one single instance in our own day: here are England and France—fifty-eight millions of men—who, united, only a few years ago, humbled the vast empire of China, with its three hundred millions of semi-civilized inhabitants.

The principles of growth and mastery in a race, a nation, or people, are the same all over the globe. The same great agencies which are needed to make a people in one quarter of the globe and in one period of time are needed here, at this time, in this American nationality. We children of Africa in this land are no way different from any other people in these respects. Many of the differences of races are slight and incidental, and oftentimes become obliterated by circumstances, position, and religion. I can take you back to a period in the history of England when its rude inhabitants lived in caves and huts, when they fed on bark and roots, when their dress was the skins of animals.

When you next look at some eminent Englishman, the personification, perchance, of everything cultivated, graceful, and refined, you may remember that his distant ancestors were wild and bloody savages, and that it has taken ten centuries to change him from the rudeness of his brutalized forefathers into an enlightened and civilized human being.

The great general laws of growth and superiority are unchangeable. The Almighty neither relaxes nor alters them for the convenience of any people. Conformity, then, to this demand for combination of forces is a necessity which we, as a people, cannot resist without loss and ruin. We cannot pay heed to it too soon; for if there has been anything for which the colored people of this country have been and now are noted, it is for disseverance, the segregation of their forces, the lack of the co-operative spirit. Neither in farming operations, nor trades, nor business, nor in mechanical employment, nor marketing, nor in attempts at grocery-keeping, do we find attempts at combination of their forces. No one hears anywhere of a company of fifty men to start a farm, to manufacture bricks, to begin a great trading business, to run a mill, or to ply a set of vessels in the coasting trade. No one sees a spontaneous movement of thirty or forty families to take possession of a tract of land for a specific monetary venture. Nowhere do we see a united movement in any State for general moral and educational improvement, whereby the masses may be delivered from inferiority and degradation. The people, as a body, seem delivered over to the same humble, servile occupations of life in which their fathers trod, because, from a lack of co-operation they are unable to step into the higher callings of business; and hence penury, poverty, inferiority, dependence, and even servility is their one general characteristic throughout the country, along with a dreadful state of mortality.

And the cause of this inferiority of purpose and of action is two-fold, and both the fault, to some extent, of unwise and unphilosophic leaders. For, since, especially emancipation, two special heresies have influenced and governed the minds of colored men in this nation: (I) The one is the dogma which I have heard frequently from the lips of leaders, personal and dear, but mistaken, friends, *that the colored people of this country should forget, as soon as possible, that they ARE colored people:*—a fact, in the first place, which is an impossibility. Forget it, forsooth, when you enter a saloon and are repulsed on account of your color! Forget it when you enter a car, South or West, and are denied a decent seat! Forget it when you enter the Church of God, and are driven to a hole in the gallery! Forget it when every child of yours would be driven ignominiously from four-fifths of the common schools of the country! Forget it, when thousands of mechanics in the large cities would make a "strike" rather than work at the same bench, in the same yard, with a black carpenter or brick-maker! Forget it, when the boyhood of our race is almost universally deprived of the opportunity of learning trades, through prejudice! Forget it, when, in one single State, twenty thousand men dare not go to the polls on election-day, through the tyranny of caste! Forget it, when one great commonwealth offers a new constitution for adoption, by which a man like *Dumas* the younger,[9] if he were a North Carolinian, could be indicted for marrying the foulest white woman in that State, and merely because she was white! Forget that you are colored, in these United States! Turn madman, and go into a lunatic asylum, and then, perchance, you may forget it! But, if you have any sense or sensibility, how is it possible for you, or me, or any other colored man, to live oblivious of a fact of so much significance in a land like this! The only place I know of in this land where you can "forget you are colored" is the grave!

But not only is this dogma folly, it is disintegrating and socially destructive. For shut out, for instance, as I am and you are from the cultivated social life of the superior classes of this country, if I forget that I am a black man, if you ignore the fact of race, and we both, ostrich-like, stick our heads in the sand, or stalk along, high-headed, oblivious of the actual distinctions which do exist in American society, what are you or I to do for our social nature? What will become of the measure of social life among ourselves which we now possess? Where are we to find our friends? Where find the circles for society and cheerful intercourse?

Why, my friends, the only way you, and I, and thousands of our people get domestic relations, marry wives and husbands, secure social relations, form good neighborhood and companionship, is by the very remembrance which we are told to scout and forswear.

2. The other dogma is the demand *that colored men should give up all distinctive effort, as colored men, in schools, churches, associations, and friendly societies.* But this, you will observe, is equivalent to a demand to the race to give up all civilization in this land and to submit to barbarism. The cry is: "Give up your special organization." "Mix in with your white fellow-citizens."

Now I waive, for the present, all discussion of abstract questions of rights and prerogatives. I direct my attention to the simple point of practicality; and I beg to say, that this is a thing which cannot be forced. Grieved, wearied and worried as humanity has been with the absurd, factitious arrangements of society in every quarter of the globe, yet men everywhere have had to wait. You can batter down oppression and tyranny with forceful implements; not so social disabilities and the exclusiveness of caste. The Saxon could not force it upon the Norman. Upon this point, if everything is not voluntary, generous, gracious, and spontaneous, the repulsive will is as icy, and as obstinate too, as Mt. Blanc.[10] I wonder that the men who talk in the style I have referred to, forget that nine-tenths of the American people have become so poisoned and stimulated by the noxious influence of caste, that, in the present day, they would resist to the utmost before they would allow the affiliations, however remote, that implied the social or domestic principle.

Nay, more than this: not only would they reject your advances, but, after they had repelled you, they would leave you to reap the fruits of your own Folly in breaking up your own distinctive and productive organisms, under the flighty stimulants of imaginative conceit.

And the disaster, undoubtedly, would be deserved; not, indeed, morally, for the inflictions of caste are unjust and cruel; but because of your unwisdom; for it is the office of common sense to see, as well the exact situation, to comprehend the real condition of things as they exist in this nation; as well as to take cognizance of the pernicious and atrocious virulence of caste!

Few things in policy are more calamitous in result than mere conceit. An unbalanced and blind imagination is one of the most destructive, most disastrous of all guides. Such I believe to be the nature of the suggestion which I reprobate. But remember, I do not condemn the men who hold them. Oppression and caste are responsible for many worse things than unwisdom, or blind speculation. How intolerable are the distinctions which hedge up our ardent, ambitious minds, on every side, I thoroughly apprehend! How the excited mind turns passionately to every fancied and plausible mode of escape, I can easily understand! But remember that the pilotage of a whole people, of an entire race, through the quicksands and the breakers of civil and social degradation, up to the plane of manly freedom and equality, while it is, by its very hazards, calculated to heighten the pulse, and to quicken the activity of the brain, is, nevertheless, just that sort of work which calls for the coolest head, and the hardest, most downright reasonableness. When you are pleading for natural rights, when men are endeavoring to throw off the yoke of oppression, you may indeed

—imitate the action of the tiger,
Stiffen the sinews, summon up the blood.[11]

But a war against a gross public sentiment, a contest with prejudices and repulsions, is a thing of a different kind, and calls for a warfare of an opposite character. You cannot destroy caste with a ten pounder! You cannot sweep away a prejudice with a park of artillery!

I know, to use the words of another, "how difficult it is to silence imagination enough to make the voice of Reason even distinctly heard in this case; as we are accustomed from our youth up to indulge that forward and delusive faculty ever obtruding beyond its sphere; of some assistance indeed to apprehension, but the author of all error; as we plainly lose ourselves in gross and crude conception of things, taking for granted that we are acquainted with what indeed we are wholly ignorant of"; so it seems to me the gravest of all duties to get rid of all delusions upon this subject; and to learn to look at it in the light of hard, serious, long-continued, painful, plodding work. It is *work*, you will observe, not abnormal disturbances, not excitement; but a mighty effort of moral and mental reconstruction, reaching over to a majestic end. And then when that is reached and secured, then all the hindrances of caste will be forever broken down!

Nothing is more idle than to talk of the invincibility of prejudice. The Gospel is sure to work out all the issues and results of brotherhood, everywhere under the sun, and in this land; but, until that day arrives, we are a nation, set apart, in this country. As such, we have got to strive—not to get rid of ourselves; not to agonize over our distinctive peculiarities; but to accept the situation as Providence allows it, and to quit "ourselves as men," in, if you say so, painful and embarrassing circumstances; determined to shift the groove of circumstance, and to reverse it.

The special duty before us is to strive for footing and for superiority in this land, *on the line of race,* as a temporary but needed expedient, for the ultimate extinction of caste, and all race distinctions. For if we do not look after our own interests, as a people, and strive for advantage, no other people will. It is folly for mere idealists to content themselves with the notion that "we are American citizens;" that, "as American citizens, ours is the common heritage and destiny of the nation;" that "special solicitude for the colored people is a superfluity;" that "there is but one tide in this land; and we shall flow with all others on it."

On the contrary, I assert, we are just now a "peculiar people" in this land; looked at, repulsed, kept apart, legislated for, criticised in journals, magazines, and scientific societies, at an insulting and intolerable distance, as a peculiar people; with the doubt against us whether or not we can hold on to vital power on this soil; or whether we have capacity to rise to manhood and superiority.

And hence I maintain that there is the greatest need for us all to hold on to the remembrance that we are "colored men," and not to forget it!

While one remnant of disadvantage abides in this land, stand by one another! While proscription in any quarter exists, maintain intact all your phalanxes! While antagonism confronts your foremost men, hold on to all the instincts of race for the support of your leaders, and the elevation of your people! While the imputation of inferiority, justly or unjustly, is cast upon you, combine for all the elements of culture, wealth, and power! While any sensitiveness or repulsion discovers itself at your approach or presence, hold on to your own self-respect, keep up, *and be satisfied with,* your own distinctive circles!

And then the "poor, forsaken ones," in the lanes and alleys and cellars of the great cities; in remote villages and hamlets; on old plantations which their fathers' blood has moistened from generation to generation; ignorant, unkempt, dirty, animal-like, repulsive, and half heathen—brutal and degraded; in some States, tens and hundreds of thousands, not slaves, indeed, according to the letter of the law, but the tools and *serfs* of would-be oppressors: stand by THEM until the school-master and preacher reach them as well as us; and the noble Christian civilization of the land transforms their features and their forms, and changes their rude huts into homes of beauty; and lifts them up into such grand superiority, that no one in the land will associate the word "Negro" with inferiority and degradation; but the whole land, yea, the whole world shall look upon them by-and-by, multitudinous in their brooding, clustered masses, "redeemed, regenerated, disenthralled,"[12] and exclaim, "Black, but comely!"[13] But, while they are low, degraded, miserable, almost beastly, don't forget that you are colored men, as well as they; "your brothers' keepers."

Do not blink at the charge of inferiority. It is not a race peculiarity; and whatever its measure or extent in this country, it has been forced upon you. Do not deny it, but neutralize and destroy it, not by shrieks, or agonies, or foolish pretense; but by culture, by probity, and industry.

I know the natural resource of some minds, under these painful circumstances, to cry out, "Agitates agitate!" But *cui bono?*[14] What advantage will agitation bring? Everything has a value, according to its relation to its own natural and specific end. But what is the bearing of agitation to a purpose which is almost entirely subjective in its nature. For, as I take it, the object we must needs have in view, in the face of the disabilities which confront our race in this land, is the attainment of such general superiority that prejudice must decline. But agitation has no such force, possesses no such value. Agitation is the expenditure of force: our end and aim is the husbandry of all our vital resources.

Character, my friends, is the grand, effective instrument which we are to use for, the destruction of caste: Character, in its broad, wide, deep, and high significance; character, as evidenced in high moral and intellectual attainments; as significant of general probity, honor, honesty, and self-restraint; as inclusive of inward might and power; as comprehending the attainments of culture, refinement, and enlightenment; as comprising the substantial results of thrift, economy, and enterprise; and as involving the forces of combined energies and enlightened cooperation. Make this, *not* the exceptional, but the common, general reality, amid the diverse, widespread populations of the colored people in this country; and then all the theories of inferiority, all the assumptions of your native and invincible degradation will pass, with wonderful rapidity, into endless forgetfulness; and the people of the very *next,* nay, multitudes, in the decline of *this* generation, when they look upon us, will wonder at the degrading facts of a past and wretched history. Only secure high, commanding, and masterly Character; and then all the problems of caste, all the enigmas of prejudice, all unreasonable and all unreasoning repulsion, will be settled forever, though you were ten times blacker than midnight! Then all false ideas concerning your nature and your qualities, all absurd notions relative to your capacity, shall vanish! Then every contemptuous fling shall be hushed, every insulting epithet be forgotten! Then, also, all the remembrances of a servile heritage, of ancestral degradation, shall be obliterated! Then all repulsive feel-ings, all evil dislikes shall fly away! Then, too, all timid disconcert shall depart from us, and all cramped and hesitant manhood shall die!

Dear brethren and friends, let there be but the clear demonstration of manly power and grand capacity in our race, in general, in this country; let there only be the wide out-flashings of art and genius, from their brains; and caste will slink, at once, oblivious to the shades. But no mere self-assertion, no strong, vociferous claims and clamor, can ever secure recognition and equal-ity, so long as inferiority and degradation, if even cruelly entailed, abide as a heritage and a cancer. And I maintain we must *organize*, to the end that we may attain such character. The whole of our future on this soil depends upon that single fact of magnitude—character. Race, color, and all the incidents thereof have but little to do with the matter; and men talk idly when they say "we must forget that we are colored men." What is needed is not that we should forget this fact, but that we should rise to such elevation that the *people of the land* be forced to forget all the facts and theories of race, when they behold our thorough equality with them, in all the lines of activity and attainment, of culture and moral grandeur. The great necessity in this land is that its white population should forget, be made to forget, that we are *colored men!* Hence there is a work ahead of us, for the overthrow of caste, which will consume the best part of a century. He, whoever he may be, commits the greatest blunder, who advises you to disband your forces, until that work is brought to its end. It was only *after* the battle of Waterloo that England and her allies broke up their armies, and scattered their huge battalions. Not until we, as a people, have fully vindicated our race; not until we have achieved to the full their rights and prerogatives; not until, by character, we challenge universal respect and consideration in the land, can we sing the song:

—Come to the sunset tree,
The day is past and gone,
The woodman's axe lies free,
And the reaper's work is done.[15]

Until that time, far distant from today, should the cry be everywhere among us: "Combine and marshal, for all the highest achievements in industry, social progress, literature, and religion!"

I hasten to conclude with two brief remarks:

First, then, let me remind and warn you, my friends, that we, as colored men, have no superfluity of powers or faculties in the work which is before us, as a race, in this country. First of all, we all start with maimed and stunted powers. And next, the work before us is so distinct, definite, and, withal, so immense, that it tolerates no erratic wanderings to out-of-the-way and foreign fields.

And yet there are men who tell us that much of our work of the day is objective, that it lies among another people. But I beg to say that we have more than we are equal to in the needs of the six millions of our ignorant and benighted people, yet crippled and paralyzed by the lingering maladies of slavery. If we address ourselves strenuously and unitedly to *their* elevation and improvement we shall have our hands full for more than one generation, without flowing over with zeal and offices to a masterful people, laden with the enlightenment of centuries.

For one, I say very candidly that I do not feel it *my* special calling to wage war with and to extirpate caste. I am no way responsible for its existence. I abominate it as an enormity. *Theirs* is the responsibility who uphold it, and theirs is the obligation to destroy it. My work is special to my own people, and it is constructive. I beg leave to differ from that class of colored men who think that ours is a special mission, to leave our camp and to go over, as it were, among the Philistines, and to destroy their idols.

For my part, I am satisfied that my field of labor is with my own race in these times. I feel I have no exuberance of powers or ability to spend in any other field, or to bestow upon any other people. I say, as said the Shunamite woman, "I DWELL AMONG MY OWN PEOPLE" (2 Kings: IV, 13); not, indeed, as mindless of the brotherhood of the entire species, not as forgetful of the sentiment of fellowship with disciples of every name and blood; but as urged by the feeling of kinship, to bind myself as "with hooks of steel"[16] to the most degraded class in the land, my own "kinsmen according to the flesh."[17] I have the most thorough and radical conviction that the very first duty of colored men, in this our day and generation, is in the large field of effort which requires the regeneration and enlightenment of the colored race in these United States.

And second, from this comes the legitimate inference suggested by the text, *i.e.,* of union and co-operation through all our ranks for effective action and for the no-blest ends. Everywhere throughout the Union wide and thorough organization of the people should be made, not for idle political logomachy, but for industrial effort, for securing trades for youth, for joint-stock companies, for manufacturing, for the production of the great staples of the land, and likewise for the higher purposes of life, i.e., for mental and moral improvement, and raising the plane of social and domestic life among us.

In every possible way these needs and duties should be pressed upon their attention, by sermons, by lectures, by organized societies, by state and national conventions; the *latter not* for political objects, but for social, industrial ends and attainments. I see naught in the future but that we shall be scattered like chaff before the wind before the organized labor of the land, the great power of capital, and the tremendous tide of emigration, unless, as a people, we fall back upon the might and mastery which come from the combination of forces and the principle of industrial co-operation. Most of your political agitation is but wind and vanity. *What this race needs in this country is* POWER—*the forces that may be felt.* And that comes from character, and character is the product of religion, intelligence, virtue, family order, superiority, wealth, and the show of industrial forces. THESE ARE FORCES WHICH WE DO NOT POSSESS. *We are the only class which, as a class,* IN THIS COUNTRY, IS WANTING IN THESE GRAND ELEMENTS. The very first effort of the colored people should be to lay hold of them; and then they will take such root in this American soil that only the convulsive upheaving of the judgment-day can throw them out!

And therefore I close, as I began, with the admonitory tones of the text. God grant they may be heeded at least by You who form this congregation, in your sacred work *here,* and in all your other relations: "They helped every one his neighbor, and every one said to his brother, Be of good courage. So the carpenter encouraged the goldsmith, and he that smootheth with the hammer him that smote the anvil, saying, It is ready for the soldering; and he fastened it with nails, that it SHOULD NOT BE MOVED!"[18]

1875

NOTES

1. On October 27, 1875, President Ulysses S. Grant issued Proclamation 226, designating Thursday, November 26, 1875, as a national day of thanksgiving.

2. The retreat, in 401 BCE, of the ten thousand Greek mercenaries back to the Black Sea at Trabzon following an unsuccessful attempt to seize the Persian throne. The episode is documented in *Anabasis,* Greek historian Xenophon's seven-volume account of these events.

3. Admiral George Anson (1697–1762) and Captain James Cook (1728–1779), English explorers noted for their pioneering voyages around the world and to the islands of the South Pacific, respectively.

4. The spread of Christianity from the Holy Land westward, during the early Christian era.

5. Jacob Merritt Howard (1805–1871), U.S. senator from Michigan, opponent of the Fugitive Slave Act of 1850 and an outspoken abolitionist, credited with helping to facilitate the passage of the Thirteenth Amendment to the Constitution, ending slavery.

6. Thomas Clarkson (1760–1846), an English abolitionist who played a critical role in the passage of the Slave Trade Act of 1807.

7. Robert Raikes (1736–1811), an English abolitionist and Anglican layman.

8. The name given to the Hawaiian Islands by English sea captain James Cook, upon his arrival there in 1778.

9. Alexandre Dumas, fils, son of the noted French author of *The Count of Monte Cristo* and *The Three Musketeers.* The novelist, Alexandre Dumas, pere, was the son of a French nobleman and an enslaved African woman.

10. The highest mountain in the Alps.

11. From Shakespeare's *King Henry V,* Act III, scene i.

12. From Mr. Chapman's description of the English poor in U.S. author Mary Henderson Eastman's popular novel, *Aunt Phillis's Cabin; or, Southern Life as It Is* (1852).

13. Song of Solomon 1:5.

14. Latin expression meaning, "to whose benefit."

15. From "Evening Song of the Tyrolese Peasants" by nineteenth-century English poet Felicia Dorothea Hemans.

16. From William Shakespeare's *Hamlet,* Act I, Scene iii.

17. Romans 9:3.

18. Isaiah 41:6–7.

HENRIETTA CORDELIA RAY
(1849-1916)

Henrietta Cordelia Ray was born in New York City to Charles Bennett Ray, a
Congregational minister and co-owner of *The Colored American* newspaper,
and Charlotte Augusta Burroughs, his second wife. She was named for her
father's deceased former wife, Henrietta Regulus Green, founder of the African
Dorcas Society, a support organization for New York's Free African Schools.
Ray would go on to earn a master of pedagogy degree from the University
of the City of New York. She was also a graduate of the Sauveur School of
Languages and was conversant in Latin, German, French, and Greek. Ray
taught English in the New York City public schools for thirty years, retiring to
Woodside, Long Island in the early 1900s. There she shared a home with
her younger sister Florence and taught lessons in languages and literature,
mathematics, and music, until her death in 1916. Writing under the name
H. Cordelia Ray, she published two books of poems as well as a biography of
her father, on which she collaborated with Florence and older sister Charlotte.
Her poems also appeared in several African American magazines and newspapers, including *The New York Age.* In the mid-1870s, she was commissioned
to compose an occasional verse to be read at the 1876 dedication of the
Freedom's Monument in Washington, DC. "Lincoln; Written for the Occasion
of the Unveiling of the Freedmen's Monument in Memory of Abraham Lincoln:
April 14, 1876" would become Ray's most popular work. The following selections also include three works from her 1910 volume, *Poems* ("To My Father,"
"Toussaint L'Ouverture," and "In Memoriam: Paul Laurence Dunbar").

LINCOLN; WRITTEN FOR THE OCCASION
OF THE UNVEILING OF THE FREEDMEN'S MONUMENT
IN MEMORY OF ABRAHAM LINCOLN: APRIL 14, 1876

To-day, O martyred chief, beneath the sun
We would unveil thy form; to thee who won
Th' applause of nations for thy soul sincere,
A loving tribute we would offer here.

'T was thine not worlds to conquer, but men's hearts;
To change to balm the sting of slavery's darts;
In lowly charity thy joy to find,
And open "gates of mercy on mankind."
And so they come, the freed, with grateful gift,
From whose sad path the shadows thou didst lift.

Eleven years have rolled their seasons round,
Since its most tragic close thy life-work found.
Yet through the vistas of the vanished days
We see thee still, responsive to our gaze,
As ever to thy country's solemn needs.
Not regal coronets, but princely deeds
Were thy chaste diadem; of truer worth
Thy modest virtues than the gems of earth.
Stanch, honest, fervent in the purest cause,
Truth was thy guide; her mandates were thy laws.

Rare heroism, spirit-purity,
The storied Spartan's stern simplicity,
Such moral strength as gleams like burnished gold
Amid the doubt of men of weaker mould,
Were thine. Called in thy country's sorest hour,
When brother knew not brother—mad for power—
To guide the helm through bloody deeps of war,
While distant nations gazed in anxious awe,
Unflinching in the task, thou didst fulfill
Thy mighty mission with a deathless will.

Born to a destiny the most sublime,
Thou wert, O Lincoln! in the march of time,
God bade thee pause and bid the oppressed go free—
Most glorious boon giv'n to humanity.
While slavery ruled the land, what deeds were done!
What tragedies enacted 'neath the sun!
Her page is blurred with records of defeat,
Of lives heroic lived in silence, meet
For the world's praise; of woe, despair and tears,
The speechless agony of weary years.

Thou utteredst the word, and Freedom fair
Rang her sweet bells on the clear winter air;
She waved her magic wand, and lo! from far
A long procession came. With many a scar
Their brows were wrinkled, in the bitter strife,
Full many had said their sad farewell to life.
But on they hastened, free, their shackles gone;
The aged, young,—e'en infancy was borne
To offer unto thee loud pæans of praise,—
Their happy tribute after saddest days.

A race set free! The deed brought joy and light!
It bade calm Justice from her sacred height,
When faith and hope and courage slowly waned,
Unfurl the stars and stripes, at last unstained!
The nations rolled acclaim from sea to sea,
And Heaven's vault rang with Freedom's harmony.
The angels 'mid the amaranths must have hushed
Their chanted cadences, as upward rushed
The hymn sublime: and as the echoes pealed,
God's ceaseless benison the action sealed.

As now we dedicate this shaft to thee,
True champion! in all humility
And solemn earnestness, we would erect
A monument invisible, undecked,
Save by our allied purpose to be true
To Freedom's loftiest precepts, so that through
The fiercest contests we may walk secure,
Fixed on foundations that may still endure,
When granite shall have crumbled to decay,
And generations passed from earth away.

Exalted patriot! Illustrious chief!
Thy life's immortal work compels belief.
To-day in radiance thy virtues shine,
And how can we a fitting garland twine?
Thy crown most glorious to a ransomed race!

High on our country's scroll we fondly trace,
In lines of fadeless light that softly blend,
Emancipator, hero, martyr, friend!
While Freedom may her holy sceptre claim,
The world shall echo with Our Lincoln's name.

1876

TO MY FATHER

A leaf from Freedom's golden chaplet fair,
We bring to thee, dear father! Near her shrine
None came with holier purpose, nor was thine
Alone the soul's mute sanction; every prayer
Thy captive brother uttered found a share
In thy wide sympathy; to every sign
That told the bondman's need thou didst incline.
No thought of guerdon hadst thou but to bear
A loving part in Freedom's strife. To see
Sad lives illumined, fetters rent in twain,
Tears dried in eyes that wept for length of days—
Ah! was not that a recompense for thee?
And now where all life's mystery is plain,
Divine approval is thy sweetest praise.

1910

TOUSSAINT L'OUVERTURE

To those fair isles where crimson sunsets burn,
We send a backward glance to gaze on thee,
Brave Toussaint! thou wast surely born to be
A hero; thy proud spirit could but spurn
Each outrage on thy race. Couldst thou unlearn
The lessons taught by instinct? Nay! and we
Who share the zeal that would make all men free,
Must e'en with pride unto thy life-work turn.

Soul-dignity was thine and purest aim;
And ah! how sad that thou wast left to mourn
In chains 'neath alien skies. On him, shame! shame!
That mighty conqueror who dared to claim
The right to bind thee. Him we heap with scorn,
And noble patriot! guard with love thy name.

1910

IN MEMORIAM: PAUL LAURENCE DUNBAR

The Muse of Poetry came down one day,
And brought with willing hands a rare, sweet gift;
She lingered near the cradle of a child,
Who first unto the sun his eyes did lift.
She touched his lips with true Olympian fire,
And at her bidding Fancies hastened there,
To flutter lovingly around the one
So favored by the Muse's gentle care.

Who was this child? The offspring of a race
That erst had toiled 'neath slavery's galling chains.
And soon he woke to utterance and sang
In sweetly cadenced and in stirring strains,
Of simple joys, and yearnings, and regrets;
Anon to loftier themes he turned his pen;
For so in tender, sympathetic mood
He caught the follies and the griefs of men.

His tones were various: we list, and lo!
"Malindy Sings,"[1] and as the echoes die,
The keynote changes and another strain
Of solemn majesty goes floating by;
And sometimes in the beauty and the grace
Of an impassioned, melancholy lay,
We seem to hear the surge, and swell, and moan
Of soft orchestral music far away.

Paul Dunbar dead! His genius cannot die!
It lives in songs that thrill, and glow, and soar;
Their pathos and their joy will fill our hearts,
And charm and satisfy e'en as of yore.
So when we would lament our poet gone,
With sorrow that his lyre is resting now,
Let us remember, with the fondest pride,
That Fame's immortal wreath has crowned his brow.

1910

NOTE

1. "When Malindy Sings," a poem by Paul Laurence Dunbar (1872–1906).

TIMOTHY THOMAS FORTUNE (1856-1928)

Timothy Thomas Fortune was born into slavery in Marianna, Florida. He received his first academic instruction from Union soldiers during the Civil War. His distinguished work as a page in the Reconstruction-era Florida legislature earned him a nomination to attend the U.S. Military Academy at West Point. At the time, however, the academy was closed to African Americans, and he was unable to enroll. Instead, Fortune attended the Stanton Institute in Jacksonville, Florida, a school for newly emancipated black students, administered by the Freedman's Bureau. In 1877 he enrolled in Howard University, which he attended for one year. In 1880, having relocated to New York, Fortune became the editor and a co-owner the *New York Globe* newspaper. In 1884 he acquired sole proprietorship of the paper, which he renamed the *New York Freeman* and, eventually, the *New York Age*. Fortune's paper would go on to become one of the most influential African American periodicals in the nation, due in part to its uncompromising perspective that all black people were entitled to equality in all quarters of American life. In 1884, Fortune outlined his political philosophy and historical vision in *Black and White: Land, Labor, and Politics in the South,* a book-length assessment of the relationship between race, property, and the structures of inequality during slavery and its aftermath. A poet as well as an essayist and reporter, Fortune published numerous poems in his own and other papers, and, in 1905, he released a collection of verse titled *Dreams of Life*. In the following excerpt from *Black and White,* Fortune analyzes the relationship between industrialization, consumer culture, and the exploitation of the working class. The poems "The Conclave," "Love's Divinest Power," and "Come Away, Love" were first published in *The New York Age*. The poem "Dreams of Life" was first published in Fortune's 1905 collection of the same name.

BLACK AND WHITE: LAND, LABOR, AND POLITICS IN THE SOUTH

Chapter XII: Civilization Degrades the Masses

There are men in all parts of the world, whose names have become synonyms of learning and genius, who proclaim it from the housetops that civilization is in a constant state of evolution to a higher, purer, nobler, happier condition of the people, the great mass of mankind, who properly make up society, and who have been styled, in derision, the *"mudsills* of society."[1] So they are, society rests upon them; society must build upon them; without them society cannot be, because they are, in the broadest sense, society itself,—not only the "mudsills" but the *superstructure* as well. They not only constitute the great producing class but the great consuming class as well. They are the bone and sinew of society.

It is therefore of the utmost importance to know the condition of the people; it is not only important to know exactly what that condition is, but it is of the very first importance to the well-being of society that there should be absolutely nothing in that condition to arouse the apprehension of the sharks who live upon the carcass of the people, or of the people who permit the sharks to so live. There is nothing more absolutely certain than that the people—who submit to be robbed through the intricate and multifarious processes devised by the cupidity of individuals and of governments—when aroused to a full sense of the wrongs inflicted upon them, will strike down their oppressors in a rage of desperation born of despair.

Modern tyrannies are far more insidious than the military despotisms of the past. These modern engines which crush society destroy the energy and vitality of the people by the slow process of starvation, sanctioned by the law, and in a majority of instances, are patiently borne by the victims. It is only when human nature can endure no more that protests are first heard; then armed resistance; then anarchy. Thus it was with the French of the eighteenth century. Thus it is with the Russian, the German, the English, the Irish peoples of to-day. The heel of the tyrant is studded with too many steel nails to be borne without excruciating pain and without earnest protest.

If in their desperate conflict with the serpent that has coiled its slimy length about the body of the people the latter resort to dynamite, and seek by savage warfare to right their wrongs, they are to be condemned and controlled, for they confound the innocent with the guilty and work ruin rather than reform. Yet there is another side to be considered, for when injustice wraps itself in the robes of virtue and of law, and calls in the assistance of armies and all the destructive machinery of modern warfare to enforce its right to enslave and starve mankind, what counter warfare can be too savage, too destructive in its operations, to compel attention to the wrong? The difficulty is that vengeance should discriminate, but that is a refinement which blind rage can hardly compass.

I believe in law and order; but I believe, as a condition precedent, that law and order should be predicated upon right and justice, pure and simple. Law is, intrinsically, a written expression of justice; if, on the contrary, it becomes instead written *injustice,* men are not, strictly speaking, bound to yield it obedience. There is no law, on the statute books of any nation of the world, which bears unjustly upon the people, which should be permitted to stand one hour. It is through the operations of law that mankind is ground to powder; it is by the prostitution of the rights of the masses, by men who pretend to be their representatives and are not, that misery, starvation and death fill the largest space in the news channels of every land.

In New York City—where the intelligence, the enterprise, the wealth and the Christianized humanity of the New World are supposed to have their highest exemplification—men, women and children die by the thousands, starved and frozen out of the world! Thousands die yearly in the city of New York from the effects of exposure and insufficient nutriment. The world, into which they had come unbidden, and the fruits of which a just God had declared they should enjoy as reward of the sweat of their brows, had refused them even a bare subsistence; and, this, when millions of food rot in the storehouses without purchasers! The harpies of trade prefer that their substance should resolve itself into the dirt and weed from which it sprung, rather than the poor and needy should eat of it and live.

I have walked through the tenement wards of New York, and I have seen enough want and crime and blasted virtue to condemn the civilization which produced them and which fosters them in its bosom.

I have looked upon the vast army of police which New York City maintains to protect life and so-called "vested rights," and I have concluded that there is something wrong in the social system which can only be kept intact by the expenditure of so much productive force, for this vast army, which stands on the street corners and lurks in the alley ways, "spotting," suspicious persons, "keeping an eye" on strangers who look "smart," this vast army contributes nothing to the production of wealth. It is, essentially, a parasite. And yet, without this army of idlers, life would be in constant danger and property would fall prey not only to the vicious and the desperate, but to the hungry men and women who have neither a place to shelter them from the storms of heaven, nor food to sustain nature's cravings from finding an eternal resting place in the Potter's Field. And, even after every precaution which selfishness can devise, courts of law and police officers are powerless to stay the hand of the pariahs whom society has outlawed—the men and women who are doomed to starve to death and be buried at the expense of society. The streets of every city in the Union are full of people who have been made desperate by social adjustments which prophets laud to the skies and which philosophers commend as "ideal," as far as they go.

One-half the producing power of the United States is to-day absolutely dependent upon the cold charity of the world; one fourth does not make sufficient to live beyond the day, while the other one-fourth only manages to live comfortably at the expense of the most parsimonious economy.

It is becoming a mooted question whether labor-saving machinery has not supplanted muscle-power in the production of every article to such a marvelous extent as to make thoughtful men tremble for the future of those who can only hope to live upon the produce of their labors. The machine has taken the place, largely, of man in the production of articles of consumption, of wear and of ornamentation; but no machine has, as yet, been invented to take the place of human wants. The markets of the world are actually glutted with articles produced by machine labor, but there are no purchasers with the means to buy, to consume the additional production caused by machinery and the consequent cheapening of processes of producing the articles of consumption, ornamentation, etc. When men have work they have money; and when men have money they spend it. Hence, when the toilers of a land have steady employment trade is brisk; when business stagnation forces them into idleness vice and crime afflict the country.

What avail the tireless labor of the machine and the mountains of material it places upon the market, if there are no purchasers? One man at a machine will do as much work in a factory to-day as required the work of fifty men fifty years ago; but the enhanced volume of production can have only one purchaser now where there was once fifty, hence the fitful existence of the one and the desperate struggle for existence of the forty-nine.[2] As iron and steel cannot compete with muscle and brain in the volume of production, so iron and steel cannot compete with muscle and brain in consumption. And, without consumption, what does production amount to? What does it avail us that our stores and granaries are overstocked, if the people are unable to buy? The thing is reduced to a cruel mockery when stores and granaries are over-gorged, while people clamor in vain for clothing and food, and drop dead within reach of these prime elements of warmth and sustentation.

What does it avail us if the balance of trade be in our favor by one, or two, or three hundred millions of dollars, if this result be obtained by the degradation and death of our own people? More; not only at the expense of the well being of our own people, but of the people of those countries in whose markets we are enabled to undersell them, by reason of the more systematic pauperization of our own producing classes.

Competition, it is declared, is the life of trade; if this be true, it is truer that it is the death of labor, of the poorer classes. For Great Britain has established herself in the markets of the world at the expense of her laboring classes. While the capitalists of that country hold up their heads among the proudest people of the world, her laboring classes are absolutely ground to powder. Because of the inhuman competition which her manufacturers have been led to adopt, and the introduction of improved labor-saving machinery, her balance of trade runs far into the millions of pounds, and political economists place their hands upon their hearts and declare that Great Britain is the most happy and prosperous country on the face of the globe. But the declaration is illusory in the extreme. No country can be happy and prosperous whose "mudsills" live in squalor, want, misery, vice and death. If Great Britain is happy and prosperous, how shall we account for the constant strikes of labor organizations for higher pay or as a protest against further reduction of wages below which man cannot live and produce? The balance of trade desire is the curse of the people of the world. It can be obtained only by underbidding other people in their own markets; and this can be done only by the maximum of production at the minimum of cost—by forcing as much labor out of the man or the machine as possible at the least possible expense.

There is death in the theory; death to our own people and death to the people with whom we compete. When a people no longer produce those articles which are absolutely necessary to sustain life the days of such people may be easily calculated.

Men talk daily of "over production," of "glutted markets," and the like; but such is not a true statement of the case. There can be no over production of anything as long as there are hungry mouths to be fed. It does not matter if the possessors of these hungry mouths are too poor to buy the bread; if they are hungry, there is no overproduction. With a balance of $150,000,000 of trade; with plethoric granaries and elevators all over the land; with millions of swine, sheep and cattle on a thousand hills; with millions of surplus revenue in the vaults of the National treasury, diverted from the regular channels of trade by an ignorant set of legislators who have not gumption enough to reduce unnecessary and burdensome taxation without upsetting the industries of the country—with all its grandiloquent exhibition of happiness and prosperity, the laboring classes of the country starve to death, or eke out an existence still more horrible.

The factories of the land run on half time, and the men, women and children who operate them grow pinch-faced, lean and haggard, from insufficient nutriment, and are old and decrepit while yet in the bud of youth; the tenements are crowded to suffocation, breeding pestilence and death; while the wages paid to labor hardly serve to satisfy the exactions of the landlord— a monstrosity in the midst of civilization, whose very existence is a crying protest against our pretensions to civilization.

Yet, "competition" is the cry of the hour. Millionaires compete with each other in the management of vast railroads and water routes, reducing labor to the verge of subsistence while exacting mints of money as tolls for transportation from the toilers of the soil and the consumers who live by their labor in other industrial enterprises; the manufacturers join in the competition, selling goods at the least possible profit to themselves and the least possible profit to those who labor for them; and, when no market can be found at home, boldly enter foreign markets and successfully compete with manufacturers who employ what our writers are pleased to style "pauper" labor. Every branch of industry is in the field *competing,* and the competition is ruining every branch of industry. The constant effort to obtain the maximum of production at the minimum of cost operates injuriously upon employer and employee alike; while the shrinkage in money circulation, caused by the competition, reduces, in every branch of industry, the wages of those who are the great consumers as well as producers; it produces those "hard times" which bear so hardly upon the poor in every walk of life. Even the laboring man has entered the race, and now competes in the labor market with his fellow for an opportunity to make a crust of bread to feed his wife and child. When things reach this stage, when the man who is working for one dollar and a half per day is underbid by a man who will work for a dollar and a quarter, then the condition of the great wealth producing and consuming class is desperate indeed. And so it is.

Frederick Douglass, the great Negro commoner, speaking at Washington, April 16, 1883, on the "Twenty-first Anniversary of Emancipation in the District of Columbia," said:

> Events are transpiring all around us that enforce respect of the oppressed classes. In one form or another, by one means or another, the ideas of a common humanity against privileged classes, of common rights against special privileges, are now rocking the world. Explosives are heard that rival the earthquake. They are causing despots to tremble, class rule to quail, thrones to shake and oppressive associated wealth to turn pale. It is for America to be wise in time.

And the black philosopher, who had by manly courage and matchless eloquence braved the mob law of the North and the organized brigandage and robbery of the South in the dark days of the past, days that tried men's souls, standing in the sunlight of rejuvenated manhood, still was the oracle of the oppressed in the sentiments above quoted.

All over the land the voice of the masses is heard. Organizations in their interests are multiplying like sands on the seashore. The fierce, hoarse mutter of the starved and starving gives unmistakable warning that America has entered upon that fierce conflict of money-power and muscle-power which now shake to their very centers the hoary-headed commonwealths of the old world. In *John Swinton's Paper*[3] of a recent date I find the following editorial arraignment of the present state of "Labor and Capital:"

The cries of the people against the oppressions of capital and monopoly are heard all over the land; but the capitalist and monopolist give them no heed, and go on their way more relentlessly than ever. Congress is fully aware of the condition of things; but you cannot get any bill through there for the relief of the people. The coal lords of Pennsylvania know how abject are the tens of thousands of blackamoors of their mines; but they grind them without mercy, and cut their days' wages again whenever they squeal. Jay Gould[4] knows of the wide-spread ruin he has wrought in piling up his hundred millions; but he drives along faster than ever in his routine of plunder. The factory Christians of Fall River see their thousands of poor spinners struggling for the bread of life amid the whirl of machinery: but they order reduction after reduction in the rate of wages, though the veins of the corporations are swollen to congestion. The "Big Four" of Chicago,[5] who corner grain and provisions, and the capitalists here and elsewhere who do the same thing, know well how the farmers suffer and the tables of the poor are ravaged by their operations; but they prosecute their work more extensively and recklessly than ever. The railroad and telegraph corporations know that, in putting on "all that the traffic will bear," they are taking from this country more than the people can stand; yet their only answer is that of the horseleech. . . .[6]

Our lawmakers know how the people are wronged through legislation in the interest of privilege and plunder; but they add statute to statute in that same interest. They know how advantageous to the producers would be the few measures asked in their name; yet they persistently refuse to adopt them. The great employers of labor, the cormorants of competition, know through what hideous injustice they enrich themselves; but speak to them of fair play, and they flout you from their presence. The wealthy corporations owning these street car lines in New York see that their drivers and conductors are kept on the rack from sixteen to eighteen hours every day of the week, including Sundays; but when a bill is brought into the State Legislature to limit the daily working hours to twelve, they order their hired agents of the lobby to defeat it. These gamblers of Wall Street know that their gains are mainly through fraud; yet forever, fast and furious, do they play with loaded dice.

The landlords of these tenement quarters know by the mortality statistics how broad is the swathe that death cuts among their victims; but they add dollar to dollar as coffin after coffin is carried into the street. . . .

These owners of the machinery of industry know how it bears upon the men who keep it flying; but they are regardless of all that, if only it fills their coffers. These owners of palaces look upon the men by whom they are built; but think all the time how to raise the rent of their hovels. These great money-lenders who hold the mortgages on countless farms know of the straits of the mortgage-bound farmers; yet they never cease to plot for higher interest and harder terms. The gilded priests of Mammon and hypocrisy cannot get away from the cries of humankind; but when do you ever hear them denouncing the guilty and responsible criminals in their velvet-cushioned pews? Harder and harder grow the exactions of capital. Harder and harder grows the lot of the millions. Louder and louder grow the cries of the sufferers. Deafer and deafer grow the ears of the millionaires. Yet, if those who cry would but use their power in action, peaceful action, they could right their wrongs, or at least the most grievous of them, before the world completes the solar circuit of this year.

Wm. Goodwin Moody (*Land and Labor in the United States,* p. 338), reverting to the difficulties which beset the pathway of labor organizations, which have so far been productive of nothing but disaster to the laboring classes, says:

Is it not time that new weapons should be adopted, and new methods introduced? . . . Will not the working men of the country learn anything from the bitter experiences they have passed through, and abandon methods that have been so uniformly followed by the ultimate failure of all their efforts. But the great evils by which we are surrounded, and that are destroying the foundations of society, can be removed by the working-men only. They form the large majority of its members, and in our country they are all-powerful. Still it is only by absolutely united action that the working-men can accomplish any good. By disunion they may achieve any amount of evil. The enemy they have to contend against, though few in number, are strong in position and possession of great capital. Nevertheless, before the united working-men of the country, seeking really national objects and noble ends, by methods that are just and in harmony with the institutions under which we live, the tyranny of capital will end. The working-men will also draw to their support a very large part of the best thought and intelligence of the country, that will be sure to keep even step with the labor of society in its attack upon the enemies of humanity and progress.

There is no fact truer than this, that the accumulated wealth of the land, and the sources of power, are fast becoming concentrated in the hands of a few men, who use that wealth and power to the debasement and enthrallment of the wage workers. Already it is almost impossible to obtain any legislation, in State or Federal legislatures, to ameliorate the condition of the laboring classes. Capital has placed its tyrant grip upon the throat of the Goddess of Liberty. The power of railroad and telegraph corporations, and associated capital invested in monopolies which oppress the many, while ministering to the wealth, the comfort and the luxury of the few, has become omnipotent in halls of legislation, courts of justice, and even in the Executive Chambers of great States, so that the poor, the oppressed and the defrauded appeal in vain for justice.

Such is the deplorable condition of the laboring classes in the west, the north and the east. They are bound to the car of capital, and are being ground to powder as fast as day follows day. They organize in vain; they protest in vain; they appeal in vain. Civilization is doing its work. "To him that hath, more shall be given; to him that hath nothing, even that shall be taken from him."

Let us turn to the South and see if a black skin has anything to do with the tyranny of capital; let us see if the cause of the laboring man is not the same in all sections, in all States, in all governments, in the Union, as it is in all the world. If this can be shown; if I can incontestably demonstrate that *the condition of the black and the white laborer is the same, and that consequently their cause is common*; that they should unite under the one banner and work upon the same platform of principles for the uplifting of labor, the more equal distribution of the products of labor and capital, I shall not have written this book in vain, and the patient reader will not have read after me without profit to himself and the common cause of a common humanity.

1884

THE CONCLAVE: TO THE LADIES OF TUSKEGEE SCHOOL

From icy Winter's rule to Summer's reign,[7]
After the lapse of years, I come again,—
From arid wastes of city brick and stone

To the fair clime where Nature claims her own!
Here dwells my heart, wherever I may roam;
No other land than this can be my home.
'Tis strange how fondly to the past will cling
The heart whatever time and change may bring,

The vernal blooms of this delicious land
Surround and charm me here on every hand;
E'en as I write the scent of orchids rare
Perfumes my room, the gift of maidens fair
And beautiful and true beyond compare,
Of women loyal as the generous earth
E'er welcomed to its sorrows and its mirth!
Their smiles have sweetened these all fragrant flowers,
Plucked within the hour from their native bowers.

And I shall wander far before I see
Maidens truer than those of Tuskegee!
For here they mold the plastic mind of youth
In ways of wisdom, virtue and of truth.
Far from the city's joys and pains and strife
They dwell apart, they dedicate their life,
To noble efforts for the needy race
With courage rare, with more than queenly grace.

                    Tuskegee, Ala., April 20, 1890.

LOVE'S DIVINEST POWER

Let mad ambition strive to gain
The cherished wish that yields but pain;
Let others seek for wealth alone,
And with its cares their lives atone;
But let me live my fleeting hour
The slave of Love's divinest power.

                    1890

COME AWAY, LOVE

Come away, love, come away
Where the men do gather hay;—
In the fruitful fields remote
Join with mine thy merry note,
In the toilsome pleasures where
Plenty drives away all care!
On the hills the flocks do browse,
And the dogs the echoes rouse;
All is life, and all is joy.
Where all hands do find employ.

1890

NOTES

1. In 1858, John Henry Hammond, U.S. senator from South Carolina, characterized African American people as "the mudsills of society," ordained to perform the menial tasks necessary to support the growth of a rising nation.

2. Wm. Goodwin Moody shows this conclusively in his work on *Land and Labor in the United States* [Fortune's note].

3. An important pro-labor weekly published from 1883 to 1887 by the former *New York Times* chief editorial writer, John Swinton (1829–1901).

4. Jason "Jay" Gould (1836–1892), railroad speculator and financier, one of the most notorious "robber barons" of the Gilded Age.

5. A likely reference to G. H. Hammond (1838–1886), Philip Danforth Armour (1832–1901), Edward Morris (1866–1913), and Gustavus Franklin Swift (1839–1903), meatpacking executives running operations in and around Chicago, each the founder of a corporation bearing his own name.

6. A reference to the figure of the *daughter of the horse-leech,* a common label for a person of insatiable or parasitic character, as in Sir Walter Scott's *Peveril the Peak,* chapter 28 ("Such and many such like were the morning attendants of the Duke of Buckingham—all genuine descendants of the daughter of the horse-leech, whose cry is 'Give, give'") or Proverbs 30:15 ("The horseleach hath two daughters, crying, 'Give, give'").

7. The Tuskegee Institute (now Tuskegee University) is a historically black college founded in 1881 by African American educator Booker T. Washington.

CHARLES WADDELL CHESNUTT (1858-1932)

Charles Waddell Chesnutt was born in Cleveland, Ohio. Both of his parents hailed from North Carolina, where they had been part of a small elite class of free African American families. In 1866, the Chesnutt family returned to North Carolina, settling in Fayetteville. There Chesnutt attended an African American school, founded by his father, until financial difficulties obliged him to abandon his formal education. Chesnutt worked as a teacher, eventually becoming the principal of the State Colored Normal School. In 1883, Chesnutt, now married, returned to Cleveland, where he found success as a stenographer. Chesnutt is best known for his short fiction, including a series of stories revolving around the character of Aun' Peggy, a free black woman and conjurer living in antebellum North Carolina. The first of the conjure-woman stories, "The Goophered Grapevine," was printed in the August 1887 issue of the *Atlantic Monthly,* the first fiction by an African American writer to appear in that publication. Less than one year later, Chesnutt published a second conjure story in the *Atlantic.* "Po' Sandy" appeared in the May 1888 issue and was followed in November 1889 by a third conjure tale, "Dave's Neckliss." Chesnutt is also remembered for his stories of the color line, a theme no doubt inspired by the complexities of his own ethnic identity. Each of his grandmothers was of mixed race, and his paternal grandfather, Waddell Cade, was a wealthy white landowner whose will divided his considerable holdings between his white offspring and the mixed-race children of his African American mistress. In works like "The Sheriff's Children" (1889) and *The House Behind the Cedars* (1900), Chesnutt explored the complicated circumstances produced by a social structure that refused to recognize the possibility of subjects who were both black *and* white. Chesnutt's most ambitious work was his fictionalized account of the 1898 Wilmington riots, *The Marrow of Tradition* (1901). Though he found a degree of acceptance in the mainstream white periodicals of his day, Chesnutt was also involved in the period's black literary culture. The conjure tale "Tobe's Tribulations" first appeared in the November 1900 issue of *The Southern Workman,* a monthly magazine published by the Hampton Institute Press. The nonfiction essay "The Free Colored People of North Carolina" was first published in *The Southern Workman* in March of 1902. The version of "The Goophered Grapevine" that appears below is as it appeared in the August 1887 issue of the *Atlantic Monthly.*

THE GOOPHERED GRAPEVINE

About ten years ago my wife was in poor health, and our family doctor, in whose skill and honesty I had implicit confidence, advised a change of climate. I was engaged in grape-culture in northern Ohio, and decided to look for a locality suitable for carrying on the same business in some Southern State. I wrote to a cousin who had gone into the turpentine business in central North Carolina, and he assured me that no better place could be found in the South than the State and neighborhood in which he lived: climate and soil were all that could be asked for, and land could be bought for a mere song. A cordial invitation to visit him while I looked into the matter was accepted. We found the weather delightful at that season, the end of the summer, and were most hospitably entertained. Our host placed a horse and buggy at our disposal, and himself acted as guide until I got somewhat familiar with the country.

I went several times to look at a place which I thought might suit me. It had been at one time a thriving plantation, but shiftless cultivation had well-nigh exhausted the soil. There had been a vineyard of some extent on the place, but it had not been attended to since the war, and had fallen into utter neglect. The vines—here partly supported by decayed and broken-down arbors, there twining themselves among the branches of the slender saplings which had sprung up among them—grew in wild and unpruned luxuriance, and the few scanty grapes which they bore were the undisputed prey of the first comer. The site was admirably adapted to grape-raising; the soil, with a little attention, could not have been better; and with the native grape, the luscious scuppernong, mainly to rely upon, I felt sure that I could introduce and cultivate successfully a number of other varieties.

One day I went over with my wife, to show her the place. We drove between the decayed gate-posts—the gate itself had long since disappeared—and up the straight, sandy lane to the open space where a dwelling-house had once stood. But the house had fallen a victim to the fortunes of war, and nothing remained of it except the brick pillars upon which the sills had rested. We alighted, and walked about the place for a while; but on Annie's complaining of weariness I led the way back to the yard, where a pine log, lying under a spreading elm, formed a shady though somewhat hard seat. One end of the log was already occupied by a venerable-looking colored man. He held on his knees a hat full of grapes, over which he was smacking his lips with great gusto, and a pile of grape-skins near him indicated that the performance was no new thing. He respectfully rose as we approached, and was moving away, when I begged him to keep his seat.

"Don't let us disturb you," I said. "There's plenty of room for us all."

He resumed his seat with somewhat of embarrassment.

"Do you live around here?" I asked, anxious to put him at his ease.

"Yas, suh. I lives des ober yander, behine de nex' san'-hill, on de Lumberton plank-road."

"Do you know anything about the time when this vineyard was cultivated?"

"Lawd bless yer, suh, I knows all about it. Dey ain' na'er a man in dis settlement w'at won' tell yer ole Julius McAdoo 'uz bawn an' raise' on dis yer same plantation. Is you de Norv'n gemman w'at's gwine ter buy de ole vimya'd?"

"I am looking at it," I replied; "but I don't know that I shall care to buy unless I can be reasonably sure of making something out of it."

"Well, suh, you is a stranger ter me, en I is a stranger ter you, en we is bofe strangers ter one anudder, but 'f I 'uz in yo' place, I wouldn' buy dis vimya'd."

"Why not?" I asked.

"Well, I dunner whe'r you b'lieves in cunj'in er not,—some er de w'ite folks don't, er says dey don't,—but de truf er de matter is dat dis yer ole vimya'd is goophered."

"Is what?" I asked, not grasping the meaning of this unfamiliar word.

"Is goophered, cunju'd, bewitch'."

He imparted this information with such solemn earnestness, and with such an air of confidential mystery, that I felt somewhat interested, while Annie was evidently much impressed, and drew closer to me.

"How do you know it is bewitched?" I asked.

"I wouldn' spec' fer you ter b'lieve me 'less you know all 'bout de fac's. But ef you en young miss dere doan' min' lis'n'in' ter a ole nigger run on a minute er two w'ile you er restin', I kin 'splain to yer how it all happen'."

We assured him that we would be glad to hear how it all happened, and he began to tell us. At first the current of his memory—or imagination—seemed somewhat sluggish; but as his embarrassment wore off, his language flowed more freely, and the story acquired perspective and coherence. As he became more and more absorbed in the narrative, his eyes assumed a dreamy expression, and he seemed to lose sight of his auditors, and to be living over again in monologue his life on the old plantation.

"Ole Mars Dugal' McAdoo bought dis place long many years befo' de wah, en I 'member well w'en he sot out all dis yer part er de plantation in scuppernon's. De vimes growed monst'us fas', en Mars Dugal' made a thousan' gallon er scuppernon'[1] wine eve'y year.

"Now, ef dey's an'thing a nigger lub, nex' ter 'possum, en chick'n, en watermillyums, it's scuppernon's. Dey ain' nuffin dat kin stan' up side'n de scuppernon' fer sweetness; sugar ain't a suckumstance ter scuppernon'. W'en de season is nigh 'bout ober, en de grapes begin ter swivel up des a little wid de wrinkles er ole age,—w'en de skin git sof' en brown,—den de scuppernon' make you smack yo' lip en roll yo' eye en wush fer mo'; so I reckon it ain' very 'stonishin' dat niggers lub scuppernon'.

"Dey wuz a sight er niggers in de naberhood er de vimya'd. Dere wuz ole Mars Henry Brayboy's niggers, en ole Mars Dunkin McLean's niggers, en Mars Dugal's own niggers; den dey wuz a settlement er free niggers en po' buckrahs down by de Wim'l'ton Road, en Mars Dugal' had de only vimya'd in de naberhood. I reckon it ain' so much so nowadays, but befo' de wah, in slab'ry times, er nigger didn' mine goin' fi' er ten mile in a night, w'en dey wuz sump'n good ter eat at de yuther een.

"So atter a w'ile Mars Dugal' begin ter miss his scuppernon's. Co'se he 'cuse' de niggers er it, but dey all 'nied it ter de las'. Mars Dugal' sot spring guns en steel traps, en he en de oberseah sot up nights once't er twice't, tel one night Mars Dugal'—he 'uz a monst'us keerless man—got his leg shot full er cow-peas. But somehow er nudder dey couldn' nebber ketch none er de niggers. I dunner how it happen, but it happen des like I tell yer, en de grapes kep' on a-goin des de same.

"But bimeby ole Mars Dugal' fix' up a plan ter stop it. Dey 'uz a cunjuh 'ooman livin' down mongs' de free niggers on de Wim'l'ton Road, en all de darkies fum Rockfish ter Beaver Crick wuz feared uv her. She could wuk de mos' powerfulles' kind er goopher,—could make people hab fits er rheumatiz, er make 'em des dwinel away en die; en dey say she went out ridin' de niggers at night, for she wuz a witch 'sides bein' a cunjuh 'ooman. Mars Dugal' hearn 'bout Aun' Peggy's doin's, en begun ter 'flect whe'r er no he could n' git her ter he'p him keep de niggers off'n de grapevimes. One day in de spring er de year, ole miss pack' up a basket er chick'n en poun'-cake, en a bottle er scuppernon' wine, en Mars Dugal' tuk it in his buggy en driv ober ter Aun' Peggy's cabin. He tuk de basket in, en had a long talk wid Aun' Peggy.

"De nex' day Aun' Peggy come up ter de vimya'd. De niggers seed her slippin' 'roun', en dey soon foun' out what she 'uz doin' dere. Mars Dugal' had hi'ed her ter goopher de grapevimes. She sa'ntered 'roun' mongs' de vimes, en tuk a leaf fum dis one, en a grape-hull fum dat one, en a grape-seed fum anudder one; en den a little twig fum here, en a little pinch er dirt fum dere,—en put it all in a big black bottle, wid a snake's toof en a speckle' hen's gall en some ha'rs fum a black cat's tail, en den fill' de bottle wid scuppernon' wine. W'en she got de goopher all ready en fix', she tuk 'n went out in de woods en buried it under de root uv a red oak tree, en den come back en tole one er de niggers she done goopher de grapevimes, en a'er a nigger w'at eat dem grapes 'ud be sho ter die inside'n twel' mont's.

"Atter dat de niggers let de scuppernon's 'lone, en Mars Dugal' did n' hab no 'casion ter fine no mo' fault; en de season wuz mos' gone, w'en a strange gemman stop at de plantation one night ter see Mars Dugal' on some business; en his coachman, seein' de scuppernon's growin' so nice en sweet, slip 'roun' behine de smoke-house, en et all de scuppernon's he could hole. No-body did n' notice it at de time, but dat night, on de way home, de gemman's hoss runned away en kill' de coachman. W'en we hearn de noos, Aun' Lucy, de cook, she up 'n say she seed de strange nigger eat'n' er de scuppernon's behine de smoke-house; en den we knowed de goopher had b'en er wukkin. Den one er de nigger chilluns runned away fum de quarters one day, en got in de scuppernon's, en died de nex' week. W'ite folks say he die' er de fevuh, but de niggers knowed it wuz de goopher. So you k'n be sho de darkies did n' hab much ter do wid dem scuppernon' vimes.

"W'en de scuppernon' season 'uz ober fer dat year, Mars Dugal' foun' he had made fifteen hund'ed gallon er wine; en one er de niggers hearn him laf-fin' wid de oberseah fit ter kill, en sayin' dem fifteen hund'ed gallon er wine wuz monst'us good intrus' on de ten dollars he laid out on de vimya'd. So I 'low ez he paid Aun' Peggy ten dollars fer to goopher de grapevimes.

"De goopher did n' wuk no mo' tel de nex' summer, w'en 'long to'ds de middle er de season one er de fiel' han's died; en ez dat lef' Mars Dugal' sho't er han's, he went off ter town fer ter buy anudder. He fotch de noo nigger home wid 'im. He wuz er ole nigger, er de color er a gingy-cake, en ball ez a hoss-apple on de top er his head. He wuz a peart ole nigger, do', en could do a big day's wuk.

"Now it happen dat one er de niggers on de nex' plantation, one er ole Mars Henry Brayboy's niggers, had runned away de day befo', en tuk ter de swamp, en ole Mars Dugal' en some er de yuther nabor w'ite folks had gone out wid dere guns en dere dogs fer ter he'p 'em hunt fer de nigger; en de han's on our own plantation wuz all so flusterated dat we fuhgot ter tell de noo han' 'bout de goopher on de scuppernon' vimes. Co'se he smell de grapes en see de vimes, an atter dahk de fus' thing he done wuz ter slip off ter de grapevimes 'dout sayin' nuffin ter nobody. Nex' mawnin' he tole some er de niggers 'bout de fine bait er scuppernon' he et de night befo'.

"W'en dey tole 'im 'bout de goopher on de grapevimes, he 'uz dat tarrified dat he turn pale, en look des like he gwine ter die right in his tracks. De oberseah come up en axed w'at 'uz de matter; en w'en dey tole 'im Henry be'n eatin' er de scuppernon's, en got de goopher on 'im, he gin Henry a big drink er w'iskey, en 'low dat de nex' rainy day he take 'im ober ter Aun' Peggy's, en see ef she would n' take de goopher off'n him, seein' ez he did n' know nuffin erbout it tel he done et de grapes.

"Sho nuff, it rain de nex' day, en de oberseah went ober ter Aun' Peggy's wid Henry. En Aun' Peggy say dat bein' ez Henry did n' know 'bout de goopher, en et de grapes in ign'ance er de quinseconces, she reckon she mought be able fer ter take de goopher off'n him. So she fotch out er bottle wid some cunjuh medicine in it, en po'd some out in a go'd fer Henry ter drink. He manage ter git it down; he say it tas'e like whiskey wid sump'n bitter in it. She 'lowed dat 'ud keep de goopher off'n him tel de spring; but w'en de sap begin ter rise in de grapevimes he ha' ter come en see her agin, en she tell him w'at e's ter do.

"Nex' spring, w'en de sap commence' ter rise in de scuppernon' vime, Henry tuk a ham one night. Whar'd he git de ham? I doan know; dey wa'nt no hams on de plantation 'cep'n' w'at 'uz in de smoke-house, but I never see Henry 'bout de smoke-house. But ez I wuz a-sayin', he tuk de ham ober ter Aun' Peggy's; en Aun' Peggy tole 'im dat w'en Mars Dugal' begin ter prume de grapevimes, he mus' go en take 'n scrape off de sap whar it ooze out'n de cut een's er de vimes, en 'n'int his ball head wid it; en ef he do dat once't a year de goopher wouldn' wuk agin 'im long ez he done it. En bein' ez he fotch her de ham, she fix' it so he kin eat all de scuppernon' he want.

"So Henry 'n'int his head wid de sap out'n de big grapevime des ha'f way 'twix' de quarters en de big house, en de goopher nebber wuk agin him dat summer. But de beatenes' thing you eber see happen ter Henry. Up ter dat time he wuz ez ball ez a sweeten' 'tater, but des ez soon ez de young leaves begun ter come out on de grapevimes de ha'r begun ter grow out on Henry's head, en by de middle er de summer he had de bigges' head er ha'r on de plantation. Befo' dat, Henry had tol'able good ha'r 'roun de aidges, but soon ez de young grapes begun ter come, Henry's ha'r begun ter quirl all up in little balls, des like dis yer reg'lar grapy ha'r, en by de time de grapes got ripe his head look des like a bunch er grapes. Combin' it did n' do no good; he wuk at it ha'f de night wid er Jim Crow,[2] en think he git it straighten' out, but in de mawnin' de grapes 'ud be dere des de same. So he gin it up, en tried ter keep de grapes down by havin' his ha'r cut sho't.

"But dat wa'nt de quares' thing 'bout de goopher. When Henry come ter de plantation, he wuz gittin' a little ole an stiff in de j'ints. But dat summer he got des ez spry en libely ez any young nigger on de plantation; fac' he got so biggity dat Mars Jackson, de oberseah, ha' ter th'eaten ter whip 'im, ef he did n' stop cuttin' up his didos en behave hisse'f. But de mos' cur'ouses' thing happen' in de fall, when de sap begin ter go down in de grapevimes. Fus', when de grapes 'uz gethered, de knots begun ter straighten out'n Henry's h'ar; en w'en de leaves begin ter fall, Henry's ha'r begin ter drap out; en w'en de vimes 'uz b'ar, Henry's head wuz baller 'n it wuz in de spring, en he begin ter git ole en stiff in de j'ints ag'in, en paid no mo' tention ter de gals dyoin' er de whole winter. En nex' spring, w'en he rub de sap on ag'in, he got young ag'in, en so soopl en libely dat none er de young niggers on de plantation couldn' jump, ner dance, ner hoe ez much cotton ez Henry. But in de fall er de year his grapes begun ter straighten out, en his j'ints ter git stiff, en his ha'r drap off, en de rheumatiz begin ter wrastle wid 'im.

"Now, ef you'd a knowed ole Mars Dugal' McAdoo, you'd a knowed dat it ha' ter be a mighty rainy day when he could n' fine sump'n fer his niggers ter do, en it ha' ter be a mighty little hole he couldn' crawl thoo, en ha' ter be a monst'us cloudy night w'en a dollar git by him in de dahkness; en w'en he see how Henry git young in de spring en ole in de fall, he 'lowed ter hisse'f ez how he could make mo' money outen Henry dan by wukkin' him in de cotton fiel'. 'Long de nex' spring, atter de sap commence' ter rise, en Henry 'n'int 'is head en commence fer ter git young en soopl, Mars Dugal' up 'n tuk Henry ter town, en sole 'im fer fifteen hunder' dollars. Co'se de man w'at bought Henry didn' know nuffin 'bout de goopher, en Mars Dugal' did n' see no 'casion fer ter tell 'im. Long to'ds de fall, w'en de sap went down, Henry begin ter git ole again same ez yuzhal, en his noo marster begin ter git skeered les'n he gwine ter lose his fifteen-hunder'-dollar nigger. He sent fer a mighty fine doctor, but de med'cine did n' 'pear ter do no good; de goopher had a good holt. Henry tole de doctor 'bout de goopher, but de doctor des laff at 'im.

"One day in de winter Mars Dugal' went ter town, en wuz santerin' 'long de Main Street, when who should he meet but Henry's noo marster. Dey said 'Hoddy,' en Mars Dugal' ax 'im ter hab a seegyar; en atter dey run on awhile 'bout de craps en de weather, Mars Dugal' ax 'im, sorter keerless, like ez ef he des thought of it,—

"'How you like de nigger I sole you las' spring?'

"Henry's marster shuck his head en knock de ashes off'n his seegyar.

"'Spec' I made a bad bahgin when I bought dat nigger. Henry done good wuk all de summer, but sence de fall set in he 'pears ter be sorter pinin' away. Dey ain' nuffin pertickler de matter wid 'im—leastways de doctor say so— 'cep'n' a tech er de rheumatiz; but his ha'r is all fell out, en ef he don't pick up his strenk mighty soon, I spec' I'm gwine ter lose 'im.'

"Dey smoked on awhile, en bimeby ole mars say, 'Well, a bahgin's a bahgin, but you en me is good fren's, en I doan wan' ter see you lose all de money you paid fer dat nigger; en ef w'at you say is so, en I ain't 'sputin' it, he ain't wuf much now. I 'spec's you wukked him too ha'd dis summer, er e'se de swamps down here don't agree wid de san'-hill nigger. So you des lemme know, en ef he gits any wusser I'll be willin' ter gib yer five hund'ed dollars fer 'im, en take my chances on his livin'.'

"Sho nuff, when Henry begun ter draw up wid de rheumatiz en it look like he gwine ter die fer sho, his noo marster sen' fer Mars Dugal', en Mars Dugal' gin him what he promus, en brung Henry home ag'in. He tuk good keer uv 'im dyoin' er de winter,—give 'im w'iskey ter rub his rheumatiz, en terbacker ter smoke, en all he want ter eat,—'caze a nigger w'at he could make a thousan' dollars a year off'n did n' grow on eve'y huckleberry bush.

"Nex' spring, w'en de sap ris en Henry's ha'r commence' ter sprout, Mars Dugal' sole 'im ag'in, down in Robeson County dis time; en he kep' dat sellin' business up fer five year er mo'. Henry nebber say nuffin 'bout de goopher ter his noo marsters, 'caze he know he gwine ter be tuk good keer uv de nex' winter, w'en Mars Dugal' buy him back. En Mars Dugal' made 'nuff money off'n Henry ter buy anudder plantation ober on Beaver Crick.

"But long 'bout de een' er dat five year dey come a stranger ter stop at de plantation. De fus' day he 'uz dere he went out wid Mars Dugal' en spent all de mawnin' lookin' ober de vimya'd, en atter dinner dey spent all de evenin' playin' kya'ds. De niggers soon 'skiver' dat he wuz a Yankee, en dat he come down ter Norf C'lina fer ter learn de w'ite folks how to raise grapes en make wine. He promus Mars Dugal' he cud make de grapevimes b'ar twice't ez many grapes, en dat de noo wine-press he wuz a-sellin' would make mo' d'n twice't ez many gallons er wine. En ole Mars Dugal' des drunk it all in, des 'peared ter be bewitched wit dat Yankee. W'en de darkies see dat Yankee runnin' 'roun de vimya'd en diggin' under de grapevimes, dey shuk dere heads, en 'lowed dat dey feared Mars Dugal' losin' his min'. Mars Dugal' had all de dirt dug away fum under de roots er all de scuppernon' vimes, an' let 'em stan' dat away fer a week er mo'. Den dat Yankee made de niggers fix up a mixtry er lime en ashes en manyo, en po' it roun' de roots er de grapevimes. Den he 'vise' Mars Dugal' fer ter trim de vimes close't, en Mars Dugal' tuck 'n done eve'ything de Yankee tole him ter do. Dyoin' all er dis time, mind yer, 'e wuz libbin' off'n de fat er de lan', at de big house, en playin' kyards wid Mars Dugal' eve'y night; en dey say Mars Dugal' los' mo'n a thousan' dollars dyoin' er de week dat Yankee wuz a runnin' de grapevimes.

"W'en de sap ris nex' spring, ole Henry 'n'inted his head ez yuzhal, en his ha'r commence' ter grow des de same ez it done eve'y year. De scuppernon' vimes growed monst's fas', en de leaves wuz greener en thicker dan dey eber be'n dyowin my rememb'ance; en Henry's ha'r growed out thicker dan eber, en he 'peared ter git younger 'n younger, en soopler 'n soopler; en seein' ez he wuz sho't er han's dat spring, havin' tuk in consid'able noo groun', Mars Dugal' 'cluded he wouldn' sell Henry 'tel he git de crap in en de cotton chop'. So he kep' Henry on de plantation.

"But 'long 'bout time fer de grapes ter come on de scuppernon' vimes, dey 'peared ter come a change ober dem; de leaves wivered en swivel' up, en de young grapes turn' yaller, en bimeby eve'ybody on de plantation could see dat de whole vimya'd wuz dyin'. Mars Dugal' tuck 'n water de vimes en done all he could, but 't wan' no use: dat Yankee done bus' de watermillyum. One time de vimes picked up a bit, en Mars Dugal' thought dey wuz gwine ter come out ag'in; but dat Yankee done dug too close unde' de roots, en prune de branches too close ter de vime, en all dat lime en ashes done burn' de life outen de vimes, en dey des kep' a with'in' en a swivelin'.

"All dis time de goopher wuz a-wukkin'. W'en de vimes commence' ter wither, Henry commence' ter complain er his rheumatiz, en when de leaves begin ter dry up his ha'r commence' ter drap out. When de vimes fresh up a bit Henry 'ud git peart agin, en when de vimes wither agin Henry 'ud git ole agin, en des kep' gittin' mo' en mo' fitten fer nuffin; he des pined away, en fine'ly tuk ter his cabin; en when de big vime whar he got de sap ter 'n'int his head withered en turned yaller en died, Henry died too,—des went out sorter like a cannel. Dey did n't 'pear ter be nuffin de matter wid 'im, 'cep'n de rheumatiz, but his strenk des dwinel' away 'tel he did n' hab ernuff lef' ter draw his bref. De goopher had got de under holt, en th'owed Henry fer good en all dat time.

"Mars Dugal' tuk on might'ly 'bout losin' his vimes en his nigger in de same year; en he swo' dat ef he could git hold er dat Yankee he'd wear 'im ter a frazzle, en den chaw up de frazzle; en he'd done it, too, for Mars Dugal' 'uz a monst'us brash man w'en he once git started. He sot de vimya'd out ober agin, but it wuz th'ee er fo' year befo' de vimes got ter b'arin' any scuppernon's.

"W'en de wah broke out, Mars Dugal' raise' a comp'ny, en went off ter fight de Yankees. He say he wuz mighty glad dat wah come, en he des want ter kill a Yankee fer eve'y dollar he los' 'long er dat grape-raisin' Yankee. En I 'spec' he would a done it, too, ef de Yankees had n' s'picioned sump'n, en killed him fus'. Atter de s'render ole miss move' ter town, de niggers all scattered 'way fum de plantation, en de vimya'd ain' be'n cultervated sence."

"Is that story true?" asked Annie, doubtfully, but seriously, as the old man concluded his narrative.

"It's des ez true ez I'm a-settin' here, miss. Dey's a easy way ter prove it: I kin lead de way right ter Henry's grave ober yander in de plantation buryin'-groun'. En I tell yer w'at, marster, I would n' 'vise yer to buy dis yer ole vimya'd, 'caze de goopher's on it yit, en dey ain' no tellin' w'en it's gwine ter crap out."

"But I thought you said all the old vines died."

"Dey did 'pear ter die, but a few ov 'em come out ag'in, en is mixed in mongs' de yuthers. I ain' skeered ter eat de grapes, 'caze I knows de old vimes fum de noo ones; but wid strangers dey ain' no tellin' w'at might happen. I would n' 'vise yer ter buy dis vimya'd."

I bought the vineyard, nevertheless, and it has been for a long time in a thriving condition, and is referred to by the local press as a striking illustration of the opportunities open to Northern capital in the development of Southern industries. The luscious scuppernong holds first rank among our grapes, though we cultivate a great many other varieties, and our income from grapes packed and shipped to the Northern markets is quite considerable. I have not noticed any developments of the goopher in the vineyard, although I have a mild suspicion that our colored assistants do not suffer from want of grapes during the season.

I found, when I bought the vineyard, that Uncle Julius had occupied a cabin on the place for many years, and derived a respectable revenue from the neglected grapevines. This, doubtless, accounted for his advice to me not to buy the vineyard, though whether it inspired the goopher story I am unable to state. I believe, however, that the wages I pay him for his services are more than an equivalent for anything he lost by the sale of the vineyard.

1887

ABOUT half a mile from our house on the North Carolina sand-hills there lay, at the foot of a vine-clad slope, and separated from my scuppernong vineyard by a rail fence, a marsh of some extent. It was drained at a somewhat later date, but at the time to which I now refer spread for half a mile in length and a quarter of a mile in breadth. Having been planted in rice many years before, it therefore contained no large trees, but was grown up chiefly in reeds and, coarse grasses, with here and there a young sycamore or cypress. Though this marsh was not visible from our house, nor from any road that we used, it was nevertheless one of the most prominent features of our environment. We might sometimes forget its existence in the day-time, but it never failed to thrust itself upon our attention after night had fallen.

It may be that other localities in our neighborhood were infested with frogs; but if so, their vocal efforts were quite overborne by the volume of sound that issued nightly from this particular marsh. As soon as the red disk of the sun had set behind the pines the performance would begin, first per- haps with occasional shrill pipings, followed by a confused chattering; then, as the number of participants increased, growing into a steady drumming, punctuated every moment by the hoarse bellowing note of some monstrous bull-frog. If the day had perchance been rainy, the volume of noise would be greater. For a while after we went to live in the neighborhood, this ceaseless, strident din made night hideous, and we would gladly have dispensed with it. But as time wore on we grew accustomed to our nocturnal concert; we began to differentiate its notes and to distinguish a sort of rude harmony in these voices of the night; and after we had become thoroughly accustomed to it, I doubt whether we could have slept comfortably without their lullaby.

But I had not been living long in the vicinity of this frog-pond before its pos- sibilities as a source of food-supply suggested themselves to my somewhat prac- tical mind. I was unable to learn that any of my white neighbors indulged in the delicate article of diet which frogs' legs might be made to supply; and strangely enough, among the Negroes, who would have found in the tender flesh of the batrachian a toothsome and bountiful addition to the coarse food that formed the staple of their diet, its use for that purpose was entirely unknown.

One day I went frog-fishing and brought home a catch of half a dozen. Our colored cook did not know how to prepare them, and looked on the whole proceeding with ill-concealed disgust. So my wife, with the aid of a cook-book, dressed the hind legs quite successfully in the old-fashioned way, and they were served at supper. We enjoyed the meal very much, and I determined that thereafter we would have the same dish often.

Our supper had been somewhat later than usual, and it was dusk before we left the table and took our seats on the piazza. We had been there but a little while when old Julius, our colored coachman, came around the house and approaching the steps asked for some instructions with reference to the stable-work. As the matter required talking over, I asked him to sit down. When we had finished our talk the old man did not go away immediately, and we all sat for a few moments without speaking. The night was warm but not sultry; there was a sort of gentle melancholy in the air, and the chorus from the distant frog-pond seemed pitched this night in something of a minor key.

"Dem frogs is makin' dey yuzh'al racket ternight," observed the old man, breaking the silence.

"Yes," I replied, "they are very much in evidence. By the way, Annie, perhaps Julius would like some of those frogs' legs. I see Nancy hasn't cleared the table yet."

"No ma'm," responded Julius quickly, "I's much obleedzd, but I doan eat no frog-laigs; no, *suh*, no *ma'm*, I doan eat no frog-laigs, not ef I knows w'at I's eatin'!"

"Why not, Julius?" I asked. "They are excellent eating."

"You listen right close, suh," he answered, "en you'll heah a pertic'ler bull-frog down yander in dat ma'sh. Listen! Dere he goes now—callin', callin', callin'! sad en mo'nful, des lak somebody w'at's los' somewhar, en can't fin' de way back."

"I hear it distinctly," said my wife after a moment. "It sounds like the lament of a lost soul."

I had never heard the vocal expression of a lost soul, but I tried, without success, to imagine that I could distinguish one individual croak from another.

"Well, what is there about that frog, Julius," I inquired, "that makes it any different from the others?"

"Dat's po' Tobe," he responded solemnly, "callin' Aun' Peggy—po' ole Aun' Peggy w'at's dead en gone ter de good Marster, yeahs en yeahs ago."

"Tell us about Tobe, Julius," I asked. I could think of no more appropriate time for one of the old man's stories. His views of life were so entirely foreign to our own, that for a time after we got acquainted with him his conversations were a never-failing source of novelty and interest. He had seen life from what was to us a new point of view—from the bottom, as it were; and there clung to his mind, like barnacles to the submerged portion of a ship, all sorts of extravagant beliefs. The simplest phenomena of life were to him fraught with hidden meaning,—some prophesy of good, some presage of evil. The source of these notions I never traced, though they doubtless could be easily accounted for. Some perhaps were dim reflections of ancestral fetishism; more were the superstitions, filtered through the Negro intellect, of the Scotch settlers who had founded their homes on Cape Fear at a time when a kelpie[3] haunted every Highland glen, and witches, like bats, darkened the air as they flew by in their nocturnal wanderings. But from his own imagination, I take it—for I never heard quite the same stories from anyone else—he gave to the raw material of folk-lore and superstition a fancifulness of touch that truly made of it, to borrow a homely phrase, a silk purse out of a sow's ear. And if perhaps, at times, his stories might turn out to have a purpose apart from any esthetic or didatic end, he probably reasoned, with a philosophy for which there is high warrant, that the laborer was worthy of his hire.

"'Bout fo'ty years ago," began Julius, "ole Mars Dugal McAdoo—*my* ole marster—useter own a man name' Tobe. Dis yer Tobe wuz a slow kind er nigger, en w'iles he'd alluz git his tas' done, he'd hafter wuk harder 'n any yuther nigger on de place ter do it. One time he had a monst'us nice 'oman fer a wife, but she got bit by a rattlesnake one summer en died, en dat lef' Tobe kind er lonesome. En mo'd'n dat, Tobe's wife had be'n cook at de big house, en eve'y night she'd fetch sump'n down ter her cabin fer Tobe; en he foun' it mighty ha'd ter go back ter bacon and co'n-bread atter libbin' off'n de fat er de lan' all dese yeahs.

"Des 'bout a mont' er so atter Tobe's wife died, dey wuz a nigger run 'way fum ole Mars Marrabo McSwayne's—de nex' plantation—en in spite er all de w'ite folks could do, dis yer nigger got clean off ter a free state in de Norf, en bimeby he writ a sassy letter back ter Mars Marrabo, en sont 'im a bill fer de wuk he done fer 'im fer twenty yeahs er mo', at a dollah en a half a day—w'at he say he wuz gittin' at de Norf. One er de gals w'at wukked roun' de big house heared de w'ite folks gwine on 'bout it, en she say Mars Marrabo cusst en swo' des tarrable, en ole missis 'mos' wep' fer ter think how ongrateful dat nigger wuz, not on'y ter run 'way, but to write back sich wick'niss ter w'ite folks w'at had alluz treated 'im good, fed 'im en clothed 'im, en nussed 'im w'en he wuz sick, en nebber let 'im suffer fer nuffin all his life.

"But Tobe heared 'bout dis yer nigger, en he tuk a notion he'd lak ter run 'way en go ter de Norf en be free en git a dollah en a half a day too. But de mo' he studied 'bout it, de ha'der it 'peared ter be. In de fus' place, de Norf wuz a monst'us long ways off, en de dawgs mought track 'im, er de patteroles[4] mought ketch 'im, er he mought sta've ter def ca'se he couldn' git nuffin ter eat on de way; en ef he wuz cotch' he wuz lakly ter be sol' so fur souf dat he'd nebber hab no chance ter git free er eber see his ole frien's nuther.

"But Tobe kep' on studyin' 'bout runnin 'way 'tel fin'lly he 'lowed he'd go en see ole Aun' Peggy, de cunjuh 'oman down by de Wim'l'ton Road, en ax her w'at wuz de bes' way fer him ter sta't. So he tuk a pa'r er pullets down ter Aun' Peggy one night en tol' her all 'bout his hank' in's en his longin's, en ax' her w'at he'd hafter do fer ter run 'way en git free.

"'W'at you wanter be free fer?' sez Aun' Peggy. 'Doan you git ernuff ter eat?'

"'Yas, I gits ernuff ter eat, but I'll hab better vittles w'en I's free.'

"'Doan you git ernuff sleep?'

"'Yas, but I'll sleep mo' w'en I's free.'

"'Does you wuk too had?'

"'No, I doan wuk too ha'd fer a slabe nigger, but ef I wuz free I wouldn' wuk a-tall 'less'n I felt lak it.'

"Aun' Peggy shuck her head. 'I dunno, nigger,' sez she, 'whuther you gwine ter fin' w'at you er huntin' fer er no. But w'at is it you wants me ter do fer you?'

"'I wants you ter tell me de bes' en easies' way fer ter git ter de Norf en be free.'

"'Well,' sez Aun' Peggy, 'I's feared dey ain' no easy way. De bes' way fer you ter do is ter fix yo' eye on de Norf Stah en sta't. You kin put some tar on yo' feet ter th'ow de houn's off'n de scent, en ef you come ter a crick you mought wade 'long fer a mile er so. I sh'd say you bettah sta't on Sad'day night, fer den mos' lakly you won' be miss' 'tel Monday mawnin', en you kin git a good sta't on yo' jou'ney. En den maybe in a mont' er so you'll retch de Norf en you'll be free, en whar you kin eat all you want, ef you kin git it, en sleep ez long ez you mineter, ef you kin 'ford it, en whar you won't hafter wuk ef you'd ruther go to jail.'

"'But w'at is I gwine ter eat dyo'in' er dis yer mont' I's trabblin'?' ax' Tobe. 'It makes me sick ef I doan git my reg'lar meals.'

"'Doan ax me,' sez Aun' Peggy. 'I ain' nebber seed de nigger yit w'at can't fin' sump'n ter eat.'

"Tobe scratch' his head. 'En whar is I gwine to sleep dyo'in' er dat mont'? I'll hafter hab my reg'lar res'.'

"'Doan ax me,' sez Aun' Peggy. 'You kin sleep in de woods in de daytime, en do yo' trabblin' at night.'

"'But s'pose'n a snake bites me?'

"'I kin gib you a cha'm fer ter kyo snake-bite.'

"'But s'pose'n' de patteroles ketch me?'

"'Look a heah, nigger,' sez Aun' Peggy, 'I's ti'ed er yo' s'pose'n', en I's was'e all de time on you I's gwine ter fer two chick'ns. I's feared you wants ter git free too easy. I s'pose you des wants ter lay down at night, do yo' trabblin' in yo' sleep, en wake free in de mawn'in. You wants ter git a thousan' dollah nigger fer nuffin' en dat's mo'd'n anybody but de sma'test w'ite folks kin do. Go 'long back ter yo' wuk, man, en doan come back ter me 'less'n you kin fetch me sump'n mo'.'

"Now, Tobe knowed well ernuff dat ole Aun' Peggy'd des be'n talkin' ter heah herse'f talk, en so two er th'ee nights later he tuk a side er bacon en kyared it down ter her cabin.

"'Uh huh,' sez Aun' Peggy, 'dat is sump'n lak it. I s'pose you still 'lows you'd lak ter be free, so you kin eat w'at you mineter, en sleep all you wanter, en res' w'eneber you feels dat erway?'

"'Yas'm, I wants ter be free, en I wants you ter fix things so I kin be sho' ter git ter de Norf widout much trouble; fer I sho'ly does hate en 'spise trouble.'

"Aun' Peggy studied fer a w'ile, en den she tuk down a go'd off'n de she'f, en sez she:—

"'I's got a goopher mixtry heah w'at 'll tu'n you ter a b'ar. You know dey use'ter be b'ars roun' heah in dem ole days.'

"Den she tuk down ernudder go'd. 'En', she went on, 'ef I puts some er dis yuther mixtry wid it, you'll tu'n back ag'in in des a week er mont' er two mont's, 'cordin' ter how much I puts in. Now, ef I tu'ns you ter a b'ar fer, say a mont', en you is keerful en keeps 'way fum de hunters, you kin feed yo'se'f ez you goes 'long, en by de een' er de mont' you'll be ter de Norf; en wen you tu'ns back you'll tu'n back ter a free nigger, whar you kin do w'at you wanter, en go whar you mineter, en sleep ez long ez you please.'

"So Tobe say all right, en Aun' Peggy mix' de goopher, en put it on Tobe en turn't 'im ter a big black b'ar.

"Tobe sta'ted out to'ds de Norf, en went fifteen er twenty miles widout stoppin'. Des befo' day in de mawnin' he come ter a 'tater patch, en bein' ez he wuz feelin' sorter hongry, he stop' fer a hour er so 'tel he got all de 'taters he could hol'. Den he sta'ted out ag'in, en bimeby he run 'cross a bee-tree en eat all de honey he could. 'Long to'ds ebenin' he come ter a holler tree, en bein' ez he felt kinder sleepy lak, he 'lowed he'd crawl in en take a nap. So he crawled in en went ter sleep.

"Meanw'ile, Monday mawn'in' w'en de niggers went out in de fiel' ter wuk, Tobe wuz missin'. All de niggers 'nied seein' 'im, en ole Mars Dugal sont up ter town en hi'ed some dawgs, en gun 'em de scent, en dey follered it ter ole Aun' Peggy's cabin. Aun' Peggy 'lowed yas, a nigger had be'n ter her cabin Sad'day night, en she had gun 'im a cha'm fer ter keep off de rheumatiz, en he had sta'ted off down to'ds de ribber, sayin' he wuz ti'ed wukkin' en wuz gwine fishin' fer a mont' er so. De w'ite folks hunted en hunted, but co'se dey did'n fin' Tobe.

"Bout a mont' atter Tobe had run 'way, en w'en Aun' Peggy had mos' fergot 'bout im, she wuz sett'n' in her cabin one night, wukkin' her roots, w'en somebody knock' at her do'.

"'Who dere?' sez she.

"'It's me, Tobe; open de do', Aun' Peggy.'

"'Sho' 'nuff, w'en Aun' Peggy tuk down de do'-bar, who sh'd be stan'in' dere but Tobe.

"'Whar is you come fum, nigger?' ax' Aun' Peggy, 'I 'lowed you mus' be ter de Norf by dis time, en free, en libbin' off'n de fat er de lan'.'

"'You must 'a s'pected me ter trabbel monst'us fas' den,' sez Tobe, 'fer I des sta'ted fum heah yistiddy mawnin', en heah I is turnt back ter a nigger ag'in befo' I'd ha'dly got useter walkin' on all-fours. Dey's sump'n de matter wid dat goopher er yo'n, fer yo' cunj'in' ain' wuk right dis time. I crawled in a holler tree 'bout six o'clock en went ter sleep, en w'en I woke up in de mawnin' I wuz tu'nt back ag'in, en bein' ez I had n' got no fu'ther 'n Rockfish Crick, I des 'lowed I'd come back en git dat goopher w'at I paid fer fix' right.'

'Aun' Peggy scratched her head en studied a minute, en den sez she:—

"'Uh huh! I sees des w'at de trouble is. I is tu'nt you ter a b'ar heah in de fall, en w'en you come ter a holler tree you crawls in en goes ter sleep fer de winter, des lak any yuther b'ar 'd do; en ef I had n' mix' dat yuther goopher in fer ter tu'n you back in a mont', you'd a slep' all th'oo de winter. I had des plum' fergot 'bout dat, so I reckon I'll hafter try sumpin' diff'ent. I 'spec' I better tu'n you ter a fox. En bein' ez a fox is a good runner, you oughter git ter de Norf in less time dan a b'ar, so I'll fix dis yer goopher so you'll tu'n back ter a nigger en des th'ee weeks, en you'll be able ter enjoy yo' freedom a week sooner.'

"So Aun' Peggy tu'nt Tobe ter a fox, en he sta'ted down de road in great has'e, en made mo'd'n ten miles, w'en he 'mence' ter feel kinder hongry. So w'en he come ter a hen-house he tuk a hen en eat it, en lay down in de woods ter git his night's res'. In de mawnin', w'en he woke up, he 'lowed he mought 'swell hab ernudder chick'n fer breakfus', so he tuk a fat pullet en eat dat.

"Now, Tobe had be'n monst's fon' er chick'n befo' he wuz tu'nt ter a fox, but he had n' nebber had ez much ez he could eat befo'. En bein' ez dere wuz so many chick'ns in dis naberhood, en dey mought be ska'se whar he wuz gwine, he 'lowed he better stay 'roun' dere 'tel he got kinder fat, so he could stan' bein' hongry a day er so ef he sh'd fin' slim pickin's fu'ther 'long. So he dug hisse'f a nice hole under a tree in de woods, en des stayed dere en eat chick'n fer a couple er weeks er so. He wuz so comf'table, eatin' w'at he laked, en restin' w'en he wa'n't eatin', he des kinder los' track er de time, 'tel befo' he notice' it his th'ee weeks wuz mos' up.

"But bimeby de people w'at own dese yer chick'ns 'mence' ter miss 'em, en dey 'lowed dey wuz a fox som'ers roun'. So dey got out dey houn's en dey hawns en dey hosses, en sta'ted off fer a fox-hunt. En sho' nuff de houn's got de scent, en wuz on po' Tobe's track in a' hour er so.

"W'en Tobe heared 'em comin' he wuz mos' skeered ter def, en he 'mence' ter run ez ha'd ez he could, en bein' ez de houn's wuz on de norf side, he run to'ds de souf, en soon foun' hisse'f back in de woods right whar he wuz bawn en raise'. He jumped a crick en doubled en twisted, en done ev'ything he could fer ter th'ow de houn's off'n de scent bu 't wa'n't no use, fer dey des kep' gittin' closeter, en closeter, en closeter.

"Ez soon ez Tobe got back to'ds home en 'skivered whar he wuz, he sta'ted fer ole Aun' Peggy's cabin fer te git her ter he'p 'im, en des ez he got ter her do', lo en behol'! he tu'nt back ter a nigger ag'in, fer de th'ee weeks wuz up des ter a minute. He knock' at de do', en hollered:—

"'Lemme in, Aun' Peggy, lemme in! De dawgs is atter me.'

"Aun' Peggy open' de do'.

"'Fer de Lawd sake! nigger, whar is you come fum dis time?' sez she. 'I 'lowed you wuz done got ter de Norf, en free long ago. W'at's de matter wid you now?'

"So Tobe up'n' tol' her 'bout how he had been stop' by dem chick'ns, en how ha'd it wuz ter git 'way fum 'em. En w'iles he wuz talkin' ter Aun' Peggy dey heared de dawgs comin' closeter, en closeter, en closeter.

"'Tu'n me ter sump'n e'se, Aun' Peggy,' sez Tobe, 'fer dat fox scent runs right up ter de do', en dey'll be 'bleedzd ter come in, en dey'll fin' me en kyar me back home, en lamb me, en mos' lakly sell me 'way. Tu'n me ter sump'n, quick, I doan keer w'at, fer I doan want dem dawgs ner dem w'ite folks ter ketch me.'

"Aun' Peggy look' 'roun' de cabin, en sez she, takin' down a go'd fum de chimbly:—

"'I ain' got no goopher made up ter-day, Tobe, but dis yer bull-frog mixtry. I'll tu'n you ter a bull-frog, en I'll put in ernuff er dis yuther mixtry fer ter take de goopher off in a day er so, en meanw'iles you kin hop down yander ter dat ma'sh en stay, en w'en de dawgs is all gone en you tu'ns back, you kin come ter me en I'll tu'n you ter a sparrer er sump'n' w'at kin fly swif', en den maybe you'll be able ter git 'way en be free widout all dis yer foolishness you's be'n goin' th'oo.'

"By dis time de dawgs wuz scratchin' at de do' en howlin', en Aun' Peggy en Tobe could heah de hawns er de hunters blowin' close behin'. All dis yer racket made Aun' Peggy sorter narvous, en w'en she went ter po' dis yuther mixtry in fer ter lif' 'de bullfrog goopher off'n Tobe in a day er so, her han' shuck so she spilt it ober de side er de yuther go'd en did n' notice dat it hadn' gone in. En Tobe wuz so busy lis'nin' en watchin' de do', dat he did n' notice nuther, en so w'en Aun' Peggy put de goopher on Tobe en tu'nt 'im inter a bull-frog, dey wa'n't none er dis yuther mixtry in it w'atsomeber.

"Tobe le'p' out'n a crack 'twix' de logs, en Aun' Peggy open' de do', en de dawgs run 'roun', en de w'ite folks come en inqui'ed, en w'en dey seed Aun' Peggy's roots en go'ds en snake-skins en yuther cunjuh-fixin's, en a big black cat wid yaller eyes, settin' on de h'a'th, dey 'lowed dey wuz wastin' dey time, so dey des cusst a little en run 'long back home widout de fox dey had come atter.

"De nex' day Aun' Peggy stayed roun' home all day, makin' a mixtry fer ter tu'n Tobe ter a sparrer, en 'spectin' 'im eve'y minute fer ter come in. But he nebber come. En bein' ez he did n' 'pear no mo', Aun' Peggy 'lowed he'd got ti'ed er dis yer animal bizness en w'en he had tu'nt back fum de bull-frog had runned 'way on his own 'sponsibility, lak she 'vised 'im at fus'. So Aun' Peggy went on 'bout her own bizness en did n' paid no mo' tention ter Tobe.

"Ez fer po' Tobe, he had hop' off down ter dat ma'sh en had jump' in de water, en had waited fer hisse'f ter tu'n back. But w'en he didn' tu'n back de fus'day, he 'lowed Aun' Peggy had put in too much er de mixtry, en bein'ez de ma'sh wuz full er minners en snails en crawfish en yuther things w'at bull-frogs laks ter eat, he 'lowed he mought's well be comf'table en enjoy hisse'f 'tel his bull-frog time wuz up.

"But bimeby, w'en a mont' roll' by, en two mont's, en thee mont's, en a yeah, Tobe kinder 'lowed dey wuz sump'n wrong 'bout dat goopher, en so he 'mence' ter go up on de dry lan' en look fer Aun' Peggy. En one day w'en she came 'long by de ma'sh, he got in front er her, en croak' en croak'; but Aun' Peggy wuz studyin' 'bout sump'n e'se; en 'sides, she 'lowed Tobe wuz done gone 'way en got free long, long befo', so she did n' pay no 'tention ter de big bull-frog she met in de path, 'cep'n ter push him out 'n de road wid her stick.

"So Tobe went back ter his ma'sh, en dere he's be'n eber sence. It's be'n fifty yeahs er mo', en Tobe mus' be 'bout ten yeahs older 'n I is. But he ain' nebber got ti'ed er wantin' ter be tu'nt back ter hisse'f, er ter sump'n w'at could run erway ter de Norf. Co'se ef he had waited lak de res' un us he'd a be'n free long ago; but he did n' know dat, en he doan know it yet. En eve'y night, w'en de frogs sta'ts up, dem w'at knows 'bout Tobe kin reco'nize his voice en heah 'im callin', callin', callin' ole Aun' Peggy fer ter come en tu'n 'im back, des ez ef Aun' Peggy had n' be'n restin' in Aberham's bosom fer fo'ty yeahs er mo'. Oncet in a w'ile I notices dat Tobe doan say nuffin fer a night er so, en so I 'lows he's gittin' ole en po'ly, en trouble' wid hoa'seness er rheumatiz er sump'n er 'nuther, fum bein' in de water so long. I doan 'spec' he's gwine to be dere many mo' yeahs; but w'iles he is dere, it 'pears ter me he oughter be 'lowed ter lib out de res' er his days in peace.

"Dat's de reason w'y," the old man concluded, "I doan lak ter see nobody eat'n frogs' laigs out'n dat ma'sh. Ouch!" he added suddenly, putting his hand to the pit of his stomach, "Ouch!"

"What's the matter, Uncle Julius?" my wife inquired with solicitude.

"Oh, nuffin, ma'm, nuffin wuf noticin'—des a little tech er mis'ry in my innards. I s'pose talkin' 'bout po' old Tobe, in dat col', wet ma'sh, wid no-body ter 'sociate wid but frogs en crawfish en water-moccasins en sich, en wid nuffin fittin' ter eat, is des sorter upsot me mo' er less. If you is anyways int'rusted in a ole nigger's feelin's, I ruther 'spec' a drap er dem bitters out'n dat little flat jimmyjohn er yo'n git me shet er dis mis'ry quicker'n anything e'se I knows."

1900

THE FREE COLORED PEOPLE OF NORTH CAROLINA

In our generalizations upon American history—and the American people are prone to loose generalization, especially where the Negro is concerned—it is ordinarily assumed that the entire colored race was set free as the result of the Civil War. While this is true in a broad, moral sense, there was, nevertheless, a very considerable technical exception in the case of several hundred thousand free people of color, a great many of whom were residents of the South-ern States. Although the emancipation of their race brought to these a larger measure of liberty than they had previously enjoyed, it did not confer upon them personal freedom, which they possessed already. These free colored people were variously distributed, being most numerous, perhaps, in Maryland, where, in the year 1850, for example, in a state with 87,189 slaves, there were 83,942 free colored people, the white population of the State being 515,918; and perhaps least numerous in Georgia, of all the slave states, where, to a slave population of 462,198, there were only 351 free people of color, or less than three-fourths of one percent, as against the about fifty percent in Maryland. Next to Maryland came Virginia, with 58,042 free colored people, North Carolina with 30,463, Louisiana with 18,647, (of whom 10,939 were in the parish of New Orleans alone), and South Carolina with 9,914. For these statistics, I have of course referred to the census reports for the years mentioned. In the year 1850, according to the same authority, there were in the state of North Carolina 553,028 white people, 288,548 slaves, and 27,463 free colored people. In 1860, the white population of the state was 631,100, slaves 331,059, free colored people, 30,463.

These figures for 1850 and 1860 show that between nine and ten percent of the colored population, and about three per cent. of the total population in each of those years, were free colored people, the ratio of increase during the intervening period being inconsiderable. In the decade preceding 1850 the ratio of increase had been somewhat different. From 1840 to 1850 the white population of the state had increased 14.05 per cent., the slave population 17.38 per cent., the free colored population 20.81 per cent. In the long period from 1790 to 1860, during which the total percentage of increase for the whole population of the state was 700.16, that of the whites was 750.30 per cent., that of the free colored people 720.65 per cent., and that of the slave population but 450 per cent., the total increase in free population being 747.56 per cent.

It seems altogether probable that but for the radical change in the character of slavery, following the invention of the cotton-gin and the consequent great demand for laborers upon the far Southern plantations, which turned the border states into breeding-grounds for slaves, the forces of freedom might in time have overcome those of slavery, and the institution might have died a natural death, as it already had in the Northern States, and as it subsequently did in Brazil and Cuba. To these changed industrial conditions was due, in all probability, in the decade following 1850, the stationary ratio of free colored people to slaves against the larger increase from 1840 to 1850. The gradual growth of the slave power had discouraged the manumission of slaves, had resulted in legislation curtailing the rights and privileges of free people of color, and had driven many of these to seek homes in the North and West, in communities where, if not warmly welcomed as citizens, they were at least tolerated as freemen.

This free colored population was by no means evenly distributed throughout the state, but was mainly found along or near the eastern seaboard, in what is now known as the "black district" of North Carolina. In Craven County, more than one-fifth of the colored population were free; in Halifax County, where the colored population was double that of the whites, one-fourth of the colored were free. In Hertford County, with 3,947 whites and 4,445 slaves, there were 1,112 free colored. Pasquotank County, with a white and colored population almost evenly balanced, one-third of the colored people were free. In some counties, for instance in that of Jackson, a mountainous county in the west of the state, where the Negroes were but an insignificant element, the population stood 5,241 whites, 268 slaves, and three free colored persons.

The growth of this considerable element of free colored people had been due to several causes. In the eighteenth century, slavery in North Carolina had been of a somewhat mild character. There had been large estates along the seaboard and the water-courses, but the larger part of the population had been composed of small planters or farmers, whose slaves were few in number, too few indeed to be herded into slave quarters, but employed largely as domestic servants, and working side by side with their masters in field and forest, and sharing with them the same rude fare. The Scotch-Irish Presbyterian strain in the white people of North Carolina brought with it a fierce love of liberty, which was strongly manifested, for example, in the Mecklenburg declaration of independence,[5] which preceded that at Philadelphia; and while this love of liberty was reconciled with slavery, the mere prejudice against race had not yet excluded all persons of Negro blood from its benign influence. Thus, in the earlier history of the state, the civil status of the inhabitants was largely regulated by condition rather than by color. To be a freeman meant to enjoy many of the fundamental rights of citizenship. Free men of color in North Carolina exercised the right of suffrage until 1835, when the constitution was amended to restrict this privilege to white men. It may be remarked, in passing, that prior to 1860, Jews could not vote in North Carolina. The right of marriage between whites and free persons of color was not restricted by law until the year 1830, though social prejudice had always discouraged it.

The mildness of slavery, which fostered kindly feelings between master and slave, often led to voluntary manumission. The superior morality which characterized the upper ranks of white women, so adequately protected by slavery, did not exist in anything like the same degree among the poorer classes, and occasional marriages, more or less legal, between free Negroes and slaves and poor white women, resulted in at least a small number of colored children, who followed the condition of their white mothers. I have personal knowledge of two free colored families of such origin, dating back to the eighteenth century, whose descendants in each case run into the hundreds. There was also a considerable Quaker element in the population, whose influence was cast against slavery, not in any fierce polemical spirit, but in such a way as to soften its rigors and promote gradual emancipation. Another source of free colored people in certain counties was the remnant of the Cherokee and Tuscarora Indians, who, mingling with the Negroes and poor whites, left more or less of their blood among the colored people of the state. By the law of partitus sequitur ventrem,[6] which is a law of nature as well as of nations, the child of a free mother was always free, no matter what its color or the status of its father, and many free colored people were of female Indian ancestry.

One of these curiously mixed people left his mark upon the history of the state—a bloody mark, too, for the Indian in him did not passively endure the things to which the Negro strain rendered him subject. Henry Berry Lowrey was what was known as a "Scuffletown mu-latto" Scuffletown being a rambling community in Robeson county, N.C., inhabited mainly by people of this origin. His father, a prosperous farmer, was impressed, like other free Negroes, during the Civil War, for service upon the Confederate public works. He resisted and was shot to death with several sons who were assisting him. A younger son, Henry Berry Lowrey, swore an oath to avenge the injury, and a few years later carried it out with true Indian persistence and ferocity. During a career of murder and robbery extending over several years, in which he was aided by an organized band of desperadoes who rendezvoused in inaccessible swamps and terrorized the county, he killed every white man concerned in his father's death, and incidentally several others who interfered with his plans, making in all a total of some thirty killings. A body of romance grew up about this swarthy Robin Hood, who, armed to the teeth, would freely walk into the towns and about the railroad stations, knowing full well that there was a price upon his head, but relying for safety upon the sympathy of the blacks and the fears of the whites. His pretty yellow wife, "Rhody," was known as "the queen of Scuffletown." Northern reporters came down to write him up. An astute Boston detective, who penetrated, under false colors, to his stronghold, is said to have been put to death with savage tortures. A state official was once conducted, by devious paths, under Lowrey's safeguard, to the outlaw's camp, in order that he might see for himself how difficult it would be to dislodge them.

A dime novel was founded upon his exploits. The state offered ten thousand, the Federal government five thousand dollars for his capture, and a regiment of Federal troops was sent to subdue him, his career resembling very much that of the picturesque Italian bandit who has recently been captured after a long career of crime. Lowrey only succumbed in the end to a bullet from the hand of a treacherous comrade, and there is even yet a tradition that he escaped and made his way to a distant state. Some years ago these mixed Indians and Negroes were recognized by the North Carolina legislature as "Croatan Indians,"[7] being supposed to have descended from a tribe of that name and the whites of the lost first white colony of Virginia. They are allowed, among other special privileges conferred by this legislation, to have separate schools of their own, being placed, in certain other respects, upon a plane somewhat above that of the Negroes and a little below that of the whites.

I may add that North Carolina was a favorite refuge for runaway slaves and indentured servants from the richer colonies north and south of it. It may thus be plainly seen how a considerable body of free colored people sprang up within the borders of the state. The status of these people, prior to the Civil War, was anomalous but tenable. Many of them, perhaps most of them, were as we have seen, persons of mixed blood, and received, with their dower of white blood, an intellectual and physical heritage of which social prejudice could not entirely rob them, and which helped them to prosperity in certain walks of life. The tie of kinship was sometimes recognized, and brought with it property, sympathy and opportunity which the black did not always enjoy. Many free colored men were skilled mechanics. The State House at Raleigh was built by colored workmen, under a foreman of the same race. I am acquainted with a family now living in the North, whose Negro grandfather was the leading tailor, in Newbern, N.C. He owned a pew on the ground floor of the church which he attended, and was buried in the cemetery where white people were laid to rest. In the town where I went to live when a child, just after the Civil War, nearly all the mechanics were men of color. One of these, a saddler by trade, had himself been the owner, before the war, of a large plantation and several slaves. He had been constrained by force of circumstances to invest in Confederate bonds, but despite this loss, he still had left a considerable tract of land, a brick store, and a handsome town residence, and was able to send one of his sons, immediately after the war, to a Northern school, where he read law, and returning to his native state, was admitted to the bar and has ever since practiced his profession. This was an old free family, descended from a free West Indian female ancestor.

For historical reasons, which applied to the whole race, slave and free, these families were, before the war, most clearly traceable through the female line.

The principal cabinet-maker and undertaker in the town was an old white man whose workmen were colored. One of these practically inherited what was left of the business after the introduction of factory-made furniture from the North, and has been for many years the leading undertaker of the town. The tailors, shoemakers, wheelwrights and blacksmiths were men of color, as were the carpenters, bricklayers and plasterers.

It is often said, as an argument for slavery, by the still numerous apologists for that institution, that these skilled artisans have not passed on to the next generation the trades acquired by them under, if not in, slavery. This failure is generally ascribed to the shiftlessness of the race in freedom, and to the indisposition of the younger men to devote themselves to hard work. But the assumption is not always correct; there are still many competent colored mechanics in the South. In the town of which I have spoken, for instance, colored men are still the barbers, blacksmiths, masons and carpenters. And while there has been such a falling off, partly due to the unsettled conditions resulting from emancipation and inseparable from so sudden and radical a change, another reason for it exists in the altered industrial conditions which confront mechanics all over the country, due mainly to the growth of manufactures and the increased ease and cheapness of transportation. The shoes which were formerly made by hand are now manufactured in Massachusetts and sold, with a portrait of the maker stamped upon the sole, for less money than the most poorly paid mechanic could afford to make them for by hand. The buggies and wagons, to produce which kept a large factory in the town where I lived in constant operation, are now made in Cincinnati and other Northern cities, and delivered in North Carolina for a price prohibitive of manufacture by hand. Furniture is made at Grand Rapids, coffins in one place, and clothing in still another. The blacksmith buys his horseshoes ready made, in assorted sizes, and has merely to trim the hoof and fasten them on with machine-made nails. The shoemaker has degenerated into the cobbler; the tinner merely keeps a shop for the sale of tinware; the undertaker merely embalms the dead and conducts funerals, and tombstones are sold by catalogue with blanks for the insertion of names and dates before delivery. In some of the new industries which have sprung up in the South, such, for instance, as cotton-milling, Negroes are not employed. Hence, in large part through the operation of social forces beyond any control on their part, they have lost their hereditary employments, and these have only in part been replaced by employment in tobacco factories and in iron mines and mills.

The general decline of the apprenticeship system which has affected black and white alike, is also in some degree responsible for the dearth of trained mechanics in the South. Even in Northern cities the finer grades of stone-cutting, bricklaying, carpentry and cabinet work, and practically all the mosaic and terra-cotta work and fine interior decorating, is done by workmen of foreign birth and training.

Many of the younger colored people who might have learned trades, have found worthy employment as teachers and preachers; but the servile occupations into which so many of the remainder have drifted by following the line of least resistance, are a poor substitute for the independent position of the skilled mechanic. The establishment, for the colored race, of such institutions as Hampton and Tuskegee, not only replaces the apprenticeship system, but fills a growing industrial want. A multiplication of such agencies will enable the "free colored people" of the next generation, who now embrace the whole race and will number some ten millions or more, to regain these lost arts, and through them, by industry and thrift, under intelligent leadership, to win that equality of citizenship of which they are now grasping, perhaps, somewhat more than the shadow but something less than the substance.

1902

NOTES

1. Scuppernongs, a variety of muscadine grape, found primarily in the coastal states of the southern United States, especially South Carolina and North Carolina, where the scuppernong is the state fruit.

2. A metal tool consisting of a wide U-shaped clamp and a thick center screw, used for bending rails.

3. An often malicious water spirit from Scottish folklore tradition, frequently appearing in the form of a horse.

4. Vernacular slang from the Standard English "patrollers," referring to groups of white men, often on horseback, appointed to patrol those communities in which enslaved laborers were held, as well as to hunt and apprehend those attempting to flee from enslavement.

5. Most often refers to the Mecklenburg Resolves, also called the Charlotte Town Resolves, in which the government of Mecklenburg County, North Carolina, effectively vacated the laws of the English Crown and state to recognize the executive powers of the Continental Congress.

6. A Latin term referring to the legal doctrine in which the child inherits the status of the mother.

7. A small community of Native American families living in the coastal areas of North Carolina at the time of first European contact with the region, now residing primarily in the Sampson County region of the state.

JOSEPHINE D. HENDERSON HEARD
(1861–1921)

Josephine Delphine Henderson Heard was born in Salisbury, North Carolina, to enslaved parents Lafayette and Annie H. Henderson. Her career as a poet began during secondary school, at which time she published several of her poems in religious periodicals. After attending local schools in Charlotte, she continued her education at Scotia Seminary (now Barber-Scotia College) in Concord, North Carolina, and at the Bethany Institute in New York City, from which she graduated with honors. After completing her education, she worked as a school teacher in North Carolina, South Carolina, and Tennessee. In 1882 she married William Henry Heard, a former representative in the South Carolina state senate and a minister in the A.M.E. Church. The two shared a love of adventure, and they went on to travel extensively, throughout much of the United States, Europe, and Africa (where they would live for more than eight years). The couple had no children. Through her husband, Heard became acquainted with the Rev. Benjamin Tucker Tanner, editor of the *A.M.E. Church Review,* who published three of her poems in his magazine. Her poems also appeared in *The New York Age, The Colored American Magazine,* and other African American periodicals of the day. *Morning Glories,* her single collection of poetry, was published in 1890. The following poems were selected from that volume.

A MOTHER'S LOVE

What sacrifice so great!
 No hour too early, or too late,
No isle too distant, no shore or strand,
 She may not reach with earnest heart, and willing hand.

What love so strong!
 It is her child, or right or wrong,
In crowded court of justice, if condemn'd,
 Her love and tearful eyes doth still defend.

What love so pure!
 Friendship oft is false, but one is sure,

That mother's love clings to us to the last,
    Wherever in life our varied lot is cast.

1890

WILBERFORCE

A quarter century ago,[1]
A March morning, bleak and wild,
The joyful news spread to and fro:
To Afro Methodist[2] is born a child;
Begotten in the time of strife,
And born in adverse circumstances,
All trembled for the young child's life,
It seemed to have so poor a chance.
But, nursed by every care,
It stronger grew, until at last
Our hearts no longer feel a fear,
The danger is forever past.
The feeble childhood's days are flown,
How swiftly speed the years away;
We hail thee now a woman grown
In regal robes and Queen's array.

Thou dark-browed beauty of the west,
Thy matchless grace is widely known;
Rich jewels sparkle on thy breast,
Thy head supports a royal crown.
And through thy veins pure Afric's blood
Flows fearlessly along its course;
Thy cheeks are mantled by the flood;
We hail thee, lovely *Wilberforce!*

Thy palace gates are open wide—
All are invited to the feast;
From frigid North or Southern side,
From every point, from West to East.
Thou holdest in thine outstretched hand
The richest, rarest gifts to youth;

From snow-capped peak to ocean strand,
Thou offerest all the words of truth.

They come! their burning thirst, quench,
For wisdom, honor, knowledge, power;
From hidden depths rich jewels wrench—
Successful effort crowns each hour.
But foul incendiary's cruel hand,
Thy Territory did invade;
By ruthless and destructive brand,
Thy lonely walls were lowly laid.

When night had hushed the birds to sleep,
Out of his covert see him creep;
The crackling flame and lurid glare,
Burst out upon the midnight air.
And what had seemed so strong and fair,
Now lay a mass of ruins there;
Triumphantly look'd all our foes,
And gloated o'er our many woes.

But men of iron nerve and will,
Looked up to God, with courage still:
Believing He their cries would heed,
And prove a friend in time of need.
The tiny seeds of kindness sown,
Into a mighty tree has grown,
And youth and maiden side by side,
Sit 'neath its spreading branches wide.

And though the seed be sown in Payne,
The trite old saying we maintain:
That whosoe'er in Payne we sow,
By faith's tears watered it shall grow.
Our trust untarnished by alloy,
We sow in tears but reap in joy;
And may thy praises never cease,
And all thy pathos be those of peace.

1890

There's a Sampson, lying, sleeping in the land,
He shall soon awake, and with avenging hand,
In an all unlooked for hour,
He will rise in mighty power;
    What dastard can his righteous rage withstand?

E'er since the chains were given at a stroke,
E'er since the dawn of Freedom's morning broke,
He has groaned, but scarcely uttered,
While his patient tongue ne'er muttered,
    Though in agony he bore the galling yoke.

O, what cruelty and torture has he felt?
Could his tears, the heart of his oppressor melt?
In his gore they bathed their hands,
Organized and lawless bands—
    And the innocent was left in blood to welt.

The mighty God of Nations doth not sleep,
His piercing eye its faithful watch doth keep,
And well nigh His mercy's spent,
To the ungodly lent:
    "They have sowed the wind, the whirlwind they shall reap."

From His nostrils issues now the angry smoke,
And asunder bursts the all-oppressive yoke;
When the prejudicial heel
Shall be lifted, we shall feel,
    That the hellish spell surrounding us is broke.

The mills are grinding slowly, slowly on,
And till the very chaff itself is gone;
Our cries for justice louder,
'Till oppression's ground to powder—
    God speed the day of retribution on!

Fair Columbia's family garments all are stained;
In her courts is blinded justice rudely chained;

The black Sampson is awaking,
And his fetters fiercely breaking;
    By his mighty arm his rights shall be obtained!

1890

AN EPITAPH

When I am gone,
Above me raise no lofty stone
Perfect in human handicraft,
No upward pointing gleaming shaft.
Say this of me, and I be content,
That in the Master's work my life was spent;
Say not that I was either great or good,
But Mary-like, "She hath done what she could."

1890

NOTES

1. Wilberforce University, a historically black college founded in 1856 by Daniel Payne, sixth bishop of the A.M.E. Church.

2. The A.M.E. Church.

ANNA JULIA COOPER (1858?-1964)

Anna Julia Haywood Cooper was born in North Carolina to Hannah Stanley, an enslaved African American woman, and her master, George Washington Haywood. In 1867, she was enrolled at St. Augustine's Normal School and Collegiate Institute in Raleigh, North Carolina. In 1881, she was admitted to Oberlin College in Ohio. There she earned a bachelor's degree, in 1884, and a master's degree in mathematics, in 1887. She would resume her studies in 1911, enrolling in a doctoral degree program at Columbia University in New York City. The death of her half-brother and her subsequent adoption of his five children forced Cooper to postpone her education. Cooper would eventually resume her studies at the University of Paris (Sorbonne), earning a PhD in French in 1925, at the age of sixty-seven. She was only the fourth African American woman to earn the doctor of philosophy degree. Her dissertation was titled "The Attitude of France Toward Slavery during the Revolution." Cooper taught at a number of secondary and post-secondary institutions, including Wilberforce University and the M Street High School in Washington, DC. A feminist activist as well as a writer, Cooper cofounded the Colored Women's League in 1892, the same year that she published *A Voice from the South,* a groundbreaking collection of essays exploring racism, sexism, and the social and political structures affecting the plight of oppressed peoples worldwide. The first essay in this collection, "Womanhood: A Vital Element in the Regeneration and Progress of a Race," was initially delivered as an address to the Fourth Annual Convocation of Colored Clergy of the Protestant Episcopalian Church, held in Washington, DC, in 1887.

A VOICE FROM THE SOUTH

Womanhood: A Vital Element in the Regeneration and Progress of a Race

The two sources from which, perhaps, modern civilization has derived its noble and ennobling ideal of woman are Christianity and the Feudal System.

In Oriental countries woman has been uniformly devoted to a life of ignorance, infamy, and complete stagnation. The Chinese shoe of to-day does not more entirely dwarf, cramp, and destroy her physical powers, than have the customs, laws, and social instincts, which from remotest ages have governed our Sister of the East, enervated and blighted her mental and moral life.

Mahomet[1] makes no account of woman whatever in his polity. The Koran, which, unlike our Bible, was a product and not a growth, tried to address itself to the needs of Arabian civilization as Mahomet with his circumscribed powers saw them. The Arab was a nomad. Home to him meant his present camping place. That deity who, according to our western ideals, makes and sanctifies the home, was to him a transient bauble to be toyed with so long as it gave pleasure and then to be thrown aside for a new one. As a personality, an individual soul, capable of eternal growth and unlimited development, and destined to mould and shape the civilization of the future to an incalculable extent, Mahomet did not know woman. There was no hereafter, no paradise for her. The heaven of the Mussulman is peopled and made gladsome not by the departed wife, or sister, or mother, but by *houri*[2]—a figment of Mahomet's brain, partaking of the ethereal qualities of angels, yet imbued with all the vices and inanity of Oriental women. The harem here, and—"dust to dust" hereafter, this was the hope, the inspiration, the *summum bonum*[3] of the Eastern woman's life! With what result on the life of the nation, the "Unspeakable Turk," the "sick man"[4] of modern Europe can to-day exemplify.

Says a certain writer: "The private life of the Turk is vilest of the vile, unprogressive, unambitious, and inconceivably low." And yet Turkey is not without her great men. She has produced most brilliant minds; men skilled in all the intricacies of diplomacy and statesmanship; men whose intellects could grapple with the deep problems of empire and manipulate the subtle agencies which check-mate kings. But these minds were not the normal outgrowth of a healthy trunk. They seemed rather ephemeral excrescencies which shoot far out with all the vigor and promise, apparently, of strong branches; but soon alas fall into decay and ugliness because there is no soundness in the root, no life-giving sap, permeating, strengthening and perpetuating the whole. There is a worm at the core! The homelife is impure! and when we look for fruit, like apples of Sodom, it crumbles within our grasp into dust and ashes.

It is pleasing to turn from this effete and immobile civilization to a society still fresh and vigorous, whose seed is in itself, and whose very name is synonymous with all that is progressive, elevating and inspiring, viz., the European bud and the American flower of modern civilization.

And here let me say parenthetically that our satisfaction in American institutions rests not on the fruition we now enjoy, but springs rather from the possibilities and promise that are inherent in the system, though as yet, perhaps, far in the future.

"Happiness," says Madame de Stael,[5] "consists not in perfections attained, but in a sense of progress, the result of our own endeavor under conspiring circumstances *toward* a goal which continually advances and broadens and deepens till it is swallowed up in the Infinite." Such conditions in embryo are all that we claim for the land of the West. We have not yet reached our ideal in American civilization. The pessimists even declare that we are not marching in that direction. But there can be no doubt that here in America is the arena in which the next triumph of civilization is to be won; and here too we find promise abundant and possibilities infinite.

Now let us see on what basis this hope for our country primarily and funda- mentally rests. Can any one doubt that it is chiefly on the homelife and on the influence of good women in those homes? Says Macaulay: "You may judge a nation's rank in the scale of civilization from the way they treat their women."[6] And Emerson, "I have thought that a sufficient measure of civilization is the influence of good women."[7] Now this high regard for woman, this germ of a prolific idea which in our own day is bearing such rich and varied fruit, was ingrafted into European civilization, we have said, from two sources, the Chris- tian Church and the Feudal System. For although the Feudal System can in no sense be said to have originated the idea, yet there can be no doubt that the habits of life and modes of thought to which Feudalism gave rise, materially fostered and developed it; for they gave us chivalry, than which no institution has more sensibly magnified and elevated woman's position in society.

Tacitus dwells on the tender regard for woman entertained by these rug- ged barbarians before they left their northern homes to overrun Europe. Old Norse legends too, and primitive poems, all breathe the same spirit of love of home and veneration for the pure and noble influence there presiding—the wife, the sister, the mother.

And when later on we see the settled life of the Middle Ages "oozing out," as M. Guizot[8] expresses it, from the plundering and pillaging life of barbarism and crystallizing into the Feudal System, the tiger of the field is brought once more within the charmed circle of the goddesses of his castle, and his imagination weaves around them a halo whose reflection possibly has not yet altogether vanished.

It is true the spirit of Christianity had not yet put the seal of catholicity on this sentiment. Chivalry, according to Bascom,[9] was but the toning down and softening of a rough and lawless period. It gave a roseate glow to a bitter winter's day. Those who looked out from castle windows reveled in its "amethyst tints." But God's poor, the weak, the unlovely, the commonplace were still freezing and starving none the less, in unpitied, unrelieved loneliness.

Respect for woman, the much lauded chivalry of the Middle Ages, meant what I fear it still means to some men in our own day—respect for the elect few among whom they expect to consort.

The idea of the radical amelioration of womankind, reverence for woman as woman regardless of rank, wealth, or culture, was to come from that rich and bounteous fountain from which flow all our liberal and universal ideas—the Gospel of Jesus Christ.

And yet the Christian Church at the time of which we have been speaking would seem to have been doing even less to protect and elevate woman than the little done by secular society. The Church as an organization committed a double offense against woman in the Middle Ages. Making of marriage a sacrament and at the same time insisting on the celibacy of the clergy and other religious orders, she gave an inferior if not an impure character to the marriage relation, especially fitted to reflect discredit on woman. Would this were all or the worst! but the Church by the licentiousness of its chosen servants invaded the household and established too often as vicious connections those relations which it forbade to assume openly and in good faith. "Thus," to use the words of our authority, "the religious corps became as numerous, as searching, and as unclean as the frogs of Egypt, which penetrated into all quarters, into the ovens and kneading troughs, leaving their filthy trail wherever they went."[10] Says Chaucer with characteristic satire, speaking of the Friars:

Women may now go safely up and doun,
In every bush, and under every tree,
Ther is non other incubus but he,
And he ne will don hem no dishonour.

Henry, Bishop of Liege, could unblushingly boast the birth of twenty-two children in fourteen years.[11]

It may help us under some of the perplexities which beset our way in "the one Catholic and Apostolic Church" to-day, to recall some of the corruptions and incongruities against which the Bride of Christ has had to struggle in her past history and in spite of which she has kept, through many vicissitudes, the faith once delivered to the saints. Individuals, organizations, whole sections of the Church militant may outrage the Christ whom they profess, may ruthlessly trample under foot both the spirit and the letter of his precepts, yet not till we hear the voices audibly saying "Come let us depart hence,"[12] shall we cease to believe and cling to the promise, *"I am with you to the end of the world."*[13]

> Yet saints their watch are keeping,
> The cry goes up 'How long!'
> And soon the night of weeping
> Shall be the morn of song.[14]

However much then the facts of any particular period of history may seem to deny it, I for one do not doubt that the source of the vitalizing principle of woman's development and amelioration is the Christian Church, so far as that church is coincident with Christianity.

Christ gave ideals not formulæ. The Gospel is a germ requiring millennia for its growth and ripening. It needs and at the same time helps to form around itself a soil enriched in civilization, and perfected in culture and insight without which the embryo can neither be unfolded or comprehended. With all the strides our civilization has made from the first to the nineteenth century, we can boast not an idea, not a principle of action, not a progressive social force but was already mutely foreshadowed, or directly enjoined in that simple tale of a meek and lowly life. The quiet face of the Nazarene[15] is ever seen a little way ahead, never too far to come down to and touch the life of the lowest in days the darkest, yet ever leading onward, still onward, the tottering childish feet of our strangely boastful civilization.

By laying down for woman the same code of morality, the same standard of purity, as for man; by refusing to countenance the shameless and equally guilty monsters who were gloating over her fall,—graciously stooping in all the majesty of his own spotlessness to wipe away the filth and grime of her guilty past and bid her go in peace and sin no more; and again in the moments of his own careworn and footsore dejection, turning trustfully and lovingly, away from the heartless snubbing and sneers, away from the cruel malignity of mobs and prelates in the dusty marts of Jerusalem to the ready sympathy, loving appreciation and unfaltering friendship of that quiet home at Bethany; and even at the last, by his dying bequest to the disciple whom he loved, signifying the protection and tender regard to be extended to that sorrowing mother and ever afterward to the sex she represented;—throughout his life and in his death he has given to men a rule and guide for the estimation of woman as an equal, as a helper, as a friend, and as a sacred charge to be sheltered and cared for with a brother's love and sympathy, lessons which nineteen centuries' gigantic strides in knowledge, arts, and sciences, in social and ethical principles have not been able to probe to their depth or to exhaust in practice.

It seems not too much to say then of the vitalizing, regenerating, and progressive influence of womanhood on the civilization of today, that, while it was foreshadowed among Germanic nations in the far away dawn of their history as a narrow, sickly and stunted growth, it yet owes its catholicity and power, the deepening of its roots and broadening of its branches to Christianity.

The union of these two forces, the Barbaric and the Christian, was not long delayed after the Fall of the Empire. The Church, which fell with Rome, finding herself in danger of being swallowed up by barbarism, with characteristic vigor and fertility of resources, addressed herself immediately to the task of conquering her conquerors. The means chosen does credit to her power of penetration and adaptability, as well as to her profound, unerring, all-compassing diplomacy; and makes us even now wonder if aught human can successfully and ultimately withstand her far-seeing designs and brilliant policy, or gainsay her well-earned claim to the word *Catholic*.[16]

She saw the barbarian, little more developed than a wild beast. She forbore to antagonize and mystify his warlike nature by a full blaze of the heart-searching and humanizing tenets of her great Head. She said little of the rule "If thy brother smite thee on one cheek, turn to him the other also;"[17] but thought it sufficient for the needs of those times, to establish the so-called "Truce of God" under which men were bound to abstain from butchering one another for three days of each week and on Church festivals. In other words, she respected their individuality: non-resistance pure and simple being for them an utter impossibility, she contented herself with less radical measures calculated to lead up finally to the full measure of the benevolence of Christ.

Next she took advantage of the barbarian's sensuous love of gaudy display and put all her magnificent garments on. She could not capture him by physical force; she would dazzle him by gorgeous spectacles. It is said that Romanism gained more in pomp and ritual during this trying period of the Dark Ages than throughout all her former history.

The result was she carried her point. Once more Rome laid her ambitious hand on the temporal power, and allied with Charlemagne, aspired to rule the world through a civilization dominated by Christianity and permeated by the traditions and instincts of those sturdy barbarians.

Here was the confluence of the two streams we have been tracing, which, united now, stretch before us as a broad majestic river. In regard to woman it was the meeting of two noble and ennobling forces, two kindred ideas the resultant of which, we doubt not, is destined to be a potent force in the betterment of the world.

Now after our appeal to history comparing nations destitute of this force and so destitute also of the principle of progress, with other nations among whom the influence of woman is prominent coupled with a brisk, progressive, satisfying civilization,—if in addition we find this strong presumptive evidence corroborated by reason and experience, we may conclude that these two equally varying concomitants are linked as cause and effect; in other words, that the position of woman in society determines the vital elements of its regeneration and progress.

Now that this is so on *a priori*[18] grounds all must admit. And this not because woman is better or stronger or wiser than man, but from the nature of the case, because it is she who must first form the man by directing the earliest impulses of his character.

Byron and Wordsworth were both geniuses and would have stamped themselves on the thought of their age under any circumstances; and yet we find the one a savor of life unto life, the other of death unto death. "Byron, like a rocket, shot his way upward with scorn and repulsion, flamed out in wild, explosive, brilliant excesses and disappeared in darkness made all the more palpable."[19]

Wordsworth lent of his gifts to reinforce that "power in the Universe which makes for righteousness"[20] by taking the harp handed him from Heaven and using it to swell the strains of angelic choirs. Two locomotives equally mighty stand facing opposite tracks; the one to rush headlong to destruction with all its precious freight, the other to toil grandly and gloriously up the steep embattlements to Heaven and to God. Who—who can say what a world of consequences hung on the first placing and starting of these enormous forces!

Woman, Mother,—your responsibility is one that might make angels tremble and fear to take hold! To trifle with it, to ignore or misuse it, is to treat lightly the most sacred and solemn trust ever confided by God to human kind. The training of children is a task on which an infinity of weal or woe depends. Who does not covet it? Yet who does not stand awe-struck before its momentous issues! It is a matter of small moment, it seems to me, whether that lovely girl in whose accomplishments you take such pride and delight, can enter the gay and crowded salon with the ease and elegance of this or that French or English gentlewoman, compared with the decision as to whether

her individuality is going to reinforce the good or the evil elements of the world. The lace and the diamonds, the dance and the theater, gain a new significance when scanned in their bearings on such issues. Their influence on the individual personality, and through her on the society and civilization which she vitalizes and inspires— all this and more must be weighed in the balance before the jury can return a just and intelligent verdict as to the innocence or banefulness of these apparently simple amusements.

Now the fact of woman's influence on society being granted, what are its practical bearings on the work which brought together this conference of colored clergy and laymen in Washington? "We come not here to talk." Life is too busy, too pregnant with meaning and far reaching consequences to allow you to come this far for mere intellectual entertainment.

The vital agency of womanhood in the regeneration and progress of a race, as a general question, is conceded almost before it is fairly stated. I confess one of the difficulties for me in the subject assigned lay in its obviousness. The plea is taken away by the opposite attorney's granting the whole question.

"Woman's influence on social progress"—who in Christendom doubts or questions it? One may as well be called on to prove that, the sun is the source of light and heat and energy to this many-sided little world.

Nor, on the other hand, could it have been intended that I should apply the position when taken and proven, to the needs and responsibilities of the women of our race in the South. For is it not written, "Cursed is he that cometh after the king?"[21] and has not the King already preceded me in "The Black Woman of the South"?[22]

They have had both Moses and the Prophets in Dr. Crummell and if they hear not him, neither would they be persuaded though one came up from the South.

I would beg, however, with the Doctor's permission, to add my plea for the *Colored Girls* of the South:—that large, bright, promising fatally beautiful class that stand shivering like a delicate plantlet before the fury of tempestuous elements, so full of promise and possibilities, yet so sure of destruction; often without a father to whom they dare apply the loving term, often without a stronger brother to espouse their cause and defend their honor with his life's blood; in the midst of pitfalls and snares, waylaid by the lower classes of white men, with no shelter, no protection nearer than the great blue vault above, which half conceals and half reveals the one Care-Taker they know so little of. Oh, save them, help them, shield, train, develop, teach, inspire them! Snatch them, in God's name, as brands from the burning! There is material in them well worth your while, the hope in germ of a staunch, helpful, regenerating womanhood on which, primarily, rests the foundation stones of our future as a race.

It is absurd to quote statistics showing the Negro's bank account and rent rolls, to point to the hundreds of newspapers edited by colored men and lists of lawyers, doctors, professors, D. D's, LL D's, etc., etc., etc., while the source from which the life-blood of the race is to flow is subject to taint and corruption in the enemy's camp.

True progress is never made by spasms. Real progress is growth. It must begin in the seed. Then, "first the blade, then the ear, after that the full corn in the ear."[23] There is something to encourage and inspire us in the advancement of individuals since their emancipation from slavery. It at least proves that there is nothing irretrievably wrong in the shape of the black man's skull, and that under given circumstances his development, downward or upward, will be similar to that of other average human beings.

But there is no time to be wasted in mere felicitation. That the Negro has his niche in the infinite purposes of the Eternal, no one who has studied the history of the last fifty years in America will deny. That much depends on his own right comprehension of his responsibility and rising to the demands of the hour, it will be good for him to see; and how best to use his present so that the structure of the future shall be stronger and higher and brighter and nobler and holier than that of the past, is a question to be decided each day by every one of us.

The race is just twenty-one years removed from the conception and experience of a chattel, just at the age of ruddy manhood. It is well enough to pause a moment for retrospection, introspection, and prospection. We look back, not to become inflated with conceit because of the depths from which we have arisen, but that we may learn wisdom from experience. We look within, that we may gather together once more our forces, and, by improved and more practical methods, address ourselves to the tasks before us. We look forward with hope and trust that the same God whose guiding hand led our fathers through and out of the gall and bitterness of oppression, will still lead and direct their children, to the honor of His name, and for their ultimate salvation.

But this survey of the failures or achievments of the past, the difficulties and embarrassments of the present, and the mingled hopes and fears for the future, must not degenerate into mere dreaming nor consume the time which belongs to the practical and effective handling of the crucial questions of the hour; and there can be no issue more vital and momentous than this of the womanhood of the race.

Here is the vulnerable point, not in the heel, but at the heart of the young Achilles; and here must the defenses be strengthened and the watch redoubled.

We are the heirs of a past which was not our fathers' moulding. "Every man the arbiter of his own destiny"[24] was not true for the American Negro of the past: and it is no fault of his that he finds himself to-day the inheritor of a manhood and womanhood impoverished and debased by two centuries and more of compression and degradation.

But weaknesses and malformations, which to-day are attributable to a vicious schoolmaster and a pernicious system, will a century hence be rightly regarded as proofs of innate corruptness and radical incurability.

Now the fundamental agency under God in the regeneration, the re-training of the race, as well as the ground work and starting point of its progress upward, must be the *black woman.*

With all the wrongs and neglects of her past, with all the weakness, the debasement, the moral thralldom of her present, the black woman of to-day stands mute and wondering at the Herculean task devolving around her. But the cycles wait for her. No other hand can move the lever. She must be loosed from her bands and set to work.

Our meager and superficial results from past efforts prove their futility; and every attempt to elevate the Negro, whether undertaken by himself or through the philanthropy of others, cannot but prove abortive unless so directed as to utilize the indispensable agency of an elevated and trained womanhood.

A race cannot be purified from without. Preachers and teachers are helps, and stimulants and conditions as necessary as the gracious rain and sunshine are to plant growth. But what are rain and dew and sunshine and cloud if there be no life in the plant germ? We must go to the root and see that it is sound and healthy and vigorous; and not deceive ourselves with waxen flowers and painted leaves of mock chlorophyll.

We too often mistake individuals' honor for race development and so are ready to substitute pretty accomplishments for sound sense and earnest purpose.

A stream cannot rise higher than its source. The atmosphere of homes is no rarer and purer and sweeter than are the mothers in those homes. A race is but a total of families. The nation is the aggregate of its homes. As the whole is sum of all its parts, so the character of the parts will determine the characteristics of the whole. These are all axioms and so evident that it seems gratuitous to remark it; and yet, unless I am greatly mistaken, most of the unsatisfaction from our past results arises from just such a radical and palpable error, as much almost on our own part as on that of our benevolent white friends.

The Negro is constitutionally hopeful and proverbially irrepressible; and naturally stands in danger of being dazzled by the shimmer and tinsel of superficials. We often mistake foliage for fruit and overestimate or wrongly estimate brilliant results.

The late Martin R. Delany, who was an unadulterated black man, used to say when honors of state fell upon him, that when he entered the council of kings the black race entered with him; meaning, I suppose, that there was no discounting his race identity and attributing his achievements to some admixture of Saxon blood. But our present record of eminent men, when placed beside the actual status of the race in America to-day, proves that no man can represent the race. Whatever the attainments of the individual may be, unless his home has moved on *pari passu*,[25] he can never be regarded as identical with or representative of the whole.

Not by pointing to sun-bathed mountain tops do we prove that Phoebus[26] warms the valleys. We must point to homes, average homes, homes of the rank and file of horny handed toiling men and women of the South (where the masses are) lighted and cheered by the good, the beautiful, and the true,—then and not till then will the whole plateau be lifted into the sunlight.

Only the BLACK WOMAN can say "when and where I enter, in the quiet, undisputed dignity of my womanhood, without violence and without suing or special patronage, then and there the whole *Negro race enters with me*." Is it not evident then that as individual workers for this race we must address ourselves with no half-hearted zeal to this feature of our mission. The need is felt and must be recognized by all. There is a call for workers, for missionaries, for men and women with the double consecration of a fundamental love of humanity and a desire for its melioration through the Gospel; but superadded to this we demand an intelligent and sympathetic comprehension of the interests and special needs of the Negro.

I see not why there should not be an organized effort for the protection and elevation of our girls such as the White Cross League in England. English women are strengthened and protected by more than twelve centuries of Christian influences, freedom and civilization; English girls are dispirited and crushed down by no such all-leveling prejudice as that supercilious caste spirit in America which cynically assumes "A Negro woman cannot be a lady." English womanhood is beset by no such snares and traps as betray the unprotected, untrained colored girl of the South, whose only crime and dire destruction often is her unconscious and marvelous beauty. Surely then if English indignation is aroused and English manhood thrilled under the leadership of a Bishop of the English church to build up bulwarks around their wronged sisters, Negro sentiment cannot remain callous and Negro effort nerveless in view of the imminent peril of the mothers of the next generation. *"I am my Sister's keeper!"* should be the hearty response of every man and woman of the race, and this conviction should purify and exalt the narrow, selfish and petty personal aims of life into a noble and sacred purpose.

We need men who can let their interest and gallantry extend outside the circle of their aesthetic appreciation; men who can be a father, a brother, a friend to every weak, struggling unshielded girl. We need women who are so sure of their own social footing that they need not fear leaning to lend a hand to a fallen or falling sister. We need men and women who do not exhaust their genius splitting hairs on aristocratic distinctions and thanking God they are not as others; but earnest, unselfish souls, who can go into the highways and byways, lifting up and leading, advising and encouraging with the truly catholic benevolence of the Gospel of Christ.

As Church workers we must confess our path of duty is less obvious; or rather our ability to adapt our machinery to our conception of the peculiar exigencies of this work as taught by experience and our own consciousness of the needs of the Negro, is as yet not demonstrable. Flexibility and aggressiveness are not such strong characteristics of the Church to-day as in the Dark Ages.

As a Mission field for the Church the Southern Negro is in some aspects most promising; in others, perplexing. Aliens neither in language and customs, nor in associations and sympathies, naturally of deeply rooted religious instincts and taking most readily and kindly to the worship and teachings of the Church, surely the task of proselytizing the American Negro is infinitely less formidable than that which confronted the Church in the Barbarians of Europe. Besides, this people already look to the Church as the hope of their race. Thinking colored men almost uniformly admit that the Protestant Episcopal Church with its quiet, chaste dignity and decorous solemnity, its instructive and elevating ritual, its bright chanting and joyous hymning, is eminently fitted to correct the peculiar faults of worship—the rank exuberance and often ludicrous demonstrativeness of their people. Yet, strange to say, the Church, claiming to be missionary and Catholic, urging that schism is sin and denominationalism inexcusable, has made in all these years almost no inroads upon this semi-civilized religionism.

Harvests from this over ripe field of home missions have been gathered in by Methodists, Baptists, and not least by Congregationalists, who were unknown to the Freedmen before their emancipation.

Our clergy numbers less than two dozen[27] priests of Negro blood, and we have hardly more than one self-supporting colored congregation in the entire Southland. While the organization known as the A. M. E. Church has 14,063 ministers, itinerant and local, 4,069 self-supporting churches, 4,275 Sunday-schools, with property valued at $7,772,284, raising yearly for church purposes $1,427,000.

Stranger and more significant than all, the leading men of this race (I do not mean demagogues and politicians, but men of intellect, heart, and race devotion, men to whom the elevation of their people means more than personal ambition and sordid gain—and the men of that stamp have not all died yet) the Christian workers for the race, of younger and more cultured growth, are noticeably drifting into sectarian churches, many of them declaring all the time that they acknowledge the historic claims of the Church, believe her apostolicity, and would experience greater personal comfort, spiritual and intellectual, in her revered communion. It is a fact which any one may verify for himself, that representative colored men, professing that in their heart of hearts they are Episcopalians, are actually working in Methodist and Baptist pulpits; while the ranks of the Episcopal clergy are left to be filled largely by men who certainly suggest the propriety of a *"perpetual* Diaconate"[28] if they cannot be said to have created the necessity for it.

Now where is the trouble? Something must be wrong. What is it?

A certain Southern Bishop of our Church reviewing the situation, whether in Godly anxiety or in "Gothic antipathy" I know not, deprecates the fact that the colored people do not seem *drawn* to the Episcopal Church, and comes to the sage conclusion that the Church is not adapted to the rude untutored minds of the Freedmen, and that they may be left to go to the Methodists and Baptists whither their racial proclivities undeniably tend. How the good Bishop can agree that all-foreseeing Wisdom, and Catholic Love would have framed his Church as typified in his seamless garment and unbroken body, and yet not leave it broad enough and deep enough and loving enough to seek and save and hold seven millions of God's poor, I cannot see.

But the doctors while discussing their scientifically conclusive diagnosis of the disease, will perhaps not think it presumptuous in the patient if he dares to suggest where at least the pain is. If this be allowed, *a Black woman of the South* would beg to point out two possible oversights in this southern work which may indicate in part both a cause and a remedy for some failure. The first is *not calculating for the Black man's personality;* not having respect, if I may so express it, to his manhood or deferring at all to his conceptions of the needs of his people. When colored persons have been employed it was too often as machines or as manikins. There has been no disposition, generally, to get the black man's ideal or to let his individuality work by its own gravity, as it were. A conference of earnest Christian men have met at regular intervals for some years past to discuss the best methods of promoting the welfare and develop-ment of colored people in this country. Yet, strange as it may seem, they have never invited a colored man or even intimated that one would be welcome to take part in their deliberations. Their remedial contrivances are purely theo-retical or empirical, therefore, and the whole machinery devoid of soul.

The second important oversight in my judgment is closely allied to this and probably grows out of it, and that is not developing Negro womanhood as an essential fundamental for the elevation of the race, and utilizing this agency in extending the work of the Church.

Of the first I have possibly already presumed to say too much since it does not strictly come within the province of my subject. However, Macaulay somewhere criticises the Church of England as not knowing how to use fanatics, and declares that had Ignatius Loyola[29] been in the Anglican instead of the Roman communion, the Jesuits would have been schismatics instead of Catholics; and if the religious awakenings of the Wesleys[30] had been in Rome, she would have shaven their heads, tied ropes around their waists, and sent them out under her own banner and blessing. Whether this be true or not, there is certainly a vast amount of force potential for Negro evangeliza-tion rendered latent, or worse, antagonistic by the halting, uncertain, I had almost said, *trimming* policy of the Church in the South. This may sound both presumptuous and ungrateful. It is mortifying, I know, to benevolent wisdom, after having spent itself in the execution of well conned theories for the ideal development of a particular work, to hear perhaps the weakest and humblest element of that work: asking "what doest thou?"

Yet so it will be in life. The "thus far and no farther" pattern cannot be fitted to any growth in God's kingdom. The universal law of development is "onward and upward." It is God-given and inviolable. From the unfolding of the germ in the acorn to reach the sturdy oak, to the growth of a human soul into the full knowledge and likeness of its Creator, the breadth and scope of the movement in each and all are too grand, too mysterious, too like God himself, to be encompassed and locked down in human molds.

After all the Southern slave owners were right: either the very alphabet of intellectual growth must be forbidden and the Negro dealt with absolutely as a chattel having neither rights nor sensibilities; or else the clamps and irons of mental and moral, as well as civil compression must be riven asunder and the truly enfranchised soul led to the entrance of that boundless vista through which it is to toil upwards to its beckoning God as the buried seed germ, to meet the sun.

A perpetual colored diaconate, carefully and kindly superintended by the white clergy; congregations of shiny faced peasants with their clean white aprons and sunbonnets catechised at regular intervals and taught to recite the creed, the Lord's prayer and the ten commandments—duty towards God and duty towards neighbor, surely such well tended sheep ought to be grateful to their shepherds and content in that station of life to which it pleased God to call them. True, like the old professor lecturing to his solitary student, we make no provision here for irregularities. "Questions must be kept till after class," or dispensed with altogether. That some do ask questions and insist on answers, in class too, must be both impertinent and annoying. Let not our spiritual pastors and masters however be grieved at such self-assertion as merely signifies we have a destiny to fulfill and as men and women we must *be about our Father's business.*

It is a mistake to suppose that the Negro is prejudiced against a white ministry. Naturally there is not a more kindly and implicit follower of a white man's guidance than the average colored peasant. What would to others be an ordinary act of friendly or pastoral interest he would be more inclined to regard gratefully as a condescension. And he never forgets such kindness. Could the Negro be brought near to his white priest or bishop, he is not suspicious. He is not only willing but often longs to unburden his soul to this intelligent guide. There are no reservations when he is convinced that you are his friend. It is a saddening satire on American history and manners that it takes something to convince him.

That our people are not "drawn" to a Church whose chief dignitaries they see only in the chancel, and whom they reverence as they would a painting or an angel, whose life never comes down to and touches theirs with the inspiration of an objective reality, may be "perplexing" truly (American caste and American Christianity both being facts) but it need not be surprising. There must be something of human nature in it, the same as that which brought about that "the Word was made flesh and dwelt among us" that He might "draw" us towards God.

Men are not "drawn" by abstractions. Only sympathy and love can draw, and until our Church in America realizes this and provides a clergy that can come in touch with our life and have a fellow feeling for our woes, without being imbedded and frozen up in their "Gothic antipathies," the good bishops are likely to continue "perplexed" by the sparsity of colored Episcopalians.

A colored priest of my acquaintance recently related to me, with tears in his eyes, how his reverend Father in God, the Bishop who had ordained him, had met him on the cars on his way to the diocesan convention and warned him, not unkindly, not to take a seat in the body of the convention with the white clergy. To avoid disturbance of their godly placidity he would of course please sit back and somewhat apart. I do not imagine that that clergyman had very much heart for the Christly (!) deliberations of that convention.

To return, however, it is not on this broader view of Church work, which I mentioned as a primary cause of its halting progress with the colored people, that I am to speak. My proper theme is the second oversight of which in my judgment our Christian propagandists have been guilty: or, the necessity of church training, protecting and uplifting our colored womanhood as indispensable to the evangelization of the race.

Apelles[31] did not disdain even that criticism of his lofty art which came from an uncouth cobbler; and may I not hope that the writer's oneness with her subject both in feeling and in being may palliate undue obtrusiveness of opinions here. That the race cannot be effectually lifted up till its women are truly elevated we take as proven. It is not for us to dwell on the needs, the neglects, and the ways of succor, pertaining to the black woman of the South. The ground has been ably discussed and an admirable and practical plan proposed by the oldest Negro priest in America, advising and urging that special organizations such as Church Sisterhoods and industrial schools be devised to meet her pressing needs in the Southland. That some such movements are vital to the life of this people and the extension of the Church among them, is not hard to see. Yet the pamphlet fell still-born from the press. So far as I am informed the Church has made no motion towards carrying out Dr. Crummell's suggestion.

The denomination which comes next our own in opposing the proverbial emotionalism of Negro worship in the South, and which in consequence like ours receives the cold shoulder from the old heads, resting as we do under the charge of not "having religion" and not believing in conversion—the Congregationalists—have quietly gone to work on the young, have established industrial and training schools, and now almost every community in the South is yearly enriched by a fresh infusion of vigorous young hearts, cultivated heads, and helpful hands that have been trained at Fisk, at Hampton, in Atlanta University, and in Tuskegee, Alabama.[32]

These young people are missionaries actual or virtual both here and in Africa. They have learned to love the methods and doctrines of the Church which trained and educated them; and so Congregationalism surely and steadily progresses.

Need I compare these well known facts with results shown by the Church in the same field and during the same or even a longer time.

The institution of the Church in the South[33] to which she mainly looks for the training of her colored clergy and for the help of the "Black Woman" and "Colored Girl" of the South, has graduated since the year 1868, when the school was founded, *five young women;*[34] and while yearly numerous young men have been kept and trained for the ministry by the charities of the Church, the number of indigent females who have here been supported, sheltered and trained, is phenomenally small. Indeed, to my mind, the attitude of the Church toward this feature of her work, is as if the solution of the problem of Negro missions depended solely on sending a quota of deacons and priests into the field, girls being a sort of *tertium quid*[35] whose development may be promoted if they can pay their way and fall in with the plans mapped out for the training of the other sex.

Now I would ask in all earnestness, does not this force potential deserve by education and stimulus to be made dynamic? Is it not a solemn duty incumbent on all colored churchmen to make it so? Will not the aid of the Church be given to prepare our girls in head, heart, and hand for the duties and responsibilities that await the intelligent wife, the Christian mother, the earnest, virtuous, helpful woman, at once both the lever and the fulcrum for uplifting the race.

As Negroes and churchmen we cannot be indifferent to these questions. They touch us most vitally on both sides. We believe in the Holy Catholic Church. We believe that however gigantic and apparently remote the consummation, the Church will go on conquering and to conquer till the kingdoms of this world, not excepting the black man and the black woman of the South, shall have become the kingdoms of the Lord and of his Christ.

That past work in this direction has been unsatisfactory we must admit. That without a change of policy results in the future will be as meagre, we greatly fear. Our life as a race is at stake. The dearest interests of our hearts are in the scales. We must either break away from dear old landmarks and plunge out in any line and every line that enables us to meet the pressing need of our people, or we must ask the Church to allow and help us, untrammeled by the prejudices and theories of individuals, to work aggressively under her direction as we alone can, with God's help, for the salvation of our people.

The time is ripe for action. Self-seeking and ambition must be laid on the altar. The battle is one of sacrifice and hardship, but our duty is plain. We have been recipients of missionary bounty in some sort for twenty-one years. Not even the senseless vegetable is content to be a mere reservoir. Receiving without giving is an anomaly in nature. Nature's cells are all little workshops for manufacturing sunbeams, the product to be *given out* to earth's inhabitants in warmth, energy, thought, action. Inanimate creation always pays back an equivalent.

Now, *How much owest thou my Lord?* [36] Will his account be overdrawn if he call for singleness of purpose and self-sacrificing labor for your brethren? Having passed through your drill school, will you refuse a general's commission even if it entail responsibility, risk and anxiety, with possibly some adverse criticism? Is it too much to ask you to step forward and direct the work for your race along those lines which you know to be of first and vital importance?

Will you allow these words of Ralph Waldo Emerson? "In ordinary," says he, "we have a snappish criticism which watches and contradicts the opposite party. We want the will which advances and dictates. Nature has made up her mind that what cannot defend itself, shall not be defended. Complaining never so loud and with never so much reason, is of no use. What cannot stand must fall; *and the measure of our sincerity and therefore of the respect of men is the amount of health and wealth we will hazard in the defense of our right.*"[37]

1892

NOTES

1. The Prophet Muhammad.

2. In Islam, the beautiful women who attend to the righteous in paradise.

3. A Latin expression meaning "the ultimate good," or "the ultimate goal."

4. Terms used during the second half of the nineteenth century to characterize Turkey and the Ottoman Empire as regions in decline.

5. Anne Louise Germaine de Staël-Holstein (1766–1817), French writer, intellectual, and socialite.

6. Attributed to English historian and politician Thomas Babington Macaulay (1800–1859).

7. In the essay "American Civilization," published in the April 1862 issue of *The Atlantic,* Ralph Waldo Emerson writes, "I have thought it a sufficient definition of civilization to say, it is the influence of good women."

8. French historian and politician François Pierre Guillaume Guizot (1787–1874).

9. Henry Bidleman Bascom (1796–1850) a bishop of the Methodist Episcopal Church, appointed in 1823 to serve as chaplain to the U.S. House of Representatives (1824–26).

10. From Bascom's *Philosophy of English Literature.*

11. Bascom [Cooper's note].

12. A possible reference to John Payne's English adaptation of the *One Thousand and One Nights,* titled *The Book of the Thousand Nights and One Night* (1882).

13. Matthew 28:20.

14. From "The Church's One Foundation," a Protestant hymn authored in 1866 by English priest Samuel John Stone.

15. An alternative name for Jesus who, in the New Testament, is described as having been raised in Nazareth, a city in northern Israel.

16. Meaning, in this context, adaptable and of diverse tastes, interests, and capacities.

17. Matthew 5:39.

18. A Latin term meaning conceived from or based on knowledge or understandings that are self-evident.

19. Bascom's Eng. Lit. p. 253 [Cooper's note].

20. Cooper paraphrases Matthew Arnold's reference, in *Literature and Dogma* (1873), to "A power not ourselves that makes for righteousness."

21. A likely reference to Ecclesiastes 2:12.

22. Pamphlet published by Dr. Alex. Crummell [Cooper's note].

23. Mark 4:28.

24. A reference to the description of Karma offered by religious philosopher Katherine Augusta Westcott Tingley (1847–1929) in *The Mysteries of the Heart Doctrine* (1902).

25. A Latin phrase meaning "on equal footing."

26. The Roman name for Apollo, the sun god of classical mythology.

27. The published report of '91 shows 26 priests for the entire country, including one not engaged in work and one a professor in a non-sectarian school, since made Dean of an Episcopal Annex to Howard University known as King Hall [Cooper's note].

28. The practice, in some denominations, of permitting deacons to serve as de facto ministers, often in areas and time periods in which ministers are in short supply.

29. St. Ignatius Loyola (1491–1556), founder of the Society of Jesus, also called the Jesuits, in 1534.

30. John (1703–1791) and Charles Wesley (1707–1788), English theologians and authors and the cofounders of Methodism.

31. A reference to the legend of Apelles of Kos, the Greek painter from the fourth century BCE, whose widely praised artistic focus is said to have been motivated in part by the criticisms of a passerby, a shoemaker who critiqued Apelles's rendering of a shoe.

32. Refers to four of the most prominent of the historically black colleges and universities.

33. A reference to Spelman College, founded in 1881 as the Atlanta Baptist Female Seminary.

34. Five have been graduated since '86, two in '91, two in '92 [Cooper's note].

35. A Latin expression referring to a third and known element in a grouping with two familiar or known elements (or individuals).

36. Luke 15:5.

37. From chapter 10, "Courage," in *Society and Solitude: Twelve Chapters* by Ralph Waldo Emerson.

DAVID BRYANT FULTON (1863?-1941)

Known to many of his readers as "Jack Thorne," David Bryant Fulton was born in Fayetteville, North Carolina, to former slaves Lavinia Robinson and Benjamin Fulton. He was educated in Wilmington, where he attended the Williston School and the Gregory Normal Institute. In 1887, Fulton left North Carolina and relocated to Brooklyn, New York, where he found work as a Pullman porter. His travels as a porter became the subject of his first published writings, a series of dispatches that appeared in the *Record,* Wilmington's African American paper. In 1892, Fulton published these sketches as a collection, titled *Recollections of a Sleeping Car Porter.* In 1907, he assembled these and other newspaper articles and opinion pieces into a longer volume, titled *Eagle Clippings.* Perhaps his most influential work, *Hanover; or The Persecution of the Lowly; A Story of the Wilmington Massacre* (1900) is a fictionalized account of the Wilmington riots of 1898. "A Hero in Ebony," one of Fulton's earlier sketches, was originally published in *Recollections of a Sleeping Car Porter.* Originally published in *The Citizen,* "Henry Berry Lowery, the North Carolina Outlaw: A Tale of the Reconstruction Period" was later reprinted in *Eagle Clippings.* The following excerpt from *Hanover* represents one of Fulton's primary goals in creating the novel, to portray the heroism of Wilmington's African American residents and the cruelty of its white aristocracy.

A HERO IN EBONY: A PULLMAN PORTER'S STORY

He was one of the many ragged little vagabonds that besiege passenger trains which stop daily at "Ashley Junction," just one mile from Charleston, S.C., which, during winter and spring months, are laden with Northern people on their way to and from Florida and congenial localities in other Southern States. He was as frolicsome, cut up as many "monkey shines" to tempt the nickels and pennies from the pockets of the tourists as any of the others. But, unlike Negro children of his age whose eyes of soft brown are so beautiful, his were the eyes of a tippler,[1] very red. He was doubtless as young as any of the others who rent the air with their songs and shouts; but his red eyes, his comical way of blinking them, knotting his face and ducking about among the others of the company of entertainers, made him appear like some old man whom nature had cheated out of his growth and confined to the companionship of children. My frequent journeyings to and from Charleston had made me a familiar figure amongst the "children of the Junction": for the twenty or thirty minutes' wait there for Southern connections I usually spent romping with them, a hearty sharer of their sport, much to the disgust and chagrin of my fellow railroad men, who scorned the idea of seeking companionship with such "uncouth and degraded specimens of the human family," as one fellow put it. But were not these "uncouth specimens" human? With the same feelings and propensities as others? What mattered it if their clothes were mere rags, their faces dirty and their hair unkempt? Smalls, Whipper, Murray[2] and others of that race in that old State who had so brilliantly demonstrated their fitness for higher things, came up from the ranks of the common people, such as these. My hero's name I could not easily remember, so I used to teasingly call him "Red Eye," and to him and all the little stripplings at the Junction I was known as "Heywood." Their barks and herbs in early spring time, their violets, water lilies and strawberries always had a ready purchaser in me. I must never leave the Junction without a bunch of fresh violets in my lapel, and a basket of choice strawberries in my locker. For they all knew that "Heywood's" return often meant a lot of cast-off clothing, old hats and old shoes to be distributed. None of these things—most of them very good—did I ever see any of them wearing at the Junction.

"I war mine ter Sundy skule; tink I gwa war um heah ter git all mummux up 'mong dese niggers?" said Red Eye, one day, in answer to my queries.

Old as Red Eye looked, he could jump higher, sing louder, and run faster than any boy or girl at the Junction. The Northerner never tires listening to "Go Down Moses,"[3] "Suwanee River,"[4] etc., and witnessing the "buck" and "wing"[5] dance so cleverly performed by these little Southern youngsters. So a performance must be given for every train-load of passengers that halted, and at these functions Red Eye was the undisputed leader. For the pennies and nickels the passengers were inclined to throw out, the little ones would cut many queer capers. At times they were unreasonable in their demands for things amusing, and trains would often pull out leaving some of the youngsters wet to their skins from diving in water for money thrown in to make the fun more enjoyable. Cruel as this part of the sport seemed, it was nevertheless an amusing spectacle. Red Eye, always apparently the least concerned, would often, while eyes were stretched watching the coin in the passenger's hand, bound into the air and seize it before it could hit the ground. Pushing the money into his pocket, he would leisurely saunter away with such a comical look of triumph in his face, that the passengers would forget the disappointment of witnessing a scramble.

One Sunday morning in early spring, before the sun had arisen to kiss away the dew from the grass, while the air was still laden with the breath of sweet flowers, I strolled out from Charleston to attend "Lovefeast"[6] at the little log meeting house at the Junction. None but those who have lived there can tell of the sweetness of a Southern spring time. A mocking bird, hidden away amid the foliage of a large oak tree, was calling to the sun to make haste, to gladden the earth with its light. Partridges, squatting beneath a clump of bushes, startled me by their sudden and hasty flight, and a serpent, aroused from its repose, scampered away, hissing angrily at me as it went. Young as was the morning, the little church was well filled with worshippers and, floating out on the perfumed air, came that old familiar hymn.

"Lawd in de mornin' dou shalt heah
My voice ascendin' high."[7]

Very much to my astonishment, in a far corner, with a look of solemnity upon his face that a priest might covet, sat Red Eye. Solemn as he tried to appear, he could not dispel the mirth-provoking expression always there upon that ebony countenance. As I momentarily observed him sitting there, looking so sober and melancholy, my thoughts flitted back to the roadside, where he was wont to be anything but worshipful; and forgetful of my surroundings, I was about to exclaim, "Hello, Red Eye," but the sad wail of the worshippers snatched me from the roadside to "The Gate of Heaven," for surely "The Lord was in that place!" An angel had come down on that beautiful morning and had troubled the waters, and those humble worshippers were laving in the life-giving stream. At the close of the meeting, a hand was gently laid upon my shoulder, and that voice I had learned to love said:

"Hello, Heywood! Wha' yo' doin' heah?"

"I came to see if you really had need of Sunday clothes," I answered, good naturedly.

"Yo see um doncher, see um?" and, thrusting his thumbs into his suspenders, he strutted off a piece that I might survey him to advantage. Turning about suddenly, his face again expressive of worshipful solemnity, he said: "An' yo' seed me in dat Amen corner, too; did'n you Heywood?"

"Yes, I saw you and was surprised to see you so worshipful, so good."

"Oh, I tells yo' ise got de deligion, shoes yo' bo'n; Ise one er gawd's lambs, an' I spec ter be dar on dat gitt'n up mawnin'.""

He had thrown his hat upon the ground, and with one hand extended above his head, was shouting and capering about in the most comical way. There was the ring of honest truth in his voice, and I believed him. The roughest piece of marble can be carved into the form of an angel. Jesus had died for this rough, uncouth, ignorant youngster as well as for the "wise and prudent," and made it possible that he, by the grace of God might be made to "shine as the brightness of the firmament, and as the stars forever."

Pausing suddenly, he caught hold of my arm and said, "Come, Heywood, gwa tek yo' home, show yo' me ma an' strawberry patch."

I followed my devoted little friend that morning to his two-roomed cabin, there to find new acquaintances and make new friends whose homely yet copious hospitality made this humble log cabin the palace of a king. Although there were knives, forks and spoons for all who sat down to dine at the humble table, Red Eye felt that I would the better enjoy my dish of delicious "garden peas," fresh from the field, if I used his favorite spoon, which he himself had polished and cleaned.

All through that balmy afternoon we wandered together through wood and field and by shady brooks in that Eden of jasmine, honey-suckles and violets, until weary and tired we sank down by the roadside to watch the spires of the distant city fade from view as the evening shadows fell around us.

On my arrival at Jersey City, I was assigned for a few trips to a Western "run," and for quite a long period was deprived of my weekly romps with the children of the Junction. Through the long stretch of country between New York and Chicago, hundreds of miles are traversed without as much as a glimpse of a single dusky face. How I did miss my little fun-makers! How void of real life were these dreary Western journeyings! Leaves, faded and dead, were flying hither and thither, blown by chill winds that heralded approaching winter, when I, with a load of Cubans, returning from Europe and Northern watering places, was again moving Southward. It was a dense foggy night, and the train having crossed the Pee Dee River into South Carolina, was slowly nearing Ashley Junction, when the engine's whistle gave a signal for "brakes," and came almost to an abrupt standstill. So quickly and suddenly were the brakes applied that the passengers were pretty severely shaken up and excited over the sudden and painful pause. As soon as quiet was restored in my car I stole out upon the platform and looked ahead, and saw, about thirty yards ahead of the engine a group of men bending over something on the track. "Poor little fellow! He has broken his leg." I heard someone exclaim, as I neared the scene. Bending over to get a closer view, the eyes of my boy met mine. In his efforts to run swiftly over the track, one of his legs had caught and snapped just above the ankle. Although his sufferings were intense, he readily recognized me, and smiling through his tears, he raised a battered lantern which, though in agony, he was still firmly grasping, and said, "Heywood, I taut yo' bin on dat train." Tenderly we lifted the little fellow and carried him to the baggage car, and there made him as comfortable as possible. But it was not until the morning sun had cleared away the mist that we fully realized why he was there upon the track at that hour, and what havoc had been averted by his being there. A blunder in the display of signals had caused a northbound freight train out of Charleston to collide with another, southbound, killing both engineers and thereby rendering others of the crews panic stricken and helpless. The boy, whose house was not far distant from the Junction, hearing the awful crash, had hastened to the scene, and seeing the others helpless, seized a lantern and ran ahead to warn the passenger train, which he knew would soon come thundering on unaware of the danger that awaited it. And although he had broken his leg before the train hove in sight, he bravely swung the lantern until the engineer saw it and stopped. Tears filled the eyes of many who bent over the little form that morning and lavishly showered money into the lap of the mother that had borne such a son; for there, upon that rude pallet, lay a hero carved in ebony.

1892

HANOVER; OR, THE PERSECUTION OF THE LOWLY; A STORY OF THE WILMINGTON MASSACRE

Chapter V: Molly Pierrepont

"Sweet and low, sweet and low
Wind of the Western sea
Low, low, breathe and blow
Wind of the Western sea
Over the rolling waters go,
Come from the dying moon and blow
Blow him again to me
While my little one, while my pretty one sleeps."[8]

This sweet old lullaby of Longfellow's, sung by a rich soprano voice floated upon the cool October air out from a beautiful and richly furnished suburban cottage in Wilmington.[9] The singer sat alone at the piano. Though vulgarly called a "Negress," her skin was almost as fair as a Saxon's; and because of the mingling of Negro blood—more beautiful in color. She was gowned in an evening dress of gossamer material, ashes of rose in color. Her hair let out to its full length hung in silky profusion down her back. There were plain old fashioned half moon rings in her ears, and bands of gold upon her bare arms enhanced their beauty. No one will deny that among the women of mixed blood in the South, there are types of surpassing beauty. The inter-mixture of Negro and Saxon, Negro and Spanish and Indian blood gives the skin a more beautiful color than exists in the unadulterated of either race. While the mulatto and octoroon[10] may reveal the Saxon in the fairness of the skin, the Negro reinforcement shows itself generally in the slight inclination of the lips toward thickness, the lustrous black of the eye and hair which is generally abundant and slightly woolly in texture. This is brought out plainly in the case of the Jew. Although centuries have passed since the Jews very extensively amalgamated with the dark races of Egypt and Canaan, their dark complexions, lustrous black eyes, and abundant woolly hair plainly reveal their Hamatic lineage.[11] To pass through the Bowery or lower Broadway in the great metropolis,[12] at an hour when the shop and factory girl is hurrying to or from her work, one is struck by the beauty of Jewish womanhood. King David's successful campaigns placed Solomon over large dominions of Moabitish and Canaanitish peoples; and for the stability of his kingdom, Solomon took wives out of all of these nationalities; and Solomon's most favored wife was his black princess, Naamah, the mother of Rehoboam, his successor. The poet describes Naamah as the "Rose of Sharon, the most excellent of her country." The marriage of Solomon to his black princess was the most notable of any of his marriages; for that wonderful poem, "Solomon's Songs," is mainly a eulogy to this one of his many wives. "I am black but comely, O ye daughters of Jerusalem as the tents of Kedar, as the curtains of Solomon. Look not upon me because I am black, because the sun hath looked upon me."[13] In the most beautiful language in the gift of the poets of that day, Solomon converses with Naamah in the following dialogue: "Return, return O Shulamite; return, return that we may look upon thee." Naamah, "What will you see in Shulamite?" Solomon, "As it were a company of two armies"[14]

We have conclusive evidence that the Southern gentleman did, and does sing such love ditties, and talk sweet nothings to the Southern black woman, and the woman of mixed blood, but unlike Solomon, he is too much of a coward to publicly extol her. During the slave period in the West Indian Islands, a child born to a slave woman shared the fortunes of its father; and if the father was free, so was the child. But the American slave holder reversed that law so that he could humble the bond-woman and damn her offspring with impunity. Upheld by the law the Southerner sold his own daughter and sister into a life of shame. The pretty Negress and the woman of mixed blood brought extortionate prices in Southern markets. Northern sympathizers may talk of the New South, and the Southern orator may harp upon the shortcomings of the "inferior race," but on this line of thought and conduct, the Southern whites have not changed one whit. Before the war, Sambo only had a quit-claim on his black or mulatto wife, and now the laws are so framed that he cannot defend the woman of his race against the encroachments of his white brother, who looks at the destruction of the Negro woman as only an indiscretion. The humble black fool is often forced away from his own wife or sweet-heart at the point of a revolver, cowed by the feeling that a manly stand against a white man might cause incalculable loss of life. Yet the advocate of Lynch Law pictures this humble fellow, this man who is afraid to attempt to defend his own home, as a reckless daredevil, keeping the whites in constant terror. How incompatible these two traits of character. No; it is not the reckless dare deviltry of the Negro that terrorizes the South, but the conscience of the white man whose wrong treatment of a defenseless people fills him with fear and intensifies his hatred. He is determined to fill to overflow his cup of iniquity. Like Macbeth, he has waded in so far, that to return were as tedious as to go over. It matters not how loud the Southerner shouts about "the good-for-nothing Nigger," he still has the same old anti-bellum liking for the women of that race. Bishop Turner is the only honest and earnest advocate of Negro Emigration; the others have only a half-hearted leaning in that direction. If it were possible for emigration to become a reality, the Southern whites would be the hardest kickers against the scheme. The only beneficiaries from this wonderful enterprise would be the steamship companies; for after the hundreds of years of transportation are over, then excursion parties would be the order of the day for time immemorial. Our Southern gentleman will not be deprived of the Negro woman. There is no ocean too wide for him to cross; no wall too high for him to scale; he'd risk the fires of hell to be in her company, intensely as he pretends to hate her. Wilmington, North Carolina, the scene of that much regretted phenomenon—the fatal clashing of races in November, 1898,[15] was not, and is not without its harems, its unholy minglings of Shem with Ham; where the soft-fingered aristocrat embraces the lowest dusky sirene in Paddy's Hollow, and thinks nothing of it. Molly Pierrepont, whom I introduce to the reader in this chapter, is a type of Negro woman whose progress along ennobling avenues is more hotly contested than any other woman in the South, because of her beauty. To decide between the honor with poverty offered by the black man and the life of ease with shame offered by the white one is her "Gethsemane." Yet where love of honor has conquered, she has made a devoted wife and a loving mother.

Such a character as Molly Pierrepont was an exclusive luxury for gentlemen. The poor white could not afford to support a mistress who of course went to the highest bidder. Ben Hartright left the Wigwam[16] before the close of the meeting in which he was so deeply interested, and proceeded directly to Molly's cottage; but he did not notice as he tipped lightly through the gate a cloaked and veiled form crouching down in the bushes a few yards away. He heard not the light footsteps as it drew nearer to be sure that there was no mistaking the visitor. Ben Hartright entered boldly; knocking was unnecessary, he was master there. The furniture and hangings were all his purchase, even the expensive jewels that the woman wore. The figure on the outside drew still closer, peered in, tip-toed upon the piazza, pressed the ear against the window to catch as much as possible of what went on within. Only a few minutes did it tarry however. As the door swung open, Molly arose from the piano and advanced with outstretched arms to meet him.

"Hello, Ben! I thought you were to be here by eight to-night." Ben Hartright sank upon a sofa and gently drew the girl down beside him before he assayed to answer her.

"Well, Molly, you must remember that I am in politics now," he said, kissing her fondly, "and I must attend the different meetings, business before pleasure you know. We are in the most exciting period of the campaign; a campaign the like of which has never before been experienced in North Carolina. We are organized and determined to save the State to the Democratic Party and make white supremacy an established fact if we have to kill every Nigger and Nigger-hearted white man in it. To make assurance doubly sure, we are arming ourselves, and seeing to it that no Nigger shall buy an ounce of powder, and every Nigger man and woman is to be searched and what weapons they have taken away that no white man's life may be endangered. There are some Niggers and white men who must be killed, and they are carefully listed."

Ben Hartright unbosomed to Molly the plots of the White Supremacy League in all its blood-curdling details, naming every man and woman who were to be the victims of the mob's fury.

"Do you think that a very brave thing to do?" asked Molly at the conclusion of Ben's recital.

"Oh, anything is fair in dealing with Niggers," answered Ben. But the look of astonishment in Molly's black eyes suddenly brought Ben Hartright to the full realization that he was revealing the secrets of his klan to one of the race he was plotting to massacre.

"Of course we don't include such as you, Molly," he said, lightly tapping her on the shoulder. "You are no Nigger, you are nearly as white as I am."

"Nearly as white," echoed Molly with a sneer. "Do you mean to try to choke it down my throat that my whiteness would save me should your people rise up against Niggers in Wilmington? Honestly, Ben Hartright, do you mean that?" Molly arose from the sofa and stood up before her lover that she might the better study his face. Hartright was silent.

In Southern legislative halls white minorities in old Reconstruction days ruled Republican majorities by appealing to the vanity of light-skinned Negro representatives.

"You are almost white, why vote with them Niggers?" Ben Hartright was using the old tactics; he had realized that he perhaps had been careless with his secrets. "What I really mean, Molly, is that you are a friend of white people—that is you are not one of those Nigger wenches who want to be er—er—ladies—that want Nigger dudes to raise their hats to them—want to be like white people you know."

"I understand," said Molly.

"We white gentlemen believe in having colored girl friends, and we always stand by them no matter what happens." Molly momentarily eyed the ceiling.

"Benny, did you ever read Uncle Tom's Cabin?"

"Yes, I have," answered Ben, "but it has been too long ago to remember very much of its contents

"Why? Everybody should read that book it seems to me; read and read again Cassie's story of her love for the man who after promising to protect and defend her, sneaked away and sold her. Cassie was almost white. Cassie was a white man's friend, and to that man she was true; but Cassie's story of betrayal, disappointment, misery at the hands of that long haired brute who afterwards became her master, would make the strongest heart weep. *You will stand by your colored girl friend*. Perhaps you think you would, but I doubt it, Ben Hartright. When that time comes that the two races are arrayed against each other, my fair complexion will be of no avail. I am a Nigger, and will be dealt with as such, even by the man who now promises me protection."

Ben Hartright quailed under Molly's biting sarcasm. He was unprepared for this change of front on the part of his mistress. His pretention of love were not sufficient to create in Molly a feeling of security.

"Then d'm it all! You as good as tell a gentleman to his teeth that he lies then?" said he doggedly.

"No; I don't mean to say that you lie. What you say to me *now,* you may earnestly mean, but under circumstances just mentioned, you would deny that you ever knew me. What you have revealed tonight concerning your aims and plots, portrays to my mind just who and what you are, and just who and what I am. Samson has revealed his secret to his Delilah, and its Delilah's duty to warn her people of the dangers that await them.[17] Men whose lives are threatened must be warned; women who are in danger of being ignominiously dealt with must be put upon their guard; must know that these defenders of virtue, these Southern gentlemen who are thirsting for the blood of a slanderer (?) of white women are hypocrites, who strain out a gnat and swallow a camel."

"By the thunder, what do you mean by such language?" and Ben Hartright arose from the sofa and glared at the girl, his eyes flashing. "Do you know that you are talking to a gentleman?"

"Be careful," said Molly, "You wouldn't have the women for whom you would be so chivalrous know who Ben Hartright *really is,* would you?"

"Why, what's the matter Molly?" said Hartright in a more subdued voice. "Have you joined the sanctified band?"

"No; but I realize as never before just who and what I am, and your trying to flatter me into the belief that I am better than black women who try to be pure, is a revelation to me who and what *you are.* There are men whom you have named to be killed whose only offense is that they are respectable and independent; and women who are hated because they are not easy victims such as I am—women who will live honestly upon bread and water. These are colored people who have so much confidence in the better class of white people, that they would not believe that such a plot is being laid for their destruction."

Ben Hartright put his arms around Molly's waist. "I thought you were a true friend of white people, Molly; but I find that you are not, so let's drop the unpleasant subject. If the Niggers keep away from the polls, and don't attempt to run a ticket, there will be no trouble; but if they persist in defying the whites, there'll be hell. But all pretty Nigger gals such as you will be all right."

"Unhand me!" said Molly, twisting herself from his grasp. "Go tell your hypocritical associates in crime that the deed they are about to commit will recoil upon their own heads, and upon the heads of their children."

"But—er—now Molly—"

"Go!" hissed Molly, pointing to the door.

Ben Hartright walked slowly to the door, paused and wistfully eyed Molly who stood with uplifted hand pointing in that direction. "Oh, you are quite full of race pride just now, but when it comes to deciding between the easy life that a white man pays for and Nigger drudgery, you'll doubtless change your tune. I leave you to reflect."

Hartright walked out. Molly sank upon the sofa and buried her face in her hands. "How true!" she sobbed. "What have I done?" but she rose and her anguish was gone in a twinkling. "Easy life! Drudgery! But *here I swear from this hour Molly Pierrepont will live no longer such a life.*"

Ben Hartright reached his home in Orange street about three o'clock, noiselessly opened the door and strode up to his apartments, thinking he would get to bed without disturbing his young wife; but she was not there. The bed remained as it was when the chambermaid left it that morning, after giving it its finishing touches. Ben Hartright looked about the room in wild amazement. He drew out his watch, scanned its face eagerly. "By ginger!" he exclaimed, "it's past three o'clock. Wonder where is Emily? This is indeed something unusual." Thinking perhaps that his child might have taken ill during the night and that his wife had remained in the nurse's room with it, he crossed the hall and rapped upon the door; a second rap brought the nurse to the door rubbing her eyes. "What's the matter, Fannie; is the baby sick?"

"No, sah!" answered the girl.

"Isn't Miss Emily in there?"

"No, sah; Mr. Benny she ain't in heah, sah."

"Where in the thunder is she then?" roared Ben Hartright, now beside himself with rage. *"Is this the way you look after your mistress?"* and he seized the already frightened girl by the shoulders and shook her vigorously, turned away before she could utter a word of excuse, and bounded down to his mother's apartments.

Mrs. Hartright, aroused by the noise above, was just emerging from her door to learn the cause of it all. "Why, what's the matter, son?" she questioned gently, as Ben, both angry and frightened, strode up to where she stood.

"Didn't you hear me asking Fannie where Emily is? Didn't you know that she hasn't been in her room, and here it is nearly four o'clock in the morning!"

"Emily went out just after tea, and I thought she had returned," answered the mother. "Perhaps she went walking with some of her girl friends, was taken ill and had to stop at one of their homes. Wait Benny, I'll dress and help you to look for her."

Ben Hartright turned and walked slowly to the door and paused to wait for his mother. There was a turn of the door latch, a vigorous twist of a key in the lock; the door flew open and Emily Hartright walked in. She apparently did not see her husband who stood and eyed her angrily as she entered and began to ascend the steps to her room.

"Emily," said Ben, following and seizing his wife by the arm. "Are you mad? If not, explain this extraordinary conduct of yours. Where have you been?" She turned, gazed into her husband's eyes for a moment, then with one vigorous tug, she wrenched her arm from his grasp and proceeded up the steps. The mother by this time had joined her son, and they both followed the young lady who had entered her room and was removing her wraps.

"What's the matter my darling?" said Mrs. Hartright, throwing her arms around her daughter's waist. "I was so troubled about you. What kept you out so late, Emily?"

"Wait, mother, until I have rested and composed myself, then I will explain," answered Emily, softly.

Ben had sank into a chair and sat with his chin resting upon the palm of his hand. Emily sat upon the side of the bed.

"Men go night after night," she said, "stay as long as they please, and return in whatever condition they please; and to queries of their wives, they are evasive in their answers; but when a woman takes the privilege of exercising her rights—"

"*Her rights,*" roared Ben, jumping to his feet. "A lady goes out of her residence, leaves her servant and relatives in ignorance of her destination, returns at four o'clock in the morning to tell anxious husband and mother about *her rights!* We'll have a direct explanation from you, Mrs. Hartright, without preambling."

"I'll not be bullied, Ben Hartright," answered the young wife calmly. "Remember that when you married *me,* you didn't marry a chambermaid or housekeeper, but a lady of one of the first families of Virginia, and such people brook *no bullying,*" and Emily arose and glared at her husband like a tigress.

Ben Hartright quailed. Never had he seen his little wife in such a state of anger and defiance.

"If you are man enough to reveal your whereabouts until the small hours of the morning, you can tell where your wife was."

Ben Hartright raised his eyes from the floor and looked at his wife in amazement.

"When you entered the house of your mistress, Molly Pierrepont, to-night, I saw you. I, your *wife,* whom *you* swore to honor and protect, saw you. She saw you embrace and kiss a Negro woman, the woman of a race whom you pretend to despise, and whom you and your pals are secretly scheming to cold bloodedly murder and drive from their homes. Take care! God knows your hypocrisy and the deeds you commit will recoil upon your own heads."

"Emily, are you mad?" gasped the elder lady who stood as if transfixed to the floor.

"Ask him," returned the young lady, "he knows whether or not I utter the truth, or whether I am a victim of a beclouded brain. He knows that he has wronged me; he knows that he has lied to me. I care not for your frowns. *You* a gentleman? You hate Niggers, yet you can embrace one so fondly. I will no longer live with such a gentleman, who night after night under the excuse of 'clubs' and 'business' spends his time away from his wife, and in company of a Negro woman. I am going home to my people."

"Now, Emily," said the elder Mrs. Hartright, "don't start a scandal; remember that you are a Southerner. Southern people do not countenance the airing of unpleasant family matters!"

"Yes," replied the young lady, "this fear of airing family troubles on the part of our women, has made us slaves, while the men are licensed to indulge in all manner of indecencies with impunity. I will be the first Southern woman to sever the chain of 'formality,' and cry aloud to the world that I leave my husband because of his unfaithfulness. It is my right, and I will exercise that right."

Ben who had again sank into his seat arose and advanced toward his wife to sue for forgiveness.

"Don't touch me!" she cried, with uplifted hand. "The cup is full. Go back to her who has monopolized the best portion of your time since you have married me."

Ben Hartright sank again into his chair and buried his face into his hands.

"Now, my darlings, let mother be the daysman between you," said the elder Mrs. Hartright, coming near caressing the young wife. "Benny knows just to what extent he has wronged you my dear, and I believe him honest enough and manly enough to acknowledge it, and sue for forgiveness. I leave you to yourselves. God grant that you may be enabled to peaceably settle your difficulties satisfactorily to you both, without giving license to Madame Gossip. God bless you." Kissing Emily, Mrs. Hartright descended to her room.

Ben Hartright succeeded in patching up matters with his wife by promising to live a more honest life, only to break it, which caused her to make good her threat and leave him.

1900

HENRY BERRY LOWERY, THE NORTH CAROLINA OUTLAW: A TALE OF THE RECONSTRUCTION PERIOD

In Robeson County, North Carolina, on the old Carolina Central Railroad, which connects the seaboard with the interior, within forty miles of Wilmington, the metropolis, and in close proximity to Lumberton, nestling among the sand hills, there is a straggling little village known for many years before the war as "Scuffle Town." The hamlet doubtless derived its name from the fact that it was a free negro settlement. In many Southern States the free colored man, shorn of the protection of a master, in many instances the object of suspicion in whom the slave-holder saw possible, if not probable, uprisings and massacres, was often looked down upon by the slave who under the protection of a master considered himself better off. Although many free negroes in North Carolina, who purchased their freedom by their own thrift and industry, lived in an enviable sphere, the shiftless among them were often referred to by the slaves as "scuffling along." Hence the name Scuffle Town. Insignificant as this obscure little hamlet may appear to the stranger with its old decayed dwellings, its neglected streets, its uneven rows of cabins, Scuffle Town less than forty years ago was the theater of some of the most exciting events, the most blood-curdling tragedies ever recorded in the history of the old North State. For this little hamlet was the home of the octoroon outlaw Henry Berry Lowery, who, with his band of bloodthirsty desperadoes, kept the entire State in terror and the eyes of the whole country settled upon Robeson County for quite a number of years. Those of us who are familiar with the history of Frank and Jesse James, who led that band of outlaws that kept the West so long in terror by their murders, train robberies and other crimes, have doubtless heard little or nothing of this man who during the same period and actuated by the same grievances terrorized North Carolina.

Just as the name of Jesse James sent an involuntary shudder through the souls of those who heard it, although far removed from the scene of his depredations, so did the name of Henry Berry Lowery awe and terrorize in North Carolina.

Lowery and his intrepid freebooters were all colored men. The James boys and their followers were armed with the most improved firearms of that day; with the exception of the carbine carried by Lowery himself, taken from a Mexican who attempted to capture him, the only weapons these men had were knives and double-barreled shotguns. Although free colored people in the South could not vote, in some States they could own property and many of them owned slaves. These Scuffler Towners, an admixture of Saxon, Indian and negro, kept aloft from the blacks, and like Santo Domingans, nursed a feeling of hostility towards the whites. In many instances during the Civil War, free mulattoes sympathized with and cast in their lot with the Confederates; in Louisiana colored people of means gave largely of their wealth to assist the Southern cause. But they were not considered as desirable fighting material until the secessionists saw defeat staring them in the face. Then every available man was pressed into service, the free negro having the first consideration. The elder Lowery, the leader and adviser of his people, and who had been outspoken in his condemnation of the South's attitude in the awful controversy, advised his people not to assist in the fight for the perpetuation of slavery. But the whites, feeling it their right to draft into the service whom they willed, invaded this free negro settlement and shot to death those who resisted them, and among the killed was the elder Lowery. Henry, then quite a young man, was an eye witness to the death of his parent. Standing over the grave of his slain father he swore never to rest until every man who participated in that dreadful tragedy paid the penalty with his life. Those who recall that dark period in Robeson County immediately following the surrender, remember how well that vow was kept. The war had ended, the defeated rebel had returned and the death of Lowery the elder was almost forgotten; when, one day, a prominent citizen of Robeson, riding along the plank road leading from Lumberton to Scuffle Town, suddenly threw up his hands and fell from his buggy, shot through the heart. This was the beginning of the work of vengeance. The death of this man, who was a recruiting officer at the time the negro stronghold was invaded, recalled to every mind the tragedy and young Lowery's vow. The whites of Lumberton and vicinity arose, invaded Scuffle Town and attempted to hunt down the murderer. But Lowery, who had laid his plans well before beginning his work of vengeance, had made for himself a secure hiding place in the fastness of the great Dismal Swamp; and the sympathy and loyalty of his people who were ready to die rather than betray him made his stronghold impregnable.

The killing of three other men within less than three months after the first tragedy threw the entire State into a panic and large rewards were offered for the capture of the murderers dead or alive. Raids by bands of armed men upon the negro settlement became frequent; and innocent men and women were in many instances beaten and killed by the man hunters, chagrined by their futile attempts to locate the outlaw and the stubborn refusal of his friends to reveal his hiding place. These cruel assaults upon the little town won to Lowery more friends and sympathizers; desperate characters began to flock to his standard until his band numbered twenty-five or more of as reckless daredevils and cutthroats as ever trod the soil of any country. Foremost among these were Stephen Lowery, brother to Henry, and—far more cruel, relentless and bloodthirsty—George Applewhite and "Boss" Strong. Murders became more frequent and train holdups and highway robberies were added to the list of crimes which intensified the feeling of dread and insecurity throughout the State. Offers of large rewards for the capture of the outlaws brought about more strenuous efforts to capture them, but they evaded the authorities for many years. Many stories became current concerning the charmed life of Henry Berry Lowery. It was averred that he was known to appear on trains running at the highest speed and to reveal his identity to awestricken passengers and trainmen, and then disappear as mysteriously as he appeared. Another tale was that, meeting a squad of soldiers on the highway one day and revealing his identity so disconcerted and demoralized them that they could not capture him. One night, carousing in the village, a raid was made upon them by constables and George Applewhite, together with a woman, supposed to be Henry's wife, were captured and taken to the Wilmington jail. The outlaw leader had, however, gained such a reputation for recklessness and bravery that a threat to enter Wilmington and burn it so terrorized the citizens that the captives were released. A Mexican, tempted by the large reward offered for the capture of the outlaws, visited Lumberton and boasted to the authorities there that he would run down and capture the leader and disperse the desperadoes within a very short time. He strutted about the streets of Lumberton for a day or two, dressed in his showy native costume, and to show his bravery entered Scuffle Town itself, and for a while chatted freely with the natives. Then he disappeared into the swamp, where he built himself a cabin and remained in hiding during the day and strolled about at night in disguise.

But in less time than he had boasted to capture the outlaw, Henry Berry Lowery himself walked into his cabin, told him it was surrounded and that there was no alternative but surrender. The Mexican was bound and escorted to the outlaw camp and told to write a farewell letter to his family. The Mexican complied and then waited calmly for his execution. But they kept him in suspense until he wearily begged the outlaws to do what they intended doing and have done with it. But bloody as had been the career of this bold and fearless outlaw, he could not do the deed nor give the order. Seeing their leader melt, all of his followers weakened except Stephen Lowery, his brother, who with an oath said to the Mexican, "Say your prayers and stand out; I'll kill you." The man complied, stepped out a few paces and dropped dead. Then a reporter for a certain great New York daily newspaper[18] contrived to enter the stronghold of the famous North Carolina outlaws in order to glean from the lips of Lowery himself the story of his uprising. Hazardous undertaking, but it was successful. The reporter having forwarded a letter that he was coming, was met at a small railroad station in the vicinity of the outlaw camp, there blindfolded and taken to their hiding place in the fastness of the Dismal Swamp.[19] And there from the lips of the leader himself he heard the story of the causes which led to the great feud during which a score or more of people had been killed, most of whom had been implicated in the murder of his father. But the only wrong thing the outlaw conceded his men had done was to kill an old defenceless man solely for the purpose of robbery. At the conclusion of the interview the visitor was again blindfolded and escorted to the village, the outlaws not permitting him to open his eyes until the railway station was reached. Following the reporters' return to New York, a glowing story of the Lowery feud was published with a flattering description of the handsome octoroon outlaw and the history and customs of his peculiar people.

The career of Jesse James[20] was brought to a sudden termination by a bullet in the back of his head from a revolver in the hands of a supposed friend. Frank James has for many years been a peaceful citizen. Those of the followers of these two daring outlaws who were not killed off have served and are serving long terms in various prisons throughout the country. The State authorities of North Carolina having utterly failed to effect the capture of Lowery and break up his stronghold, for many months after the release of George Applewhite from Wilmington jail, all attempts to capture the outlaws were apparently abandoned. Excepting Henry Berry Lowery himself, who was ever cautious and wary, the outlaws with their many friends enjoyed the freedom of their native town where they met to divide the spoils from train holdups and robberies. Stephen Lowery was a banjo player, and often his love for music and whiskey had cost his comrades many serious encounters and hairbreadth escapes, and in their flight for safety, very frequently Stephen had to be taken up bodily by his companions and carried. In the back woods of North Carolina, upon the old county roads, journeying from settlement to settlement, can still be seen the quaint old white-covered, sway-backed wagon of the "trader." After the breaking out of the Lowery feud, traders evaded Scuffle Town and vicinity, but the tempting prizes offered for the capture of the outlaws often during that long season of terror caused the more venturesome ones to pause upon the village streets to trade and run the risk of being killed and robbed. One day as Stephen Lowery sat half drunk by the roadside on the outskirts of the village, slowly running his fingers over the strings of his banjo, a trader's wagon in passing paused and one of the occupants engaged him in conversation. "Fine banjer yo got thar," said the trader. "Straight'n up, ol' man, an' giv' us a tune; I know yo' kin do it." Stephen, flattered by the compliment, assayed to comply. A shot rang out and the bandit fell over dead. Two men jumped out, severed Stephen's head from the trunk and hastened away. The next victim of this feeling of security was Boss Strong: he was shot through a crack in the wall of a house one night while lying on his back playing a Jew's harp during a frolic. But the murderers failed to get his body, which was immediately removed by his friends and all traces of the murder cleared away. Of all this band of over twenty-five outlaws, none was captured and but few were killed. While the feud was on they were relentless and cruel in their treatment of enemies. But when the last person under suspicion of having part in the death of the elder Lowery had been killed off, the authorities had ceased to harass them and their leader had called off the feud; as calmly and as peaceful as lambs they returned to their farms. George Applewhite, whose reputation for daring was far worse than that of Lowery himself, finally surrendered to the authorities of his State, and has for many years been a peaceful citizen of Goldsboro. But the fate of the undaunted leader himself remains a mystery to this day. Among the many stories of his fate is the one in which it is alleged that he had himself stored away in a tool chest in which he was shipped West, where he joined the army. On visiting Scuffle Town a few years ago I found it still a settlement of Ishmaelites with their fists shut against the outside world, cherishing the old aversion for social mingling or intermarriage with blacks. I found them open to social chats, however, the grandson of one of the outlaws furnishing the material for the foregoing story. Some of the men who two decades ago thought nothing of snuffing out the lives of their fellows are to-day grizzled old law-abiding citizens, their faces the index of genuine piety. Still men tremble as they recall that awful bloody period in the history of Robeson County and speak the name of Henry Berry Lowery with bated breath.

1907

NOTES

1. A consumer of alcoholic beverages, most often a heavy drinker.

2. Robert Smalls (1839–1915), William James Whipper (1834–1907), and George Washington Murray (1853–1926) were African American South Carolina residents who held elected office during the period of Reconstruction. Smalls and Murray were elected to the House of Representatives, each from the state's Seventh District. Whipper was elected to participate in the state's postwar constitutional convention and, later, to serve in the South Carolina State legislature.

3. An African American spiritual.

4. A minstrel-show standard, written in 1851 by Stephen Foster and made famous by the blackface performers of Christy's Minstrel's, a popular mid-nineteenth-century performance troupe.

5. A popular nineteenth-century dance incorporating elements of African American and Irish folk traditions for both humorous and acrobatic effect, often performed by white dancers in traveling blackface minstrel troupes.

6. In many African American churches, a monthly gathering that combines food with prayer and religious testimony.

7. "Lord, in the Morning Thou Shalt Hear," a hymn written in 1719 by English lyricist Isaac Watts (1674–1748).

8. Commonly known as the "Cradle Song," from the 1847 narrative poem *The Princess* by English poet Alfred, Lord Tennyson (1809–1892).

9. A port city in southeastern North Carolina.

10. A term used during (and for some decades after) slavery for people one-eighth of whose ancestry was believed to be African or African American.

11. A reference to the belief, pervasive throughout much of the nineteenth century, that people of African ancestry are the descendents of Ham, the second of three sons of the biblical patriarch Noah, whose children were, according to tradition, believed to have migrated to Africa and whose skin was turned dark by a curse on their father.

12. New York City.

13. Song of Solomon 1:5–6.

14. Song of Solomon 6:13.

15. A reference to the Wilmington riots of 1898, in which more than 1,500 white residents overthrew the existing city government and chased more than 2,100 black residents from their homes.

16. An Anglicized reference to any Native American residential or ceremonial structure that is round in structure and constructed of bark, animal skins, or cloth laid over a wooden frame. The term can also be applied to any structure that resembles that shape and construction.

17. A reference to the Biblical account (Judges 16) of Samson, the strongman of the Israelites, who faced defeat at the hands of Delilah and the Philistines.

18. *The New York Times.*

19. A marshy wetland along the coast of southeastern Virginia and northeastern North Carolina, spanning an area of more than one million acres.

20. Jesse Woodson James (1847–1882), notorious white American outlaw and member of the James-Younger gang.

IDA B. WELLS-BARNETT (1862-1931)

Ida Bell Wells-Barnett was born in Holly Springs, Mississippi, to enslaved parents Elizabeth Warrenton and Jim Wells. After the yellow fever epidemic of 1878, during which Wells-Barnett lost both of her parents and two of her eight siblings, she took on the care of the remaining children. Educated at Shaw University (later renamed Rust College), Wells-Barnett was able to earn sufficient income as a teacher to support her family. In 1883, after relocating to Memphis, Wells-Barnett began submitting articles and editorials to local African American newspapers, eventually becoming part owner of the *Free Speech and Headlight*. In addition, reprints of her locally published articles began appearing in *The New York Age, The Indianapolis Freeman, The Chicago Conservator,* and other black papers and magazines. Her dismissal from her teaching position for writing and publishing articles critical of the city's African American schools foreshadowed the toll that her journalism would take on her life in Memphis. In 1892, after three of her friends were lynched, Wells-Barnett called on the city's African Americans to save their money and, as she wrote in the *Free Speech,* "leave a town which will neither protect our lives and property, nor give us a fair trial in the courts." At great risk to her own safety, she stepped up her anti-lynching campaign, publishing the pamphlet *Southern Horrors: Lynch Law in All its Phases.* In 1893, Wells-Barnett relocated to Chicago, where she continued to agitate for stronger penalties against the perpetrators of racist violence. She spoke out on other civil rights issues as well. In that same year, she published *The Reason Why the Colored American Is Not in the World's Columbian Exposition,* a collection of writings by prominent activists, compiled in response to the near total exclusion of African Americans from participation in the Chicago-based event. She was also deeply involved in antiracist organizations, including W. E. B. Du Bois's Niagara Movement, the Chicago Negro Fellowship League, and the Anti-Lynching Bureau. Wells-Barnett would continue to report on lynching throughout the rest of her life, publishing *The Arkansas Race Riot* in 1920 and beginning an autobiography, which was edited and published by her daughter, following the author's death.

Preface

The greater part of what is contained in these pages was published in the *New York Age*[1] June 25, 1892, in explanation of the editorial which the Memphis whites considered sufficiently infamous to justify the destruction of my paper, the *Free Speech*.[2]

Since the appearance of that statement, requests have come from all parts of the country that "Exiled" (the name under which it then appeared) be issued in pamphlet form. Some donations were made, but not enough for that purpose. The noble effort of the ladies of New York and Brooklyn Oct. 5 have enabled me to comply with this request and give the world a true, unvarnished account of the causes of lynch law in the South.

This statement is not a shield for the despoiler of virtue, nor altogether a defense for the poor blind Afro-American Sampsons who suffer themselves to be betrayed by white Delilahs. It is a contribution to truth, an array of facts, the perusal of which it is hoped will stimulate this great American Republic to demand that justice be done though the heavens fall.

It is with no pleasure I have dipped my hands in the corruption here exposed. Somebody must show that the Afro-American race is more sinned against than sinning, and it seems to have fallen upon me to do so. The awful death-roll that Judge Lynch is calling every week is appalling, not only because of the lives it takes, the rank cruelty and outrage to the victims, but because of the prejudice it fosters and the stain it places against the good name of a weak race.

The Afro-American is not a bestial race. If this work can contribute in any way toward proving this, and at the same time arouse the conscience of the American people to a demand for justice to every citizen, and punishment by law for the lawless, I shall feel I have done my race a service. Other considerations are of minor importance.

IDA B. WELLS
New York City, Oct. 26, 1892

The Offense

Wednesday evening May 24, 1892, the city of Memphis was filled with excitement. Editorials in the daily papers of that date caused a meeting to be held in the Cotton Exchange Building; a committee was sent for the editors of the *Free Speech* an Afro-American journal published in that city, and the only reason the open threats of lynching that were made were not carried out was because they could not be found. The cause of all this commotion was the following editorial published in the *Free Speech* May 21, 1892, the Saturday previous.

> Eight negroes lynched since last issue of the *Free Speech,* one at Little Rock, Ark., last Saturday morning where the citizens broke (?) into the penitentiary and got their man; three near Anniston, Ala., one near New Orleans; and three at Clarksville, Ga., the last three for killing a white man, and five on the same old racket—the new alarm about raping white women. The same programme of hanging, then shooting bullets into the lifeless bodies was carried out to the letter.
>
> Nobody in this section of the country believes the old thread-bare lie that Negro men rape white women. If Southern white men are not careful, they will overreach themselves and public sentiment will have a reaction; a conclusion will then be reached which will be very damaging to the moral reputation of their women.

The *Daily Commercial*[3] of Wednesday following, May 25, contained the following leader:

> Those negroes who are attempting to make the lynching of individuals of their race a means for arousing the worst passions of their kind are playing with a dangerous sentiment. The negroes may as well understand that there is no mercy for the negro rapist and little patience with his defenders. A negro organ printed in this city, in a recent issue publishes the following atrocious paragraph: "Nobody in this section of the country believes the old thread-bare lie that negro men rape white women. If Southern white men are not careful they will overreach themselves, and public sentiment will have a reaction; and a conclusion will be reached which will be very damaging to the moral reputation of their women."
>
> The fact that a black scoundrel is allowed to live and utter such loathsome and repulsive calumnies is a volume of evidence as to the wonderful patience of Southern whites. But we have had enough of it.

There are some things that the Southern white man will not tolerate, and the obscene intimations of the foregoing have brought the writer to the very outermost limit of public patience. We hope we have said enough.

The *Evening Scimitar*[4] of same date copied the *Commercial's* editorial with these words of comment:

> Patience under such circumstances is not a virtue. If the negroes themselves do not apply the remedy without delay it will be the duty of those whom

he has attacked to tie the wretch who utters these calumnies to a stake at the intersection of Main and Madison Sts., brand him in the forehead with a hot iron and perform upon him a surgical operation with a pair of tailor's shears.

Acting upon this advice, the leading citizens met in the Cotton Exchange Building the same evening, and threats of lynching were freely indulged, not by the lawless element upon which the deviltry of the South is usually saddled—but by the leading business men, in their leading business centre. Mr. Fleming, the business manager and owning a half interest in the *Free Speech,* had to leave town to escape the mob, and was afterwards ordered not to return; letters and telegrams sent me in New York where I was spending my vacation advised me that bodily harm awaited my return. Creditors took possession of the office and sold the outfit, and the *Free Speech* was as if it had never been.

The editorial in question was prompted by the many inhuman and fiendish lynchings of Afro-Americans which have recently taken place and was meant as a warning. Eight lynched in one week and five of them charged with rape! The thinking public will not easily believe freedom and education more brutalizing than slavery, and the world knows that the crime of rape was unknown during four years of civil war, when the white women of the South were at the mercy of the race which is all at once charged with being a bestial one.

Since my business has been destroyed and I am an exile from home because of that editorial, the issue has been forced, and as the writer of it I feel that the race and the public generally should have a statement of the facts as they exist. They will serve at the same time as a defense for the Afro-American Sampsons who suffer themselves to be betrayed by white Delilahs.

The whites of Montgomery, Ala., knew J. C. Duke sounded the keynote of the situation—which they would gladly hide from the world, when he said in his paper, the *Herald,* five years ago: "Why is it that white women attract negro men now more than in former days? There was a time when such a thing was unheard of. There is a secret to this thing, and we greatly suspect it is the growing appreciation of white Juliets for colored Romeos." Mr. Duke, like the *Free Speech* proprietors, was forced to leave the city for reflecting on the "honah" of white women and his paper suppressed; but the truth remains that Afro-American men do not always rape (?) white women without their consent.

Mr. Duke, before leaving Montgomery, signed a card disclaiming any intention of slandering Southern white women. The editor of the *Free Speech* has no disclaimer to enter, but asserts instead that there are many white women in the South who would marry colored men if such an act would not place them at once beyond the pale of society and within the clutches of the law.

The miscegnation laws of the South only operate against the legitimate union of the races; they leave the white man free to seduce all the colored girls he can, but it is death to the colored man who yields to the force and advances of a similar attraction in white women. White men lynch the offending Afro-American, not because he is a despoiler of virtue, but because he succumbs to the smiles of white women.

The Black and White of It

The *Cleveland Gazette* of January 16, 1892, publishes a case in point. Mrs. J. S. Underwood, the wife of a minister of Elyria, Ohio, accused an Afro-American of rape. She told her husband that during his absence in 1888, stumping the State for the Prohibition Party, the man came to the kitchen door, forced his way in the house and insulted her. She tried to drive him out with a heavy poker, but he overpowered and chloroformed her, and when she revived, her clothing was torn and she was in a horrible condition. She did not know the man but could identify him. She pointed out William Offett, a married man, who was arrested and, being in Ohio, was granted a trial.

The prisoner vehemently denied the charge of rape, but confessed he went to Mrs. Underwood's residence at her invitation and was criminally intimate with her at her request. This availed him nothing against the sworn testimony of a minister's wife, a lady of the highest respectability. He was found guilty, and entered the penitentiary, December 14, 1888, for fifteen years. Some time afterwards the woman's remorse led her to confess to her husband that the man was innocent.

These are her words:

> I met Offett at the Post Office. It was raining. He was polite to me, and as I had several bundles in my arms he offered to carry them home for me, which he did. He had a strange fascination for me, and I invited him to call on me. He called, bringing chestnuts and candy for the children. By this means we got them to leave us alone in the room. Then I sat on his lap. He made a proposal to me and I readily consented. Why I did so, I do not know, but that I did is true. He visited me several times after that and each time I was indiscreet. I did not care after the first time. In fact I could not have resisted, and had no desire to resist.

When asked by her husband why she told him she had been outraged, she said: "I had several reasons for telling you. One was the neighbors saw the fellows here, another was, I was afraid I had contracted a loathsome disease, and still another was that I feared I might give birth to a Negro baby. I hoped to save my reputation by telling you a deliberate lie." Her husband, horrified by the confession, had Offett, who had already served four years, released and secured a divorce.

There are thousands of such cases throughout the South, with the difference that the Southern white men in insatiate fury wreak their vengeance without intervention of law upon the Afro-Americans who consort with their women. A few instances to substantiate the assertion that some white women love the company of the Afro-American will not be out of place. Most of these cases were reported by the daily papers of the South.

In the winter of 1885–86 the wife of a practicing physician in Memphis, in good social standing whose name has escaped me, left home, husband and children, and ran away with her black coachman. She was with him a month before her husband found and brought her home. The coachman could not be found. The doctor moved his family away from Memphis, and is living in another city under an assumed name.

In the same city last year a white girl in the dusk of evening screamed at the approach of some parties that a Negro had assaulted her on the street. He was captured, tried by a white judge and jury, that acquitted him of the charge. It is needless to add if there had been a scrap of evidence on which to convict him of so grave a charge he would have been convicted.

Sarah Clark of Memphis loved a black man and lived openly with him. When she was indicted last spring for miscegenation, she swore in court that she was *not* a white woman. This she did to escape the penitentiary and continued her illicit relation undisturbed. That she is of the lower class of whites does not disturb the fact that she is a white woman. "The leading citizens" of Memphis are defending the "honor" of *all* white women, *demi-monde* included.

Since the manager of the *Free Speech* has been run away from Memphis by the guardians of the honor of Southern white women, a young girl living on Poplar St., who was discovered in intimate relations with a handsome mulatto young colored man, Will Morgan by name, stole her father's money to send the young fellow away from that father's wrath. She has since joined him in Chicago.

The *Memphis Ledger* for June 8 has the following:

> If Lillie Bailey, a rather pretty white girl seventeen years of age, who is now at the City Hospital, would be somewhat less reserved about her disgrace there would be some very nauseating details in the story of her life. She is the mother of a little coon.[5] The truth might reveal fearful depravity or it might

reveal the evidence of a rank outrage. She will not divulge the name of the man who has left such black evidence of her disgrace, and, in fact, says it is a matter in which there can be no interest to the outside world. She came to Memphis nearly three months ago and was taken in at the Woman's Refuge in the southern part of the city. She remained there until a few weeks ago, when the child was born. The ladies in charge of the Refuge were horrified. The girl was at once sent to the City Hospital, where she has been since May 30. She is a country girl. She came to Memphis from her father's farm, a short distance from Hernando, Miss. Just when she left there she would not say. In fact she says she came to Memphis from Arkansas, and says her home is in that State. She is rather good looking, has blue eyes, a low forehead and dark red hair. The ladies at the Woman's Refuge do not know anything about the girl further than what they learned when she was an inmate of the institution; and she would not tell much. When the child was born an attempt was made to get the girl to reveal the name of the Negro who had disgraced her, she obstinately refused and it was impossible to elicit any information from her on the subject.

Note the wording. "The truth might reveal fearful depravity or rank outrage." If it had been a white child or Lillie Bailey had told a pitiful story of Negro outrage, it would have been a case of woman's weakness or assault and she could have remained at the Woman's Refuge. But a Negro child and to withhold its father's name and thus prevent the killing of another Negro "rapist." A case of "fearful depravity."

The very week the "leading citizens" of Memphis were making a spectacle of themselves in defense of all white women of every kind, an Afro-American, M. Stricklin, was found in a white woman's room in that city. Although she made no outcry of rape, he was jailed and would have been lynched, but the woman stated she bought curtains of him (he was a furniture dealer) and his business in her room that night was to put them up. A white woman's word was taken as absolutely in this case as when the cry of rape is made, and he was freed.

What is true of Memphis is true of the entire South. The daily papers last year reported a farmer's wife in Alabama had given birth to a Negro child. When the Negro farm hand who was plowing in the field heard it he took the mule from the plow and fled. The dispatches also told of a woman in South Carolina who gave birth to a Negro child and charged three men with being its father, *every one of whom has since disappeared.* In Tuscumbia, Ala., the colored boy who was lynched there last year for assaulting a white girl told her before his accusers that he had met her there in the woods often before.

Frank Weems of Chattanooga who was not lynched in May only because the prominent citizens became his body guard until the doors of the penitentiary closed on him, had letters in his pocket from the white woman in the case, making the appointment with him. Edward Coy who was burned alive in Texarkana, January 1, 1892, died protesting his innocence. Investigation since as given by the Bystander in the *Chicago Inter Ocean,* October 1, proves:

1. The woman who was paraded as a victim of violence was of bad character; her husband was a drunkard and a gambler.
2. She was publicly reported and generally known to have been criminally intimate with Coy for more than a year previous.
3. She was compelled by threats, if not by violence, to make the charge against the victim.
4. When she came to apply the match Coy asked her if she would burn him after they had "been sweethearting" so long.
5. A large majority of the "superior" white men prominent in the affair are the reputed fathers of mulatto children.

These are not pleasant facts, but they are illustrative of the vital phase of the so-called race question, which should properly be designated an earnest inquiry as to the best methods by which religion, science, law and political power may be employed to excuse injustice, barbarity and crime done to a people because of race and color. There can be no possible belief that these people were inspired by any consuming zeal to vindicate God's law against miscegnationists of the most practical sort. The woman was a willing partner in the victim's guilt, and being of the "superior" race must naturally have been more guilty.

In Natchez, Miss., Mrs. Marshall, one of the *creme de la creme* of the city, created a tremendous sensation several years ago. She has a black coachman who was married, and had been in her employ several years. During this time she gave birth to a child whose color was remarked, but traced to some brunette ancestor, and one of the fashionable dames of the city was its godmother. Mrs. Marshall's social position was unquestioned, and wealth showered every dainty on this child which was idolized with its brothers and sisters by its white papa. In course of time another child appeared on the scene, but it was unmistakably dark. All were alarmed, and "rush of blood, strangulation" were the conjectures, but the doctor, when asked the cause, grimly told them it was a Negro child. There was a family conclave, the coachman heard of it and, leaving his own family, went west, and has never returned. As soon as Mrs. Marshall was able to travel she was sent away in deep disgrace. Her husband died within the year of a broken heart.

Ebenezer Fowler, the wealthiest colored man in Issaquena County, Miss., was shot down on the street in Mayersville, January 30, 1885, just before dark by an armed body of white men who filled his body with bullets. They charged him with writing a note to a white woman of the place, which they intercepted and which proved there was an intimacy existing between them.

Hundreds of such cases might be cited, but enough have been given to prove the assertion that there are white women in the South who love the Afro-American's company even as there are white men notorious for their preference for Afro-American women.

There is hardly a town in the South which has not an instance of the kind which is well known, and hence the assertion is reiterated that "nobody in the South believes the old thread bare lie that negro men rape white women." Hence there is a growing demand among Afro-Americans that the guilt or innocence of parties accused of rape be fully established. They know the men of the section of the country who refuse this are not so desirous of punishing rapists as they pretend. The utterances of the leading white men show that with them it is not the crime but the *class*. Bishop Fitzgerald has become apologist for lynchers of the rapists of *white* women only. Governor Tillman, of South Carolina, in the month of June, standing under the tree in Barnwell, S.C., on which eight Afro-Americans were hung last year, declared that he would lead a mob to lynch a *negro* who raped a *white* woman. So say the pulpits, officials and newspapers of the South. But when the victim is a colored woman it is different.

Last winter in Baltimore, Md., three white ruffians assaulted a Miss Camphor, a young Afro-American girl, while out walking with a young man of her own race. They held her escort and outraged the girl. It was a deed dastardly enough to arouse Southern blood, which gives its horror of rape as excuse for lawlessness, but she was an Afro-American. The case went to the courts, an Afro-American lawyer defended the men and they were acquitted.

In Nashville, Tenn., there is a white man, Pat Hanifan, who outraged a little Afro-American girl, and, from the physical injuries received, she has been ruined for life. He was jailed for six months, discharged, and is now a detective in that city. In the same city, last May, a white man outraged an Afro-American girl in a drug store. He was arrested, and released on bail at the trial. It was rumored that five hundred Afro-Americans had organized to lynch him. Two hundred and fifty white citizens armed themselves with

Winchesters and guarded him. A cannon was placed in front of his home, and the Buchanan Rifles (State Militia) ordered to the scene for his protection. The Afro-American mob did not materialize. Only two weeks before Eph. Grizzard, who had only been *charged* with rape upon a white woman, had been taken from the jail, with Governor Buchanan and the police and militia standing by, dragged through the streets in broad daylight, knives plunged into him at every step, and with every fiendish cruelty a frenzied mob could devise, he was at last swung out on the bridge with hands cut to pieces as he tried to climb up the stanchions. A naked, bloody example of the blood-thirstiness of the nineteenth-century civilization of the Athens of the South! No cannon or military was called out in his defense. He dared to visit a white woman.

At the very moment these civilized whites were announcing their determination "to protect their wives and daughters," by murdering Grizzard, a white man was in the same jail for raping eight-year-old Maggie Reese, an Afro-American girl. He was not harmed. The "honor" of grown women who were glad enough to be supported by the Grizzard boys and Ed Coy, as long as the liaison was not known, needed protection; they were white. The outrage upon helpless childhood needed no avenging in this case; she was black.

A white man in Guthrie, Oklahoma Territory, two months ago inflicted such injuries upon another Afro-American child that she died. He was not punished, but an attempt was made in the same town in the month of June to lynch an Afro-American who visited a white woman.

In Memphis, Tenn., in the month of June, Ellerton L. Dorr, who is the husband of Russell Hancock's widow, was arrested for attempted rape on Mattie Cole, a neighbor's cook; he was only prevented from accomplishing his purpose, by the appearance of Mattie's employer. Dorr's friends say he was drunk and not responsible for his actions. The grand jury refused to indict him and he was discharged.

1892

NOTES

1. An African American newspaper, founded in 1880 as the *New York Globe*. The paper remained in circulation until 1953, when it was renamed the *New York Age Defender* and published as a weekly until 1960.

2. Founded in 1888 as the *Memphis Free Speech* and renamed the *Free Speech and Headlight*, the paper was co-owned by Ida B. Wells Barnett, Rev. Taylor Nightingale of the First Baptist Church, and J. L. Fleming, a local businessman. The paper received national

attention for its outspoken opposition to lynching and mob rule, led by Ida B. Wells-Barnett's investigative journalism.

3. One of two mainstream, majority-owned newspapers in the Memphis region during the late nineteenth century, published from 1889 to 1891, before it merged with the *Appeal* to become the daily *Commercial Appeal*.

4. A Memphis area daily that ceased publication in 1904.

5. A pejorative term for an African American person.

FANNIE BARRIER WILLIAMS (1855-1944)

Fannie Barrier Williams was born in Brockport, New York, to Harriet and Anthony Barrier. Her father was a barber and coal merchant, and her mother taught Bible classes at the city's First Baptist Church. After graduating from the local public school, Williams enrolled in the New York Normal School in her region (now the State University of New York at Brockport), and in 1870 she became its first African American graduate. Influenced by the beliefs of Frederick Douglass, a family friend, Williams moved south to teach the children of newly freed blacks, eventually returning to the North to study piano performance at Boston's New England Conservatory of Music. Her stay was cut short when complaints from southern white students compelled administrators to expel her. In 1887, the newly married Williams moved to Chicago, where she became deeply involved in local reform movements. She was a founding member of the National League of Colored Women and the National Federation of Afro-American Women; and in 1895 she became the first African American woman admitted to the previously all-white Chicago Women's Club. Williams' greatest notoriety, however, came as a result of her leadership in securing black women's inclusion in Chicago's Columbian Exposition of 1893. Williams herself delivered two speeches at the event, one to the World's Parliament of Religions and the other to the World Congress of Representative Women. It was the latter address, titled "The Intellectual Progress of Colored Women in the United States Since the Emancipation Proclamation," that secured her legacy as one of the period's most charismatic and persuasive speakers. The excerpts below are reprinted from the The World Congress of Representative Women: A Historical Résumé, published in 1894.

THE INTELLECTUAL PROGRESS OF COLORED WOMEN SINCE THE EMANCIPATION PROCLAMATION

Less than thirty years ago the term progress as applied to colored women of African descent in the United States would have been an anomaly. The recognition of that term to-day as appropriate is a fact full of interesting significance. That the discussion of progressive womanhood in this great assemblage of the representative women of the world is considered incomplete without some account of the colored women's status is a most noteworthy evidence that we have not failed to impress ourselves on the higher side of American life.

Less is known of our women than of any other class of Americans.

No organization of far-reaching influence for their special advancement, no conventions of women to take note of their progress, and no special literature reciting the incidents, the events, and all things interesting and instructive concerning them are to be found among the agencies directing their career. There has been no special interest in their peculiar condition as native-born American women. Their power to affect the social life of America, either for good or for ill, has excited not even a speculative interest.

Though there is much that is sorrowful, much that is wonderfully heroic, and much that is romantic in a peculiar way in their history, none of it has as yet been told as evidence of what is possible for these women. How few of the happy, prosperous, and eager living Americans can appreciate what it all means to be suddenly changed from irresponsible bondage to the responsibility of freedom and citizenship!

The distress of it all can never be told, and the pain of it all can never be felt except by the victims, and by those saintly women of the white race who for thirty years have been consecrated to the uplifting of a whole race of women from a long-enforced degradation.

The American people have always been impatient of ignorance and poverty. They believe with Emerson that "America is another word for opportunity," and for that reason success is a virtue and poverty and ignorance are inexcusable. This may account for the fact that our women have excited no general sympathy in the struggle to emancipate themselves from the demoralization of slavery. This new life of freedom, with its far-reaching responsibilities, had to be learned by these children of darkness mostly without a guide, a teacher, or a friend. In the mean vocabulary of slavery there was no definition of any of the virtues of life. The meaning of such precious terms as marriage, wife, family, and home could not be learned in a school-house. The blue-back speller, the arithmetic, and the copy-book contain no magical cures for inherited inaptitudes for the moralities. Yet it must ever be counted as one of the most wonderful things in human history how promptly and eagerly these suddenly liberated women tried to lay hold upon all that there is in human excellence. There is a touching pathos in the eagerness of these millions of new home-makers to taste the blessedness of intelligent womanhood. The path of progress in the picture is enlarged so as to bring to view these trustful and zealous students of freedom and civilization striving to overtake and keep pace with women whose emancipation has been a slow and painful process for a thousand years. The longing to be something better than they were when freedom found them has been the most notable characteristic in the development of these women. This constant striving for equality has given an upward direction to all the activities of colored women.

Freedom at once widened their vision beyond the mean cabin life of their bondage. Their native gentleness, good cheer, and hopefulness made them susceptible to those teachings that make for intelligence and righteousness. Sullenness of disposition, hatefulness, and revenge against the master class because of two centuries of ill-treatment are not in the nature of our women.

But a better view of what our women are doing and what their present status is may be had by noticing some lines of progress that are easily verifiable.

First it should be noticed that separate facts and figures relative to colored women are not easily obtainable. Among the white women of the country, independence, progressive intelligence, and definite interests have done so much that nearly every fact and item illustrative of their progress and status is classified and easily accessible. Our women, on the contrary, have had no advantage of interests peculiar and distinct and separable from those of men that have yet excited public attention and kindly recognition.

In their religious life, however, our women show a progressiveness parallel in every important particular to that of white women in all Christian churches. It has always been a circumstance of the highest satisfaction to the missionary efforts of the Christian church that the colored people are so susceptible to a religion that marks the highest point of blessedness in human history.

Instead of finding witchcraft, sensual fetiches, and the coarse superstitions of savagery possessing our women, Christianity found them with hearts singularly tender, sympathetic, and fit for the reception of its doctrines. Their superstitions were not deeply ingrained, but were of the same sort and nature that characterize the devotees of the Christian faith everywhere.

While there has been but little progress toward the growing rationalism in the Christian creeds, there has been a marked advance toward a greater refinement of conception, good taste, and the proprieties. It is our young women coming out of the schools and academies that have been insisting upon a more godly and cultivated ministry. It is the young women of a new generation and new inspirations that are making tramps of the ministers who once dominated the colored church, and whose intelligence and piety were mostly in their lungs. In this new and growing religious life the colored people have laid hold of those sweeter influences of the King's Daughters, of the Christian Endeavor and Helping Hand societies,[1] which are doing much to elevate the tone of worship and to magnify all that there is blessed in religion.

Another evidence of growing intelligence is a sense of religious discrimination among our women. Like the nineteenth century woman generally, our women find congeniality in all the creeds, from the Catholic creed to the no-creed of Emerson. There is a constant increase of this interesting variety in the religious life of our women.

Closely allied to this religious development is their progress in the work of education in schools and colleges. For thirty years education has been the magic word among the colored people of this country. That their greatest need was education in its broadest sense was understood by these people more strongly than it could be taught to them. It is the unvarying testimony of every teacher in the South that the mental development of the colored women as well as men has been little less than phenomenal. In twenty-five years, and under conditions discouraging in the extreme, thousands of our women have been educated as teachers. They have adapted themselves to the work of mentally lifting a whole race of people so eagerly and readily that they afford an apt illustration of the power of self-help. Not only have these women become good teachers in less than twenty-five years, but many of them are the prize teachers in the mixed schools of nearly every Northern city.

These women have also so fired the hearts of the race for education that colleges, normal schools, industrial schools, and universities have been reared by a generous public to meet the requirements of these eager students of intelligent citizenship. As American women generally are fighting against the nineteenth century narrowness that still keeps women out of the higher institutions of learning, so our women are eagerly demanding the best of education open to their race. They continually verify what President Rankin of Howard University recently said, "Any theory of educating the Afro-American that does not throw open the golden gates of the highest culture will fail on the ethical and spiritual side."

It is thus seen that our women have the same spirit and mettle that characterize the best of American women. Everywhere they are following in the tracks of those women who are swiftest in the race for higher knowledge.

To-day they feel strong enough to ask for but one thing, and that is the same opportunity for the acquisition of all kinds of knowledge that may be accorded to other women. This granted, in the next generation these progressive women will be found successfully occupying every field where the highest intelligence alone is admissible. In less than another generation American literature, American art, and American music will be enriched by productions having new and peculiar features of interest and excellence.

The exceptional career of our women will yet stamp itself indelibly upon the thought of this country.

American literature needs for its greater variety and its deeper soundings that which will be written into it out of the hearts of these self-emancipating women.

The great problems of social reform that are now so engaging the highest intelligence of American women will soon need for their solution the reinforcement of that new intelligence which our women are developing. In short, our women are ambitious to be contributors to all the great moral and intellectual forces that make for the greater weal of our common country.

If this hope seems too extravagant to those of you who know these women only in their humbler capacities, I would remind you that all that we hope for and will certainly achieve in authorship and practical intelligence is more than prophesied by what has already been done, and more that can be done, by hundreds of Afro-American women whose talents are now being expended in the struggle against race resistance.

The power of organized womanhood is one of the most interesting studies of modern sociology. Formerly women knew so little of each other mentally, their common interests were so sentimental and gossipy, and their knowledge of all the larger affairs of human society was so meager that organization among them, in the modern sense, was impossible. Now their liberal intelligence, their contact in all the great interests of education, and their increasing influence for good in all the great reformatory movements of the age has created in them a greater respect for each other, and furnished the elements of organization for large and splendid purposes. The highest ascendancy of woman's development has been reached when they have become mentally strong enough to find bonds of association interwoven with sympathy, loyalty, and mutual trustfulness. To-day union is the watchword of woman's onward march.

If it be a fact that this spirit of organization among women generally is the distinguishing mark of the nineteenth century woman, dare we ask if the colored women of the United States have made any progress in this respect?

For peculiar and painful reasons the great lessons of fraternity and altruism are hard for the colored women to learn. Emancipation found the colored Americans of the South with no sentiments of association. It will be admitted that race misfortune could scarcely go further when the terms fraternity, friendship, and unity had no meaning for its men and women.

If within thirty years they have begun to recognize the blessed significance of these vital terms of human society, confidence in their social development should be strengthened. In this important work of bringing the race together to know itself and to unite in work for a common destiny, the women have taken a leading part.

Benevolence is the essence of most of the colored women's organizations. The humane side of their natures has been cultivated to recognize the duties they owe to the sick, the indigent and ill-fortuned. No church, school, or charitable institution for the special use of colored people has been allowed to languish or fail when the associated efforts of the women could save it.

It is highly significant and interesting to note that these women, whose hearts have been wrung by all kinds of sorrows, are abundantly manifesting those gracious qualities of heart that characterize women of the best type. These kinder sentiments arising from mutual interests that are lifting our women into purer and tenderer relationship to each other, and are making the meager joys and larger griefs of our conditions known to each other, have been a large part of their education.

The hearts of Afro-American women are too warm and too large for race hatred. Long suffering has so chastened them that they are developing a special sense of sympathy for all who suffer and fail of justice. All the associated interests of church, temperance, and social reform in which American women are winning distinction can be wonderfully advanced when our women shall be welcomed as co-workers, and estimated solely by what they are worth to the moral elevation of all the people.

I regret the necessity of speaking to the question of the moral progress of our women, because the morality of our home life has been commented upon so disparagingly and meanly that we are placed in the unfortunate position of being defenders of our name.

It is proper to state, with as much emphasis as possible, that all questions relative to the moral progress of the colored women of America are impertinent and unjustly suggestive when they relate to the thousands of colored women in the North who were free from the vicious influences of slavery. They are also meanly suggestive as regards thousands of our women in the South whose force of character enabled them to escape the slavery taints of immorality. The question of the moral progress of colored women in the United States has force and meaning in this discussion only so far as it tells the story of how the once enslaved women have been struggling for twenty-five years to emancipate themselves from the demoralization of their enslavement.

While I duly appreciate the offensiveness of all references to American slavery, it is unavoidable to charge to that system every moral imperfection that mars the character of the colored American. The whole life and power of slavery depended upon an enforced degradation of everything human in the slaves. The slave code recognized only animal distinctions between the sexes, and ruthlessly ignored those ordinary separations that belong to the social state.

It is a great wonder that two centuries of such demoralization did not work a complete extinction of all the moral instincts. But the recuperative power of these women to regain their moral instincts and to establish a respectable relationship to American womanhood is among the earlier evidences of their moral ability to rise above their conditions. In spite of a cursed heredity that bound them to the lowest social level, in spite of everything that is unfortunate and unfavorable, these women have continually shown an increasing degree of teachableness as to the meaning of woman's relationship to man.

Out of this social purification and moral uplift have come a chivalric sentiment and regard from the young men of the race that give to the young women a new sense of protection. I do not wish to disturb the serenity of this conference by suggesting why this protection is needed and the kind of men against whom it is needed.

It is sufficient for us to know that the daughters of women who thirty years ago were not allowed to be modest, not allowed to follow the instincts of moral rectitude, who could cry for protection to no living man, have so elevated the moral tone of their social life that new and purer standards of personal worth have been created, and new ideals of womanhood, instinct with grace and delicacy, are everywhere recognized and emulated.

This moral regeneration of a whole race of women is no idle sentiment—it is a serious business; and everywhere there is witnessed a feverish anxiety to be free from the mean suspicions that have so long underestimated the character strength of our women.

These women are not satisfied with the unmistakable fact that moral progress has been made, but they are fervently impatient and stirred by a sense of outrage under the vile imputations of a diseased public opinion.

Loves that are free from the dross of coarseness, affections that are unsullied, and a proper sense of all the sanctities of human intercourse felt by thousands of these women all over the land plead for the recognition of their fitness to be judged, not by the standards of slavery, but by the higher standards of freedom and of twenty-five years of education, culture, and moral contact.

The moral aptitudes of our women are just as strong and just as weak as those of any other American women with like advantages of intelligence and environment.

It may now perhaps be fittingly asked, "What mean all these evidences of mental, social, and moral progress of a class of American women of whom you know so little?"Certainly you cannot be indifferent to the growing needs and importance of women who are demonstrating their intelligence and capacity for the highest privileges of freedom.

The most important thing to be noted is the fact that the colored people of America have reached a distinctly new era in their career so quickly that the American mind has scarcely had time to recognize the fact, and adjust itself to the new requirements of the people in all things that pertain to citizenship.

Thirty years ago public opinion recognized no differences in the colored race. To our great misfortune public opinion has changed but slightly. History is full of examples of the great injustice resulting from the perversity of public opinion, and its tardiness in recognizing new conditions.

It seems to daze the understanding of the ordinary citizen that there are thousands of men and women everywhere among us who in twenty-five years have progressed as far away from the non-progressive peasants of the "black belt" of the South as the highest social life in New England is above the lowest levels of American civilization.

This general failure of the American people to know the new generation of colored people, and to recognize this important change in them, is the cause of more injustice to our women than can well be estimated. Further progress is everywhere seriously hindered by this ignoring of their improvement.

Our exclusion from the benefits of the fair play sentiment of the country is little less than a crime against the ambitions and aspirations of a whole race of women. The American people are but repeating the common folly of history in thus attempting to repress the yearnings of progressive humanity.

In the item of employment, colored women bear a distressing burden of mean and unreasonable discrimination. A Southern teacher of thirty years' experience in the South writes that "one million possibilities of good through black womanhood all depend upon an opportunity to make a living."

It is almost literally true that, except teaching in colored schools and menial work, colored women can find no employment in this free America. They are the only women in the country for whom real ability, virtue, and special talents count for nothing when they become applicants for respectable employment. Taught everywhere in ethics and social economy that merit always wins, colored women carefully prepare themselves for all kinds of occupation only to meet with stern refusal, rebuff, and disappointment. One of countless instances will show how the best as well as the meanest of American society are responsible for the special injustice to our women.

Not long ago I presented the case of a bright young woman to a well-known bank president of Chicago, who was in need of a thoroughly competent stenographer and typewriter. The president was fully satisfied with the young woman as exceptionally qualified for the position, and manifested much pleasure in commending her to the directors for appointment, and at the same time disclaimed that there could be any opposition on account of the slight tinge of African blood that identified her as a colored woman. Yet, when the matter was brought before the directors for action, these mighty men of money and business, these men whose prominence in all the great interests of the city would seem to lift them above all narrowness and foolishness, scented the African taint, and at once bravely came to the rescue of the bank and of society by dashing the hopes of this capable yet helpless young woman. No other question but that of color determined the action of these men, many of whom are probably foremost members of the humane society and heavy contributors to foreign missions and church extension work.

This question of employment for the trained talents of our women is a most serious one. Refusal of such employment because of color belies every maxim of justice and fair play. Such refusal takes the blessed meaning out of all the teachings of our civilization, and sadly confuses our conceptions of what is just, humane, and moral.

Can the people of this country afford to single out the women of a whole race of people as objects of their special contempt? Do these women not belong to a race that has never faltered in its support of the country's flag in every war since Attucks[2] fell in Boston's streets?

Are they not the daughters of men who have always been true as steel against treason to everything fundamental and splendid in the republic? In short, are these women not as thoroughly American in all the circumstances of citizenship as the best citizens of our country?

If it be so, are we not justified in a feeling of desperation against that peculiar form of Americanism that shows respect for our women as servants and contempt for them when they become women of culture? We have never been taught to understand why the unwritten law of chivalry, protection, and fair play that are everywhere the conservators of women's welfare must exclude every woman of a dark complexion.

We believe that the world always needs the influence of every good and capable woman, and this rule recognizes no exceptions based on complexion. In their complaint against hindrances to their employment colored women ask for no special favors.

They are even willing to bring to every position fifty per cent more of ability than is required of any other class of women. They plead for opportunities untrammeled by prejudice. They plead for the right of the individual to be judged, not by tradition and race estimate, but by the present evidences of individual worth. We believe this country is large enough and the opportunities for all kinds of success are great enough to afford our women a fair chance to earn a respectable living, and to win every prize within the reach of their capabilities.

Another, and perhaps more serious, hindrance to our women is that nightmare known as "social equality." The term equality is the most inspiring word in the vocabulary of citizenship. It expresses the leveling quality in all the splendid possibilities of American life. It is this idea of equality that has made room in this country for all kinds and conditions of men, and made personal merit the supreme requisite for all kinds of achievement.

When the colored people became citizens, and found it written deep in the organic law of the land that they too had the right to life, liberty, and the pursuit of happiness, they were at once suspected of wishing to interpret this maxim of equality as meaning social equality.

Everywhere the public mind has been filled with constant alarm lest in some way our women shall approach the social sphere of the dominant race in this country. Men and women, wise and perfectly sane in all things else, become instantly unwise and foolish at the remotest suggestion of social contact with colored men and women. At every turn in our lives we meet this fear, and are humiliated by its aggressiveness and meanness. If we seek the sanctities of religion, the enlightenment of the university, the honors of politics, and the natural recreations of our common country, the social equality alarm is instantly given, and our aspirations are insulted. "Beware of social equality with the colored American" is thus written on all places, sacred or profane, in this blessed land of liberty. The most discouraging and demoralizing effect of this false sentiment concerning us is that it utterly ignores individual merit and discredits the sensibilities of intelligent womanhood. The sorrows and heartaches of a whole race of women seem to be matters of no concern to the people who so dread the social possibilities of these colored women.

On the other hand, our women have been wonderfully indifferent and unconcerned about the matter. The dread inspired by the growing intelligence of colored women has interested us almost to the point of amusement. It has given to colored women a new sense of importance to witness how easily their emancipation and steady advancement is disturbing all classes of American people. It may not be a discouraging circumstance that colored women can command some sort of attention, even though they be misunderstood. We believe in the law of reaction, and it is reasonably certain that the forces of intelligence and character being developed in our women will yet change mistrustfulness into confidence and contempt into sympathy and respect. It will soon appear to those who are not hopelessly monomaniacs on the subject that the colored people are in no way responsible for the social equality nonsense. We shall yet be credited with knowing better than our enemies that social equality can neither be enforced by law nor prevented by oppression. Though not philosophers, we long since learned that equality before the law, equality in the best sense of that term under our institutions, is totally different from social equality.

We know, without being exceptional students of history, that the social relationship of the two races will be adjusted equitably in spite of all fear and injustice, and that there is a social gravitation in human affairs that eventually overwhelms and crushes into nothingness all resistance based on prejudice and selfishness.

Our chief concern in this false social sentiment is that it attempts to hinder our further progress toward the higher spheres of womanhood. On account of it, young colored women of ambition and means are compelled in many instances to leave the country for training and education in the salons and studios of Europe. On many of the railroads of this country, women of refinement and culture are driven like cattle into human cattle-cars lest the occupying of an individual seat paid for in a first-class car may result in social equality. This social quarantine on all means of travel in certain parts of the country is guarded and enforced more rigidly against us than the quarantine regulations against cholera.

Without further particularizing as to how this social question opposes our advancement, it may be stated that the contentions of colored women are in kind like those of other American women for greater freedom of development. Liberty to be all that we can be, without artificial hindrances, is a thing no less precious to us than to women generally.

We come before this assemblage of women feeling confident that our progress has been along high levels and rooted deeply in the essentials of intelligent humanity. We are so essentially American in speech, in instincts, in sentiments and destiny that the things that interest you equally interest us.

We believe that social evils are dangerously contagious. The fixed policy of persecution and injustice against a class of women who are weak and defenseless will be necessarily hurtful to the cause of all women. Colored women are becoming more and more a part of the social forces that must help to determine the questions that so concern women generally. In this Congress we ask to be known and recognized for what we are worth. If it be the high purpose of these deliberations to lessen the resistance to woman's progress, you cannot fail to be interested in our struggles against the many oppositions that harass us.

Women who are tender enough in heart to be active in humane societies, to be foremost in all charitable activities, who are loving enough to unite Christian womanhood everywhere against the sin of intemperance, ought to be instantly concerned in the plea of colored women for justice and humane treatment. Women of the dominant race cannot afford to be responsible for the wrongs we suffer, since those who do injustice cannot escape a certain penalty.

But there is no wish to overstate the obstacles to colored women or to picture their status as hopeless. There is no disposition to take our place in this Congress as faultfinders or suppliants for mercy. As women of a common country, with common interests, and a destiny that will certainly bring us closer to each other, we come to this altar with our contribution of hopefulness as well as with our complaints.

When you learn that womanhood everywhere among us is blossoming out into greater fullness of everything that is sweet, beautiful, and good in woman; when you learn that the bitterness of our experience as citizen-women has not hardened our finer feelings of love and pity for our enemies; when you learn that fierce opposition to the widening spheres of our employment has not abated the aspirations of our women to enter successfully into all the professions and arts open only to intelligence, and that everywhere in the wake of enlightened womanhood our women are seen and felt for the good they diffuse, this Congress will at once see the fullness of our fellowship, and help us to avert the arrows of prejudice that pierce the soul because of the color of our bodies.

If the love of humanity more than the love of races and sex shall pulsate throughout all the grand results that shall issue to the world from this parliament of women, women of African descent in the United States will for the first time begin to feel the sweet release from the blighting thrall of prejudice.

The colored women, as well as all women, will realize that the inalienable right to life, liberty, and the pursuit of happiness is a maxim that will become more blessed in its significance when the hand of woman shall take it from its sepulchre in books and make it the gospel of every-day life and the unerring guide in the relations of all men, women, and children.

1893

NOTES

1. The International Order of the King's Daughters, the Young People's Society of the Christian Endeavor, and the Ladies' Helping Hand Society, religiously affiliated service organizations for women and children.

2. Crispus Attucks, an African American man and the first person to die in the American Revolutionary War, killed in the Boston Massacre by a shot through the chest.

AMANDA SMITH (1837-1915)

Amanda Berry Smith was born into slavery in Long Green, Maryland. Her parents, Samuel and Mariam Berry, lived on adjacent farms. Both were literate, and both were committed to their children's education. Though Smith had less than four months of formal schooling, her mother taught her to read and encouraged her to educate herself. Selling the brooms and straw mats that he was able to make in the evenings, her father was able to purchase the freedom of his entire family, including himself, his wife, and his five children. In time, the family would move to York County, Pennsylvania, where Smith experienced a religious conversion and became deeply involved in the activities of her church. Smith would marry and be widowed twice. She had two children with her first husband and three with her second; but only Mazie, a daughter, survived to adulthood. Due to strict rules barring the ordination of women, and despite her growing popularity as a preacher, Smith was forced to remain an itinerate evangelist, supporting herself and her daughter through her work as a washerwoman. It was not until after her second husband's death that she began the missionary work that would define much of her later life. Between 1878 and 1894, Smith traveled and preached in England, India, and Liberia (where she lived for eight years). By 1894, Smith had returned to the United States permanently, having decided to commit the remainder of her life to addressing the needs of black people in the U.S. In 1899, she founded the Amanda Smith Industrial Orphan Home for Colored Children, in Harvey, Illinois. Though she was a regular correspondent for several Christian magazines and newspapers, Smith is best known for her spiritual narrative, *An Autobiography: The Story of the Lord's Dealings with Mrs. Amanda Smith, the Colored Evangelist.* Published in 1893, the volume provides a lengthy account of the author's upbringing, conversion, evangelism, and missionary work. The book was very well received in the United States, England, and Liberia, and went through several editions. In the following excerpt, Smith describes her experiences in West Africa, emphasizing the challenges she experienced as she slowly adjusted to the preindustrial setting, the tropical climate, and the unique characters she encountered there.

Chapter XXXI

Emigrants going to Liberia think they can rent a small house, or rooms, as they can in this country. People will come there, who have left a comfortable home behind, and think they will rent a small house for six months or a year, till they can get their own house built; but this they can seldom do. The reason of this, I think is, the climate is very hard on timber, and a house standing unoccupied for any length of time will soon be destroyed.

The bug-a-bug is a very large ant, which eats the wood to a perfect hull, and the most destructive insect in that regard in the country. If they get into a trunk or chest of clothes, and are not discovered in time, they will go through everything, books, papers, etc.; nothing stands before them. After you know this, a little watching may save you a great deal of trouble.

So that the most of the people in Liberia, or anywhere else in the republic, build, and live in their own houses. Houses that are built of stone or brick are the most durable; and the best houses there are thus built. But the frame houses have the hardest time.

Slate roofing, in one sense, would be better than shingles, especially for the rainy season, for the reason that the rain and sun do not affect it so much as they do the shingles.

During the rainy season there, it literally pours. I have often thought of Noah in the ark when I have seen the rain pour down without mercy for two or three days in succession, with just a little intervals of a slight break between. Then the sun would come out, sometimes for a half day, perhaps in the morning or afternoon, then it would rain at night; but these little intervals help the people to get about and do their work. Nobody seems to stop especially. After you have been here awhile you do not seem to mind it. It is rather comfortable, for it is not so warm then, and you can stand a good little fire in the house to absorb the dampness.

As a rule there is a good deal of sickness and fever among the natives during this season; but people having comfortable houses suffer but very little inconvenience.

When the rainy season is over, and the blazing, hot sun beats down, the shingles curl right up and split, so that almost every year it is necessary to go through some repairing. On the other hand, the slate roof gets so hot that it makes sleeping almost impossible, unless the roof is high, and well lined under the slate.

There are some large houses, for stores; these are occupied by white merchants, or traders, so that if there chance to her a good house of any size to rent, they generally have the preference, for they always have the money, and that is the first consideration in Africa as well as elsewhere.

Now, in this regard Sierra Leone is different. There are almost always good houses to rent there; they build houses for that purpose. And so if you want a house with a store underneath, or a large private house, or one not so large, it can be got at a reasonable price, as a rule, and on a good, wide street.

The Sierra Leone houses are very substantially built, but generally of stone or brick, with yards enclosed by a good, high wall, after the English style, and nicely furnished inside. I have seen some as finely finished houses in Sierra Leone and Lagos as I have seen in America or England.

The people of Sierra Leone are greatly mixed, as to tribes; so much so, that I think it would be difficult to tell to just what particular tribe they really belong.

They have no real, distinct language. They speak a lingo of broken English, which all seem to understand; and when two or three dozen of them are together, especially the women and girls in the market places, it would remind one unaccustomed to it of the chattering of a thousand swallows. My! but they can talk. But there are hundreds who speak good English.

There are many wealthy merchants, both in Sierra Leone and Lagos, who often send their sons and daughters to England, and sometimes to France, to be educated. But somehow they never seem to lose this peculiar Sierra Leone idiom; so that they are just as distinct in their customs and manners of speech from Liberians and Americans, as Italians are different from Americans in this country; so they do not assimilate easily. They intermarry occasionally, but not often, and when they do, they seldom get on well together; their training and education are so entirely different.

But the country is no better off for this education. Of course they don't come home to do missionary work among the people; they belong to the upper rank; and so those of the same rank are a society among themselves; and the second and third classes of their own people are never the better for their higher education, only as they may serve them, as servants, or otherwise.

If it is a lady, she is either engaged, before she comes home, to be married to some rich gentleman, or very soon after she gets home you may hear that she has had an offer; sometimes there will be rival suitors for her hand, and you will wait with the greatest interest, for you are sure to hear of it, which of these has won the suit. As much of this depends on the weight of their pockets as anything else.

And then, when one of these weddings comes off, it will give you a little idea of what real black aristocracy is. It would compare favorably with the same kind of an event on Fifth Avenue New York, or in Washington, D.C. Fine cards and wedding presents, and all the outfits for four or five bridesmaids, as well as bride and groom, and best man, etc., etc., all imported from England and France. These people are not ignorant in regard to the highest style, and the greatest etiquette.

As a rule, I think the Sierra Leone people are generally industrious; there are merchants, tailors, carpenters, etc., among them. They have large markets where you can go and get, two or three times a week, all sorts of produce, at a good price. Then they have regular beef markets, from which they supply Government House, and the large barracks of English soldiers.

They are great traders, men, women, boys and girls; the women often surpass the men. They will go up and down the rivers, and in the interior, buying palm oil, rubber, camwood, and boys and girls, if necessary. I was told they do this sometimes, but for the purpose of setting them free, as the English law does not allow anyone to own slaves, when it is really known. Thank God for that.

Formerly they had good schools in Freetown.[1] This is one thing I admire in the English government; she generally looks well after the education of her colonists. Of course there is room for much improvement, even in Sierra Leone and Lagos.

All up and down the coast, wherever you go where the English flag waves, and there has been any civilization at all, you will find scores and hundreds who have a liberal education, and are fitted for most all professions and callings.

The Wesleyan Girls' High School, at Freetown, was once a beautiful build-ing, with well furnished dormitories, and a staff of first-class teachers; but it has seen its best days, without a great change takes place. For several years it has been sadly declining in power and influence, being almost entirely under the control of one or two parties. I was told that when it was first founded, it was under the management of white people; the lady principal and teachers were all white, and they did a grand work. And then the boys' high school, which I also visited, and had the privilege, through the invitation of the prin-cipal, Mr. M., of addressing, was not what it once was, or should be. The

Episcopal school, both for girls and boys, is good. The boys have a fine, large, commodious building, and a good staff of teachers.

Several of the Liberian families, who have not been able to send their sons and daughters as far as England to be educated, sent them to Freetown. I had the pleasure of going all through this building, on the day of the dedication of the new dormitory and recitation rooms, which had been added to the main building, accommodating, I think, probably two hundred in all. His lordship the Bishop, was in the chair, and gave a most excellent address, as did also Mr. N., who, I think, at that time had charge of the theological department, and who was a noble, Christian gentleman. His sister was the lady principal of the girls' high school, which I also visited, and had the pleasure of speaking a few words to the young ladies. Everything was in good order.

I was greatly delighted with this school, especially the house-keeping department, where, in connection with their studies, each girl took her turn in the sweeping, dusting, making bread, biscuit, pie, or cake, and in washing dishes and attending the dining room. This, it seemed to me, was the most essential of all; it would certainly be one of the "one needful things." For if, having the intellectual qualifications, the girls in Africa are remiss in this, the former is as good as lost, to a great extent, as their homes would not be what they might be otherwise.

Then, there are private schools. I visited a Mr. Leapol's school, which was a very nice school for boys. I suppose he accommodated about forty. Mr. L. was a very high type of a Christian gentleman; I think, a West Indian by birth. This school was of the higher grade. Teachers and helpers, I believe, were all colored.

There was a good government school, which, according to my American ideas, should have continued to exist. But when the new Bishop came, he, being a very conservative English gentleman, and invested with power, thought it best, as I was told, to disband the government school, and build a large parish school. So that many of the poor children, who were not able to pay, were shut out. This opened a good harvest for the Roman Catholics, which they lost no time in securing.

I am often asked if I think that missionary work in Africa prospers and develops better when under the entire control of colored people, or do I think it is better under the control of white people.

To answer this as best I can I will give my experience and observation at the several places I have been.

The schools at Old Calabar under the Scotch Presbyterian Missionary Society, and the schools and missions at Lagos, and the Episcopal, Baptist and Wesleyan Schools in the Republic of Liberia; and then in Sierra Leone the United Free Methodists, the Episcopals, the Lady Huntington Society, the U. B. Mission, and the English Baptist Mission, all were established, supported and superintended by white missionaries; but just in proportion as they have died, or on account of poor health have had to retire from the work, the schools and mission property have declined.

Many of them in the work have developed good native teachers and preachers, who are loyal, and faithful, and true; and the white missionary feels that he, or she, could not do without these native helpers. But when the whole work is left to them the interest seems to flag, and the natives themselves seem to lose their interest, which the teacher feels, but cannot help.

I do not attempt to make any explanation of this; I simply state the facts as I met them. And as I mingled with the people, old and young, and as the older people, who knew more about it, would tell me what it had been in former years, the remains of which were left, in the mission house and grounds, it was not difficult to see the difference.

Then, the white missionaries, as a rule, give better satisfaction, both to the natives and to the church or society which sends them out.

I suppose no church or society ever gave a salary to a colored man, no matter how efficient he was, as large as they give to a white man or woman, no matter how inefficient he or she may be in the start; and I think they are generally expected to do more work. This I think is a great mistake.

I believe that the death of the grandest black missionary I ever knew, Rev. Joseph Gomer, of the Shanghai Mission, was hastened through over-work and pressing need, and salary and means for work being cut down, and great anxiety because of the urgent demand for the work.

For pure Christian integrity and untarnished moral character, and fatherly sympathy and love for the poor heathen, he had but few equals in Africa, if any.

"Then you think, Mrs. Smith, it is better that white missionaries should go to Africa."

Yes, if they are the right kind. If they are thoroughly converted and fully consecrated and wholly sanctified to God, so that till their prejudices are completely killed out, and their hearts are full of love and sympathy, and they have firmness of character, and good, broad, level-headed common sense, and are possessed of great patience and strong, persistent, persevering faith, and then keep up the spirit of earnest prayer to Almighty God, day and night. I do not say that it is necessary to be under a dead strain all the time, not at all; but my own personal experience is that the more one prays and trusts in God, the better he can get on, especially in Africa.

Everything is so different from what you have it at home, that this is an absolute necessity; and the person that has not got the stick-to-itiveness on these lines, especially, whatever else he may have, will not make a good missionary in Africa, whether he be white or black.

I have known some white missionaries who have gone to Africa, who were just as full of prejudice against black people as they are in this country, and did not have grace enough to hide it; but they seemed to think they were in Africa, and there was no society that they cared for, and that the black people had but little sense, so they would never know if they did act mean and do mean things.

And I have known some who have done disreputable things, and it has had its effect on the motives and principles of the good missionaries, until they have had time enough patiently to live it down, and have proved to the Liberians and natives that there is a difference, even in white missionaries.

But thank God, He has sent some who have fully answered to what I have said before. There are one or two who come to my mind now, who, I believe, in every particular fill the bill. I refer to Miss Lizzie McNeil, who, it seems to me, is a born missionary, and to Miss Whitfield. There are numbers of others; but I speak of these because I know them personally, and know their work.

I remember the first party of Bishop Taylor's[2] missionaries that came to Cape Palmas while I was there. The steamer got in on Saturday afternoon; six of the men came ashore Saturday evening; the others, with their families, remained till morning, and they all got ashore in time for church Sunday morning.

Dear Brother Harnard preached a grand sermon. He was the leader, or bishop, of the party. They were all so full of hope and cheer. How bright and happy they all seemed to be. Brother Harnard had two beautiful children, about two and four years of age, I suppose; and the people, natives and all, were so delighted with them. Some of them have never seen white children so young; and then they were so beautifully trained; and Brother and Sister Harnard were so good and kind to every one.

Brother Pratt, Bishop Taylor's agent in Cape Palmas, whatever he may be now, was certainly the best man that Bishop Taylor could have got anywhere to fill the position, at the time. Oh, how faithfully that man worked. How he sacrificed his home, and everything for the work. His poor wife was sick all the time; suffered—Oh! what a sufferer she was; but she was second in everything for the success and good of Bishop Taylor's work.

He took Brother Harnard and his wife and two children, and two of the other men, Brother Johnson and Brother Miller, to his house. Sister Harmon and I had arranged to take care of three of the brethren—Brother Cadle, Brother Ortlit, and Brother Garwood. I gave them breakfast and tea, and Sister Harmon lodged them, and gave them dinner.

On Monday afternoon I invited Brother Johnson and Brother Miller to take tea with the other brethren. Of course, these were my own country people; they had left their home and went to work among my people in Africa. So we did our best for them.

I got Sister Harmon to make some nice, old-fashioned, Maryland biscuit (which she knew as well how to do as I did myself, and I used to be considered an expert, once upon a time), and we had nice fried chicken, and all else we could get, and that in abundance, that is the way we generally had it in Africa, when we were in for a big thing!

Of course, we could not go at that speed every day. But thank God, I never saw a day in Africa that I did not have plenty to eat. And when at Ma Payne's, in Monrovia, for days my meals would be sent to me in my room, when I was not able to go down, and as nicely served on a waiter as if I had been at a nice boarding house, or at my own home in America.

After tea was over we were all talking and having a pleasant time; the brethren seemed so to have enjoyed their tea, and we were all pleased.

Brother Johnson had been expressing in the most flattering terms his delight and appreciation of the splendid tea, and especially the biscuit. He said the lady who made them must have been a wonderfully nice lady, and if she was not married, she ought to be; for a lady that could make such biscuit ought to have a good husband. Well, we all laughed, and passed it off in a joking manner. I felt pretty safe, as I had not made the biscuit.

Sister Harmon was a nice looking woman, but was older than I, and had sons grown and married, and grandchildren; so she had no fear of anything, save the embarrassment of the question and answer, if it really came to that. So Brother Johnson said to me:

"Mrs. Smith, I would like to speak to you privately."

"Very well," I said; "we will excuse these brethren, and you can see me just here."

So the three brethren arose and withdrew to the parlor. I had watched and listened to Brother Johnson, and had taken his measure pretty thoroughly while he was talking, and I felt in my mind that he was going to play the fool.

"Now, Brother Johnson," said I, "proceed. What is it you want to say?"

He straightened up and smiled, and acted a little embarrassed; then got red in the face and all down his neck, till his beautiful white necktie seemed as though it was about to get pink, too.

I thought, "Dearie me, what will he say?" For I looked him squarely in the eye, and with the look of the rock of Gibraltar, if Gibraltar ever looked. I said, "It cannot mean that he is going to propose to me; he has just come; has not been here three days." After clearing his throat, he said:

"Well, Sister Smith, or Mrs. Smith," (emphasizing the Mrs.).

"Yes," I said.

"Well, I have come to Africa, and expect to make it my future home. I have not come to go back. I expect to die here."

Then I spoke and said, "I don't think you need die here any sooner than you would in the United States. One need only use his common sense, and go a little slow while he is acclimating." Then I waited for the next shot.

"I thought," he continued, "I would ask you if you knew of any nice colored woman that you think would make me a good wife. I could have married before I left my country, or America," (he was a Swede); "but I chose to wait till I got here; and I thought it would be better for me to marry a woman of the country, who is already acclimated. If I were to marry a white woman, she would all the time be crying to go home to see her aunt or uncle, or her mother," with a pretty smile.

I groaned, being burdened, to give vent to my mingled feelings. But then I controlled myself; for, during the time he talked, I was reading him, and I said to myself: "There is nothing in this man; he is as full of self as he can be, and he is going to be a failure, if not a disgrace, to Bishop Taylor's mission here." For the work was just starting, and was new, and needed much careful guiding and management, with all the American and African prejudices against this new, self-supporting movement.

"Mr. Johnson, I know some very nice women here, who, I think would make good wives for somebody; but I would not recommend anyone that I know, to do what I would not do myself; and I, myself, would not marry you, or any other man, if you were gold; a rank stranger, just come from another country, and have not been here three days; no one knows anything about you; you know nothing about the people. You are entirely premature. You will need to be here some time, and know Africa and the people. Then, besides, Bishop Taylor's self-supporting mission is in its infancy, and every eye is upon these first missionaries, both here and at home, and we must be careful that we do nothing that will hinder or hurt it in the start."

I saw that my version of things did not take very well with Brother Johnson. But I did not know until Wednesday what had gone before.

Mr. Pratt's wife's sister, a very nice girl, had gone to help in the house, as Mrs. Pratt was sick. She took a great fancy to Mrs. Harnard and the children, and had offered herself to Mrs. Harnard, to go with her, to take care of the children.

It appeared that when Mr. Johnson came ashore on Saturday, and saw this girl at Mrs. Pratt's, he was struck clear through at first sight, and had proposed; and she, poor thing, thought it was splendid. She judged from outside appearances; for Mr. Johnson was a very nice looking man, nicely dressed, patent leather boots, shirt collar and necktie exquisitely beautiful, and she thought she had a fish of the first water. I suppose she had; but it was bony.

They were to be married on Thursday, and would have been, if Mr. Pratt had allowed it. When he found it out, he sent the girl home to her father, and managed to hold Brother Johnson in check for two weeks.

So that was the meaning of the private conversation that Mr. Johnson wanted with me Monday evening. But he did not come straight out and tell me. I was glad afterward that I did not know anything about it, and that I talked just as I did. And, notwithstanding all that, they tried to say that I was favorable to it.

They were married at the Methodist Church, by somebody, I don't remember now by whom; but I know Brother Harnard did not marry them. I never went near; because I was so busy with my sick missionaries, and I did not care anyhow, to see the beginning of the thing; I was more interested about how it was going to come out.

Well, it turned out just as I said. After a week or so he carried the poor thing up into the country to their station. She had nothing, and he had nothing, only his mission supplies; and they had used the best part of those for their marriage feast, no one made them any feast, or gave them any presents, as they do in this country. In this they both seemed to be greatly disappointed.

Mr. Johnson seemed to think if he only married a colored girl, he being a white man, it would be such a standing proof to the colored people that he really loved them, that they would take him right into their arms, and lavish upon them their wealth and gifts; especially as he had married into one of the most respectable families in Cape Palmas; the daughter of the Hon. Mr. H. Gibson. My! he thought he had it. And so he had.

Poor girl! I knew her well. She had been converted and sanctified in one of the meetings that I had held, and had grown in grace, and was developing so nicely, and was one of our good workers in the Band of Hope Temperance work.

When I knew that the decree was passed to marry Mr. Johnson, I confess I was disappointed in her; for I really gave her credit for having more sense. So I never opened my head to her on the subject.

Her joy and delight were of short duration. He got fever and was down sick. They came back to the Cape. I went to see him, and did what I could.

When he got better they went again up to their station. The natives received them gladly, and gave them a bullock. They had their mission house built to go into. But everything was so different from what it was in America. He got down with fever again, and again they returned to the Cape. I, with Brother Pratt, did everything I could for him till I left.

After some months of going back and forth, and getting down with fever, he came back to the Cape again, and took the first steamer for home, and left his wife there, to live or die. Poor thing! In less than a year she died.

And Brother Johnson—though everything was done for him that could be done, I saw him after this in Monrovia, going about from house to house, and the worst thing he could say of Bishop Taylor and his self-supporting mission was too good.

Of course, he and Mr. Hillman, and Mr. Astley, had all gone over to the Episcopal Church; and, it seems that one of the surest marks of true fidelity to that church is to ignore and denounce everybody and everything in the church that has fitted them for this church to receive.

The last time I saw Brother Johnson, was in July, '91, at the Episcopal Mission at Cape Mount; and of all the poor, forlorn looking creatures that I had seen for some time, he seemed most to be pitied.

I have said it was not always a matter of having the cash, in order to get on in Africa, for there were times when you couldn't get things even with the cash.

"Then what would we do when we couldn't get the things we wanted at the stores?"

Well, we would just have to wait, and do the best we could, till a steamer came, or an American vessel; sometimes it would be a week, or two, or three, just as it happened.

"How did we get on?"

Well, that is a difficult question to answer—how we got on. But we did get on; we would just call up the old mother of invention, and she always had some plan to help us out; so there was no necessity of getting homesick or backsliding.

I never was homesick but about five minutes the whole eight years I was in Africa; and that was one day when I was reading an account in the "Christian Standard" of a wonderful holiness meeting held at old John Street, New York, and I was so hungry for such a spiritual feast; and as I read I found myself saying, "How I wish I were there."

When I thought of what I had said I sprang to my feet and cried out, "Now, Lord, help me, for I know I am right in the place where you want me, and it is all right." And in a moment the homesick feeling left me.

Then once, while I was at Miss Sharpe's, I was very nearly homesick. I was just going through my first attack of fever, and suffered for a drink of cool water. Being accustomed to having ice in this country, or going to a spring or pump and getting a cool drink, I felt I must have some ice. In India they make ice; so while there I could get ice water; but they don't make it in Africa. Sometimes we could get a piece off the steamer; but only a small piece, which could not last very long; and generally when one wanted it most, there would be no steamer in; so one must do without it.

And the water is always warm. The only time you get it cool is very early in the morning, or during the rainy season. In the morning it would be a little cool, but if you drink it so very early you will be very apt to have a chill; so you must be careful on that line.

I was pretty well scorched with fever, and as the days and nights went on, and nothing cool to drink, and no appetite to eat anything I could get to eat, I craved what I could not get.

Plenty could be got, but not what I wanted. I wanted a nice broiled mutton chop, basted with some nice hard butter, not that soft, oily stuff that was in the tins. I wanted a nice baker's roll, with hard butter off the ice, and a nice cup of tea, with some fresh cream, not condensed milk.

All the nice things that I ever did for sick people when I lived in a rich gentleman's family came into my mind. I knew exactly how to do it; I had done it for others. And when I would shut my eyes there would be all the things right before me. I could see them just as plain as could be. When I fell into a little doze of sleep they would haunt me. When I would wake, Oh! how hungry I would be for just that; I wanted nothing else.

It was not the question of money; I had a little, and would have got all these things, but they were not there to be got.

So one night I prayed nearly all night, and asked the Lord to take all desire out of me for everything I could not get, and help me to like and relish just what I could get. About four o'clock in the morning I fell asleep, and woke about six; and every bit of desire for mutton chop, and rolls, and hard butter, and fresh cream was gone, and I was as free from the desire as if I had never had it. I laughed, and cried, and praised the Lord for His loving mercy.

No one who has not had the experience can tell anything about what it means to be weak, and sick, and hungry, and where you cannot get a little of what your appetite craves. But our God is a wonderful deliverer. And then the grand old text that He gave me when I first started, "My God will supply all of your need,"—how true. Praise His name. Amen.

1893

NOTES

1. The capital of Sierra Leone.

2. William Taylor (1821–1902) of the Methodist Episcopal Church, elected Missionary Bishop of Africa in 1884.

KATHERINE DAVIS TILLMAN (1870-?)

Katherine Davis Chapman Tillman was born in Mound City, Illinois, to parents Charles and Laura Chapman Tillman. Her formal education began at the age of twelve, around which time her family relocated to Yanktown, South Dakota. It was during this period that she published some of her earliest short fiction, in the journal *Our Women and Children,* an early black women's magazine of which there are no known surviving copies. In 1889, at the age of eighteen, her first published poem appeared in the *Christian Recorder,* thus beginning a personal and professional relationship with the A.M.E. Church that would last for the rest of her life. Tillman attended the State University of Louisville in Kentucky and Wilberforce University in Ohio. After her marriage to A.M.E. Minister George Tillman, she became increasingly involved in the church, supporting its publications with her frequent contributions of poetry, fiction, and historical essays. Her two novellas, *Beryl Weston's Ambition: The Story of an African American Girl's Life* (1893) and *Clancy Street* (1898–99), were serialized in the *A.M.E. Church Review.* In 1902, Tillman released her first and only collection of poetry, *Recitations,* published by the A.M.E. Book Concern, who also published her three plays, *Aunt Betsy's Thanksgiving* (date unknown), *Thirty Years of Freedom* (1902), and *Fifty Years of Freedom, or From Cabin to Congress* (1910). Although the date of Tillman's death is unknown, it is likely that she lived at least until 1922, when her last written work, a play titled *The Spirit of Allen: A Pageant of African Methodism,* was published. The following selections first appeared in *The Christian Recorder Magazine.*

THE NEWSBOY

Through the streets the newsboy goes
With a waggish smile for well he knows,
That merchant, lawyer, preacher and all,
Anxiously wait his cheery call.

The merchant looks for his flaming "ad,"
And hopes he has made his rival mad,

While the lawyer hums a merry tune
As he reads of the weddings to be in June.

The preacher reads of the sermon grand.
Delivered all over our sunny land,
His brave heart catches the hallowed fire,
And he longs his own little flock to inspire.

The laborer searches the paper through,
In quest of news and pictures too,
The paper's the boon of each weary night,
And the newsboy's coming he hails with delight.

Hurray for the newsboy, the pen and the Press,
In all of their traffic, we wish them success.
The newsboy's a king, and his subjects are we,
And our joy at his coming he plainly can see.

1893

AFRO-AMERICAN BOY

Afro-American boy whose face
Africa's sun hath fondly kissed
Though by American prejudice hissed
With her proudest sons take thy rightful place.

Lift to the breeze thy thoughtful brow
Heir of America's lands and schools,
God, above men forever rules
He has a care for such as thou.

Thou art as dear to His great heart
Who cannot be mocked by outward show,
As any soul whom thou dost know
In the busy streets of the world's great mart.

Only be brave and do thy task
Purity of life mayst thou possess,
Thou canst not succeed in life with less
This alone doth thy Father ask.

1897

THE WARRIOR'S LAY

Sometimes like wee tired children
We wish for restful place
To cuddle and rest our worn selves
Ere duties new we face.

But the need of the world is great
And Duty clamors strong
And off we are at work again,
Battling against the wrong.

And the hardest battle we wage
Is the war that's within
Where the soul must wield its armour
Against the hosts of sin.

For no true success in battle
Can come to warriors bold
Until our foes within,
The victor's place they hold.

1897

SOUL VISIONS

Have you ever seen a vision
    In the day or in the night
Of what you might, if you dared to be
    And you shrank back in affright?

And accepted a lower purpose
    Or lived by a weaker thought
And sacrificed your ideals
    For earth-things that you sought?

We call our visions madness
    And cast our ideals away
And are ever less that we should be
    Had we bade our visions stay.

For those who most helped the world
   In its onward march to roll
Have cherished day and night
   The visions of the soul.

                                   1897

THE SUPERANNUATE

Watch him totter down the street,
Haste the dear old man to greet;
From his steps so very slow
And his voice so weak and low
Nature doth to us relate
Leaveth our superannuate!

But yesterday quite in his frame
The foremost preacher of his time,
Warning in love old age and youth
To choose the blessed ways of truth.
How time did all his powers abate
And left him—Superannuate.

But still he loves the Sacred Word,
And often shouts "Praise ye the Lord,"
And bids the younger men go on
And win the prize as he has won.
He is no railer 'gainst his fate,
Though he is superannuated!

Yet when fell first the dreaded word,
His inmost soul within him stirred
To lay his precious life work by,
And like all worn out things to die,
He felt so old, so out of date
To be a superannuate!

And now he's ling' ring by death's stream
Across the wave comes silvery gleams

Of waters still, of pastures green
And forms arrayed in dazzled sheen,
Mansion and crown from him await,
Thrice blessed! Superannuate!

1899

RICHARD THEODORE GREENER (1844–1922)

Richard Theodore Greener was born in Philadelphia, to Mary Ann Le Brune and Richard Wesley Greener, a sailor. Raised in Boston, he attended the Broadway Grammar School in Cambridge, Massachusetts, until the age of twelve. Then, as in the case of so many African Americans of his day, family hardship compelled him to leave school and find full-time employment. It was under the advice of one his employers, Boston-based importer Augustus E. Batchelder, that Greener resumed his education. After completing two years in the preparatory program at Oberlin College, Greener enrolled at Phillips Academy in Andover, Massachusetts. In 1865, after graduating from Andover, he enrolled at Harvard College, where gaps in his preparation compelled him to repeat his freshman year. In 1870, he became the college's first African American graduate. He earned a law degree in 1876, from the University of South Carolina. In 1878, Greener was appointed dean of the Howard University Law School, a position that he held for two years. Greener served for seven years as a representative of the U.S. State Department, first in India and later in Russia. He returned to the United States in 1905, where he became a strong supporter of W. E. B. Du Bois's Niagara Movement and, eventually, a member of the NAACP. Throughout his life, Greener was a consistent advocate for African American rights and freedoms, often through letters and essays submitted to the nation's African American newspapers and magazines. "The White Problem," Greener's incisive critique of individual and institutional racism in the United States, was serialized in three consecutive issues of the *Cleveland Gazette* weekly newspaper, beginning on September 22, 1894.

THE WHITE PROBLEM

If one wishes to observe eccentricity, vagary, platitude, and idiosyncrasy all combined, let him only read the literary effusions of the so called "Caucasian" intellect from Thomas Jefferson's "Notes on Virginia" down to the recent contributions to the Forum, when discussing any phase of the "Negro Problem." Jefferson, fresh from Hume, uttered some platitudes about the two races living together in freedom, treading very cautiously, as is his custom, when not too sure of his premises. Imlay and Abbé Grégoire routed him at once, and, as if to complete the poetic irony, the Negro almanac maker, Benjamin Banneker, who had, from 1792 until 1800, calculated alone the only almanacs printed for Maryland, Delaware, District of Columbia, and Virginia, sent him a copy, with an autograph letter, couched in as choice English as Jefferson ever penned and of equal chirography. Nevertheless, the special Negro hate went on. Nott & Glidden,[1] De Leon,[2] De Bow,[3] alius alii,[4] quoting, rehashing Jefferson, supplementing him with modern discoveries.

A phase of the white problem is seen in the determination, not only to treat the Negro as a member of a child-like race, but the grim determination to keep him a child or a ward. In every advance since emancipation, it has, with true Caucasian gall, been assumed that everything must be done for him, and under no circumstances must he be allowed to do for himself. In religion, in politics, in civil and social life, he must be developed in a pen, staked off from the rest of mankind, and nursed, coddled, fed, and trained by aid of the longest spoons, forks, and rakes obtainable. All along there has been heard the solemn, low refrain of doubt, small hope, and feeble expectation as to the probable survival of this black infant. Indeed, nothing has so weighed upon the average American Christian heart as the precarious health of this infant, whom no one had the heart exactly to kill, were it possible, but whose noiseless and peaceful departure to a better world, would have been hailed with smothered sighs of intense relief.

This feeling obtains North as well as South: scalawag, native, carpet-bagger or sand-hiller, democrat, republican, or independent, seem to think that for some occult reason this infant must not be allowed to grow in any one of the social, religious, or political ways, in which other American citizens grow and develop healthfully for the good of their country. All the traditions seem against the Negro, all the arguments surely were. He was rarely given a real chance, as here, to talk freely for himself, and when such opportunity was afforded, he generally took his cue from his audience, and talked to the jury, and usually with bated breath. When he spoke humbly, apologetically, deprecatingly, he was an intelligent, sensible fellow, a milder form of "good nigger" before the war. Among, the *novi homines*[5] of the Republic it is so self-satisfying to have some one to look down upon and despise, just perhaps; —as you have emerged from the mire yourself, and before, indeed, the evidence of "previous condition" has been thoroughly obliterated.

Wut *is* there lef I'd like to know,
Ef't ain't the difference o' color,
To keep up self-respec' an show
The human natur' of a fullah?
Wut good in bein' white, onless
It's fixed by law, nut lef to guess,
That we are smarter, an' they duller.[6]

Another difficulty of this white problem is the universal belief that somehow the Negro race began its career with President Lincoln's proclamation.
All such novices would do well to look up their old histories, newspapers,
and pamphlets. Next to the Indian, he is probably of the purest racial stock
in the country, and as has been stated, whatever accession has come to him,
has been from the "choicest" blood of the country. He has been thoroughly
identified with it from the beginning. He was the agricultural laborer and
the artisan at the South, the trusted servant and companion; at the North
he took part in all mechanical pursuits, helped build the houses, worked on
the first newspaper, made the first wood cuts, and was the best pressman at
Charleston, Philadelphia, and Boston. In every industrial, social, and political movement, as well as in the different warlike struggles, he has borne an
honorable part, which to profess ignorance of, is not creditable, or, if denied,
shows willful prejudice. He was on the heights of Abraham with Wolfe; in
the French and Indian wars with Braddock; the first martyr of the Revolution
is seen in Trumbull's picture retreating with the patriots from Bunker Hill,
musket in hand; Washington did not disdain to share a blanket with him on
the cold ground at Valley Forge; at the South with Marion and Greene; at the
North with Washington and Gates, with Wayne and Allen. On account of
the injury to the United States through him, the war of 1812 was begun, and
his fertile brain suggested the defence of New Orleans, and, after the battle,
led Andrew Jackson to say in public proclamation:

> I expected much: I knew well how you loved your native country . . . You
> have done much more than I expected . . . The President of the United States
> shall hear how praiseworthy was your conduct in the hour of danger . . . The
> American people, I doubt not, will give you the praise your exploits entitle
> you to. Do we not know how they fought with Lawrence in the Chesapeake,
> and formed more than half of the crew of Old Ironsides, were with Scott
> and Taylor in Mexico, as they were with Grant and Sherman, and Sheridan

and Butler, with Farragut and Foote and Porter, at Port Hudson and Battery Wagner? He who doubts the record can read it from the pen of Negro historians, from Nell or Williams or Wilson, for "of those who perform the deeds. and those who write, many such are praised."

No sneer of race, no assumption of superiority, no incrusted prejudice will ever obscure this record, much less obliterate it, and while it stands, it is the Negro's passport to every right and privilege of every other American.

Not alone a soldier and a sailor, the Negro was a citizen, under colonial and proprietary governments, under the Articles of Confederation,[7] and in most of the original thirteen states, was an honorable part of "we people," who ordained and established this constitution for the United States of America. Long before Calhoun and Taney,[8] he fought, lived, voted, and acted like any other citizen; and if many of his race were enslaved, he was not alone. There were "free willers," "indentured servants," and "apprentices," many of them to bear him company. Not a few of these, as records show, white men, Irishmen, Scotchmen, Englishmen, Moors, Palatines, were ruthlessly sold into slavery as the exactions of the traffic became more pressing. At the earliest period there was always a class of black freemen, and they were found at the South as well as at the North—at New Orleans, Mobile, Charleston, and Virginia, as well as at Washington, Baltimore, Philadelphia, New York" and Boston, where in business, in social life, in church and in politics, they were active, enterprising, and respected. In rare instances, with acquired wealth, like some "free willers," and "indentured servants," they went West or North, as the case might be, and mingled and blended into the new surroundings and developed civilization, where, but for names and traditions, all traces of them would be lost. There come to mind, of such men, three United States senators of distinction, at least ten representatives in Congress before the war, five eminent officers of the United States Army, two cabinet officers, three eminent Catholic prelates, four prominent divines of the Episcopal Church, while in the other churches, in medicine and in law, the list is too long for enumeration.

But of those who were content to remain chafing under the indignities and ostracism, which increased from 1820, it is time it should be clearly, emphatically and proudly stated that instead of being a pauper pariah class, as is supposed, there was no movement looking to the amelioration of their condition, from 1808 until John Brown's raid in 1859—nothing which tended to unshackle the slave or remove the clogs from the free colored man, in which he was not the foremost, active, intelligent participant, never a suppliant, never a mere recipient. On the contrary, he was first to organize for his own emancipation; among the first to speak, and write, and print in his own behalf. From Benezet and Gregoire, Condorcet, Brissat de Warville;[9] from Franklin, Rush and Rittenhouse,[10] and more than all, from that "glorious communion of the saints," the Friends, he had early learned the value of his own manhood, was willing to fight for it, and acquired the art of putting his complaint into pretty choice English, at a time, too, when Abbé Raynal, 1779, thought it a matter of astonishment that America had not a good poet, an able mathematician, or a man of genius, in any single art or science, and "not one of them shows any decisive talent for one in particular."[11]

When Fisher Ames was saying, 1807, "Excepting the authors of two able books on our politics, we have no authors; shall we match Joel Barlow against Homer or Hesiod? Can Tom Paine contend against Plato?" When Sydney Smith, 1818, wrote, "There does not seem to be in America, at this moment, one man of any considerable talent," a Negro astronomer[12] was calculating logarithms, studying all alone, in the woods of Maryland, Ferguson's Astronomy, making valuable observations, viewing the stars, and computing his almanacs. During this period, 1780–1810, the Negro had his churches, literary societies, abolition societies, and, later on, newspapers, with educated editors, and active agents for the assertion of their rights and privileges, before Lundy and Garrison.

Mr. Howell looks up the streets of "Nigger Hill," Boston and sees only a few straggling Negroes. They are of no interest, and of course have "no story, bless you, to tell." And yet there are many stories, many traditions, much history clustering about that hill, from Cambridge Street to the Common, from Charles to Hancock. Big Dick, the boxer, the precursor of Jackson;[13] the Blind Preacher, Raymond, Prince Hall, and Easton, Master Paul and his church and school,[14] in which the first American anti-slavery society was organized, Jan. 6, 1832.[15]

"On that dismal night, and in the face of public opinion, fiercer far than the tempest, or wind and hail that beat upon the windows of that 'nigger school-house' were laid the foundations of an organized movement against American slavery that at last became too mighty to be resisted."[16] Mr. Garrison might have told Mr. Howells, he certainly could have learned that among colored men of that dear old town, the first patrons of "The Liberator" were found who supported it the first year, when it had not fifty white subscribers. Mr. Garrison, at Exeter Hall in London, sixty years ago said;

I am proud to say that the funds for my mission . . . were principally made up by the voluntary contributions of my free colored brethren at very short notice . . . Many of their number are in the most affluent circumstances, and distinguished for their refinement, enterprise, and talents . . . They have flourishing churches, temperance and other societies . . . Among them is taken a large number of daily and weekly papers, and of literary and scientific periodicals, from the popular monthlies up to the grave and erudite North American and American Quarterly Reviews. I have, at this moment, to my own paper, 'The Liberator,' one thousand subscribers among this people; and from an occupancy of the editorial chair of more than seven years, I can testify that they are more punctual in their payments than any five hundred white subscribers whose names I ever placed indiscriminately in my subscription book.

Not alone William Lloyd Garrison. Long before Frederick Douglass began "to pray with his legs" and look toward the "north star," the leading colored men of Washington, Carey, and Fleet, and Cook; of Philadelphia, Forten, Allen, Burr, and Purvis; of Baltimore, Grice, Greener, and Watkins; of Boston, Paul, Easton, Barbadoes, and Walker corresponded with, aided, lodged and fed the apostle Lundy in his mysterious journeyings through the southern states, and circulated his Genius of Universal Emancipation.

My account is from Isaac Carey,[17] who knew "the little, pale, thin man," and he says Lundy never departed empty handed.

It was in Master Paul's Church, Belknap Street, that the abolitionists, driven from Tremont Temple, in 1860,[18] found refuge, and preserved there free speech for Boston and America. Master Paul himself was a college graduate, accompanied Mr. Garrison to England, and won praise from Daniel O'Connell for his scholarship and eloquence.

Before emancipation in New York State, Freedom's Journal, edited by Cornish and Russwurm, a graduate of Bowdoin, I am told, afterwards President of Liberia demonstrated the public spirit, intelligence, and literary character of the American Negro. If David Walker's Appeal, issued in 1829, had been printed in 1765 or '70, and had been about the rights of the colonies, it would long since have attracted attention. But it was written by one of the "old clo' merchants" of Brattle Street—an extinct guild—and is the voice of a black John the Baptist, crying in the wilderness. It attained the honor of legislative attention, and a reward set for the author's head; but it is an American classic, and forever answers all hints at Negro contentment under oppression. By law of heredity, thanks to Governor Butler, Walker's son became a lawyer and a municipal judge in Boston.

These facts taken at random would tend to show that the American Negro has tradition—far more, and more honorable than many of his traducers; they are of services, ancestry, interests in public affairs in his own future. Now traditions of blood and training and achievement can never be permanently repressed. Pile Etna upon them, they will break forth, no matter how long or persistently kept down. As a help to the solution of the White Problem, this article is to show that they exist, and if they have not hitherto asserted themselves, it is because they could afford to wait, not because they are not cherished and kept for inspiration. Some complacent critics of the Negro, who analyze, weigh, measure him with their little poles, discuss his removal to Africa, debate his admission to trade unions, into the ranks of business, into the literary circle, into social life, would save themselves much unrest if they knew his motto, *J'y suis, j'y reste*.[19]

He is a reader of the Census. He calmly contemplates either horn of the politico-economic problem—absorption, all he asks to be is an actual American citizen; repression and fifty years of race isolation,—one of the ruling force of this Republic, the arbiter of the South. For, in fifty years, he will be nearly 100,000,000 strong, and, judging solely by the advance since 1863, in thrift, in education, in race development, in equipoise, in aspiration, all that tend to consolidate and strengthen, he will have no fear of the few white chips which will here and there attempt to stem the rush of this black Niagara. Truly he can afford to wait. One of the worst phases of the White Problem is the fatuous clinging to certain ideas, especially the good done to the Negro by bringing him to America. As well tell the descendants of Virginia convicts, the progeny of the kidnapped Irish, 1645–52; the proud descendants of Dutch, Scotch and English poor-houses, shambles and heaths, of the benefits which have accrued to them.

For the presence of all these, the Negro included, America is the gainer, humanity the debtor. The value of his contribution far out-weighs any benefit he may be supposed to have received. He has reaped down the fields, developed new ideas, preserved the ark of the Nation's inheritance, and, if Fletcher of Saltoun, and Dr. Dvořák[20] have any weight, he is to become greater than the lawgiver, he is to found the American music of the future.

> The future music of this country must be founded upon what are called Negro melodies . . . They are American. They are the folk songs of America, and your composers must turn to them. . . . In the Negro melodies of America, I discover all that is needed for a great and noble school of music. There

is nothing in the whole range of composition that cannot find a thematic source here.—Dvořák[21]

The Negro has no tears to shed over that "wonderful school of slavery, under Providence,"[22] so often quoted. He is no such hypocrite as to go through the pretense of believing that slavery is ever a good, a necessary, or beneficial school. Much less does he grant that any phase of that school, at any stage, affected him morally, socially, or physically, except adversely, while he does, know from bitter experience how utterly pharisaical, how absurdly hypocritical, and how thoroughly unchristian the entire system was in practice, example, and influence.

Whatever of intelligence, Christianity, or civilization the Negro possesses today, let it be remembered he retains in spite of slavery, and its relic, caste. Whatever of honesty or morality or thrift has survived the charnel-house, comes from that excellent stock—better than the Indian—which Galton says is now farther behind the best English brain of today than it is behind the brain of Athens! It is due to a brain that slavery could not disintegrate, to a happy heart, an abiding faith.

I am at loss to observe how close the race maintains its hold on orthodox Christianity, when it is remembered how even maxims of the common law were set aside, at its behests—partus sequitur patiem—how Virginia (Hening, v.II, 491) declared that those imported thither, "except Turks and Moors in amity," shall be accounted slaves, "not withstanding a conversion to Christianity after their importation." How far from solution seems the white problem, when the Negro reflects how powerless is Christianity even to repress race prejudice; how often indifferent to real brotherhood, while affecting deep denominational interest. Indeed, while an emasculated religion has been preached to the Negro, each denomination has seemed to shirk the main question of, "Who is my Neighbor?" A premium has been offered every self-respecting Negro to repudiate Christianity as it is taught. Why speak of the Christian? Take the cultured editor, W.H. Page (a North Carolinian) in the Forum, the moulder of public opinion. How despairing the "white problem," when this is the high water mark of culture.

Consider him at his best. I cite the case of a manly and accomplished gentleman of the race. His life has no background. What we mean by ancestry is lacking to him; and not only is it lacking, but its lack is proclaimed by his color, and he is always reminded of it. Be who he may and do what he may, when the personal test comes he finds himself a man set apart, a marked man. There is a difference between the discrimination against him in one part of the country (the South) and in another part (the North), but it is a difference in degree only. He is not any where in a fellowship in complete equipoise with men of the other race. Nor does this end it. The boundless sweep of opportunity which is the inheritance of every white citizen of the Republic, falls to him curtailed, hemmed in, a mere pathway to a few permissible endeavors. A sublime reliance on the ultimate coming of justice may give him the philosophic temper. But his life will bring chiefly opportunities to cultivate it. And for his children what better? To those that solve great social problems with professional ease, I commend this remark that Mr. Lowell is said to have made: 'I am glad I was not born a Jew; but if I had been a Jew, I should be prouder of that fact than any other.' You can find men who are glad that they were not born Negroes; but can you find a man who, if he had been born a Negro, would be prouder of that fact than of any other? When you have found many men of this mind, then this race problem will, owing to some change in human nature, have become less tough, but till then, patience and tolerance.[23]

Here is a paragraph which most people will acquiesce in; which bears the air of hard sense, stern reality, deep philosophic insight, keen analysis and delicate humor. It is already winging its way, and will be quoted as solid fact. If it were true then Schopenhauer reigns in America; religion and culture have failed to soften the manners but have hardened and intensified the small prejudices of two centuries ago. If the statements were true, acquiescence in such condition would show the utmost callousness, a more than heathen indifference, a heartlessness, and inhumanity, unworthy of the century. If character, reputation, manly accomplishments, the heights reached, the palm won, still find any black hero a "marked man," because of no fault of his own, and church and society, home and club, united in thus ostracising him and his children, then is it not demonstrated that it is not the Black but the White Problem, which needs most serious attention in this country?

Mr. Lowell,[24] as always, was wisely terse. No trace of the snob was in him; he was no panderer to caste. Of course he was not anxious to be born a Jew, for he knew unreasoning and unreasonable pride of race still pecked often at its superior; but Lowell, knowing the history of the race, and what its sons had accomplished in spite of persecution, felt he "would be prouder of that fact if he were a Jew than any other." Nor is it true that every social avenue is closed to the aspiring and manly Negro of today. Professor Washington, of Tuskegee, the leader in perhaps the greatest work of the race, is received among the best people of Boston, Philadelphia, and New York. The late Professor Price[25] of North Carolina, was the recipient of exceptional attention at home and abroad, on account of his talents and rare eloquence. Professor Scarborough,[26] the best Greek scholar of the race, meets the members of the American Philological Association on terms of equality, and Mr. Du Bois,[27] who won a travelling scholarship at Harvard, read a paper before the American Historical Society, and has been offered a professorship in a white college. It is surely no unusual thing in New York City to see educated colored men, at various social functions, collegiate, theological, political, literary, professional. These are sporadic cases, of course; but so are the cases of the bright farmer boys from Vermont, North Carolina, Michigan, Connecticut, and New York State, who have, by virtue of study or talent, gained entree to the same salons. The fact springs from the new ozone of equality, or better liberality, which is in the air, and is prompted and encouraged by those who have a clear notion of the fitness of things. Here at least, it is not a race, nor color, nor creed line.

Against that flippancy which draws too hasty conclusions, which cannot conquer its early prejudices, or ignore its limitations, there looms up a quiet unobtrusive but persistent force, which is determined not to give way to caste distinctions; but to see to it that there is a career open to all, despite sex, or creed, or race, in order that no atom of intellectual force shall be lost to our common country, and it is this which tends to the solution of our problem. Once in a while the great utterance of some broad-souled, warm-hearted American, determined to give his testimony, comes to us. Bishop Potter, broader than his entire church, says tersely, "What the Negro needs more than anything else is, opportunity." Or, it is Cable: "I must repeat my conviction that if the unconscious habit of oppression were not already there, a scheme so gross, irrational, unjust and inefficient as our present caste distinctions could not find a place among a people so generally intelligent and high-minded . . . We hear much about race instinct. The most of it, I fear, is pure twaddle. It may be there is such a thing. We do not know. It is not proved. And even if it were established, it would not necessarily be a proper moral guide."

Then, it is Bishop Dudley, bravely fighting his way through traditions: "The time may come and will, when the prejudices now apparently invincible shall have been conquered. Society then as now organized upon the basis of community of interests, congeniality of tastes, and equality of position, will exclude the multitude who cannot speak its shibboleth; but there will be no color line of separation . . . Such a social revolution as will open wide the drawing-rooms of Washington to the black men who have been honored guests in the palaces of England and France. . . . Capacity is not lacking, but help is needed, the help, I repeat, which the intelligence of the superior race must give by careful selection and personal contact with the selected. Does not our mother Nature teach us that this is the only process offering prospect of success, such being her method of procedure, working under the Creator's law?"[28]

Not on the Protestant side alone. Here this clearer blast from the leader of the Catholic cause in the Northwest, Archbishop Ireland of Minnesota: "The right way. There is a work for us. Slavery has been abolished in America; the trail of the serpent, however, yet marks the ground. We do not accord to our black brother all the rights and privileges of freedom and of a common humanity. They are the victims of an unreasonable and unjustifiable ostracism. . . . It looks as if we had grudgingly granted to them emancipation, as if we fain still would be masters, and hold them in servitude.

"What do I claim for the black men? That which I claim for the white men, neither more nor less. I would blot out the color line. White men have their estrangements. They separate on lines of wealth, of intelligence, of culture, of ancestry. Those differences and estrangements I do not now discuss, and will not complain if the barriers they erect are placed on the pathway of the black man. But let there be no barrier against mere color. Treat Negroes who are intellectually inferior to us as we treat inferior whites, and I shall not complain. The Negro problem is upon us, and there is no other solution to it, peaceful and permanent, than to grant to our colored citizens practical and effective equality with white citizens." Here are men whose words shed some rays of light upon the solution of this terrible White Problem, which I may lay some slight claim to the distinction of having discovered, though it would be presumptuous for me to say the solution is clear to me. If it could properly be stated, perhaps, Edmund Burke's *"timid prudence with which a tame circumspection so frequently enervates the work of beneficence,"* and of all things being "afraid of being too much in the right," might be found its salient point on the positive side, while, as I have hinted, the absolute ignorance about the Negro presents the negative side.

> Slaves of Gold! whose sordid dealings
> Tarnish all your boasted powers,
> Prove that you have human feelings
> Ere you proudly question ours.[29]

We earn from the *Forum* editor that there are members of this race who are "accomplished"—and "manly." He is mistaken in supposing they have "no background;" some of them have several, three generations of education, sufficient, according to Emerson, to make a scholar. Some have proved their capacity, not in contests with Negroes alone, but with representatives of all races; some have, it is true, from training and heredity, the philosophic temperament. Like Hebrews, who look not back to Jerusalem, or await a Messiah; like Irishmen, who do not dream alone of a resuscitated Irish monarchy, or see visions of an Irish Parliament at Dublin, they are painfully aware what disadvantages still hedge the members of any proscribed race, in ordinary pursuits, and in daily life; but they see no reason because of this, why they should feel ashamed of the fact, seek to deny it, or attempt to ignore it. They feel that they are first of all American citizens, and secondarily Negroes. From their reading, observation, and reflection, they are not sure but that the very fact of their origin may have been the means, under God's guidance of the Universe, of saving them from illiberal prejudices, from over-weening race-pride, from utter disregard of other races' rights, feelings and privileges, and from intellectual narrowness and bigotry.

1894

NOTES

1. Josiah Clark Nott and George Robert Glidden, coauthors of the 1854 *Types of Mankind*, which posits separate evolutionary paths for white Europeans and people of African descent.

2. Edwin De Leon (1818–1891), proslavery journalist and author of the Civil War-era pamphlet *The Truth about the Confederate States of America*, a defense of slavery and secession.

3. James Dunwoody Brownson De Bow (1820–1867), publisher of the proslavery and secessionist monthly, *De Bow's Review*.

4. A Latin term meaning "one to the other."

5. A Latin term meaning "new man."

6. From "Hosea on Reconstruction" by American Romantic poet James Russell Lowell (1819–1891).

7. A preliminary constitution establishing the United States as a union of thirteen independent states, adopted in 1777.

8. Roger Brook Taney (1777–1864), the fifth chief justice of the U.S. Supreme Court, under whose leadership the court ruled in favor of slaveholder John F. A. Sanford in the infamous Dred Scott decision.

9. In 1788, only thirteen years after French-born American abolitionist Anthony Benezet founded the Society for the Relief of Free Negroes Unlawfully Held in Bondage,

Parisian activists Henri Abbé Grégoire (1750–1831) and Marquis de Condorcet (1743–1794) helped establish the Société des Amis des Noirs (Society of the Friends of the Blacks), with Jacques Pierre Brissot (de Warville) as the group leader.

10. Benjamin Franklin (1706–1790), Benjamin Rush (1746–1813), and David Rittenhouse (1732–1796), prominent scholars, antislavery advocates, and lifelong residents of Philadelphia.

11. From *A Philosophical and Political History of the Settlements and Trade of the Europeans in the East and West Indies, Vol. III,* one of the most widely read antislavery books of the age, by French cleric and historian Abbé Guillaume-Thomas-François Raynal (1711–1796).

12. African American astronomer and mathematician Benjamin Banneker (1731–1806).

13. African American boxer and boxing school owner Richard Crafus (possibly Cephas or Seaver), born in the late eighteenth century in the United States or Haiti, known throughout the Boston area and beyond for his size, skill, and strength in boxing and other combat sports, described here as the predecessor of Peter Jackson, popular African American boxing champion of the late nineteenth century.

14. Thomas Paul (1773–1831), the founding minister of the First African Meeting House, home of the Boston's first school for black children.

15. Greener erroneously names the New England Anti-Slavery Society as the first abolitionist organization in the United States. This organization, founded at a gathering of prominent white abolitionists in the basement of the First African Meeting House, was, in fact, preceded by a number of other antislavery organizations, beginning as early as the 1770s.

16. From *William Lloyd Garrison and His Times, Or, Sketches of the Anti-slavery Movement in America* (1881) by Oliver Johnson (1809–1889), a cofounder (with Garrison) of the New England Anti-Slavery Society, and editor and staff member for several abolitionist papers, including Garrison's *The Liberator.*

17. Rev. Isaac Eddy Carey, a Presbyterian minister from Freeport, Illinois, whose June 1, 1865, sermon, "Abraham Lincoln: The Value to the Nation of His Exalted Character," was widely distributed in pamphlet form.

18. On December 3, 1860, a mob of proslavery agitators overwhelmed and expelled a crowd of black and white abolitionists gathered at Boston's Tremont Temple to hear Frederick Douglass's address on the first anniversary of the execution of antislavery activist John Brown.

19. A French expression meaning "here I am, here I stay."

20. Refers to Scottish writer and statesman Andrew Fletcher of Saltoun (1655–1716), to whom is attributed the observation, "I knew a very wise man that believed that, if a man were permitted to make all the ballads he need not care who should make the laws of a nation"; and noted composer Antonín Leopold Dvořák (1841–1904), who openly espoused the superiority of African American music over that of other U.S. traditions.

21. As quoted in "Dvořák on Negro Music," in the July 1893 issue of the Boston-based *Musical Record* monthly. The issue also includes the article "An African-American School of Music," reprinted from the *London Music News* and consisting of a detailed consideration of the implications of Dvořák's assertions.

22. The most widely recognized promoter of this view was the African American author and educator Booker T. Washington, founder of the Tuskegee Institute in Alabama.

23. From "The Last Hold of the Southern Bully," by Walter Hines Pages, in *Forum Magazine,* November 1893.

24. Poet James Russell Lowell.

25. Joseph C. Price (1854–1893), founding president of Livingstone College, in Salisbury, North Carolina.

26. William S. Scarborough (1852–1926), professor of Latin and Greek and later president of Wilberforce University, in Xenia, Ohio.

27. William Edward Burghardt Du Bois (1868–1963), the first African American to earn a PhD at Harvard University (in 1895) and one of the first African Americans to teach at the University of Pennsylvania.

28. Thomas Dudley Underwood (1837–1904), Episcopal Bishop of the State of Kentucky and Confederate veteran of the Civil War, in "How Shall We Help the Negro," an essay that appeared in *The Century Illustrated Monthly Magazine* in June of 1885.

29. From "The Negro's Complaint" (1835), a poem by African American abolitionist and orator Maria Stewart (1803–1880).

VICTORIA EARLE MATTHEWS (1861-1907)

Victoria Earle Matthews was born in Fort Valley, Georgia. Her mother, Caroline Smith, was enslaved. Her father, William Smith, is believed to have been her mother's owner. During the Civil War, Matthews' mother escaped to the North. In 1873, she returned to Georgia to reclaim her children, and thus reunited, the family settled in New York City. There Matthews briefly attended Grammar School 48, until financial constraints compelled her to leave. Largely self-taught, Matthews made use of the resources available to educate herself in literature, history, and social thought. Working as a household servant, she attended free lectures and symposia throughout the city and made avid use of the libraries of her employers. By the 1880s, she was publishing articles and opinion pieces in mainstream newspapers like the *New York Times,* the *Herald,* and the *Sunday Mercury,* as well as several prominent African American papers, including the *Boston Advocate* and the *New York Globe.* Matthews also produced several pieces of fiction, for young readers as well as adults. In 1898, she edited and published *Black Belt Diamonds,* a collection of speeches by Booker T. Washington. An activist as well as a writer, Matthews was not only a founding member of the Women's Loyal Union of New York and Brooklyn, but also its first president. A noted speaker on a range of social justice issues, Matthews is best known to twenty-first-century readers for her landmark speech, "The Value of Race Literature," in which she became one of the earliest African American thinkers to call for the preservation of any and all written evidence of African American literary and intellectual achievement. Matthews delivered this address in 1895, at the First Congress of Colored Women, held in Boston.

THE VALUE OF RACE LITERATURE: AN ADDRESS DELIVERED AT THE FIRST CONGRESS OF COLORED WOMEN OF THE UNITED STATES

By race literature, we mean ordinarily all the writings emanating from a distinct class—not necessarily race matter; but a general collection of what has been written by the men and women of that Race: History, Biographies,

Scientific Treatises, Sermons, Addresses, Novels, Poems, Books of Travel, miscellaneous essays and the contributions to magazines and newspapers.

Literature, according to Webster, is learning; acquaintance with books or letters: the collective body of literary productions, embracing the entire results of knowledge and fancy, preserved in writing, *also the whole body of literature,* productions or writings upon any given subject, or in reference to a particular science, a branch of knowledge, as the Literature of Biblical Customs, the Literature of Chemistry, Etc.

In the light of this definition, many persons may object to the term, Race Literature, questioning seriously the need, doubting if there be any, or indeed whether there can be a Race Literature in a country like ours apart from the general American Literature. Others may question the correctness of the term American Literature, since our civilization in its essential features is a reproduction of all that is most desirable in the civilizations of the Old World. English being the language of America, they argue in favor of the general term, English Literature.

While I have great respect for the projectors of this theory, yet it is a limited definition; it does not express the idea in terms sufficiently clear.

The conditions which govern the people of African descent in the United States have been and still are, such as create a very marked difference in the limitations, characteristics, aspirations and ambitions of this class of people, in decidedly strong contrast with the more or less powerful races which dominate it.

Laws were enacted denying and restricting their mental development in such pursuits, which engendered servility and begot ox-like endurance; and though statutes were carefully, painstakingly prepared by the most advanced and learned American jurists to perpetuate ignorance, yet they were powerless to keep all the race out from the Temple of Learning. Many though in chains mastered the common rudiments and others possessing talent of higher order—like the gifted Phyllis Wheatley, who dared to express her meditations in poetic elegance which won recognition in England and America, from persons distinguished in letters and statesmanship—dared to seek the sources of knowledge and wield a pen.

While oppressive legislation, aided by grossly inhuman customs, successfully retarded all general efforts toward improvement, the race suffered physically and mentally under a great wrong, an appalling evil, in contrast with which the religious caste prejudice of India appears as a glimmering torch to a vast consuming flame.

The prejudice of color! Not condition, not character, not capacity for artistic development, not the possibility of emerging from savagery into Christianity, not these, but the "Prejudice of Color." Washington Irving's *Life of Columbus* contains a translation from the contemporaries of Las Casas,[1] in which this prejudice is plainly evident. Since our reception on this continent, men have cried out against this inhuman prejudice; granting that, a man may improve his condition, accumulate wealth, become wise and upright, merciful and just as an infidel or Christian, but they despair because he cannot change his color, as if it were possible for the victim to change his organic structure, and impossible for the oppressor to change his wicked heart.

But all this impious wrong has made a Race Literature a possibility, even a necessity to dissipate the odium conjured up by the term "colored" persons, not originally perhaps designed to humiliate, but unfortunately still used to express not only an inferior order, but to accentuate and call unfavorable attention to the most ineradicable difference between the races.

So well was this understood and deplored by liberal minded men, regardless of affiliation, that the editor of *"Freedom's Journal,"* published in New York City in 1827, the first paper published in this country by Americans of African descent, calls special attention to this prejudice by quoting from the great Clarkson, where he speaks of a master not only looking with disdain upon a slave's features, but hating his very color.

The effect of this unchristian disposition was like the merciless scalpel about the very heart of the people, a sword of Damocles, at all times hanging above and threatening all that makes life worth living. Why they should not develop and transmit stealthy, vicious and barbaric natures under such conditions, is a question that able metaphysicians, ethnologists and scientists will, most probably in the future, investigate with a view of solving what to-day is considered in all quarters a profound mystery, the Negro's many-sided, happy, hopeful, enduring character.

Future investigations may lead to the discovery of what to-day seems lacking, what has deformed the manhood and womanhood in the Negro. What is bright, hopeful and encouraging is in reality the source of an original school of race literature, of racial psychology, of potent possibilities, an amalgam needed for this great American race of the future.

Dr. Dvorak claims this for the original Negro melodies of the South, as every student of music is well aware. On this subject he says,

> I am now satisfied that the future music of this continent must be founded
> upon what are called the Negro melodies. This can be the foundation of a

serious and original school of composition to be developed in the United States.

When I first came here, I was impressed with this idea, and it has developed into a settled conviction. The beautiful and varied themes are the product of the soil. *They are American, they are the folk songs of America, and our composers must turn to them.* All of the great musicians have borrowed from the songs of the common people.

Beethoven's most charming *scherzo* is based upon what might now be considered a skillfully handled Negro melody. I have myself gone to the simple half-forgotten tunes of the Bohemian peasants for hints in my most serious work. Only in this way can a musician express the true sentiment of a people. He gets into touch with common humanity of the country.

In the Negro melodies of America I discover all that is needed for a great and noble school of music. They are pathetic, tender, passionate and melancholy, solemn, religious, bold, merry, gay, gracious, or what you will. It is music that suits itself to any work or any purpose. There is nothing in the whole range of composition that cannot find a thematic source here.

When the literature of our race is developed, it will of necessity be different in all essential points of greatness, true heroism and real Christianity from what we may at the present time, for convenience, call American Literature. When some master hand writes the stories as Dr. Dvorak has caught the melodies, when, amid the hearts of the people, there shall live a George Eliot, moving this human world by the simple portrayal of the scenes of our ordinary existence; or when the pure, ennobling touch of a black Hannah More shall rightly interpret our unappreciated contribution to Christianity and make it into universal literature, such writers will attain and hold imperishable fame.

The novelists most read at the present time in this country find a remunerative source for their doubtful literary productions based upon the wrongly interpreted and too often grossly exaggerated frailties. This is patent to all intelligent people. The Negro need not envy such reputation, nor feel lost at not reveling in its ill-gotten wealth or repute. We are the only people most distinctive from those who have civilized and governed this country, who have become typical Americans, and we rank next to the Indians in originality of soil, and yet remain a distinct people.

In this connection, Joseph Wilson, in the "Black Phalanx," says: "The Negro race is the only race that has ever come in contact with the European race that has proved itself able to withstand its atrocities and oppression. All others like the Indians whom they could not make subservient to their use they have destroyed."

Prof. Sampson in his "Mixed Races" says, "The American Negro is a new race, and is not the direct descent of any people that has ever flourished."[2]

On this supposition, and relying upon finely developed, native imaginative powers, and humane tendencies, I base my expectation that our Race Literature when developed will not only compare favorably with many, but will stand out preeminent, not only in the limited history of colored people, but in the broader field of universal literature.

Though Race Literature be founded upon the traditionary history of a people, yet its fullest and largest development ought not to be circumscribed by the narrow limits of race or creed, for the simple reason that literature in its loftiest development reaches out to the utmost limits of soul enlargement and outstrips all earthly limitations. Our history and individuality as a people not only provides material for masterly treatment; but would seem to make a Race Literature a necessity as an outlet for the unnaturally suppressed inner lives which our people have been compelled to lead.

The literature of any people of varied nationality who have won a place in the literature of the world, presents certain cardinal points. French literature for instance, is said to be "not the wisest, not the weightiest, not certainly the purest and loftiest, but by odds the most brilliant and the most interesting literature in the world."

Ours, when brought out, and we must admit in reverence to truth that, as yet, we have done nothing distinctive, but may when we have built upon our own individuality, win a place by the simplicity of the story, thrown into strong relief by the multiplicity of its dramatic situations; the spirit of romance, and even tragedy, shadowy and as yet ill-defined, but from which our race on this continent can never be disassociated.

When the foundations of such a literature shall have been properly laid, the benefit to be derived will be at once apparent. There will be a revelation to our people, and it will enlarge our scope, make us better known wherever real lasting culture exists, will undermine and utterly drive out the traditional Negro in dialect,—the subordinate, the servant as the type representing a race whose numbers are now far into the millions. It would suggest to the world the wrong and contempt with which the lion viewed the picture that the hunter and a famous painter besides, had drawn of the King of the Forest.

As a matter of history, the only high-type Negro that has been put before the American people by a famous writer is the character Dred founded upon the deeds of Nat Turner, in Mrs. Stowe's novel.

Except the characters sketched by the writers of folk-lore, I know of none more representative of the spirit of the writers of to-day, wherein is infiltrated in the public mind that false sense of the Negro's meaning of inalienable rights, so far as actual practice is concerned, than is found in a story in *"Harper's Magazine"* some years ago. Here a pathetic picture is drawn of a character generally known as the typical "Darkey."

The man, old and decrepit, had labored through long years to pay for an humble cabin and garden patch; in fact, he had paid double and treble the original price, but dashing "Marse Wilyum" quieted his own conscience by believing, so the writer claimed, that the old Darkey should be left free to pay him all he felt the cabin was worth to him. The old man looked up to him, trusted him implicitly, and when he found at last he had been deceived, the moment he acknowledged to himself that "Marse Wilyum" had cheated him, a dejected listlessness settled upon him, an expression weak and vacant came in his dull eyes and hung around his capacious but characterless mouth, an exasperatingly meek smile trembled upon his features, and casting a helpless look around the cabin that he thought his own, nay, knew it was, with dragging steps he left the place! "Why did you not stand out for your rights?" a sympathizing friend questioned some years afterwards. To this the writer makes the old man say:

"Wid white folks dat's de way, but wid niggers it's dif'unt."

Here the reader is left to infer whatever his or her predilection will incline to accept, as to the meaning of the old man's words. The most general view is that the old man had no manhood, not the sense, nothing to even suggest to his inner conscience aught that could awaken a comprehension of the word man, much less its rightful price; no moral responsibility, no spirit or, as the Negro-hating Mark Twain would say, no capacity of kicking at real or imaginary wrongs, which in his estimation makes the superior clan. In a word, there was nothing within the old man's range of understanding to make him feel his inalienable rights.

We know the true analysis of the old man's words was that faith, once destroyed, can never be regained, and the blow to his faith in the individual and the wound to his honest esteem so overwhelming, rendered it out of the question to engage further with a fallen idol.

With one sweep of mind he had seen the utter futility of even hoping for justice from a people who would take advantage of an aged honest man. That is the point, and this reveals a neglected subject for analytical writers to dissect in the interest of truth the real meaning of the so-called cowardice, self-negation and lack of responsibility so freely referred to by those in positions calculated to make lasting impressions on the public, that by custom scoffs at the meaning introduced in Mrs. Stowe's burning words, when she repeated a question before answering;—"What can any individual do?" There is one thing every individual can do. They can see to it that they feel right—an atmosphere of sympathetic influence encircles every human being; and the man or woman who feels strongly, healthily and justly on the great interests of humanity, is a constant benefactor to the human race."

Think of the moral status of the Negro, that Mr. Ridpath in his history degrades before the world.[3] Consider the political outline of the Negro, sketched with extreme care in "Bryce's Commonwealth,"[4] and the diatribes of Mr. Froude.[5] From these, turn to the play, where impressions are made upon a heterogeneous assemblage—Mark Twain's "Pudd'n Head Wilson," which Beaumount Fletcher claims as "among the very best of those productions which gives us hope for a distinctive American drama."

In this story we have education and fair environment attended by the most deplorable results, an educated octoroon is made out to be a most despicable, cowardly villain. "The one compensation for all this," my friend, Professor Greener wittily remarks, "is that the 'white nigger' in the story though actually a pure white man, is indescribably worse in all his characteristics than the 'real nigger,' using the vernacular of the play, was ever known to be, and just here Mark Twain unconsciously avenges the Negro while trying his best to disparage him."

In "Imperative Duty," Mr. Howells laboriously establishes for certain minds, the belief that the Negro possesses an Othello like charm in his ignorance which education and refinement destroys, or at best makes repulsive.[6]

In explaining why Dr. Olney loves Rhoda, whose training was imparted by good taste, refined by wealth, and polished by foreign travel, he says:

> It was the elder world, the beauty of antiquity which appealed to him in the luster and sparkle of this girl, and the *remote taint* of her servile and savage origin, *gave her a fascination* which refuses to let itself be put in words, it was the grace of a limp, the occult, indefinable, lovableness of deformity, but transcending these by its allurements, in indefinite degree, and going for the

reason of its effect deep into the mysterious places of being, where the spirit and animal meet and part in us.

The mood was of his emotional nature alone, it sought and could have won no justification from the moral sense which indeed it simply submerged, and blotted out for all time.

All this tergiversation and labored explanation of how a white man came to love a girl with a remote tinge of Negro blood! But he must have recourse to this tortuous jugglery of words, because one of his characters in the story had taken pains to assert, "That so far as society in the society sense is concerned we have frankly simplified the matter, and no more consort with the Negroes than we do with lower animals, so that one would be quite as likely to meet a cow or a horse in an American drawing-room, as a person of color." This is the height of enlightenment! and from Dean Howells too, litterateur, diplomat, journalist, altruist!

Art, goodness, and beauty are assaulted in order to stimulate or apologize for prejudice against the educated Negro!

In Dr. Huguet, we have as a type a man pitifully trying to be self-conscious, struggling to feel within himself, what prejudice and custom demand that he feel.[7]

In "A Question of Color"[8] the type is a man of splendid English training, that of an English gentleman, surrounded from his birth by wealth, and accepted in the most polished society, married to a white girl, who sells herself for money, and after the ceremony like an angelic Sunday-school child, shudders and admits the truth, that she can never forget that he is a Negro, and he is cad enough to say, so says the writer, that he will say his prayers at her feet night and morning notwithstanding!

We all know, no man, negro or other, ever enacted such a part; it is wholly inconsistent with anything short of a natural-born idiot! And yet a reputable house offers this trash to the public, but thanks to a sensible public, it has been received with jeers. And so stuff like this comes apace, influencing the reading-world, not indeed thinkers and scholars; but the indiscriminate reading world, upon whom rests, unfortunately, the bulk of senseless prejudice.

Conan Doyle, like Howells, also pays his thoughtful attention to the educated negro—making him in this case more bloodthirsty and treacherous and savage than the Seminole. One more, and these are mentioned only to show the kind of types of Negro characters eminent writers have taken exceeding care to place before the world as representing us.

In the "Condition of Women in the United States," Mme. Blanc, in a volume of 285 pages, devotes less than 100 words to negro women; after telling ironically of a "Black Damsel" in New York engaged in teaching Latin, she describes her attire, the arrangement of her hair, and concludes, "I also saw a class of little Negro girls with faces like monkeys studying Greek, and the disgust expressed by their former masters seemed quite justified."

Her knowledge of history is as imperfect so far as veracity goes, as her avowal in the same book of her freedom from prejudice against the Negro. The "little girls" must have been over thirty years old to have had any former masters even at their birth! And all this is the outcome in the nineteenth century of the highest expressions of Anglo-Saxon acumen, criticism and understanding of the powers of Negroes of America!

The point of all this, is the indubitable evidence of the need of thoughtful, well-defined and intelligently placed efforts on our part, to serve as counter-irritants against all such writing that shall stand, having as an aim the supplying of influential and accurate information, on all subjects relating to the Negro and his environments, to inform the American mind at least, for literary purposes.

We cannot afford any more than any other people to be indifferent to the fact that the surest road to real fame is through literature. Who is so well known and appreciated by the cultured minds as Dumas of France, and Pushkin[9] of Russia? I need not say to this thoughtful and intelligent gathering that, any people without a literature is valued lightly the world round. Who knows or can judge of our intrinsic worth, without actual evidences of our breadth of mind, our boundless humanity. Appearing well and weighted with many degrees of titles, will not raise us in our own estimation while color is the white elephant in America. Yet, America is but a patch on the universe: if she ever produces a race out of her cosmopolitan population that can look beyond mere money-getting to more permanent qualities of true greatness as a nation, it will call this age her unbalanced stage.

No one thinks of mere color when looking upon the Chinese, but the dignified character of the literature of his race, and he for monotony of expression, color and undesirable individual habits is far inferior in these points to the ever-varying American Negro. So our people must awaken to the fact, that our task is a conquest for a place for ourselves, and is a legitimate ground for action for us, if we shall resolve to conquer it. While we of to-day view with increasing dissatisfaction the trend of the literary productions of this country, concerning us, yet are we standing squarely on the foundation laid for us by our immediate predecessors?

This is the question I would bring to your minds. Are we adding to the structure planned for us by our pioneers? Do we know our dwelling and those who under many hardships, at least, gathered the material for its upbuilding? Knowing them do we honor—do we love them—what have they done that we should love? Your own Emerson says—"To judge the production of a people you must transplant the spirit of the times in which they lived."

In the ten volumes of American Literature edited by H. L. Stoddard only Phyllis Wheatley and George W. Williams[10] find a place. This does not show that we have done nothing in literature; far from it, but it does show that we have done nothing so brilliant, so effective, so startling as to attract the attention of these editors. Now it is a fact that thoughtful, scholarly white people do not look for literature in its highest sense from us any more than they look for high scholarship, profound and critical learning on any one point, nor for any eminent judicial acumen or profound insight into causes and effects.

These are properly regarded as the results only of matured intellectual growth or abundant leisure and opportunity, when united with exceptional talents, and this is the world's view, and it is in the main a correct one. Even the instances of precocious geniuses and the rare examples of extraordinary talent appearing from humble and unpromising parentage and unfortuitous surroundings, are always recognized as brilliant, sporadic cases, exceptions.

Consequently our success in Race Literature will be looked upon with curiosity and only a series of projected enterprises in various directions—history, poetry, novel writing, speeches, orations, forensic effort, sermons, and so on, will have the result of gaining for us recognition.

You recall Poteghine's remark in Turgenev's novel of "Smoke." How well it applies to us.

> For heaven's sake do not spread the idea in Russia that we can achieve success without preparation. No, if your brow be seven spans in width study, begin with the alphabet or else remain quiet and say nothing. Oh! it excites me to think of these things.

Dr. Blyden's essays, Dr. Crummell's sermons and addresses, and Professor Greener's orations, all are high specimens of sustained English, good enough for any one to read, and able to bear critical examination, and reflect the highest credit on the race.

Your good city of Boston deserves well for having given us our first real historian, William C. Nell—his history of "The Colored Patriots of the Revolution"—not sufficiently read nowadays or appreciated by the present generation; a scholarly, able, accurate book, second to none written by any other colored man.

William Wells Brown's "Black Man" was a worthy tribute in its day, the precursor of more elaborate books, and should be carefully studied now; his "Sights and Scenes Abroad" was probably the first book of travel written by an American Negro. The same is doubtless true of his novel, "Clotilde."[11] The "Anglo-African" magazine published in New York City in 1859, is adjudged by competent authority to be the highest, best, most scholarly written of all the literature published by us in fifty years.

We have but to read the graphic descriptions and eloquent passages in the first edition of the "Life and Times" of Frederick Douglass to see the high literary qualities of which the race is capable. "Light and Truth," a valuable volume published many years ago; Dr. Perry's "Cushite!"[12] "Bond and Free, or Under the Yoke," by John S. Ladue;[13] "The Life of William Lloyd Garrison," by Archibald Grimké;[14] Joseph Wilson's "Black Phalanx," and "Men of Mark," by Rev. W. J. Simmons; "Noted Women," by Dr. Scruggs;[15] "The Negro Press and Its Editors," by I. Garland Penn; "Paul Dunbar's Dialect Poems," which have lately received high praise from the Hoosier Poet James Whitcomb Reilly, "Johnson's School History;" "From a Virginia Cabin to the Capitol," by Hon. J. M. Langston; "Iola Leroy," by Mrs. F. E. W. Harper; "Music and Some Highly Musical People," by James M. Trotter, are specimen books within easy reach of the public, that will increase in interest with time.

Professor R. T. Greener as a metaphysician, logician, orator, and prize essayist, holds an undisputed position in the annals of our literature second to none. His defense of the Negro in the "National Quarterly Review," 1880, in reply to Mr. Parton's strictures, has been an arsenal from which many have since supplied their armor. It was quoted extensively in this country and England.

And it is not generally known that one of the most valuable contributions to Race Literature, has appeared in the form of a scientific treatise on "Incandescent Lighting" published by Van Nostrand of New York, and thus another tribute is laid to Boston's credit by Lewis H. Latimer.

In the ecclesiastical line we have besides those already mentioned, the writings of the learned Dr. Pennington, Bishops Payne and Tanner of the A.M.E. Church.

The poems, songs and addresses by our veteran literary women F. E. W. Harper, Charlotte Forten Grimké, H. Cordelia Ray, Gertrude Mossell, "Clarence and Corinne," "The Hazeltone Family" by Mrs. G. E. Johnson, and "Appointed" by W. H. Stowers, and W. H. Anderson are a few of the publications on similar subjects; all should be read and placed in our libraries, as first beginnings it is true, but they compare favorably with similar work of the most advanced people.

Our journalism has accomplished more than can now be estimated; in fact not until careful biographers make special studies drawn from the lives of the pioneer journalists, shall we or those contemporary with them ever know the actual meed of good work accomplished by them under almost insurmountable difficulties.

Beginning with the editors of the first newspapers published in this country by colored men, we New Yorkers take pride in the fact that Messrs. Cornish and Russwurm of "Freedom's Journal," New York City, 1827, edited the first paper in this country devoted to the upbuilding of the Negro. Philip A. Bell of the "Weekly Advocate," 1837, was named by contemporaries "the Nestor of African American journalists." The gifted Dr. James McCune Smith was associated with him. The "Weekly Advocate" later became the "Colored American." And in 1839, on Mr. Bell's retirement Dr. Charles Ray assumed the editorial chair, continued until 1842, making an enviable record for zeal on all matters of race interest. These men were in very truth the Pioneers of Race Journalism.

Their lives and record should be zealously guarded for the future use of our children, for they familiarized the public with the idea of the Negro owning and doing the brain work of a newspaper. The people of other sections became active in establishing journals, which did good work all along the line. Even the superficial mind must accept the modest claim that "These journals proved a powerful lever in diverting public opinion, public sympathy, and public support towards the liberation of the slave."

Papers were edited by such men as Dr. H. H. Garnet, David Ruggles, W. A. Hodges and T. Van Rensselaer, of the "Ram's Horn." In 1847 our beloved and lofty minded Frederick Douglass edited his own paper "The North Star," in the City of Rochester, where his mortal remains now peacefully rest. His paper was noted for its high class matter—and it had the effect of raising the plane of journalism thereafter. About this time Samuel Ringold Ward of the Impartial Citizen, published in Syracuse, N.Y., "forged to the front," winning in after years from Mr. Douglass a most flattering tribute. "Samuel Ringold Ward," the sage of Anacostia once said to the writer, "was one of the smartest men I ever knew if not the smartest."

The prevailing sentiment at that time was sympathy for the ambitious Negro. At a most opportune time, "The Anglo African," the finest effort in the way of a newspaper made by the race up to that time, was established in January of

1859 in New York City, with Thomas Hamilton as editor and proprietor. The columns were opened to the most experienced writers of the day. Martin R. Delaney contributed many important papers on astronomy, among which was one on "Comets," another on "The Attraction of the Planets." George B. Vashon wrote "The Successive Advances of Astronomy," James McCune Smith wrote his comments "On the Fourteenth Query of Thomas Jefferson's Notes on Virginia" and his "German Invasion"—every number contained gems that to-day are beyond price. In these pages also appeared "Afric-American Picture Gallery," by "Ethiope"—Wm. J. Wilson; Robert Gordon's "Personality of the First Cause;" Dr. Pennington on "The Self-Redeeming Power of the Colored Races of the World;" Dr. Blyden on "The Slave Traffic;" and on the current questions of the day, such brave minds as Frederick Douglass, William C. Nell, John Mercer Langston, Theodore Holly, J. Sella Martin, Frances Ellen Watkins, Jane Rustic,[16] Sarah M. Douglass, and Grace A. Mapps! What a galaxy! The result was a genuine race newspaper, one that had the courage to eliminate everything of personal interest, and battle for the rights of the whole people, and while its history, like many other laudable enterprises, may be little known beyond the journalistic fraternity, to such men as Wendell Phillips and William Lloyd Garrison, the paper and staff were well known and appreciated. In those days, the Negro in literature was looked upon as a prodigy; he was encouraged in many ways by white people particularly, as he was useful in serving the cause of philanthropic agitators for the liberation of the slave. The earnest, upright character and thoughtful minds of the early pioneers acted as a standing argument in favor of the cause for which the abolitionists were then bending every nerve when the slave was liberated and the Civil War brought to a close. The spirit of Mr. Lincoln's interview with a committee of colored citizens of the District of Columbia, in August, 1862, as told by William Wells Brown, in which Mr. Lincoln said, "But for your people among us, there would be no war," reacted upon the public, and from that time until the present, a vigorous system of oppression, under the name of natural prejudice, has succeeded immeasurably in retarding our progress.

As a matter of history, we have nothing to compare with the weekly publications of 25 or 30 years ago. The unequal contest waged between Negro journals and their white contemporaries is lost sight of by the people, as only those connected with various publications are aware of the condition and difficulties surrounding the managements of such journals.

Our struggling journalists not only find themselves on the losing side, but as if to add to their thankless labor, they oftentimes receive the contemptuous regard of the people who should enthusiastically rally to their support. The journalist is spurred with the common sense idea that every enterprise undertaken and carried on by members of the race is making a point in history for that entire race, and the historians of the future will not stop to consider our discontented and sentimental whys and wherefores, when they critically examine our race enterprises; but they will simply record their estimate of what the men and women journalists of to-day not only represented, but actually accomplished.

It is so often claimed that colored newspapers do not amount to anything. People even who boast of superior attainments, voice such sentiments with the most ill-placed indifference; the most discreditable phase of race disloyalty imaginable—one that future historians will have no alternative but to censure.

If our newspapers and magazines do not amount to anything, it is because our people do not demand anything of better quality from their own. It is because they strain their purses supporting those white papers that are and always will be independent of any income derived from us. Our contributions to such journals are spasmodic and uncertain, like fluctuating stocks, and are but an excess of surplus. It is hard for the bulk of our people to see this; it is even hard to prove to them that in supporting such journals, published by the dominant class, we often pay for what are not only vehicles of insult to our manhood and womanhood, but we assist in propagating or supporting false impressions of ourselves or our less fortunate brothers.

Our journalistic leader is unquestionably T. Thomas Fortune, Editor of "The New York Age," and a regular contributor of signed articles to the "New York Sun," one of the oldest and ablest daily newspapers in the United States, noted on two continents for its rare excellence.

For many years Mr. Fortune has given his best efforts to the cause of race advancement, and the splendid opportunities now opening to him on the great journals of the day, attest the esteem in which he is held by men who create public opinion in this country.

If John E. Bruce, "Bruce-Grit," "John Mitchell, Jr." W. H. A. Moore, Augustus M. Hodge [sic] "B Square," were members of any other race, they would be famous the country over. Joe Howard or "Bill Nye" have in reality done no more for their respective clientage than these bright minds and corresponding wits have done for theirs.

T. T. Fortune of "The Age," Ida Wells-Barnett of the "Free Speech," and John Mitchell of the "Richmond Planet," have made a nobler fight than the brilliant Parnell in his championship of Ireland's cause, for the reason that the people for whom he battled, better knew and utilized more the strength

obtained only by systematic organization, not so is the case with the constituents of the distinguished journalists I have mentioned.

Depressing as this fact is, it should not deter those who know that Race
Literature should be cultivated for the sake of the formation of habits. First
efforts are always crude, each succeeding one becomes better or should be
so. Each generation by the law of heredity receives the impulse or impression
for good or ill from its predecessors, and since this is the law, we must begin
to form habits of observation and commence to build a plan for posterity by
synthesis, analysis, ourselves aiming and striving after the highest, whether
we attain it or not. Such are the attempts of our journalists of to-day, and
they shall reap if they faint not.

Race Literature does not mean things uttered in praise, thoughtless praise
of ourselves, wherein each goose thinks her gosling a swan. We have had
too much of this, too much that is crude, rude, pompous, and literary nothings, which ought to have been strangled before they were written much
less printed; and this does not only apply to us; for it is safe to say that, only
an infinitesimal percentage of the so-called literature filling the book shelves
today, will survive a half century.

In the words of a distinguished critic, "It is simply amazing how little of
all that is written and printed in these days that makes for literature; how
small a part is permanent, how much purely ephemeral, famous to-day on
account of judicious advertising, forgotten tomorrow. We should clear away
the under-brush of self-deception which makes the novice think because
sentences are strung together and ordinary ideas evolved, dilated upon and
printed, that such trash is literature." If this is claimed for the more favored
class, it should have a tendency with us to encourage our work, even though
the results do not appear at once.

It should serve the student by guarding him against the fulsome praise
of "great men," "great writers," "great lawyers," "great ministers," who in
reality have never done one really great or meritorious thing.

Rather should the student contemplate the success of such as Prof.
Du Bois who won the traveling fellowship at Harvard on metaphysical studies, and has just received his Ph.D., at the last commencement, on account
of his work. For such facts demonstrate that it is the character of the work
we do, rather than the quantity of it, which counts for real Race Literature.

Race Literature does mean though the preserving of all the records of a
Race, and thus cherishing the materials saving from destruction and obliteration what is good, helpful and stimulating. But for our Race Literature,

how will future generations know of the pioneers in Literature, our states-men, soldiers, divines, musicians, artists, lawyers, critics, and scholars? True culture in Race Literature will enable us to discriminate and not to write hasty thoughts and unjust and ungenerous criticism often of our superiors in knowledge and judgment.

And now comes the question, What part shall we women play in the Race Literature of the future? I shall best answer that question by calling your atten-tion to the glorious part which they have already performed in the columns of the *"Woman's Era,"* edited by Josephine St. P. Ruffin.

Here within the compass of one small journal we have struck out a new line of departure—a journal, a record of Race interests gathered from all parts of the United States, carefully selected, moistened, winnowed and garnered by the ablest intellects of educated colored women, shrinking at no lofty theme, shirking no serious duty, aiming at every possible excellence, and determined to do their part in the future uplifting of the race.

If twenty women, by their concentrated efforts in one literary movement, can meet with such success as has engendered, planned out, and so success-fully consummated this convention, what much more glorious results, what wider spread success, what grander diffusion of mental light will not come forth at the bidding of the enlarged hosts of women writers, already called into being by the stimulus of your efforts?

And here let me speak one word for my journalistic sisters who have already entered the broad arena of journalism. Before the "Woman's Era" had come into existence, no one except themselves can appreciate the bitter experience and sore disappointments under which they have at all times been compelled to pursue their chosen vocations.

If their brothers of the press have had their difficulties to contend with, I am here as a sister journalist to state, from the fullness of knowledge, that their task has been an easy one compared with that of the colored woman in journalism.

Woman's part in Race Literature, as in Race building, is the most important part and has been so in all ages. It is for her to receive impressions and transmit them. All through the most remote epochs she has done her share in literature. When not an active singer like Sappho, she has been the means of producing poets, statesmen, and historians, understandingly as Napoleon's mother worked on Homeric tapestry while bearing the future conqueror of the world.

When living up to her highest development, woman has done much to make lasting history, by her stimulating influence and there can be no greater responsibility than that, and this is the highest privilege granted to her by the Creator of the Universe.

Such are some brief outlines of the vast problem of Race Literature. Never was the outlook for Race Literature brighter. Questions of vast importance to succeeding generations on all lines are now looming up to be dissected and elucidated.

Among the students of the occult, certain powers are said to be fully developed innately in certain types of the Negro, powers that when understood and properly directed will rival if not transcend those of Du Maurier's Svengali.[17]

The medical world recognizes this especially when investigating the science of neurology,—by the merest chance it was discovered that certain types of our nurses—male and female—possessed invaluable qualities for quieting and controlling patients afflicted with the self-destructive mania. This should lead our physicians to explore and investigate so promising a field.

American artists find it easy to caricature the Negro, but find themselves baffled when striving to depict the highest characteristics of a Sojourner Truth. If he lacks the required temperament, there is thus offered a field for the race-loving Negro artist to compete with his elder brother in art, and succeed where the other has failed.

American and even European historians have often proved themselves much enchained by narrow local prejudice, hence there is a field for the unbiased historian of this closing century.

The advance made during the last fifteen or twenty years in mechanical science is of the most encouraging nature possible for our own ever-increasing class of scientific students.

The scholars of the race, linguists and masters of the dead languages have a wide field before them, which when fully explored, will be of incalculable interest to the whole people—I mean particularly the translators of the writings of the ancient world, on all that pertains to the exact estimate in which our African ancestors were held by contemporaries. This will be of interest to all classes, and especially to our own.

Until our scholars shall apply themselves to these greatly neglected fields, we must accept the perverted and indifferent translations of those prejudiced against us.

Dr. Le Plongeon, an eminent explorer and archaeologist, in his Central American studies, has made startling discoveries, which, if he succeeds in proving, will mean that the cradle of man's primitive condition is situated in Yucatan, and the primitive race was the ancestor of the Negro.

The "Review of Reviews," of July has this to say: "That such a tradition should have been handed down to the modern Negro is not so improbable in view of the fact that the inhabitants of Africa appear certainly to have had communication with the people of the Western world up to the destruction of the Island of Atlanta, concerning which events Dr. Le Plongeon has much to tell us."

Think of it! What a scope for our scholars not only in archaeology, but in everything that goes to make up literature!

Another avenue of research that commands dignified attention is the possibility that Negroes were among those who embarked with Columbus. Prominent educators are giving serious attention to this. Prof. Wright, of Georgia, lately sailed to England with the express purpose of investigating the subject, during his vacation, in some of the famous old libraries of Europe.

The lesson to be drawn from this cursory glance at what I may call the past, present and future of our Race Literature, apart from its value as first beginnings, not only to us as a people but literature in general, is that unless earnest and systematic effort be made to procure and preserve for transmission to our successors, the records, books and various publications already produced by us, not only will the sturdy pioneers who paved the way and laid the foundation for our Race Literature, be robbed of their just due, but an irretrievable wrong will be inflicted upon the generations that shall come after us.

1895

NOTES

1. Bartolomé de las Casas (1484–1566), historian, Dominican friar, early Spanish colonist, and the first bishop of the Chiapas region of Mexico.

2. A reference to *Temperament and Phrenology of Mixed Races* (1884), by African American abolitionist, educator, and attorney John Patterson Sampson (1837–1928).

3. A reference to *Ridpath's Universal History* (1895) by John Clark Ridpath (1840–1900).

4. *The American Commonwealth* (1888) by English historian and statesman James Bryce (1838–1922).

5. English historian, novelist, and magazine editor James Anthony Froude (1818–1894), an outspoken advocate for the dominion of the English over the Irish, the Xhosa, the people of India, and other colonial subjects.

6. A novel of racial passing, published in 1891 by American author and long-time editor of the *Atlantic Monthly* William Dean Howells (1837–1920).

7. A reference to *Doctor Huguet: A Novel* (1891) by novelist Ignatius Loyola Donnelly (1831–1901), a U.S. representative from Minnesota.

8. Refers to *A Question of Color* (1895), a novel of racial passing and hidden identities by English novelist, actor, and dramatist Francis Charles Phillips (1849–1921).

9. Alexander Sergeyevich Pushkin (1799–1837), a Russian poet of the Romantic era, best known as the author of *Eugene Onegin*, a novel written in verse. Pushkin was frequently referenced in nineteenth-century black print culture as an example of the creative achievements of people of African descent; a maternal great-grandfather was an Ethiopian businessman, first brought to Russia as a slave.

10. African American author, historian, naval officer, and politician George Washington Williams (1849–1891).

11. A reference to William Wells Brown's *Clotel; or, The President's Daughter.*

12. *The Cushite; or, The Children of Ham* (1887) by African American scientist, author, and Baptist minister Rufus L. Perry (ca. 1845–1895).

13. *Under the Yoke; or, Bond and Free* (1876), a play by African American dramatist John S. Ladue (birth and death dates unknown).

14. African American attorney, diplomat, and antiracist activist Archibald Henry Grimké (1849–1930).

15. *Noted Women* was one of two books on African American women published by black physicians in the year 1893. It was not, however, written by Dr. Scruggs. Dr. Lawson A. Scruggs was the author of *Women of Distinction* while *Noted Negro Women* was penned by Dr. Monroe A. Majors.

16. A pseudonym under which the author Frances E. W. Harper published a series of sketches in *The Anglo-African Magazine*, in 1859 and 1860.

17. A reference to the character Svengali in the 1895 novel *Trilby* by French-born British novelist and humorist George Du Maurier (1834–1896).

DANIEL WEBSTER DAVIS (1862-1913)

Daniel Webster Davis was born in Caroline Country, Virginia, to enslaved parents, John and Charlotte Ann. Davis was raised in Richmond, Virginia, where he graduated from high school in 1878, earning the Essayist Medal for his skill and creativity as a writer. From 1880 to the early 1890s, Davis worked as a schoolteacher. By the time he married, in 1893, he had returned to school, studying for the ministry at Lynchburg Baptist Seminary. After his ordination, in 1896, he assumed the pastorate at South Richmond's Second Baptist Church. Davis published his first collection of poems, *Idle Moments,* in 1895. His second and final volume, *Weh Down Souf,* would follow in 1897. Though alternately praised and condemned for his reliance on a stylized version of southern black dialect, Davis frequently uses this and other conventions of the plantation tradition as a means to subvert prevailing anti-black stereotypes and racist beliefs. The following poems are selected from *Weh Down Souf* and from the *A.M.E. Church Review,* to which he was an occasional contributor.

DE LININ' UB DE HYMNS

Dars a mighty *row* in Zion an' de *debbil's gittin' high,*
An' de *saints* done beat de *sinners, a-cussin' on de sly;*
What for it am? you reckon, well, I'll tell how it 'gin
Twuz 'bout a *mighty leetle thing, de linin' ub de hyms.*[1]

De *young folks* say *taint stylish* to *lin' out* no mo',
Dat *dey's* got *edikashun,* an' dey wants us all to know
Dat *dey* likes to hab dar *singin' books* a-holin' fore dar eyes,
An *sing de hymns right straight along* to mansion in de skies.

Dat it am *awful fogy* to gin um out *by lin',*
An' ef de ole folks will kumplain 'cause dey is ole an' blin
An' slabry's chain don kep dem back from larnin how to read,
Dat *dey* mus' take a *corner seat,* and let de *young folks* lead.

We *bin* peatin' *hine* de pastor when he sez dat lubly pray'r
Cause some un us *don kno' it* an' kin not say it squar,
But dey *sez* we *mus' peat wid* him, an' ef we kan keep time,
De gospel train will drap us off from follin' long behin'.

Well p'haps dez's right, I kin not say, my lims is growin' ole,
But I likes to sing dem dear ole hymns 'tis *music to my soul,*
An' 'pears to me twon't do *much* harm to gin um out *by lin'*,
So we *ole folk* dat *kin not read* kin *foller long behin'*.

But few ub us am lef here now dat bore de slabry's chain,
We don edekate our boys an' gals we'd do de sam' agin
An *Zion's* all dat's lef us now to cheer us wid its song,
Dey *mought* 'low us to *sing wid dem,* it kin not be fur long.

De *sarmons* high-falutin' an' de *chuch* am mighty fin',
We trus' dat *God still understans* ez he did in olden times;
When we do ign'ant po an' mean still worshiped wid de soul
Do oft akross our peac'ful breas' de wabes ub trouble rolled.

De ole time *groans* an' *shouts* an' *moans* am passin' out ub sight,
Edikashun changed all dat, and we beleive [sic] *it right*:
We *should* serb God *wid 'telligence* but fur dis thing I plead,
Jes lebe a leetle place in chuch fur dem as kin not read.

1895

STICKIN' TO DE HOE

Dar's mighty things agwine on,
Sense de days when I wuz young;
An' folks don' do ez dey did once,
Sense dese new times is kum;
Dey gals dey dresses pow'ful fin',
An all am fur a show;
But enny how dis nigger
Am a-stickin' to de hoe.

Larnin is a blessed thing,
An' good cloze mighty fin',

But I likes to see de cullud gal
What knows jes how to ine,
Gimme de gal to wash an' scrub,
An' keep things white an' clean,
An' kin den go in de kitchin,
An' cook de ham an' greens.

I ain't got no edekashun,
But dis I know am true,
Dat raisin' gals too good to wuck,
Ain't never gwine to do;
De boys dat look good nuf to eat,
But too good to saw de logs,
Am karrin us ez fas' ez smoke
To lan us at de dogs.

I spoze dat I'm ole fashun,
But God made man to plow,
An git his libbin by de sweat
Dat trickles down his brow;
While larnin an' all dem things
Am mighty good for sho',
De bes way we kin make our pints,
Is—stickin' to de hoe.

1895

NOTE

1. A practice in many rural churches in the southern United States and believed to have originated in Scotland, in which a song leader chants or speaks each line of the hymn as the line is to be sung, enabling the congregation to worship together in song, without the need of hymnals.

PAUL LAURENCE DUNBAR (1872-1906)

Paul Laurence Dunbar was born in Dayton, Ohio, to Matilda and Joshua Dunbar, formerly enslaved African Americans, each of whom had escaped from bondage in Kentucky. Though neither had any formal education, Dunbar's parents instilled in their son a love of language and storytelling. Taught basic reading skills by his mother and raised on colorful stories of southern life told by his father, Dunbar brought the influence of his parents' lives and words to life and light in all of his work, but most especially in his dialect poetry. Dunbar's dialect poems bear the markings of his keen understanding of the impact of pronunciation and cadence both on the meanings of individual words and phrases and on the emotions of his readers. Dunbar was educated at Dayton Central High School, where he was editor of the school paper and president of the literary society. Selected as class poet, Dunbar was also the class valedictorian. His poems appeared in many of the most widely circulated periodicals of his time, including the *New York Times,* the *Saturday Evening Post, Lippincott's Monthly, Century,* and the *Atlantic Monthly.* In 1893, just two years after completing high school, Dunbar published *Oak and Ivy,* his first collection of poetry. In subsequent years he would publish five more volumes of poetry and five novels. Though he wrote much of his poetry in standard English, he is best known for his skillfully crafted dialect poems, many of which offer a considerably more complicated view of black southern life than readers might encounter in the work of his white counterparts (most notably Joel Chandler Harris, creator of the character Uncle Remus). In 1898, Dunbar married writer Alice Ruth Moore. The couple would divorce in 1902, four years before the poet's death from tuberculosis. The following Dunbar selections include five of the standard English poems that were reprinted in the *Colored American Magazine*—"Compensation," "The Colored Soldiers," "Dawn," "Frederick Douglass," and "If"—as well as three of his most beloved dialect poems. They are: "Little Brown Baby," from *Poems of Cabin and Field* (1899), and "A Negro Love Song" and "When Malindy Sings," from *Lyrics of Lowly Life* (1896).

UNEXPRESSED

Deep in my heart that aches with the repression,
    And strives with plenitude of bitter pain,
There lives a thought that clamors for expression,
    And spends its undelivered force in vain.

What boots it that some other may have thought it?
    The right of thoughts' expression is divine;
The price of pain I pay for it has bought it,
    I care not who lays claim to it—'t is mine!

And yet not mine until it be delivered;
    The manner of its birth shall prove the test.
Alas, alas, my rock of pride is shivered—
    I beat my brow—the thought still unexpressed.

1896

FREDERICK DOUGLASS

A hush is over all the teeming lists,
    And there is pause, a breath-space in the strife;
A spirit brave has passed beyond the mists
    And vapors that obscure the sun of life.
And Ethiopia, with bosom torn,
Laments the passing of her noblest born.

She weeps for him a mother's burning tears—
    She loved him with a mother's deepest love.
He was her champion thro' direful years,
    And held her weal all other ends above.
When Bondage held her bleeding in the dust,
He raised her up and whispered, "Hope and Trust."

For her his voice, a fearless clarion, rung
    That broke in warning on the ears of men;
For her the strong bow of his power he strung,
    And sent his arrows to the very den
Where grim Oppression held his bloody place
And gloated o'er the mis'ries of a race.

And he was no soft-tongued apologist;
    He spoke straightforward, fearlessly uncowed;
The sunlight of his truth dispelled the mist,
    And set in bold relief each dark-hued cloud;
To sin and crime he gave their proper hue,
And hurled at evil what was evil's due.

Through good and ill report he cleaved his way
    Right onward, with his face set toward the heights,
Nor feared to face the foeman's dread array,—
    The lash of scorn, the sting of petty spites.
He dared the lightning in the lightning's track,
And answered thunder with his thunder back.

When men maligned him, and their torrent wrath
    In furious imprecations o'er him broke,
He kept his counsel as he kept his path;
    'Twas for his race, not for himself, he spoke.
He knew the import of his Master's call,
And felt himself too mighty to be small.

No miser in the good he held was he,—
    His kindness followed his horizon's rim.
His heart, his talents, and his hands were free
    To all who truly needed aught of him.
Where poverty and ignorance were rife,
He gave his bounty as he gave his life.

The place and cause that first aroused his might
    Still proved its power until his latest day.
In Freedom's lists and for the aid of Right
    Still in the foremost rank he waged the fray;
Wrong lived; his occupation was not gone.
He died in action with his armor on!

We weep for him, but we have touched his hand,
    And felt the magic of his presence nigh,
The current that he sent throughout the land,
    The kindling spirit of his battle-cry.
O'er all that holds us we shall triumph yet,
And place our banner where his hopes were set!

Oh, Douglass, thou hast passed beyond the shore,
    But still thy voice is ringing o'er the gale!
Thou'st taught thy race how high her hopes may soar,
    And bade her seek the heights, nor faint, nor fail.
She will not fail, she heeds thy stirring cry,
She knows thy guardian spirit will be nigh,
And, rising from beneath the chast'ning rod,
She stretches out her bleeding hands to God!

1896

WHEN MALINDY SINGS

G'way an' quit dat noise, Miss Lucy—
    Put dat music book away;
What's de use to keep on tryin'?
    Ef you practise twell you're gray,
You cain't sta't no notes a-flyin'
    Lak de ones dat rants and rings
F'om de kitchen to be big woods
    When Malindy sings.

You ain't got de nachel o'gans
    Fu' to make de soun' come right,
You ain't got de tu'ns an' twistin's
    Fu' to make it sweet an' light.
Tell you one thing now, Miss Lucy,
    An' I'm tellin' you fu' true,
When hit comes to raal right singin',
    'T ain't no easy thing to do.

Easy 'nough fu' folks to hollah,
    Lookin' at de lines an' dots,
When dey ain't no one kin sence it,
    An' de chune comes in, in spots;
But fu' real melojous music,
    Dat jes' strikes yo' hea't and clings,
Jes' you stan' an' listen wif me
    When Malindy sings.

Ain't you nevah hyeahd Malindy?
    Blessed soul, tek up de cross!
Look hyeah, ain't you jokin', honey?
    Well, you don't know whut you los'.
Y' ought to hyeah dat gal a-wa'blin',
    Robins, la'ks, an' all dem things,
Heish dey moufs an' hides dey faces
    When Malindy sings.

Fiddlin' man jes' stop his fiddlin',
    Lay his fiddle on de she'f;
Mockin'-bird quit tryin' to whistle,
    'Cause he jes' so shamed hisse'f.
Folks a-playin' on de banjo
    Draps dey fingahs on de strings—
Bless yo' soul—fu'gits to move 'em,
    When Malindy sings.

She jes' spreads huh mouf and hollahs,
    "Come to Jesus," twell you hyeah
Sinnahs' tremblin' steps and voices,
    Timid-lak a-drawin' neah;
Den she tu'ns to "Rock of Ages,"
    Simply to de cross she clings,
An' you fin' yo' teahs a-drappin'
    When Malindy sings.

Who dat says dat humble praises
    Wif de Master nevah counts?
Heish yo' mouf, I hyeah dat music,
    Ez hit rises up an' mounts—
Floatin' by de hills an' valleys,
    Way above dis buryin' sod,
Ez hit makes its way in glory
    To de very gates of God!

Oh, hit's sweetah dan de music
    Of an edicated band;
An' hit's dearah dan de battle's
    Song o' triumph in de lan'.

It seems holier dan evenin'
 When de solemn chu'ch bell rings,
Ez I sit an' ca'mly listen
 While Malindy sings.

Towsah, stop dat ba'kin', hyeah me!
 Mandy, mek dat chile keep still;
Don't you hyeah de echoes callin'
 F'om de valley to de hill?
Let me listen, I can hyeah it,
 Th'oo de bresh of angels' wings,
Sof' an' sweet, "Swing Low, Sweet Chariot,"
 Ez Malindy sings.

        1896

A NEGRO LOVE SONG

Seen my lady home las' night,
 Jump back, honey, jump back.
Hel' huh han' an' sque'z it tight,
 Jump back, honey, jump back.
Hyeahd huh sigh a little sigh,
Seen a light gleam f'om huh eye,
An' a smile go flittin' by—
 Jump back, honey, jump back.

Hyeahd de win' blow thoo de pine,
 Jump back, honey, jump back.
Mockin'-bird was singin' fine,
 Jump back, honey, jump back.
An' my hea't was beatin' so,
When I reached my lady's do',
Dat I could n't ba' to go—
 Jump back, honey, jump back.

Put my ahm aroun' huh wais',
 Jump back, honey, jump back.
Raised huh lips an' took a tase,
 Jump back, honey, jump back.

Love me, honey, love me true?
Love me well ez I love you?
An' she answe'd, "'Cose I do"—
    Jump back, honey, jump back.

                    1896

LITTLE BROWN BABY

Little brown baby wif spa'klin' eyes,
    Come to yo' pappy an' set on his knee.
What you been doin', suh—makin' san' pies?
    Look at dat bib—you's ez du'ty ez me.
Look at dat mouf—dat's merlasses, I bet;
    Come hyeah, Maria, an' wipe off his han's.
Bees gwine to ketch you an' eat you up yit,
    Bein' so sticky an sweet—goodness lan's!

Little brown baby wif spa'klin' eyes,
    Who's pappy's darlin' an' who's pappy's chile?
Who is it all de day nevah once tries
    Fu' to be cross, er once loses dat smile?
Whah did you git dem teef? My, you's a scamp!
    Whah did dat dimple come f'om in yo' chin?
Pappy do' know you—I b'lieves you's a tramp;
    Mammy, dis hyeah's some ol' straggler got in!

Let's th'ow him outen de do' in de san',
    We do' want stragglers a-layin' 'roun' hyeah;
Let's gin him 'way to de big buggah-man;
    I know he's hidin' erroun' hyeah right neah.
Buggah-man, buggah-man, come in de do',
    Hyeah's a bad boy you kin have fu' to eat.
Mammy an' pappy do' want him no mo',
    Swaller him down f'om his haid to his feet!

Dah, now, I t'ought dat you'd hug me up close.
    Go back, ol' buggah, you sha'n't have dis boy.
He ain't no tramp, ner no straggler, of co'se;
    He's pappy's pa'dner an' playmate an' joy.

Come to you' pallet now—go to yo' res';
    Wisht you could allus know ease an' cleah skies;
Wisht you could stay jes' a chile on my breas'—
    Little brown baby wif spa'klin' eyes!

1899

DAWN

An angel, robed in spotless white,
Bent down and kissed the sleeping Night.
Night woke to blush; the sprite was gone.
Men saw the blush and called it Dawn.

1900

COMPENSATION

Because I had loved so deeply,
    Because I had loved so long,
God in His great compassion
    Gave me the gift of song.

Because I have loved so vainly,
    And sung with such faltering breath,
The Master in infinite mercy
    Offers the boon of Death.

1901

OLIVIA WARD BUSH-BANKS
(1869-1944)

Olivia Ward Bush-Banks was born to Eliza Draper and Abraham Ward, in Sag Harbor, Long Island, New York. Both of her parents were the descendants of long-emancipated mixed-race families of Native American (Montauk) and African American ancestry. Educated in Providence, Rhode Island, Bush-Banks began writing poetry in high school. Twice wed, first to Frank Bush and later to Anthony Banks, she published her first collection, *Original Poems,* in 1899, shortly after the end of her first marriage. As recognition of her work grew, so too did her involvement in the African American literary community; but her increasingly frequent contributions to black periodicals like the *Boston Transcript* and *Voice of the Negro* did not preclude her deep involvement in the Mohawk nation, and she served for several years as its official historian. Bush-Banks published her second collection of poems, *Driftwood,* in 1914. In later life, she would return to New York and become an active participant in the Harlem Renaissance, befriending the poets Countee Cullen and Langston Hughes and participating in the Works Progress Administration (WPA) writers' project. The following poems are from her first collection, *Original Poems,* and from the *Colored American* magazine.

VOICES

I stand upon the haunted plain
   Of vanished day and year,
And ever o'er its gloomy waste
   Some strange, sad voice I hear.
Some voice from out the shadowed Past;
   And one I call Regret,
And one I know is Misspent Hours,
   Whose memory lingers yet.

Then Failure speaks in bitter tones,
   And Grief, with all its woes;

Remorse, whose deep and cruel stings
    My painful thoughts disclose.
Thus do these voices speak to me,
    And flit like shadows past;
My spirit falters in despair,
    And tears flow thick and fast.

But when, within the wide domain
    Of Future Day and Year
I stand, and o'er its sunlit Plain
    A sweeter Voice I hear,
Which bids me leave the darkened Past
    And crush its memory,—
I'll listen gladly, and obey
    The Voice of Opportunity.

                                    1898

HEART-THROBS

We suffer and ye know it not,
Nor yet can ever know,
What depth of bitterness is ours,
Or why we suffer so;—

If we would know what anguish la,
Ask of the dark-skinned race,
Ay! ask of him who loves to know
The color of his face.

Then plead as he has often pled
For manhood among men,
And feel the pain of rights denied;
Thou canst not know till then.

Or share with him for one brief space,
Ambition's fond desire,
Reach out, and strive, as he has striven,
And aim for something higher.

Let knowledge cultivate, refine,
Let culture feed the mind,
Then fondly dream of hopes fulfilled,
And dreaming wake to find;—

That merit worth or patient toil
Does not suffice to win.
Then learn the cause of this defeat,
The color of the skin.

The mother of the dusky babe,
Surveys with aching heart
Bright prospects, knowing all the while,
Her off-spring shares no part.

The child attains to manhood's years,
Still conscious of the same,
While others boast of Life's success,
He knows it but in name.

Yes, aim, reach out, aspire and strive
And know, 'Twere all in vain,
And e'en in Freedom's name appeal,
Then ye can sense our pain.

We suffer and ye know it not,
Nor yet can ever know,
What depth of bitterness is ours,
Or why we suffer so.

1904

THE NATION'S EVIL

A sound is heard throughout our land,
A moaning, yearning, pleading cry;
"O mighty Arm of Right stretch forth,
Crush out our hopeless misery.
I see a weary dark-skinned race
Bend low beneath Oppression's weight,

I hear their off-spring wailing out,
O, "Save us from our father's fate!"

I see a fierce, blood-thirsty mob,
Add torture to a quivering frame.
I hear an agonizing cry
Hushed by the cruel fiery flame.
I see the home left desolate,
I see a father forced to die,
I hear a mother's anguished groan,
I hear their children's piteous cry.

How long I ask shall these things be?
How long shall men have hearts of stone?
My soul grown sick and faint within,
Cries out in supplicating tone,
"Great God, send forth thy swift demand,
Declare this evil shall not be,
That man give justice unto man,
And cease this inhumanity."

1904

SUTTON E. GRIGGS (1872-1933)

Sutton Elbert Griggs was born in Chatfield, Texas. The son of a Baptist minister, Griggs began his education in the Dallas public schools. A graduate of Bishop College in Marshall, Texas, and the Richmond Theological Seminary in Virginia, he was ordained as a minister in 1893. Committed to the uplift of the African American people, Griggs used his talent as a writer and his authority in the pulpit to advocate for the rights of black people. While serving as a Baptist pastor—first in Berkeley, Virginia, and later in Nashville, Tennessee—Griggs published over thirty-five pamphlets and books, including five novels. As an author, Griggs actively courted the African American audience, selling his books from door to door in black neighborhoods. The following selections from Griggs's most famous novel, *Imperium in Imperio,* include the four opening chapters in which are introduced the protagonists, best friends and rivals, Bernard Belgrave and Belton Piedmont.

IMPERIUM IN IMPERIO

Chapter I: A Small Beginning

"Cum er long hunny an' let yer mammy fix yer 'spectabul, so yer ken go to skule. Yer mammy is 'tarmined ter gib yer all de book larning dar is ter be had eben ef she has ter lib on bred an' herrin's, an' die en de a'ms house."

These words came from the lips of a poor, ignorant negro woman, and yet the determined course of action which they reveal vitally affected the destiny of a nation and saved the sun of the Nineteenth Century, proud and glorious, from passing through, near its setting, the blackest and thickest and ugliest clouds of all its journey; saved it from ending the most brilliant of brilliant careers by setting, with a shudder of horror, in a sea of human blood.

Those who doubt that such power could emanate from such weakness; or, to change the figure, that such a tiny star could have dimensions greater than those of earth, may have every vestige of doubt removed by a perusal of this simple narrative.

Let us now acquaint ourselves with the circumstances under which the opening words of our story were spoken. To do this, we must need lead our readers into humble and commonplace surroundings, a fact that will not come in the nature of a surprise to those who have traced the proud, rushing, swelling river to the mountain whence it comes trickling forth, meekly and humbly enough.

The place was Winchester, an antiquated town, located near the north-western corner of the State of Virginia.

In October of the year 1867, the year in which our story begins, a white man by the name of Tiberius Gracchus Leonard had arrived in Winchester, and was employed as teacher of the school for colored children.

Mrs. Hannah Piedmont, the colored woman whom we have presented to our readers as addressing her little boy, was the mother of five children—three girls and two boys. In the order of their ages, the names of her children were: James Henry, aged fifteen, Amanda Ann, aged thirteen, Eliza Jane, aged eleven, Belton, aged eight, and Celestine, aged five. Several years previous to the opening of our history, Mr. Piedmont had abandoned his wife and left her to rear the children alone.

School opened in October, and as fast as she could get books and clothing Mrs. Piedmont sent her children to school. James Henry, Amanda Ann, and Eliza Jane were sent at about a week's interval. Belton and Celestine were then left—Celestine being regarded as too young to go. This morning we find Belton's mother preparing him for school, and we shall stand by and watch the preparations.

The house was low and squatty and was built of rock. It consisted of one room only, and over this there was a loft, the hole to climb into which was in plain view of any one in the room. There was only one window to the house and that one was only four feet square. Two panes of this were broken out and the holes were stuffed with rags. In one corner of the room there stood a bed in which Mrs. Piedmont and Amanda Ann slept. Under this was a trundle bed in which Eliza Jane and Celestine slept at the head, while Belton slept at the foot. James Henry climbed into the loft and slept there on a pallet of straw. The cooking was done in a fireplace which was on the side of the house opposite the window. Three chairs, two of which had no backs to them, completed the articles in the room.

In one of these chairs Mrs. Piedmont was sitting, while Belton stood be-fore her all dressed and ready to go to school, excepting that his face was not washed.

It might be interesting to note his costume. The white lady for whom Mrs. Piedmont washed each week had given her two much-torn pairs of trousers, discarded by her young son. One pair was of linen and the other of navy blue. A leg from each pair was missing; so Mrs. Piedmont simply transferred the good leg of the linen pair to the suit of the navy blue, and dressed the happy Belton in that suit thus amended. His coat was literally a conglomeration of patches of varying sizes and colors. If you attempted to describe the coat by calling it by the name of the color that you thought predominated, at least a half dozen aspirants could present equal claims to the honor. One of Belton's feet was encased in a worn-out slipper from the dainty foot of some young woman, while the other wore a turned over boot left in town by some farmer lad who had gotten himself a new pair. His hat was in good condition, being the summer straw last worn by a little white playfellow (when fall came on, this little fellow kindly willed his hat to Belton, who, in return for this favor, was to black the boy's shoes each morning during the winter).

Belton's mother now held in her hand a wet cloth with which she wished to cleanse his face, the bacon skin which he gnawed at the conclusion of his meal having left a circle of grease around his lips. Belton did not relish the face washing part of the programme (of course hair combing was not even considered). Belton had one characteristic similar to that of oil. He did not like to mix with water, especially cold water, such as was on that wet cloth in his mother's hand. However, a hint in reference to a certain well-known leather strap, combined with the offer of a lump of sugar, brought him to terms.

His face being washed, he and his mother marched forth to school, where he laid the foundation of the education that served him so well in after life.

A man of tact, intelligence, and superior education moving in the midst of a mass of ignorant people, ofttimes has a sway more absolute than that of monarchs.

Belton now entered the school-room, which in his case proves to be the royal court, whence he emerges an uncrowned king.

Chapter II: The School

The house in which the colored school was held was, in former times, a house of worship for the white Baptists of Winchester. It was a long, plain, frame structure, painted white. Many years prior to the opening of the colored school it had been condemned as unsafe by the town authorities, whereupon the white Baptists had abandoned it for a more beautiful modern structure.

The church tendered the use of the building to the town for a public school for the colored children. The roof was patched and iron rods were used to hold together the twisting walls. These improvements being made, school was in due time opened. The building was located on the outskirts of the town, and a large open field surrounded it on all sides.

As Mrs. Piedmont and her son drew near to this building the teacher was standing on the door-steps ringing his little hand bell, calling the children in from their recess. They came running at full speed, helter skelter. By the time they were all in Mrs. Piedmont and Belton had arrived at the step. When Mr. Leonard saw them about to enter the building an angry scowl passed over his face, and he muttered half aloud: "Another black nigger brat for me to teach."

The steps were about four feet high and he was standing on the top step. To emphasize his disgust, he drew back so that Mrs. Piedmont would pass him with no danger of brushing him. He drew back rather too far and began falling off the end of the steps. He clutched at the door and made such a scrambling noise that the children turned in their seats just in time to see his body rapidly disappearing in a manner to leave his feet where his head ought to be.

Such a yell of laughter as went up from the throats of the children! It had in it a universal, spontaneous ring of savage delight which plainly told that the teacher was not beloved by his pupils.

The back of the teacher's head struck the edge of a stone, and when he clambered up from his rather undignified position his back was covered with blood. Deep silence reigned in the school-room as he walked down the aisle, glaring fiercely right and left. Getting his hat he left the school-room and went to a near-by drug store to have his wounds dressed.

While he was gone, the children took charge of the school-room and played pranks of every description. Abe Lincoln took the teacher's chair and played "'fessor."

"'Sallie Ann ain't yer got wax in yer mouf?"

"Yes ser." "Den take dis stick and prop yer mouf opun fur half hour. Dat'll teach yer a lesson."

"Billy Smith, yer didn't know yer lessun," says teacher Abe. "Yer may stan' on one leg de ballunce ob de ebenning."

"Henry Jones, yer sassed a white boy ter day. Pull off yer jacket. I'll gib yer a lessun dat yer'll not furgit soon. Neber buck up to yer s'periors."

"John Jones, yer black, nappy head rascal, I'll crack yer skull if yer doan keep quiut."

"Cum year, yer black, cross-eyed little wench, yen I'll teach yer to go to sleep in here." Annie Moore was the little girl thus addressed.

After each sally from Abe there was a hearty roar of laughter, he imitated the absent teacher so perfectly in look, voice, manner, sentiment, and method of punishment.

Taking down the cowhide used for flogging purposes Abe left his seat and was passing to and fro, pretending to flog those who most frequently fell heir to the teacher's wrath. While he was doing this Billy Smith stealthily crept to the teacher's chair and placed a crooked pin in it in order to catch Abe when he returned to sit down.

Before Abe had gone much further the teacher's face appeared at the door, and all scrambled to get into their right places and to assume studious attitudes. Billy Smith thought of his crooked pin and had the "cold sweats." Those who had seen Billy put the pin in the chair were torn between two conflicting emotions. They wanted the pin to do its work, and therefore hoped. They feared Billy's detection and therefore despaired.

However, the teacher did not proceed at once to take his seat. He approached Mrs. Piedmont and Belton, who had taken seats midway the room and were interested spectators of all that had been going on. Speaking to Mrs. Piedmont, he said: "What is your name?" She replied: "Hannah Lizabeth Piedmont."

"Well, Hannah, what is your brat's name?"

"His name am Belton Piedmont, arter his grandaddy."

"Well, Hannah, I am very pleased to receive your brat. He shall not want for attention," he added, in a tone accompanied by a lurking look of hate that made Mrs. Piedmont shudder and long to have her boy at home again. Her desire for his training was so great that she surmounted her misgivings and carried out her purposes to have him enrolled.

As the teacher was turning to go to his desk, hearing a rustling noise toward the door, he turned to look. He was, so to speak, petrified with astonishment. There stood on the threshold of the door a woman whose beauty was such as he had never seen surpassed. She held a boy by the hand. She was a mulatto woman, tall and graceful. Her hair was raven black and was combed away from as beautiful a forehead as nature could chisel. Her eyes were a brown hazel, large and intelligent, tinged with a slight look of melancholy. Her complexion was a rich olive, and seemed especially adapted to her face, that revealed not a flaw.

The teacher quickly pulled off his hat, which he had not up to that time removed since his return from the drug store. As the lady moved up the aisle toward him, he was taken with stage fright. He recovered self-possession enough to escort her and the boy to the front and give them seats. The whole school divided its attention between the beautiful woman and the discomfited teacher. They had not known that he was so full of smiles and smirks.

"What is your name?" he enquired in his most suave manner.

"Fairfax Belgrave," replied the visitor.

"May I be of any service to you, madam?"

At the mention of the word madam, she colored slightly. "I desire to have my son enter your school and I trust that you may see your way clear to admit him."

"Most assuredly madam, most assuredly." Saying this, he hastened to his desk, opened it and took out his register. He then sat down, but the next instant leapt several feet into the air, knocking over his desk. He danced around the floor, reaching toward the rear of his pants, yelling: "Pull it out! pull it out! pull it out!"

The children hid their faces behind their books and chuckled most gleefully. Billy Smith was struck dumb with terror. Abe was rolling on the floor, bellowing with uncontrollable laughter.

The teacher finally succeeded in extricating the offending steel and stood scratching his head in chagrin at the spectacle he had made of himself before his charming visitor. He took an internal oath to get his revenge out of Mrs. Piedmont and her son, who had been the innocent means of his double downfall that day.

His desk was arranged in a proper manner and the teacher took his pen and wrote two names, now famous the world over.

"Bernard Belgrave, age 9 years."

"Belton Piedmont, age 8 years."

Under such circumstances Belton began his school career.

Chapter III: The Parson's Advice

With heavy heart and with eyes cast upon the ground, Mrs. Piedmont walked back home after leaving Belton with his teacher. She had intended to make a special plea for her boy, who had all along displayed such precociousness as to fill her bosom with the liveliest hopes. But the teacher was so repulsive in manner that she did not have the heart to speak to him as she had intended.

She saw that the happenings of the morning had had the effect of deepening a contemptuous prejudice into hatred, and she felt that her child's school life was to be embittered by the harshest of maltreatment.

No restraint was put upon the flogging of colored children by their white teachers, and in Belton's case his mother expected the worst. During the whole week she revolved the matter in her mind. There was a conflict in her bosom between her love and her ambition. Love prompted her to return and take her son away from school. Ambition bade her to let him stay. She finally decided to submit the whole matter to her parson, whom she would invite to dinner on the coming Sunday.

The Sabbath came and Mrs. Piedmont aroused her family bright and early, for the coming of the parson to take dinner was a great event in any negro household. The house was swept as clean as a broom of weeds tied together could make it. Along with the family breakfast, a skillet of biscuits was cooked and a young chicken nicely baked.

Belton was very active in helping his mother that morning, and she promised to give him a biscuit and a piece of chicken as a reward after the preacher was through eating his dinner. The thought of this coming happiness buoyed Belton up, and often he fancied himself munching that biscuit and biting that piece of chicken. These were items of food rarely found in that household.

Breakfast over, the whole family made preparations for going to Sunday school. Preparations always went on peacefully until it came to combing hair. The older members of the family endured the ordeal very well; but little "Lessie" always screamed as if she was being tortured, and James Henry received many kicks and scratches from Belton before he was through combing Belton's hair.

The Sunday school and church were always held in the day-school building. The Sunday school scholars were all in one class and recited out of the "blue back spelling book." When that was over, members of the school were allowed to ask general questions on the Bible, which were answered by anyone volunteering to do so. Everyone who had in any way caught a new light on a passage of scripture endeavored, by questioning, to find out as to whether others were as wise as he, and if such was not the case, he gladly enlightened the rest.

The Sunday school being over, the people stood in groups on the ground surrounding the church waiting for the arrival of the parson from his home, Berryville, a town twelve miles distant. He was pastor of three other churches besides the one at Winchester, and he preached at each one Sunday in the month. After a while he put in his appearance. He was rather small in stature, and held his head somewhat to one side and looked at you with that knowing look of the parrot. He wore a pair of trousers that had been black, but were now sleet from much wear. They lacked two inches of reaching down to the feet of his high-heeled boots. He had on a long linen duster that reached below his knees. Beneath this was a faded Prince Albert coat and a vest much too small. On his head there sat, slightly tipped, a high-topped beaver that seemed to have been hidden between two mattresses all the week and taken out and straightened for Sunday wear. In his hand he held a walking cane.

Thus clad he came toward the church, his body thrown slightly back, walking leisurely with the air of quiet dignity possessed by the man sure of his standing, and not under the necessity of asserting it overmuch in his carriage.

The brothers pulled off their hats and the sisters put on their best smiles as the parson approached. After a cordial handshake all around, the preacher entered the church to begin the services. After singing a hymn and praying, he took for his text the following "passige of scripter:"

"It air harder fur a camel to git through de eye of a cambric needle den fur a rich man to enter de kingdom of heben." This was one of the parson's favorite texts, and the members all settled themselves back to have a good "speritual" time.

The preacher began his sermon in a somewhat quiet way, but the members knew that he would "warm up bye and bye." He pictured all rich men as trying to get into heaven, but, he asserted, they invariably found themselves with Dives. He exhorted his hearers to stick to Jesus. Here he pulled off his collar, and the sisters stirred and looked about them. A little later on, the preacher getting "warmer," pulled off his cuffs. The brethren laughed with a sort of joyous jumping up and down all the while—one crying "Gib me Jesus," another "Oh I am gwine home,"[1] and so on.

One sister who had a white lady's baby in her arms got happy[2] and flung it entirely across the room, it falling into Mrs. Piedmont's lap, while the frenzied woman who threw the child climbed over benches, rushed into the pulpit, and swung to the preacher's neck, crying—"Glory! Glory! Glory! "In the meanwhile Belton had dropped down under one of the benches and was watching the proceedings with an eye of terror.

The sermon over and quiet restored, a collection was taken and given to the pastor. Mrs. Piedmont went forward to put some money on the table and took occasion to step to the pulpit and invite the pastor to dinner. Knowing that this meant chicken, the pastor unhesitatingly accepted the invitation, and when church was over accompanied Mrs. Piedmont and her family home.

The preacher caught hold of Belton's hand as they walked along. This mark of attention, esteemed by Belton as a signal honor, filled his little soul with joy. As he thought of the manner in which the preacher stirred up the people, the amount of the collection that had been given him, and the biscuits and chicken that now awaited him, Belton decided that he, too, would like to become a preacher.

Just before reaching home, according to a preconcerted plan, Belton and James Henry broke from the group and ran into the house. When the others appeared a little later on, these two were not to be seen. However, no question was asked and no search made. All things were ready and the parson sat down to eat, while the three girls stood about, glancing now and then at the table. The preacher was very voracious and began his meal as though he "meant business."

We can now reveal the whereabouts of Belton and James Henry. They had clambered into the loft for the purpose of watching the progress of the preacher's meal, calculating at each step how much he would probably leave. James Henry found a little hole in the loft directly over the table, and through this hole he did his spying. Belton took his position at the larger entrance hole, lying flat on his stomach. He poked his head down far enough to see the preacher, but held it in readiness to be snatched back, if the preacher's eyes seemed to be about to wander his way.

He was kept in a state of feverish excitement, on the one hand, by fear of detection, and on the other, by a desire to watch the meal. When about half of the biscuits were gone, and the preacher seemed as fresh as ever, Belton began to be afraid for his promised biscuit and piece of chicken. He crawled to James Henry and said hastily—"James, dees haf gone," and hurriedly resumed his watch. A moment later he called out in a whisper, "He's tuck anudder." Down goes Belton's head to resume his watch. Every time the preacher took another biscuit Belton called out the fact to James.

All of the chicken was at last destroyed and only one biscuit remained; and Belton's whole soul was now centered on that biscuit. In his eagerness to watch he leaned a good distance out, and when the preacher reached forth his hand to take the last one Belton was so overcome that he lost his balance and tumbled out of his hole on the floor, kicking, and crying over and over again: "I knowed I wuzunt goin' to git naren dem biscuits."

The startled preacher hastily arose from the table and gazed on the little fellow in bewilderment. As soon as it dawned upon him what the trouble was, he hastily got the remaining biscuit and gave it to Belton. He also discovered that his voracity had made enemies of the rest of the children, and he very adroitly passed a five cent piece around to each.

James Henry, forgetting his altitude and anxious not to lose his recompense, cried out loudly from the loft: "Amanda Ann you git mine fur me."

The preacher looked up but saw no one. Seeing that his request did not have the desired effect, James Henry soon tumbled down full of dust, straw and cobwebs, and came into possession of his appeasing money. The preacher laughed heartily and seemed to enjoy his experience highly.

The table was cleared, and the preacher and Mrs. Piedmont dismissed the children in order to discuss unmolested the subject which had prompted her to extend an invitation to the parson. In view of the intense dislike the teacher had conceived for Belton, she desired to know if it were not best to withdraw him from school altogether, rather than to subject him to the harsh treatment sure to come.

"Let me gib yer my advis, sistah Hannah. De greatest t'ing in de wul is edification. Ef our race ken git dat we ken git ebery t'ing else. Dat is de key. Git de key an' yer ken go in de house to go where you please. As fur his beatin' de brat, yer musn't kick agin dat. He'll beat de brat to make him larn, and won't dat be a blessed t'ing? See dis scar on side my head? Old marse Sampson knocked me down wid a single-tree tryin' to make me stop larning, and God is so fixed it dat white folks is knocking es down ef we don't larn. Ef yer take Belton out of school yer'll be fighting 'genst de providence of God."

Being thus advised by her shepherd, Mrs. Piedmont decided to keep Belton in school. So on Monday Belton went back to his brutal teacher, and thither we follow him.

Chapter IV: The Turning of a Worm

As to who Mr. Tiberius Gracchus Leonard was, or as to where he came from, nobody in Winchester, save himself, knew.

Immediately following the close of the Civil War, Rev. Samuel Christian, a poor but honorable retired minister of the M. E. Church, South, was the first teacher employed to instruct the colored children of the town.

He was one of those Southerners who had never believed in the morality of slavery, but regarded it as a deep rooted evil beyond human power to uproot. When the manacles fell from the hands of the Negroes he gladly accepted the task of removing the scales of ignorance from the blinded eyes of the race.

Tenderly he labored, valiantly he toiled in the midst of the mass of ignorance that came surging around him. But only one brief year was given to this saintly soul to endeavor to blast the mountains of stupidity which centuries of oppression had reared. He fell asleep.

The white men who were trustees of the colored school were sorely puzzled as to what to do for a successor. A Negro, capable of teaching a school, was nowhere near. White young men of the South, generally, looked upon the work of teaching "niggers" with the utmost contempt; and any man who suggested the name of a white young lady of Southern birth as a teacher for the colored children was actually in danger of being shot by any member of the insulted family who could handle a pistol.

An advertisement was inserted in the Washington Post to the effect that a teacher was wanted. In answer to this advertisement Mr. Leonard came. He was a man above the medium height, and possessed a frame not large but compactly built. His forehead was low and narrow; while the back of his head looked exceedingly intellectual. Looking at him from the front you would involuntarily exclaim: "What an infamous scoundrel." Looking at him from the rear you would say: "There certainly is brain power in that head."

The glance of Mr. Leonard's eye was furtive, and his face was sour looking indeed. At times when he felt that no one was watching him, his whole countenance and attitude betokened the rage of despair.

Most people who looked at him felt that he carried in his bosom a dark secret. As to scholarship, he was unquestionably proficient. No white man in all the neighboring section, ranked with him intellectually. Despite the lack of all knowledge of his moral character and previous life, he was pronounced as much too good a man to fritter away his time on "niggers."

Such was the character of the man into whose hands was committed the destiny of the colored children of Winchester.

As his mother foresaw would be the case, Belton was singled out by the teacher as a special object on which he might expend his spleen.[3] For a man to be as spiteful as he was, there must have been something gnawing at his heart. But toward Bernard none of this evil spirit was manifested. He seemed to have chosen Bernard for his pet, and Belton for his "pet aversion." To the one he was all kindness; while to the other he was cruel in the extreme. Often he would purchase flowers from the florist and give to Bernard to bear home to his mother. On these days he would seemingly take pains to give Belton fresh bruises to take home to his mother. When he had a particularly good dinner he would invite Bernard to dine with him, and would be sure to find some pretext for forbidding Belton to partake of his own common meal. Belton was by no means insensible to all these acts of discrimination. Nor did Bernard fail to perceive that he, himself, was the teacher's pet. He clambered on to the teacher's knees, played with his mustache, and often took his watch and wore it. The teacher seemed to be truly fond of him.

The children all ascribed this partiality to the color of Bernard's skin, and they all, except Belton, began to envy and despise Bernard. Of course they told their parents of the teacher's partiality and their parents thus became embittered against the teacher. But however much they might object to him and desire his removal, their united protests would not have had the weight of a feather. So the teacher remained at Winchester for twelve years. During all these years he instructed our young friends Belton and Bernard.

Strangely enough, his ardent love for Bernard and his bitter hatred of Belton accomplished the very same result in respect to their acquirements. The teacher soon discovered that both boys were talented far beyond the ordinary, and that both were ambitious. He saw that the way to wound and humiliate Belton was to make Bernard excel him. Thus he bent all of his energies to improve Bernard's mind. Whenever he heard Belton recite he brought all of his talents to bear to point out his failures, hoping thus to exalt Bernard, out of whose work he strove to keep all blemishes. Thus Belton became accustomed to the closest scrutiny, and prepared himself accordingly. The result was that Bernard did not gain an inch on him.

The teacher introduced the two boys into every needed field of knowledge, as they grew older, hoping always to find some branch in which Bernard might display unquestioned superiority. There were two studies in which the two rivals dug deep to see which could bring forth the richest treasures; and these gave coloring to the whole of their after lives. One was the History of the United States, and the other, Rhetoric.

In history, that portion that charmed them most was the story of the rebellion against the yoke of England. Far and wide they went in search of everything that would throw light on this epoch. They became immersed in the spirit of that heroic age.

As a part of their rhetorical training they were taught to declaim. Thanks to their absorption in the history of the Revolution, their minds ran to the sublime in literature; and they strove to secure pieces to declaim that recited the most heroic deeds of man, of whatever nationality.

Leonidas,[4] Marco Bozarris,[5] Arnold Winklereid,[6] Lajos Kossuth,[7] Robert Emmett,[8] Martin Luther, Patrick Henry and such characters furnished the pieces almost invariably declaimed. They threw their whole souls into these, and the only natural thing resulted. No human soul can breathe the atmosphere of heroes and read with bated breath their deeds of daring without craving for the opportunity to do the like. Thus the education of these two young men went on.

At the expiration of twelve years they had acquired an academic education that could not be surpassed anywhere in the land. Their reputation as brilliant students and eloquent speakers had spread over the whole surrounding country.

The teacher decided to graduate the young men; and he thought to utilize the occasion as a lasting humiliation of Belton and exaltation of his favorite, Bernard Belgrave. Belton felt this.

In the first part of this last school year of the boys, he had told them to prepare for a grand commencement exercise, and they acted accordingly. Each one chose his subject and began the preparation of his oration early in the session, each keeping his subject and treatment secret from the other.

The teacher had announced that numerous white citizens would be present; among them the congressman from the district and the mayor of the town. Belton determined upon two things, away down in his soul. He determined to win in the oratorical contest, and to get his revenge on his teacher on the day that the teacher had planned for his (Belton's) humiliation. Bernard did not have the incentive that Belton did; but defeat was ever galling to him, and he, too, had determined to win.

The teacher often reviewed the progress made by Bernard on his oration, but did not notice Belton's at all. He strove to make Bernard's oration as nearly perfect as labor and skill could make it. But Belton was not asleep as to either of the resolutions he had formed. Some nights he could be seen stealing away from the congressman's residence. On others he could be seen leaving the neighborhood of the school, with a spade in one hand and a few carpenter's tools in the other.

He went to the congressman, who was a polished orator with a national reputation, in order that he might purge his oration from its impurities of speech. As the congressman read the oration and perceived the depth of thought, the logical arrangement, the beauty and rhythm of language, and the wide research displayed, he opened his eyes wide with astonishment. He was amazed that a young man of such uncommon talents could have grown up in his town and he not know it. Belton's marvelous talents won his respect and admiration, and he gave him access to his library and criticized his oration whenever needed.

Secretly and silently preparations went on for the grand conflict. At last the day came. The colored men and women of the place laid aside all work to attend the exercises. The forward section of seats was reserved for the white people. The congressman, the mayor, the school trustees and various other men of standing came, accompanied by their wives and daughters.

Scholars of various grades had parts to perform on the programme, but the eyes of all sought the bottom of the page where were printed the names of the two oratorical gladiators:

"BELTON PIEDMONT.
BERNARD BELGRAVE."

The teacher had given Bernard the last place, deeming that the more advantageous. He appointed the congressman, the mayor, and one of the school trustees to act as judges, to decide to whom he should award a beautiful gold medal for the more excellent oration. The congressman politely declined and named another trustee in his stead. Then the contest began. As Belton walked up on the platform the children greeted him with applause. He announced as his subject: "The Contribution of the Anglo-Saxon to the Cause of Human Liberty." In his strong, earnest voice, he began to roll off his well turned periods. The whole audience seemed as if in a trance. His words made their hearts burn, and time and again he made them burst forth in applause.

The white people who sat and listened to his speech looked upon it as a very revelation to them, they themselves not having had as clear a conception of the glory of their race as this Negro now revealed. When he had finished, white men and women crowded to the front to congratulate him upon his effort, and it was many minutes before quiet was restored sufficiently to allow the programme to proceed.

Bernard took his position on the platform, announcing as his subject: "Robert Emmett." His voice was sweet and well modulated and never failed to charm. Admiration was plainly depicted on every face as he proceeded. He brought to bear all the graces of a polished orator, and more than once tears came into the eyes of his listeners. Particularly affecting was his description of Emmett's death. At the conclusion it was evident that his audience felt that it would have been difficult to have handled that subject better.

The judges now retired to deliberate as to whom to give the prize. While they are out, let us examine Belton's plans for carrying out the second thing, upon the accomplishment of which he was determined; viz., revenge.

In the rear of the schoolhouse, there stood an old wood-shed. For some slight offense the teacher had, two or three years back, made Belton the fire-maker for the balance of his school life instead of passing the task around according to custom. Thus the care of the woodhouse had fallen permanently to Belton's lot.

During the last year Belton had dug a large hole running from the floor of the wood-shed to a point under the platform of the school room. The dirt from this underground channel he cast into a deep old unused well, not far distant. Once under the platform, he kept on digging, making the hole larger by far. Numerous rocks abounded in the neighborhood, and these he used to wall up his underground room, so that it would hold water. Just in the middle of the school-room platform he cut, from beneath, a square hole, taking in the spot where the teacher invariably stood when addressing the school. He cut the boards until they lacked but a very little, indeed, of being cut through. All looked well above, but a baby would not be safe standing thereon. Belton contrived a kind of prop with a weight attached. This prop would serve to keep the cut section from breaking through. The attached weight was at rest in a hole left in the wall of the cavity near its top. If you dislocated the weight, the momentum that it would gather in the fall would pull down the prop to which it was attached.

Finally, Belton fastened a strong rope to the weight, and ran the rope under the schoolhouse floor until it was immediately beneath his seat.

With an auger he made a hole in the floor and brought the end through. He managed to keep this bit of rope concealed, while at the same time he had perfect command of his trap door.

For two or three nights previous to commencement day Belton had worked until nearly morning filling this cistern with water. Now when through delivering his oration, he had returned to his seat to await the proper moment for the payment of his teacher. The judges were out debating the question as to who had won. They seemed to be unable to decide who was victorious and beckoned for the teacher to step outside.

They said: "That black nigger has beat the yellow one all to pieces this time, but we don't like to see nigger blood triumph over any Anglo-Saxon blood. Ain't there any loop-hole where we can give it to Bernard, anyhow?"

"Well, yes," said the teacher eagerly, "on the ground of good behavior."

"There you hit it," said the Mayor. "So we all decide."

The judges filed in, and the Mayor arose to announce their decision. "We award," said to the breathless audience, "the prize to Bernard Belgrave."

"No! no! no!" burst forth from persons all over the house. The congressman arose and went up to Belton and congratulated him upon his triumph over oratory, and lamented his defeat by prejudice. This action caused a perceptible stir in the entire audience.

The teacher went to his desk and produced a large gold medal. He took his accustomed place on the platform and began thus:

"Ladies and Gentlemen, this is the proudest moment of my life." He got no further. Belton had pulled the rope, the rope had caused the weight to fall, and the weight had pulled the prop and down had gone the teacher into a well of water.

"Murder! Murder! Murder!" he cried "Help ! Help! Help! I am drowning. Take me out, it is cold. "

The audience rushed forward expecting to find the teacher in a dangerous situation; but they found him standing, apparently unharmed, in a cistern, the water being a little more than waist deep. Their fright gave way to humor and a merry shout went up from the throats of the scholars.

The colored men and women laughed to one side, while the white people smiled as though they had admired the feat as a fine specimen of falling from the sublime to the ridiculous. Bending down over the well, the larger students caught hold of the teacher's arms and lifted him out.

He stood before the audience wet and shivering, his clothes sticking to him, and water dripping from his hair. The medal was gone. The teacher dismissed the audience, drew his last month's pay and left that night for parts unknown.

Sometimes, even a worm will turn when trodden upon.

1899

NOTES

1. The titles of two popular African American spirituals.

2. To be overcome with religious fervor, often expressed through uncontrolled dancing, jumping, stomping, gesticulating, or speaking in tongues.

3. To express anger, especially at a person who is not the source of that anger.

4. Leonidas I (540 BCE-480 BCE), King of Sparta and commander of Spartan forces, remembered for his heroic sacrifice during the Battle of Thermopylae.

5. Markos Botsaris (ca. 1788–1823), military leader and hero of the Greek War for Independence.

6. Swiss patriot of the fourteenth century, remembered for his heroic death at the Battle of Sempach, Switzerland, in 1386.

7. Lajos Kossuth de Udvard et Kossuthfalva (1802–1894), regent-president of Hungary during that nation's war for independence, hailed worldwide as a freedom fighter and advocate for democracy.

8. Irish nationalist and leader of a failed bid for independence from Britain, captured and convicted of high treason and executed in 1803.

WILLIAM HANNIBAL THOMAS (1843–1935)

William Hannibal Thomas was born to free black parents in Pickaway County, Ohio. As a boy, he worked as a manual laborer and attended school only sporadically. In 1859, the largely self-educated Thomas became the first African American admitted to Ohio's Otterbein University. His time on that campus was short-lived, however, as his presence sparked racially motivated harassment and vandalism. During the next seventy-six years, Thomas worked in a number of occupations. He served briefly as the principal of a vocational training school, as a Civil War combat sergeant in an all-black regiment, and as an attorney, a minister, a politician, and a writer, in cities and towns from Massachusetts to Georgia. Thomas also worked as a journalist, publishing several articles in the *Christian Recorder* and the *A.M.E. Church Review.* In 1886, he founded his own magazine, *The Negro,* which folded after only two issues. Thomas's greatest notoriety, however, came in response to his 1901 volume, *The American Negro: What He Was, What He Is, and What He May Become.* Deeply critical of both the intellect and morality of African Americans, and of black women in particular, *The American Negro* was widely condemned by Thomas's African American contemporaries. Radical white segregationists embraced his text as welcome affirmation of their antiblack stereotypes and sentiments; but Thomas drew criticism from the black literary and intellectual establishment, led by figures like Booker T. Washington, Charles Chesnutt, and W. E. B. Du Bois. Eventually, the voices of protest against Thomas's antiblack sentiments overwhelmed those of his supporters, and he disappeared from the public's attention almost as swiftly as he had entered it. Thomas lived out the remainder of his years in virtual obscurity, working as a janitor in eastern Ohio in the years leading up to his death.

THE AMERICAN NEGRO: WHAT HE WAS, WHAT HE IS, AND WHAT HE MAY BECOME

Chapter VII: Moral Lapses

Man is not a law to himself; on the contrary, he is both the product and subject of law. He is a rational being, and as such is cognizant of the existence of moral and physical laws. He further understands that conformity to these laws constitutes a sane attitude of mind, that non-conformity is followed by pains and penalties above and beyond human infliction. From these fundamental principles of life, which apply to all men and are equally obligatory upon all, man has derived a feasible and comprehensive standard of right and wrong conduct,—one by which the civilization and morality of men is measured. When men have agreed upon a normal standard of living, and fixed the boundaries of right and wrong, it is obvious that henceforth the social status of a race is to be determined by the degree of conformity or resistance with which a majority of its people evince toward such established rules of conduct. The sum of racial greatness is never more than the whole product of individual power minus the sum of individual weakness.

A man, we say, is good or bad, according as he conforms to or departs from the spirit of sound ethical deportment. But it cannot be assumed that he is good or bad in an absolute sense. In like manner a person is said to be ignorant or learned, notwithstanding the fact that no human being is so untaught as to be entirely devoid of some degree of intelligence, and that the greatest human erudition is limited by insurmountable mystery. What these relative terms are meant to indicate is that a manifest excess of immoral inclinations in a given individual is evidence of vicious intent, just as a preponderance of rectitude is indicative of ethical obedience. There is no other criterion, and by such discriminations, the dividing line between the vicious and virtuous of mankind is ascertained. Such endeavors are not only landmarks of growth or monuments of folly in any people, but it is absolutely true that the actual condition of any given portion of mankind is nowhere more clearly exemplified than in their moral conceptions, their ideals of truth and duty in everyday living, and the character and aim of their social and civic institutions.

But no intelligent comprehension of social subjects will be reached, unless it is fully realized that the home life of a people is the most vital of all civic or social institutions. We need, therefore, in order to secure trustworthy results when dealing with inferior types of people, to ascertain correctly the drift of the moral impulse of that people, and what social order they sanction in their family life. In any examination into the moral condition of the freedmen, these observations are to be kept in mind. To know the negro people in any comprehensive and inclusive way, one must dwell with them and be one of them in outward sentiment and sympathy. There is no other way by which a clear insight into their domestic living can be acquired. The freedmen, like all submerged classes, have an exterior and an interior code of conduct, and the superficial knowledge of their social life acquired through public contact is altogether misleading and worse than useless as an agency for bettering them. We are therefore led to believe, by reason of the current misapprehension concerning the freed people, that every essential fact of negro life and living should without evasion or concealment be brought to light. We also trust that this brief recital of racial shortcomings may not only induce an awakening, but will enable those charged with the education of the black people to devise adequate measures for their enlightenment.

Now, to persons reared in an atmosphere of domestic privacy and chaste living, the well-attested facts connected with the actual conditions of negro life may appear incredible statements; but, if so, it will be largely for the reason that the cultured among us have but slight knowledge of the habits, disposition, and social conduct of those inferior to them in point of development. Nor is it possible for our higher classes, with their formal methods and masterful ways, to acquire an accurate insight into the actual life and living of those beneath them, since visible contempt on the one side and resentful distrust on the other effectually block the way to any mutual understanding. In this explanation lies the key to the usual inconclusive results achieved by reformatory agencies. In what is attempted, there is rarely any honest effort to get at the core of the matter by ascertaining, with precision, the instincts, impulses, and aspirations of the people whom we undertake to serve. Humanitarian efforts for the amelioration of mankind are, therefore, often futile. Nor does the matter end there, for philanthropy becomes discouraged and ceases to interest itself in human betterment while those of inferior social attainments cling with greater obstinacy to environing conditions. In most cases such results might be averted if a clearer understanding of actual conditions were acquired before attempts at social uplifting were begun.

No one will deny that our freed people occupy an anomalous and unique relation to American society; consequently, in any serious study of this subject, the question which naturally arises is, "What are the chief besetments which hinder negro recognition, as an equal member of our social fraternity?" There are four characteristic phases which we shall note, as having a pronounced bearing on his exclusion from well-ordered social intercourse. He is regarded as a creature of lascivious habits, personal vanity, mental density, and physical laziness. All who know the negro recognize, however, that the chief and overpowering element in his make-up is an imperious sexual impulse, which, aroused at the slightest incentive, sweeps aside all restraints in the pursuit of physical gratification. We may say now that this element of negro character constitutes the main incitement to the degeneracy of the race, and is the chief hindrance to its social uplifting.

We have elsewhere referred to the cleavage between high and low degrees of social development. In well-ordered homes, the conduct of the members, male and female, is environed with certain reservations, and their personal intercourse is governed by a self-respecting courtesy that neither invades individual privacy nor invites wanton liberties. In negro homes, on the contrary, their inmates, devoid of either modesty or discretion, indulge in the utmost freedom of speech and action, and the female members, regardless of the presence of their male relatives and friends, go about in scanty clothing which invites a familiar caress that is rarely forbidden or resented as an insult. Not only does the semi-nude attire of the adult negresses invite lascivious carousal at home, but their young daughters are permitted to parade the streets and visit their associates clad in a scantiness of attire that ought never to be seen outside a bedroom. With a knowledge of these facts, it will not require a very keen discernment to discover that negroes have not learned the elementary principles of moral conduct, nor acquired sobriety of speech, nor delicacy of manner in daily intercourse, and domestic seclusion.

But what else could be expected of a people, among whom vulgarisms of speech are staple topics of conversation, where obscene allusions are listened to with avidious relish by the young and old of both sexes, and where there is such moral laxity among all classes as to transcend every semblance of decency? It is fair to say, however, that much of the temptation and wrong-doing which beset the freedmen arises from the fact that negroes are preëminently social in their instincts. To be sure, their illiterate loquacity is fatal to enduring friendship; but, as their puerile gossip chiefly concerns each other's dress, color, hair, male and female associates, and domestic living, it seldom foments enduring discord among themselves, though not infrequently their craze for social excitement involves them in serious crimes.

To understand intelligently the subject, we must realize that the great mass of the negro people are implacably arrayed against social distinctions, and seek to reduce all higher grades of race living to its own debasing level. Hence, the most heinous infringement of the moral law is no bar to social recognition among a people where individual intercourse is regulated by personal likes or dislikes. So triumphantly entrenched are they in insuperable vanity, and so surrounded by a rampart of ceaseless indiscretions, that it is no rare thing to see prostitution lock arms with chastity, and cultured libertinism outrank illiterate purity in their most notable social gatherings. We shall be grossly deceived, however, if we conclude that the negro has no code of morality. He has, and one that in many respects is rigorously enforced. For instance, the negro's ethical code sternly reprobates dancing, theatre attendance, and all social games of chance. It does not, however, forbid lying, rum-drinking, or stealing. Furthermore, a man may trail his loathsome form into the sanctity of private homes, seduce a wife, sister, or daughter with impunity, and be the father of a score of illegitimate children by as many mothers, and yet be a disciple of holiness and honored with public confidence. So bestial are negro men that we have known them to lead wives, mothers, sisters, and daughters to the sensuous embraces of white men as readily as it is said the Irish peasants led their virgin daughters to the arms of their English conquerors during the early conquest of that country.

So lacking in moral rectitude are the men of the negro race that we have known them to take strange women into their homes and cohabit with them with the knowledge, but without protest, from their wives and children. So great is their moral putridity that it is no uncommon thing for stepfathers to have children by their step-daughters with the consent of the wife and mother of the girl. Nor do other ties of relationship interpose moral barriers; for fathers and daughters, brothers and sisters, oblivious of decent social restrictions, abandon themselves without attempt at self-restraint to sexual gratification whenever desire and opportunity arises. That such licentiousness is prevalent is not surprising, when we reflect that animal impulse is the sole master, to which both sexes yield unquestioned obedience. Not only is negro immorality without shame, remorse, or contrition, but their unchaste men and women are perfidious, malevolent, and cowardly in their relations, and with reckless obliviousness to consequences, eagerly gloat over each other's frailties and readily betray the indiscretions of their companions in guilt. Moreover, the contradictions of the freedman's nature are such that, while imputations of personal impurity are resented by the known impure, there is a common disposition to question each other's morals, and rarely is either male or female accorded a clean bill of approval. Soberly speaking, negro nature is so craven and sensuous in every fibre of its being that a negro manhood with decent respect for chaste womanhood does not exist.

These conclusions are reached because the facts show that the negro is slowly and steadily undergoing moral deterioration; not, however, because he cannot keep pace with the advancing strides of an environing superior civilization, but because he has no ethical integrity, no inbred determination for right-doing, and consequently no clearly defined and steadfast aversion to wrong-doing.

The American negro never had a conscientious and intelligent appreciation of the law of obedience, and for that reason either does not clearly apprehend, or else wantonly ignores, essential facts. In any critical analysis of this subject, we shall easily discover that the groundwork of negro degeneration rests on mental frivolity and physical pleasure, and that, owing to these characteristic traits, his confusion of mind is such that he fails to realize that between good and evil conduct there is a great gulf. He has yet to discern that there is such a thing as moral inexorableness, with every sin shadowed by its own penalty. The simple truth is that there is going on, side by side in the negro people, a minimum progress with a maximum regress; or, in other words, an awakening of a minority of them, with an increasing degradation of the majority.

One of the most reprehensible features leading to the ruin of negro men is their foolish imitations of the vices of the whites. For instance, negro attendants in hotels frequently wait on prominent white men who have resorted thither for carousal with lewd female companions. The example thus set they readily follow, and speedily make a business of what white men do for pastime. When rebuked for their folly, they set up the excuse that they are no worse than their superiors in vicious indulgence. Likely enough this is true; nevertheless, not only do white men come out of their debaucheries in a better condition than their imitators, but it is also true that, so long as the latter do not realize their moral degradation, moral betterment is impossible. Moreover, as long as the negro is heedless as to act and thoughtless as to consequences, his disposition to imitate white folly will be the source of much evil-doing within the race. It may be, however, that the negro cannot acquire an inflexible determination for the realities of right living. While he can state with absolute precision the distinction between right and wrong, and is outspoken in condemnation of the immoralities of others, we find no evidence of the existence of moral aversion to wrong-doing within himself. Furthermore, the negro's attitude toward personal wrong-doing is always childish, and in many respects borders on imbecility; for, when actual misdeeds are brought home to him in a way that admits of no denial, instead of confessing his guilt and attempting its eradication, he merely seeks condonation and justification by pointing to the evil-doings of other people. But what, we ask, has the negro to do with the crimes of the white man, and in what respect can white heinousness efface negro guilt? Cannot the freedman realize that he alone is responsible for his own act?—that his crimes are to be considered and treated as if they were the only misdeeds in the universe, and he the only criminal? One thing is certain, his infamy will never be blotted out by contrast.

But, while the negro is thoroughly imbruted with lascivious instincts, there are many contributory causes which accelerate libidinous acts. For instance, the practice of masturbation is common among the children of both sexes, and the physical desire awakened and stimulated by organic manipulation inevitably leads to sexual intercourse. It is, therefore, almost impossible to find a person of either sex, over fifteen years of age, who has not had actual carnal knowledge. But not only do the young negro girls who grow up in idleness become prematurely old in viciousness, but even those better reared are amazingly yielding to licentious overtures, especially if a proposed meeting-place is sufficiently secluded to render detection improbable. For although abashed by discovery and chagrined by publicity, such girls are not easily deterred from following their inclinations, inasmuch as the greatest immoralities rarely disturb their social status or exclude them from church associations. Innate modesty is not a characteristic of the American negro women. On the contrary, there is observable among them a willing susceptibility to the blandishments of licentious men, together with a widespread distribution of physical favors among their male friends. The great majority of them, to be sure, are not bold and avaricious like the abandoned women of other races, though they are becoming that, especially in the North. Nevertheless, the grossly depraved among them exhibit considerable animal affection, and readily yield to caresses that consciously lead them to destruction.

Marriage is no barrier to illicit sexual indulgence, and both men and women maintain such relations in utter disregard of their plighted troth. In fact, so deeply rooted in immorality are our negro people that they turn in aversion from any sexual relation which does not invite sensuous embraces, and seize with feverish avidity upon every opportunity that promises personal gratification. Women unresistingly betray their wifely honor to satisfy a bestial instinct, and though there may be times when a morbid sentimental remorse reminds them for a brief period of their folly, yet every notion of marital duty and fidelity is cast to the winds when the next moment of passion arrives.

Most negro women marry young; when they do not their spinsterhood is due either to physical disease, or sexual morbidity, or a desire for unrestrained sexual freedom. But, even in the latter case, there are but few freedwomen who do not have particular male friends, to whom they are more or less constant. Negro women, however, have but dim notions of the nature and obligations of wifehood; for, as we have observed, the leading thoughts which actuate them are to be free from parental control, to secure idle maintenance, and to indulge in unbridled sexual freedom. Nor is female ante-nuptial knowledge a bar to marriage among negroes, especially in the alliance of a fair woman to a black man, while illegitimate motherhood is rather a recommendation in the eyes of a prospective husband.

Marital immoralities, however, are not confined to the poor, the ignorant, and the degraded among the freed people, but are equally common among those who presume to be educated and refined. We have personal knowledge of more than a score of negro preachers of high repute who are married to women of known impurity, and of whose immorality they were fully cognizant before marriage. In more than one instance we have heard such a preacher privately denounce a woman publicly known as the mistress of white men, and afterward found that that particular woman had become the wife of that identical preacher and a leader in negro society. We have convincing proof that many negro ministers owe their prominence in pastoral appointment to the fact that their wives have prostituted themselves with their official superiors. We know of others who have been thrust into conspicuous churches for no other reason than because they had knowledge of, or were purveyors for, the licentious instincts of their clerical superiors. But while a large majority of our negro ministry is conspicuous for its licentious indulgence with female members of negro churches, there are not wanting instances where church debts have been created, and schemes concocted for procuring money from philanthropic white people, in order that a black preacher might have means to win the favor of white women of lewd morals.

All of the negro schools in the South are not moral sanctuaries, and it is but in keeping with well-known facts to say that many of those in authority, who were entrusted to guide into paths of truth and righteousness the humble beings committed to their charge, have wantonly betrayed their trust. This has been notably true of the schools in charge of the black people themselves, though there are others that equally deserve censure. We have knowledge of many unmentionable features incident to the educational work among the freedmen that have greatly hampered the inculcation of sound moral distinctions, but such is the cravenness of white and black institutional poverty that it has not dared to exact from its attendants genuine moral sobriety. The consequence is that there is no school of prominence in negro training which has not had among its pupils young freedwomen sustaining immoral relations with white men, whose school expenses have been, in many instances, defrayed by such persons with the knowledge and consent of the school authorities. It is also a significant and suggestive fact, that it is always the good-looking, light-colored girl who is favored, both as a student and as an applicant for a position in the public schools. But however regrettable these things may be, it is needful to know that, for causes which need not be specified, the complex conditions of the Southern social system have from the beginning exercised a pernicious influence on the educational work among the freedmen.

Vice, never wanting in emissaries, is propagated among the freedmen in many ways. One is the habit they have of betaking themselves to the villages on Saturdays, where their wives and daughters, congregated around the stores and other public places, are the subjects of obscene speech and the victims of immoral advances. The railroad excursions, so extensively indulged in by the negro preachers of the South for the benefit of their churches, are another prolific cause of immorality, and many young girls are brought to grief and ruin by them. Nor is it surprising that such should be the case, when hundreds of them, allured, by the cheap rates, will crowd the cars and travel long distances, only to find themselves in a strange city, where, without means or friends, they are compelled to spend a night as best they can. Negro religionists have much to answer for in the way of commission as well as omission; but their culpability becomes specially heinous when abandoned courtesans can directly trace their downfall to a religious picnic and a clerical seducer. Another incentive to negro degradation is that nondescript order of social clubs in which every city abounds; for, while these social rendezvous are ostensibly of a literary nature, they are in reality devoted to gambling, drinking, and dancing. Their most conspicuous attractions, however, are young women dressed *décolleté*,[1] who are under the impression that they are like white society when permitting their nude charms to be openly caressed at the pleasure of their male companions. Knowledge of social decorum among these young women has been mainly derived from questionable novels and salacious theatricals. Besides, in the North, their real or affected prudery would put them at a serious disadvantage in competing for the favor of their male companions owing to the fact that lewd white women resort to such places and become the coveted prizes of the most desirable negro men.

A despicable source of moral corruption is that class of negro men infesting all of our large cities who never engage in honest work, but eke out a precarious existence by their wits. These men are the systematic corrupters of black womanhood, their chosen prey being those employed in domestic service. On these girls they levy a species of blackmail for idle maintenance, though none escape their licentious overtures. There are also negro men and women, of good repute in their churches in the North, who make periodical visits to the South for the purpose of procuring handsome-looking negro girls for infamous purposes. They are ostensibly engaged for domestic service, but in reality to be consigned to the lowest dens of infamy. No large city in the North is free from this degrading traffic, because there are but few of these religious "saints," who will not sell the chastity of any young girl for a moderate sum of money. There are other negro men and women, of good social standing in their own race, who make a business of providing furnished rooms for the transient cohabitation of men and women, and live in comparative affluence on their ill-gotten gains. But, notwithstanding their universal licentiousness, the negro women as a whole are superior in many respects to negro men. The force of this conclusion rests on the fact that in all of our cities, North and South, there is a large class of freedwomen who, by their unaided efforts, pay their house rent and feed and clothe their children, while their dissolute husbands roam about in wanton idleness. The latter are usually great braggarts but arrant cowards, and decidedly inferior to their slave forbears in every semblance of manhood.

Negro social conditions will, however, be but dimly understood, even in their more conspicuous phases unless we are prepared to realize at every step in our investigation that physical excitation is the chief and foremost craving of the freedman's nature. We see evidence of this in his manner of eating, drinking, and indulgence in social pleasures, from which we may gather some notion of the boundless obstacles which stand in the way of his immediate or remote regeneration. It is as much a quest for physical excitement as the promise of pecuniary gain which impels the negro to indulge in petty gambling and makes him the chief "policy-player"[2] of the community, in every city, North and South. So deeply rooted is this impulse, that both "saints and sinners," the leaders and the led of the negro men and women, constantly haunt such gambling-places, and, notwithstanding arrest, imprisonment, and disgrace are not rare incidents in their experience, they continue to be the most persistent supporters of "policy" promoters. It is chiefly a desire for physical sensation which causes snuff-dipping[3] to be such a prevalent custom among black people. Even the children at their mothers' breasts are taught to use it; and the bleared eyes and blotched cheeks of men and women sodden with the use of tobacco betokens but too well to what excess they have gone in the use of loathsome narcotics. For like reasons, rum-drinking is also universal among both sexes; and all grades of negro society, preachers and laity seem to vie with each other in the use of intoxicating liquors. So excessive is their indulgence in these two vices that it has been reliably estimated that the freedmen spend over sixty millions of dollars annually for rum and tobacco.

A deplorable fact to be noted is that, while venereal diseases, especially those of a syphilitic nature, were almost unknown among the negroes during slavery, since their freedom these diseases have overspread the entire South. This is specially true of syphilis; and while it rarely assumes the malignant form so often exhibited in cold climates, owing to its peculiar amenability to tropical and subtropical temperatures, yet so deep-seated is it among the negroes that it threatens to baffle the skill of the medical profession. So firmly rooted are these venereal diseases among the freed people of the cities that many persons, especially women, are unconscious of the nature of their ailments, and, when chance apprises them of their misfortune, false notions of modesty or innate cowardice leads them to seek relief through quack medicines rather than through the advice and treatment of capable physicians. These physical disorders are extending to the plantation negroes, and are largely brought about through rural freedwomen, who have been permitted to indulge briefly in the allurements of city life, to whose attractions they have readily yielded. On return to their homes they become the ignorant disseminators of loathsome diseases.

Our statements concerning the immoral tendencies of the freed people may shock the sensibilities of those persons who are ignorant of their physical inclinations. It is altogether likely that they will wound the vanity of the race inculpated. Nevertheless, the certainty of our conclusions is as demonstrable as any problem of Euclid. We shall, however, cite some facts which will go toward substantiating our conclusions. For example, a noted teacher in a Southern negro school, who has charge of several hundred children, ranging in age from six to fifteen, has informed us that it was well-nigh impossible to keep the boys and girls from indulging in immoral practices even while together in the schoolyard, and that several instances of carnal contact had taken place despite the presence of numerous onlooking companions. This is not an exceptional experience. Co-sexual assemblages of negroes, whether of children or adults, in the schoolroom or sanctuary, would, if the light were turned on, disclose an equal degree of moral turpitude. We have also been informed by a trustworthy physician, who has had an exceptionally large female practice, that he had professionally examined over nine hundred negro girls ranging in age from ten to twenty-five years, and that, out of that number, only two furnished proofs of virginity, while most of the others exhibited indisputable

evidence of unchastity. He further stated that he found the greatest manifestation of sexual desire in those girls who were under twenty years of age.

We anticipate that these statements may be controverted, and the averment
made that evidence of female immorality is lacking where its usual fruitage
is invisible. Such an objection is groundless, for, while wifeless maternity is
decreasing among negroes, ante-nuptial infanticide is increasing at an alarming rate. Besides, the fact is not to be overlooked that early sexual indulgence
precipitates an internal derangement of the physical organs which renders
conception difficult, if not improbable. When it does take place, however,
the young negro woman is not without adequate resources, for in the South
the fields around her cabin supply her with a potent remedy of whose peculiar efficacy she is fully aware. Then, again, in the cities and towns of either section she can and does have recourse to criminal operations with the
knowledge and approval of her parents. Criminal malpractice is not rare, as
all well-informed people know. For example, we have in mind a prominent
white physician residing in a leading Southern city, who has in a confidential
way privately acknowledged to having been instrumental in effecting over
two hundred abortions among young negro women at the instance of their
white paramours. This is not an exceptional medical experience, but one
that can be duplicated in every Southern city, and in not a few of those of
the North. So widespreading is this disorder that, if not arrested, American
negro women are likely to become as infertile as the Greek courtesans, and
it is needless to say that the people of any race is doomed to extinction when
the women cease to become mothers.

This reference to criminal operations for the destruction of sexual fruitage calls up another phase of social conditions that cannot be ignored in any
attempted uplifting of the race. We refer to the well-nigh universal custom
in the South, as well as in many sections of the North, of white men keeping
negro mistresses. This shameless prostitution of an inferior people by the men
of a superior race offers the most forcible obstacle to be encountered in any
effort for the moral regeneration of the freed people. Not only are the inherent lascivious instincts of the race to be met and overcome, but the subtle and
powerful machinations of an adroit libertinism, interested in perpetuating
negro degradation, must be courageously reckoned with. That such grave
social complications exist is well attested by the fact that Southern grand
juries, composed of reputable white citizens have been outspoken in their
condemnation of the prevalent negro concubinage of their section, and their
presentments to the courts of their vicinage have repeatedly affirmed that

their young white men are not marrying, and would not marry, their social peers, so long as they were permitted to keep negro mistresses. The causes which have brought about this anomalous social phase are not far to seek. They will be found in the lax morality, the love of luxury, and that material greed which so largely permeates our civilization, and which are doing for us what the same influences wrought in the French people,—that is, producing a class of voluptuous white celibates, who will not create conjugal homes and rear legitimate families, because they have greater freedom and less expense in a misalliance with an inferior and subjective female class. We may, to be sure, blindly ignore existing facts, and be oblivious to the drift of events, but any sane forecast of the future will reveal impending evils of prodigious magnitude to a people who are neither "marrying nor given in marriage."

There may be a disposition by well-intentioned persons who have more or less knowledge of this matter to question the facts underlying our statements concerning negro social conditions. If so, they are advised in advance that no conclusive evidence to the contrary exists; furthermore, to all who are disposed to challenge the veracity of these statements, we suggest a simple method by which they may reasonably ascertain for themselves the correctness of what we say. For example, let those interested in this subject make out, from among their immediate acquaintances, a random list of one hundred female negroes; then scan the list critically, and we venture the assertion that they will be amazed and mortified at the number of moral lapses which a mere inspection of the list will disclose. Of course an adequate and authoritative comprehension of this question can only be reached in this, as in other departments of knowledge, from facts, from analytical investigation and verified data. We shall, however, in view of all the known facts at our command, be justified in assuming that not only are fully ninety per cent of the negro women of America lascivious by instinct and in bondage to physical pleasure, but that the social degradation of our freedwomen is without a parallel in modern civilization.

In advancing this conclusion we shall briefly note, in addition to what has already been said in this connection, that the leading causes which have wrought their downfall and which perpetuate their shame, are an aversion for manual labor, the desire for physical ease, a craving for gaudy display in dress, the lack of conception or knowledge of the fundamental duties, obligations, and social requirements of womankind, and the consciousness of white superiority and negro debasement. These incitements to personal degradation are supplemented and overshadowed by the racial distinctions instilled in the minds of negro girls by many mothers, who not only bring them up in an atmosphere of lax morality, but in many instances, with positive aversion to their own race and color, thereby effecting their early transition from purity to concubinage. While these social statements fairly indicate the status and trend of negro development, the question arises again: Is it instinct, impulse, or will, or all of them combined, which leads the negro to prefer darkness to light, vice to virtue, crime to innocence, death to life? To our mind the answer lies in a sentence,—it is an insatiate craving for physical sensations, an impulse that constitutes the supreme motif of negroid activity. In order to apprehend the significance of this statement in all its bearings, there is need to realize that the psychical endowment of the negro has not developed adequate mental and spiritual forces. He is lacking in continuity of purpose, in abstract endeavor, and seeks satisfaction in such concrete sensations as taste and feeling.

It was not deemed necessary to the verification of our statements that special incidents should be related in detail, either as to person or act. Such disclosures could serve no useful end; besides, the characteristic data of which we have made use is everywhere present in the negro people, and readily accessible to the observant public. It is hardly necessary to add that these animadversions of negro shortcomings are not indulged in for the sake of denunciation. Wherefore, then, it may be questioned, are these revelations, this exhibit of frailty, this analysis of weakness? For this: to arouse moral apathy into earnest discontent, to protest against bigotry, to stimulate upris- ing against ignorance, to revolt against infamy,—to the end that hoary men- dacities, sacerdotal hypocrisies, the ghastly corpses of servile mummeries, and all other duplicities which shackle the conscience and blur the vision of enthralled souls shall be tossed aside and trampled under foot, and that the dross be utterly consumed in the indignation of reclaimed men and women.

The moral status of a race is fixed by the character of its women; but, as moral rectitude is not a predominant trait in negro nature, female chastity is not one of its endowments. Nor has negro womankind any strong incen- tive for virtuous living when the pure and the impure are received on an equal footing in social intercourse, and the ability to wear good clothes is the sole criterion of individual social standing. The manifest disposition of the negro people to blot out all moral distinctions in social intercourse has had its inevitable fruits. The women of that race are evading honest toil to live in licentious ease. Moreover, as fine clothes are the open sesame to social recognition, a craze for dress and personal adornment has aroused within the freedmen a passionate discontent that urges them to resort to all sorts of reprehensible follies, and even crime, to obtain their desire. This greed and unrest among their women, which would be laudable if it led them to honest labor and thrifty forethought, is a strong incitement to immoral vices,—so much so that, without remorse or shame, for the sake of obtaining luxuries without labor, they will traffic in their bodies, which is the most marketable commodity they possess.

So visibly universal is the strife for personal adornment that negro mothers cannot be held blameless for the immoralities of their daughters, and there is at least ground for believing that sexual impurity is deliberately inculcated in them, since, in many instances, their maternal guardians appear to be never so pleased as when the physical charms of their daughters have procured for them dress and jewels beyond the ability of their parents to provide. Nor do the girls themselves appear to be abashed by any publicity of their immoralities. On the contrary, they are conspicuous in the social gatherings of their people, and parade with shameless audacity their wanton finery before their envious and less successful female friends. These facts would be incredible did we not realize that negro women are admittedly weak in purpose, timid in execution, superstitious in thought, lascivious in conduct, and signally lacking in those enduring qualities which make for morality, thrift, and industry. Therefore, as they are seldom animated by high aspirations and noble purposes, the common-sense lessons of life which universal experience teaches are rarely heeded by them.

So far as we can discern, negro motherhood is not animated with profound convictions of truth and duty. The freedwomen evidently do not realize that they are the custodians of the souls as well as the bodies of their children, and the first and chief teachers in life of purity in speech and action, of right-doing in all its phases, and the God-ordained creators of true manhood and womanhood. On the contrary, they bring to the discharge of their domestic duties illiterate minds, unskilled hands, impetuous tempers, untidy deportment, and shiftless methods. Moreover, as their chief defects are ignorance and laziness, filth and squalor, these advance agents of intemperance and vice pervade and dominate their domestic endeavors, and such conditions are increasingly perpetuated as the negro children come into being. Where such conditions exist it is obvious that any uplifting movement begun for the race must attack every point of life and character requiring amendment or improvement; though, first and foremost, let us realize that it is example and environment which make for the good or ill of mankind. We see that vice propagates vice, that wholesome surroundings induce virtuous living, and nothing more strongly exemplifies this fact, either in the direction of upward or downward growth, than the law of habit. Obviously we build solid characters of truth and righteousness mainly through pure association and the steady repetition of good deeds. On the other hand, evil contact and vicious example has certainly led to vice and infamy. We shall therefore make no mistake in saying that until an all-pervading desire for cleanliness, sobriety, industry, and chastity awakens within the freedwomen and arouses them to reformatory action, no amount of theoretical knowledge will be of the slightest value to them, solely because knowledge is valuable only in proportion as it is applied to the actual needs of life.

These observations lead us to note that, whether considered as units of contrasts or as inclusive aggregates of type characteristics, there is a fundamental difference in the racial character, habits, integrity, courage, and strength of negro and white Americans. What makes it? The answer lies in one word—their women. But while that fact is obvious, it furnishes no solution of another equally patent, which is this: Girls of the two races will grow up side by side, attend the same schools, go through the same course of study, and enjoy equal mental advantages, yet the chances are two to one that the negro girl at twenty will be a giggling idiot and lascivious wreck, while her white companion in school and church, of the same age, has blossomed out into chaste womanhood, intelligent in mind and accomplished in manner. This difference between them becomes of fundamental significance when we reflect that each girl represents the future maternal life-blood of her respective people, and that the wives and mothers of a race are its earliest and most convincing teachers. How important, then, that negro women should comprehend and uphold, under all circumstances and in all places, the purity, dignity, and worth of chaste living. Is it not obvious that the negro people will never become great, wise, or true, until its women become the qualified teachers of infant life and the moral censors of mature existence, until they institute such safeguards and assurances of chaste maidenhood as characterize Hebrew social life?

So far as the questions of marriage and divorce relate to the freedman we are confronted by conditions that no amount of common-sense pleading will eliminate. Marriage rites are held by negroes to effect a mystical union between two persons of opposite sex, in much the same sense that regeneration is understood to operate upon their spiritual natures. That is to say, no matter how divergent in character, sentiment, habit, or inclination two persons may be, they are by some supernatural process made one through a ceremonial incantation uttered by clerical lips. Ceremonial marriage, therefore, with the negroes, is invested with a superstitious halo, notwithstanding the fact that the nature, purpose, duties, and obligations of marital relations are unknown to most of those contracting connubial ties, and when known to them are frequently unheeded. In the presence of such beliefs it would be a waste of time and words to say that true marriage is a complete union of the aims, ideals, purposes, and interests of two persons, of such consummate oneness as to shut out all variant individual interests and compel personal selfishness to give way to dual welfare; that actual marriage is neither mercenary nor sensuous, but replete with sacrifice and service, with a constant preference of another for self, and that when these do not exist, the essentials of wedded life are wanting.

Concurrent with the freedman's notion concerning marriage there is a disposition among many of the leading negro societies to discredit the legitimate function of divorce, some of which have even gone so far as to usurp functions belonging to the state by not only undertaking to regulate marriage among their followers, but to pass in review the mandates of the state and impeach the legality of its acts. The consequence is that, should a man or woman of these societies when mated with an impure companion procure a severance of marital ties through divorce, and to live a decent life thereafter marry another, he or she is liable to be adjudged guilty of bigamy. The negro conjugal maxim is, once married always married; to which doubtless he has been led by his creed, which is, once in Christ always in Christ. In each condition, however, he is sadly derelict in conjoining practice with belief, and chiefly because he is more concerned with the form than with the facts of morality. The religious negro often expresses an abhorrence of divorces, while he freely indulges in conjugal separation, and exhibits a decided preference for sexual alliances free from legal restraint.

For ourselves, we believe in maintaining, wherever it is possible, the integrity of marriage, the purity of home, the fidelity of husband and wife to all the duties and requirements imposed by marital obligations. But we as firmly believe, when these duties are disregarded, when family honor is imperiled and home life desecrated with nuptial infidelity, that the legitimate and honorable step for self-respect and conscious rectitude to take is immediate separation and divorce. Marriage, as all intelligent people know, is a civil compact, consummated by two individuals of opposite sex, under such limitations and restrictions as the civic organism has made and provided. It is a civil contract between persons capable of making a legal agreement; the sanction of the state is necessary to its validity; it is annullable for cause through judicial process. Hence a decree for divorce from a court having jurisdiction is *prima facie*[4] evidence of the annulment of the previously contracted marriage, and, unless it can be clearly established before a competent judicial tribunal that such decree was obtained through collusion and fraud, it will not be set aside. These are facts of which it appears the negro is willfully ignorant, or to which he opposes obstinate indifference.

The question naturally arises, What can be done to ameliorate the condition of these negro people? We have but one solution to offer, and that is an amenable family supervision of such a character as will impart to its old and young useful knowledge of immediate needs, and induce one and all to strive for sincere social betterment. As we see this question, the one supreme need of negro family life is regenerated fathers and mothers and wholesome living. Evidently, then, as long as these are lacking, the moral and social redemption of badly reared, poorly nurtured, and viciously environed boys and girls is impossible, unless the reformatory discipline to which they are subjected extends to their homes and includes their parents. The value of this suggestion lies in the fact that any adequate family supervision would awaken in parents a desire for social betterment, and open the way for a sympathetic development of their children. Moreover, as there is a perceptible awakening to the evils of immoral degradation among negroes themselves, it is reasonable to believe that the more self-respecting freedmen would welcome corrective oversight, and be fairly amenable to any agency which, in a helpful spirit, undertook to improve their social condition. As matters now stand, they cannot effect their own extrication.

But such lessons in living as the negro needs cannot be imparted through any process of mental abstraction. Memorized precepts will not leaven sinful humanity with truth and righteousness; neither will verbal gymnastics bring about moral transformation. What the negro stands in absolute need of is such a renovating education as will implant within his untutored nature high ideals of sound sentiments respecting manhood and womanhood, and, at the same time, will train his mind, enlighten his soul, and discipline his body in every essential function of wholesome living. Already something has been accomplished in this direction, and both the flower and fruitage of racial evolution may be seen in that class of men and women among the freedmen who are honestly striving to free themselves from immoral entanglement. Nevertheless, it is obviously impossible for a fraction of regenerated negroes, with neither faith nor force behind them,—not to mention a lack of other essential endowments,—to change the habits and ideals of those from whom they have emerged, and who, in consequence, are bound to regard them as not a whit better than themselves.

The duty of all serious promoters of negro enlightenment is to apply to racial viciousness such correctives as the soundest experience has demonstrated to be the most efficacious in promoting the social bettering of mankind. Present methods will not regenerate the negro race; neither sobriety nor stability is ever attained by a homeless people. The negro needs to be taught how to create and maintain a home in honor and purity, and to that end he requires the influence of wholesome example and the inspiration of supervising contact. But no substantial moral elevation of the negro is possible without the intervention and coöperation of highly qualified women, such as are thoroughly capable, painstaking, and God-fearing teachers of truth and righteousness. This is a common-sense suggestion, and it is in line with conditions of aid which now exist. Negroes are accustomed to industrial control, and have been for centuries in abject submission to the white people of the South, who know, as no others can, all their good and bad qualities. We are therefore constrained to believe that, were the best representatives of Southern white civilization to lay aside their exclusive race arrogance, there is little doubt but that prodigious results would follow any candid and serious purpose on their part to accomplish the freedman's regeneration.

It ought, moreover, to be said that this duty is fairly incumbent upon those who have so interminably dominated an inferior race, and with whom, through vicious sexual alliance, they have become inextricably entangled in blood, lineage, speech, and habits. Candidly speaking, the white people of the South owe it to our civilization and Christianity, as well as to themselves and their posterity, to purify, by chaste speech and wholesome example, the homes of the blacks whom they and their ancestors have so wantonly debauched. It is no less a matter of moral preservation than their imperative duty, to arrest the degeneracy of that race with whom their future is inseparably bound up. But, whether or not this work is taken up by the white men and women of the South, the fetidness of negro sensuality must be eradicated. It can only be done, however, through an army of good and true women; and as no sufficient number of such women are to be found within the race itself, they must be sought from without. Where can such divinely consecrated teachers and exemplars of righteousness as this work requires be found? The only feasible hope for such a consummation centres in such white women of the

North as may be aroused to a sense of the needs and wants of a degraded black sisterhood, and who, by going to its relief, shall train the young negro women into abhorrence for immorality, and lead them to chaste living.

The freedmen require in this, as in other respects, not benevolent pandering nor lordly oversight, but genuine service unstintedly rendered for helpful and wholesome race improvement. To blunder in the face of such opportunities would be criminal, and it would be an unpardonable blunder to exploit any half-hearted measures for the freedman's redemption. The conscience of the negro is imperfectly developed, and he needs constant drill in moral endeavor, under such guidance and surrounded by such influences as will reduce the possibilities of immoral relapse to a minimum. Such training should begin at the cradle. Never, until this is done, shall we succeed in inculcating in this people such ideals as will develop characters grounded on integrity and consecrated to service and duty. Despite their vanity, sensuous follies, and instability of temperament, our freed men and women have within them an unfathomed wealth of sentiment, which only awaits the deft hand of moral tactfulness to be moulded into serious and steady response to the demands of life.

1901

NOTES

1. Wearing a low-cut neckline.
2. A gambler.
3. Using tobacco in powdered form.
4. A Latin term meaning, "on first impression" or "at first sight."

A GUDE DEEKUN (?-?)

In 1901 and 1902, a handful of short stories appeared in the *Colored American Magazine* under the pseudonym "A Gude Deekun." The selection included here was published in May of 1901. In this story, the African American characters meet the violent attacks of their white oppressors with their own defensive actions. While the identity of this writer is unknown, the irony that the author of these elaborately conceived fantasies of black revenge would adopt so righteous an appellation (pronounced "a good deacon") leaves the impression of one whose creative imagination was comprised of equal parts sarcasm and rage.

A GEORGIA EPISODE

"Say, Jonce, that's a fine girl you've got in there, that one ironing. Who is she? Don't think I've seen her before."

The man addressed carefully examined a cigar he had taken from his pocket and after lighting it, turned to his friend with a half smile as he said, "You mean that good-looking coon?"

"No, I hope you don't call any of those coons in there good-looking. I'm talking about that new girl at the ironing machine nearest the door."

"Well, I understood you. She's a darky."

"She's the devil!"

"O no, she's not the devil," sarcastically, "for she told me, last night that she was a 'respectable colored girl' and wished to be treated as such," said the other with a grin on his coarse, sensual face at the recollection, and he continued, "Want to look at her again? Come inside and go out through the office."

The speakers were standing at the door of the Alabastine Laundry of L——, a small but progressive town of Southern Georgia, which had lately experienced a boom in the business world on account of important discoveries of coal and iron deposits.

The two men were Johnson Smith, son of the proprietor of the Laundry, and his friend, William Lawson. Johnson, or 'Jonce' Smith, was a short rather stout young man about twenty-five, good-looking in a coarse, sensual way, and always dressed in the height of fashion according to certain standards. He was a thorough sporting man and very popular in the younger set. His father was self-made and he had done the job well, being of ample means, and according to a facetious remark of his son, he did not take after the latter at all. The elder man was away just now on business and as the younger, in spite of his gay proclivities, thoroughly understood the management of the laundry, he was now in charge, though for the first time.

The employees of the establishment consisted of about ten young women, white and colored, and they, with an old Negro man, who was engineer, janitor and general utility man, comprised the entire force.

No wagons were kept, and as a rule there was no need for any, as the laundry having no opposition, required its patrons to both bring and call for their linen.

As the two men re-entered the building the workers in the large room looked up and while the manager turned to speak to an employee, his visitor was closely scrutinizing the subject of their late discussion, but the latter not relishing his stare, gathered up a pile of work and carried it from the room.

As the office door closed behind the two, Lawson exclaimed, "Well I'll be ——if I would take her for a nigger! She's as white as they make 'em. How long have you had her?"

"About four days. She's the daughter of old Delhi Hall, that used to belong to my grandfather. I've a notion that we are related, but I haven't claimed kinship yet." The idea seemed to please him and after a hearty laugh, which to his friend did not seem entirely necessary, he relighted his cigar, with the remark, "Sorry I haven't another smoke, Laws, but you can watch me enjoy this one. Oh yes, speaking of the girl in there, her name is Smith, too, a sort of step-cousin-in-law, you see." And then more seriously he went on, "The old man will be gone for about five weeks up in Troy and a lot of other places looking up new wrinkles in machinery and such stuff, and while he's away I'm in for some fun here. He has always frowned on my having anything to say to the girls; says it interferes with biz, but you can gamble on it. I'm running these works now for a while."

Lawson did not make any comment, and after a pause Smith continued:

"That girl came in the other day looking for a job and I took her on at once, though the old man won't allow it when he gets back, as we're already full handed. But say, don't you know, she's trying to act white and says she's a lady if she is black. I laughed when she told me that, but if she won't have sense enough to be friendly with me why she will have to take what comes."

"Better be careful, Jonce, she might make you trouble," Lawson ventured.

"Trouble for me? Not much. She's nothing but a coon anyway, and you can always handle them if you go about it right, and even supposing there was some row, why the old man would hush it up quick on account of the business. O no, she's mine anyway it goes," and he laughed and rubbed his hands over the pleasant anticipation.

"Well, I wish you success with your black beauty, but some of the coons are getting mighty uppish nowadays trying to 'assert their rights,' as they say. So long, old man, don't forget to be on hand tonight."

For a while Johnson Smith stood in his office door smoking and jollying the old black engineer, who had come up from his warm quarters to enjoy his pipe. Presently the old fellow moved a little nearer to his employer and taking his stubby pipe from his mouth, pointed with it down the street, as he said, "Mr. Jonce, jist look at dis boy coming up the street and see 'f you knows him."

The boy in question was a neatly attired young colored man who was walking along carefully scanning the buildings as he passed. On reaching the laundry, he paused an instant as he read the large signs, and after carefully scrutinizing the building, passed on without noticing the two men watching him.

"No, I don't know him, Uncle Tom. New coon in town, isn't he?"

The old man chuckled, as he answered, "I 'lowed you wouldn't know him. He's old 'Brickbat' Simpson's daughter's boy, Russell Woodleigh. Sont hisself to school up Norf fer a long time an' now he's home visitin'. Teachin' school somewheres in Ferginny an' I hears he's sweet on that new gal you hired 'tother day. Spect dey'll git married 'fore he goes back."

The young man frowned severely and then with a short suggestive laugh, he said. "Going to get married, are they? Well I'll treat the bride fine," and he turned and went back into the office whistling the latest popular air.

On the next morning the new ironer gave notice that she would leave at the end of the week, and on being pressed for a reason she said she expected to leave town shortly, but more than that would not say: so Mr. Johnson Smith said he would be sorry to part with her but supposed he would have to let her go.

Russell Woodleigh, the young colored man, said to be engaged to marry the laundry girl, Emma Smith, had left L—— seven years before, and after graduating from a widely known educational institution at Washington, had recently secured a position as public school teacher in a Virginia town near the Capital City. He was a tall, well-built, pleasant faced young man, of an olive complexion, and with his dark curly hair and mustache was readily mistaken for a foreigner. As the engineer had said, he was the son of Brickbat Simpson's daughter, and his maternal grandfather was reputed to have been a well known State official, his father not being in evidence. The fact that his Caucasian ancestry was greatly predominant did not matter in the least as regards his racial classification, for unquestionably he had some Negro blood in his veins and no matter how little, it was sufficient to make him a 'coon'—and all that name implies.

With his sweetheart it was the same, only in her case her sex and good looks made it much worse for her.

The young teacher had come home proud of his success in his school work, expecting to spend a few weeks at his old home and then return with his bride to the scene of his new labors, but when Emma told him of the obnoxious attentions her employer had been paying her, it was decided that it would be the wisest and best plan for the marriage to take place at once.

The girl had hoped to work at the laundry for some little time, but on Thursday she gave notice that she would leave at the end of the week.

The next evening—Friday—the two were out calling on friends, and as they were returning home along the main street of the town, they passed a group of young men, among whom were Johnson Smith and his friend, Lawson.

As they passed under the glare of an electric light, Lawson called the attention of his companions to the couple, and turning to Smith, slapped him on the shoulder and remarked, "Jonce, old man, you have a rival with your African belle, and say, fellows, what do you think that darky's name is? Russell Woodleigh!"

"Woodleigh? Russell Woodleigh? Why that is the name of our last governor!"

"The same name all right, and the same blood, too, I guess, for it is said that his Excellency was rather gay when he was young. Guess the name was given this fellow for a joke, and it's a pretty good one in this case on the ex-Governor."

They continued to smoke and to banter for a while, and after visiting a neighboring saloon for a "leave-taker," the crowd broke up, several of them going down the street together. As luck would have it, they had proceeded but a short distance when they met Woodleigh on his way home. Lawson immediately began to jolly Smith again, and that estimable young man, already much provoked and being somewhat under the influence of the various potations indulged in, promptly hailed the unoffending Woodleigh.

"Look here, you! You half-white nigger! You want to get out of this town, and out quick!"

The young man, while very angry at this gratuitous insult, did not stop or give any sign that he heard. He was anxious to avoid trouble and knew the odds were overwhelmingly against him, so he endeavored to pass on. But it was not so to be. Johnson Smith broke from his companions and barring his way, shook his fist in Woodleigh's face and shouted, "I'm talking to you, you yellow ——," applying a most vile epithet to him, "and I want you to understand me. You want to keep away from Emma Smith, too."

At this allusion to his sweetheart, Woodleigh's wrath burst beyond all control and he struck his tormentor full in the face with all his might.

The man fell like a log, but before the blow could be followed up, his assailant was seized by the fallen man's friends and they all joined in a most brutal assault on him. He would doubtless have been killed had not a policeman, who had all the time been standing near with his back discreetly turned, now advanced and placed the colored man under arrest. He was too badly injured to walk, and was placed in a wagon and conveyed to the station house.

The next morning, owing to influence his friends had been able to secure for him, he escaped a chain gang sentence and was allowed to go free after paying a heavy fine, which took his last dollar.

Sick and sore in body and mind, he made his way home and, after sending a note to Emma, he lay down, determined to leave town the next night and have Emma follow if she could not accompany him then.

On Saturday night at the laundry all the employees were promptly paid off except Emma Smith. The girl was somewhat uneasy and was about to ask for her wages when Johnson Smith rose from his desk and with "just a minute," went back through the work rooms and down into the engine room below, where he could be heard talking with the engineer.

The interior of the office could not be seen from the street and Emma began to be alarmed; as she knew it was her employer's habit to remain in the office very late Saturday nights to arrange the books for the week, and she could not imagine why she was detained. In a very short time Smith returned, accompanied by the engineer, who received his money and was at once dismissed.

As the door closed behind him, Smith turned to the waiting girl, who had risen from her seat, and with an evil smile on his face, said to her, "Do you know Russell Woodleigh, Emma?"

She did not reply, but frightened by his strange actions, stood regarding him in terrified silence. The fact that he had deliberately sent away everyone else and that she was alone in the building with him, now dawned on her with full force, and she turned toward the door, intending to rush out and escape, but he divined her intention and, moving between her and the door, addressed her with a sneer: "Ah, I see you do know him. Well, I met him last night and he gave me this mark on my face and now I'm going to make you pay for it," and he advanced toward her.

With a piercing scream she sprang aside and darted for the door. But the man reached it first.

— — —

The Monday evening issue of the local paper contained the following news item:

> Found Dead in Her Room.
> A Mullatto Woman Named Emma Smith
> From an Overdose of Morphine, to Which She
> Was Said to be Addicted.—She Had Been Working
> At the Alabastine Laundry for About a Week,
> But Did Not Give Satisfaction.

The following Saturday night, half an hour before the laundry closed, there was a tap at the door of the engine room, which opened on a narrow alley. The engineer opened it and was about to gruffly stop the disreputable object that started to enter, when the light fell on it and he started back with a cry.

"Good Gawd! Russell, is dis you? O Lordy, what does you want? You mustn't stay yere."

The wild eyed, haggard and unkempt man with a terribly bruised and battered face stared at him and then with a finger on his lips, said in a low tone, "Hush, Uncle Tom, I'm cold and just want to get warm by your fire."

He crept in and stood for a minute looking around at everything in the room, while the old man regarded him fearfully, and then went over by the furnace and leaned against the wall with one hand over his injured face.

The old man gazed at him and then crossed the room and placed a grimy hand on his shoulder and for a moment the two were silent.

Suddenly Woodleigh raised his head and his eyes were dull and listless, and he said, "Well, Uncle Tom, I'm almost done for, and this is all I live on now," and taking a flask of liquor from his pocket he placed it to his lips.

After the first exclamation of alarmed surprise at Woodleigh's unexpected appearance, the engineer had said nothing. He did not like to turn him away, but knowing of the recent tragic events feared to let him stay, dreading lest someone should come in and discover his presence, but the sight of the tempting bottle overshadowed his fears and he promptly accepted the proffered drink.

The whisky seemed to have a great effect on Woodleigh. He brightened up and began to ask questions about the place and the management of the boiler and engine. The engineer under the potent influence of the freely offered stimulant, began to wax eloquent. Still carefully speaking in a subdued tone, with some pride, he explained how the building was heated in cold weather, how he could get up steam quickly in the boiler, which was high pressure, the amount it would safely carry and showed how when necessary the boiler could be emptied of water and then filled again.

His visitor listened very attentively and then got him to explain everything over again, meanwhile generously sharing the liquor.

The women overhead could be heard moving about getting ready to leave and the old man was going to show how he banked his fire to let it go gradually out, but Russell stopped him by saying he was not quite warm yet. He continued to make a pretense of drinking and strongly plied the old man.

Presently it was evident from the silence that, the other employees had gone and Johnson Smith's voice called down the speaking tube to know if the engineer didn't want any money that night.

He replied huskily that he would come right up and then asked his visitor for one more drink and told him he must go.

As the old man turned his head for an instant the other drew a second partly filled bottle from another pocket and placed it in the outstretched hand.

The engineer drank greedily and then as he turned to bank the fire he reeled and would have fallen but the younger man caught him and carefully stretched him on the floor.

Instantly Russell Woodleigh's demeanor changed from its former apathy and listlessness to that of the fiercest activity. He sprang to the furnace and rapidly and noiselessly renewed the fire under the boiler, carefully coaxing it to an intense heat. The escape valve was then wired down tightly and part of the water was slowly drawn from the boiler.

In a few minutes the steam began to shoot up rapidly and the indicator of the steam gauge moved round the dial face by jumps under the increased pressure, when the worker paused for an instant and going to the alley door peered cautiously out. He seemed satisfied, for leaving the door open, he returned to the unconscious man and taking him by the shoulders, slowly dragged him outside, and then placed the bottle of whisky in his hands.

By the time this was accomplished and he returned to the furnace, the indicator had completed the circuit of the dial face and was lodged against the brass pin at the zero mark, and inside the boiler there was an ominous humming.

With an almost diabolical grin, the man stood watching the result of his work, when he heard Johnson Smith moving about in the office overhead.

For a second he bowed his head with hands clasped, and then with set face, opened the valve that emptied the boiler.

The joints in the pipes were beginning to hiss and as the last of the water disappeared from the tube, he opened wide the cold water supply pipe.

On the front page of the local paper on Monday were the following scare head-lines:

ALABASTINE LAUNDRY WRECKED BY EXPLOSION.

Son of Proprietor Killed.
Explosion of Boiler Due to Drunkenness
of Negro Engineer, Whose
Body was Found with
Bottle of Whisky
by its Side.
Portions of another Body were Found,
Supposed to be that of a Tramp.
Loss to Building Fully Covered by Insurance.

1901

PAULINE HOPKINS (1859-1930)

Pauline Elizabeth Hopkins was born in Portland, Maine, to free black parents Sarah Allen and Northrup Hopkins. Her mother was descended from a noted New England family of African American writers, performers, and clergymen. Hopkins herself was the great-grandniece of noted poet and antislavery activist James Monroe Whitfield. Raised and educated in Boston, she was a graduate of the city's prestigious Girls High School. Her success as a writer began when, at the age of fifteen, Hopkins won a citywide writing contest for her original essay on temperance. The contest was cosponsored by the Congregational Publishing Society of Boston and William Wells Brown, the noted black novelist and historian. Shortly afterward, she began writing drama, and in 1880 Hopkins performed in a stage production of her first play, *Slave's Escape: or, the Underground Railroad.* She continued to act and to write for the theater until 1895, when she began a brief career as stenographer for the U.S. Census Bureau. In 1900, she joined the staff of the *Colored American Magazine* and became a regular contributor, publishing short stories and serialized novels as well as biographical sketches of notable African American figures. In 1916, she founded *New Era Magazine* with Walter Wallace, cofounder of the *Colored American.* Financial issues drove the magazine out of print after only two issues. Little is known about Hopkins' life after *New Era.* She is believed to have resumed her career as a stenographer, taking a position at the Massachusetts Institute of Technology. Pauline Hopkins is best known to contemporary readers for her first novel, *Contending Forces: A Romance Illustrative of Negro Life North and South,* published in 1900. It was followed soon after by the short story "The Mystery Within," published in the May 1900 issue of the *Colored American.* Several short works and three serialized novels would follow, the first of which, *Hagar's Daughter: A Story of Southern Caste Prejudice,* is excerpted here. Published in the *Colored American* under the pseudonym "Sarah A. Allen," the novel was released in thirteen monthly installments, beginning in March of 1901. In the following excerpt, Hagar and Ellis Enson, a wealthy white Washington, DC, couple, learn that Mrs. Enson is, in fact, a woman of mixed-race descent.

Chapter IV

The morning sun poured its golden light upon the picturesque old house standing in its own grounds in one of the suburban towns adjacent to Baltimore—the Baltimore of 1858 or 1860.

The old house seemed to command one to render homage to its beauty and stateliness. It was a sturdy brick building flanked with offices and having outbuildings touching the very edge of the deep, mysterious woods where the trees waved their beckoning arms in every soft breeze that came to revel in their rich foliage. This was Enson Hall. The Hall was reached through a long dim stretch of these woods—locusts and beeches—from ten to twelve acres in extent; its mellow, red-brick walls framed by a background of beech trees reminded one of English residences with their immense extent of private grounds. In the rear of the mansion was the garden, with its huge conservatories gay with shrubs and flowers. Piazzas and porticoes promised delightful retreats for sultry weather. The interior of the house was in the style that came in after the Revolution. An immense hall with outer door standing invitingly open gave greeting to the guest. The stairs wound from the lower floor to the rooms above. The grand stairway was richly embellished with carving, and overhead a graceful, arch added much to the impressive beauty which met the stranger's first view. The rooms, spacious and designed for entertaining largely, had paneled wainscoting and carved chimney-pieces.

Ellis Enson, the master of the Hall was a well-made man, verging on forty. "Born with a silver spoon in his mouth," for the vast estate and all invested money was absolutely at his disposal, he was the envy of the men of his class and the despair of the ladies. He was extremely good-looking, slight, elegant, with wavy dark hair, and an air of distinction. Since his father's death he had lived at the Hall, surrounded by his slaves in lonely meditation, fancy free. This handsome recluse had earned the reputation of being morose, so little had he mixed with society, so cold had been his politeness to the fair sex. His farms, his lonely rides, his favorite books, had sufficed for him. He was a good manager, and what was more wonderful, considering his Southern temperament, a thorough man of business. His crops, his poultry, his dairy products, were of the very first quality. Sure it was that his plantation was a paying investment. Meanwhile the great house, with all its beautiful rooms and fine furniture, remained closed to the public, and was the despair of managing mammas with many daughters to provide with eligible husbands. Enson was second to none as a "catch," but he was utterly indifferent to women.

Just about this time when to quarry the master of Enson Hall seemed a hopeless task, Hagar Sargeant came home from a four years' sojourn at the North in a young ladies' seminary.

The Sargeant estate was the one next adjoining Enson Hall; not so large and imposing, but a valuable patrimony that had descended in a long line of Sargeants and was well preserved. For many years before Hagar's birth the estate had been rented because of financial misfortunes, and they had lived in St. Louis, where Mr. Sargeant had engaged in trade so successfully that when Hagar was six years old they were enabled to return to their ancestral home and resume a life of luxurious leisure. Since that time Mr. Sargeant had died. On a trip to St. Louis, where he had gone to settle his business affairs, he contracted cholera, then ravaging many large cities of the Southwest, and had finally succumbed to the scourge. Hagar, their only child, then became her mother's sole joy and inspiration. Determined to cultivate her daughter's rare intellectual gifts, she had sent her North to school when every throb of her heart demanded her presence at home. She had developed into a beautiful girl, the admiration and delight of the neighborhood to which she returned, almost a stranger after her long absence.

A golden May morning poured its light through the open window of the Sargeant breakfast-room. A pleasanter room could scarcely be found, though the furniture was not of latest fashion, and the carpet slightly faded. There was a bay window that opened on the terrace, below which was a garden; there was a table in the recess spread with dainty china and silver, and the remains of breakfast; honeysuckles played hide-and-seek at the open window. Aunt Henny, a coal-black Negress of kindly face, brought in the little brass-bound oaken tub filled with hot water and soap, and the linen towel., Hagar stood at the window contemplating the scene before her. It was her duty to wash the heirlooms of colonial china and silver. From their bath they were dried only by her dainty fingers, and carefully replaced in the corner cupboard. Not for the world would she have dropped one of these treasures. Her care for them, and the placing of every one in its proper niche, was wonderful to behold. Not the royal jewels of Victoria were evermore carefully guarded than these family heirlooms.

This morning Hagar was filled with a delicious excitement, caused by she knew not what. The china and silver were an anxiety unusual to her. She felt a physical exhilaration, inspired, no doubt, by the delicious weather. She always lamented at this season of the year the lost privileges of the house of

Sargeant, when their right of way led directly from the house to the shining waters of the bay. There was a path that led to the water still, but it was across the land of their neighbor Enson. Sometimes Hagar would trespass; would cross the park-like stretch of pasture, bordered by the woodland through which it ran, and sit on the edge of the remnant of a wharf, by which ran a small, rapid river, an arm of Chesapeake Bay, chafing among wet stones and leaping gaily over rocky barriers. There she would dream of life before the Revolution, and in these dreams participate in the joys of the colonial dames. She longed to mix and mingle with the gay world; she had a feeling that her own talents, if developed, would end in something far different from the calm routine, the housekeeping and churchgoing which stretched before her. Sometimes softer thoughts possessed her, and she speculated about love and lovers. This peaceful life was too tranquil and uneventful. Oh, for a break in the humdrum recurral of the same events day after day.

She had never met Ellis Enson. He was away a great part of the time before she left home for school, and since she had returned. If she remembered him at all, it was with the thought of a girl just past her eighteenth birthday for a man forty.

This morning Hagar washed the silver with the sleeves of her morning robe turned up to the shoulder, giving a view of rosy, dimpled arms. "A fairer vision was never seen," thought the man who paused a moment at the open window to gaze again upon the pretty, homelike scene. As Hagar turned from replacing the last of the china, she was startled out of her usual gay indifference at the sight of a handsome pair of dark eyes regarding her intently from the open window. A quick wonder flashed in the eyes that met hers; the color deepened in his face as he saw he was observed. The girl's beauty startled him so, that for a moment he lost the self-control that convention dictates. Then he bared his head in courteous acknowledgment of youth and beauty, with an apology for his seeming intrusion.

"I beg pardon," Enson said in his soft, musical tones; "is Mrs. Sargeant at home? I did not know she had company."

"I am not company; I am Hagar. Yes, mamma is at home; if you will come in, I will take you to her." He turned and entered the hall door and followed her through the dark, cool hall to the small morning-room, where Mrs. Sargeant spent her mornings in semi-invalid fashion. Then a proper introduction followed, and Ellis Enson and Hagar Sargeant were duly acquainted.

At forty Enson still retained his faith in womanhood, although he had been so persistently pursued by all the women of the vicinity. He believed there were women in the world capable of loving a man for himself alone, without a thought of worldly advantage, only he had not been fortunate enough to meet them. He had a very poor opinion of himself. Adulation had not made him vain. His face indicated strong passions and much pride; but it was pride of caste, not self. There was great tenderness of the eye and lip, and signs of a sensitive nature that could not bear disgrace or downfall that might touch his ancient name. After he left the Sargeant home Hagar's face haunted him; the pure, creamy skin, the curved crimson lips ready to smile,—lips sweet and firm,—the broad, low brow, and great, lustrous, long-lashed eyes of brilliant black—soft as velvet, and full of light with the earnest, cloudless gaze of childhood; and there was heart and soul and mind in this countenance of a mere girl. Such beauty as this was a perpetual delight to feast the eyes and charm the senses—aye, to witch a man's heart from him; for here there was not only the glory of form and tints, but more besides—heart that could throb; soul that could aspire, mind that could think. She was not shy and self-conscious as young girls so often are; she seemed quite at her ease, as one who has no thought of self. He was conscious of his own enthrallment. He knew that he had set his feet in the perilous path of love at a late day, but knowing this, he none the less went forward to his fate.

After that the young girl and the man met frequently. She did not realize when the time came, that she had grown to look for his coming. There were walks and drives and accidental meetings in the woods. The sun was brighter and the songs of the birds sweeter that summer than ever before.

Ellis fell to day-dreaming, and the dreams were tinged with gold, bringing a flush to his face and a thrill to his heart. Still he would have denied, if accused; that this was love at first sight—bah! That was a well-exploded theory. And yet if it was not love that had suddenly come into his being for this slender, dark-eyed girl, what was it? A change had come into Ellis Enson's life. The greatest changes, too, are always unexpected.

It was a sultry day; there was absolutely no chance to catch a refreshing breeze within four walls. It was one of the rare occasions when Mrs. Sargeant felt obliged to make a business call alone. From the fields came the sound of voices singing: the voices of slaves. Aunt Henny's good-natured laugh occasionally broke the stillness.

"Now I shall have a nice quiet afternoon," thought Hagar, as she left the house for the shadow of the trees. Under the strong, straight branches of a beech she tied three old shawls, hammock-like, one under another, for strength and safety. It was not very far from the ground. If it should come down, she might be bruised slightly, but not killed. She crawled cautiously into her nest; she had let down the long braids of her hair, and as she lolled back in her retreat, they fell over the sides of the hammock and swept the top of the long, soft grass. Lying there, with nothing in sight but the leafy branches of the trees high above her head, through which gleams of the deep blue sky came softly, she felt as if she had left the world, and was floating, Ariel-like, in midair.

After an hour of tranquility, footsteps were audible on the soft grass. There was a momentary pause; then someone came to a standstill beside her fairy couch.

"Back so soon, mamma? I wish you could come up here with me; it is just heavenly."

"Then I suppose you must be one of the heavenly inhabitants, an angel, but I never can pay compliments as I ought," said a voice.

"Mr. Enson!" Hagar was conscious of a distinct quickening of heart-action and a rush of crimson to her cheeks; with a pretty, hurried movement she rose to a sitting posture in her hammock; "I really am ashamed of myself. I thought you were mamma."

"Yes," he answered, smiling at her dainty confusion.

"Mr. Enson," she said again, this time gravely," politeness demands that I receive you properly, but decency forbids I should do it unless you will kindly turn your back to me while I step to earth once more."

The man was inwardly shaking with laughter at the grave importance with which she viewed the business in hand, but not for worlds would he have had her conscious of his mirth.

"I can help you out all right," he said.

"No, I am too heavy. I think I will stay here until you go."

"Oh—but—say now, Miss Hagar, that is hard to drive me away when I have just come; and such an afternoon, too, hot enough to kill a darkey. Do let me help you down."

"No; I can get out myself if I must. Please turn your back."

Thus entreated, he turned his back and commenced an exhaustive study of the landscape. Hagar arose; the hammock turned up, and Ellis was just in time to receive her in his arms as she fell.

"Hagar—my darling—you are not hurt?" he asks anxiously, still holding her in a close embrace.

"No; of course not. It is so good of you to be by to care for me so nicely," she said in some confusion.

"Hagar—my darling," he said again, with a desperate resolve to let her know the state of his feelings, "will you marry me?" She trembled as his lips pressed passionate kisses on hers. The veil was drawn away. She understood—this was the realization of the dreams that had come to her dimly all the tender springtime. Never in all her young life had she felt so happy, so strangely happy. A soft flush mounted to cheek and brow under his caresses.

"I don't understand," murmured the girl, trembling with excitement.

"My darling, I think I have said it more plainly than most men do. Hagar, I think you must know it; I have made no secret of my love for you. Have you not understood me all the days of the spring and summer?"

"Are you quite sure that you love me? You are so old and wise, and I so ignorant to be the wife of so grand a man as you."

"She glanced up fleetingly, and flushed more deeply under the look she met. He folded her closer still in his arms. His next words were whispered:

"My love! lift your eyes to mine, and say you love me."

Hagar had not dreamed that such passion as this existed in the world. It seemed to take the breath of her Inner life and leave her powerless, with no separate existence, no distinct mental utterance.

Gently Ellis drew back the bright head against him, and bent over the sweet lips that half sought his kiss; and so for one long moment he knew a lifetime of happiness. Then he released her.

"Heaven helping me, you shall be so loved and shielded that sorrow shall never touch you. You shall never repent trusting your young life to me. May I speak to your mother tonight?"

"Yes," she whispered.

And so they were betrothed. Ellis felt and meant all that he said under the stress of the emotion of the moment; but who calculates the effect of time and cruel circumstance? Mrs. Sargeant was more than pleased at the turn of events. Soon Ellis was taking the bulk of the business of managing her estates upon his own strong shoulders. These two seemed favored children of the gods all that long, happy summer. She was his, and he was hers.

The days glided by like a dream, and soon brought the early fall which was fixed for the wedding festivities. All was sunshine. The wedding day was set for October. On the morning of the day before, Hagar entered her mother's room as was her usual custom, to give her a loving morning greeting, and found nothing but the cold, unresponsive body, from which the spirit had fled. Then followed days that were a nightmare to Hagar, but under Ellis' protecting care the storm of grief spent itself and settled into quiet sadness. There was no one at the Sargeant home but the bereaved girl and her servants. At the end of a month Ellis put the case plainly before her, and she yielded to his persuasions to have the marriage solemnized at once, so that he might assume his place as her rightful protector. A month later than the time originally set there was a quiet wedding, very different from the gay celebration originally planned by a loving mother, and the young mistress took her place in the stately rooms of Enson Hall. When a twelve-month had passed there was a little queen born—the heiress of the hall. Ellis' happiness was complete.

Chapter V

It was past the breakfast hour in the Hall kitchen, but Marthy still lingered. It was cold outside; snow had fallen the night before; the clouds were dull and threatening. The raw northern blasts cut like bits of ice; the change was very sudden from the pleasant coolness of autumn. The kitchen was an inviting place; the blaze shot up gleefully from between the logs, played hide-and-seek in dark corners and sported merrily across the faces of the pickaninnies[1] sprawling on the floor and constantly under Aunt Henny's feet.

Aunt Henny now reigned supreme in the culinary department of the Hall. Her head was held a little higher, if possible, in honor of the new dignity that had come to the family from the union of the houses of Enson and Sargeant.

"'Twarn't my 'sires fer a weddin' so close to a fun'ral, but Lor', chile, dars a diffurunce in doin' things, an' it 'pears dis weddin's comin' out all right. Dem two is a sight fer sore eyes, an' as fer de baby"—Aunt Henny rolled up her eyes in silent ecstasy.

"Look hyar, mammy," said Marthy, Mrs. Enson's maid and Aunt Henny's daughter, "why don' you sec Unc' Demus? He'd guv you a charm fer Miss Hagar to wear; she needn't know nuthin' 'bout it."

"Sho, honey, wha' you take me fo? I done went down to Demus soon as dat weddin' wus brung up."

"Wha' he say, mammy?"

"Let me 'lone now tell I tells you." Aunt Henny was singeing pin-feathers from a pile of birds on the floor in front of the fire. She dropped her task to give emphasis to her words. " I carried him Miss Hagar's pocket-hankercher and he guv me a bag made outen de skin ob a rattlesnake, an' he put in it a rabbit's foot an' er sarpint's toof, an' er squorerpin's tail wid a leetle dust outen de graveyard an' he sewed up de bag. Den he tied all dat up in de hankercher an' tell me solemn: 'Long as yer mistis keep dis 'bout her, trouble'll neber stay so long dat joy won't conquer him in de end.' So, honey, I done put dat charm in Missee Hagar draw 'long wid her tickler fixins an' I wants yer Marthy, to take keer ob it," she concluded, with a grave shake of her turbanned head. Marthy was duly impressed, and stood looking at her mother with awe in every feature of her little brown face.

"'Deed an' I will, mammy."

"My young Miss will be all right ef dat St. Clair Enson keeps 'way from hyar," continued the woman reflectively.

"Who's St. Clar Enson?" asked Marthy.

"Nemmin' 'bout him. Sometime I'll tell you when you gits older. All you got ter do now is ter take mighty good keer o' your mistis and de baby," replied her mother, with a knowing wag of her head. "Fling anudder chunk on dat fire!" she called to one of the boys playing on the floor. "Girtin' mighty cole fer dis time ob year, de a'r smell pow'rful lack mo' snow."

A shadow fell across the doorsill shutting out the light for a moment, that came through the half-open doorway. Marthy gave a shriek that ended in a giggle as a young Negro, tall, black, smiling, sauntered into the kitchen; it was Isaac. Aunt Henny threw her arms high above her head in unbounded astonishment. "

"En de name ob de Lawd! Isaac! What's gwine ter happen ter dis fambly now, Ike, dat you's come sneakin' home?"

Isaac grinned. "Isn't you pow'rful glad ter see me, Aunt Henny? I is ter see you an Marthy. Marfy's a mighty likely lookin' gal, I 'low." He gave a sly roll of his eye in the direction where the girl stood regarding the athletic young Negro with undisguised admiration.

"None o' dat," sputtered Aunt Henny. "Don' you go tryin' ter fool wid dat gal, you lim' ob de debbil. Take yo'sef right off! What yer doin' hyar, enyhow? Dis ain't no place fer you."

My marse tell'd me ter come," replied Isaac, not at all ruffled by his reception. "I ain't gwine ter go right off; ain't tell'd none o' de folks howdy yit."

"*Your marse tell'd you ter come!* What fer he tell'd yer to come?" stormed Aunt Henny, with a derisive snort. "Dat's what I want ter know. *My* marse'll have somethin' ter say I reckon, ef *yer* marse *did* tell'd yer ter come. An' I b'lieve you's a liar, 'deed I do. I don' b'lieve yer marser knows whar you is at, dis blessid minnit."

Isaac chuckled. "I've come home ter see de new mistis an' de leetle baby; I cert'n'y hopes dey is well. Marse St. Clar'll be hyar hisself bimeby."

Aunt Henny stood a moment silently regarding the boy. Fear, amazement and curiosity were blended in her honest face. Plainly, she was puzzled. "De

debbil turn sain'," she muttered to herself, with a long look at the unconscious Isaac; who sat toasting his cold bare toes before the roaring fire. "Dis
house got mo' peace in it, an' Marse Ellis happier den he been sence his mar,
ol' Missee Enson, died; but," and she shook her turbanned head ominously,
"'tain't fer long. I ain't fergit nuffin'; I isn't lived nex' dis Enson Hall so many
years fer nuffin."

"I'se walk'd a long way slipping officers"—began Isaac.

"Um!" grunted Aunt Henny, with the look of alarm still in her eyes, "officers! dat's what's de matter."

"Dey'll hab ter see Marse St. Clar, tain't me. He sol' me. I runned 'way. I
come home, dat's all. Kain't I hab suthin' to eat?"

"Ef 'tain't one it's t'odder. Befo' God, I 'lieve you an' yo' marse bof onhu-
man. Been sol'! runned 'way! hump!" again grunted Aunt Henny.

Meanwhile Marthy had made coffee and baked a corncake in the hot ashes.
Isaac sniffed the aroma of the fragrant coffee hungrily. There was chicken and
rice, too, he noticed as she placed food on the end of a table and motioned
him to help himself. Isaac needed no pressing, and in a moment was eating
ravenously.

"Tell you de troof, Aunt Henny," he said at last, as he waited for a fourth
help, "Marse St. Clar git hard up de oder night in a little play comin' up de
bay an' he sell me to a gempleman fer sixteen hundred dollars. But, Lor', dat
don' hol' Isaac, chile, while he's got legs."

"Dat's jes' what I thought. No use yer lyin' ter me, Isaac, yer Aunt Henny
was born wif a veil.[3] I knows a heap o' things by seein' 'em fo' dey happens. I
don' tell all I sees, but I keeps up a steddyin' 'bout it."

"Dar's no mon can keep me, I don' keer how much Marse St. Clar sells
me; he's my onlies' marser," continued Isaac, as he kept on devouring food
a little more slowly than at first.

"Lawd sakes, honey; you's de mos' pow'rfulles' eater I'se seed fer many a
day. Don' reckon you's had a good meal sence yer was home five years ago.
Dog my cats ef I don' hope Marse Ellis will jes' make yer trot."

"He kin sen' me back, but I isn't gwine stay wid 'em," replied Isaac, with
his mouth full of food.

"You cain't he'p yo'se'f."

"I kin walk," persisted Isaac doggedly.

"Put you in de caboose an' give yer hundred lashes," Aunt Henny called
back, as she waddled out of the kitchen to find her master.

"Don' keer fer dat, nudder."

Isaac improved the time between the going and coming of Aunt Henny by making fierce love to Marthy, who was willing to meet him more than half way.

The breakfast-room was redolent with the scent of flowers, freshly cut from the greenhouses; the waxed floor gleamed like polished glass beneath the fur rugs scattered over it, and the table, with its service for two, was drawn in front of the cheerful fire that crackled and sparkled in the open fireplace. All the luxuries that wealth could give were gathered about the young matron. It was a happy household, the hurry and rush of warlike preparations had not reached its members, and the sting of slavery, with its demoralizing brutality, was unknown on these plantations so recently joined. Happiness was everywhere, from the master in his carriage to the slave singing in the fields at his humble task. Breakfast was over, and as Ellis glanced over the top of his morning paper at his wife and baby, he felt a thrill of intense pride and love.

As compared with her girlhood, Hagar's married life had been one round of excitement. Washington and many other large cities had been visited on their brief honeymoon. They were royally entertained by all the friends and relatives of both families, and the beautiful bride had been the belle of every assembly. Ellis was wrapped up in her; intimate acquaintance but deepened his love. Her nature was pure, spiritual, and open as the day. Gowned in spotless white, her slender form lost in a large armchair, she sat opposite him, dandling the baby in her arms. She looked across at him and smiled.

"Well, pet," he smiled back at her, "going to ride?"

She shook her head and set every little curl in motion."I won't go out today, it is so cold; we are so comfortable here before the fire, baby and I."

"What a lazy little woman it is," he laughed, rising from his seat and going over to stand behind her chair, stroke the bright hair, and clasp mother and child in his arms. Hagar rested her head against him, and held the infant at arm's length for his admiration.

"Isn't she a darling? See, Ellis, she knows you," as the child cooed and laughed and gurgled at them both, in a vain effort to clinch something in her little red fists.

"This little beggar has spoiled our honeymoon with a vengeance," he replied with a laugh. "I cannot realize that it is indeed over, and we have settled down to the humdrum life of old married folk."

"Can anything ever spoil that and its memories?" she asked, with a sweet upward look into his face. "Indeed, I often wonder if I am too happy; is it right for any human being to be so favored in life as I have been."

"Gather your roses while you may, there will be dark clouds enough in life, heaven knows. No gloomy thoughts, Mignon; let us be happy in the present." He kissed the lips raised so temptingly for his caress, and then one for the child. He thought humbly of his own career beside the spotless creature he had won for life. While not given to excesses, yet there were things in the past that he regretted. Since the birth of their child, the days had been full of emotion for these two people, who were, perhaps, endowed with over-sensitive natures given to making too much of the commonplace happenings of life. Now, as he watched the head of the child resting against the mother's breast, he ran the gamut of human feelings in his sensations. Love and thanksgiving for these unspeakable gifts of God—his wife, and child—swept the inmost recesses of his heart.

"Please, Marse Ellis!" cried Aunt Henny's voice from the doorway, "please, sah, Marse St. Clar's Isaac done jes' dis minnit come home. What's I gwine ter do wid him?"

"What, Henny!" Ellis cried in astonishment; "St. Clair's Isaac? Where's his master?"

"Dunno, Marse Ellis, but dar's allers truble, sho, when dat lim' o' Satan turns up; 'deed dar is."

Ellis left the room hurriedly, followed by Aunt Henny. Hagar sat there, fondling the child, a perfect picture of sweet womanhood. She had matured wonderfully in the few months of married life; her girlish manner had dropped from her like a garment. Eve's perfect daughter, she accomplished her destiny in sweet content. Presently the door opened, and her husband stood beside her chair again; his face wore a troubled look.

"What is it?" she asked, with a sweeping upward glance that noted every change of his countenance.

"St. Clair's Isaac."

"Well, and is he so serious a matter that you must look so grave?"

"My dear, the slaves all look upon him as a bird of evil omen; for myself, I look upon it as mere ignorant superstition, but still I have a feeling of uneasiness. They have neither of them been at the Hall for five years. Isaac says his master is coming—that he expected to find him here. What brings them is the puzzler."

"News of your marriage, Ellis; a natural desire, to see his new relative. I see nothing strange in that, dear."

"He can't feel very happy about it, according to the terms of the will; probably he has been counting on my not marrying, and now, being disappointed, comes for me to pay his debts, or perform some impossible favor."

"Why impossible?"

"St. Clair is an unsavory fellow, and his desires are not likely to appeal to a man of honor," replied Ellis, with a short, bitter laugh.

"So bad as that?" said his wife regretfully; it was the first shadow since the beginning of their honeymoon. She continued: "Promise me, Ellis, to bear with him kindly and grant him anything in reason, in memory of our happiness."

In the kitchen Aunt Henny, with little braids of hair sticking out from under her turban, talked to Marthy.

"Ef Marse Ellis listen to me, he gwine ter make dat Isaac quit dese diggin's."

"Law, mammy," laughed Marthy, showing her tiny white teeth and tossing her head, "you don' want ter drive de po' boy 'way from whar he was born, does yer?" Marthy was a born coquette, and Isaac was very gallant to her.

"Dat all I gwine ter say. Nobody knows dat Marse St. Clar an' his Isaac better'n I does. I done part raise 'em bof. I reckon my ha'r'd all turn plum' white ef dem two hadn't done lef' dese parts."

"How you come to raise 'em, mammy, an' what made 'em try ter turn yo' ha'r plum' white?"

"Dev'ment, honey, pur' dev'ment! It 'pears lack 'twas only yisterday dat I was a gal wurkin' right yere in dis same ol' kitchen. Marse Sargeant he lose heap money, an' all ob dem move ter St. Louis ter 'trench an' git rich ergin; Marse Enson he want me fer ol' Miss, an' so Marse Sargeant done leave me hyar at Enson Hall. While I was hyar bof ob dem imps was born, but Marse St. Clar he good bit older dan Isaac. Many's de time he run me all ober dis plantation when he no bigger'n dat Thomus Jefferson, 'cause I wouldn't give dat Isaac fus' help from de chickuns jes' roasted fer dinner befo' de fambly done seed nary leg ob 'em. Chase me, chile, wid a pissle pinted plum' at me."

"Lordy! wha' you reckon he do ef he come back hyar now?"

"I don' reckon on nuffin but dev'ment, jes' same as he done time an' time agin when he were a boy—jes' dev'ment."

"Mammy, you say oder day when Missee Hagar git merried to Marse Ellis: 'Now dat St. Clar'll stan' no chance ob gittin' de property'; what you mean by dat?"

"Didn't mean nuffin," snapped her mother, with a suspicious look at her.

"G' 'long 'bout yo' bisness; you's gittin' mighty pert sence you git to be Miss Hagar's maid; you's axin' too many questions."

In a day or so the family settled down to Isaac's presence as a matter of course. Aunt Henny's predictions about the weather were verified, and the week was unpleasant. The wind blew the bare branches of the trees against the veranda posts and roared down the wide fireplaces; snowflakes were in the air. Hagar and Ellis had just come in from a canter over the country roads; she went immediately to her room to dress for dinner, but Ellis tarried a moment in the inviting room which seemed to command his admiration. The luxuries addressed themselves to his physical sense, and he was conscious of complete satisfaction in the knowledge that his wealth could procure a fitting setting for the gem he had won. Other thoughts, too, crept in, aroused by the talk of a friend where they had called on the way home. He had not thought of war, and was not interested in politics; still, if it were true that complications were arising that demanded a settlement by a trial of arms, he was ready. "Perhaps we are too happy for it to last," he muttered; "but, come what will, I have been blessed." His gaze followed Marthy's movements mechanically, as she lighted the wax candles and let fall the heavy curtains, shutting the gloom outside in the gathering darkness. He was aroused from the deep reverie into which he had fallen by the sound of wheels on the carriage drive. In a moment before he could cross the room, the door opened and St. Clair Enson entered, followed by the slave-trader, Walker.

"St. Clair! Is it possible!" he cried, striding forward to grasp his brother's hand. "Is it really you? Welcome home!" They shook hands warmly, and then Ellis threw his arm about St. Clair's shoulders, and for a moment the two men gazed in the depths of each other's eyes with emotion too deep for words. The younger man *did* feel for an instant a wave of fraternal love for this elder brother against whom he meditated an evil deed.

"Why, Ellis, I do believe you're glad to see me. You're ready to kill the fatted calf to feast the prodigal," St. Clair said, as they fell apart. "My friend, Mr. Walker—Walker, my brother."

"Glad to see you and welcome you to Enson Hall," said Ellis in cordial greeting, his hospitable nature overcoming his repugnance for this man of unsavory reputation.

"Thanky thanky," said Walker, as he awkwardly accepted the armchair Ellis offered him, and drew near the blazing fire.

"Just in time for dinner; you will dine with us, Mr. Walker." Walker nodded assent.

"Well, Ellis, how's the world using you? You're married, lucky dog. Got your letter while I was at the nominating convention; it must have followed me about for more than a month. Thought I'd come up and make the acquaintance of my new sister and niece," remarked St. Clair, with careless ease.

"Yes," replied Ellis. Somehow his brother's nonchalant air and careless words jarred upon his ear. "You are always welcome to come when you like and stay as long as you please. This is your home."

"Home with a difference," replied St. Clair, as an evil smile for an instant marred his perfect features.

"He won't stand much show of gittin' eny of this prop'ty now you's got a missus, Mr. Enson," ventured Walker, with a grin. "He's been mighty anxious to meet your missus. Most fellers isn't so oneasy about a sister-in-law, but I reckon this one is different, being report says she's a high-stepper," said Walker, as he grinned at Ellis and cleared his mouth by spitting foul tobacco juice on the polished hearth. Ellis bowed coldly in acknowledgment of his words.

"Mrs. Enson will be down presently. This certainly is a joyful surprise," he said turning to St. Clair; "Why didn't you send word, and the carriage would have met you at the station?"

"Oh, we came out all right in Walker's trap.

"I'll have it put up." Ellis rose as he spoke.

"No, no; my man will drive me back to the city shortly," Walker broke in.

"I hope you are doing well, St. Clair; where are you from now?"

"Just from Charleston, where I have made a place for myself at last. Politics," he added significantly.

"Ah!"

"Great doin's down to Charleston; great doin's," Walker broke in again.

"No doubt of it; how do you think this matter will end?"

"It's goin' to be the greatest time the world ever saw, Mr. Enson. When we git a-goin' thar'll be no holdin' us. The whole South, sah, is full of sodjers, er-gittin ready to whup the Yanks t'uther side of nex' week. That's how it's goin' to end."

"Then it will really be war?"

"The greatest one the worl' ever seen, sah, unless the Yanks git on their knees and asks our pardon, and gives up this govinment to their natral rulers.

Why, man, ain't yer heard? You's a patriot, ain't you? Yer a son of the sunny South, ain't yer?"

Ellis smiled at his enthusiasm, although filled with disgust for the man.

"When one has his family to think of, there are times when he forgets the world and thinks of nothing but his home. Be that as it may, I am no recreant son of the South. I stand by her with all I possess. I can imagine nothing that would turn me a traitor to my section."

"Spoken like a man. That's the talk, eh, Enson?" he said, appealing to St. Clair, who nodded in approval. "Do all you can, I say, for the Confederate States of America, from givin' 'em yer money down to helpin' 'em cuss."

"When the time comes I shall not be found wanting. By the way, St. Clair, your boy Isaac is here. Came on us suddenly the other day."

"Ha, ha, ha! the little black rascal. Didn't I tell you he'd do Johnson out of that money? He's the very devil, that boy."

"Like master, like man," replied St. Clair, with a shrug of his handsome shoulders.

"What is it?" asked Ellis sternly; "no cheating or swindling, is there?"

"He's a runaway. I sold him to a gentleman about a week ago," was St. Clair's careless answer.

"What is the man's name, and where is he to be found? He must be re-imbursed or Isaac returned to him," said Ellis, looking sternly at his brother. "Enson Hall is no party to fraudulent dealings."

"I'm glad to hear you say that, Mr. Enson; I'm up here lookin' for a piece of property belonging to me, and said to be stopping on this very plantation."

"Impossible, sir; all our slaves have been here from childhood, or have grown old with us. You have been misinformed."

"I reckon not. As I was tellin' your brother here, it's a mighty onpleasant job I've got before me, but I must do my dooty." Walker put on a sardonic smile, and continued:

"I see, sah, that you don' understan' me. Let me explain further: Fourteen years ago I bought a slave child from a man in St. Louis, and not being able to find a ready sale for her on account of her white complexion, I lent her to a Mr. Sargeant. I understand that you have her in your employ. I've come to get her." Here the slave-trader took out his large sheepskin pocketbook, and took from it a paper which he handed to Ellis.

Ellis gazed at Walker in bewilderment; he took the paper in his hand and mechanically glanced at it. "Still your meaning is not clear to me, Mr. Walker.

I tell you we have no slave of yours on this plantation," but his face had grown white, and large drops of perspiration stood on his forehead.

"Well, sah, I'll explain a leetle more. Mr. and Mrs. Sargeant lived a number of years in St. Louis; they took a female child from me to bring up—*a nigger*—and they passed her off on the commoonity here as their own, and you have *married* her. Is my meaning clear now, sah?"

"Good God!" exclaimed Ellis, as he fell back against the wainscoting,[2] "then this paper, if it means anything, must mean my wife."

"I can't help who it means or what it means," replied Walker, "this yer's the bill of sale, an' there's an officer outside there in the cart to git me my nigger."

"This paper proves nothing. You'll take no property from this house without proper authority," replied Ellis with ominous calm. Walker lost his temper, apparently.

"I hold you in my hand, sah!" he stormed; "you are a brave man to try to face me down with stolen property."

Ellis rose slowly to his feet. Pale, teeth set, lips half parted, eyes flashing lightning—furious, terrible, superb in his wrath. His eyes were fixed on Walker, who, frightened at his desperate look, rose to his feet also, with his hand on his pistol. "You would murder me," he gasped.

Ellis laughed a strange, discordant laugh.

"There is, there must be some mistake here. My wife was the daughter of Mr. Sargeant. There is not a drop of Negro blood in her veins; I doubt, sir, if you have ever seen her. And, Mr. Walker, if you do not prove the charges you have this day insulted me by making, your life shall pay the penalty."

"Well, sah, fetch her in the room here; I reckon she'll know me. She warn't so leetle as to fergit me altogether."

Just at this moment Hagar opened the door, pausing on the threshold, a fair vision in purest white; seeing her husband's visitors, she hesitated. Ellis stepped quickly to her side and took her hand.

"My dear, are you acquainted with this gentleman? Do you remember ever seeing him before?"

She looked a moment, hesitated, and then said: "I think not."

Walker stepped to the mantel where the wax-light would fall full upon his face, and said:

"Why, Hagar, have you forgotten me? It's only about fourteen years ago that I bought you, a leetle shaver, from Rose Valley, and lent you to Mrs. Sargeant, ha, ha, ha!"

Hagar put her hand to her head in a dazed way as she heard the coarse laugh of the rough, brutal slave-trader. She looked at Ellis, put out her hand to him in a blind way, and with a heartrending shriek fell fainting to the floor.

"I thought she'd remember," exclaimed Walker.

Ellis raised his wife in his arms and placed her upon a sofa. St. Clair stood watching the scene with a countenance in which curiosity and satisfaction struggled for the mastery.

"Throw a leetle water in her face, and that'll bring her to. I've seen 'em faint befo', but they allers come to."

Ellis was deathly white; he turned his flaming eyes upon the trader:

"The less you say, the better. By God! I have a mind to put a ball in you now, you infernal hound!"

"Yes, but she's mine; I want to see that she's all right," and Walker shrank away from the infuriated man.

Ellis took his wife in his arms and bore her from the room. Shortly, Aunt Henny brought them word to dine without him, their rooms were ready, and he would see Mr. Walker in the morning after he had communicated with his lawyer. The officer was dismissed, and drove back to the town. As they sat at the table enjoying the sumptuous fare and perfect appointments, St. Clair said to Walker:

"Is this thing true?"

"True as gospel. The only man who could prove the girl's birth is the one I took her from, and he's dead."

"Well, you've done me a mighty good turn, blame me if you have'nt. I shan't forget it. Here's to our future prosperity," and he touched his wineglass to his friend's.

"I don't mean you shall forget," was Walker's reply as he sat his glass down empty. "Now, siree, you hang about here for a spell and watch the movements. He'll pay me all right, but you mustn't let him snake her off or anything. Ef things look queer, jes' touch the wires and I'll be with you instanter."

On the following morning Ellis Enson's lawyer, one of the ablest men of the Maryland Bar, pronounced the bill of sale genuine, for it had been drawn up by a justice, and witnessed by men who sent their affidavits under oath.

"There is but one thing to be done, Mr. Walker," Ellis said, after listening to his lawyer's words. "What do you want? How much money will it take to satisfy you to say no more about the matter?"

"I don't bear you any malice for nothing you've said ter me; perhaps I'd do about the same as you have ef it was my case. Five thou, cash, will git her, though ef I toted her to New Orleans market, a handsome polished wench like her would bring me any gentleman's seven or eight thou, without a remark. As for the pickaninny—"

"What!" thundered Ellis, "the child, too?"

"In course," replied Walker, drawing his fingers in and out his scraggy whiskers, the child follows the condition of the mother, so I scoop the pile."

Ellis groaned aloud.

"As I was sayin'," continued Walker, "the pickaninny will cost you another thou, and cheap at that."

"I would willingly give the money twice over, even my whole fortune, if it did not prove my wife to be of Negro blood," replied Ellis, with such despair in his tones that even these men, inured to such scenes from infancy, were touched with awe.

The money was paid, and within the hour the house had resumed its wonted quiet and all was apparently as before; but the happiness of Enson Hall had fled forever.

1901–1902

NOTES

1. A derogatory term for black children.

2. Wooden paneling, traditionally made from oak boards, applied to the lower walls of a room.

3. Refers to the belief, common among many African Americans, that children born with all or part of the amniotic sac intact were endowed with special powers, including foresight, the ability to see ghosts, mindreading, and good luck.

JAMES D. CORROTHERS (1869-1917)

James David Corrothers was born in Cass County, Michigan. Raised by his grandfather in South Haven, Michigan, he was often the only African American child to regularly attend the city's public schools. By the age of 14, Corrothers was the primary wage earner in his household. After the death of his grandfather, when Corrothers was 16, he sought employment in the neighboring states of Indiana, Ohio, and Illinois, finding work as a janitor, a sawyer, a lumberjack, a waiter, and even a boxer. It was through his work as the attendant at a white barbershop in Chicago that he met and befriended some of the city's most influential journalists and reformers. With the support of friends Henry Demarest Lloyd, a muckraking journalist, and Frances Willard, a temperance activist, he was able to attend the preparatory program at Northwestern University. Corrothers went on to attend Bennett College in North Carolina before eventually joining the clergy of the A.M.E. Church. A minister as well as a journalist, poet, and prose writer, he published articles in several of the major Chicago dailies. His poetry appeared in the *Colored American* and other black periodicals of his time, as well as in book form; his autobiography, *In Spite of the Handicap,* was published in 1916, a year before his death. Corrothers's poetry developed in two distinct phases. Most of his dialect writing was produced during the earlier part of his career, including *The Black Cat Club* (1902), a unique collection of humorous poems and sketches using as a frame the fictional "Black Cat Literary Club," a society of African American, southern-born migrants living on Chicago's South Side. "The Club Introduced" is an excerpt from this volume. Beginning in 1901, Corrothers's work began to rely more and more on Standard English as he increasingly turned to poetry as a medium for expressing antiracist sentiments. The dialect and Standard English poems included here were originally published in the *Colored American* magazine.

THE SNAPPING OF THE BOW

> The toad beneath the harrow knows
> Exactly where each harrow-tooth goes;
> The butterfly upon the road,
> Preaches contentment to that toad.
> —Kipling[1]

I dreamed a dream, and, in my dream, I heard
One wail at midnight by a convent's walls.
And, as he wailed, he clutched the stars, and shook
The pillars of the firmament of God,
And rolled the thunders of Olympus down
On men; and they besought their holy ones
To plead with him—lest he might spoil the world.

His face was bronze; his limbs were bronze but steel;
His mane was blacker than the Steeds of Night.[2]
And his great eyes flashed warnings from beneath
A citadel where daring thoughts abode.—
A comely youth—why needed he to weep?

Alas! upon his brow he wore the brand
Of degradation, and upon his neck
A circlet galling as a crime!—And from
The cursèd thing a chain of hate e'er bound
Him where he stood. His hands were manacled;
His limbs wore thongs that cut the flesh agape,
Until, for the pure pain, he writhed and wept,—
As weeps a conquered god—the prisoner of Despair!

He flung himself upon his knees, and burst into a prayer:
"O God, and hast
Thou made me for these miseries? I feel
Myself a man—I have the spirit and
The hopes of one. O, why, then, must I strive
And fail?—No lake is clearer than my soul;
No ship is prouder; none more tempest tost.
'Tis true my brow is dark; but, in the night,
My spirit walks the stars, and lightly spurns

Its kinship to this world!—Lord, I have tried;
The burden of the failure rests with thee."
So fell he tranced.

    But, on the plain there rose
A phantom of the silent sphinx—the grim,
Spell-casting thought of some deep master dead.
And lo! beside its ancient, crumbling base,
Napoleon, fresh from mighty deeds of war,
Halted his band, and spoke in tones of awe.—
All this I saw, and dreamed that yet—aye, yet!—
The race might rise that built the awful thing
That holds its secret still in Egypt's sands.

                    1901

ME 'N' DUNBAR

One day when me 'n' Dunbar wuz a-hoein' in de co'n,
Bofe uv us tried an' anxious foh to heah de dinnah—ho'n.—
Him in his fiel', an' me in mine, a-wo'kin' on togeddah,
A-sweatin' lak de mischief in de hottes' kine o' weddah,
A debblish notion tuck me 't Paul wuz gittin' on too fast:
But, thainks I: "Wait untwel he git 'mongst all dem weeds an' grass,
'N' I'll make him ne'ly kill his se'f, an' den come out de las'."

Tuck off ma coat, rolled up ma slebes, spit on ma han's an' say:
"Ef God'll he'p me—'n' not he'p him—I beats ma man today!"
S'I: "Paul, come on, le's have a race!—I see you achin' foh it"—
S'e: "All right, Jeems, ma son: strack out—I sho' admire yo' spurrit."
S'I: "Son er father. I'm yo' match—jes' ketch me, ef you ken!"
S'I: "You'd gib up now, ef you'd take advice f'om yo' bes' fr'en"—
An' den de way dem two hoes flew wuz scand'l'us—gen-'l'men!

De sun shone on us br'ilin' hot: but, now an' den de breeze
Blowed fresh, f'om 'cross de maddah lot, de fragrance ob de trees
In de ole orchard, jes' beyon'. De birds sung clear an' sweet:
De tree toad wuz a-callin' out his 'pinion ob de heat:
De fahm-house looked invitin', an', erbout a mile away.

De town gleamed white—across de road, de fahmers made dey hay:—
But me 'n' Paul was hustlin': 'ca'se dat wuz ouh "busy day."

By'm-by, I got so tired dat I thought ma soul I'd die—
An' all de time a-watchin' Paul, out one side ob ma eye.—
I walks up to de fence, an, le'nt upon ma hoe a spell,
An' say: "Paul, how you mekin' out?" S'e: "Putty middlin' well."
"Dat so?" sez I, you lookin' weak!" Sez he "Am dat a fack?—
Who wuz it lef' his hoein' fuss? You bettah go on back,—
An' go to wo'k, 'r I'll be so fur dat you cain't fine ma track!"

'N' back I went, an' slashed about, an' to'e up mo' good co'n—
An' missed mo' weeds den airy othah mo'tal evah bo'n.
An' all de time a-thinkin' thoughts, untwel I come to see
Dat, dat ah' kine o' foolishness wa'n't he'pin' him ner me.
S'I: "Hole on, Paul, le's stop awhile, an' talk an' git ouh breff—
'Ca'se bofe uv us has got to hoe his own patch foh his se'f."
Sez he: "Dat's right; hey ain't no use to wo'k ouhse'fs to deff."

1901

JUNY AT THE GATE

Beside a gate rudely possessed
   By clambering vines of ivy now,
Once, as the sun sunk in the west,
   A young girl stood with anxious brow.

A fair, dark girl from whose deep eyes
   The love-light beamed so tenderly,
And dripped like moonbeams from the skies,
   When summer skies from clouds are free.

Her soft curls clustered 'round her head,
   And clasped her fair form tenderly;
And her full lips were ripe and red
   As cherries on their native tree.

Beneath her feet a river flowed—
   Kissing its silent shores adieu;

Beyond, adown a dusky road,
    She watched a dim form fade from view.

Her brother! he had kissed her cheek,
    And whispered: "Wait down here for me."
She pressed his hand, but did not speak,
    And waited for him silently.

The gathering night frowned black and grim,
    Like glaring eyes the red stars burned;
And still she waited there for him,
    Who never, nevermore returned.

The wind moaned like a restless ghost,
    The stream sobbed like a broken heart;
And still she lingered at her post,
    With fluttering breast and lips apart.

Ah well would they who checked his pace,
    In other days than slavery's reign,
Have loosed him, had they seen the face
    Of Juny waiting him in vain.

But O! fell Slavery's cruel chain
    Loosed not a captive that it bound;
But tightened at each cry of pain,
    To goad its victim's rankling wound.

Moons waxed and waned—long years rolled on,
    Long, cruel years of toil and pain—
Seed-time and harvest-time had gone,
    And yet he never came again.

And yet, with melancholy face,
    And massy, dark, disheveled hair,
Each night, in the old meeting place,
    Stood lovely Juny, waiting there.

O that was in the long ago,
    And love, remembering, sadly weeps!
Now, by the yellow, swift Yazoo,
    Where long she watched, sweet Juny sleeps.

The warm sun shines, the grasses wave,
    Ivy and musk-grape haunt the spot;
Wild songsters sing above the grave,
    But the lone sleeper waketh not.

No troublous thoughts nor earthly care
    Shall pain that gentle heart again;—
The only sigh that murmurs there
    Is "Peace on earth, good will to men."

Fail, song of mine, our leave we take;
    Alas! O cruel slavery!
The tenderest heart that ever brake [*sic*],
    And none to tell the tale but me.

When long my rhyme shall be forgot,
    Some bard this story will relate.
And master hands will paint the spot,
    With Juny waiting at the gate.

1902

THE BLACK CAT CLUB: NEGRO HUMOR & FOLK-LORE

Chapter I: The Club Introduced

Sandy Jenkins, alias "Doc," president of the "Black Cat Club" and poet-laureate of the Chicago levee,[3] strolled contentedly along Clark Street one sunny afternoon—the proudest and happiest mortal in the universe.

Sandy was "dressed to kill": His linen was spotless; his clothing faultless; his cane, chrysanthemum, diamonds, and "patent leathers" matchless; while his "Jockey Club" perfume proclaimed his presence quite as much as they. Sandy was satisfied.

Under one arm he carried an immense black cat with which to "hoodoo" his enemies, while in his inside coat pocket reposed securely his precious rabbit's foot, together with the manuscript of his famous poem, "De Cahvin" —an effusion which never failed to delight his Negro constituents of the levee, whenever the poet condescended to read it to them.

But Sandy had still other reasons to be proud.

It had been indeed a great day for him. He had perfected the organization of the "Black Cat Literary Club" on the night before, and the morning papers had all published glowing accounts of the affair, in which Sandy came in for the lion's share of the glory. Five morning papers had each devoted a column of space to an elaborate description of the club, and Sandy's name had appeared with amazing frequency in each report. The thought of it overcame the poet, and he repaired to the nearest saloon and called for "whisky straight."

"You black people bin raisin' san' wid yo' Shakespeare ack!" observed "Billy" Spooks, the bartender, pouring out Sandy's drinks, as a number of the great man's admirers filed into the place. "See whut de papahs said 'bout you dis mo'nin', Doc?"

"Nevah pays no 'tention to sich small mattahs," answered Sandy; "might, ef I wuz raised pickin' cotton in de backwoods down South, lak you. I'se a genamun, mase'f."

"You'll be gen'ler 'n' dat 'fo' I gits th'u' wid you," replied the bartender with a laugh.

Sandy drew his razor.

"Come on wid yo' cutlery; but foh de Laud sake hol' dat cat!" exclaimed Spooks, with feigned excitement. "I thought you could take a *joke!*"

"G'way!" said Sandy hotly; "I 'member when you rid into town on a hay-wagon, too hongry to cas' a shadder, an' struck me fur two bits to git yo'se'f somethin' t'eat wid! Don't tell *me!* Knowed you when de mice built nests in yo' wool!"

"Doan' let me down so hahd, Doc," said Spooks, with a laugh. Then he prepared the drinks, and, while the crowd was enjoying the treat, picked up a morning paper that lay behind the counter, and read the following, punctuating his monologue with an occasional laugh and witticism:

DE BLACK CAT CLUB

ALL SORTS OF WEIRD NOTIONS HAUNT ITS MEMBERS

Sandy Jenkins, Poet-Laureate of the Levee, Writes Stirring Epics which have Made Him Famous "Down de Line," and Gained Him the Presidency of the New Society.

"Sandy Jenkins, the colored poet-laureate of the levee, and his friends have organized a literary society which will henceforth be known to fame as the 'Black Cat Club.' "The club is the most peculiar literary society on earth. It is founded on a pretended belief in the old Negro superstition that black cats are the children of his Satanic majesty, and that all kinds of bad luck await the unfortunate individual whose luck is crossed by one of these sable disturbers of the midnight peace. Nothing but the possession of a rabbit's foot and a silver spoon can thwart the power of the black cat's hoodoo. These things the learned Sandy possesses. Moreover he has captured a big black cat with which to hoodoo a dozen literary rivals who have dared to evidence their existence since Jenkins leaped into popularity as the author of his pathetic poem, 'De Cahvin.' Sandy's friends have taken up the spirit of the fun, and the 'Black Cat Club' is the result.

"There are but nine members in the club—one for each of the cat's alleged nine lives. New members are never taken in—old ones are not allowed to withdraw. College graduates are not eligible to membership, and no member is allowed to become too familiar with the classics or to speak disrespectfully of Jenkins' black cat. In fact, the club members are expected to learn all they can concerning cats, witches, ghosts, quaint Negro sayings and plantation stories and melodies, and to impart them in an original manner at the meetings of the club. Swell banquets will be given at all meetings of the society, where watermelons, 'possum, sweeten 'tatahs, pie, co'n pone, po'k chops, chicken, and intoxicating liquors will be very much in evidence. This is one of the main objects of the organization.

"The club has, as yet, no regular headquarters. It was organized in a levee saloon, and thus far its meetings have been held in the private rooms of its members.

"All the members of the club are well-known characters about the levee, but in the club assumed names are adopted. None but the imperial Jenkins himself is allowed to retain his usual cognomen. Henry Harris is the club's chaplain. In the club he is known as the 'Rev. Dark Loudmouth.' He opens up the meetings with a prayer to the black cat. The club has no secretary. It doesn't need any, so its members say; but 'K. C. Brighteyes' looks after its funds. Jenkins is both its president and poet-laureate. The club has no critic. It couldn't stand one. 'Bad Bob Sampson' is its sergeant-at-arms. Other members of the society are: 'Johnny Yellowshort,' 'Saskatchewan Jones,' 'Prof. Lightfoot Johnsing,' 'Roustabout Thompson,' and 'Slippery Simon.' The club has no honorary members; but, by virtue of its constitution, it is allowed to have 999. Contrary to general usage, however, these members will not be chosen because of their brilliancy or the honor they are expected to reflect upon the club; nor will they be called honorary members at all. They will be denominated 'onry members,' and will be chosen because they are considered too 'onry' to belong to the club—"

"Dat's whah *you* comes in, Billy," interrupted Sandy. And amid the laugh that followed, "Billy" good-naturedly treated the crowd. Then he continued his reading:

"The club meets every Friday night, and none but members are admitted to its rooms. Upon the walls of the club, ornamented by a skull and cross-bones, will hang a coffin-shaped motto:

'Death to eavesdroppers, policemen, and reporters.
By order of MESMERIZER and the CLUB.'

"The club does not believe in woman's rights, and none of its members are allowed to marry.

"One of its most unique and laughable features is its farcical worship of Jenkins' black cat, 'Mesmerizer,' who is supposed to bring good luck to members of the organization, but to be a deadly 'hoodoo' to their enemies. Mesmerizer is alleged to be as old as the universe, and to be the child of Satan himself. He is closely related to the 'original sin,' and delights in doing evil.

"Jenkins, the originator and moving spirit of the club, is a jolly fellow who has knocked about the levee for the last ten years. Among his companions he is affectionately known as 'Doc.' He is an interesting character, chic and up-to-date in everything except the trivial matter of a little schooling—"

"Say, Doc," exclaimed the bartender, breaking off from his reading, "I wouldn't stan' dat—dog-goned ef I would! I'd cahve dat kid reporter on sight! Here you done paid him yo' good money to write you up, an' he's cas'in' reflections on yo' intelligence!"

"Yes, but he squares evahthing right there below—read on an' see."

Then the bartender read: "Doc has more than filled up the deficiency, however, with a stock of ideas, original and inherited, which he hopes to promulgate through the medium of the 'Black Cat Club'—"

"Dat makes it all right, don' it, Billy?"

"Sho' thing," remarked Spooks.

"Den keep yo' mouf shet," returned Sandy. And Spooks continued his perusal of the paper:

"Doc dresses well and is not bad-looking. He is tall and rather slender, but has a good figure and an erect carriage that give him an air of importance. His complexion is a clear, light brown. He has glowing black eyes, and he wears a small mustache which he curls in a manner which must make him a beau-ideal among the belles of colored swelldom.[4] He is a musician as well as a poet. He plays a half-dozen instruments, and has a silvery tenor voice that makes him good company almost anywhere. He is pledged to furnish an original poem at every meeting of the club, among the members of which and around the levee generally he is lionized, and is considered the peer of

Burns, Milton, Shakespere, and Tennyson, and, in levee vernacular, of 'any literary monkey dat evah push' a pen!'"

"Doc," was Billy Spooks' comment, "you sho' has got yo'se'f a record! Tetch ma flesh!" he added, grasping Sandy's hand.

"Doc," exclaimed Saskatchewan Jones, "de repo'tah dat written *dat* wuz smaht, foh true! Here! I'm got a dollah—evahbody hab a drink—ain't nothin' small 'bout me! Here's to de kid!"

"He's a bo'n genamun whut ought to be dead drunk dis minute," said Sandy, gulping down his liquor.

"Ought to ketch him, Sandy, an' cahve yo' monograph in him, so' you'd know him when you need him 'g'in," suggested Billy Spooks; "'tain't evah-body splashes ink lak dat. He cain't tetch you, tho', Doc, 'ca'se you's done got Shakespere hangin' ovah de ropes! Read dat piece o' yo's once mo' an' let me die a listenin' to it!"

Then the room grew still, and a look of happy expectancy lighted up the faces of the crowd as the learned man drew out his manuscript, and, with a grandiloquent sweep of the hand, began:

"Jim Johnson lubbed a yallah girl
Until his brain began to whirl;
But Sambo Brown he lubbed huh, too,
An' out o' dat a quarrel grew.
So Jimmy Johnson comes to town
A-purpose to cahve Sambo Brown.
Along about de hour ob noon,
He fines him down in Smiff's saloon;
'Fo' Sambo knowed whut he wuz 'bout,
Jim Johnson drawed him razah out,
An' cut him all around de face—
All up de back, an' evah place!
He cut him low, he cut him high—
Cleah f'om his ankle to his eye—
He clipped bofe ears off f'om Sam's head—
It was a sin how po' Sam bled!
He dislocated Sambo's jaw—
He cahved him to de bone—oh, Law!
I tell you whut, it wuz a sight
De way he slashed him lef' an' right!

He spoiled Sam's go-to-meetin' clothes,
He whacked de end off f'om Sam's nose,
He cut him 'twel he hel' his breff—
He like to cut de coon to deff!
When, suddenly, Sam tu'ns about,
An' draws a bran' new razah out,
An' whacks Jim Johnson jes' lak dat!
He sp'iled his ketch-me-quick plug hat⁵—
He cut his head, he cut his feet,
An' den he made de two cuts meet—
He cut out Johnson's bes'es eye—
He cut his tongue out, putty nigh!
He cut his name in Johnson's cheek—
He cut him 'twel he couldn't speak.
He cut de po' man jes' foh fun—
Good Laud, I thought Jim's time had come!
But Johnson rallied, 'bout dis time,
An, swo' dat he'd make Sambo climb!
Den, oh! de way dem two did fight,
No man kin tell in black an' white:—
Slashin' one 'nother all to slashes,
An' gashin' each other all to gashes!
Dey fit an' mixed an' mixed an' fit—
Seemed lak dem fellahs wouldn't quit!
And co'se we didn't nah one staht 'em;
An' didn't feel disposed to paht 'em;
An' Smiff say: "Let 'em fight it out;
Dey's got de grit you reads about."
Alas! how I regrets to tell
How bofe at last in mincemeat fell.
But, in de midst ob dat brown hash,
De razahs still contrived to clash,
As ef de souls ob dem two shades⁶
Still struggled in de razah blades!
We sent around an' got some glue,
An' done de bes' dat we could do—
We tried; but, man, we tried in vain

To make 'em stick together again—
All we could do wuz git a broom,
An' sweep 'em bofe out ob de room."

"Out o' sight!" yelled a dozen voices, as the poem was concluded.

"Say, Doc," added Saskatchewan Jones, "dat head o' yo'n belongs in Washington! Ef I had yo' sense, I wouldn't stay here ner no whah else!"

This remark was followed by the gurgling of a dozen dusky throats.

"Say, Doc," inquired Spooks, "when yo' club meet ag'in?"

"Friday night," returned the poet, preparing to leave. "Well, ef you'll 'sep' uv it, I'm got a back room you kin use."

"Thankee, Billy," returned Sandy, "you's a good fellah," And, sauntering out, he continued his triumphal march down the street.

1902

NOTES

1. The epigraph is from the poem "Pagett, M.P.," by English prose writer and poet Joseph Rudyard Kipling (1865–1936).

2. In Norse mythology, Hrimfaxi (frost-mane) is the horse of night, riding across the heavens every evening, bringing darkness in its wake. Skinfaxi (shining-mane) follows each morning, bringing the day.

3. Refers to the Levee District of Chicago, in what is now the South Loop area and which served as the city's red light district from the 1880s through 1912.

4. Elite or high society.

5. The term "plug hat" refers to a shaped, hard-brimmed felt hat with a small brim, most often a bowler or top hat. "Catch-me-quick" refers to any hat adorned with ornamental streamers attached in the back.

6. A derogatory slang term for black people.

BENJAMIN GRIFFITH BRAWLEY (1882-1939)

Benjamin Griffith Brawley was born in Columbia, South Carolina, to parents Margaret Dickerson Brawley and Edward McKnight Brawley, the president of a small Alabama college. As a young man, Brawley's father had been the first African American student to graduate from Pennsylvania's Bucknell University. As a child, Benjamin Brawley was academically precocious, and his mother tutored him at home for several years before enrolling him in school. A gifted student of classical languages, he divided his summer days between odd jobs in the agricultural sector and studying Latin and Greek on his own. At the age of thirteen, he enrolled in the preparatory program at Atlanta Baptist College (now Morehouse University). Brawley would go on to earn baccalaureate degrees from Morehouse (1901) and the University of Chicago (1906), as well as a master's degree from Harvard (1908). He held teaching posts at Howard University, Shaw University, and Morehouse, where he was appointed the institution's first dean. A prolific writer of both poetry and scholarship, Brawley published a number of poems in the period's black magazines and newspapers. His books include three collections of poetry and numerous volumes on African American literature and history, most notably, *A Short History of the American Negro* (1913), *The Negro in Literature and Art in the United States* (1918), *A Short History of the English Drama* (1921), and *Paul Laurence Dunbar: Poet of His People* (1936). The poems "The Path of Life" and "The Battleground" first appeared in the *Colored American* magazine in the year 1902. "The Problem" was published in Brawley's 1905 collection of the same name.

THE PATH OF LIFE

The opening bud of a flower,
　　Its incense borne on the air,
The curve of a graceful petal,
　　An answering image there—
The love of a life awaking,
　　The peal of an ancient reign—

Some say that it leads to Passion,
   And some that it leads to Pain.

The stifling odor of battle,
   The sound of answering guns,
The slaughter of men in trenches
   For a flag that onward runs,
The wail of far-off kindred,
   A night when the dirges swell—
Some say that it leads to Glory,
   And some that it leads to Hell.

A scholar sitting at midnight,
   And pondering mystic lore;
A woman toiling and suffering
   After the day is o'er;
Hopes that over the wrecking
   Up to the stairs set aim—
Some say that it leads to Heart-breaks,
   And some that it leads to Fame.

A youth in the glare of temples,
   A maid in a crowded town,
A mart where the blaze of splendor
   Goes glittering up and down,
A woman eating an apple,
   A man that burns within—
Some say that it leads to Knowledge,
   And some that it leads to Sin.

O, this mazy existence,
   O, these passionate years,
When the heart is full and restless,
   And the life we know not nears;
After the toiling is over,
   What of the path we have trod?
Some say that it leads to Exile,
   And some that it leads to God.

1902

THE BATTLEGROUND

Let me live close to men's hearts. In the years
When youth is full, let me know men and grow
Into the knowledge of their pulsing souls.
Not on some distant peak where in the veil
Fame tapers and the siren temples blaze,
May my days pass, but on a lower ground,
Where men of might brave dubious circumstance
Where sorrow wears the heart, would lose the soul,
Where strenuous life demands high ideals.
In lusty labor and the fight with fire,
Or sin, unlovable benightedness,
May I know men, and knowing learn to love,
And loving learn to help them in their toil.

1902

THE PROBLEM

Ye who have the vision, ye who know the plan
Of the stretch of empire o'er the haunts of man,

Ye who claim dominion far as man may reach,
What are these wild doctrines that at home ye teach?

What is this new notion of the lust of laws,
Sheltered by your ensign, bargained for your cause?

Farther yet and farther spreads the eagle's wing.
Louder yet your triumph bids the heathen sing;

Farther yet and farther do your footsteps go,
Each new day a harvest of the seed ye sow:

Ye who day by day are seeking for your need,
What is this ye harbor, what is this ye breed,

This the hope of glory, this the great desire,
Daily growing fatter 'neath your altar-fire?

What are these decrees your legislators make,
Striving all the founding of your code to shake?

What is this proscription, what these brazen bars,
What this fearful phantom of the jim-crow cars?[1]

Whence these gods of fury at whose feet ye bow,
Relics of the darkness, superseded now?

Was it then for this ye sank the Merrimac,
Or is this the whole wild fabric going back—

Back across the ages to the river-brink
Where the man meets slave, where young slave-children drink?

One of your strong poets, virile and of sight,
Saw the fearful image, piteous in its plight,

Of a man of might, with muffled undertone,
Rolling, rolling, rolling up a hill a stone.

All the agitation, all the strife and woe,
All the stress and tumult forty years ago,

Left this ancient problem, reared at your command,
Shall ye try to crush this man, or bid him stand?

Was it idle speaking, was it platitude,
Do we bend the meaning, stretch the magnitude,

Of the Declaration—all the hope it meant,
That "We hold these truths to be self-evident?"

Were the fathers wrong, or did they say too much?
Was oppression such but when they felt its touch?

What are all the words here that ye fail to heed?
Can it be that folly satisfied your need;

Or is this the God-sent oracle of truth,
Purchased with your blood for all the world forsooth?

Hearts are still unchanging; what ye craved for then
Burns within the bosoms of a million men;

All ye fain would teach us by a sterner hand
Do our minds full-seeing fail to understand.

Ye who have the vision, ye who know the way,
Hear the mighty millions singing as they pray;

Heed the word the dubious present prophesies,
List the music-making as the toilers rise,

Toiling with their face full-turned upon the sun,
Rising yet and higher when each day is done.

Ye who claim the gospel, ye who know the law,
Worship ye the night, or what your fathers saw?

1905

NOTE

1. The name applied to the blacks-only sections of segregated trains and trolley cars.

RUTH D. TODD (1878–?)

Much of the life of African American short-fiction writer Ruth D. Todd remains unknown. Literary historian Yolanda Williams Page reports locating census records that indicate the author was born in the state of Virginia, to Mattie and Edward P. Todd. In 1900, Todd was employed as a domestic servant in Philadelphia, in the home of Dr. George M. Cooper. At some point she left this position, however, and by 1910 she was working as a seamstress and sharing living quarters with a chambermaid named Alice Byers, also from Virginia. To date, no further documentation of her life has been uncovered. The dearth of biographical information is counterbalanced, however, by the compelling body of literary work that she left behind in the pages of the *Colored American* magazine. During the period between 1902 and 1904, Todd published three short stories and a serialized novella, all of which use inversion and humor to challenge the trope of the "tragic mulatto." Todd flouts convention by creating refreshingly ironic narratives in which the condition of being mixed-race is neither tragic nor a marker of superiority (over darker-skinned black people). "The Octoroon's Revenge," published in March of 1902, is characteristic of the author's engagement with questions of race and color, using the familiar theme of passing to offer a vision of multiracial identity and multiethnic community that defies the familiar characterization of the so-called "white negro" as victim and outcast.

THE OCTOROON'S REVENGE

He was a tall young fellow, with the figure of an athlete, extremely handsome, with short, black curls and dark eyes.

His companion was a beautiful girl, tall and slight, though exceedingly graceful, with masses of silken hair of a raven blackness, and with eyes large and dreamy, of a deep violet blue.

But while she was the daughter of one of Virginia's royal blue bloods, he was simply a young mulatto coachman in her father's employ.

The young girl was sitting on a mossy bank by the side of a shady brook, while the young man lay at her feet. A carriage with a pair of fine horses stood just at the edge of the wood, across the roadway.

At last the young man spoke, looking up at the girl as he did so, and there was a world of anguish in his sad, dark eyes.

"Lillian, dearest, I am afraid that this must be our last day alone with each other."

"Oh, Harry dear, why so, what has happened? Does any one suspect us?" exclaimed the young girl as she moved swiftly from her seat and knelt by his side. He caught both her hands in his and covered them with kisses before he replied.

"No, dearest, nothing has happened as yet, but something may at any moment, Lillian darling." And the young man raised himself up and clasped the girl passionately to his heart. "It almost drives me mad to tell you, but I must go away."

"Oh, no! no! no! Harry, dear Harry surely you do not mean what you are saying."

"Yes, darling, I must go! For your sake; for both of our sakes. Think dear one, it is quite possible that we may be found out some day, and then think of the shame and disgrace it will bring to you. Think what a blow it would give your father; what a blight it would cast upon an old and honored name. Shunned and despised by your most intimate friends, you would be a social outcast. They would lynch me, of course, but for myself I care not. It is of you that I must think, and your father who has been so very kind to me. Dear heart, I would gladly lay down my life to save your pure and spotless name."

"Harry, dearest, although a few drops of Negro blood flows through your veins, your heart is as noble and your soul as pure as that of any one of my race. I would fain take you by the hand as my own, defying friends, father—defying the world, Harry, for I love you; and if you leave me I shall surely go mad! It would break my heart; it would kill me!" cried the girl, with frantic sobs.

"Oh, God! why was I ever born to wreck so pure and beautiful a heart as this? Why, oh, why is it such a crime for one of Negro lineage to dare to love the woman of his choice?"

"Darling, I wish that we had never met—that I had died before seeing your beautiful face—and then dear one you would be free to love and honor one of your class; one who would be more worthy of you; at least, worthier than I, a Negro."

"To me, Harry, you are the noblest man on earth, and Negro that you are, I would not have you changed. I only wish, dear, that I also was possessed of Negro lineage, so that you would not think of me so far above you. As it is dear—perhaps it is but the teaching of Mammie Nell—but I feel something as though I belonged to your race, at any rate I shall very soon, for whither you go, there too I shall be."

"My darling—what strange words—what do you mean?" he asked anxiously.

"Simply this, that we can elope!"

"Oh Lillian, dear one, you forget that you are the daughter of one of Virginia's oldest aristocrats!"

"Do not reproach me for that Harry. Have I not thought, and wept, and prayed over it until my eyes were dim and my heart ached? I tell you there is no other way. We could go to Europe. I have always longed to visit Italy and France. Oh, Harry! We could be so happy together!"

"Lillian! Lillian! oh, my dearest!" he cried as he drew her closer within his embrace and pressed passionate kisses on her upturned face. Then he as suddenly put her from him.

"No! No! I am but mortal; do not tempt me. It would be worse than cowardly to do this. I cannot! Oh God! I cannot!"

But the girl wound her beautiful arms around his neck and asked tenderly: "Not even for my sake, Harry? Not even if it was the only thing on earth that would make me happy?"

The soft arms clinging about his neck, the pleading eyes gazing into his, completely stole his senses. He could not draw her closer to him, but his voice shook with emotion as he answered:

"Lillian, I have said that I would die for you, if it would but make you happy. And the thought of taking you away—of making you my wife—drives me wild with joy. Will you trust yourself with me?"

"I am yours—take me to your heart." Was her reply.

And he kissed her again passionately, almost madly; he called her sweetheart, wife, and many other endearing names.

— — —

A week later the country for miles around was ringing with the news of Lillian Westland's elopement with her father's Negro coachman.

A posse of men and women scoured the country for miles around hoping to find the young people established in some dainty cottage. Cries of "lynch the Nigger, lynch the Nigger!" rang through the woods, and many were the comments, innuendoes and slighting words bestowed upon the young girl, who had been such a pet, but who had now outraged society so grossly.

It was a terrible shock to Lillian's white-haired aristocrat father. He had loved and worshipped his beautiful daughter and only child. But this madness, this ignominious conduct that his well beloved and petted darling had shown, crushed and dazed him, and placed him in a stupor from which it was impossible to arouse him. He shut himself up and refused to see even his most intimate friends.

The short, imploring, pitiful letter received from Lillian, confessing all, and begging that in time her father would look upon her conduct a little less harshly, failed to animate him.

A month later, the news of the Hon. Jack Westland's death from suicide was announced by the entire press of that section. A deep mystery was connected with the suicide, of which vague hints were published in the daily papers. But nothing definite being known, the Westland mystery was soon forgotten by the world in general.

By only one person was the key of the mystery held, and she was a servant, who had been in the Westland's employ for many years.

This servant was an octoroon woman of about thirty-five years of age. Her eyes were the most remarkable feature about her. They were large and dark: at times wild and flashing, and again gentle and appealing, which fact conveyed to one the idea of a most romantic history. Her straight nose, well cut mouth and graceful poise of her head and neck showed that she was once a very beautiful creature, as well as an ill-used one, to judge from her story which was as follows:

It was twenty years ago that I first took the position as chambermaid at Westland Towers; I was just sixteen years of age that day—June 17th, 1875. My mother I never knew, but I was told by an aunt, an only relative of mine, that my mother had been a beautiful quadroon woman, and my father a member of one of Virginia's best families. My aunt having died while I was as yet but ten years old, the hardships and misery I experienced during my wretched existence between ten and sixteen, can better be imagined then described.

The filth and degradation of the low class Negroes among whom, for lack of means, I was forced to live, disgusted me so that I grew to despise them. I held aloof from them and refused to take part in the vulgar frivolities which they indulged in, and occupied my spare moments in study, thereby evoking a torrent of anger and abuse upon my head, from the lowest Negroes. It was therefore with great relief that I accepted a position as chambermaid at Westland Towers, preferring to live as a servant with white people than to be the most honored guest of the Negroes among whom I lived. I was young then, and the blood of my father who was a great artist, was stronger in me than that of my mother. Naturally I hated all things dark, loathsome and disagreeable, and my soul thirsted and hungered for the bright sunshine, and the brilliancy and splendor of all things beautiful, which I found at Westland Towers. It was one of the most magnificently beautiful places in Virginia.

The Westland family were of old and proud descent, and consisted of a father, son and a wizened old housekeeper. The son was a handsome man. In fact I will describe him as I saw him for the first time in my life. I was in the act of dusting his private sitting room, when I turned and saw this handsome young man standing in the doorway. The expression on his face was one of ardent admiration. His violet blue eyes, as they gazed into mine seeming to read my very soul, had a charm about them which drew me to him in spite of myself. His short curls, which lay about his high aristocratic forehead shone like bright gold, and a soft, light mustache hid a mouth which was better acquainted with a smile than a sneer. His figure was tall and stalwart, though as graceful as a woman's, and altogether, he impressed me as being by far the most handsome man I have ever seen.

He spoke to me pleasantly, kindly, and with a gentleness which seemed to thrill my very soul. I was young and foolish, unused to the ways of the world and of men, and when his blue eyes looked into mine, so appealingly, and his gentle, musical voice spoke to me so tenderly, telling me that I was the most beautiful girl in all the world, and that he loved me passionately, nay madly, adding that if I would only be his, he would place me in a beautiful house with servants, horses, and carriages; telling me that I should have beautiful dresses and jewelry and that all within the household should worship me, I laid my head upon his breast and told him I would be his.

But when I asked him if we could not marry he replied that it was impossible. That if he ever married one of colored blood, his father's anger would be so great as to cause his disinheritance, and that then he could not place his darling in a high position, adding that being born a gentleman, it would go hard with him to try to earn his own livelihood, all of which seemed to me a very fitting excuse. He also told me that it was not a marriage certificate or the words of a ceremony which made us man and wife. That marriages were made in Heaven, and if we loved each other and lived together, God would look down on us and bless our union, adding that he would always love me and never leave me. Oh, God! That was a bitter trial! I had no mother to advise me; no friend to go to for assistance, and the very thought of giving him up for the filth and degradation from which I came, tortured me for days, during which time my great love for him overcame all obstacles, and on the 4th of July, I found myself living in a luxury of love.

We lived together for eighteen months, during which time no sorrow came to me, save the death of a baby boy. Oh, they were happy days! I was assuredly the happiest girl in all Virginia. But there came evil times. His father died, and of course he had to leave me for a time to attend to important duties.

I was sorry for his father's death and I was also glad, thinking that now no obstacle being in the way, he would surely marry me. But in this I was doomed to bitter disappointment.

A young and beautiful lady, a distant cousin of his, stole his heart from me, and when I received a letter from him telling me that grave duties confronted him, and though it broke his heart to say it, he must part from me, offering me an annuity of five hundred dollars, a great lump rose in my throat which seemed to choke me. I felt my heart breaking. The things before my eyes began to dance and gloat at my anguish. Then everything grew dark and I knew no more for several weeks. When I regained consciousness, my first impulse was to kill myself, but remembering that in a few months I would become a mother for the second time, I stayed my hand. I also accepted the annuity of five hundred dollars, thinking that if my little one lived, it would amount to a small fortune when of age. My love died, and in it instead lived hatred and thirst for vengeance. I thought constantly of the words:

"Hell hath no fury like a woman scorned."

And likened them unto myself. I was young; I could be patient for years, but an opportunity presented itself sooner than I expected. Eight months before the birth of my child, which was a girl, Jack Westland married and one year after his marriage, his beautiful young wife was called away by death, the cause of which was a tiny baby girl. The death of his young wife caused him such anguish that he shut himself up and would see no one. He would not even look upon the face of the poor motherless babe. He bade the housekeeper to procure a wet nurse for the infant, which was a delicate little thing, and as there were no other to be obtained, they sought me out and begged me to take the position as nurse.

I obstinately refused at first, but on learning that Jack would soon go abroad to try to divert his mind, I accepted; for an idea that would suit my purpose exactly flashed through my brain. The two babies were almost exactly alike, both having violet blue eyes and dark hair. Indeed the only difference between them was that my baby was four months older. Supposing that the young heiress should die? Could I not deftly change the babies? I would try at all events.

All things went as I had hoped for. The young heiress as I expected died, and I mourned her death as that of my own, and when I returned to Westland Towers, no one noticed any change, but that the sea air had improved the baby's health wonderfully.

When Jack returned home two years later, he saw a beautiful, blue eyed baby girl, with jet black curls about her little neck. He greeted me kindly, but there was no touch of passion in his voice. In fact he treated me as an exalted servant which made me hate him all the more.

"He was glad," he said "that I took such an interest in the welfare of little Lillian," and he asked me if there was any special thing that he could do to repay me. There was one thing I desired above all others, and that was the education of a mulatto lad of ten years of age, who worked about the stables. I asked him if he would send the lad to some industrial institution, which request he readily granted. There is but little more to tell. My little girl grew up to be a beautiful young lady, the pet and leader among Virginia's most exclusive circle. But the teachings of her old Mammie Nellie, she never forgot.

Her sympathy was always for the poor and lowly, and though there were scores of young men of aristocratic blood seeking in her heart and hand, she preferred, as I intended she should, the colored youth, Harry Stanley.

"It was the result of this little episode of the change in the babies, which I related to Jack Westland, after the elopement, that caused him to commit suicide, and as he leaves everything to his daughter Lillian, I hope we shall live happily hereafter," said Mammie Nellie, as she arose and rung for lights.

"My poor abused mother!" exclaimed both Harry and Lillian simultaneously, who had just joined her in New York City, so both threw a loving arm tenderly around her neck. "And now," said Lillian, "your revenge is complete. Let us close up the house, and go abroad. We can remain away several years, traveling and enjoying the beauties of the Old World. What do you say to his?"

"A capital idea," said Harry.

"As well as a practical one, for even here in New York race feeling sometimes runs very high!" exclaimed the octoroon avenger, with a curl of scorn about her mouth and a triumphant light flashing from her beautiful dark eyes.

1902

WILLIAM STANLEY BRAITHWAITE
(1878-1962)

Boston native William Stanley Beaumont Braithwaite was one of five children born to a Guianese immigrant father and a formerly enslaved African American mother, both of mixed-race descent. The value of literature was instilled in the Braithwaite children through the efforts of their father, who tutored them in a range of academic subjects. Braithwaite's father died when the author was only seven years old, at which point he sought to continue his education in the local public school. When he was thirteen, his family's desperate financial circumstances forced him out of the classroom and into the workforce. Braithwaite began writing poetry around the age of sixteen, when he took a position at a publishing house. In addition to two volumes of his own poems, *Lyrics of Life and Love* (1904) and *The House of Falling Leaves and Other Poems* (1908), Braithwaite published a number of anthologies of British and American literature, most notably the aptly titled *Anthology of Magazine Verse,* which appeared in 1913. The poems below were originally published in *Alexander's Magazine*, the *Colored American* magazine, and Braithwaite's second collection of poetry, *The House of Falling Leaves.*

LOVE'S WAYFARING

Do you remember, love—
    How long ago it seems—
When by the pebbled cove,
    Our sweet, fair dreams
Took wing?

Alas, how long it is—
    What wasted years between;
What untouched hours of bliss;
    And unlived dream—
Time's sting!

Were not the high tides sweet!
    The sails upon the stream—

The billows' bounding beat,
    The sea-gull's scream
And swing.

What murmuring music rose
    From zephyr's low-tuned chords,
To which in love's repose
    Our hearts made words
To sing.

Ah, sweet, where is Love gone?
    To what bourne, east or west,
Shall you and I alone
    Bide his behest
Wand'ring?

                                1902

GOLDEN MOONRISE

When your eyes gaze seaward
Piercing through the dim
Slow descending nightfall,
On the outer rim

Where the deep blue silence
Touches sky and sea,
Hast thou seen the golden
Moon, rise silently?

Seen the great battalions
Of the stars grow pale—
Melting in the magic
Of her silver veil?

I have seen the wonder,
I have felt the balm
Of the golden moonrise
Turn to silver calm.

                                1908

IN THE ATHENAEUM LOOKING OUT ON THE GRANARY BURYING GROUND ON A RAINY DAY IN NOVEMBER

Here in this ancient, dusty room[1]
Filled with the rain-washed chill and gloom,
The wistful books stand 'round in hosts—
Familiar friends of forgotten ghosts
Who sleep in their narrow beds below
When daylight walks, and by them go
The unremembering city throng.
Here where dust and silence belong
I feel their presence in each nook
As if they too would stand and look
With me, out where the motley city lies,
With timid, unrecollecting eyes.

I feel the damp creep round my heart
Because my thoughts have grown a part
Of the infinite, ancient sense of pain
Echoing voices in the rain.
How long its unassuaging cry
Has filled man's memory with a sigh
When wind and rain among bare trees
Has made even joy feel ill at ease!
Joy!—where that tortuous winding coil
Of slaves to duty, sweat and toil—
Does joy dwell there? this monotone
Of rain is far more dumb of groan.

How old the world is—yet I think
No man has yet had his full drink
Of joy, while life flowed in his veins
Or disillusion racked his brains.
How like a picture shadow-bound,
That street is 'cross the burial ground!
And from this room those forms out there
Are not so real as ghosts in here.

1908

NOTE

1. An athenaeum is an institution for the transmission, creation, or storage of knowledge, often a library or an archive.

AUGUSTUS HODGES (1854–?)

The Brooklyn-based writer "B Square" (or "B Square Bluster") was born Augustus Michael Hodges, in Williamsburg, Virginia. He was the founding editor of the *Brooklyn Sentinel* newspaper and a founding member of the Invincible Sons and Daughters of Commerce, a secret society dedicated to supporting black businesses. The son of Willis Augustus Hodges, a prominent African American journalist and writer, and a graduate of Hampton University (1874), his articles, poetry, and short fiction appeared in *Waverly Magazine, The New York Globe, The Indianapolis Freeman,* and other publications. His novel, *Fred Jackson's Vow; or As Good as His Word,* was serialized in the *Christian Recorder* beginning in April of 1881. A number of his humorous poems and stories appeared in *The Colored American Magazine,* including "What Happened to Scott: An Episode of Election Day," first published in August of 1903.

WHAT HAPPENED TO SCOTT: AN EPISODE OF ELECTION DAY

Mr. George Washington Scott did not vote the Democratic ticket on election day. The reader must not thereby conclude that he voted the Republican ticket, as Mr. Scott did not vote at all. It was not our hero's fault that he did not "put one in" for the Democratic ticket. Circumstances he could not timely curb prevented him from exercising that great constitutional right of every citizen of New York State. Circumstances were greatly aided in the plot to deprive Mr. Scott from voting by Mrs. Scott, or, in other words, "there was a woman in it," and she stayed deeply in it until the end of the chapter. When Mrs. Scott learned that her husband was going to vote the Democratic ticket she "reasoried" with him until he saw, or more properly speaking, felt the political error he was about to make, and repented just before it was too late.

Mr. George Washington Scott, known to his friends as "Scottie," was an Afro-American, a past officer of "Never Sweat Lodge, No. 41144" of The Ancient Order of Parasites, and like all members of the order, he worked by proxy; his wife Hannah and his sixteen-year-old daughter Sadie, took his place in the battle for bread, mixed ale, whiskey, tobacco, and now and then an odd dollar for the back rent. Still "Scottie" was as happy as a clam at high tide, or a dog with two tails, or a small boy after he has broken a window, or a five-year-old girl with a new doll, or a twenty-five-year-old girl with a new Easter bonnet, or—a New York State Republican on the morning of November 9th.

It is a great wear and tear upon the minds of pater familias[1] to be obliged, day in and day out, to hustle out in the cold or rain to work for the bread, mixed ale, whiskey, tobacco, etc. The graveyards are full of overworked fathers, sent to untimely graves by cruel, lazy mothers who openly refused to go out and work for the bread, mixed ale, etc. Statistics show that the number of these worthless females is growing to such an alarming degree that young men of the day stop and think one hundred times before entering the bonds of wedlock. There appears to be something wrong of late, either in our young women or their education, as you will often hear them say that they would not marry a man who would not work and let them sit in the house and do nothing.

Mrs. Hannah Scott, however, belonged to the good old school of females and had been working hard for seven years, while our hero was waiting either in the house or the barber shop for some one to come along and offer him a job with good pay and little work.

It was on the morning of November 8th that Mr. George Washington Scott awoke from his peaceful slumber at half-past seven. He sniffed the air several times, before he opened his eyes "to see" if he could detect the smell of pork chops cooking in the next room (Mr. G. Washington Scott, like many of his race, was very fond of pork chops). He was greatly surprised by not being able to detect the fragrance of his favorite repast, as he had "ordered" some pork chops the night before. When he opened his eyes, he was treated to a greater surprise, for there lay his wife, on the front of the bed, sleeping as quietly as if it were midnight. It was a bright morning, the sun was shining and all nature feeling gay. In fact, it was a regular Republican victory day. As soon as Mr. Scott recovered from his surprise—which was several minutes, as he could hardly believe his eyes, and concluded he was dreaming—he gave his better half a kick and yelled out.

"Hannah! You Hannah! Why, what in the duce's the matter with you? Are you crazy? Why here it is almost eight o'clock and you ain't gone to work yet. Git up! Git up, I say! Do you hear me? Git up! Well, as I live! Sleeping till this hour! What's the matter with you? Do you want to lose all your good places?"

Why, to-day's 'lection day. I'se not goin' ter work, Scott. Leastmore, I needs a little rest, I thinks," replied his wife.

"Well, if you are not going to work, get up and make the fire and git my breakfast. Did you get them pork chops?"

"No, I forgot them, but I'se—"

"Well, what in the world is getting in you of late, anyway? Hannah, some of these days you'll forgit your head. Git up, make the fire and send Sadie after them pork chops."

Poor Mrs. Scott got up, made the fire, sent for the chops, cooked them, and informed her dusky lord and master that breakfast was ready. Mr. G. W. Scott arose at once, and commenced to fix his toilet, and was soon ready for breakfast. He took his proper place at the head of the table and said "grace." Mrs. Scott sat opposite, his daughter Sadie, was seated on his right and his little five-year-old son, Geo. W. Scott, Jr., on his left. There were five pork chops in the dish, and Mr. Scott helped himself to three. As he did so, his little son, in childish surprise remarked: "Why, Pop's goin' ter eat all ther meat up." Mr. Scott gave the boy a slap that almost knocked the child from the chair. "Well, as I live, if that boy ain't gitting too sassy to live. Now Hannah, you want to learn that boy some manners."

Mrs. Scott made no reply, but snatched the other two chops from the dish and placed one upon Sadie's plate, and commenced to cut the other one up for little George who was crying bitterly. After she had finished, she pulled the dish over to herself and soaked a piece of bread in the gravy and commenced to eat it with a relish. When Mr. Scott looked up after he had devoured one chop, he remarked with some surprise, "Why, Hannah, you haven't given me anything to drink. How the duce do you expect me to eat my breakfast without something to drink?"

"Will you have a cup of tea, Scott?" she asked.

"Tea be—. Give Sadie ten cents right way, and let her go out and git er pint of beer. Don't get mixed ale, Sadie, 'cause it's too warm for ale, and hurry up. Give her the money! Whatin the 'll's the matter with you, Hannah? You set there looking like er fool! Give her the money." As Mr. Scott yelled out this injunction, poor Mrs. S., who had been dreaming—dreaming of the better days before she met her "better half"—was recalled to life. With her usual fear, she jumped up from the table, and rushed in the bedroom and brought out "the price of a pint," and gave it to her daughter, who hurried out to fill the can for her beloved father. She returned in a few minutes, and placed the can and the only glass in the house before our hero, who at once got on the outside of half the beer. The breakfast was finished without any other noteworthy incident, and Mrs. Scott went out, leaving Sadie to wash up the dishes. Mr. Scott felt in his coat pocket and found his half-stem old clay pipe and walked over to the mantelpiece, and looked into an old collar box in which he kept his tobacco. He was surprised to find the box empty. It was a day of unpleasant surprises for Mr. Scott, as the reader will learn if he continues to the end of the chapter.

"Well, I sware! Well, if your mother hasn't forgot my tobacco. Where is she? Call her here!"

"She's gone out," replied Sadie.

"Gone out! Did she leave any money for beer or tobacco?"

"No, sir."

"Well, I swear, if your mother ain't going crazy. I don't know what's gitting in her of late," Mr. Scott remarked as he felt in his coat pocket and found a few crumbs of tobacco, which he put in his pipe, and taking a seat by the window, commenced smoking and wondering what strange thing his wife would do next.

In a few minutes Mrs. Scott rushed in, puffing and blowing, with a paper of Honest Short Sliced tobacco, and remarked: "Oh, Scott, I forgot your tobacco, so I run'd back ter—"

"Well say, Hannah! Well say, what's gitting in you of late? I say woman, you are going crazy; bring that tobacco here!"

"Scottie," to give him his due, had never beaten his wife, although the other members of Never Sweat Lodge had often been forced to correct their wives with fist or club. Our hero was something of a moral suasionist, and up to the time our story begins, he had little or no trouble in making Mrs. Scott obey him or go out to work. He used hard words instead of hard blows.

As near as he ever got to the common mode of punishment inflicted upon lazy and unruly wives by members of Never Sweat Lodge, was to throw a shoe at Mrs. S's head, one night about a year before the historic morning of November 8th, 1898. At that time his better half got a little bit too "sassy" and he felt inclined to "punish her a la Never Sweat Lodge.

Mr. Scott was a "yaller" man just a very little below the average, and would have weighed upon the historic morning about one hundred and thirty-five pounds before breakfast and about one hundred and forty-two after breakfast. He was born at Oyster Bay, L.I. (local pride should have made him vote the Republican ticket). He had never been further South than South Beach, Staten Island. Mrs. Scott was born "way down Souf in Norf Caroliny" in the historic town of Wilmington, some forty-odd years before our opening. She left Wilmington, N.C., and came North to find a fortune and Mr. George Washington Scott was a part of "the find." In complexion Mrs. Scott was a running mate to starless midnight; in weight, she would have tipped the scales in her night robe (if she had owned one) at one hundred and eighty-seven pounds of solid flesh in good fighting condition. Her friends had often said that she married our hero because he was a "yaller" man, and worked for him for the same illogical reason. We do not know why she married him, but the reason why she worked indirectly for him was because she did not want to see her family starve or go to the county poorhouse at Flatbush.[2] She had the meekness of a lamb and the strength of a lion, together with an iron constitution. The Scotts lived upon the top floor of a little "ram-shackled" old two-story frame house, which was located sixty-odd feet from the street in a tenth-class section of the Borough of Brooklyn. This fact gave Mr. Scott an opportunity to see all comers and to be "not at home" to those he did not want to see.

He was sitting at the window about ten o'clock smoking, when he saw three brother members of the Never Sweat Lodge coming up the alley from the street. They were Mr. Geo. Washington, better known as "Big Wash," Mr. Sam Sykes, better known as "Crap Sam," and "Capt." Joe Jones.

"Hurry up and kinder fix things up, Hannah! Hurry up, here comes some friends. Sadie, you run downstairs quick to Mrs. Johnson's and try to borrow two chairs. Git er move on you, hurry up!" yelled out Mr. Scott. His wife and daughter obeyed in time. The three friends entered in a few minutes, and received a friendly greeting from the head of the house, or at least, the head of the two little cheerless rooms. Mr. Scott then asked his friends what they would "have." Upon learning that their pleasure was mixed ale, he told his daughter, Sadie, to get a pint of that soul-stirring nectar. When she returned, her father winked at her and remarked: "Sadie, run downstairs and tell Mrs. Johnson to give you them three glasses she borrowed the other day; that's the worse of lending these common niggers anything, for they never return nothing."

Sadie took the hint, and went downstairs and borrowed three glasses, and our hero dished out four glasses of mixed ale. The contents of the can were soon a thing of the past. "I don't like O'Brien's ale, boys; what do you say if we have some whiskey?" The suggestion was carried by a large majority.

"Hannah, give Sadie that bottle and a quarter, and let her git some good whiskey,"

"Can I speak to you a minute, Scott?" asked his wife, as she led the way into the bedroom. "What's the matter now, no money?" asked Mr. Scott, as he poked his head in the bedroom.

"I've only one dollar left an I must give that to Mr. Wheeden, the landlord, on last month's rent. You know he'll be here to-night."

"Wheeden be d——? he's got to wait. I'll see him myself and give him a stand off—tell him I expect a job next week sure. Why, say, Hannah, do you suppose we must give that old duffer our last dollar? Well, I guess nit. Give me that dollar! Hurry up; give me the dollar!"

"But Scott, you know—"

"No buts, give me the dollar!"

Poor Mrs. Scott gave up the dollar with a sad heart, then threw herself across the bed and cried. The whiskey was sent for, and soon followed the downward course of the mixed ale, when "Big Wash," remarked, "Scottie, you have given us such a good time that we almost forgot our business. You see today is 'lection, and Mike Clancy the Democratic leader of the ward, is givin' all the boys two dollars to vote the straight Democratic ticket, and he says if this 'lection district goes Democratic (you know all the colored folks is in this district) he'll give all we boys what voted the Democratic ticket, five dollars extra. You can't bet on the five, but you've got the two dead. Most all of the boys is voted and got the dust. We are going now, and thought we'd run in and give you the tip, so you could make a couple of bones. You know 'lection day comes but once a year, and you are foolish, Scottie, if you miss this graft, 'cause 'lection days is not like they used to be before this here new 'lection ballot came in."

"Now boys, I'm much obliged to you for telling me. I'll slip on my coat right er way, and go out and vote and get the money," said Mr. Scott.

"What! You-ain't-goin-ter-vote-ther-Dimmercrat-ticket-is-you-Scott?' asked our hero's wife in a surprised tone.

"Mind your own business, Hannah, and git me my coat and hat!"

"Well, as I live! Well, well, but this is too much, George Scott. It's more dan I kin stan' or will stan'. I have worked like er slave for years while you sot in ther house and done nothin'; I didn't say nothin' 'bout you taken' every extra cent I has made for beer an' policy numbers; I've never sed nothin' when you slept all day in bed, while I went out in the snow an' rain ter work; I has never sed nothin' when you sold or pawned everything in the house that you could git any money on. I've borne all these things like er fool, but when you tell me to my face that you is goin' to vote their Demmecrat ticket after all the Demmecrats is done to low rate our people, and is still goin' ter do (for yistiddy I got a letter from Cousin Jane down in my old home in Wilmington, Norf Carliny, an' she say the white folks—the Demmecrats, is goin' to kill all the black folks up this day, yes this day.) An' then when you think what "Abe Lincoln an' the 'Publican party done for us, freed us an' give us all we have, an' how they all is our friends, an' how them black solgers fit an'—"

"Oh, shut up! You make me tired; the Republican Party never freed me; I was born free, and some of you ignorant fools of contrabands was only fit to be slaves, and should be slaves now. (I mean the women, the men is O.K.)" remarked Mr. Scott. The left-hand apology was tacked on in honor of "Big Wash" and the "Capt."

Mr. George Washington Scott reached for his hat and coat, intent upon making a couple of Democratic dollars. Mrs. George Washington Scott reached for the rolling pin, and got to the door first, intent upon cheating the ballot box out of one Democratic vote.

"George Scott, you'll not vote ther Demmecrat ticket till you walk over my dead body," said Mrs. Scott, as she stood, arms akimbo, in the doorway.

"Are you going to let your wife rule you, and queer your game, Scottie?" asked "Big Wash."

"I thought you was ther man; Scottie, and wore the pants?" added the "Capt."

"Well, I guess I run this house, boys, Git out of the way, Hannah. Or I'll knock you down!" remarked the hero of this story.

"No, I will not!" was the reply.

"Then take that!" and Mr. Scott dealt his wife a slap on the face.

It was like sticking a three-inch hat pin into the flank of a sleeping lioness. Mrs. Scott grabbed her politically erring husband by the neck with an iron-like grasp, holding shirt collar and coat; her hard knuckles stuck in his neck as she gave him a combination jerk and pull, then a cross between a push and shove, during which she struck Mr. Scott's right eye against the door, causing it to turn black. She then held him out at arm's length, then whirled him around the room several times at the rate of 603 revolutions per half-minute, remarking: "You nasty, good-fer-nothin', lazy nigger! So you can't be talked to or reasoned to, hey? You's goin ter vote there Dimmycrat ticket, hey? Well, I don't think you will."

As round and round he went, our hero thought he was the roughest kind of a rough rider, seated upon a "merry-go-round," the motive power of which had run riot. A drowning man, it is said, will catch at a straw, and a man in Mr. Scott's position would catch at almost anything he concluded would stop his circular ride around the room, against table and borrowed chairs. The only thing catchable was the misfit antediluvian stove pipe. The joints of the pipe had, for a long time, been waiting, for some excuse to break the unhappy union between themselves, so when their owner grabbed hold of them, they separated sine die. One of them fell on Mr. Scott's face, cutting his felt eye to the bone and covering him not with glory but with soot, until he was dark black instead of a light yellow. By superhuman pull he broke away from his mooring, and made for the bedroom on a dead run, with Mrs. Scott a close second in the race. His foot got caught in a hole in the old carpet, and he fell on his face, but turned over on his back just in time to receive Mrs. Scott's full weight, as she also fell. Her anger had not fallen, however, for she grabbed her better half by the ears and knocked his head against the floor, while she "reasoned" with him and tried to convince him it was wrong, Oh, very, very wrong for a colored man to vote the Democratic ticket that election morning—or any other election morning, noon or night. "So you's (bang) goin' ter (bang) vote ther (bang) Demmer (bang, bang, bang) cratic ticket (bang) is you, Scott?" (bang, bang, bang.)

"Oh, Hannah; Don't kill me! No, I'll never, if I live, vote the Democratic ticket again; and if you don't kill me, I'll promise to look for work, get a good job and move in a nice house. Oh, don't kill me! I'll do what's right! Oh, murder! Don't kill me! Don't kill me, Hannah dear."

Mrs. Scott was only a woman, so she let up on Mr. Scott, bathed his wounds, put him to bed, made him some hot whiskey to drink and then went out in the living room and cried.

What became of the three friends? Why, they rushed out pell mell, when the debate got hot and rushed around the corner to the barber shop and told the boys that Scottie's wife was killing him. The doctor said that, with care, Mr. Scott will be as good as new by the following Christmas. His wife convinced him that it was wrong for a sane Negro to vote the Democratic ticket.

This, kind reader, is What Happened to Scott!!

1903

NOTES

1. The patriarch of the household or, colloquially, the man of the house.
2. A neighborhood in Brooklyn, New York.

MARIE LOUISE BURGESS-WARE (CA. 1870-?)

Little is known about the life of Marie Louise Burgess-Ware. Existing records identify a Marie Louise Burgess as the first head nurse at the St. Agnes Hospital in Raleigh, North Carolina, one of the region's earliest African American health facilities. It is believed that she took on the hyphenated surname Burgess-Ware after she married. Educated at the New England Hospital for Women and Children in Boston, she published both fiction and nonfiction works (including tracts on nursing and healthcare) for *The Women's Era,* a Boston-based magazine for African Americans. She is also the likely author of *Ave Maria: A Tale,* a novella published in 1895 by the Boston-based Press of the Monthly Review. The following short story was serialized in two consecutive issues of the *Colored American* magazine, in August and September of 1903.

BERNICE, THE OCTOROON

I

Learn to dissemble wrongs, to smile at injuries,
And suffer crimes thou want'st the power to punish;
Be easy, affable, familiar, friendly;
Search and know all mankind's mysterious ways,
But trust the secret of thy soul to none;
This is the way,
This only, to be safe in such a world as
this is.

—Rowe's Ulysses[1]

"I'll not grieve longer over what may never be. Sometimes I think my lot hard, cruel, and unjust, then I remember that others suffer as keenly, if not more, than I."

These words were spoken by a beautiful girl, scarcely out of her teens. Her evenly developed head was covered with golden curls that reminded me of burnished gold, as the rays of sunlight fell upon them. Her blonde complexion, dainty mouth, and deep blue eyes completed one of the loveliest faces.

She lifted her tear-stained face, so like a Madonna's, filled with unutterable love. Rising, she exclaimed, "I must attend to my duties. I want no traces of tears on my face. Inquisitive little children may ask questions that perhaps will make my heart bleed," She bathed her swollen eyes, brushed back the curls from for her forehead, and rang the bell which told the children recess was over. About forty little ones came marching into the school-room, all sizes and ages, and of every conceivable shade peculiar to the Negro race. Such bright faces, sparkling eyes and pretty teeth!

"Miss Bernice," as they called her, seemed to have good command of these little ones, although she appeared to be of a gentle, yielding temperament. Could you have looked into this country school-house, with its rude benches, ragged children and great inconveniences, you would have wondered what this college-bred lady was doing in the back woods of a Southern State, when a teacher less tenderly reared would have answered as well. Was it for money? Was it love of the race? The latter was the reason. This cultured octoroon, refined and fair as an Anglo-Saxon, was one of a despised rate, and had only recently learned it.

Bernice Silva was a native of Ohio. Her father, a man of wealth and position, had married Pauline Blanchard twenty years before this story opens. She was the daughter of a wealthy Kentucky planter, and had been educated in a Western college, together with her sister, Mrs. Gadsden. The young couple were very happy, and when Bernice came with her wealth of golden curls, she was called "papa's sunbeam" by the delighted young father, whose life she crowned with joy.

All that wealth could bestow was lavished upon this child, and at a proper age, she, too, was sent to college. She became a great favorite with teacher and classmates, because of her winsome disposition and brilliant gifts as a student, her musical talent being of a very high order.

Mrs. Gadsden had a daughter Lenore who was also at college with Bernice. The two cousins were exact opposites in all things,—Lenore was as dark as Bernice was fair, as envious as Bernice was generous; she had a heart filled with jealousy and hatred for her beautiful cousin. Beautiful herself, her haughtiness repelled those who aspired to her friendship. This was more the result of over-indulgence, for after Mr. Gadsden's death, the child was given her own will in all things.

The winter after the girls were graduated was spent by both families in the picturesque town of St. Augustine, Florida. Society there was made up of many Northern and Southern aristocrats, who greeted with open arms two beautiful and accomplished young women, possessed of wealth and prestige.

There was a flutter of expectancy throughout the little colony when cards were issued for a reception of Thanksgiving evening by Mrs. Silva, and the fortunate recipients counted themselves very lucky.

It was a night long remembered in St. Augustine. The spacious rooms were crowded by brave men and fair women. Flowers filled the air with fragrance, birds sang in gilded cages, fountains played, their perfumed waters falling in prismatic shades under constantly changing colored electric lights: the dreamy, pulsing notes of the band were a welcome accompaniment to romantic conversation.

It was a memorable reception for all, but for Garrett Purnello life took a sudden change. The promising young barrister never again had eyes for a woman's fair face. He was much impressed by Bernice's beauty and modesty. He, with his passionate Spanish blood, loved her then and forever; she, with her pure heart returned his love unconsciously.

II

Several days later, Bernice saw her father coming towards the house, accompanied by Mr. Purnello. They came immediately to the drawing-room where Mrs. Silva and her daughter were sitting. After the usual greetings, Mr. Silva said: "I brought Mr. Purnello home to lunch, and we have been having a lively discussion of the race question. This recent disfranchisement and the attitude taken by the majority of our sound citizens towards the black men of this country, appears unjust to me. To be sure, the ignorant vote of any people is not fit to be counted, but still the Negro excites my pity. Ushered out of slavery into an unknown sphere of life, many have made themselves worthy to bear the name of citizen. And wholesale disfranchisement is to rob him almost of life itself. One wonders if mob law is not a stigma on our loved republic; this sweet land of liberty, the land of the noble free. It is as if the fatherhood of God and the brotherhood of man existed only in legends of Holy Writ. Peaceful black citizens are driven from their homes because a mob decides that they must leave a community. Is there no panacea for this evil, for evil it is?"

"To my mind, there is, but one remedy," replied the younger man "and that is being applied by Booker T. Washington and other advocates of Industrial Education. The masses of the blacks and the poor whites of our Southland must be educated, not only in books, but in trades and all those other things which crush out idleness and keep down vice. If we consider the matter seriously, we find that all this disturbance arises between the poor whites and the illiterate blacks. The intelligent Negro does not clamor for social equality; he is satisfied to be a leader of his people."

"What you say is true," replied Mr. Silva, "but it is an outrage to know that men are driven from their homes because they are Negroes. Debarred from all things which protect the white laborer, yet in spite of all this they multiply and grow in mental and physical strength. Like the Jews they are favored of God although despised by men. But this is dull conversation for the ladies; we will change the subject."

"But papa," exclaimed Bernice, "I have read much concerning this matter; do not discontinue the conversation because mamma and I here. I am sure that what involves the welfare of our country is interesting to us, and must be to all true women."

Garrett listened eagerly; it was rare to find so sweet a girl and one so young finding attraction in words of wisdom and discretion. A pleasant hour was spent about the social board, and then the two gentlemen spent another enjoyable hour in the music room. Garrett was entranced by the wonderful gifts possessed by Bernice. Thus sped many pleasant days, merging into weeks, and it was soon plain to the onlooking world that the young people loved each other. It was the old, old story, ever fresh, ever new.

Lenore looked on with a heart swelling with envy and indignation. She was beautiful too; why was it that the only man she had ever felt she could love, found no attraction in her? That Bernice should take him from her filled her heart with most bitter thoughts. She clinched her hands in rage as she walked the floor of her room, and swore to part them.

Very soon the engagement of these popular young people was announced. Mr. Silva reluctantly consented to give his treasure to Garrett. All his affection was centered in this beautiful child, and he could not bear to think of trusting her happiness in a stranger's hands; but he smiled as he said to his wife—

"Thus it is our daughters leave us, those we love and those who love us."

III

About six weeks after the betrothal, Mrs. Purnello and Garrett took tea with Bernice. Mr. and Mrs. Silva had taken a trip to Tuskegee Institute. They had given considerable money for the education of the Freedmen, and so wished to see this school of schools. Mrs. Gadsden was acting hostess, and had planned a very pretty tea. Lenore had changed greatly during the past few weeks, and everyone attributed it to ill-health. In spite of this, she tried to assume her usual manner.

While they were enjoying the tea an old Negro servant came into the room, with some tea cakes which had been forgotten. Bernice smiled at her, and admired the pretty bandana 'kerchief which she wore.

Mrs. Purnello, with a scornful smile, said quickly, "Bernice don't admire these Negroes; they get beside themselves. I despise them; it were not for their labor, I would be glad to have them swept out of existence."

Bernice was startled at such language from a lady's lips. Garrett was mortified; he knew his mother hated Negroes, and was oftentimes very eccentric about them. But such an outburst startled him.

Bernice glanced at Mrs. Purnello and said. "You surely could not have had a good old mammy for your nurse. Why not let these people live and thrive? We are taught, and pretend to believe that God created all alike; that Christ died for all, and commands us as Christians to love our fellow man. We are taught next to our duty to God, to love our neighbor as ourselves. How can you entertain such a feeling in your bosom, and be a member of Christ's Church?"

"Law, Honey you'se a Christian. Don' yer waste yer bref; she ain't got no 'ligion uv any kind. My sole dis minute am heap whiter'n her face," and the old woman shrugged her shoulders, and withdrew from the dining room.

Bernice looked pained. She was about to say something when Mrs. Purnello said in her haughtiest manner, "Bernice, we will not discuss this subject further: you must relinquish some of your strange ideas about this matter. My son's future wife cannot hold such views. You have much to learn; I hope never to hear such expressions again in my presence."

"But, my dear madam, I have no desire to lay aside my good breeding nor my own convictions. I can never learn to be cruel to a race of people, who have never injured me. We have become rich through their toil," replied Bernice. "Their faults have not blinded me to their nobler qualities. They have hearts as tender as my own. All my life my heart has gone out to them, and when my parents have received appeals for help from their various homes and institutions of learning, I have longed to help them myself in some way."

Lenore had sat a silent spectator of the scene. Now she spoke.

"You can have your wish; nothing is easier, for you are one of them. Do you not know that your mother is of Negro ancestry?"

For a moment dead silence followed her words. Bernice turned white to the lips. Garrett overcame his first anger and consternation with a laugh. He had seen through Lenore's jealousy for some time. But Mrs. Purnello held up both hands in horror. She moved away from Bernice, as if the air were contaminated.

Recovering herself by a great effort, Bernice smiled. She was not now the little girl whom every one thought so meek and gentle; her eyes sparkled, her air breathed defiance.

"How long have you known this, Lenore?"

"My parents have always known it?" replied Lenore, now somewhat frightened at what she had done.

"Then if one drop of that despised blood flows in my veins, loyal to that race I wilt be. I did not expect such a blow from you, Lenore."

The latter made no reply, but left the room, apparently satisfied with the mischief done.

"Garrett," said Mrs. Purnello, greatly agitated, "Bernice cannot expect you to fulfill your engagement under these unfortunate conditions. You cannot marry a Negro."

Garrett had been silent all through the storm aroused by Lenore's assertion. He faced his mother with unusual sternness on his handsome face.

"Mother, you have said enough; if you have no respect for us, have a little for yourself. Do not hide all that is womanly in you. Remember, Bernice is a woman, and has a woman's tender feelings, and it is not necessary to try to crush her. She is dearer to me than ever, because if she be really a Negro, she will need me more than ever. She may be good and pure, but she will be counted by many as no better than the most common type of her race. I will stand by her until death. I see in her all that is pure and lovely in woman. I love her with a love devoid of prejudice; it is too late for that to separate us."

"Then you are no longer my son."

"As you say, mother. A man's word is his bond. I am strong; she is weak. I will protect her. I am willing to give up even you because you are wrong. Where is the warm feeling which should fill your bosom as a woman? I fear, mother, there is a touch of something unnatural and inhuman in your conduct."

"Bernice, let me appeal to you. Garrett is unreasonable and Quixotic. After the first few months of married life, he would become dissatisfied and unhappy. But if you will keep this matter secret, perhaps we can hide it from the world; but if you persist in allying your fortunes with Negroes, then our friendship must end. I love Garrett; I would like to see him happy, but I love my good name too well to wish him to marry into an alien race. As you value your future happiness, think well before you decide."

Bernice smiled. "My dear Mrs. Purnello, I see no difference between you and me; my tastes are as refined and cultured as yours. My skin is fairer than many of our acquaintances. My parents as cultured. Why should I be persecuted because mamma is of mixed origin? Did not God create all in His own image? Are we not taught that He is the father of all mankind? Because the despised blood of the Negro chances to flow through my veins, must I be trampled upon and persecuted? Let me ask you, how did it happen that your ancestors, whom you claim were so chivalrous and aristocratic, stooped to mix with an inferior race, and thus flood the country with the mulattoes, quadroons, and octoroons that are so bitterly despised by many of both races? Well may you blush when you think of such chivalry! My heart warms to the inferior race, and I will give all that I have in learning and culture, to follow in the footsteps of the great Teacher, who said,—Inasmuch as ye have done it unto the least of these my brethren, ye have done it unto me."

Mrs. Purnello left the room without replying to Bernice.

Turning to Bernice, Garrett ex-claimed passionately, "Think, Bernice, all that this means. Can you stand the snubs, insults, and temptations? My dear girl, you know not what you will have to encounter. Many will think you an Anglo-Saxon, and will treat you kindly, but if they find out what you really are, there is no ignorant Negro who will be treated more contemptuously. I cannot bear to think of it. Marry me, and forget all that has just happened."

"Garrett, I appreciate your kind thoughts for my welfare. I could not agree to anything but the right. Were I to accept your proposition, I would feel like a woman wearing a mask. There is too much at stake. The sins of the fathers are surely visited upon the children. The Negro blood would show itself, if not in my children, in some of the coming generations. The so-called curse will follow us and I would not blight your life. I know I have been beyond recognition all these years; others have been and others will be," replied Bernice sadly.

"I admire and love you more than ever; do not come to a hasty conclusion, even though you are right; you must not injure yourself. Talk with your parents, be guided by them; to-morrow we may be better able to decide what is best to be done under the circumstances. You are mine; I will never give you up this side of eternity."

He was sincere; this was no passing fancy. He loved her. He began to wonder why the white man should be the dominant race and considered so far above his educated Negro brother. In his heart, he thought it unjust. He was deeply grieved and sorely perplexed in spirit. He thought of the passage of Scripture, "God is no respecter of persons." He wondered what it meant. His own sorrow was not to be compared with his sympathy for Bernice. When he thought of what she had been subjected to, the muscles of his face became rigid. The veins became prominent; his countenance showed the great anguish through which he was passing.

When Mr. Silva learned of the unwomanly conduct of Lenore, he was shocked; first of all, because of her treachery; secondly, because of the Negro blood in his wife's veins. It was true that Mrs. Silva and Mrs. Gadsden were only half-sisters. They were originally from Kentucky. Their father Joseph Blanchard had been a wealthy slave owner. He had educated them at the same college, and when, by accident, Beatrice had learned that Pauline's mother was her "mammy," she too was horrified to expose it. She loved her sister, and as the world was none the wiser, it was quietly covered up, and both daughters married well. Had Garrett Purnello loved Lenore, this story would never have been written.

Mr. and Mrs. Silva were grieved for Bernice. They cared nothing for themselves, but to have her life clouded in its springtime caused them much pain. They knew they could return to their Western home unmolested. But Bernice had determined not to sail under false colors, and had made up her mind to teach her people. She had a deep sense of right and wrong, and then, knowing the depth of the chasm existing between the two races, was not willing to remain in a false position. She knew nothing of her people, their manners and customs, nor the hardships which many had to endure. She did not dream of the discouragements awaiting her. She saw only their needs and her ability to help them. The ragged, ignorant, or unclean of either race, she had never come in contact with. She was ignorant of the vice that existed in the world, and when she entered upon this work, you can imagine her consternation at the sights she saw. After much persuasion, her parents consented to let her go to Maryland, to teach a parish school. When our story opens she is in the schoolroom, trying to teach forty mischievous little children.

IV

"Fairlily, sit down my dear," Bernice said, pointing to a little picanniny as black as midnight. Her head was covered with short, knotty hair, that looked as if a comb had never passed through it.

What a name for such a looking child. "Fairlily." She wondered where the mother got the name. Then there was a little boy named "Esther." He had an unusually large head and beautiful black eyes. His body was small and badly nourished, and the little creature seemed to have what is known as the "rickets." The next one that attracted her attention was as white as the others were black. Her face was freckled, her hair sandy and stringy. She looked very much out of place. Looking about her, Bernie noticed similar children, scattered here and there. She thought this the most motley crowd she had ever seen; there were no two alike.

"And these are my people," she mused, "indeed it is a mixture. Where did they come from, and how did they become like this? It never entered her pure mind that many of these knew no father; it did not dawn upon her that a race despising hers was at every opportunity flooding the country with children, born to be despised and persecuted. Some of these little ones were ragged and hungry, whose fathers lived in luxury, while their mothers were ignorant women who knew nothing of the development of their intellectual being, but allowed their animal natures to predominate, and brought forth children regardless of the laws of God or man. Immorality to these people had no meaning, and thus these poor little children's opportunities to become noble men and women, were very limited.

Bernice was the picture of a modern Priscilla in her simple black gown, white cuffs and apron. Her eyes were red from excessive weeping; her heart cried out in its loneliness, her task was very hard. Her boarding place was unlike her comfortable home. The log cabin had only three rooms, two of which were unfinished. Her room was the best in the house, and had a clean bare floor an old-fashioned bed covered with brilliantly colored quilts of various designs, a strip of home-made rag carpet answered for a mat, and two pine chairs and a table. The people around her were very sensitive, and she had to guard against hurting anyone's feelings, for they soon would brand her as an "eddicated and stuck-up yaller nigger." The food was coarse, the greens, which she ate very often, were a new article of food to her; the corn pones seemed heavy; the biscuits were a sure trial to her digestive organs, for she was used to home-made, light bread, and had never eaten very many biscuits. She had longed for a porterhouse steak, broiled and juicy, but that was unheard-of fare.

In spite of the many disadvantages, she labored on, teaching a Sabbath School in connection with her other work. It pleased her to see the children eagerly listening to the story she told them about the first Christmas. One little fellow with bright eyes, said, "Law, Miss Bernice, I never knew Christmas meant a thing more'n hanging up yer stockin's and gittin' presents. No one ever tole us anything else. Why, we gits up and runs across to Aunt Nancy and hollers,—'Christmas Gift!' She grins and says, 'You der same, honey,' and we all has a big time. Ma comes home from de white folks, and den we hear de chickens holler, and de eggs a beatin', and Miss Nicey, yer kin smell de egg nogg way down de road. I tastes de poun' cake right now."

Bernice smiled. She thought that there was no need of going to Africa to do missionary work, there was plenty right here. Her sewing school was enjoyed not only by the little girls, but their mothers came also. One day each week she taught them how to cook and prepare food for the table in a scientific manner. Such poverty, ignorance and superstition as she saw among the lowest types! Christian education was sadly needed to save both soul and body. The public schools kept open only three or four months during the year, then to the pea-picking and other farming! Parents barely received money enough to provide for their large families, and the people were types of illiteracy. There were many strange customs which Bernice had never heard of, such as wakes. When the people died, in the dead hours of the night you would hear wild shrieks go up in the air, which would make you shudder, and then again you would hear a weird melody, followed by a loud prayer over the dead. Everyone at the wakes did not partake of the spirits of Frumenti,[2] which almost always was there, but enough drank of it to give much life to the occasion.

The spiritual condition was bad; preachers were almost always called of God, but not very often educated and fitted for the work. The preacher was judged by the strength of his lungs, and oftentimes the number of big words which he used. A revival meant great excitement, exhortations, great shouting and much hilarity. Mourners went to the mourners' bench under the heat of a sermon which had vividly painted a picture of a burning lake, and his satanic majesty and his fiendish host standing ready with their cloven feet and pitchforks to throw the victims into the lake before them. People who mourned often, wrestled for several days before Satan would leave their bodies, and when they felt him as he departed, they arose and made known their experiences to the remaining sinners.

Many might have thought this ludicrous, but Bernice thought it a sad sight in a Christian land. The Negroes whom she had seen during her life were not of this type; they were people whom education and Christianity had made intelligent men and women. She felt certain that religion scared into a person could not last after the excitement was over, and how she longed to instill into the little hearts under her control that God's Holy Word and His Spirit would make them better, if they would quietly ask him, and make up their little minds to do His will.

This town was twenty miles from any railroads, hence its backwardness.

Bernice had imported an organ. The little voices were so sweet and mellow, she often likened them to the mocking birds which warbled before her school door. Many of the people had never seen or heard an organ. How they did enjoy the music. It was not long before she learned to accompany their beautiful plantation melodies, although to a listener they are much sweeter without an instrument.

There was an interesting old lady who never missed a Sabbath. She led the melodies, and the children joined in with much fervor. Bernice could not help being touched by the weird tones and the soul-stirring words.

One Sabbath morning there was a funeral, and dear Aunt Martha led the music at the graveyard. They had all assembled around the grave; the air was filled with unearthly shrieks, the mourners were determined that everybody should know they were bereaved. Even in the midst of all the sorrow, there was something most amusing. One of the mourners had a red bandana handkerchief, wiping her eyes under a heavy crape veil. The minister committed the body to the ground, with a voice loud and trembling. Old Aunt Martha raised her tune.

> Mother an' father, pray for me,
> Mother an' father, pray for me,
> Mother an' father, pray for me,
> I've got a home in Galilee.

CHORUS.

> Can't yer live humble? Praise King Jesus,
> Can't yer live humble? Dying Lamb.

The mourners wailed, the brothers shouted. Such a scene! Bernice had never witnessed the like before nor since. She looked towards her friend, Aunt Martha. Great drops of perspiration were rolling off her face, the tears were streaming down her cheeks, as she sang,

> When you hear my coffin sound,
> When you hear my coffin sound,
> When you hear my coffin sound,
> You may know I've gone around.

CHORUS.

> Can't yer live humble? Praise King Jesus,
> Can't yer live humble? Dying Lamb.[3]

There stood the old lady, under the shade of the trees, singing with all her might. Eighty-one years old, the mother of twenty-one children, unlettered, but trilling like a bird.

V

Bernice was an earnest Christian; she believed above all things in the preservation of the purity of womanhood. She wanted to make every woman the highest type of truth, beauty, and goodness. The scenes which she witnessed in her new surroundings were strange to her, and yet they were real. What had she known of temptation—she who had been surrounded by all that was pure and lovely, whose moral and religious training had been of the highest order? She was unacquainted with the ways of the outside world; her life had been lived among those whose every thought had been for her and of her. She knew nothing of the life of the lowly, of the sin which surrounded them everywhere, of the temptations which they resisted as well as yielded to. In her weak way she tried to reach the hearts of the women to teach them by her example, as well as by talks in her mothers' meetings, that if they overcame temptation and repented of their sins then would come real strength of character and true religion.

She had heard lectures by people engaged in work among the black men. She had thought much of the degradation and ignorance mentioned was exaggeration. She was entirely unprepared for the scenes which she encountered. Superstition prevailed. There were signs for everything. The guinea hens could not "holler" unless fallen weather was sure to follow. An owl could not hoot in the tree before the house unless it must be followed by a death in that family. The rooster could not crow before the door unless hasty news followed, and if he dared to strut away from the door and crow as he was leaving what would be the result? Why, the news of a death would soon reach the family. The dog must not howl, if so, the neighborhood all wondered to whom this death warning had been sent. These are only a very few of the many strange signs Bernice listened to.

She visited the homes of the children, and when sickness came it was she who knew just what to do for them, and how to do it. She showed the old people many things that they might do for the comfort of their suffering ones. She spent many nights by the bedsides of the sick ones; she prayed for them, comforted those who mourned, and in numerous ways brought sunshine into the homes.

There was one old mammy, "Aunt Lizzie," by name. She was one of those tall, well-built Negro women of pure blood, perfect in physique and handsome in features. Her black skin was as smooth as satin, her teeth, like pearl. She had a little daughter wasting away with consumption. Nor was it to be wondered at, for they lived in a two-room house, unfit for renting. There was a family of nine. Tina, the oldest, lay dying. The parents were what is known as "hardshell Baptists." They believed in foot-washing, and many other strange customs, known only to that set of Baptists. When Bernice came to care for her pupil, they looked on in wonder. Their house was very humble; it boasted of two beds in the front room and one in the kitchen. On one of the beds in the front room Tina lay, on the brink of eternity. The mother was washing, trying to obtain the means to provide extra comforts for Tina, the father working hard to earn the regular support of four dollars a week. Bernice made the room tidy, bathed the feverish child, and made her little delicacies. Tina grasped Bernice's hands as she lay dying, and exclaimed, "Oh, Miss Bernice, you've done tole me 'bout heaven, Jesus and the angels; tell Mammy too." And with Bernice's hands on her burning brow the child's spirit went into Paradise.

Bernice helped prepare her for burial, and if you can picture that family in its poverty and sorrow, the pine coffin, costing the paltry sum of seven dollars, the golden-rod and daisies which covered the coffin that contained the loving mother's child, you would feel that it is only too true that one-half the world knows not how the other half lives. The love in that ignorant yet tender heart would put to shame some of our more intelligent mothers. Then if you could have looked into that church, and seen Bernice and her pupils with their hands clasped, their heads bowed in prayer, and the sweet voices chanting,

My God, my father, while I stray,
Far from my home on life's rough way,
O teach me from my heart to say,
Thy will be done.[4]

All these scenes reached Bernice's sensitive nature, and drew her nearer to God and bound her more closely to her poor, despised and ignorant people.

VI

Three years rolled by, and Bernice longed for a change of scene. She had not been away from Leeville since she came there, and had it not been for the many periodicals which she received weekly she would not have known what was happening in the outside world. Many of her classmates had corresponded with her, and were much interested in what they termed "her pious freak." She had been urged to spend Christmas in Baltimore. After much consideration, she decided to go. She thought she would enjoy a farewell peep into the world where once she had figured so prominently. Rita Payne was delighted to see her; although she did not approve of Bernice teaching in a Negro school, her love for her thus far had remained unchanged. Any one who has lived in a gay Southern city and seen its many beautiful women, and enjoyed their hospitality, can realize what a delightful time Bernice had.

She met the fashionable young men of the large Southern metropolis, and received much attention from them. She smiled as she thought of the stigma resting upon her. Such chivalry, such gallantry, but let it be even whispered that one drop of that blood coursed through her veins, she would be scorned and disgraced. This was only one of many instances which have happened in America.

She accepted the compliments and courtesy, smiling inwardly; her father's wealth was a great incentive to those who possessed good blood and small incomes.

During her stay, Rita gave a musicale. She wished her friends to hear Bernice sing. The young ladies in her circle wondered if she were really as talented as they had heard. They were obliged to admit that she was wondrously fair, but they did not wish to see anything above the ordinary in her music. But her voice was an exceedingly well-trained contralto, and when she stood before the cultured assemblage, even the most critical person had to admit the superior quality of her voice, and every one begged for an encore. Rita then placed "My Rosary" on the music stand, and Bernice began:

The hours I spend with thee, dear heart,
    Are like a string of pearls to me,
I count them over, every one apart,
    My Rosary, my Rosary.

Each hour a pearl, each pearl a prayer,
    To still a heart in absence wrung,
I tell each bead unto the end,
    And there a cross is hung!

O memories that bless and burn!
    O barren gain and bitter loss!

I kiss each bead, and strive at last to learn
    To kiss the cross, Sweetheart! to kiss the cross!⁵

The pathos of her voice touched the hearts of nearly everyone who listened, and Bernice could barely finish. The memories within her soul did bless and burn, and she thought of how many times she had bowed her head and kissed the cross she bore. There passed before her mind's eye a picture of all that had transpired since she and Rita had practised together at college. She grew sick and faint at heart. Her visit was no longer pleasant to her; it was only a ghost of a happier past. Taking leave of Rita, after ten days' rest, she returned to Leeville, fully determined that Bernice Silva in that world could be no more, and she never intended to wear the mask again.

Returning to Leeville, she took up the old duties with renewed strength. The children were delighted to have her back again. There were times when she became discouraged and wished she might enter some convent and get away from everyone and everything; then she thought how cowardly it would be to shrink from life's duties.

The old people had planned to give her a party. It was equal to the one of which the talented Dunbar wrote in verse.⁶ Everybody came to the party, old and young, dressed in their best clothes. The cape bonnets were all done up freshly for the occasion, and the men's bosoms were ironed to a finish. Refreshments were served—fried chicken, Maryland biscuit, pound cake, potato custards, and 'possum, too, was there, fat and cooked to perfection. The people feasted, then they sang. How Bernice enjoyed the melodies! The tears rolled down her cheeks. They seemed so earnest; their rich voices, though untrained, were full of real music.

After they had sung to their hearts' content, speechmaking was next in order. The old men expressed themselves in the most elaborate manner, while the women when their turn came, made many informal gestures and courtesies. Bernice responded, and thanked them for the warm expression of their regard for her. She begged them to send their children to school regularly, and thus help her in her efforts to educate their children. She told them of the struggles of the race, the condition of the masses, and the necessity of improving their mental conditions in order to make them morally good. There was much headshaking and bowing, with an occasional "Amen." The old men thought her a godsend to their community.

VII

The busy days grew into weeks. Summer passed and another winter. She attended strictly to her duties; nothing was left undone that would tend to the elevation of her people. Alas, like all human beings, she began to feel the great nervous strain. Instead of taking the rest she required, she often spent nights planning work for her girls and boys. One September evening she broke down with high fever and severe congestion of the brain. The doctor pronounced it typhoid fever. Each day the fever grew higher, until she became delirious and unmanageable. The cruel ravages of typhoid fever were visible in her beautiful countenance; her golden hair which her father had loved to smooth, had to be shaved off, and now, in spite of all this, her life was despaired of.

Many an humble heart prayed for her recovery; more than one little barefoot child came to inquire for her. The people sent her fresh eggs, chickens, and anything that they thought tempting, but she tasted nothing. She was not even conscious of their existence. They sent for her parents; death seemed inevitable. Two colored trained nurses had come from Charleston, and she was being cared for by skilled hands.

No one knew anything of her past life. The doctor thought her one of God's missionaries, who had given her life to this work. The crisis was at hand; twenty-four hours would decide her condition. The doctor feared her parents would never see her alive; her beautiful, useful life seemed at an end, and he dreaded to impart the tidings to them.

Mr. and Mrs. Silva were at Newport, R.I., when they received the news. Garrett was with them; he had just arrived from his Southern home, and was anxious to learn Bernice's whereabouts. When the telegram was received, Mr. Silva was shocked. Mrs. Silva uttered no words, but collapsed completely. Garrett Purnello shook his head gravely as he said, "God is just, man is unjust. What a world of suffering man's injustice has caused right here."

When they arrived at Leeville the hack rolled up to the hotel and the strangers alighted. The whole village knew in an hour that the visitors had arrived. The hotel was only an apology, but they deposited their luggage, and repaired to Bernice's boarding place. The doctor, although a country physician, had graduated from Bellevue, and thoroughly understood his profession. He told them she had overdone, and had for several days before she had taken her bed, a kind of walking typhoid fever. The nurses were untiring in their efforts and all they could depend upon was Divine power.

Mr. Silva grew old in a few hours. He almost idolized his only child.

Garrett looked at Bernice; he was overcome. He knelt by the bedside, took the hot, feverish hand in his, pressed it to his lips.

"This is the result of Lenore's work. I wish she might see it," he murmured.

Mrs. Silva said nothing. She silently prayed for the preservation of her only child. "Thy will, not mine," she prayed, but her grief was intolerable.

Garrett bent over the sufferer, and as he watched the unconscious face, a spirit of rebellion swelled in his bosom. It was soon replaced by a feeling of humble submission to Divine providence. He bathed her forehead with cool spring water, hoping to see her eyelids unclose. For hours he sat there, his heart filled with suspense. Finally his patience was rewarded. She opened her large blue eyes, tears rolled down her cheeks; she recognized him. It was the first intelligent expression that had been on her face for weeks. The doctor smiled. Garrett pressed her hand, and assured her that it were really he.

As yet Bernice had no knowledge of her parents' presence, and not until the next morning did they come to her. They feared the nervous shock would be too great. Sleep returned to the weary eyelids; she was on the road to recovery. Her joy at seeing her parents once more was boundless. They found no words to express their feelings. Her pale face showed how intensely she had suffered, but they were thankful that her life had been spared.

When she was able to be propped up on pillows, Garrett had a long story to tell her, and one evening as she was looking at the mountains in the distance, he drew his chair near her and began to tell her that which he had longed to tell her days before.

"Bernice," he began, "when we parted, I had a strange presentiment that my mother had not the character that stamped the caste of noble birth. I feared there was a mystery about her which ought to be fathomed. She was never able or willing to tell anything of her mother, only of her wealthy father. After her unwomanly conduct towards you, I decided to investigate the matter. She is my mother, but I could not overlook her unnecessary treatment of you. I have found that Negro blood flows in her veins; she is a mulatto, and has a living mother, whom she has cruelly ignored and disowned.

"I found my grandmother in Alabama, a smart old woman who has brought into this world three beautiful daughters, whose father was her master. One was dead, the second is married to the principal of a large Negro school, and the third is my own mother. Her father sent her away to college, and during one of her vacations she met my father, a foreigner, who had not long been in America. She has never visited her mother since; her father gave her a large sum of money when she married. She was his favorite child, exactly like him in appearance and manners, and he was satisfied to see her well provided for. She inherited his arrogant ways, and very little, if any, of her mother's disposition."

"Did the old lady know she married well?" questioned Bernice.

"She knew it only too well, and many have been her heartaches, when she knew that her own child was no longer identified with her black kin-people. That child, Olivia, is my own mother. I asked my grandmother, for she is mine, if she would know Olivia if she saw her after all these years.

"Course I'd know my own child, honey. She is the image of her father, and 'though it's nearly thirty years since I've seen her, I'd neber fergit her.

"I took the old lady to Florida," he continued, "and when my mother saw her she fainted. I needed no further proof of the truthfulness of the statements. I was ashamed of the cruel treatment which the dear old soul had received at her hands. I provided for her temporarily, and hastened to impart the tidings to you. You cannot imagine my sadness when I found you in this condition. But

> There's never a day so sunny
> But a little cloud appears;
> There's never a life so happy
> But has had its time of tears;
> Yet the sun shines out the brighter
>   When the stormy tempest clears.[7]

"God grant that the sun may smile graciously upon us after these years of sorrow."

Bernice had listened eagerly to his rehearsal, and in her heart pitied the woman who wished to lose her identity in this world, but would have to answer for living a lie, before Him who shall judge all folks righteously.

The doctor had told her that her teaching days were over; her health would permit it no longer. They decided to turn the work over to a mission board, and assist them to get someone to continue the work. The people wept when they learned that she would leave them,—the children flocked to see her. She was loath to leave them; her work had grown very dear to her. They succeeded in obtaining a graduate of an Industrial School, and after everything was satisfactorily arranged, Bernice, her parents and Garrett left the little village.

Bernice and Garrett were quietly married. He is a lawyer of much repute, and greatly beloved for the good he does for the race with which they are identified.

Lenore buried herself in a convent to atone for the wickedness she had done, if possible. She is known as Sister Jessie; she is no longer the haughty woman whom we knew, but a sweet Sister of Mercy. Bernice forgave her long ago. Mrs. Purnello never consented to be recognized as the old mammy's daughter; she continues to live in seclusion, while Garrett and Bernice have the old lady with them, who does all she can for "her dear chilluns," as she calls them.

1903

NOTES

1. From *Ulysses: A Tragedy* (1705) by English poet and dramatist Nicholas Rowe (1674–1718).

2. A term for whiskey, most often written "spiritus frumenti."

3. Lines from "Can't You Live Humble," an African American spiritual.

4. From the hymn "My God and Father! While I Stray," by English lyricist Charlotte Elliott (1789–1871) from *The Invalid's Hymnbook* (1834).

5. From "The Rosary," lyrics written and published by poet Robert Cameron Rogers, in 1894, with music written and published by Ethelbert Nevin, in 1898.

6. A reference to "The Party," a poem by Paul Laurence Dunbar (1872–1906), from his popular breakthrough collection, *Lyrics of Lowly Life*, published in 1896.

7. Authorship of the poem from which this excerpt was taken was claimed by two different writers, Lilien Wise, who published it in 1887 under the title "The Silver Lining," and Mary B. Colby, who published the poem in 1872 under the title "Clouds with Silver Linings."

W. E. B. DU BOIS (1868-1963)

The foremost African American intellectual of his time, with more than twenty books to his credit, William Edward Burghardt Du Bois was born in Great Barrington, Massachusetts. His father, Alfred, left the family when his son was a young child, and Du Bois was raised by his mother, Mary Burghardt Du Bois. He attended the local schools in his community and was named the valedictorian of his high school graduating class. Du Bois earned bachelor's degrees from Fisk University and Harvard University. He went on to study at the University of Berlin before returning to Harvard to complete his PhD in history, in 1895. In so doing, he became the first African American in the history of that institution to earn its highest degree. A prolific writer and respected black community leader, Du Bois authored numerous articles and books on topics ranging from race relations to African American history to the sociology of race. In addition, he also published fiction and poetry, including five novels. In 1910, Du Bois became the founding editor of *The Crisis*, the nation's largest African American magazine and the official journal of the NAACP. During his twenty-four years at its helm, he remained one of the most powerful figures in U.S. black literature, shaping African American aesthetics and political sensibilities through his support for and, alternatively, his rejection of specific topics, themes, and writing styles. Although Du Bois is known to twenty-first-century readers primarily for *The Souls of Black Folk* (1903), his groundbreaking treatise on race in the U.S., his shorter works appeared in a range of both African American and mainstream, white-owned newspapers and magazines. Before they were reprinted in *The Colored American* and other African American periodicals, the following poems were first published in popular progressive magazines, all during the years immediately following *The Souls of Black Folk*. "Credo" first appeared in the October 6, 1904, issue of *The Independent;* and "A Litany for Atlanta," written in response to the 1906 race riot in that city, was published in *The Independent* two years later (on October 11, 1906). "The Burden of Black Women" and "My Country 'Tis of Thee" first appeared in the November 1907 issue of *Horizon Magazine*.

CREDO

I believe in God who made of one blood all races that dwell on earth. I believe that all men, black and brown and white, are brothers, varying, through Time and Opportunity, in form and gift and feature, but differing in no essential particular, and alike in soul and in the possibility of infinite development.

Especially do I believe in the Negro Race; in the beauty of its genius, the sweetness of its soul, and its strength in that meekness which shall yet inherit this turbulent earth.

I believe in pride of race and lineage and self; in pride of self so deep as to scorn injustice to other selves; in pride of lineage so great as to despise no man's father; in pride of race so chivalrous as neither to offer bastardy to the weak nor beg wedlock of the strong, knowing that men may be brothers in Christ, even tho they be not brothers-in-law.

I believe in Service—humble reverent service, from the blackening of boots to the whitening of souls; for Work is Heaven, Idleness Hell, and Wage is the "Well done!" of the Master, who summoned all them that labor and are heavy laden, making no distinction between the black sweating cotton hands of Georgia and the First Families of Virginia, since all distinction not based on deed is devilish and not divine.

I believe in the Devil and his angels, who wantonly work to narrow the opportunity of struggling human beings, especially if they be black; who spit in the faces of the fallen, strike them that cannot strike again, believe the worst and work to prove it, hating the image which their Maker stamped on a brother's soul.

I believe in the Prince of Peace.[1] I believe that War is Murder. I believe that armies and navies are at bottom the tinsel and braggadocio of oppression and wrong; and I believe that the wicked conquest of weaker and darker nations by nations whiter and stronger but foreshadows the death of that strength.

I believe in Liberty for all men; the space to stretch their arms and their souls; the right to breathe and the right to vote, the freedom to choose their friends, enjoy the sunshine and ride on the railroads, uncursed by color; thinking, dreaming, working as they will in a kingdom of God and love.

I believe in the training of children black even as white; the leading out of little souls into the green pastures and beside the still waters, not for pelf or peace, but for Life lit by some large vision of beauty and goodness and truth; lest we forget, and the sons of the fathers, like Esau, for mere meat barter their birthright in a mighty nation.

Finally, I believe in Patience—patience with the weakness of the Weak and the strength of the Strong, the prejudice of the Ignorant and the ignorance of the Blind; patience with the tardy triumph of Joy and the mad chastening of Sorrow—patience with God.

ATLANTA UNIVERSITY, ATLANTA, GA.

1904

A LITANY OF ATLANTA

O Silent God, Thou whose voice afar in mist and mystery hath left our ears a-hungered in these fearful days—

Hear us, good Lord!

Listen to us, Thy children: our faces dark with doubt, are made a mockery in Thy sanctuary. With uplifted hands we front Thy heaven, O God, crying:

We beseech Thee to hear us, good Lord!

We are not better than our fellows, Lord; we are but weak and human men. When our devils do deviltry, curse Thou the doer and the deed: curse them as we curse them, do to them all and more that ever they have done to innocence and weakness, to womanhood and home.

Have mercy upon us, miserable sinners!

And yet whose is the deeper guilt? Who made these devils? Who nursed them in crime and fed them on injustice? Who ravished and debauched their mothers and their grandmothers? Who bought and sold their crime, and waxed fat and rich on public iniquity?

Thou knowest, good God!

Is this Thy justice, O Father, that guilt be easier than innocence, and the innocent crucified for the guilt of the untouched guilty?

Justice, O Judge of men!

Wherefore do we pray? Is not the God of the fathers dead? Have not seers seen in Heaven's halls Thine hearsed and lifeless form stark amidst the black and rolling smoke of sin, where all along bow bitter forms of endless dead?

Awake, Thou that sleepest!

Thou art not dead, but flown afar, up hills of endless light, thru blazing corridors of suns, where worlds do swing of good and gentle men, of women strong and free—far from the cozeage, black hypocrisy and chaste prostitution of this shameful speck of dust!

Turn again, O Lord, leave us not to perish in our sin!

From lust of body and lust of blood
Great God deliver us!

From lust of powers and lust of gold
Great God deliver us!

From the leagued lying of despot and of brute,
Great God deliver us!

A city lay in travail, God our Lord, and from her loins sprang twin Murder and Black Hate. Red was the midnight; clang, crack and cry of death and fury filled the air and trembled underneath the stars when church spires pointed silently to Thee. And all this was to sate the greed of greedy men who hide behind the veil of vengeance!

Bend us Thine, ear, O Lord!

In the pale, still morning we looked upon the deed. We stopped our ears and held our leaping hands, but they—did not wag their heads and leer and cry with bloody jaws: *Cease from Crime!* The word was mockery, for thus they train a hundred crimes while we do cure one.

Turn again our captivity, O Lord!

Behold this maimed and broken thing; dear God it was an humble black man who toiled and sweat to save a bit from the pittance paid him. They told him: *Work and Rise.* He worked. Did this man sin? Nay, but some one told how some one said another did—one whom he had never seen nor known. Yet for that man's crime this man lieth maimed and murdered, his wife naked to shame, his children, to poverty and evil.

Hear us, O heavenly Father!

Doth not this justice of hell stink in Thy nostrils, O God? How long shall the mounting flood of innocent blood roar in Thine ears and pound in our hearts for vengeance? Pile the pale frenzy of blood-crazed brutes who do such deeds high on Thine altar, Jehovah Jireh,[2] and burn it in hell forever and forever!

Forgive us, good Lord; we know not what we say!

Bewildered we are, and passion-tost, mad with the madness of a mobbed and mocked and murdered people; straining at the armposts of Thy Throne, we raise our shackled hands and charge Thee, God, by the bones of our stolen fathers, by the tears of our dead mothers, by the very blood of Thy crucified Christ: *What meaneth this?* Tell us the Plan; give us the Sign!

Keep not thou silent, O God!

Sit no longer blind, Lord God, deaf to our prayer and dumb to our dumb suffering. Surely Thou too are not white, O Lord, a pale, bloodless, heartless thing?

Ah! Christ of all the Pities!

Forgive the thought! Forgive these wild, blasphemous words. Thou art still the God of our black fathers, and in Thy soul's soul sit some soft darkenings of the evening, some shadowings of the velvet night.

But whisper—speak—call, great God, for Thy silence is white terror to our hearts! The way, O God, show us the way and point us the path.

Whither? North is greed and South is blood; within, the coward, and without, the liar. Whither? To death?

Amen! Welcome dark sleep!

Whither? To life? But not this life, dear God, not this. Let the cup pass from us, tempt us not beyond our strength, for there is that clamoring and clawing within, to whose voice we would not listen, yet shudder lest we must, and it is red, Ah! God! It is a red and awful shape.

Selah!

In yonder East trembles a star.

Vengeance is mine; I will repay, saith the Lord!

Thy will, O Lord, be done!

Kyrie Eleison![3]

Lord, we have done these pleading, wavering words.

We beseech Thee to hear us, good Lord!

We bow our heads and hearken soft to the sobbing of women and little children.

We beseech Thee to hear us, good Lord!

Our voices sink in silence and in night.

Hear us, good Lord!

In night, O God of a godless land!

Amen!

In silence, O Silent God.
Selah!

Done at Atlanta, in the Day of Death, 1906.

1906

THE BURDEN OF BLACK WOMEN

Dark daughter of the lotus leaves that watch the southern sea,
Wan spirit of a prisoned soul a-panting to be free;
  The muttered music of thy streams, the whispers of the deep
  Have kissed each other in God's name and kissed a world to sleep.

The will of the world is a whistling wind sweeping a cloud-cast sky,
And not from the east and not from the west knelled its soul-searing cry;
But out of the past of the Past's grey past, it yelled from the top
  of the sky;
  Crying: Awake, O ancient race! Wailing: O woman arise!
  And crying and sighing and crying again as a voice
    in the midnight cries;
  But the burden of white men bore her back,
    and the white world stifled her sighs.

The White World's vermin and filth:
  All the dirt of London,
  All the scum of New York;
  Valiant spoilers of women
  And conquerors of unarmed men;
  Shameless breeders of bastards
  Drunk with the greed of gold,
  Baiting their blood-stained hooks
  With cant for the souls of the simple,
  Bearing the White Man's Burden
  Of Liquor and Lust and Lies!
  Unthankful we wince in the East,
  Unthankful we wail from the westward,
  Unthankfully thankful we sing,
  In the un-won wastes of the wild:
    I hate them, Oh!

I hate them well,
I hate them, Christ!
As I hate Hell,
If I were God
I'd sound their knell
This day!
Who raised the fools to their glory
But Black men of Egypt and Ind?
Ethiopia's sons of the evening,
Chaldeans⁴ and Yellow Chinese?
The Hebrew children of Morning
And mongrels of Rome and Greece?
    Ah, well!

And they that raised the boasters
Shall drag them down again:
Down with the theft of their thieving
And murder and mocking of men,
Down with their barter of women
And laying and lying of creeds,
Down with their cheating of childhood,
And drunken orgies of war—
    down,
        down,
            deep down,
Till the Devil's strength be shorn,
Till some dim, darker David a-hoeing of his corn,
And married maiden, Mother of God,
Bid the Black Christ be born!

Then shall the burden of manhood,
Be it yellow or black or white,
And Poverty, Justice and Sorrow—
The Humble and Simple and Strong,
Shall sing with the Songs of Morning
And Daughters of Evensong:

Black mother of the iron hills that guard the blazing sea,
Wild spirit of a storm-swept soul a-struggling to be free,

Where 'neath the bloody finger marks, thy riven bosom quakes,
Thicken the thunders of God's voice, and lo! A world awakes!

1907

MY COUNTRY, 'TIS OF THEE

Of course you have faced the dilemma: it is announced, they all smirk and rise. If they are *ultra,* they remove their hats and look ecstatic; then they look at you. What shall you do? *Noblesse oblige;*[5] you cannot be boorish, or ungracious; and too, after all it is your country and you *do* love its ideals if not all of its realities. Now, then, I have thought of a way out: Arise, gracefully remove your hat, and tilt your head. Then sing as follows, powerfully and with deep unction. They'll hardly note the little changes and their feelings and your conscience will thus be saved:

My country 'tis of thee,
Late land of slavery,
   Of thee I sing.
Land where my father's pride
Slept where my mother died,
From every mountain side
   Let freedom ring!

My native country thee
Land of the slave set free,
   Thy fame I love.
I love thy rocks and rills
And o'er thy hate which chills,
My heart with purpose thrills,
   To *rise* above.

Let laments swell the breeze
And wring from all the trees
   Sweet freedom's song.
Let laggard tongues awake,
Let all who hear partake,
Let Southern silence quake,
   The sound prolong.

Our fathers' God to thee
Author of Liberty,
    To thee we sing
Soon may our land be bright,
With Freedom's happy light
Protect us by Thy might,
    Great God our King.

1907

NOTES

1. A name for Jesus Christ.

2. A compound name for the God of the Judeo-Christian tradition, from the Hebrew, literally meaning "the Lord will provide."

3. From the Greek, meaning "Lord have mercy."

4. Refers to an ethnic Assyrian minority community, primarily concentrated in the regions of northern Iraq, northeast Syria, northwest Iran, and southeast Turkey, and with growing communities in the United States, Australia, and Western Europe.

5. A French term meaning "nobility obligates," commonly used in English to refer to the belief that those with economic or other forms of privilege have an obligation to help those who are marginalized.

EFFIE WALLER SMITH (1879-1960)

Effie Waller Smith was born in Chloe Creek, Kentucky, a small community on the Cumberland River. Her parents, former slaves Frank Waller and Sibbie Ratliff, had four children, all of whom completed the highest level of education available for black students in the local segregated school system. Smith and her two older siblings pursued further training at Kentucky Normal School for Colored Persons. Smith began writing poetry during her teen years and, in 1904, she released *Songs of the Months,* her first collection of poems. During this same period, she was also able to publish her work in mainstream periodicals, including *Putnam's,* a white-owned general-interest magazine. In 1909, Smith published her last two volumes, *Rhymes from the Cumberland* and *Rosemary and Pansies.* In 1917, she published the sonnet "Autumn Winds." She is believed to have ended her writing career with this final achievement. The following selections are reprinted from her first and second collections. "The Preacher's Wife" and "Apple Sauce and Chicken Fried" first appeared in *Songs of the Months.* "To a Spring in the Cumberlands" and "The Bachelor Girl" were first published in *Rhymes from the Cumberland.* These poems address several of Smith's most common themes, including women's rights, religious faith, and her beloved Kentucky landscape.

THE PREACHER'S WIFE, DEDICATED TO THE WIVES OF THE ITINERANT PREACHERS OF THE M.E. CHURCH

God bless his wife, the preacher's wife,
    Wherever she may be;
A cheerful joy, a comfort and
    A blessing, all is she.

Whether from humble cottage, or
    From mansion great and grand,
Where ease and luxury she left
    To travel o'er the land,

With him, her Christlike husband,
    Who doth labor for the cause,
And faithfully doth bear aloft
    The banner of the Cross.

In village and in town is he,
    And on the hill and plain,
Through forests vast, through swollen streams,
    He goes in sun and rain.

Oft persecuted, oft despised,
    His fare is rough and hard,
But God he seeks to please, not man,
    In God is his reward.

And tho' it may not be the lot
    Of her, the preacher's wife,
To mingle as her husband does
    In ruder ways of life,

But hers it is to visit and
    Cherish the sick and weak;
And nurse them in affliction's hour
    And words of comfort speak.

And other's burdens nobly bear,
    The sorrowing hearts to soothe,
And with affection's loving hand
    The dying pillows smooth;

And in the Sabbath school repeat
    The story's oft been told;
And lovingly and gently lead
    The lambs to Jesus's fold.

What tho' her life may trials have,
    Her pathway checkered be,
Will not a golden crown of life
    Be giv'n to such as she?

Far, far away from childhood's home,
    'Mongst other scenes and skies,

These pure and unfamed women live,
    And for their Master die.

All over our dear land to-day
    Are graves where rest their dust;
With their work done they dreamless wait,
    The Rising of the just.

                                        1904

APPLE SAUCE AND CHICKEN FRIED

You may talk about the knowledge
Which our farmers' girls have gained
From cooking-schools and cook-books,
(Where all modern cooks are trained);
But I would rather know just how,
(Though vainly I have tried)
To prepare, as mother used to,
Apple sauce and chicken fried.

Our modern cooks know how to fix
Their dainty dishes rare,
But, friend, just let me tell you what!—
None of them can compare
With what my mother used to fix,
And for which I've often cried,
When I was but a little tot,—
Apple sauce and chicken fried.

Chicken a la Française,
And also fricassee,
Served with some new fangled sauce
Is plenty good for me,
Till I get to thinking of the home
Where once I used to 'bide,
And where I used to eat,—um, my!
Apple sauce and chicken fried.

We always had it once a week,
Sometimes we had it twice;
And I have even known the time
When we have had it thrice.
Our good, yet jolly pastor,
During his circuit's ride
With us once each week gave grateful thanks
For apple sauce and chicken fried.

Why, it seems like I can smell it,
And even taste it, too,
And see it with my natural eyes,
Though of course it can't be true;
And it seems like I'm a child again,
Standing by mother's side,
Pulling at her dress and asking
For apple sauce and chicken fried.

1904

TO A SPRING IN THE CUMBERLANDS

Gurgling spring in sylvan beauty[1]
Almost hid away from view;
From your own bright sparkling water
I will drink a health to you.

Beach and oak tree reaching skyward
Guard you from the sunlight's heat;
And from this overhanging stone
Comes a breath of flowers sweet.

In your water clear and cold
Warbling birds their plumage lave;
From your brink o'ergrown with mosses
Dainty fern fronds gently wave.

Huntmen here have often lingered
Drinking of your water clear;

And you've often quenched the thirst
Of the agile, antlered deer.

So here's health dear sparkling spring
Gurgling from the mountain's side,
With a wish that in your beauty
You will ever here abide.

1909

THE BACHELOR GIRL

She's no "old maid," she's not afraid
To let you know she's her own "boss,"
She's easy pleased, she's not diseased,
She is not nervous, is not cross.

She's no desire whatever for
Mrs. to precede her name,
The blessedness of singleness
She all her life will proudly claim.

She does not sit around and knit
On baby caps and mittens,
She does not play her time away
With puggy dogs and kittens.

And if a mouse about the house
She sees, she will not jump and scream;
Of handsome beaux and billet doux[2]
The "bachelor girl" does never dream.

She does not puff and frizz and fluff
Her hair, nor squeeze and pad her form.
With painted face, affected grace,
The "bachelor girl" ne'er seeks to charm.

She reads history, biography,
Tales of adventure far and near,
On sea or land, but poetry and
Love stories rarely interest her.

She's lots of wit, and uses it,
Of "horse sense," too, she has a store;
The latest news she always knows,
She scans the daily papers o'er.

Of politics and all the tricks
And schemes that politicians use,
She knows full well and she can tell
With eloquence of them her views.

An athlete that's hard to beat
The "bachelor girl" surely is,
When playing games she makes good aims
And always strictly minds her "biz."

Amid the hurry and the flurry
Of this life she goes alone,
No matter where you may see her
She seldom has a chaperon.

But when you meet her on the street
At night she has a "32,"
And she can shoot you, bet your boots,
When necessity demands her to.

Her heart is kind and you will find
Her often scattering sunshine bright
Among the poor, and she is sure
To always advocate the right.

On her pater and her mater
For her support she does not lean,
She talks and writes of "Woman's Rights"
In language forceful and clean.

She does not shirk, but does her work,
Amid the world's fast hustling whirl,
And come what may, she's here to stay,
The self-supporting "bachelor girl."

1909

NOTES

1. The Cumberland Mountain range runs 131 miles through the Appalachian regions of West Virginia, Virginia, Kentucky, and Tennessee.
2. A love letter.

MARY CHURCH TERRELL (1863-1954)

Mary Eliza Church Terrell was born in Memphis, Tennessee, to former slaves Louisa Ayers and Robert Church. Terrell's father was an affluent member of the city's black community, having earned a sizeable fortune through his skillful investments in area real estate. For her primary and secondary education, Terrell attended the Model School at Antioch College in Yellow Springs, Ohio. She remained in Ohio for her post-secondary studies, earning both a bachelor's degree and a master's degree at Oberlin College (in 1884 and 1888, respectively). Defying her father's hope that she would embrace the genteel ladyhood that awaited her as a member of the African American elite, Terrell instead sought out work as a teacher, first at Ohio's Wilberforce University and later at the M Street School in Washington, DC. In 1888, she traveled to Europe, where she spent two years traveling and studying languages. In 1890, she returned to the United States, where she married Robert H. Terrell, a young attorney who would go on to become the first African American judge in the District of Columbia. Though married women were barred from teaching, Terrell had no trouble identifying a use for her considerable energies. A cofounder as well as the first president of the National Association of Colored Women (NACW), she was a lifelong advocate for women's equality and black civil rights. A charter member of the NAACP, Terrell was for many years vice-president of the organization's Washington, DC, branch. A prolific writer, Terrell wrote essays, short stories, and opinion pieces for a variety of African American publications, though she is best known for her compelling speeches, many of which were printed and distributed in pamphlet form. In 1940, at the age of seventy-seven, she published her autobiography, *A Colored Woman in a White World.* Terrell remained politically active throughout her life, participating in sit-ins and other protests, well into her eighties. The following speech, delivered on October 10, 1906, at the United Women's Club in Washington, DC, was reprinted in the January 24, 1907 issue of *The Independent.*

WHAT IT MEANS TO BE COLORED IN THE CAPITAL
OF THE UNITED STATES

Washington, D.C., has been called "The Colored Man's Paradise." Whether this sobriquet was given to the national capital in bitter irony by a member of the handicapped race, as he reviewed some of his own persecutions and rebuffs, or whether it was given immediately after the war by an ex-slave-holder who for the first time in his life saw colored people walking about like freemen, minus the overseer and his whip, history saith not. It is certain that it would be difficult to find a worse misnomer for Washington than "The Colored Man's Paradise" if so prosaic a consideration as veracity is to determine the appropriateness of a name.

For fifteen years I have resided in Washington, and while it was far from being a paradise for colored people, when I first touched these shores, it has been doing its level best ever since to make conditions for us intolerable. As a colored woman I might enter Washington any night, a stranger in a strange land, and walk miles without finding a place to lay my head. Unless I happened to know colored people who live here or ran across a chance acquaintance who could recommend a colored boarding house to me, I should be obliged to spend the entire night wandering about. Indians, Chinamen, Filipinos, Japanese and representatives of any other dark race can find hotel accommodations, if they can pay for them. The colored man alone is thrust out of the hotels of the national capital like a leper.

As a colored woman I may walk from the Capitol to the White House, ravenously hungry and abundantly supplied with money with which to purchase a meal, without finding a single restaurant in which I would be permitted to take a morsel of food, if it was patronized by white people, unless I were willing to sit behind a screen. As a colored woman I cannot visit the tomb of the Father of this country, which owes its very existence to the love of freedom in the human heart and which stands for equal opportunity to all, without being forced to sit in the Jim Crow section of an electric car which starts from the very heart of the city—midway between the Capitol and the White House. If I refuse thus to be humiliated, I am cast into jail and forced to pay a fine for violating the Virginia laws. Every hour in the day Jim Crow cars filled with colored people, many of whom are intelligent and well to do, enter and leave the national capital.

As a colored woman I may enter more than one white church in Washington without receiving that welcome which as a human being I have a right to expect in the sanctuary of God. Sometimes the color blindness of the usher takes on that peculiar form which prevents a dark face from making any impression whatsoever upon his retina, so that it is impossible for him to see colored people at all. If he is not so afflicted, after keeping a colored man or woman waiting a long time, he will ungraciously show these dusky Christians who have had the temerity to thrust themselves into a temple where only the fair of face are expected to worship God to a seat in the rear, which is named in honor of a certain personage, well known in this country, and commonly called Jim Crow.

Unless I am willing to engage in a few menial occupations, in which the pay for my services would be very poor, there is no way for me to earn an honest living, if I am not a trained nurse or a dressmaker or can secure a position as teacher in the public schools, which is exceedingly difficult to do. It matters not what my intellectual attainments may be or how great is the need of the services of a competent person, if I try to enter many of the numerous vocations in which my white sisters are allowed to engage, the door is shut in my face.

From one Washington theater I am excluded altogether. In the remainder certain seats are set aside for colored people, and it is almost impossible to secure others. I once telephoned to the ticket seller just before a matinee and asked if a neat appearing colored nurse would be allowed to sit in the parquet with her little white charge, and the answer rushed quickly and positively thru the receiver—NO. When I remonstrated a bit and told him that in some of the theaters colored nurses were allowed to sit with the white Children for whom they cared, the ticket seller told me that in Washington it was very poor policy to employ colored nurses, for they were excluded from many places where white girls would be allowed to take children for pleasure.

If I possess artistic talent, there is not a single art school of repute which will admit me. A few years ago a colored woman who possessed great talent submitted some drawings to the Corcoran Art School, of Washington, which were accepted by the committee of awards, who sent her a ticket entitling her to a course in this school. But when the committee discovered that the young woman was colored, they declined to admit her, and told her that if they had suspected that her drawings had been made by a colored woman, they would not have examined them at all. The efforts of Frederick Douglass and a lawyer of great repute who took a keen interest in the affair were unavailing. In order to cultivate her talent this young woman was forced to leave her comfortable home in Washington and incur the expense of going to New York. Having entered the Woman's Art School of Cooper Union, she graduated with honor, and then went to Paris to continue her studies, where she achieved signal success and was complimented by some of the greatest living artists in France.

With the exception of the Catholic University,[1] there is not a single white college in the national capital to which colored people are admitted, no matter how great their ability, how lofty their ambition, how unexceptionable their character or how great their thirst for knowledge may be.

A few years ago the Columbian Law School admitted colored students, but in deference to the Southern white students the authorities have decided to exclude them altogether.

Some time ago a young woman who had already attracted some attention in the literary world by her volume of short stories answered an advertisement which appeared in a Washington newspaper, which called for the services of a skilled stenographer and expert typewriter. It is unnecessary to state the reasons why a young woman whose literary ability was so great as that possessed by the one referred to should decide to earn money in this way. The applicants were requested to send specimens of their work and answer certain questions concerning their experience and their speed before they called in person. In reply to her application the young colored woman, who, by the way, is very fair and attractive indeed, received a letter from the firm stating that her references and experience were the most satisfactory that had been sent and requesting her to call. When she presented herself there was some doubt in the mind of the man to whom she was directed concerning her racial pedigree, so he asked her point blank whether she was colored or white. When she confessed the truth the merchant expressed great sorrow and deep regret that he could not avail himself of the services of so competent a person, but frankly admitted that employing a colored woman in his establishment in any except a menial position was simply out of the question.

Another young friend had an experience which, for some reasons, was still more disheartening and bitter than the one just mentioned. In order to secure lucrative employment she left Washington and went to New York. There she worked her way up in one of the largest dry goods stores till she was placed as saleswoman in the cloak department. Tired of being separated from her family, she decided to return to Washington, feeling sure that, with her experience and her fine recommendation from the New York firm, she could easily secure employment. Nor was she overconfident, for the proprietor of one of the largest dry goods stores in her native city was glad to secure the services of a young woman who brought such hearty credentials from New York. She had not been in this store very long, however, before she called upon me one day and asked me to intercede with the proprietor in her behalf, saying that she had been discharged that afternoon because it had been discovered that she was colored. When I called upon my young friend's employer he made no effort to avoid the issue, as I feared he would. He did not say he had discharged the young saleswoman because she had not given satisfaction, as he might easily have done. On the contrary, he admitted without the slightest hesitation that the young woman he had just discharged was one of the best clerks he had ever had. In the cloak department, where she had been assigned, she had been a brilliant success, he said. "But I cannot keep Miss Smith in my employ," he concluded. "Are you not master of your own store?" I ventured to inquire. The proprietor of this store was a Jew, and I felt that it was particularly cruel, unnatural and cold-blooded for the representative of one oppressed and persecuted race to deal so harshly and unjustly with a member of another. I had intended to make this point when I decided to intercede for my young friend, but when I thought how a reference to the persecution of his own race would wound his feelings, the words froze on my lips. "When I first heard your friend was colored," he explained, "I did not believe it and said so to the clerks who made the statement. Finally, the girls who had been most pronounced in their opposition to working in a store with a colored girl came to me in a body and threatened to strike. 'Strike away,' said I, 'your places will be easily filled.' Then they started on another tack. Delegation after delegation began to file down to my office, some of the women my very best customers, to protest against my employing a colored girl. Moreover, they threatened to boycott my store if I did not discharge her at once. Then it became a question of bread and butter and I yielded to the inevitable—that's all. Now," said he, concluding, "if I lived in a great, cosmopolitan city like New York, I should do as I pleased, and refuse to discharge a girl simply because she was colored." But I thought of a similar incident that happened in New York. I remembered that a colored woman, as fair as a lily and as beautiful as a Madonna, who was the head saleswoman in a large department store in New York, had been discharged, after she had held this position for years, when the proprietor accidentally discovered that a fatal drop of African blood was percolating somewhere thru her veins.

Not only can colored women secure no employment in the Washington stores, department and otherwise, except as menials, and such positions, of course, are few, but even as customers they are not infrequently treated with discourtesy both by the clerks and the proprietor himself. Following the trend of the times, the senior partner of the largest and best department store in Washington, who originally hailed from Boston, once the home of William Lloyd Garrison, Wendell Phillips, and Charles Sumner,[2] if my memory serves me right, decided to open a restaurant in his store. Tired and hungry after her morning's shopping a colored school teacher, whose relation to her African progenitors is so remote as scarcely to be discernible to the naked eye, took a seat at one of the tables in the restaurant of this Boston store. After sitting unnoticed a long time the colored teacher asked a waiter who passed her by if she would not take her order. She was quickly informed that colored people could not be served in that restaurant and was obliged to leave in confusion and shame, much to the amusement of the waiters and the guests who had noticed the incident. Shortly after that a teacher in Howard University, one of the best schools for colored youth in the country, was similarly insulted in the restaurant of the same store.

In one of the Washington theaters from which colored people are excluded altogether, members of the race have been viciously assaulted several times, for the proprietor well knows that colored people have no redress for such discriminations against them in the District courts. Not long ago a colored clerk in one of the departments who looks more like his paternal ancestors who fought for the lost cause than his grandmothers who were the victims of the peculiar institution, bought a ticket for the parquet of this theater in which colored people are nowhere welcome, for himself and mother, whose complexion is a bit swarthy. The usher refused to allow the young man to take the seats for which his tickets called and tried to snatch from him the coupons. A scuffle ensued and both mother and son were ejected by force. A suit was brought against the proprietor and the damages awarded the injured man and his mother amounted to the munificent sum of one cent. One of the teachers in the Colored High School received similar treatment in the same theater.

Not long ago one of my little daughter's bosom friends figured in one of the most pathetic instances of which I have ever heard. A gentleman who is very fond of children promised to take six little girls in his neighborhood to a matinee. It happened that he himself and five of his little friends were so fair that they easily passed muster, as they stood in judgment before the ticket seller and the ticket taker. Three of the little girls were sisters, two of whom were very fair and the other a bit brown. Just as this little girl, who happened to be last in the procession, went by the ticket taker, that Argus-eyed, sophisticated gentleman detected something which caused a deep, dark frown to mantle his brow and he did not allow her to pass. "I guess you have made a mistake," he called to the host of this theater party. "Those little girls," pointing to the fair ones, "may be admitted, but this one," designating the brown one, "can't." But the colored man was quite equal to the emergency. Fairly frothing at the mouth with anger, he asked the ticket taker what he meant, what he was trying to insinuate about that particular little girl. "Do you mean to tell me," he shouted in rage, "that I must go clear to the Philippine Islands to bring this child to the United States and then I can't take her to the theater in the National Capital?" The little ruse succeeded brilliantly, as he knew it would. "Beg your pardon," said the ticket taker, "don't know what I was thinking about. Of course she can go in."

"What was the matter with me this afternoon, mother," asked the little brown girl innocently, when she mentioned the affair at home. "Why did the man at the theater let my two sisters and the other girls in and try to keep me out?" In relating this incident, the child's mother told me her little girl's question, which showed such blissful ignorance of the depressing, cruel conditions which confronted her, completely unnerved her for a time.

Altho' white and colored teachers are under the same Board of Education and the system for the children of both races is said to be uniform, prejudice against the colored teachers in the public schools is manifested in a variety of ways. From 1870 to 1900 there was a colored superintendent at the head of the colored schools. During all that time the directors of the cooking, sewing, physical culture, manual training, music and art departments were colored people. Six years ago a change was inaugurated. The colored superintendent was legislated out of office and the directorships, without a single exception, were taken from colored teachers and given to the whites. There was no complaint about the work done by the colored directors, no more than is heard about every officer in every school. The directors of the art and physical culture departments were particularly fine. Now, no matter how competent or superior the colored teachers in our public schools may be, they know that they can never rise to the height of a directorship, can never hope to be more than an assistant and receive the meager salary therefore, unless the present regime is radically changed.

Not long ago one of the most distinguished kindergartners in the country came to deliver a course of lectures in Washington. The colored teachers were eager to attend, but they could not buy the coveted privilege for love or money. When they appealed to the director of kindergartens, they were told that the expert kindergartner had come to Washington under the auspices of private individuals, so that she could not possibly have them admitted. Realizing what a loss colored teachers had sustained in being deprived of the information and inspiration which these lectures afforded, one of the white teachers volunteered to repeat them as best she could for the benefit of her colored co-laborers for half the price she herself had paid, and the proposition was eagerly accepted by some.

Strenuous efforts are being made to run Jim Crow streetcars in the national capital. "Resolved, that a Jim Crow law should be adopted and enforced in the District of Columbia," was the subject of a discussion engaged in last January by the Columbian Debating Society of the George Washington University in our national capital, and the decision was rendered in favor of the affirmative. Representative Heflin, of Alabama, who introduced a bill providing for Jim Crow street cars in the District of Columbia last winter, has just received a letter from the president of the East Brookland Citizens' Association "endorsing the movement for separate street cars and sincerely hoping that you will be successful in getting this enacted into a law as soon as possible." (Brookland is a suburb of Washington.)

The colored laborer's path to a decent livelihood is by no means smooth. Into some of the trades unions here he is admitted, while from others he is excluded altogether. By the union men this is denied, altho' I am personally acquainted with skilled workmen who tell me they are not admitted into the unions because they are colored. But even when they are allowed to join the unions they frequently derive little benefit, owing to certain tricks of the trade. When the word passes round that help is needed and colored laborers apply, they are often told by the union officials that they have secured all the men they needed, because the places are reserved for white men, until they have been provided with jobs, and colored men must remain idle, unless the supply of white men is too small.

I am personally acquainted with one of the most skilful laborers in the hardware business in Washington. For thirty years he has been working for the same firm. He told me he could not join the union, and that his employer had been almost forced to discharge him, because the union men threatened to boycott his store if he did not. If another man could have been found at the time to take his place he would have lost his job, he said. When no other human being can bring a refractory chimney or stove to its senses, this colored man is called upon as the court of last appeal. If he fails to subdue it, it is pronounced a hopeless case at once. And yet this expert workman receives much less for his services than do white men who cannot compare with him in skill.

And so I might go on citing instance after instance to show the variety of ways in which our people are sacrificed on the altar of prejudice in the Capital of the United States and how almost insurmountable are the obstacles which block his path to success. Early in life many a colored youth is so appalled by the helplessness and the hopelessness of his situation in this country that, in a sort of stoical despair he resigns himself to his fate. "What is the good of our trying to acquire an education? We can't all be preachers, teachers, doctors and lawyers. Besides those professions, there is almost nothing for colored people to do but engage in the most menial occupations, and we do not need an education for that." More than once such remarks, uttered by young men and women in our public schools who possess brilliant intellects, have wrung my heart.

It is impossible for any white person in the United States, no matter how sympathetic and broad, to realize what life would mean to him if his incentive to effort were suddenly snatched away. To the lack of incentive to effort, which is the awful shadow under which we live, may be traced the wreck and ruin of scores of colored youth. And surely nowhere in the world do oppression and persecution based solely on the color of the skin appear more hateful and hideous than in the capital of the United States, because the chasm between the principles upon which this Government was founded, in which it still professes to believe, and those which are daily practiced under the protection of the flag, yawns so wide and deep.

1906

NOTES

1. The Catholic University of America, the national university of the Catholic Church in the United States, founded in 1887.

2. A U.S. senator from Massachusetts, best remembered for "The Crime against Kansas," his powerful antislavery speech, delivered on the floor of the Senate in 1856.

KELLY MILLER (1863–1939)

Writer, mathematician, and founding member of the American Negro Academy Kelly Miller was born in Winnsboro, South Carolina. His father was a free black Confederate soldier in the Civil War, and his mother was enslaved. Miller began his education in a local school established for free black students. His instructors encouraged him to continue his studies, and he went on to spend two years at Winnsboro's Fairfield Institute. In 1880 he enrolled in the college preparatory program at Howard University, completing the three-year curriculum in just twenty-four months. He graduated from Howard's baccalaureate program in 1886. In 1887, Miller became the first African American to enroll at Johns Hopkins University, where he spent two years in the mathematics doctoral program before returning to Howard to complete his postgraduate studies. In 1890, he was appointed to the Howard faculty. Though he served for a time as professor of mathematics, Miller's greatest contribution to the university came when he introduced sociology to the Howard curriculum. In 1895, Miller was appointed Howard's first professor of sociology. He would remain in that post until 1934. A prolific writer and an antiracist activist, Miller produced many essays on racism, equality, and civil rights, as well as numerous articles in his doctoral field of mathematics. During the 1920s, his weekly column appeared in more than one hundred newspapers. The following piece is excerpted from Miller's 1905 pamphlet, *As To the Leopard's Spots, an Open Letter to Thomas Dixon, Jr.* The pamphlet was Miller's response to *The Leopard's Spots,* the first of three novels in Thomas Dixon's Ku Klux Klan trilogy, a series in which the white, segregationist author advocated lynching and racial terrorism as a means for limiting African American freedom and self-determination in the South.

FROM *AS TO THE LEOPARD'S SPOTS: AN OPEN LETTER TO THOMAS DIXON, JR.*

Your fundamental thesis is that "no amount of education of any kind, industrious, classical or religious, can make a Negro a white man or bridge the chasm of the centuries which separates him from the white man in the evolution of human history." This doctrine is as old as human oppression. Calhoun made it the arch stone in the defense of Negro slavery—and lost.

This is but a recrudescence of the doctrine which was exploited and exploded during the anti-slavery struggle. Do you recall the school of pro-slavery scientists who demonstrated beyond doubt that the Negro's skull was too thick to comprehend the substance of Aryan knowledge? Have you not read in the discredited scientific books of that period, with what triumphant acclaim it was shown that the Negro's shape and size of skull, facial angle, and cephalic configuration rendered him forever impervious to the white man's civilization? But all enlightened minds are now as ashamed of that doctrine as they are of the one time dogma that the Negro had no soul. We become aware of mind through its manifestations. Within forty years of only partial opportunity, while playing as it were in the back yard of civilization, the American Negro has cut down his illiteracy by over fifty percent; has produced a professional class, some fifty thousand strong, including ministers, teachers, doctors, lawyers, editors, authors, architects, engineers, and all higher lines of listed pursuits in which white men are engaged; some three thousand Negroes have taken collegiate degrees, over three hundred being from the best institutions in the North and West established for the most favored white youth; there is scarcely a first-class institution in America, excepting some three or four in the South, that is without colored students who pursue their studies generally with success, and sometimes with distinction; Negro inventors have taken out four hundred patents as a contribution to the mechanical genius of America; there are scores of Negroes who, for conceded ability and achievements, take respectable rank in the company of distinguished Americans.

It devolves upon you, Mr. Dixon, to point out some standard, either of intelligence, character or conduct to which the Negro can not conform. Will you please tell a waiting world just what is the psychological difference between the races? No reputable authority, either of the old or the new school of psychology, has yet pointed out any sharp psychic discriminant. There is not a single intellectual, moral or spiritual excellence attained by the white race to which the Negro does not yield an appreciative response. If you could show that the Negro was incapable of mastering the intricacies of Aryan speech, that he could not comprehend the intellectual basis of European culture, or apply the apparatus of practical knowledge, that he could not be made amenable to the white man's ethical code or appreciate his spiritual motive, then your case would be proved. But in default of such demonstration, we must relegate your eloquent pronouncement to the realm of generalization and prophecy, an easy and agreeable exercise of the mind in which the romancer is ever prone to indulge.

The inherent, essential and unchangeable inferiority of the Negro to the white man lies at the basis of your social philosophy. You disdain to examine the validity of your fondly cherished hope. You follow closely in the wake of Tom Watson,[1] in the June number of his homonymous magazine. You both hurl your thesis of innate racial inferiority at the head of Booker T. Washington. You use the same illustrations, the same arguments, set forth in the same order of recital, and for the most part in identical language. This seems to be an instance of great minds, or at least of minds of the same grade, running in the same channel.

These are your words: "What contribution to human progress have the millions of Africa, who inhabit this planet made during the past four thousand years? Absolutely nothing." These are the words of Thomas Watson spoken some two months previous: "What does civilization owe to the Negro race? Nothing! Nothing!! Nothing!!!" You answer the query with the most emphatic negative noun and the strongest qualifying adjective in the language. Mr. Watson, of a more ecstatic temperament, replies with the same noun and six exclamation points. One rarely meets, outside of yellow journalism, with such lavishness of language, wasted upon a hoary dogma. A discredited dictum that has been bandied about the world from the time of Canaan to Calhoun is revamped and set forth with as much ardor and fervency of feeling as if discovered for the first time and proclaimed for the illumination of a waiting world.

But neither boastful asseveration on your part nor indignant denial on mine will affect the facts of the case. That Negroes in the average are not equal in developed capacity to the white race, is a proposition which it would be as simple to affirm as it is silly to deny. The Negro represents a backward race which has not yet taken a commanding part in the progressive movement of the world. In the great cosmic scheme of things, some races reach the lime light of civilization ahead of others. But that temporary, forwardness does not argue inherent superiority is as evident as any fact of history. An unfriendly environment may hinder and impede the one, while fortunate circumstances may quicken and spur the other. Relative superiority is only a transient phase of human development. You tell us that: "The Jew had achieved a civilization—had his poets, prophets, priests and kings, when our Germanic ancestors were still in the woods cracking cocoanuts and hickory nuts with the monkeys." Fancy some learned Jew at that day citing your query about the contribution of the Germanic races to the culture of the human spirit, during the thousands of years of their existence! Does the progress of history not prove that races may lie dormant and fallow for ages and then break suddenly into prestige and power? Fifty years ago you doubtless would have ranked Japan among the benighted nations and hurled at their heathen heads some derogatory query as to their contribution to civilization. But since the happenings at Mukden and Port Arthur, and Portsmouth,[2] I suppose that you are ready to change your mind. Or maybe since the Jap has proved himself "a first class fighting man," and able to cope on equal terms with the best breeds of Europe, you will claim him as belonging to the white race, notwithstanding his pig eye and yellow pigment.

In the course of history the ascendency of the various races and nations of men is subject to strange variability. The Egyptian, the Jew, the Indian, the Greek, the Roman, the Arab, has each had his turn at domination. When the earlier nations were in their zenith of art and thought and song, Franks and Britains, and Germans were roaming through dense forests, groveling in subterranean caves, practicing barbarous rites, and chanting horrid incantations to graven gods. In the proud days of Aristotle, the ancestors of Newton and Shakespeare and Bacon could not count beyond the ten fingers. As compared with the developed civilization of the period, they were a backward, though as subsequent development has shown, by no means an inferior race. There were hasty philosophers in that day who branded these people with the everlasting stamp of inferiority. The brand of philosophy portrayed in *Tom Watson's Magazine*[3] has flourished in all ages of the world.

The individuals of a backward race are not, as such, necessarily inferior to those of a more advanced people. The vast majority of any race is composed of ordinary and inferior folk. To use President Roosevelt's expression, they cannot pull their own weight. It is only the few choice individuals, reinforced by a high standard of social efficiency, that are capable of adding to the civilization of the world.

There is no hard and fast line dividing the two races on the scale of capacity. There is the widest possible range of variation within the limits of each. A philosopher and a fool may not only be members of the same race but of the same family. No scheme of classification is possible which will include all white men and shut out all Negroes. According to any test of excellence that yours and Mr. Watson's ingenuity can devise, some Negroes will be superior to most white men; no stretch of ingenuity or strain of conscience has yet devised a plan of franchise which includes all of the members of one race and excludes all those of the other. Learned opinion on the other side ought, at least, to weigh as much against your thesis as your own fulminations count in favor of it. You surely have high respect for the authority of Thomas Jefferson.—In a letter to Benjamin Banneker, the Negro astronomer, the author of the great declaration wrote: "Nobody wishes more than I do to see such proofs as you exhibit that nature has given to our black brethren talents equal to those of the other colors of men, and that the apparent want of them is owing merely to the degraded condition of their existence, both in Africa and America."

Mr. William Mathews, a noted author, writing some time ago in the *North American Review*, asserts: "We affirm that the inferiority of the Negro has never been proven, nor is there any good ground to suppose that he is forever to maintain his relative position, or that he is inferior to the white man in any other sense than some white races are inferior to each other."[4]

Prof. N. S. Shaler,[5] a native of the South, and Professor in Harvard University, writes in the Arena: "There are hundreds and thousands of black men who in capacity, are to be ranked with the superior persons of the dominant race, and it is hard to say that in any evident feature of mind they characteristically differ from their white fellow citizens."

Benjamin Kidd,[6] in his work on *Social Evolution* declares that the Negro child shows no inferiority, and that the deficiency which he seems to manifest in after life is due to his dwarfing and benumbing environment. Prof. John Spencer Bassett, of Trinity College, North Carolina, has had the courage to state the belief that the Negro would gain equality some day. He also tells us that Dr. Booker Washington, whom Mr. Watson takes so sharply to task for hinting that the Negro may be superior to some white men, is the greatest man with a single exception, that the South has produced in a hundred years. This is indeed a suggestion of Negro superiority, with a vengeance. In the judgment of this distinguished Southerner, one Negro, at least, is superior to millions of his white fellow citizens, including the editor of *Tom Watson's Magazine* and the author of *The Leopard's Spots*.

But, rejoins the objector: "if the Negro possesses this inherent capacity, why has he not given the world the benefit of it during the course of history?" Capacity is potential rather than a dynamic mode of energy. Whatever native capacity the mind may possess, it must be stimulated and reinforced by social accomplishments before it can show great achievements. In arithmetic a number has an inherent and local value, the latter being by far the more powerful function in numerical calculation. The individual may count for much but the social efficiency counts for most. It is absolutely impossible for a Bacon[7] to thrive among the Bushmen[8] or a Herbert Spencer[9] among the Hottentots.[10] The great names of the world always arise among the people who, for the time being are in the forefront of the world's movements. We do not expect names of the first degree of lustre to arise among suppressed and submerged classes.

In confirmation of this view let us turn for a moment to the pages of history. Mr. Lecky[11] tells us in his "History of European Morals":

> I regard it as one of anomalies of history that within the narrow limits and scanty population of the Greek states should have arisen men who in almost every conceivable form of genius, in philosophy, in ethics, in dramatic and lyric poetry, in written and spoken eloquence, in statesmanship, in sculpture, in painting, and probably also in music, should have attained almost or altogether the highest limits of human perfection.

Mr. Galton[12] in his "Hereditary Genius" tells us: "We have no men to put beside Socrates and Phidias. The millions of Europe breeding as they have done for the subsequent two thousand years have never produced their equals. It follows from all this that the average ability of the Athenian race is, on the lowest estimate, very nearly two grades higher than our own, that is about as much as our race is above that of the African Negro." And yet this intellectual race, this race of Phidias[13] and Homer, of Plato and Socrates, has continued for two thousand years in a state of complete intellectual stagnation. When they lost their political nationality and become submerged beneath the heavy weight of oppression, to use the language of MacCaulay, "their people have degenerated into timid slaves and their language into a barbarous jargon." Can there be any stronger proof of the fact that great achievements depend upon environment and social stimulus rather than innate capacity?

Where now is the boasted glory of Egypt and Babylon, of Nineveh and Tyre?[14] Expeditions from distant continents are sent to unearth the achievements of renowned ancestors beneath the very feet of their degenerate descendants, as a mute reminder to the world of the transiency of human greatness.

The Jews seem to form an exception to this rule, but the exception is seeming rather than real. While they have lost their political integrity, they have preserved their spiritual nationality. The race of Moses and Paul and Jesus still produces great names though not of the same grade of glory as their prototypes of old.

Our own country has not escaped the odium of intellectual inferiority. The generation has scarcely passed away in whose ears used to ring the standing sneer "Who reads an American Book?" It was in the day of Thomas Jefferson that a learned European declared: "America has not produced one good poet, one able mathematician, one man of genius in a single art or science." In response to this charge, Jefferson enters an eloquent special plea. He says: "When we shall have existed as a people as long as the Greeks did before they produced a Homer, the Romans a Virgil, the French a Racine,[15] the English a Shakespeare and Milton, should this reproach be still true, we will inquire from what unfriendly cause it has proceeded." How analogous to this is the reproach which you and Mr. Watson, treading the track of Thomas Nelson Page, and those of his school of thought, now hurl against the Negro race? The response of Jefferson defending the American colonies from the reproach of innate inferiority will apply with augmented emphasis to ward off similar charges against the despised and rejected Negro. A learned authority tells us that—"Hardly two centuries have passed since Russia was covered with a horde of barbarians among whom it would have been as difficult to find any example of intellectual cultivation and refinement as at this day to find the same phenomenon at Timbuctoo or among the Negroes of Georgia or Alabama." It is well for the good fame of the Russian people that *Tom Watson's Magazine* did not exist in those days.

According to a study of the distribution of ability in the United States by Hon. Henry Cabot Lodge, the little State of Massachusetts has produced more men of distinction and achievement than all the South combined. "In architecture, agriculture, manufactures, finance, legislation, sculpture, religion, organization, painting, music, literature, science, the wedding of the fine arts to religion," the South is relatively backward as compared with other sections of the country. But this lack of comparative achievement is not due at all to innate inferiority of Southern white men to their brethren in higher latitudes. Mr. Thomas Nelson Page in his famous book on the Old South,[16] accepts this derogatory fact and explains its cause with much ingenuity. The white people of the South claim, or rather boast of, a race prepotency and inheritance as great as that of any breed of men in the world. But they clearly fail to show like attainment.

It would evidently be unfair to conclude that the white race in Georgia is inherently inferior to the people of New England because it has failed to produce names of like renown. The difference in wealth, culture and bracing tone of environments are quite sufficient to account for the difference in results. I think that you and Mr. Watson will be generous enough to concede to the Negro the benefit of the same argument which the defenders of the South resort to in justification of its own relative backwardness. The Negro has never, during the whole course of history, been surrounded by those influences which tend to strengthen and develop the mind. To expect the Negroes of Georgia to produce a great general like Napoleon when they are not even allowed to carry arms, or to deride them for not producing scholars like those of the Renaissance when a few years ago they were forbidden the use of letters, verges closely upon the outer rim of absurdity. Do you look for great Negro statesmen in States where black men are not allowed to vote? Mr. Watson can tell something about the difficulty of being a statesman in Georgia, against the protest of the ruling political ring. He tried it. Above all, for Southern white men to berate the Negro for failing to gain the highest rounds of distinction, reaches the climax of cruel inconsistency. One is reminded of the barbarous Teutons, in *Titus Andronicus*,[17] who, after cutting out the tongue and hacking off the hands of the lovely Lavinia, ghoulishly chided her for not calling for sweet water with which to wash her delicate hands.

Here is another specimen of the grade of reasoning to which the readers of *Tom Watson's Magazine* are treated:

"Let me repeat to you, Doctor, the unvarnished truth, for it may do you good. The advance made by your race in America is the reflection of the white man's civilization. Just that and nothing more. The Negro lives in the light of the white man's civilization and reflects a part of that light."

Here again we come across the thread bare argument of the advocates of suppression and subordination of the Negro. The aptitude of any people for progress is tested by the readiness with which they absorb and assimilate the environment of which they form a part. I wonder if Mr. Watson would contend that the red Indian shows capacity for civilization because he neither borrows nor imitates. Civilization is not a spontaneous generation with any race or nation known to history, but the torch is handed down from race to race and from age to age, and gains in brilliancy as it goes. The progress made by the Negro has been natural and inevitable. Does Mr. Watson expect the American Negro to invent an alphabet before he learns to read? The Negro has advanced in exactly the same fashion that the white race has advanced, by taking advantage of all that has gone before. Other men have labored and we have entered into their labors. The Japanese did not invent the battleship, modern artillery, or the modern manual of arms, but they used them pretty effectively. A young race, just like the individual, must first appropriate and apply what has already gone before. The white male has no exclusive proprietorship in civilization. White man's civilization is as much a misnomer as the white man's multiplication table. It is the equal inheritance of any one who can appropriate and apply it. This is the only practicable test of a people's capacity.

I have no doubt that Mr. Watson would say that the million white people of Georgia are a very capable folk. And yet how many of them have added anything to the processes of civilization? They have simply entered into, and carried on the processes already established. When Mr. Watson concedes the Negro's ability to do this much he negatives the whole argument of inferiority.

1905

NOTES

1. Georgia attorney Thomas Edward Watson (1856–1922), whose failed 1908 presidential campaign emphasized his embrace of white supremacist beliefs; he was elected to the U.S. Senate in 1920.

2. Refers to the Battle of Mukden (fought in February and March of 1905) and the Battle of Port Arthur (fought in February of 1904), key battles in the Russo-Japanese War; and the Portsmouth Peace Conference, at which the two nations signed the Treaty of Portsmouth (on September 5, 1905), ending the conflict.

3. Published by Georgia attorney and 1908 presidential candidate Thomas Edward Watson, who used the periodical as an instrument for the dissemination of antiblack, white-supremacist propaganda.

4. Attorney William Matthews, writing in the July 1889 issue of the *North American Review*.

5. Nathaniel Southgate Shaler (1841–1906), professor of geology and dean of the Lawrence Scientific School, Harvard University.

6. English sociologist Benjamin Kidd (1858–1916).

7. English philosopher, author, scientist, and statesman Francis Bacon (1561–1626).

8. Derogatory colonial name for the indigenous hunter-gatherer peoples of Southern Africa, including the !Kung, Naro, Tsoa, Gua, and others.

9. English philosopher, scientist, anthropologist, and author Herbert Spencer (1820–1903).

10. Derogatory colonial term for the Khoekhoe or Khoikhoi, the cattle-herding people of Southern Africa, especially the Cape region of South Africa.

11. Irish poet, historian, and political theorist William Edward Hartpole Lecky (1838–1903).

12. English psychologist, anthropologist, author, and inventor Francis Galton (1822–1911).

13. Greek sculptor and architect, designer of Athena Parthenos (480 BCE–430 BCE).

14. Ancient cities on the Tigris River and the Mediterranean Sea, respectively. These cities symbolized the lost grandeur of fallen empires for many writers of the Victorian era, as exemplified in Kipling's "Recessional": "Lo, all our pomp of yesterday / Is one with Nineveh and Tyre!"

15. French dramatist Jean-Baptiste Racine (1639–1699).

16. *The Old South: Essays Social and Political*, published in 1893.

17. An early tragedy by the playwright William Shakespeare (1564–1616).

THOMAS HORATIUS MALONE (CA. 1872-?)

A native of Augusta, Georgia, Thomas Horatius Malone was educated at Atlanta University and the University of Michigan Law School. In the 1890s, after completing his legal studies, Malone relocated to Atlanta, where he opened a law firm with African American attorney and Republican Party activist William A. Pledger, the founder of several black newspapers. Like Pledger, Malone was involved in both regional and national politics, serving twice as a presidential elector for the state Republican Party. A writer as well as attorney and political activist, Malone published fiction and poetry in a number of African American newspapers and magazines, including *Voice of the Negro, The New York Age,* the Washington, DC-based *Colored American* newspaper, and the Boston-based *Colored American* magazine. Malone's poems address popular themes (love, the changing seasons) and stylistic trends (dialect and local color), while his fiction is more directly focused on civil rights and social justice issues. The short story "An Unheeded Signal," first published in the May 1902 issue of the *Colored American* magazine, explores the role of personal values and individual action in either sustaining or resisting racial violence.

AN UNHEEDED SIGNAL

It was eight o'clock and the last passenger train for the night, due to stop, had just left the little station of Cameron. The rapid puffing of the engine was fast being lost to hearing in the distance. The passengers who had just arrived and the curious crowd that always gathered to witness the arrival were slowly wending their way up the wide street toward the center of the town. Presently all were gone except John Sanderson, the telegraph operator and agent, and his friend, Will Compton who frequently dropped in to talk with John in the evenings. The two were preparing to leave when Sanderson was attracted to the telegraph instrument by an unusual clicking. He was in time to catch this message: "Special with soldiers and prisoner passes Cameron at 10. No. 29 has orders." Turning to Compton he informed him of the message, concluding "What do you suppose it means Bill?"

"I dunno an' yes I do too; The truth is that the boys have jes' about caught that nigger at Doratown that burned that barn an' stock an' wanted to put a few bullets in his carcass when up comes the governor an' orders out them soldiers an' a special train to take him to some other place for safe keepin'."

"That's just about what it is" came the reply. Then they both were silent for several minutes. It was the operator who next spoke:

"What are you thinking about so hard Bill?"

"Nothin' 't all. What you thinkin' 'bout yo'self?"

"Nothing much. Let's see! Number 29, the local freight, pulls up here at 9:30 and takes the siding for 38, the limited express, and then—why 29 is due to pull out at 10; guess her orders are to wait on the special." Again there was silence.

"Penny for your thoughts Bill."

"You kin have 'em for less than that an' since you are a white man I don't mind telling 'em. I was jest a thinkin' how much coal the railroad would save ef some thoughtful man should hang out a red lantern close to the middle of the main line jest about four or five minutes before that special comes along an' let it stay there until the man in the cab saw it. They don't run over red lights, do they John?"

"Not much; but go on with your story; It's beginning to be interesting."

"Well she'd be apt to stop good an' hard an' then the conductor would be a nosing aroun' askin' what's the trouble, an' swearin' and them cigarette smokin' soldiers would be falling over each other to get out an' see what the matter was, since they had orders not to stop an' specially since the conductor was cussing so loud an' the nigger—well he'd be lonesome unless some of the town boys here that was hid in the bushes went in an' took him out of the back door. Then there wouldn't be any use for that special to burn any coal further down the road. It takes smart men to run this country I tell you."

"I'm in the service of the railroad," came from the operator, with emphasis on the "I'm."

"I aint, an' come to think about it, I s'pose it's time for to be movin'. Good night John, be a good boy because you're in the service of the railroad an' I aint. Go home and go to bed an' take yo' rest. They didn't say for you to meet that special" and Compton hurried from the place without taking time to say good night to his friend.

"I wonder if he really means to do it," muttered the operator aloud. "Oh well what's the odds any how, but Mister Sanderson, for your part, you must be at home when that special runs and you must be able to prove that you were there in case proof is necessary," and having finished checking his accounts and assorting some papers the operator locked the door and left.

Scarcely had the sound of his footstep become inaudible in the distance when a rustling noise was heard behind the benches and boxes in the corner of the little station building.

--- ---

"Reckon dey forgot dat ole Mose stayed in dis place at night. Anyhow he wasn't 'sleep an' he ain't too deaf to heah what's gwine on eroun' him. Mister Will Compton, you er mighty bully, you is, al ovah dis county, an' Mister John San'erson, I always 'steemed you might high, long as I been 'quainted wid you, but I done learn something tonight. Reckon I'll go out an' take a little walk an' git some fresh air."

The clock in the little court house had just struck nine and all was quiet in Cameron. A close observer might have discovered forms stealthily gliding toward the station in groups of twos and threes. A light that had been burning dimly in a hardware store suddenly went out and two men walked out of the door, one carrying a rope that was not even concealed.

The clock struck the half hour and a great puffing engine, pulling a long string of freight cars, ran up to the station and changed to a side track. In ten minutes a red light in the sky, gradually getting nearer and brighter, marked the approach of No. 38, the limited express. In five minutes more it thundered past the station. The freight train still kept the side track. A hundred yards above the station, in a little clump of bushes and trees, were gathered the forms that had been so mysteriously flitting to and for a short while before. Five minutes of ten and a man, tall and wiry, stepped up on the tracks in front of the station carrying a glowing red lantern.

"What's up?" shouted the engineer of the freight to him.

"Nothin' jest going to flag the limited to see if they'll stop an' take me down to Monterey."

"Friend, she's gone full twelve minutes and by this she's due to be past Monterey, and guess she is; by the way, she passed us."

"Alright," said the man with the lantern, "I'll jest wait erwhile for one of the boys that promised to be here to give me a package for a friend of his down the road. 'Pears like he's powerful long time gitting here. Why ain't you pulled out?"

"Got orders to let some sort of special pass me here. Some of them big guns, I suppose, going down to Florida to cut up."

"Reckon so," retorted the lantern carrier, "lots of 'em ought to be put to plowin' and I'd love to be the overseer of 'em. Reckon I'd learn 'em a right smart about what honest folks ought to do."

Two miles up the track the special was dashing on toward Cameron. Suddenly the engineer saw ahead a red lantern slowly moving near the track. Cautiously he peered through the little window in front of him to see if his eyes were true. He realized that he was being signalled.

"What have we yonder?" he called to his fireman.

Cap, on my life it's a red light and they're signaling us to stop."

"Well, I have never yet run over that sort of signal, and I will hardly do so to-night," replied the man at the throttle, while the train gradually slowed down and stopped. And just as Will Compton had predicted, in his conversation with the operator in the early part of the night, when train had been stopped by the danger signal, the conductor jumped down and ran ahead, while close behind him scampered all of the military, almost every man without his gun and all bent on finding out the trouble. If there had been any that called for their services they would have been little prepared to meet it.

"Who stopped this train?" demanded the conductor in an angry tone.

"Me, Cap'n, jes' me, and ef you'll be so pleased to 'low me to tell you, I'll 'splain mah reason fer so doin'. You got a man on dis train what done some great crime somewhar up de road, so dey say, and to-night I overheard a gen'man talk like he was gwine to stop dis train, which I believes is de special he was talkin' about, an' he said how it would be er good thing to wave you down wid er danger lamp. I heard ev'y word he had ter say an' I tell you, Cap'n, he's er man dat don't stand in fear of nothin' when he wants ter do a thing, mo' specially ef its er bad thing. Yas sah, I know in reason dat he's er layin' fer dis train and dat he' s got mo men wid him, beca'se somehow it look like he's got er way of leadin' men into trouble who wouldn't think of such er thing ef it wasn't fer him an' his argyments 'bout things. I aint meddlin' in yo' business, Cap'n, but I jest couldn't he'p f'om stoppin' you beca'se I'm sartain dat he's gwine ter fling out dat danger lamp."

"Throw it out where?" asked the the Captain of the company impatiently. "Why don't you come down to the point? Where is this to happen at and how many men are in the crowd, and are they armed?"

"Mind you, sah, I hab not 'seen dese men and I don' t know zac'ly dat dey is dar, but to best of my belief dey is right dar waitin'. Yes, sah, dey object is to throw out dat signal at Cameron, an' with er heap of other men, as I said befo', wid guns, take de man you got on board what dey say done dat great crime, an' I s'posed dey would be trouble fer you all, and maybe somebody might git hurt. Yas, sah, I don't take no sides wid nobody what does dese great crimes, fer I'm er man for peace; but it didn't look right ter me ter hav a great killin' befo' knowin' dat a man was guilty, an' dat's de reason Mose stopped dis train."

The conductor went back to the engine and related the engineer what had been told to him, venturing the opinion that there might be trouble ahead and that there was need of caution.

"You and your soldiers go on back to the train and get aboard," was all that the man in the cab had to say. Turning to his fireman he said: "Partner, you've been putting in coal in 98 for three years while I've been on this box and you've never seen me run over a red light yet; but you'll see me do it to-night, danger or no danger. That's a cowardly way of murdering people, by flagging my engine, and it looks like they want to make me a party to it. They may take me out of this cab to-morrow but I'll break one rule of the road to-night. Now, let her have all the coal that you can give her."

A mile and three-quarters down the track another light was burning; behind the bushes and trees rifles were being lifted and handled, while nearer came the roar of the train. Up in the signal station the white light of safety was glowing, and telling the rapidly approaching train to go on, for all was safe; down near the track the red light of danger was waving frantically, warning the train to stop. Did the man in the engine see it? Surely; for how could he fail to? If he did was he deliberately running over it? Evidently, for the speed was not decreasing, and in a few seconds the train tore wildly past the station and, with a shriek from the whistle that was piercing, left Cameron behind.

"What was the trouble, Bill?" came from a hundred throats.

"I dunno, but I hope she'll turn over on Turpin trestle and land somebody in hell, and I don't care much if it ain't the nigger."

In a little cottage about half a mile from the station a young man looking haggard and nervous had just heard the blast of the passing engine. He sprang up from his chair. "Thank God she didn't stop. After all I'm glad of it, but I wonder if Bill's nerve failed him."

Three days afterward, when the afternoon newspapers had been put off the train, Will Compton glanced over the headlines. He managed to make out these words: "The Wrong Man. Negro Arrested at Doratown for Barn Burning Clearly Shown to be Innocent."

"Did yon meet the special the other night?" he inquired of the operator.

"Not much. I was too sleepy and went to bed as soon as I got home," came the reply.

"Same here," said Compton, as he dropped the paper and looked out of the window.

"Look out heah, boss, I don't want to run ovah none of my white folks wid dis truck of cotton. Ole Mose like to do good in dis worl' an' not harm de short time he got to stay heah."

"John," said the engineer of engine 98 to the operator one day, "there's an old Negro in this town who deserves a life saving medal. I'll tell you all about it some time if you'll promise not to say anything about it."

"All right," said Sanderson; "I promise, and when you tell me about this Negro I'll tell you about an engineer friend of mine who deserves the same sort of adornment; but you musn't tell about this either, because I promised the faithful old black man who can't keep anything from me that I would never mention it."

1905

PRISCILLA JANE THOMPSON (1871-1942)

Priscilla Jane Thompson was one of six children born in Rossmoyne, Ohio, to Clara Jane and John Henry Thompson, former slaves from Virginia. The sister of poets Clara Ann and Aaron Belford Thompson, she lived all of her childhood and at least a portion of her adult life in the town of her birth. Neither she nor her sister Clara ever married. Thompson published two collections of her poetry, *Ethiope Lays,* in 1900, and *Gleanings of Quiet Hours,* in 1907. Like her sister, she produced poems in Standard English and in the stylized dialect form that was popular in her day. Of the following selections, "Freedom at McNealy's" first appeared in her earlier collection. "The Husband's Return" and "A Home Greeting" were both published in *Gleanings of Quiet Hours.*

FREEDOM AT MCNEALY'S

All around old Chattanooga,
   War had left his wasteful trace;
And the rebels, quelled and baffled,
   Freed reluctantly their slaves.

On his spacious, cool, veranda—
   Stood McNealy, gaunt and tall,
With bowed head, and long arms folded,
   Pond'ring on his blacks, enthralled.

Years and years, he'd been their master,
   Harsh and stern his reign had been;
Many an undeserving lashing,
   He had rudely given them.

All his life he'd been a despot;
   Ruling all with iron hand;
Never till this deadly conflict,
   Had he e'er brooked one command.

But his lately rich plantation,
    Sacked by Union men he see;
And the bitter dregs stand waiting:
    He must set his bondmen free.

From their work, they come together,
    At their master's last command,
And at length, well-nigh two hundred,
    'Fore the large veranda stand.

Oh! that motley crowd before him,
    Speaks the wrong one man has done;
For his constant, dire oppression,
    Can be seen on every one.

Men of middle age all palsied,
    By hard work and sorrow's pain;
Blighted youths and orphaned infants;
    All had felt his cruel reign.

There were women fair who knew him,
    To be more of brute than man;
There were children clinging to them,
    Through whose veins his own blood ran.

Widowed hearts in swarthy bosoms,
    Ever bled in patient pain,
O'er their loved ones, sold before them,
    To increase McNealy's gain.

All of this preys on McNealy,
    As before his slaves he stands;
And his low'ring, dogged, expression,
    Speaks the power that's left his hands.

And, with quivering voice and husky,
    Tells he that each one is free;
Tells them of his heavy losses,
    Meanly seeking sympathy.

And the soft hearts of his vassals,
    Melt, as only Ethiopes' can;
As with brimming eyes and kind words,
    Each one grasps his tyrant's hand.

One by one, they've all departed;
    Man and woman, boy and girl;
Void of learning, inexperienced,
    Launched upon the crafty world.

But one cabin is not empty,
    Two old souls are kneeling there;
In the throes of desolation,
    They have sought their Lord in prayer.

They have never tasted freedom,
    And their youthful hopes are fled;
Now, the freedom they are seeking,
    Is with Jesus and the dead.

Poor aunt Jude and uncle Simon!
    Freedom brings to them no cheer;
They have served McNealy's fam'ly—
    For threescore, or more of years.

Steep and rough, the road they've traveled,
    Many were their heart felt [sic] groans—
Yet they cleave unto their tyrant,
    For his lash, is all they've known.

Like a bird of long confinement,
    Cleaves unto his open cage,
These two wretched slaves, benighted,
    Clave to bondage, in their age.

And they sought McNealy humbly,
    With their hearts filled to the brim;
Told him, all their days remaining,
    They would gladly give to him.

And McNealy, pleased and flattered,
　　With no feeling of remorse,
Takes them back into his service,
　　As you would a faithful horse.

1900

THE HUSBAND'S RETURN

The proud, majestic Southern sun,
　　Let fall a golden gleam;
It flickered through a leafy bower,
And fell aslant a traveler's brow,
　　And roused him from his dream.

A finer specimen of man,
　　Was never cast in clay;
A swarthy Hercules was he,
With that rash intrepidity,
　　Of manhood's earliest day.

He, an emancipated slave,
　　From Rappahanock's[1] side;
Assured by Lincoln's strong decree,
Had journeyed southward, bold and free,
　　To claim his stolen bride.

From many a camp of Union men,
　　He'd found his rations free;
And by their kindly guiding hand,
He now locates the plundered land,
　　Where his young wife must be.

A three hours' tramp 'cross rugged hills,
　　Footsore, yet full of life;
Now brings him to the handsome gate,
Where flowers, bedeck a mansion great,
　　The prison of his wife.

And as he boldly seeks the porch,
    On entering through the gate,
The master, from his wicker chair,
With grim forebodings, wildly glare,
    As he his errand wait.

Advancing nearer, now at hand,
    He recognize the face,
The same firm mouth, the flashing eye,
The trouble wrought in days gone by,
    Comes back with no good grace.

"Well Steve, you scoundrel, what's to pay?"
    He said, with rising fear;
"You've run away, that is a fact,
I'll have you flogged, and shipped right back,
    What do you want back here?"

Young Stephen, to keep down his wrath,
    His strongest will employ;
He simply says, "All slaves are free,
The news is heard where e'er I be;
    I want my wife and boy."

A white rage lights the planter's face,
    His oaths are fierce and wild;
He calls on demons from below,
To take him if a will he'd show,
    To yield the wife and child.

The rash young freedman with one bound,
    Had seized his deadly foe,
But Providence sent "second thought,"
Before the murderous deed was wrought,
    He loosed his hold to go.

There played about that swarthy youth,
    As he strode down the path,
A threat'ning storm from rights bereft,

That stayed the planter's gasping breath,
    And took away his wrath.

"Stop, Steve! where are you going now?"
    He cried with deadly fear;
"Come, boy, now let me hear your plan,
Come, let us talk as man to man!
    Your wife is happy here."

Young Stephen flung an answer back,
    With fury in his eye,
That suddenly did take his breath,
And paled his face, as if grim death
    Had dropped down from the sky.

"I'm a-goin' to the barracks,
    An' fetch the "blue-coats"[2] here;
I swear this day I'll claim my wife,
Or you will pay it with your life,
    Long 'fore the night appear."

Swift to the dairy house hard by,
    A summon speeds the while;
A slender girl, with, sweet, dark eyes,
Comes quickly forth in glad surprise,
    Dangling a heavy child.

Young Stephen's wrath is all forgot,
    As with a cry of joy,
With kisses sweet and sighs of love,
The bright sun smiling from above,
    He clasps his wife and boy.

And, as he strained them to his breast,
    Where tumult late held sway,
A peace suffused his storm tossed heart,
That bade all gloomy moods depart,
    And lit with joy his way.

1907

A HOME GREETING

A pair of soft, black eyes,
    A velvet, dusky, cheek,
A flash of dazzling pearls,
    An Eden for me speak.

And next a soft embrace;
    My eyes drink to their fill,
The tender, liquid, depth,
    Of orbs that ever thrill.

A long, ecstatic, kiss,
    That drowns all earthly strife:
What gift can e'er exceed,
    A pure, confiding, wife?

1907

NOTES

1. A river in eastern Virginia, running from the Blue Ridge Mountains to the Chesapeake Bay.

2. Union soldiers.

CLARA ANN THOMPSON (1869–1949)

Poet Clara Ann Thompson was one of six children born in Rossmoyne, Ohio, to Virginia-born ex-slaves Clara Jane and John Henry Thompson. She was educated in the Rossmoyne public schools as well under the guidance of private tutors. Though she was trained for a career in teaching, Thompson spent much of her life working as a speaker and writer in Cincinnati, Ohio. She was active in many local and national organizations, including the NAACP. Two of Thompson's siblings were also poets, sister Priscilla Jane and brother Aaron Belford Thompson. Clara Thompson never married, and she lived at least part of her adult life with siblings Priscilla Jane and Garland Yancey Thompson her oldest sibling. She published her first volume of poetry, *Songs from the Wayside,* in 1908. The collection included works written in both Standard English and the popular dialect style. This collection was followed in 1926 by one additional volume, *A Garland of Poems.* The following selections were first published in her earlier collection.

JOHNNY'S PET SUPERSTITION

Teacher, Jimmie's toe is bleedin';
Stumped it, comin' down the road;
I jest knowed that he would do it,
'Cause he went an' killed a toad.

Teacher, you jest ought to see it;
Oh, the blood's jest spurtin' out!
You won't ketch me killin' toad-frogs,
When I see them hoppin' 'bout.

"Oh, now, Johnny, that's all nonsense!
I told you sometime ago,
That the killing of a hop-toad
Wouldn't make you hurt your toe;

"Who told you that silly story?"
Grandma said that it is so;
She's much older than you, teacher,
An' I guess she ought to know.

"Come, now, Johnny, don't be saucy;"
Teacher, grandma did say so,
An' she says: 'You No'thern cullud,
Don't b'lieve nothin' any mo'.

'Cause you say there ain't no speerits,
'Tain't bad luck to kill a cat,
Dog a-howlin' ain't no death-sign,
An' you've made me b'lieve all that.

But I jest can't b'lieve this, teacher,
'Cause I'm 'fraid to—Don't you see?
Bet you wouldn't b'lieve it either,
Ef you went barefoot, like me.

1908

MRS. JOHNSON OBJECTS

Come right in this house, Will Johnson!
Kin I teach you dignity?
Chasin' aft' them po' white children,
Jest because you wan' to play.

Whut does po' white trash keer fah you?
Want you keep away fum them,
Next, they'll be-a-doin' meanness,
An' a-givin' you the blame.

Don't come mumblin' 'bout their playthings,
Yourn is good enough fah you;
'Twus the best that I could git you,
An' you've got to make them do.

Go'n' to break you fum that habit,
Yes, I am! An' mighty soon,

Next, you'll grow up like the white-folks,
All time whinin' fah the moon.

Runnin' with them po' white children—
Go'n' to break it up, I say!—
Pickin' up their triflin' habits,
Soon, you'll be as spilte as they.

Come on here, an' take the baby—
Mind now! Don't you let her fall—
'Fo' I'll have you runnin' with them,
I won't let you play at all.

Jest set there, an' mind the baby
Till I tell you—You may go;
An'jest let me ketch you chasin'
Aft' them white trash any mo'.

                                    1908

THE EASTER BONNET

John, look what Mis' Nelson give me,
When I cleaned for her today;
Mean, close-fisted, old white woman!
'Clare, I'll throw the thing away!

You may just say I've gone crazy,
When I wear a thing like that;
Just look at that 'bomination!
Who would call that thing a hat?

What say? 'Beggars can't be choosers?'
Didn't ask her for the thing—
Only said that Easter's coming,
An' I'd need a hat this spring.

Then she went upstairs a-prancing,
And I looked for something grand;
Next I knew, she come down, grinning,
With this fool thing in her hand.

Guess she knew I didn't like it,
For I just made out to say:
Much obliged to you Mis' Nelson,—
Got right up and come away.

John, I saw hats in her closet,
That she only bought last year,
An' says now they're out of fashion,
That I'd be too glad to wear.

But she would'nt give them to me,
'Fraid I'd hold my head too high;
Giving me this old-time bonnet!
'Clare, I'm mad enough to cry.

"Oh, don't mind old Mrs. Nelson,
Been an old fool all her life;
I'll buy you your Easter bonnet;
She don't have to clothe my wife.

"But I can't help laughing, Jennie,
When I see that turned-up nose;
Ha! ha! ha! guess you'll quit hinting
For the white-folks cast-off clothes."

                                    1908

A LULLABY

Hush ye, hush ye! honey, darlin',
Hush ye, now, an' go to sleep;
Mammy's got to wash them dishes,
An' she's got this floor to sweep.

You must think I'm made uv money,
An's got nothin' else to do,
But to set here, in this rocker,
Like a lady, holdin' you.

Now you's gone to laughin' at me;
Little rascal! Hush! I say,

Mammy's got to wash them dishes,
She ain't got no time to play.

Ef you don't quit lookin' at me,
With that little sassy eye,
I declare, I'll tell your daddy,
An' tonight, he'll make you fly.

Now jest look how you's a-laughin'!
See you's bound to have your way,
I'll jest have to set an' hold you;
Won't git nothin' done today.

                              1908

S. LAING WILLIAMS (1863-?)

Attorney and essayist Samuel Laing Williams Jr. was born in Savannah, Georgia, to parents Nancy and Samuel Laing Williams Sr. A graduate of the University of Michigan and the Columbian Law School in Washington, DC (now
George Washington University Law School), Williams was admitted to the
Illinois Bar in 1885. In 1887, he married lecturer and activist Fannie Barrier
Williams, and the two became fixtures in Chicago's African American activist
and literary circles. In addition to his work in private practice, Williams also
served for several years as the assistant U.S. attorney for the Northern District
of Illinois. In the following essay, published in *Alexander's Magazine* in November of 1908, Williams argues that the 20th century has ushered in a new
breed of black citizen, one whose departure from the previous generation's
alienation, poverty, and perceived stasis is manifest in his academic achievements, professional advancement, and economic gains.[1]

THE NEW NEGRO

The rise of man from a low estate to a high estate, from dependence to
independence, from ignorance to intelligence and self-sufficiency, is always
interesting, always important and always more or less disturbing. The immediate problem of this man is to get himself known, respected, and believed
in. He may be worthy, he may be aspiring, he may be competent for high
service, but he is mistrusted and even hated because he is aspiring. It is a
tremendously difficult thing for this new applicant for citizenship to gain the
good will and confidence of a whole nation of people who are in undisputed
power and control.

The difficulty is enhanced when this new man comes in the visage of
Othello and in the condition of dependence.

The new man merely asks for standing room, yet he is crowded back.
He asks to be heard and is silenced. He asks to be trusted and he is denied.
He pleads to be tested by his intelligence and his honor as a man, and he is
scorned. In short, he "asks for bread and is given a stone." His presence is a
menace, his proffered service is ignored. Indeed, all the higher laws of God and

man are set aside when this new man comes with his undisputed credentials of worth and sufficiency. Yet this new man, conscious of his worth, persists in his quest for recognition. He knows that what is right must eventually prevail.

No country can afford to deny the right of any man to be respected. Men of character and force are the chief assets of a nation. The greatest nations are those who have the highest uses for their best men. While this is true, yet the passion for keeping some men down is everywhere in evidence. This is so because the fixed opinion of men and things is hard to change. Give a man a bad name and it will pass current in spite of his innocence and his virtues.

In this great country of ours we freely judge and misjudge men according to our feelings. The worth of a man is not always a shield of protection against bad opinions of him. Whether we are liked or disliked, trusted or mistrusted, often depends upon such superficial things as race, color, intelligence, ignorance, poverty or wealth. The most unyielding of all separating causes between man and man is race prejudice. Race prejudice needs no definition. The sting of it, the mean force of it, and the cruelty of it are a part of our common experience. No race of men has been entirely free from opposition due to race prejudice, and the Negro race in America is conspicuously no exception to the rule.

For over two hundred years the force of race prejudice in this country has overridden justice, morality and religion, in keeping our people below the level of men of white complexion. By a strange perversity of human nature our very uprising in intelligence, moral worth and economic efficiency has been regarded as a menace to American civilization.

There is nothing to be gained by reopening this dark chapter in our nation's history. If we have suffered many things because of our worthy aspiration to deserve well of the American people, the American people have also suffered by violating the laws of God and man in their effort to establish two standards of righteousness, one black and one white. There are some things about which there can be no compromise. A righteous man is neither white nor black. He is simply a righteous man. To hate him because he is either white or black is wicked; to mistrust him is folly; to be afraid of him is cowardly. Somewhere and at some time or place in this great world of human beings such a man is needed and will find his place. It is sometimes said that the Negro race in America is on trial and it might be as fittingly added that the jury is packed and the verdict made up even before the evidence is heard. Hence the burden of our plea always is, hear the evidence. The evidence is more interesting than the possible verdict.

Some great things have been going on in this country of ours during the past forty years. Much of it is unseen, unknown and not believed, but is more or less distinctly felt in the social and economic life of the American people.

As a result of it all we have in this country today what may be fittingly called a "new Negro," and the race problem may be defined as the failure of the American people to recognize this new Negro. So hard and uncompromising has been the separation between the races that this new and well-equipped man of the hour has had no chance to reveal himself to those who still have in their minds types of the cotton field and log cabin Negro of fifty years ago. It seems to be human nature to dislike people we don't know. The Negro people of this country have moved on and up at such a wonderful pace that their splendid worth has dazed the American people.

It is not too much to say that the average American knows more about the Japanese and Chinese, who are separated from them by almost impossible barriers of differences, than he does about the race that for over two hundred years has been helping to build up a great nation. It is a long and weary distance from Jamestown to Tuskegee, and the pathway is strewn with suffering and madness, yet the journey has been made and all we ask of the American people is to turn around and at least recognize the size of our burden.

The New Negro is not a fictitious man. He is not a child of fortune—a man without a history—without an expanding soul and without a destiny. There have been two emancipations of the Negro race. The one was physical and was consummated in 1865; the other has been a continuous emancipation from slavish heritages of conditions and instincts, to a persistence and extent that few Americans can understand. The drastic and uncompromising laws of separations have made it impossible for the people in whose midst we live and move to feel the extent of this second emancipation. No recitals of mere facts and figures can tell the whole story of this wonderful self-emancipation. The test of a race's worth is the kind of men it is capable of producing. An Indian chief is merely stronger but not ethically better than the rest of his tribe. There are no distinguished Esquimaux. They are all on the low level of an ice-enduring existence. Out of such races no civilization develops, but its people are held everlastingly to the primal instincts of animalism.

The significant and compelling thing about the Negro race is that it has always shown a capacity for the highest and best things in our national life. As an illustration some facts and figures are significant. Emerson says somewhere that "it is inhuman not to believe in education, since amelioration is the law of life." Education has been the controlling passion of the Negro race. Within forty years they have overcome quite sixty percent of their illiteracy. Thousands of young Colored men and women have won academic degrees in many of the best colleges and universities of America and Europe. The Negro that most Americans picture as mendicant, shiftless and unenterprising, now pays taxes on over $300,000,000 worth of real estate. This race that is so greatly feared as a menace to Anglo-Saxon social morality has been busy since 1865 building churches, schools, colleges, hospitals, home for the aged, some thirty banks and taking a conspicuous part in all those movements that indicate an increase in civic virtue and individual morality. In other words, the man who forty-five years ago was a chattel has become in some instances a lawyer, a physician, a theologian, an artist, a poet, a journalist, a banker, a diplomat, a linguist, a soldier unafraid, an ardent patriot and a man who dares to have courage in the midst of discouragements. Who can afford not to respect men of this kind? Surely there must be some real soul, something heroic, in the man who can thus honorably give an account of himself. The chattel of the cotton field has become a gentleman in spirit and in fact. He is a self-made man and challenges the respect of all mankind. He asks to be respected for what he is and stands for in his new status and not for what the American people meanly think he is.

This new man has been wonderfully tested and has borne himself with heroic patience. He is a man of distinctly American spirit, in language, in religion, in democratic instincts, in enterprise, in his ethical impulses and patriotism, the most ardent of Americans, ready at all times to fight or work for our national security. He lives in the present, in spite of the people who think of him and treat him as a backward race.

Civilization has been defined as "the power of good men." Is this aphorism large enough to include men and women of African descent? Within two generations at least, five Negro men have added to the glory of American annals: Frederick Douglass, the orator; Booker T. Washington, the educator; Dunbar, the poet; Du Bois, the sociologist; Tanner, the artist;[2] Kelly Miller, the teacher, and Frank J. Grimke, the preacher.[3] A race that can produce a group of men such as these in a single generation cannot be forever written down as a race without an interesting future.

This new Negro is an optimist in spite of the wrongs that he endures. Formerly he complained without hope; now he hopes without complaint. The American who cannot see and appreciate this new man is himself blind and need not be feared. No race that has the power to redeem itself can be kept in an inferior position. When you can pity the man who wantonly hates you, you have achieved the mastery over him and his tribe.

The race problem of today, in spite of the people who think, feel and act as if it were the same as it was in 1860, is a new problem and may be defined: What shall be the status of this educated, high-spirited, ambitious and deserving man of the Negro race or this new Negro? He knocks and knocks persistently at the door of opportunity. Shall it be opened? Justice and fair play say, yes; race prejudice, in the spirit of 1860, says no. The American Negro has become well accustomed to the American "No." In a sort of triumphant spirit, the noble Frederick Douglass used to say, when beset on all sides by evil forces, in the dark days of the '60s: "I sometimes forget the color of my skin and remember that I am a man; I sometimes forget that I am hated of men and remember that I am loved of God." And so these black men of today, in spite of the recurrent fury of race prejudice, keep their faith in God and the growing spirit of tolerance of all mankind. Bad laws may be written and enforced to prevent a good man from being an uncontested citizen, but we feel strong in the fact that before man made us citizens, great nature made us men, and the man behind the citizen is more important than a man-made citizen. Let us be tested by what we deserve and the problem is solved. Let us not make the mistake of believing it is possible to compel any class of freemen in this Republic "to keep his place." A man's place in this country should be wherever he himself can make it.

Every Colored man or woman in this country who has come into prominence because of his or her worth has done so in defiance of all the evil forces that for two hundred years have insisted that this is a "white man's country." The Negro people have forces that for two hundred years have performed a great service by proving that you cannot found a great civilization on complexion alone. It is scarcely worthy a great nation of people to be afraid and become hysterical for fear of losing their social exclusiveness. While this new Negro is struggling upward through cruel repression to become a God-fearing and man-loving citizen of the world of mankind, our white friends are continuously haunted by the unworthy bugbear of "social equality." This new Negro asks for nothing that he dares not deserve and it is inhuman to expect him to be satisfied with less. If the right to vote, if the right to pay taxes, if the right to defend our position as American citizens and deserve the good opinion of the Lincolns and the Sumners of the past make for social equality, the fault must be theirs who feel so insecure of their social status. Certainly the tide of progress of one race of people must not be kept back until some other race can make itself socially impregnable. In the name of this social equality mania more sins have been committed by our white friends than can be expiated in a century of good will. To the new Negro this social equality terror is both amusing and exasperating. His character, his culture, his good sense and fine manners are an offence and a menace to people who are so sure of their unapproachable superiority. Certainly there must be something fundamentally wrong with the man or woman who becomes meanly afraid because I can read and appreciate Emerson and Herbert Spencer, and can be stirred by an ambition to serve well my country. Ah, my friends, there is a wrong in all this that goes to the heart of our national honor. It discounts our religion, it cheapens our patriotism and casts a shadow of falsehood over our pretended national greatness.

Some forty years ago the people of this country became so alarmed over the multitude of freedmen at the close of the Civil War that they established a Freedmen's Bureau to aid the freedmen in their transition from slavery to freedom. That was a great service and was inspired by true love of humanity. The ignorant, uncivilized and empty-handed man of 1865 has become a man of culture, a man of force and a man of independence. We shall have to look to this new man to complete this great work of reconstruction. In other words, the new Negro people have a race problem on their hands which is both interesting and far reaching in its consequences, and that is to teach white Americans how possible it is to be both just and respectable towards this expanding race of ours without their loss of anything worth having.

We must save the American people from the debilitating effects of the fears they have that our increase of intelligence and independence means their own loss of social prestige. Let me enjoy all the rights I deserve—who will suffer? To this end let us be confident as to these things:

1. The rise of the Negro people in intelligence, in social efficiency, in self-pride, in the power to add its share toward the wealth and social uplift of the nation must not be hindered or prevented by race prejudice.
2. Injustice, race hatred, discrimination in the matter of fundamental rights will never solve the race problem.
3. The fear of social equality has become a national fetish. It is a fear that was born in the dark days of slavery out of a guilty conscience, and is today fostered and nourished by people who have not yet been touched by the expanding thought of this new era of national growth.
4. In the conflict between race prejudice and the Negro's advancement I am satisfied that whatever is fundamentally right will finally triumph.
5. A state built on the foolish fear of social equality will remain where it began, and will make no history worth reading.

This new Negro only asks and fights for a chance. He sees about him men from all Europe and Asia. Every shop, factory, office and honor is open to this man from across the sea. The descendants of the man who fought under Jackson at New Orleans,[4] with Perry on Lake Erie,[5] who triumphantly died at Fort Wagner,[6] who helped Custer in the West to make room for the Norwegians and Swedes who planted our conquering flag at El Caney[7] are asked to step aside and be satisfied to blacken the shoes of these newcomers.

The new Negro who sees and feels all this is asked to be patient—simply to wait and watch. And so he has watched and waited patiently, heroically and confidently. But he now begins to feel that his heroic patience has invited contempt rather than praise. This new Negro, unlike his grandfather, is sensitive to wrongs, writhes under injustice and is fretful under discriminations copied from South Carolina and Alabama.

This country of ours is a country teeming with opportunities. The man of thorough education, the man of technical training, the inventor, the man skilled in law, medicine, diplomacy and statesmanship can find here his opportunity. This new Negro that I have been talking about is here and ready for all kinds of service. His worth is admitted: why not give him a chance? By everything we pretend to be in this country, in religion, in morals, democracy and spirit of fair play, the ambitions of this well-equipped man should be honored and he be given the chance he deserves. There are never too many fit men to do the high services of a great and ever expanding nation.

Here, then, is our new race problem that has been brought to the nation by this new and ambitious Negro.

What shall be done for or with this new man with a black face? Here in America we have a wide-open civilization. We are made up of all kinds and conditions of people, and we are alike ambitious to do the low and high services of the nation and to be rewarded according to our worth.

The new Negro today offers himself as a fit man for everything that comes within the range of superior intelligence and worthy ambition. Shall he be encouraged, or shall he be turned away hopeless and discouraged? Can this nation, with its limitless opportunities, afford to fix a limitation to the ambitions of any of its people?

Thanks to the progress of humane sentiment in this country, this new man who asks the question can help to answer it. There was a time when all the questions asked as to what should be the status of the Negro were asked and answered by the same man. Thanks to the growth of intelligence and the manhood spirit of the race, no question concerning us is completely answered without our participation in the answer. This shows progress.

This new Negro is an aggressive man, and he will be increasingly heard, and deserves to be increasingly respected. This new Negro may be impatient, as he has a right to be, but he is not altogether discouraged. He is strong in the faith that he is right and fit, and what is right will some day be the unchallenged law of conduct everywhere.

The race problem of today is not one of social equality, but rather one of recognized moral and mental equality—of the right to aspire, of the right to serve our common country in times of peace as well as in times of war. There never can be too many good men and good women in the world, come they from whatever country or race.

The United States is a nation of great problems, and the nation cannot afford to make it impossible for some men to serve the nation in their solution. In spite of unworthy fears of some Americans concerning the new Negro of today and tomorrow, the unfolding of new opportunities for men of brawn, brain and courage will need us. This new Negro will be wanted. In this growing nation of ours there is to be a new political economy to meet the new conditions of our ever expanding nation. A new social ethics that will enable all men to respect each other without fear or loss of social prestige. A new spirit of politics that shall make public office a public trust. A new spirit of brotherhood when it will be more honorable for men to be just to each other than to be socially equal, and a new awakening of all the higher senses of man to his duty to man. Such a consummation is devoutly to be wished. But none of this "vision splendid" can be realized until our interest in mankind shall be greater than our interest in some men.

Today we are fettered by the spirit of the tribe and those who claim to be most free are most fettered. It is not the things we own and the power we have and misuse that make our nation truly great. Why cannot we afford to be just and patient to a race that daily grows in independence and power of self-hood? Who cannot respect a man of worth, even though he be brown or black? Who cannot afford to be just and have faith that what is just will hurt no man? All of us are ready to say yes to these questions, yet we all painfully know that it is easier to live below our ideals. The man who compels me to pay a first class fare for worse than a second class accommodation in a "Jim Crow" car from Chicago to Tuskegee is often a churchman who gives liberal alms to the poor and needy. The man who thinks most of Thomas Jefferson because he stood for the great idea of equality is apt to be the man who is the most violent in insisting that this is "a white man's country." The man who thinks he is a Christian and who pretends to conform his life to the Golden Rule of the Bible is too often the man who practices the iron rule of justice.

This new Negro knows all this and feels this and yet he is a man of faith and courage. Though held down he continues to look up and in all honorable ways struggles for his rights. He submits heroically to the things he cannot overcome. Opposition has made him heroic, and his love of justice has made him optimistic. His ambition is to deserve what he claims, and his high privilege is to pity the man who merely stands in the way of progress.

The new Negro is approaching an era of great things. Tremendous are the problems of tomorrow. In the larger world of higher politics, in the new ideals of higher citizenship, in the social atmosphere of the new ethics of fellowship and in a more exalted religious sense, this new man of our republic will be needed and will find his place, and will be honored for what he is and can do for the world of mankind.

1908

NOTES

1. Williams' essay was published a full sixteen years before Harlem Renaissance writer Alain Locke's similarly themed essay of the same name. Published in 1925, Locke's essay is the introduction to his anthology of the same name. Locke's assembled works are offered as evidence of a new phase in the development of African American identity, community, literature, and social and political thought. See Alain Locke, "The New Negro," in *The New Negro: An Interpretation.*

2. African American visual artist Henry Ossawa Tanner (1859–1937).

3. African American Presbyterian minister Francis James Grimké (1852–1937), a founding member of the National Association for the Advancement of Colored People (NAACP).

4. The Battle of New Orleans, the last major battle of the War of 1812.

5. The Battle of Lake Erie, a key battle in the War of 1812, in which the United States was led to victory over Britain by Master Commandant Oliver Hazard Perry (1785–1819).

6. Located on Morris Island, South Carolina, site of the Union Army Operations against the Defenses of Charleston, during the American Civil War, in 1863.

7. The Battle of El Caney, fought in El Caney, Cuba, 1898, resulting in a Cuba-U.S. allied victory over Spain.

JOSEPH SEAMON COTTER (1861–1949)

Joseph Seamon Cotter was born near Bardstown, Kentucky. His mother taught him how to read and enrolled him in a local school, but economic circumstances forced him to abandon his education at the age of eight, and for the next fourteen years he worked as a laborer in various industries. Cotter was not able to return to school until the age of twenty-two, when he enrolled in a Louisville-area night school. His aptitude and discipline were such that he was promoted to a teaching post after only two terms of study. Cotter would remain in education for the rest of his life, founding the Paul Laurence Dunbar School in Louisville, Kentucky, and eventually serving as the principal of the Samuel Coleridge-Taylor School, also in Louisville, from 1911 to 1942. Cotter was a prolific writer, publishing drama and fiction as well as the poetry for which he is most often remembered. In both his dialect and his Standard English poems, Cotter expresses his views on African American culture, black-white race relations, and the path to upward mobility and equal rights. A staunch supporter of Booker T. Washington's moderate path to black self-sufficiency, Cotter wrote poems in praise of Tuskegee and the ideals of its creator. The following were selected from Cotter's 1909 collection, *A White Song and a Black One*.

GRANT AND LEE

The South's the sin? The North's the glory?[1]
Laugh out of court the hackneyed story.
The sin took root in the nation's heart.
And North and South played a dual part.

The North and the South wore a cheek of shame,
Till a life of woe wrought an earth of flame.
And who were the heroes? All who fell,
Whether North or South, in the nation's hell.

And who were the heroes? Great souls who fed
The nation's maw with the nation's dead
Till the nation's blood slew the nation's curse,
And made man free as the universe.

Neither Grant of the North nor Lee of the South
Shall link his name with the cannon's mouth.
Neither Lee of the South nor Grant of the North
Shall stand accused when the blame goes forth.

In the South's warm heart, on the North's just tongue,
A dual epic of peace is sung
With regret for the bond and hope for the free,
And a God-like love for Grant and Lee.

1909

UNCLE REMUS TO MASSA JOEL

Listen, Massa Joel;[2]
    I'se er callin' ter you;
Callin' in de sunlight,
    Callin' in de dew,
Callin' whar you uster be,
    An' callin' whar you ain't.
'Specks de Lawd dun called you blessed,
    An' de angels calls you saint.

Heah me, Massa Joel;
    I'se er mournin' fer you;
Mournin' when de day is old,
    Mournin' when it's new,
Mournin' whar you uster sing,
    An' whar you uster pray.
'Specks de worl' is full ob mournin',
    But de heabens, dey is gay.

Meet me, Massa Joel;
    I'se er comin' ter you;

Comin' wid er load ob sin
　　Fer de sinner's due;
Comin' whar I sho' kin borrer
　　'Er-little loan ob grace.
'Specks de Lawd gwine call us brudders
　　When He sees us face ter face.

1909

THE CONFEDERATE VETERAN AND THE OLD-TIME DARKY

I seed him on de corner dar
Er-lookin' lak he's gwine to war.
I wondered ef he thought it sin
Ter fight dem battles ober ergin.

De way he greeted de passers-by
Showed me de kindness in his eye.
De way he listened ter my woes
Tuk all de fight outen his clo'es.

1909

NEGRO LOVE SONG

I lobes your hands, gal; yes I do.
　　(I'se gwine ter wed ter-morro'.)
I lobes your earnings thro' an' thro'.
　　(I'se gwine ter wed ter-morro'.)
Now, heah de truf. I'se mos' nigh broke;
I wants ter take you fer my yoke;
　　So let's go wed ter-morro'.

Now, don't look shy, an' don't say no.
　　(I'se gwine ter wed ter-morro'.)
I hope you don't expects er sho'
　　When we two weds ter-morro'.
I needs er licends—you knows I do—
I'll borrow de price ob de same frum you,
　　An' den we weds ter-morro'.

How pay you back? In de reg'ler way.
   When you becomes my honey
You'll habe myself fer de princ'pal pay,
   An' my faults fer de interes' money.
Dat suits you well? Dis cash is right.
So we two weds ter-morro' night,
   An' you wuks all de ter-morro's.

1909

NOTE

  1. The title refers to Civil War generals Ulysses S. Grant (1822–1885), commander of the Union Army, and Robert E. Lee (1807–1870), commander of the Confederate Army.

  2. The poem is presented as a message to plantation tradition writer and folklorist Joel Chandler Harris (1845–1908), from his most popular character, the fictional Uncle Remus, a jovial black storyteller, content with his status in the racial hierarchy of the postbellum-era South.

MAGGIE POGUE JOHNSON
(1880?-1957?)

A native of Fincastle, Virginia, poet Maggie Pogue Johnson was one of twelve children born to Lucie Jane Banister Pogue and the Rev. Samuel Pogue, an early pastor of Fincastle's First Baptist Church. Her parents' commitment to education was reflected in their children's pursuits. Of the ten who survived to adulthood, five would go on to become teachers, two would become physicians, one would join the ministry, one would become a pharmacist, and one a farmer. A teacher by training, Johnson was educated at the Virginia Normal and Industrial Institute in Petersburg. She married physician Walter Weston Johnson in 1904, and the two had one son, Walter Jr. After the death of her first husband, she married Dr. John Wesley Shellcroft, a native of Antigua, British West Indies. Described by Harold Bloom as a "coterie poet," perhaps in the fashion of John Donne or Aphra Behn, she wrote verse in both Standard English and the popular southern-inspired dialect of the day. A prolific writer whose career spanned from the post-Reconstruction era through the Harlem Renaissance and well into the post-World War II era, Johnson published at least four books during her lifetime. Her first collection of poems, *Virginia Dreams: Lyrics for the Idle Hour,* was released in 1910. Her second collection, *Thoughts for Idle Hours,* followed in 1915. After a long gap, Johnson published *Fallen Blossoms,* a compendium of her first two collections and several of her more recent works, in 1951. Her last known volume, *Childhood Hours: With Songs for Little Tots,* was published in 1952. The following poems are reprinted from her first collection, *Virginia Dreams.* These dialect poems are notable for, among other things, their frequent reliance on female speaking subjects whose ideas and opinions challenge traditional women's roles. Such works appropriate the conventions of the plantation tradition while subverting its themes of white supremacy and nostalgia for the antebellum years.

I'se been upon de karpet,
    Fo' lo, dese many days;
De men folks seem to sneer me,
    In der kin' ob way.

But I don't min' der foolin',
    Case I sho' is jis as fine
As any Kershaw pumpkin[1]
    A hangin on de vine.

I looks at dem sometimes,
    But hol's my head up high,
Case I is fer above dem
    As de moon is in de sky.

Dey sho' do t'ink dey's so much,
    But I sho' is jis as fine
As eny sweet potato
    Dat's growd up from de vine.

Dey needn't t'ink I's liken dem,
    Case my match am hard to fin',
En I don't want de watermillion
    Dat's lef' upon de vine.

Case I ain't no spring chicken,
    Dis am solid talk,
En I don't want anything
    Dat's foun' upon de walk.

Case ef I'd wanted anything,
    I'd hitched up years ago,
En had my sher ob trouble.
    But my min' tol' me no.

I'd rader be a single maid,
    A wanderin' bout de town,
Wid skercely way to earn my bread,
    En face all made ob frowns,—

Den hitched up to some numbskull,
 Wid skercely sense to die,
En I know I cud'n kill him,
 Dar'd be no use to try.

So don't let ol' maids boder you,
 I'll fin' a match some day,
Or else I'll sho' 'main single,
 You hear me what I say!

I specs to hol' my head up high
 En always feel as free
As any orange blossom
 A hangin' on de tree.

1910

WHAT'S MO' TEMPTIN' TO THE PALATE

What's mo' temptin' to de palate,
 When you's wuked so hard all day,
En cum in home at ebentime
 Widout a wud to say,—
En see a stewin' in de stove
 A possum crisp en brown,
Wid great big sweet potaters,
 A layin' all aroun'.

What's mo' temptin' to de palate,
 Den a chicken bilin' hot,
En plenty ob good dumplin's,
 A bubblin' in de pot;
To set right down to eat dem,
 En 'pease yo' hunger dar,
'Tis nuffin' mo' enjoyin',
 I sho'ly do declar.

What's mo' temptin' to de palate
 Den a dish ob good baked beans,

En what is still mo' temptin'
    Den a pot brimfull ob greens;
Jis biled down low wid bacon,
    Almos' 'til dey's fried,
En a plate ob good ol' co'n cakes
    A layin' on de side.

What's mo' temptin' to de palate
    Den on Thanksgibin' Day
To hab a good ol' tuckey
    Fixed some kin' o' way;
Wid cranber'y sauce en celery,
    All settin' on de side,
En eat jis' til yo' appetite
    Is sho' full satisfied.

What's mo' temptin' to de palate,
    Den in de Summer time,
To bus' a watermillion
    Right from off de vine;
En set right down to eat it
    In de coolin breeze,
Wif nuffin' to moles' you,
    Settin' neaf de apple trees.

What's mo' temptin' to de palate,
    Den poke chops, also lam',
En what is still mo' temptin'
    Den good ol' col' biled ham;
Veal chops dey ain't bad,
    Put de mutton chops in line,
I tell you my ol' appetite,
    Fo' all dese t'ings do pine.

What' mo' temptin' to de palate,
    When you cum from wuk at night,
To set down to de fiah,
    A shinin' jis so bright,

De ol' 'oman walks in,—
    Wid supper brilin' hot,
En a good ol' cup ob coffee,
    Jis steamin' out de pot.

'Tis den I kin enjoy myse'f,
    En eat dar by de fiah,
Case puttin' way good eatin's
    Is sho'ly my desire;
Dar's nuffin dat's so temptin',
    Dat to me is a treat,
Den settin' at a table
    Wid plenty good to eat.

1910

NOTE

1. A large, green squash grown in the mid-South, also called a Cushaw pumpkin or a Tennessee Sweet Potato Squash, used for soups and pies.

BIBLIOGRAPHY OF INCLUDED WORKS

Beman, Amos. "The Tears of a Slave." *Freedom's Journal,* March 14, 1828. *Accessible Archives.* Web. Accessed July 16, 2009.

Braithwaite, William Stanley. "Golden Moonrise." *The House of Falling Leaves: With Other Poems.* Boston: John W. Luce, 1908. 27. Print.

———. "In the Athenaeum Looking out on the Granary Burying Ground on a Rainy Day in November." *The House of Falling Leaves: With Other Poems.* Boston: John W. Luce, 1908. 92–93. Print.

———. "Love's Wayfaring." *Colored American Magazine* 5 (August 1902). 243–44. Rpt. New York: Negro Universities P, 1969. Print.

Brawley, Benjamin Griffith. "The Battleground." *The Problem: And Other Poems.* Atlanta: Atlanta Baptist College, 1905. 3. Print.

———. "The Path of Life." *Colored American Magazine* 5 (August 1902): 283–84. Rpt. New York: Negro Universities P, 1969. Print.

———. "The Problem." *The Problem: And Other Poems.* Atlanta: Atlanta Baptist College, 1905. 1–2. Print.

Brown, Solomon G. "The New York Riot." *Christian Recorder,* August 22, 1863. *Accessible Archives.* Web. Accessed June 11, 2009.

Brown, William Wells. *Clotel; or, The President's Daughter: A Narrative of Slave Life in the United States.* London: Partridge & Oakley, 1853. Print.

———. "Letter from William Wells Brown, Adelphi Hotel, York, March 26, 1851." *The North Star,* March 26, 1851. *Accessible Archives.* Web. Accessed June 14, 2009.

———. "Letter from Williams Wells Brown, Oxford, September 10th, 1851." *The North Star,* April 17, 1851. *Accessible Archives.* Web. Accessed June 14, 2009.

———. *My Southern Home: or, The South and Its People.* Boston: A. G. Brown & Co., 1880. Print.

———. "Visit of a Fugitive Slave to the Grave of Wilberforce." *Autographs for Freedom.* Ed. Julia Griffiths. Rochester, NY: Beardsley, Wanzer &, 1854. 70–76. Print.

Burgess-Ware, Marie Louise. "Bernice, the Octoroon." *Colored American Magazine* 6.8 (August 1903): 607–16; 6.9 (September 1903): 652–56. Rpt. New York: Negro Universities P, 1969. Print.

Bush-Banks, Olivia Ward. "Heart-Throbs." *Colored American Magazine* 2.1 (May 1904): n.p. Rpt. New York: Negro Universities P, 1969. Print.

———. "The Nation's Evil." *Colored American Magazine* 2.1 (May 1904): n.p. Rpt. New York: Negro Universities P, 1969. Print.

———. "Voices." Original Poems. Providence, RI: P of Louis A. Basinet, 1899. 17–19. Print.

Chesnutt, Charles Waddell. "The Free Colored People of North Carolina." *Southern Workman* 31.3 (March 1902): 136–41. Print.

———. "The Goophered Grapevine." *The Conjure Woman.* Boston: Houghton Mifflin, 1899. 1–35. Print.

————. "Tobe's Tribulations." *Southern Workman* 29.11 (November 1900): 656–64. Print.

Cooper, Anna Julia. "Womanhood: A Vital Element in the Regeneration and Progress of a Race." *A Voice From the South*. Xenia: Aldine, 1892. 9–47. Print.

Cornish, Samuel, and John Russwurm. "To Our Patrons." *Freedom's Journal*, March 16, 1827. *Accessible Archives*. Web. Accessed July 16, 2009.

Corrothers, James D. *The Black Cat Club: Negro Humor & Folklore*. New York: Funk & Wagnalls, 1902. Print.

————. "Juny at the Gate." *Colored American Magazine* 5.1 (May 1902): 3–4. Rpt. New York: Negro Universities P, 1969. Print.

————. "Me 'n' Dubnar." *Colored American Magazine* 3 (July 1901): 163–64. Rpt. New York: Negro Universities P, 1969. Print.

————. "The Snapping of the Bow. *Colored American Magazine* 3 (May 1901): 23–24. Rpt. New York: Negro Universities P, 1969. Print.

Cotter, Joseph S. "The Confederate Veteran and the Old-Time Darky." *A White Song and a Black One*. Louisville: Bradley & Gilbert, 1901. 16. Print.

————. "Grant and Lee." *A White Song and a Black One*. Louisville: Bradley & Gilbert, 1901. 13. Print.

————. "Negro Love Song." *A White Song and a Black One*. Louisville: Bradley & Gilbert, 1901. 48. Print.

————. "Uncle Remus to Massa Joel." *A White Song and a Black One*. Louisville: Bradley & Gilbert, 1901. 15. Print.

Crummell, Alexander. "The Social Principle Among a People and Its Bearing on Their Progress and Development, Thanksgiving Day, 1875." *The Greatness of Christ and Other Sermons*. New York: Thomas Whittaker, 1882. 285–311. Print.

Davis, Daniel Webster. "De Linin' ub de Hymns." *'Weh Down Souf and Other Poems*. Cleveland: Helman-Taylor, 1897. 54–56. Print.

————. "Stickin' to de Hoe." *'Weh Down Souf and Other Poems*. Cleveland: Helman-Taylor, 1897. 57–59.

Delany, Martin R. *Blake; or, the Huts of America*. January 1959–July 1959. Rpt. New York: Arno P and *The New York Times*, 1968. Print.

Douglass, Frederick. "The Heroic Slave." *Frederick Douglass' Paper*, March 4 and 11, 1853. *Accessible Archives*. Web. Accessed August 1, 2009.

————. "To My Old Master." *The North Star*, September 8, 1848: 1. *Accessible Archives*. Web. Accessed June 14, 2009.

————. "What Are the Colored People Doing for Themselves?" *The North Star*, July 14, 1848: 1. *Accessible Archives*. Web. Accessed July 14, 2009.

Douglass, Sarah Mapps. "Ella: A Sketch." *Liberator*, August 4, 1832: 123. *Accessible Archives*. Web. Accessed July 17, 2009.

————. "Family Worship." *Liberator*, September 8, 1832: 143. *Accessible Archives*. Web. Accessed July 17, 2009.

Du Bois, W. E. B. "The Burden of Black Women." *Horizon* 2 (November 1907): 3–5. Print.

————. "Credo." *Independent* 57 (October 6, 1904): 787. Print.

————. "The Litany of Atlanta." *Independent* 5.1 (October 11, 1906): 856–58. Print.

————. "My Country, 'Tis of Thee." *Horizon* 2 (November 1907): 5–6. Print.

Dunbar, Paul Laurence. "Compensation." *Lyrics of Sunshine and Shadow*. New York: Century Co., 1901. 60–61. Print.

————. "Dawn." *Lyrics of Lowly Life*. New York: Dodd, Mead and Co., 1896. 153. Print.

———. "Frederick Douglass." *Lyrics of Lowly Life*. New York: Dodd, Mead and Co., 1896. 8–11. Print.

———. "Little Brown Baby." *Poems of Cabin and Field*. New York: Dodd, Mead and Co., 1896. 43–54. Print.

———. "A Negro Love Song." *Lyrics of Lowly Life*. New York: Dodd, Mead and Co., 1896. 110. Print.

———. "Unexpressed." *Lyrics of Lowly Life*. New York: Dodd, Mead and Co., 1896. 55. Print.

———. "When Malindy Sings." *Lyrics of Lowly Life*. New York: Dodd, Mead and Co., 1896. 195–99. Print.

Forten, James. "Letters from a Man of Colour, on a Late Bill before the Senate of Pennsylvania: Letter I." *Freedom's Journal* (February 22, 1828): 190. *Accessible Archives*. Web. Accessed July 16, 2009.

Fortune, T. Thomas. *Black and White: Land, Labor, and Freedom*. New York: Fords, Howard, & Hulbert, 1884. Print.

———. "Come Away, Love." *Dreams of Life*. New York: n.p., 1905. 20. *American Verse Project*. Web. Accessed April 8, 2008.

———. "The Conclave: To the Ladies of Tuskegee School." *New York Age* 3.32 (May 3, 1890): 2. Microfilm. *Library of Congress: Committee on Negro Studies of the American Council of Learned Societies* (November 2, 1889–September 12, 1891): reel 3.

———. "Love's Divinest Power." *New York Age* 3.47 (August 16, 1890): 2. Microfilm. *Library of Congress: Committee on Negro Studies of the American Council of Learned Societies* (November 2, 1889–September 12, 1891): reel 3.

Fulton, David Bryant. *Hanover; or The Persecution of the Lowly; A Story of the Wilmington Massacre*. Philadelphia: M. C. L. Hill, 1901. Print.

———. "Henry Berry Lowery, the North Carolina Outlaw: A Tale of the Reconstruction Period." *"Eagle Clippings" by Jack Thorne, Newspaper Correspondent and Story Teller: A Collection of His Writings to Various Newspapers*. Brooklyn, NY: David B. Fulton, 1907. 65–71. Print.

———. "A Hero in Ebony." *"Eagle Clippings" by Jack Thorne, Newspaper Correspondent and Story Teller: A Collection of His Writings to Various Newspapers*. Brooklyn, NY: David B. Fulton, 1907. 89–93. Print.

Greener, Richard T. "The White Problem." *Cleveland Gazette* 12.7 (September 22–October 6, 1894). *Library of Congress: The African-American Experience in Ohio*. Web. Accessed May 14, 2008.

Griggs, Sutton E. *Imperium in Imperio*. Cincinnati: Editor Publishing Co., 1899. Rpt. New York: AMS P, 1969. Print.

A Gude Deekun. "A Georgia Episode." *Colored American Magazine* 3.1 (May 1901): 3–8. Rpt. New York: Negro Universities P, 1969. Print.

Harper, Frances Ellen Watkins. "Bury Me in a Free Land." *Liberator*, January 14, 1864. *Accessible Archives*. Web. Accessed June 9, 2009.

———. "Eliza Harris." *Frederick Douglass' Paper*, December 23, 1853: 4. *Accessible Archives*. Web. Accessed May 22, 2009.

———. "Enlightened Motherhood: An Address by Mrs. Frances E. W. Harper, Before the Brooklyn Literary Society, November 15, 1892." New York: Brooklyn Literary Society, 1892. *Daniel Murray Collection*. Web. Accessed May 22, 2008.

———. "The Slave Auction." *Poems on Miscellaneous Subjects*. Boston: J. B. Yerrinton & Son, 1855. PDF.

Heard, Josephine D. Henderson. "The Black Samson." *Morning Glories*. Philadelphia: n.p., 1890. 89–90. Print.

———. "An Epitaph." *Morning Glories*. Philadelphia, 1890. Print.

———. "A Mother's Love." *Morning Glories*. Philadelphia, 1890. 68. Print.

———. "Wilberforce." *Morning Glories*. Philadelphia, 1890. 78–80. Print.

Highgate, Edmonia Goodelle. "Neglected Opportunities." *Christian Recorder*, July 15, 1866. *Accessible Archives*. Web. Accessed June 14, 2009.

———. "On Horse Back—Saddle Dash. No.1." *Christian Recorder*, November 3, 1866. *Accessible Archives*. Web. Accessed June 14, 2009.

Hodges, Augustus. "What Happened to Scott: An Episode of Election Day." *Colored American Magazine* 6 (August 1903): 574–79. Rpt. New York: Negro Universities P, 1969. Print.

Holly, Joseph C. "An Epitaph." *Freedom's Offering, a Collection of Poems*. Rochester, NY: Chas. H. McDonnell, 1853. 9. *Chadwyck-Healy*. Web. Accessed January 30, 2008.

———. "On the Death of My Sister Cecilia—The Last of Five Members of the Family, Who Died Successively." *Freedom's Offering, a Collection of Poems*. Rochester, NY: Chas. H. McDonnell, 1853. 14. *Chadwyck-Healy*. Web. Accessed January 30, 2008.

——— "To Mrs. Harriet B. Stowe." *Freedom's Offering, a Collection of Poems*. Rochester, NY: Chas. H. McDonnell, 1853. 36. *Chadwyck-Healy*. Web. Accessed January 30, 2008.

Hopkins, Pauline. *Hagar's Daughter: A Story of Southern Caste Prejudice*. Colored American Magazine 2.5 (March 1901)–5.6 (October 1902). Rpt. New York: Negro Universities P, 1969. Print.

Horton, George Moses. "Forbidden to Ride on the Street Cars." *Christian Recorder* 177 (1866). *Accessible Archives*. Web. Accessed June 8, 2009.

———. "Gratitude." *Freedom's Journal*, September 5, 1828. *Accessible Archives*. Web. Accessed July 16, 2009.

———. "Lines on the Evening and the Morning." *Freedom's Journal*, August 15, 1828: 166. *Accessible Archives*. Web. Accessed June 8, 2009.

———. "Slavery." *Freedom's Journal*, September 5, 1828: 135. *Accessible Archives*. Web. Accessed June 8, 2009.

Jacobs, Harriet. *Incidents in the Life of a Slave Girl. Written by Herself.* Ed. Lydia Maria Child. Boston, 1861.

Johnson, Maggie Pogue. "The Old Maid's Soliloquy." *Virginia Dreams: Lyrics for the Idle Hour, Tales of Time Told in Rhyme*. Virginia: John M. Leonard, 1910. 10–12. *American Verse Project*. Web. Accessed May 3, 2007.

———. "What's Mo' Temptin' to the Palate." *Virginia Dreams: Lyrics for the Idle Hour, Tales of Time Told in Rhyme*. Virginia: John M. Leonard, 1910. 30–31. *American Verse Project*. Web. Accessed May 3, 2007.

Jones, Absolom. *A Thanksgiving Sermon, Preached January 1, 1808, in St. Thomas's, or the African Episcopal Church, Philadelphia: on Account of the Abolition of the African Slave Trade, on That Day by the Congress of the United States*. Philadelphia: Fry and Kammerer, 1808. PDF.

Loguen, Rev. Jermaine Wesley. "Letter to Rev. J. W. Loguen, from his Old Mistress, and Mr. Loguen's Reply." *The Liberator*, April 27, 1860: 65. *Accessible Archives*. Web. Accessed October 7, 2009.

————. *The Rev. J. W. Loguen, as a Slave and as a Freeman. A Narrative of Real Life.* Syracuse, NY: J. G. K. Truair & Co., 1859. PDF.

Malone, Thomas Horatius. "The Unheeded Signal." *Colored American Magazine,* May 1908: 281–85. Rpt. New York: Negro Universities P, 1969. Print.

Matthews, Victoria Earle. "The Value of Race Literature." Address, First Congress of Colored Women of the United States. Boston, July 30, 1895.

Menard, John Willis. "Liberia." *Christian Recorder,* March 7, 1863. *Accessible Archives.* Web. Accessed October 14, 2009.

————. "To Madame Selika." *Lays in Summer Lands.* Washington, DC: Enterprise, 1879. 34. Print.

Miller, Kelly. *As to the Leopard's Spots: An Open Letter to Thomas Dixon, Jr.* Washington, DC: Howard, 1905. Print.

Plato, Ann. "Advice to Young Ladies." *Essays; Including Biographies and Miscellaneous Pieces, in Prose and Poetry.* Hartford, CT, 1841. 93. *Women Writers Project.* Web. Accessed January 11, 2009.

————. "The Infant Class, Written in School." *Essays; Including Biographies and Miscellaneous Pieces, in Prose and Poetry.* Hartford, CT, 1841. 102–3. *Women Writers Project.* Web. Accessed January 11, 2009.

————. "Lines, upon Being Examined in School Studies for the Preparation of a Teacher." *Essays; Including Biographies and Miscellaneous Pieces, in Prose and Poetry.* Hartford, CT, 1841. 94. *Women Writers Project.* Web. Accessed January 11, 2009.

Randolph, Peter. *Sketches of Slave Life: Or, Illustration of the "Peculiar Institution."* Boston: the author, 1855. *Documenting the American South (DocSouth).* Web. Accessed September 6, 2009.

Ray, Henrietta Cordelia. "In Memoriam: Paul Laurence Dunbar." *Poems.* New York: Grafton, 1910. 166–67. *Digital Schomburg African American Women Writers of the 19th Century.* Web. Accessed October 18, 2007.

————. "Lincoln: Written for the Occasion of the Unveiling of the Freedman's Monument in Memory of Abraham Lincoln." *Oration by Frederick Douglass, Delivered on the Occasion of the Unveiling of the Freedman's Monument in Memory of Abraham Lincoln, in Lincoln Park, Washington, D.C., April 14, 1876. With an Appendix. Appendix Contains Account of the Ceremonies, with Poem by Miss Cordelia Ray.* Washington, DC: Gilsar Brothers, 1876. 17–21. Print.

————. "To My Father." *Poems.* New York: Grafton, 1910. 86. *Digital Schomburg African American Women Writers of the 19th Century.* Web. Accessed October 18, 2007.

————. "Toussaint L'Overture." *Poems.* New York: Grafton, 1910. 88. *Digital Schomburg African American Women Writers of the 19th Century.* Web. Accessed October 18, 2007.

Raymond, J. Anderson. "The Critic (Concluded)." *Christian Recorder,* November 12, 1864: 181. *Accessible Archives.* Web. Accessed June 8, 2009.

————. "Poetry and Poets: Part I." *Christian Recorder,* July 30, 1864: 121. *Accessible Archives.* Web. Accessed June 7, 2009.

————. "Poetry and Poets: Part II." *Christian Recorder,* August 6, 1864: 25. *Accessible Archives.* Web. Accessed June 7, 2009.

————. "Poetry and Poets: Part IV." *Christian Recorder,* August 27, 1864: 137. *Accessible Archives.* Web. Accessed June 7, 2009.

Rogers, Elymas Payson. "Loguen's Position." *The Rev. J. W. Loguen, as a Slave and as a Freeman. A Narrative of Real Life.* Syracuse, NY: J. G. K. Truair & Co., 1859. 449–50. PDF.

———. *The Repeal of the Missouri Compromise Considered.* Newark, NJ: A. Stephen Holbrook, 1856. *University of Virginia Library.* Web. Accessed July 27, 2009.

S. "Theresa,—A Haytien Tale." *Freedom's Journal,* January 18, 1828–February 15, 1828. *Accessible Archives.* Web. Accessed July 16, 2009.

Smith, Amanda. *An Autobiography: The Story of the Lord's Dealings with Mrs. Amanda Smith, the Colored Evangelist; Containing an Account of Her Life Work of Faith, and Her Travels in America, England, Ireland, Scotland, India, and Africa, as an Independent Missionary.* Chicago: Meyer & Brother, 1893. PDF.

Smith, Effie Waller. "Apple Sauce and Chicken Fried." *Songs of the Months.* New York: Broadway Publishing Co., 1904. 120–31. *Digital Schomburg African American Women Writers of the 19th Century.* Web. Accessed June 27, 2007.

———. "The Bachelor Girl." *Rhymes from the Cumberland.* New York: Broadway Publishing Co., 1909. 49–51. *Digital Schomburg African American Women Writers of the 19th Century.* Web. Accessed June 27, 2007.

———. "The Preacher's Wife, Dedicated to the Wives of the Itinerant Preachers of the M.E. Church." *Songs of the Months.* New York: Broadway Publishing Co., 1904. 82–83. *Digital Schomburg African American Women Writers of the 19th Century.* Web. Accessed June 27, 2007.

———. "To a Spring in the Cumberlands." *Rhymes from the Cumberland.* New York: Broadway Publishing Co., 1909. 17–18. *Digital Schomburg African American Women Writers of the 19th Century.* Web. Accessed June 27, 2007.

Smith, James McCune. "Heads of the Colored People, Done with a Whitewash Brush." *Frederick Douglass' Paper,* March 25, 1852. *Accessible Archives.* Web. Accessed July 17, 2009.

———. "Heads of the Colored People: The Black News-Vender." *Frederick Douglass' Paper,* March 25, 1852. *Accessible Archives.* Web. Accessed July 17, 2009.

———. "Heads of the Colored People: The Schoolmaster." *Frederick Douglass' Paper,* November 3, 1854. *Accessible Archives.* Web. Accessed July 7, 2009.

———. "Heads of the Colored People: The Sexton." *Frederick Douglass' Paper,* July 16, 1852. *Accessible Archives.* Web. Accessed July 7, 2009.

———. "Heads of the Colored People: The Washerwoman." *Frederick Douglass' Paper,* June 17, 1852. *Accessible Archives.* Web. Accessed July 7, 2009.

Stewart, Maria W. "An Address, Delivered at the African Masonic Hall, Boston, February 27, 1833. *Meditations from the Pen of Mrs. Maria W. Stewart (Widow of the Late James W. Stewart), Now Matron of the Freedman's Hospital, and Presented in 1832 to the First African Baptist Church and Society of Boston, Mass.* Washington, DC: Enterprise, 1879. 66–72. PDF.

Terrell, Mary Church. "What it Means to be Colored in the Capital of the United States." *Independent,* January 24, 1907: 181–86. Print.

Thomas, William Hannibal. *The American Negro: What He Was, What He Is, and What He May Become.* New York: Macmillan, 1901. Print.

Thompson, Clara Ann. "The Easter Bonnet." *Songs from the Wayside.* Rossmoyne, OH: n.p., 1908. 91–93. *Digital Schomburg African American Women Writers of the 19th Century.* Web. Accessed October 14, 2005.

———. "Johnny's Pet Superstition." *Songs from the Wayside*. Rossmoyne, OH: n.p.,
1908. 7–8. *Digital Schomburg African American Women Writers of the 19th Century*. Web.
Accessed October 14, 2005.

———. "A Lullaby." *Songs from the Wayside*. Rossmoyne, OH: n.p., 1908. 63–65. *Digital
Schomburg African American Women Writers of the 19th Century*. Web. Accessed October 14, 2005.

———. "Mrs. Johnson Objects." *Songs from the Wayside*. Rossmoyne, OH: n.p., 1908.
17–18. *Digital Schomburg African American Women Writers of the 19th Century*. Web.
Accessed October 14, 2005.

Thompson, Priscilla Jane. "Freedom at McNealy's." *Ethiope Lays*. Rossmoyne, OH: n.p.,
1900. 69–73. *Digital Schomburg African American Women Writers of the 19th Century*.
Web. Accessed October 15, 2005.

———. "A Home Greeting." *Gleanings of Quiet Hours*. Rossmoyne, OH: n.p., 1907. 22.
Digital Schomburg African American Women Writers of the 19th Century. Web. Accessed
October 15, 2005.

———. "The Husband's Return." *Gleanings of Quiet Hours*. Rossmoyne, OH: n.p., 1907.
13–16. *Digital Schomburg African American Women Writers of the 19th Century*. Web.
Accessed October 15, 2005.

Tillman, Katherine Davis. "Afro-American Boy." *Christian Recorder*, June 24, 1897: 1.
Accessible Archives. Web. Accessed July 22, 2009.

———. "The Newsboy." *Christian Recorder*, December 7, 1893: 1. Web *Accessible Archives*.
Web. Accessed July 22, 2009.

———. "Soul Visions." *Christian Recorder*, August 21, 1902: 2. Web. Accessed July 22, 2009.

———. "The Superannuate." *Christian Recorder*, March 16, 1899: 1. Web. Accessed
July 22, 2009.

———. "The Warriors Lay." *Christian Recorder*, October 22, 1902: 1. *Accessible Archives*.
Web. Accessed July 22, 2009.

Todd. Ruth D. "The Octoroon's Revenge." *Colored American Magazine* 4 (March 1902):
291–95. Rpt. New York: Negro Universities P, 1969. Print.

Walker, David. *Walker's Appeal, in Four Articles; Together With a Preamble, to the Coloured
Citizens of the World, but in Particular, and Very Expressly, to Those of the United States
of America*. 3rd ed. Boston, 1830. *Documenting the American South (DocSouth)*. Web.
Accessed July 6, 2008.

Wells-Barnett, Ida B. *Southern Horrors: Lynch Law in All Its Phases*. Aberdeen, Scotland:
Thomson & Duncan, 1892. *History of Scholarly Societies: LSE Selected Pamphlets*. Web.
Accessed May 16, 2009.

Whitfield, James Monroe. "America." *America and Other Poems*. Buffalo, NY: James S.
Leavitt, 1853. 9–16. *Internet Archive*. Web. Accessed June 5, 2009.

———. "A Poem." San Francisco: *The Elevator*, 1867. *U of Virginia Library*. Web. Accessed
June 12, 2009.

———. "Prayer of the Oppressed." *America and Other Poems*. Buffalo, NY: James S.
Leavitt, 1853. 61–63. *Internet Archive*. Web. Accessed June 5, 2009.

Williams, Fannie Barrier. "The Intellectual Progress of Colored Women Since the
Emancipation Proclamation." *The World's Congress of Representative Women: A
Historical Résumé for Popular Circulation of the World's Congress of Representative
Women, Convened in Chicago on May 15, and Adjourned on May 22, 1893, under the Auspices*

of the Woman's Brach of the World's Congress Auxiliary. Ed. May Wright Sewall. Vol. 2.
New York: Rand, McNally & Co., 1894. 696–711. PDF.

Williams, Peter. *An Oration on the Abolition of the Slave Trade; Delivered in the African Church in the City of New York, January 1, 1808.* New York: Samuel Wood, 1808.

Williams, S. Laing. "The New Negro." *Alexander's Magazine* 7 (November 1908): 17–22. Rpt. New York: Negro Universities P, 1969. Print.

Wilson, Harriet. *Our Nig: Sketches from the Life of a Free Black.* Boston: George C. Rand & Avery, 1859. *U of Virginia Library.* Web. Accessed December 17, 2007.

Wilson, William J. "Afric–American Picture Gallery: Number 1." *Anglo–African Magazine* 1 (February 1859): 52–55. *Hathi Trust Digital Archive.* Web. Accessed October 3, 2009.

———. "From Our Brooklyn Correspondent, May 13, 1852." *Frederick Douglass' Paper,* May 13, 1852. *Accessible Archives.* Web. Accessed July 17, 2009.

BIOGRAPHICAL SOURCES

Beman, Amos

Bruce, Dickson D. *The Origins of African American Literature, 1680–1865*. Richmond: U of Virginia P, 2001. Print.

Freeman, Amos N. "A Trip to New Haven." *The Colored American*, May 22, 1841: 2. *Accesible Archives*. Web. Accessed November 5, 2009.

Swift, David E. *Black Prophets of Justice: Activist Clergy Before the Civil War*. Baton Rouge: Louisiana State UP, 1898. Print.

Braithwaite, William Stanley

Butcher, Philip. "Introduction." *The William Stanley Braithwaite Reader*. Ann Arbor: U of Michigan P, 1972. 1–7. Print.

Cullen, Counteem, ed. "William Stanley Braithwaite." *Caroling Dusk: An Anthology of Verse by Negro Poets*. New York: Harper, 1927. 31. Print.

Nuss, Kirk. "William Stanley Braithwaite (1878–1962)." *African American Authors, 1745–1945: A Bio-Bibliographical Critical Sourcebook*. Ed. Emmanuel Sampath Nelson. Westport, CT: Greenwood, 2000. 44–49. Print.

Brawley, Benjamin Griffith.

Parker, John W. "Benjamin Brawley and the American Cultural Tradition." *Phylon* 16.2 (Summer 1955): 183–94. Print.

Perry, Patsy B. "Benjamin Griffith Brawley (1882–1939)." *Southern Writers: A New Biographical Dictionary*. Ed. Joseph M. Flora, Amber Vogel, and Gryan Giemza. 41–42. Print.

Schuppert, Roger A. "Brawley, Benjamin Griffith." *African American Lives*. Ed. Henry Louis Gates and Evelyn Brooks Higginbotham. New York: Oxford UP, 2004. 97–98. Print.

Brown, Solomon G.

Dall, William Healey. *Spencer Fullerton Baird: A Biography, Including Selections from His Correspondence with Audubon, Agassiz, Dana, and Others*. New York: J. B. Lippincott, 1915. Print.

Holland, Jesse J. *Black Men Built the Capitol: Discovering African American History in and Around Washington, Part 3*. Guilford: Globe Pequot, 2007. Print.

Simmons, William J. Henry McNeal Turner. "Hon. Solomon G. Brown." *Men of Mark: Eminent, Progressive and Rising*. Cleveland: G. M. Rewell, 1887. 302–13. Print.

Brown, William Wells

Adams, H. G., ed. "William Wells Brown." *God's Image in Ebony: Being a Series of Biographical Sketches, Facts, Anecdotes, Etc., Demonstrative of the Mental Powers and Intellectual Capacities of the Negro Race*. London: Partridge and Oakey, 1854. 121–24. Print.

Brown, Josephine. *Biography of an American Bondman.* Boston: R. F. Walcutt, 1856. Print.

Greenspan, Ezra, ed. *William Wells Brown: A Reader.* Athens: U of Georgia P, 2010. Print.

Sekora, John. "William Wells Brown." *Fifty Southern Writers before 1900: A Bio-Bibliographical Sourcebook.* Ed. Robert Bain and Joseph M. Flora. Westport, CT: Greenwood, 1987. 44–54. Print.

Burgess-Ware, Marie Louise

Browne, Thea Joy. "To Follow in Their Train: The St. Agnes Hospital and Training School for Colored Nurses." *Deeper Joy: Lay Women and Vocation in the 20th Century Episcopal Church.* Ed. Sheryl Kujawa-Holbrook and Fredrica Harris Thompsett. New York: Church Publishing, 2005. 73–96. Print.

Burgess, Marie Louise. "Women at Home: Notes on Nursing, Paper No. II." *The Woman's Era* 1.4 (1894): 14. Print.

Cobb, W. Montague. "St. Agnes Hospital, Raleigh, North Carolina, 1896–1961." *Journal of the National Medical Association* 53.5 (1861): 439–46. Print.

"Organizing the Profession for African American Nurses." *St. Agnes School of Nursing—1896.* UNC-TV. Web. Accessed November 12, 2010.

Bush-Banks, Olivia Ward

"Editorial and Publishers' Announcements." *Colored American Magazine* 1.2 (June 1900): 127. Rpt. New York: Negro Universities P, 1969. Print.

Guillaume, Bernice F., ed. *The Collected Works of Olivia Ward Bush-Banks.* New York: Oxford UP, 1991.

Sollars, Michael D. "Bush-Banks, Olivia Ward (1869–1944)." *Writing African American Women.* Ed. Elizabeth Ann Beaulieu. Vol. 1. Westport, CT: Greenwood, 2006. Print.

Stone, Susan M. "Olivia Ward Bush-Banks (1869–1944)." *Encyclopedia of African American Women Writers.* Ed. Yolanda Williams Page. Vol. 1. Westport, CT: Greenwood, 2007. Print.

Chesnutt, Charles Waddell

Andrews, William L. *The Literary Career of Charles W. Chesnutt.* Baton Rouge: Louisiana State UP, 1980. Print.

Brodhead, Richard H. "Introduction." *The Conjure Woman, and Other Conjure Tales.* Charles Chesnutt. Durham, NC: Duke UP, 1993. 1–22. Print.

Du Bois, W. E. B. "Postscript: Chesnutt." *The Crisis* 40.1 (January 1933): 20. Print.

Obituary. *The Crisis* 40.1 (January 1933): 19. Print.

Redding, Jay Saunders. *To Make a Poet Black.* Chapel Hill: U of North Carolina P, 1939. Print.

Cooper, Anna Julia

Gordon, Lewis R. *An Introduction to Africana Philosophy.* New York: Cambridge UP, 2008. Print.

Logan, Shirley Wilson. *We Are Coming: The Persuasive Discourse of Nineteenth-Century Black Women.* Carbondale: Southern Illinois UP, 1999. Print.

Springer, Kimberly. "Cooper, Anna Julia Haywood." *African American Lives.* Ed. Henry Louis Gates and Evelyn Brooks Higginbotham. New York: Oxford UP, 2004. 190–91. Print.

Cornish, Samuel

Bacon, Jacqueline. *Freedom's Journal: The First African American Newspaper.* New York: Lexington, 2007. Print.

Hutton, Frankie. *The Early Black Press in America, 1827–1860.* Westport, CT: Greenwood, 1993. Print.

Moses, Wilson Jeremiah. *Alexander Crummell: A Study of Civilization and Discontent.* New York: Oxford UP, 1989. Print.

Rummel, Jack. *African-American Social Leaders and Activists.* New York: Infobase, 2003. Print.

Corrothers, James David

Corrothers, James David. *In Spite of the Handicap: An Autobiography.* New York: George H. Doran, 1916. Print.

Guzman, Richard. *Black Writing from Chicago: In the World, Not of It?* Carbondale: Southern Illinois UP, 2006. Print.

Johnson, James Weldon. *The Book of American Negro Poetry.* New York: Harcourt, 1922. Print.

Cotter, Joseph Seamon, Sr.

Cotter, Joseph Seamon, Sr. *Negro Tales.* New York: Cosmopolitan, 1912. Print.

Hall, Wade H. *The Kentucky Anthology: Two Hundred Years of Writing in the Bluegrass State.* Lexington: U of Kentucky P, 2010. Print.

O'Gorman, W. Farrell. "Cotter, Joseph Seamon, Sr." *Harlem Renaissance Lives: From the African American National Biography.* Ed. Henry Louis Gates Jr. and Evelyn Brooks Higginbotham. New York: Oxford UP, 2009. 129–30. Print.

Crummell, Alexander

Fish, Cheryl J., and Farah J. Griffin, eds. "Alexander Crummell." *A Stranger in the Village.* Boston: Beacon, 1999. 124–36. Print.

Moses, Wilson Jeremiah. *Alexander Crummell: A Study of Civilization and Discontent.* New York: Oxford UP, 1989. Print.

Wahle, Kathleen O'Mara. "Alexander Crummell: Black Evangelist and Pan-Negro Nationalist." *Phylon* 29.4 (Winter 1968): 388–95. Print.

Walls, Andrew F.. *Biographical Dictionary of Christian Missions.* Ed. Gerald H. Anderson. Grand Rapids, MI: Eerdmans, 1999. 161–62. Print.

Davis, Daniel Webster

Culp, Daniel Wallace. "Daniel Webster Davis." *Twentieth Century Negro Literature: Or, A Cyclopedia of Thought on the Vital Topics Relating to the American Negro.* Naperville, IL: J. L. Nichols, 1902. 38. Print.

Jackson, Walter Clinton, and Newman Ivey White. "Daniel Webster Davis." *Anthology of Verse by American Negroes.* Clinton and Newman. Durham: Trinity College P, 1924. 98–103. Print.

Johnson, James Weldon. *The Book of American Negro Poetry.* New York: Harcourt, 1922. Print.

Sherman, Joan R. "Daniel Webster Davis: A Black Virginia Poet in the Age of Accommodation." *The Virginia Magazine of History and Biography* 81.4 (October 1973): 457–78. Print.

Delany, Martin R.

Rollin, Frank A. *Life and Public Services of Martin R. Delany: Sub-Assistant Commissioner, Bureau Relief of Refugees, Freedmen, and of Abandoned Lands, and the Late Major 104th U.S. Colored Troops.* Boston: Lee and Shepard, 1883. Print.

Simmons, William J. Henry McNeal Turner. "Major Martin R. Delaney, M.D. [*sic*]." *Men of Mark: Eminent, Progressive and Rising.* Cleveland: G. M. Rewell, 1887. 1007–15. Print.

Douglass, Frederick

Gregory, James Monroe. *Frederick Douglass The Orator: Containing and Account of His Life; His Eminent Public Services; His Brilliant Career as Orator; Selections from His Speeches and Writings.* Springfield, MA: Willey, 1893. Print.

Meier, August. *Negro Thought in America, 1880–1915: Racial Indeologies in the Age of Booker T. Washington, Issue 2.* Ann Arbor: U Michigan P, 1988. Print.

Quarles, Benjamin. *Frederick Douglass.* Englewood Cliffs, NJ: Prentice Hall, 1968. Print.

Ryan, Barbara. "Frederick Douglass (c. 1817–1895)." *Slavery in the United States: A Social, Political, and Historical Encyclopedia.* Ed. Junius P. Rodriguez. Vol. 2. Santa Barbara, CA: ABC-CLIO, 2007. 264–65. Print.

Douglass, Sarah Mapps

Alex-Assensoh, Yvette. "Grace Bustill Douglass." *Notable Black Women.* Ed. Jessie Carney Smith. Book 2. Westport, CT: Gale, 1996. 189–90. Print.

Bond, Cynthia D. and Jean Fagan Yellin, Eds. *The Pen Is Ours: A Listing of Writings by and about African American Women before 1910 with Secondary Bibliography to the Present.* New York: Oxford UP, 1991. Print.

Jones, Martha S. *All Bound Up Together: The Woman Question in African American Public Culture, 1830–1900.* Chapel Hill: U of North Carolina P, 2009. Print.

Wright, Michelle Diane. *Broken Utterances: A Selected Anthology of 19th Century Black Women's Social Thought.* Baltimore: Three Sistahs P, 2007. Print.

Du Bois, W. E. B.

Du Bois, W. E. B. *The Autobiography of W. E. B. Du Bois. A Soliloquy on Viewing My Life from the Last Decade of Its First Century.* New York: International Publishers, 1968. Print.

Lewis, David Levering. *W. E. B. Du Bois: A Biography.* New York: Macmillan, 2009. Print.

Marable, Manning. *W. E. B. Du Bois: Black Radical Democrat.* Boulder, CO: Paradigm, 2005. Print.

Dunbar, Paul Laurence

Braxton, Joanne M. "Dunbar, Paul Laurence." *The Concise Oxford Companion to African American Literature.* Ed. William L. Andrews, Frances Smith Foster, and Trudier Harris. New York: Oxford UP, 1997. 119–20. Print.

Dunbar, Paul Laurence. *The Collected Poetry of Paul Laurence Dunbar.* Ed. Joanne M. Braxton. Print.

Dunbar-Nelson, Alice Moore, Reverdy C. Ransom, and William S. Scarborough. *Paul Laurence Dunbar, Poet Laureate of the Negro Race.* Philadelphia: Reverdy C. Ransom, 1914. Print.

Wiggins, Lida Keck. *The Life and Works of Paul Laurence Dunbar: Containing His Complete Poetical Works, His Best Short Stories, Numerous Anecdotes and a Complete Biography of the Famous Poet*. New York: Dodd, Mead & Co., 1907. Print.

Forten, James

Bacon, Jacqueline. *Freedom's Journal: The First African American Newspaper*. New York: Lexington, 2007. Print.

Child, Lydia Maria Francis. "James Forten." *The Freedmen's Book*. Ed. Lydia Maria Francis Child. Boston: Ticknor and Fields, 1866. 101–3. Print.

Dorof, Al. "James Forten (1766–1842)." *Southwark Historical Society*, August 19, 2012. Web. Accessed October 18, 2009.

Jackson, Eric. R. "James Forten, Sr. (1766–1842)." *Slavery in the United States: A Social, Political, and Historical Encyclopedia*. Ed. Junius P. Rodriguez. Vol. 2. Santa Barbara, CA: ABC-CLIO, 2007. Print.

Nell, William Cooper. *The Colored Patriots of the American Revolution: With Sketches of Several Distinguished Colored Persons: To Which Is Added a Brief Survey of the Condition and Prospects of Colored Americans*. Boston: Wallcut, 1855. Print.

Winch, Julie. *A Gentleman of Color: The Life of James Forten*. New York: Oxford UP, 2002. Print.

Fortune, T. Thomas

Alexander, Shawn Leigh. *T. Thomas Fortune, the Afro-American Agitator*. Gainesville: UP of Florida, 2010. Print.

Calloway-Thomas, Carolyn, and Thurmon Garner. "Fortune, Timothy Thomas." *Encyclopedia of the Harlem Renaissance*. Ed. Paul Finkelman and Cary D. Wintz. Vol. 1. New York: Taylor & Francis, 2004. 405–6. Print.

Penn, Irvine Garland. *The Afro-American Press and Its Editors*. Springfield, MA: Willey, 1891. Print.

Fulton, David Bryant

Andrews, William L., ed. *The North Carolina Roots of African American Literature: An Anthology*. Chapel Hill: U North Carolina P, 2006. Print.

Bruce, Dickson, D. *Black Writing from the Nadir: The Evolution of a Literary Tradition*. Baton Rouge: Louisiana State UP, 1992. Print.

Gunning, Sandta. *Race, Rape, and Lynching: The Red Record of American Literature, 1890–1912*. New York: Oxford UP, 1996. Print.

Greener, Richard T.

"The First Black Harvard College Graduate: For Good Government & Urban Politics." 1964. *Blacks at Harvard: A Documentary History of African-American Experience at Harvard and Radcliffe*. Ed. Werner Sollors, Caldwell Titcomb, and Thomas A. Underwood. New York: New York UP, 1993. 36–41. Print.

Hoogenboom, Olive. "Greener, Richard Theodore." *African American Lives*. Ed. Henry Louis Gates and Evelyn Brooks Higginbotham. New York: Oxford UP, 2004. 350–52. Print.

Mounter, Michael Robert. "A Brief Biography of Richard Greener." *The White Problem: The Fascinating, Ironic Life of Richard Theodore Greener.* 2001 Web. Accessed October 20, 2009.

Griggs, Sutton E.

Elder, Arlene A. "Griggs, Sutton E." *The Concise Oxford Companion to African American Literature.* Ed. William L. Andrews, Frances Smith Foster, and Trudier Harris. New York: Oxford UP, 1997. 178–80. Print.

Joyce, Donald F. "Orion Publishing Company." *Black Book Publishers in the United States: A Historical Dictionary of the Presses, 1817–1990.* Ed. Donald F. Joyce. Westport, CT. Greenwood, 1991. 175–79. Print.

Kay, Roy. "Sutton E. Griggs (1872–1933)." *African American Authors, 1745–1945: A Bio-Bibliographical Critical Sourcebook.* Ed. Emmanuel Sampath Nelson. Westport, CT: Greenwood, 2000. 44–49. Print.

Taylor, Michelle. "Griggs, Sutton E." *Encyclopedia of the Harlem Renaissance.* Ed. Paul Finkelman and Cary D. Wintz. Vol. 1. New York: Taylor & Francis, 2004. 448–49. Print.

A Gude Deekun

Bruce, Dickson, D. *Black Writing from the Nadir: The Evolution of a Literary Tradition.* Baton Rouge: Louisiana State UP, 1992. Print.

Wallinger, Hanna. *Pauline E. Hopkins: A Literary Biography.* Athens: U of Georgia P, 2012. Print.

Harper, Frances Ellen Watkins

Brown, Hallie Q. *Homespun Heroines and Other Women of Distinction.* Xenia, OH: Aldine, 1926. Print.

Graham, Maryemma, ed. New York: Oxford UP, 1988. Print.

Richings, G. F. *Evidences of Progress Among Colored People.* Philadelphia: Geo. S. Ferguson, 1903. Print.

Sklar, Kathryn Kish, and James Brewer Stewart. *Women's Rights and Transatlantic Antislavery in the Era of Emancipation.* New Haven, CT: Yale UP, 2007. Print.

Haynes, Lemuel

Branham, Robert James and Philip Sheldon Foner, eds. *Lift Every Voice: African American Oratory, 1787–1900.* Tuscaloosa: U of Alabama P, 1998. Print.

Cooley, Timothy Mather. *Sketches of the Life and Character of the Rev. Lemuel Haynes, A.M., for Many Years Pastor of a Church in Rutland, VT., and Later in Granville, New York.* New York: Harper, 1837. Print.

Franklin, Benjamin, V. *Research Guide to American Literature: Colonial Literature, 1607–1776.* New York: Facts on File, 2010. Print.

McLam, Helen. "Introduction: Black Puritan on the Northern Frontier." *Black Preacher to White America: The Collected Writing of Lemuel Haynes, 1774–1833.* New York: Carlson, 1990. viii–xxxi. Print.

Heard, Josephine D. Henderson

Heard, Josephine D. Henderson. *Morning Glories.* 1890. *Collected Black Women's Poetry.* Ed. Joan R. Sherman. Vol. 4. New York: Oxford UP, 1988. Print.

Sherman, Joan R. "Afro-American Women Poets of the Nineteenth Century: A Guide to Research and Bio-Bibliographies of the Poets." *All the Women Are White, All the Blacks Are Men, but Some of Us Are Brave: Black Women's Studies.* Ed. Patricia Bell-Scott, Gloria T. Hull, and Barbara Smith. New York: Feminist P, 1982. 245–60. Print.

Wright, Richard R. "Heard, Bishop William H." *Centennial Encyclopaedia of the African Methodist Episcopal Church, Containing Principally the Biographies of the Men and Women, Both Ministers and laymen, Whose Labors During a Hundred Years, Helped Make the A.M.E. Church What It Is.* Ed. Richard R. Wright. Philadelphia: Book Concern of the A.M.E. Church, 1916. III. Print.

Highgate, Edmonia Goodelle

Butchart, Ronald E. "Edmonia G. and Caroline V. Highgate: Black Teachers, Freed Slaves, and the Betrayal of Black Hearts." *Portraits of African American Life Since 1865.* Ed. Nina Mjagkij. Lanham, MD: Rowman & Littlefield, 2003. 1–14. Print.

Logan, Shirley Wilson. *We Are Coming: The Persuasive Discourse of Nineteenth-Century Black Women.* Carbondale: Southern Illinois UP, 1999. Print.

Sernett, Milton C. *North Start Country: Upstate new York and the Crusade for African American Freedom.* Syracuse, NY: Syracuse UP, 2002. Print.

Hodges, Augustus M.

Gatewood, Willard B. *Aristocrats of Color: The Black Elite, 1880–1920.* Fayetteville: U of Arkansas P, 1990. Print.

Gossett, Thomas F. "Imperialism and the Anglo-Saxon." *Race and the U.S. Foreign Policy in the Ages of Territorial and Market Expansion.* Ed. Nathaniel Gates. New York: Routledge, 1998. 208–40. Print.

"Personal Notes." *The Southern Workman* 30.1 (January 1901): 785. Print.

Wallinger, Hanna. *Pauline E. Hopkins: A Literary Biography.* Athens: U of Georgia P, 2012. Print.

Holly, Joseph C.

Douglass, Frederick. "Death of Joseph C. Holly." *Frederick Douglass' Paper,* January 4, 1855: 2. Print.

Sherman, Joan R. *African-American Poetry of the Nineteenth Century.* Champaign: U of Illinois P, 1992. Print.

Wickman, Donald. "African American Vermonters." *The Vermont Encyclopedia.* Ed. John J. Duffy, Samuel B. Hand, Ralph H. Orth. Lebanon, NH: UP of New England, 2003. 33–34. Print.

Hopkins, Pauline E.

Davidson, Adenike Marie. "Pauline Elizabeth Hopkins (1859–1930)." *African American Authors, 1745–1945: A Bio-Bibliographical Critical Sourcebook.* Ed. Emmanuel Sampath Nelson. Westport, CT: Greenwood, 2000. 231–38. Print.

Hopkins, Pauline. *Daughter of the Revolution: The Major Nonfiction Works of Pauline E. Hopkins.* Ed. Ira Dworkin. New Brunswick, NJ: Rutgers UP, 2007. Print.

Wallinger, Hanna. *Pauline E. Hopkins: A Literary Biography.* Athens: U of Georgia P, 2012. Print.

Horton, George Moses

Horton, George Moses. "Life of George Moses Horton, The Colored Bard of North Carolina." *The Poetical Works of George M. Horton, The Colored Bard of North Carolina.* Hillsborough, NC: Heartt, 1845. 1–8. Print.

Johnson, Lonnell E. "George Moses Horton (1797–1883?)." *African American Authors, 1745–1945: A Bio-Bibliographical Critical Sourcebook.* Ed. Emmanuel Sampath Nelson. Westport, CT: Greenwood, 2000. 239–43. Print.

Walser, Richard. "Horton, George Moses." *Dictionary of North Carolina Biography.* Vol. 3. Ed. William S. Powell. Chapel Hill: UNC, 2000. Print.

Jacobs, Harriet

Douglass, Frederick, and Harriet Jacobs. *Incidents in the Life of a Slave Girl, Written by Herself* and *Narrative of the Life of Frederick Douglass, an American Slave.* Introd. Kwame Anthology Appiah. New York: Modern Library, 2000. Print.

Yellin, Jean Fagan. *Harriet Jacobs: A Life.* New York: Basic Civitas, 2004. Print.

Johnson, Maggie Pogue

Bennett, Paula Bennett. "Rewriting Dunbar: Realism, Black Women Poets, and the Genteel." *African-American Poets.* Ed. Harold Bloom. New York: Infobase, 2009. 133–47. Print.

"Deaths: Dr. John Wesley Shellcroft." *Journal of the National Medical Association,* March 1955: 138. Print.

Johnson, Maggie Pogue. *Virginia Dreams.* 1910. *Collected Black Women's Poetry.* Ed. Joan R. Sherman. Vol. 4. New York: Oxford UP, 1988. Print.

"Johnson, Maggie Pogue." *Who's Who of the Colored Race: A General Biographical Dictionary of Men and Women of African Descent.* Ed. Frank Lincoln Mather. Vol. 1. Chicago, 1915. 157. Print.

"Johnson, Walter Werston." *Who's Who of the Colored Race: A General Biographical Dictionary of Men and Women of African Descent.* Ed. Frank Lincoln Mather. Vol. 1. Chicago, 1915. 158. Print.

Jones, Absalom

Brawley, Benjamin. *Negro Builders and Heroes.* Chapel Hill: U of North Carolina P, 1937. Print.

Lapansky, Philip, Richard S. Newman, and Patrick Rael, eds. *Pamphlets of Protest: An Anthology of Early African-American Protest Literature, 1790–1860.* New York: Psychology P, 2001. Print.

Ulle, Robert F. "A History of St. Thomas' African Episcopal Church, 1784–1865 (Philadelphia, Pennsylvania, Afro-American)." PhD diss. U of Pennsylvania, 1986. Ann Arbor: UMI, 1986. Print.

Loguen, Rev. Jermaine Wesley

Hunter, Carol M. *To Set the Captives Free: Reverend Jermain Wesley Loguen and the Struggle for Freedom in Central New York, 1835–1872.* New York: Garland, 1993. Print.

Kubisch, Linda Brown. *The Queen's Bush Settlement: Black Pioneers, 1839–1865.* Toronto: Natural Heritage Books, 2004. Print.

Loguen, Rev. Jermaine Wesley. *The Rev. J. W. Loguen, as a Slave and as a Freeman, A Narrative of Real Life.* Syracuse, NY: J. G. K. Truair, 1859. Print.

Malone, Thomas Horatius

Africana Criminal Justice Project. *Africana Criminal Justice: A Working Annotated Bibiography.* New York: Center for Contemporary Black History, Columbia U. PDF.

Atlanta University. *Catalogue of the Officers and Students of Atlanta University, Atlanta, Georgia, 1879–80.* Atlanta: Atlanta Constitution Power Book and Job P, 1880. Print.

Mason, Herman, Jr. *Politics, Civil Rights, and Law in Black Atlanta, 1870–1970.* Charleston, SC: Acadia, 2000. Print.

P. W. "Politics, Poetry, Law." *The Colored American,* Feburary 15, 1902: 10. Print.

Matthews, Victoria Earle

Branham, Robert James, and Philip Sheldon Foner, eds. *Lift Every Voice: African American Oratory, 1787–1900.* Tuscaloosa: U of Alabama P, 1998. Print.

Logan, Shirley Wilson, ed. *With Pen and Voice: A Critical Anthology of Nineteenth-Century African-American Women.* Carbondale: Southern Illinois UP, 1995. Print.

Wallinger, Hanna. "'Shrinking at No Lofty Theme': The Race Literature of Victoria Earle Matthews, Gertrude Mossell, and Katherine Tillman." *Loopholes and Retreats: African American Writers and the Nineteenth Century.* Berlin: Lit Verlag, 2009. 189–203. Print.

Menard, John Willis

Hirsch, Arnold Richard. *Creole New Orleans: Race and Americanization.* Louisiana State UP, 1992. Print.

Houzeau, Jean-Charles. *My Passage at the New Orleans Tribune.* Ed. David C. Rankin. Trans. Gerard F. Denault. Baton Rouge: Louisiana State UP, 2001. Print.

Wood, Forrest G. *Black Scare: The Racist Response to Emancipation and Reconstruction.* Berkeley: U of California P, 1968. Print.

Miller, Kelly

"Kelly Miller." *Men of Mark in America: Ideals of American Life Told in Biographies of Eminent Living Americans.* Ed. Merrill Edwards Gates. Washington, DC: Men of Mark, 1906. 181–83. Print.

McGruder, Larry. "Kelly Miller: The Life and Thought of a Black Intellectual, 1863–1939." PhD diss. Miami U, 1984. Print.

"Prof. Kelly Miller." *The Baptist Home Mission Monthly* 23.8 (August 1901): 222. Print.

Plato, Ann

Bassard, Katherine Clay. *Spiritual Interrogations: Culture, Gender, and Community in Early African American Women's Writing.* Princeton, NJ: Princeton UP, 1999. Print.

Fluker, Walter E. *The Stones That the Builders Rejected: The Development of Ethical Leadership from the Black Church Tradition.* Harrisburg, PA: Trinity, 1998. Print.

Wright, Michelle Diane. *Broken Utterances: A Selected Anthology of 19th Century Black Women's Social Thought.* Baltimore: Three Sistahs P, 2007. Print.

Randolph, Peter

Bassard, Katherine Clay. "Crossing Over: Free Space, Sacred Place and Intertextual Geographies in Peter Randolph's 'Sketches of Slave Life.'" *Religion & Literature* 35.2–3 (Summer–Autumn 2003): 113–41. Print.

Randolph, Peter. *From Slave Cabin to the Pulpit: The Autobiography of Rev. Peter Randolph: The Southern Question Illustrated; and, Sketches of Slave Life.* Boston: J. H. Earle, 1893. Print.

"Tombstones of the Allen Family, at Claremont Surry Co. *William and Mary College Quarterly Historical Magazine* 3.2 (October 1899): 112–15. Print.

Ray, Henrietta Cordelia

Banks, Marva Osborne. "Henrietta Cordelia Ray." *African American Authors, 1745–1945: A Bio-Bibliographical Critical Sourcebook.* Ed. Emmanuel Sampath Nelson. Westport, CT: Greenwood, 2000. 366–70. Print.

Bennett, Paula. *Nineteenth-Century American Women Poets: An Anthology.* Malden, MA: Blackwell, 1998. Print.

Brawley, Benjamin Griffith. *The Negro Genius: A New Appraisal of the Achievement of the American Negro in Literature and the Fine Arts.* New York: Dodd, Mead & Co., 1937. Print.

Walker, Cheryl. *American Women Poets of the Nineteenth Century: An Anthology.* New Brunswick, NJ: Rutgers UP, 1992. Print.

Raymond, J. Anderson

McPherson, James M. *The Negro's Civil War: How American Negroes Felt and Acted During the War for the Union.* New York: Vintage, 2008. Print.

"Mr. J. Anderson Raymond." *The Christian Recorder,* October 14, 1865: 1. Print.

"Notice." *The Christian Recorder,* January 7, 1865. 1. Print.

Rogers, Elymas Payson

Barbour, Lucius Barnes. *Families of Early Hartford, Connecticut.* Baltimore: Genealogical, 1977. Print.

Brown, William Wells. *The Black Man: His Antecedents, His Genius, and His Achievements.* 1863. New York: Johnson, 1968. Print.

Sernett, Milton C. *Abolition's Axe: Beriah Green, Oneida Institute, and the Black Freedom Struggle.* Syracuse, NY: Syracuse UP, 1986. Print.

Sherman, Joan R. *African-American Poetry of the Nineteenth Century.* Champaign: U of Illinois P, 1992. Print.

Strong, James L. "Rogers, Elymas P." *Cyclopedia of Biblical, Theological, and Ecclesiastical Literature.* Ed. Rev. John M'Clintock and James Strong. Vol. 9. New York: Harper, 1880. 62. Print.

Russwurm, John Brown

Bacon, Jacqueline. *Freedom's Journal: The First African American Newspaper.* New York: Lexington, 2007. Print.

Brewer, William M. "John B. Russwurm." *Journal of Negro History* 13.4 (October 1928): 413–22. Print.

Hutton, Frankie. *The Early Black Press in America, 1827–1860.* Westport, CT: Greenwood, 1993. Print.

James, Winston. *The Struggles of John Brown Russwurm: The Life and Writings of a Pan-Africanist Pioneer, 1799–1851.* New York: New York UP, 2010. Print.

S.

Bacon, Jacqueline. *Freedom's Journal: The First African American Newspaper.* New York: Lexington, 2007. Print.

Bruce, Dickson D. *The Origins of African American Literature, 1680–1865.* Richmond: U of Virginia P, 2001. Print.

Turner, Lorenzo Dow. *Anti-Slavery Sentiment in American Literature Prior to 1865.* Port Washington, NY: Kennikat, 1966. Print.

Smith, Amanda

Bogin, Ruth, and Bert James Loewenberg. *Black Women in Nineteenth-Century American Life: Their Words, Their Thoughts, and Their Feelings.* University Park: Pennsylvania State UP, 1976. Print.

Brown, Hallie Q. *Homespun Heroines and Other Women of Distinction.* Xenia, OH: Aldine, 1926. Print.

Crogman, William Henry and Henry F. Kletzing. *Progress of a Race: Or, The Remarkable Advancement of the Afro-American Negro from the Bondage of Slavery, Ignorance and Poverty, to the Freedom of Citizenship, Intelligence, Affluence, Honor and Trust.* Naperville, IL: J. L. Nichols, 1903. Print.

Smith, Effie Waller

Deskins, David. "Effie Waller Smith." *Beyond Hill and Hollow: Original Readings in Appalachian Women's Studies.* Athens: Ohio UP, 2005. 212–31. Print.

———, and Jennifer Kovach. "Introduction." *The Collected Works of Effie Waller Smith.* New York: Oxford UP, 1991. 3–26. Print.

Obermiller, Phillip J., and Thomas E. Wagner. *African American Miners and Migrants: The Eastern Kentucky Social Club.* Urbana: U of Illinois P, 2004. Print.

Smith, James McCune

Delany, Martin R. *The Condition, Elevation, Emigration, and Destiny of the Colored People of the United States.* 1852. New York: Arno P, 1968. Print.

Smith, James McCune. *The Works of James McCune Smith: Black Intellectual and Abolitionist.* Ed. John Stauffer. New York: Oxford UP, 2007. Print.

Stauffer, John. *The Black Hearts of Men: Radical Abolitionists and the Transformation of Race.* Cambridge, MA: Harvard UP, 2009. Print.

Washington, Booker T. *The Story of the Negro: The Rise of the Race from Slavery.* Vol. 2. New York: Association P, 1909. Print.

Stewart, Maria W.

Branham, Robert James, and Philip Sheldon Foner, eds. *Lift Every Voice: African American Oratory, 1787–1900.* Tuscaloosa: U of Alabama P, 1998. Print.

Lapansky, Philip, Richard S. Newman, and Patrick Rael, eds. *Pamphlets of Protest: An Anthology of Early African-American Protest Literature, 1790–1860*. New York: Psychology P, 2001. Print.

Stewart, Maria W. *Maria W. Stewart, America's First Black Woman Political Writers: Essays and Speeches*. Ed. Marilyn Richardson. Bloomington: Indiana UP, 1987. Print.

———. "Preface." *Meditations from the Pen of Mrs. Maria W. Stewart: (Widow of the late James W. Stewart) Now Matron of the Freedman's Hospital, and Presented in 1832 to the First African Baptist Church and Society of Boston, Mass.* Washington, DC, 1879. Print.

Terrell, Mary Church

Harley, Sharon. "Mary Church Terrell: Genteel Militant." *Black Leaders of the Nineteenth Century.* Ed. Leon Litwack and August Meier. Urbana: U of Illinois P, 1988. 291–307. Print.

Hine, Darlene Clark, William C. Hine, and Stanley Harrold, eds. *The African-American Odyssey.* Saddle River, NJ: Prentice Hall, 2005. Print.

Marable, Manning, and Leith Mullings. *Let Nobody Turn Us Around: Voices of Resistance, Reform, and Renewal.* Lanham, MD: Rowman & Littlefield, 2009. Print.

McCallum, Shara. " Mary Eliza Church Terrell (1863–1954)." *African American Authors, 1745–1945: A Bio-Bibliographical Critical Sourcebook.* Ed. Emmanuel Sampath Nelson. Westport, CT: Greenwood, 2000. 379–83. Print.

Wheeler, Marjorie Spruill. *Votes for Women! The Woman Suffrage Movement in Tennessee, the South, and the Nation.* Knoxville: U of Tennessee P, 1995. Print.

Thomas, William Hannibal

Bannister, Robert C. *Social Darwinism: Science and Myth in Anglo-American Social Thought.* Philadelphia: Temple UP, 2010. Print.

Cole, Johnetta B., and Beverly Guy-Sheftall. *Gender Talk: The Struggle for Women's Equality in African American Communities.* New York: Ballantine, 2003. Print.

Smith, John D. *Black Judas: William Hannibal Thomas and the American Negro.* Athens: U of Georgia P, 2000. Print.

Thompson, Clara Ann

Honey, Maureen. *Shadowed Dreams: Women's Poetry of the Harlem Renaissance.* New Brunswick, NJ: Rutgers UP, 2006. Print.

Jackson, Walter Clinton, and Newman Ivey White. "Clara Ann Thompson." *Anthology of Verse by American Negroes.* Durham, NC: Trinity College P, 1924. 132–34. Print.

Sherman, Joan R. "Introduction." *Collected Black Women's Poetry.* Ed. Joan R. Sherman. Vol. 2. New York: Oxford UP, 1988. Print.

Thompson, Priscilla Jane

Maffly-Kipp, Laurie F. *Setting Down the Sacred Past: African-American Race Histories.* Cambridge, MA: Harvard UP, 2010. Print.

Mance, Ajuan M. *Inventing Black Women: African American Women's Poetry and Self-Representation, 1877–2000.* Knoxville: U of Tennessee P, 2007. Print.

Sherman, Joan R. "Introduction." *Collected Black Women's Poetry*. Ed. Joan R. Sherman. Vol. 2. New York: Oxford UP, 1988. Print.

Tillman, Katherine Davis

Higginbotham, Evelyn Brooks. *Righteous Discontent: The Women's Movement in the Black Baptist Church*. Cambridge, MA: Harvard UP, 1994. Print.

Saunders, Kirsten. "Katherine Davis Chapman Tillman (1870–?)." *African American Authors, 1745–1945: A Bio-Bibliographical Critical Sourcebook*. Ed. Emmanuel Sampath Nelson. Westport, CT: Greenwood, 2000. 396–99. Print.

Tate, Claudia. "Introduction." *The Works of Katherine Davis Chapman Tillman*. New York: Oxford UP, 1991. Print.

Todd, Ruth D.

Blair, Amy L. "Ruth D. Todd (1878?–?)." *Encyclopedia of African American Women Writers*. Ed. Yolanda Williams Page. Vol. 2. Westport, CT: Greenwood, 2007. 567–68. Print.

Bond, Cynthia D. and Jean Fagan Yellin, eds. *The Pen Is Ours: A Listing of Writings by and about African American Women before 1910 with Secondary Bibliography to the Present*. New York: Oxford UP, 1991. Print.

Bruce, Dickson, D. *Black Writing from the Nadir: The Evolution of a Literary Tradition*. Baton Rouge: Louisiana State UP, 1992. Print.

Walker, David

Burrow, Rufus. *God and Human Responsibility: David Walker and Ethical Prophecy*. Macon, GA: Mercer UP, 2003. Print.

Walker, David. *David Walker's Appeal: To the Colored Citizens of the World, But in Particular, and Very Expressly, to Those of the United States of America*. Ed. James Turner. Baltimore: Black Classic, 1993. Print.

———. *David Walker's Appeal: To the Colored Citizens of the World*. Ed. Peter P. Hinks. University Park: Pennsylvania State UP, 2000. Print.

Wells-Barnett, Ida B.

Franklin, V. P. *Living Our Stories, Telling Our Truths: Autobiography and the Making of the African-American Intellectual Tradition*. New York: Scribner, 1995. Print.

Schechter, Patricia Ann. *Ida B. Wells-Barnett and American Reform, 1880–1930*. Chapel Hill: U of North Carolina P, 2001. Print.

Wells-Barnett, Ida B. *Selected Works of Ida B. Wells-Barnett*. Ed. Trudier Harris. New York: Oxford UP, 1991. Print.

Whitfield, James Monroe

Brown, William Wells. *The Black Man: His Antecedents, His Genius, and His Achievements*. 1863. Rpt. New York: Johnson, 1968. Print.

Hill, James L. "James Monroe Whitfield (1822–1871)."*African American Authors, 1745–1945: A Bio-Bibliographical Critical Sourcebook*. Ed. Emmanuel Sampath Nelson. Westport, CT: Greenwood, 2000. 474–78. Print.

Levine, Robert Steven, and Ivy G. Wilson. *The Works of James M. Whitfield: "America" and Other Writings by a Nineteenth-Century African American Poet*. Chapel Hill: U of North Carolina P, 2011. Print.

Williams, Fannie Barrier

Branham, Robert James, and Philip Sheldon Foner, eds. *Lift Every Voice: African American Oratory, 1787–1900*. Tuscaloosa: U of Alabama P, 1998. Print.

Chesnutt, Charles Waddell. *The Marrow of Tradition*. Ed. Nancy Bentley and Sandra Gunning. Boston: Bedford/St. Martin's, 2002. Print.

Deegan, Mary Jo., ed. *The New Woman of Color: The Collected Writings of Fannie Barrier Williams, 1893–1918*. DeKalb: Northern Illinois UP, 2002. Print.

Edwards, June. "Fannie Barrier Williams." *Dictionary of Unitarian Universalist Biography*. 1999. Web. Accessed October 2, 2009.

Williams, S. Laing

Reed, Christopher Robert. *Black Chicago's First Century, Volume 1, 1833–1900*. Columbia: U of Missouri P, 2005. Print.

"Samuel Laing Williams." *Who's Who of the Colored Race: A General Biographical Dictionary of Men and Women of African Descent*. Ed. Frank Lincoln Mather. Vol. 1. Chicago: n.p., 1915. 286. Print.

Smith, J. Clay. *Emancipation: The Making of the Black Lawyer, 1844–1944*. Philadelphia: U of Pennsylvania P, 1999. Print.

Wilson, Harriet

Brown, William Wells, Frederick Douglass, and Harriet E. Wilson. *Three Classic African-American Novels*. Ed. William L. Andrews. New York: Vintage, 1990. Print.

Ellis, R. J. *Harriet Wilson's Our Nig: A Cultural Biography of a "Two-Story" African American*. New York: Rodopi, 2003. Print.

Gates, Henry Louis, Jr. *Figures in Black: Words, Signs, and the "Racial" Self*. New York: Oxford UP, 1987. Print.

Grasso, Linda M. *The Artistry of Anger: Black and White Women's Literature in America, 1820–1860*. Chapel Hill: U of North Carolina P, 2002. Print.

Wilson, William J.

Brown, William Wells. *The Black Man: His Antecedents, His Genius, and His Achievements*. 1863. New York: Johnson, 1968. Print.

Levine, Robert Steven. *Martin Delany, Frederick Douglass, an the Politics of Representative Identity*. Chapel Hill: U of North Carolina P, 1997. Print.

Roediger, David R. *Black on White: Black Writers on What It Means to Be White*. New York: Schocken, 1998. Print.

Smith, James McCune. *The Works of James McCune Smith: Black Intellectual and Abolitionist*. Ed. John Stauffer. New York: Oxford UP, 2007. Print.

Wilder, Craig Steven. *A Covenant with Color: Race and Social Power in Brooklyn*. New York: Columbia UP, 2000. Print.

Yacovone, Donald. *Freedom's Journey: African American Voices of the Civil War*. Chicago: Lawrence Hill, 2004. Print.

SECONDARY SOURCES

Andrews, William L., ed. *The North Carolina Roots of African American Literature*. Chapel Hill: U of North Carolina P, 2006. Print.

Boers, David. *History of American Education*. New York: Peter Lang, 2007. Print.

Brooks, Gwendolyn. "A Bronzeville Mother Loiters in Mississippi. Meanwhile, a Mississippi Mother Burns Bacon." *The Bean Eaters*. New York: Harper & Row, 1960. Print.

Collier, Eugenia and Richard A. Long. , *Afro-American Writing: An Anthology of Prose and Poetry*. University Park: Penn State UP, 1985. Print.

Deck, Alice. "A Response to Elizabeth McHenry." *American Literary History*. 19.2 (Summer 2007): 402-405. *Project Muse*. Web. 13 September 2010.

Du Bois, W.E. Burghardt. *The Souls of Black Folk: Essays and Sketches*. Chicago: A.C. McClurg, 1903.

Faulkner, William. "Dry September." *The Faulkner Reader*. New York: Radom House, 1977. Print.

Finkelman, Paul and Cary D. Wintz. *Encyclopedia of the Harlem Renaissance*. New York: Routledge, 2004. Print.

Flora, Joseph M., Lucinda Hardwick KacKethan, and Todd W. Taylor. *The Companion to Southern Literature: Themes, Genres, Places, People, Movements, and Motifs*. Baton Rouge: Louisiana State UP, 2001. Print.

Fox, Robert Elliot. "Shaping an African American Literary Canon: Review of the *Norton Anthology of African American Literature* and *Call and Response: The Riverside Anthology of the African American Literary Tradition*" *Postmodern Culture*. 9.1. (September 1998): n. pag. Web. 20 June 2008.

Frere. "To Rosa." *Freedom's Journal*. 21 March 1828: n. page. *Accessible* Archives. Web. 6 June 2009.

Gates, Henry Louis, Jr. and Evelyn Brooks Higginbotham, eds. *Harlem Renaissance Lives from the African American National Biography*. New York: Oxford UP, 2009. Print.

———.and Nellie McKay. "From the Soil of Suffering." Interview by Jim Lehrer. *NewsHour*. PBS. Washington, D.C. 7 March 1997. Transcript. Web. 12 April 2010.

———. *The Norton Anthology of African American Literature*. New York: W.W. Norton, 1996. Print.

Glazener, Nancy. *Reading for Realism:The History of a U.S. Literary Institution, 1850–1910*. Durham: Duke University Press, 1997. Print.

Hill, Patricia Liggins, et al. *Call & Response: The Riverside Anthology of African American Literature*. New York: Houghton Mifflin Harcourt, 1997. Print.

Hobsbawn, Eric. *The Age of Capital, 1848–1875*. London: Weidenfeld & Nicholson, 1975. Print.

———. *The Age of Empire, 1875–1914*. London: Weidenfeld & Nicholson, 1987. Print.

————. *The Age of Revolution, 1789–1848*. London: Weidenfeld & Nicholson, 1962. Print.

Logan, Shirley Wilson. *With Pen and Voice: A Critical Anthology of Nineteenth Century African American Women*. Carbondale: Southern Illinois UP, 1995. Print.

Marable, Manning and Leith Mullings. *Let Nobody Turn Us Around: Voices of Resistance, Reform, and Renewal*. New York: Rowman & Littlefield, 2003. Print.

McHenry, Elizabeth. *Forgotten Readers: Recovering the Lost History of African American Literary Societies*. Durham: Duke UP, 2002. Print.

————"Rereading Literary Legacy: New Considerations of the 19th-Century African-American Reader and Writer." *Callaloo*. 22.2 (Spring 1999): 477-482. Print.

————. "Toward a History of Access: The Case of Mary Church Terrell." *American Literary History*, 19.2 (Summer 2007): 381-401. Print.

Norment, Mary. *The Lowrie History, as Acted in Part by Henry Berry Lowrie, the Great North Carolina Bandit, with Biographical Sketch of His Associates*. Lumberton: Lumbee Publishing Co., 1909. Print.

Norton, Michael. *The Dialect of Modernism: Race, Language, and Twentieth-Century Literature*. New York: Oxford UP, 1994. Print.

Ritche, Donald A. *American Journalists: Getting the Story*. New York: Oxford UP, 1997. Print.

Sherman, Joan R. *African American Poetry of the Nineteenth Century*. Urbana: U of Illinois Press, 1992. Print.

Steward, Theophilus Gould. *Memoirs of Rebecca Steward*. Philadelphia: A.M.E. Church, 1877.

Steward, William. *John Blye: or Triumphs and Trials of a Whitewasher's Son. The Christian Recorder*. 11 July 1878-12 November 1878. *Accessible Archives*. Web. 12 June 2009.

Thelin, John R. *A History of American High Education*. Baltimore: John Hopkins U Press, 2013. Print.

Townsend, George. *The Swamp Outlaws: or, the North Carolina Bandits. Being a Complete History of the Modern Rob Roys and Robin Hoods*. New York: Robert M. De Witt, 1872. Print.

Wright, Michelle Diane. *Broken Utterances: A Selected Anthology of 19th Century Black Women's Social Thought*. Baltimore: Three Sistahs Press, 2007. Print.

INDEX

Entries in **boldface** refer to authors, entries in *italics* refer to titles, and entries in roman type refer to first lines.